E. H. ZEYDEL
LUDWIG TIECK, THE GERMAN ROMANTICIST

EDWIN H. ZEYDEL

LUDWIG TIECK,
THE
GERMAN ROMANTICIST

A CRITICAL STUDY

WITH A PREFACE TO THE SECOND EDITION
BY THE AUTHOR

1971

GEORG OLMS VERLAG
HILDESHEIM · NEW YORK

Dem Nachdruck liegt das Exemplar des Autors zugrunde.

C

Reprografischer Nachdruck der Ausgabe Princeton 1935
Printed in Germany
Herstellung: Druckerei Lokay, 6101 Reinheim / Odw.
ISBN 3 487 04144 8

Preface to the Second Edition

A new edition in Germany of a book first published in the United States by the Princeton University Press for the University of Cincinnati over thirty-three years ago and long out of print, requires some comment. This is especially true since the work is reappearing in the language of the original edition. Two principal reasons have prompted this republication by the firm of Georg Olms in Hildesheim, to whom the author would express his gratitude at the outset. One is the fact that political conditions in Europa were such during the second quinquennium of the 'thirties and its sequel, that an American work, though appealing primarily to scholars and general readers of Central Europe, went almost unnoticed. The other reason is that some of the source material upon which it is based was either destroyed during the War or is no longer readily accessible.

Research since 1935 in the field of German Romanticism, specifically insofar as it affects Tieck and his writings, while not voluminous, has thrown new light upon some of the many problems involved. This would not be the proper place to review these investigations in detail.* Nevertheless it is appropriate to call attention to some of the more important publications which have appeared during the years that have elapsed.

The comprehensive five hundred page French doctoral thesis of Robert Minder, *Un poète romantique allemand, Ludwig Tieck* (1936), which never received proper attention outside of France, is a searching, carefully reasoned and independent analysis of the poet and his entire literary production, rather than a biography.

---

* See Marianne Thalmann, "Hundert Jahre Tieckforschung", *Monatshefte* (Madison, Wisconsin) XLV, 113—123.

Dr. Minder and the present writer were in close touch while working on their respective studies, and their results, although not their objectives, are very similar. Two other more or less general investigations of later date are the volumes of Marianne Thalmann, *Ludwig Tieck, der romantische Weltmann aus Berlin* (Dalp-Taschenbücher, Munich, 1955), and *Ludwig Tieck, der Heilige von Dresden: Aus der Blütezeit der Novelle* (Quellen und Forschungen, N. F. 3, Berlin, 1960). They stress the human side of Tieck's character and the basis for his fame during his lifetime. More specialized is James Trainer's important study *Ludwig Tieck. From Gothic to Romantic* (The Hague, 1964). Though brief, it makes stimulating reading but fails to adduce sufficient evidence from *William Lovell* and the earlier "novellen" such as *Der blonde Eckbert* to explain and clarify Tieck's transition from the Gothic to the Romantic manner. Valuable too are the various investigations of Raymond Immerwahr, e. g. the study *The esthetic Intent of Tieck's fantastic Comedy* (Washington University Studies, N. S., Language and Literature 22, St. Louis, 1953) and the article *"Der blonde Eckbert" as Poetic Confession* (German Quarterly, 34, 113–117). The monograph of Anneliese Bodensohn *Ludwig Tiecks "Kaiser Octavianus" als romantische Dichtung* (Frankfurt, 1937) deserves mention as a perceptive study of this "all-in-one" pronunciamento of Tieck's Romantic creed. A sequel to the present writer's monograph *Ludwig Tieck and England* (Princeton, 1931) is Percy Matenko's *Ludwig Tieck and America* (Chapel Hill, 1954). Highly valuable too are several recent articles by William J. Lillyman on *Der blonde Eckbert, Der Runenberg, Sternbald* and *Vittoria Accorombona* (in *Seminar*, 1971; *Monatshefte*, 1970; *Germanisch-Romanische Monatsschrift*, 1972; and *Journal of English and Germanic Philology*, 1971, respectively), the study of F. G. Klussmann in Benno von Wiese's *Deutsche Dichter des 19. Jahrhunderts*, 1969, and the *Studienausgabe* of *Sternbald* by A. Anger, 1966.

As for textual criticism, little progress has been made. The twenty-eight volumes of *Schriften* (Berlin, 1828–1854), now reprinted by de Gruyter (Berlin, 1966), is still indispensable as far as it goes. A step forward, textually speaking, was made by Marianne Thalmann in her four-volume edition of *Werke* "unter Berücksichtigung der Erstdrucke ... mit Nachworten und Anmerkungen" (Munich, 1963–

1966). The ambitious Reclam collection offers among its blue series now editions of *Sternbald* (Reihe 17, Band 6), *Blaubart* and *Genoveva* (Band 8), *Der gestiefelte Kater, Zerbino,* and *Der neue Herkules* (Band 9).

Of transcending importance as regards biography and "Stoffgeschichte" are two volumes of letters. The first is *"Letters of Ludwig Tieck hitherto unpublished, 1792–1853,* collected and edited by Edwin H. Zeydel, Percy Matenko and Robert Herndon Fife, with the cooperation of the Department of Germanic Languages, Columbia University" (Modern Language Association of America, New York, 1937). This contains some five hundred previously unknown letters in the original texts and with an English commentary. Still available, this volume should be used in conjunction with the present book, which quotes extensively from these letters, two years before their publication. As but two examples among scores, see the present volume, note 4 to Chapter Five, page 354 (letter to Nicolai of July 5, 1797: *Letters of Ludwig Tieck,* p. 21) and note 8 to Chapter Six, page 357 (*Letters,* pp. 173, 256, 369). In these *Letters* the entire Tieck correspondence with Nicolai, Frommann, Cotta, Reimer, Winkler, and almost 125 relatives and other friends is contained. Wherever the notes of the present volumes refer to "unpublished letters", the *Letters of Ludwig Tieck* should be consulted. Whatever flaws this edition of *Letters* may have as to an occasional misreading of carelessly written manuscripts, or as to excessive information in the Notes, familiar to "Germanisten" in Europe, it is invaluable today because many of the original letters have since been destroyed by acts of war or are beyond the reach of many.

The second volume, *Letters to and from Ludwig Tieck and his Circle* by Percy Matenko, Edwin H. Zeydel, and Bertha Masche (Chapel Hill, University of North Carolina Press, 1967), presents over 160 new letters by more than sixty correspondents, chiefly written to Tieck but extending on to 1871, and includes for the first time his complete available correspondence with his sister Sophie. This correspondence fills in the picture of the relationship of these problematical siblings, which is not without interest to literary scholarship as well as to psychiatry. On the whole, however, Tieck's letters are not personally revealing.

Finally three unpublished typewritten theses in the Library of the University of Cincinnati offer texts and studies of seven unedited early dramas of Tieck, *Der neue Don Carlos, eine Posse in drei Akten,* by Alfred Puhan (Master's thesis, 1937), *Anna Boleyn* by Frank Preuninger (Master's thesis, 1941), and *Medea, Der alte Meiners, Gotthold, Siward,* and *Braddeck,* by Albert B. Halley (doctoral thesis, 1959). The manuscripts of all seven were photostated in 1932 in the Preußische Staatsbibliothek (now known as Deutsche Staatsbibliothek, in East Berlin).

A survey of this research on Tieck since 1935 leaves the impression that although new light has been shed upon many dark corners, the principal problems which face Tieck scholarship may not yet have been solved. They are indicated in the article of Marianne Thalmann referred to in the footnote above. Tieck research has been too much concerned, she charges, with questions of whence the material *(Woher des Stoffes)* and too little with those of whither does this lead *(Wohin des Weges),* so that what may be timelessly applicable to his work has been overlooked. Mere temporal questions having to do with fashions of the day were deemed more appropriate. Nor has the central focus of the man — his *geistige Einheit* — been clearly defined, having been clouded by old, oft-repeated clichés about Romanticism. These clichés must be laid to rest. The evaluation of Tieck as a man must be undertaken afresh. Discussion must be encouraged again whether he actually was inferior as an artist to almost all his contemporaries, as German literary historians now believe pretty generally. Of importance in this connection is also the more recent article of Robert Minder "Das gewandelte Tieck-Bild" in the *Festschrift für Klaus Ziegler,* ed. Catholy and Hellmann, Tübingen, 1968, pp. 181—204.

These are difficult and vexing problems in a writer who struggled against self-revelation by all the means at his disposal, and who donned so many masks to hide his real personality. It is hoped that the present volume will at least give future critics some of the necessary facts upon which to build their interpretation.

To return to the present book, the original edition was generously financed by the Charles Phelps Taft Memorial Fund of the

University of Cincinnati (a fund donated by Mrs. Taft in memory of her husband, who was an older half-brother of William Howard Taft, twenty-seventh President of the United States). The volume was enthusiastically received by such authorities in the field of Romanticism as Julius Petersen of Berlin, who followed its writing with interest, Josef Körner in Prague, A. Gillies in England, R. Minder in France, and H. W. Hewett-Thayer and H. W. Nordmeyer in America. Critics who received it unfavorably did so because of basic differences in interpretation, because they felt that, in spite of the plethora of critical apparatus of fifty closely printed pages, and numerous footnotes in the text, it was not credited and documented fully enough (especially insofar as Witkowski and Gundolf are concerned), and because they thought that inherent weaknesses in Tieck, the man and the writer, here clearly revealed, did not entitle him to such full treatment as he is given. This point of view overlooks the fact that literary criticism judges some writers by the seeds they planted, the fruits of which they could not harvest but left to others to glean.

However that may be, the writer would repeat what was said in the original Preface of 1935, that he aimed to produce "ein aufschließendes," not "ein abschließendes Werk," and that he has viewed many facts through better eyes than his own. Moreover, to stress again what was said at the beginning of this new Preface, many of the documents upon which the work is based are now irretrievably lost.

To conclude, the writer expresses his thanks to the University of Cincinnati and its Taft Fund, as well as to the Princeton University Press, which held the original copyright, for their courteous permission to make this new edition possible. Gratitude to Herrn Georg Olms and his firm has already been noted. And so, after a generation and a half this story of Ludwig Tieck, the German Romanticist, whatever may be its shortcomings, and the actors who participated in the drama of his life, from his humble parents who lived behind the rope-maker's shop in the old Ross-Straße in downtown Berlin, to King Frederick William IV of Prussia, the "Romanticist on the throne," is unfolded again.

Ihr naht euch wieder, schwankende Gestalten.

Cincinnati, Ohio, USA.   Edwin H. Zeydel

LUDWIG TIECK,
THE GERMAN
ROMANTICIST

❦

PUBLISHED WITH THE AID OF
THE CHARLES PHELPS TAFT MEMORIAL FUND

LONDON: HUMPHREY MILFORD
OXFORD UNIVERSITY PRESS

LUDWIG TIECK, THE GERMAN ROMANTICIST

A Critical Study

BY

EDWIN H. ZEYDEL

Professor of German, University of Cincinnati

PRINCETON: PRINCETON UNIVERSITY PRESS
FOR THE UNIVERSITY OF CINCINNATI
1935

PRINTED AT PRINCETON UNIVERSITY PRESS
PRINCETON, NEW JERSEY, U.S.A.

PREFACE

IN THE course of the past few generations, particularly in the last two decades, hundreds of books on various phases of German Romanticism have appeared. Yet we find nothing approaching a satisfactory study of Ludwig Tieck among them, although it is recognized that with all his limitations he was the earliest, most prolific and most versatile practical exponent of the movement and that the extent of his influence, not only upon succeeding Romanticists but upon German literature, scholarship and criticism can hardly be measured. In discussing him, writers on Romanticism have with few exceptions been content to copy their predecessors and to pass judgment upon him which does not rest upon full knowledge of the man and his works.

A rapid survey of biographical works on Tieck since his death gives the following results. Köpke's book (1855), the one and only full biography, will always retain unique value. It is based upon conversations with Tieck himself and upon a wealth of source material, some of which is now lost. But besides containing numerous factual errors, many of which have been copied again and again, it lays more emphasis upon trivial anecdotes than upon critical appraisal. Worse still, Köpke proves a very one-sided advocate instead of an unbiased judge. Facts unfavorable to Tieck which we know were familiar to him were suppressed, partly, no doubt, because Tieck's daughter Agnes was still living. Moreover, some time after finishing his work he confessed to Varnhagen von Ense that at the time of writing he had no inkling of a mass of other circumstances surrounding Tieck's private life and casting a flood of light upon his character. Most of these, of course, Tieck himself could not have been expected to divulge.

Friesen's contribution (1871) is not a biography in any sense, but a series of casual reminiscences of the Dresden period, with a critique of some of the later writings added as an afterthought. Haym's admirable treatment in his work on early Romanticism, in some respects still standard, has one weakness. It is more severe on the author than the facts warrant. Besides, it necessarily takes into account only the first thirty years of his life, leaving very important aspects, such as his shift to the "new manner" after 1810, his voluminous output after Octavian, and his critical work in Dresden entirely out of consideration. Bernhardi (1894) and Goedeke (1898) have merely presented random materials for a biography.

[v]

PREFACE

*The biographical introductions of Klee (1892), Witkowski (1904)
and Berend (1908), though valuable, are not biographies, but prefaces
to eclectic editions. Gundolf's long essay on Tieck (1929), finally, reveals all of its author's strong points. It is original in thought, remarkably revealing, clever, stimulating and even brilliant. But it contains
misstatements, distortions and evidence that Gundolf died before he gave
it the finishing touch. The latter part is very sketchy and seems almost
like a set of lecture notes still in the rough. Of more importance, generally speaking, are some of the special studies, such as those of Minor
and Petrich and, more recently, those of Thalmann, Donat, and Lüdeke.*

*In offering the first full-length account of Tieck's life and works
since Köpke, as well as the first which attempts to set him off against
the background of his time and to accord him a critical appraisal, the
present writer realizes that he has undertaken a labor of tremendous
difficulty. Many reasons have deterred more able predecessors from ac-
complishing the task. Among them are the vastness of Tieck's literary
output, of which a not inconsiderable part is still unpublished; the fact
that his correspondence (an edition of which was prematurely announced by Klee in 1882) is widely scattered, in part inaccessible and
in part lost; the impersonal nature of most of his available letters; his
extremely enigmatical character and peculiar development; his puz-
zling position between Rationalism and Irrationalism, and consequently
his complicated transitional relationship to the Enlightenment, Storm
and Stress, Romanticism and Realism, which explains why almost all the
threads forming the woof of German literature between 1790 and 1840
find one of their centers in him; his extremely diverse activities and
influence as a poet, critic, editor, translator, commentator, dramatic
expert and arbiter of taste; and finally the absence of any biography of
the Schlegels.*

*These multifarious obstacles have helped cause the writer to approach
his task with humility. That he has carried it out at all is due less to
self-confidence than to the eventual realization that the time has come
when generalities about Tieck, however glittering they may be, are a
menace to literary criticism. While a definitive work—"ein abschlie-
ssendes Werk"—can at present not be written about Tieck (or about any
author of the past few hundred years), the present writer hopes to offer
at least a helpful contribution to a better knowledge of the German
Romanticist—"ein aufschliessendes Werk."*

*Had the writer not enjoyed certain important advantages, his work
would not have been finished. To Professor R. H. Fife of Columbia University and Dr. Percy Matenko of Brooklyn College, who are collabo-*

PREFACE

rating with him on an edition of Tieck's unedited letters, he owes valuable suggestions, as well as knowledge of five hundred letters, largely unfamiliar to scholarship and scattered in a score of libraries from London to Leningrad and from Copenhagen to Vienna. To Professor Fife and Columbia University he is indebted for the opportunity to use photostats of all these letters. To the Germanic Seminar of Columbia, which under Professor Fife's guidance has recently devoted several semesters to special studies on Tieck, and particularly to Miss Bertha Masche of Hunter College, he owes helpful information. To Professor Josef Körner of the University of Prague he is indebted for many valuable hints and a chance to inspect his priceless notes on Tieck. Robert Minder of the University of Strassburg has also given useful information. To the John Simon Guggenheim Memorial Foundation, which awarded him a fellowship for the year 1932-1933, and the University of Cincinnati he owes the opportunity of a year's study abroad under unusually favorable circumstances, particularly in Berlin and Dresden, where over thirty works of Tieck still lie unpublished. He owes Dean Louis T. More of Cincinnati gratitude for helpful criticism. He is indebted to the Charles Phelps Taft Memorial Fund for the Humanities at the University of Cincinnati for material aid in pursuing his researches and in publishing this volume, and to the Carl Schurz Memorial Foundation for encouraging support. An expression of gratitude is also due, last but not least, to the authorities of the many libraries that have extended courtesies, among them those of the University of Cincinnati and Columbia University, the New York Public Library, the Preussische Staatsbibliothek, the municipal libraries in Berlin and Dresden, the Sächsische Landesbibliothek and the Nationalbibliothek in Vienna.

The researches of previous workers in the field of Tieck studies have of course been drawn upon heavily. In the words of Voltaire, "il y a des faits que j'ai vus par mes yeux, et d'autres par des yeux meilleurs." Acknowledgment to these predecessors will be found in the notes which follow the text and are referred to in the body of the book by superior numerals.

All prose quotations from Tieck, which are given in English translation in the body of the book, are quoted in the notes in the original German. The English renderings of poetical passages, the original of which is always cited at the bottom of the same page, are by the present writer. Only one exception is to be noted. The quotations from Tieck's Die Sommernacht *in chapter two are from the translation of that work by Mary C. Rumsey (London, 1854).*

TABLE OF CONTENTS

CONTENTS

THE BACKGROUND

WITH the rise of the German middle class during the late Middle Ages, its struggle for intellectual supremacy began. By the end of the fifteenth century this contest had practically ended in victory. Ever since that time German literature has been largely the product and instrument of the middle class and has issued from the spiritual needs of this class. In the age of the so-called Reformation poetry served one part of the bourgeoisie as the expression of a strong undaunted self-consciousness, of a passionate adoption of the faith purified and propagated by Luther; to the other part it was a bulwark against this new faith and a means of buttressing and revivifying the old faith as it had survived the attacks from the cold rationalist north.

Then, during the century of the Thirty Years' War, when religious differences again came to a head, poetry guided the burgher away from the grim present into the calm depths of mysticism and supplied him with a vehicle for carrying his newly awakened scholarly interests. Gradually, almost imperceptibly, the Germans lifted their heads from under the ruins which the besom of war had piled high during those thirty years of misery.

Much was found changed. The Holy Roman Empire had become even more shadowy and impotent. The Gallicized princely courts had lost some of their lustre. Art and literature were turning baroque. The German language was at last coming into its own, after being hopelessly submerged by Latin and French influences.

Political impotence and disenfranchisement, however, remained the lot of the masses, as did the oppression and intellectual helotism which weighed down even those most buoyant of spirit. Deprived of a centralized government with any semblance of power, cursed with a cumbersome and archaic judicial procedure, lorded over by rulers to whom the life of the individual was a mockery, and robbed of every chance to acquire an elementary smattering of practical political sense, the people did not even realize their plight nor miss the leaders to whom they would have been entitled.

Meanwhile the philosophy of the age, particularly that of Leibnitz, endeavored to prove that this was the best of all possible worlds, and the intellect of the age accepted this doctrine. It was the era of the so-called Enlightenment, or Rationalism, which, coming from France, took an extreme form in Germany and in time bid fair to deaden the national soul. But, a foreign importation and out of harmony with the deepest essence of the German spirit, it never became more than a "movement," though it took a hundred years to run its course. That it had a salutary influence cannot be gainsaid. It liberated and clarified men's minds and helped to obliterate a mass of superstitions and false beliefs which had persisted ever since the Dark Ages. By 1780 it had served its purpose and was a dead letter in Germany; only in Berlin it survived for almost another generation. In the other Western European countries it has remained at least a force to this day.

Even in the heyday of Rationalism the German heart continued to seek the fulfilment of its yearning for liberty and happiness in a dream-world, in religion, or in the venerable but academic heritage of antiquity.

It is no accident, then, that modern German literature began with the Messianic odes and cantos of Klopstock (born in 1724), who breathed the spirit of Milton and the Bible, liberated German literature from imitative slavery, fathered modern lyric poetry and shaped the language of the German classics.

What was conjured up in hazy, uncertain forms by Klopstock's "sentimental" poetry received shape from the children of the Enlightenment. Foremost among them was Lessing, whose keen intellect strove for clearness, simplicity and truth. This stern Aristotelian expositor was not a man of flexible moods or tender emotions. His interest lay in many fields—theology, philosophy, philology, antiquity, esthetics and literature. He was a champion of the freedom of the spirit and of humanity. So far as he was concerned with the feeling of his time, he saw it concentrated in the doleful joy of compassion. To stir the emotion of pity, he urged, is the chief formal function of Melpomene, the loftiest of the Muses.

Still ruled by despots who at best were benevolent, but self-willed and unchecked by a strong central power, and excluded from participation in political life, the German burgher was able to indulge in politics only in the rôle of an individual theorist. As such he was innocuous enough. Within the massive walls of his dingy house or favorite beer hall all his interest in reality was confined, even after the French Revolution. And he was content to remain in a condition of mute servility, so long as his sovran spirit could rise aloft and give vent to his emotions in limitless space.

History proves that he acted wisely. Instead of shedding his blood upon the altar of civil rights, he bided his time and, if he was a potential poet, spent happy days in the land of poets and thinkers. From that incorporeal point of vantage he gained influence soon enough over the courts and the nobility, which had too long been cribbed, cabined and confined by a stale, senescent French culture producing no more spiritual values for Germany.

Wieland, an epic writer, definitely won the ruling classes over to the infantile though rugged German art of letters by abandoning Klopstock's obtrusively religious and moral-didactic sentiment, so characteristic of the bourgeoisie, and by substituting a mundane materialism, glorified by a sense of artistic values and by a winsome, polished style. Here upper and middle classes could meet on common ground.

But the age of Klopstock and Wieland was also that of nascent German idealism. Hamann, the Rousellian apostle of feeling and individuality, taught that the poet is the "vessel of the creative deity," a seer guided by the rhythm of his own nature. The more emotional and individualistic Spinoza was called upon to supplement Kant's pure reason. Jacobi's pantheism was deepened by the historical consciousness of Herder, Winckelmann and Lessing. Fichte's subjective idealism proclaimed that the ego is supreme and the phenomenal world its creation, and Schleiermacher, Schelling and Hegel strove to complete the grand synthesis of *Rationalismus* and *Irrationalismus*. Goethe is the shining exemplar of this fusion in action. With him and Schiller the spirit of German burgherdom attained its noblest fulfilment and maturity in literature. The "German Movement," as it is now often called, pervaded the whole period from 1770 to 1830. Through Storm and Stress and the great classical era it was carried to its final stages by German Romanticism, which at the end of the eighteenth century endeavored to render this latest and noblest flowering of poetry and philosophy the common property of ever wider circles, thus realizing a new ideal of culture in life.[1]*

Romanticism enjoyed no small measure of success, though soon growing decadent and superficially popular. Insofar as it was successful in the hands of its nobler exponents, it represents the first clarified, and perhaps the most grandiose, expression of the German national soul. It contributed to a deepening of men's feeling, not only for nature, but for the more subtle processes in the life of the individual.

Of course the spirit of Romanticism was not born with the German Romanticists. It is an offshoot of another "ism"—modern idealism as manifested in the field of esthetics. The germ of this idealism, characterized by a striving for the infinite in form and content, was conceived

*The notes follow the text. See pp. 343 *ff*.

in the Neoplatonism of late Imperial Rome. It was foreboded by Vergil's *Aeneid*, a "Bildungsepos" in the sense that *Wilhelm Meister* is a "Bildungsroman," and became articulate in such writers as Commodianus (*Carmen Apologeticum*, A.D. 249), Plotinus (*ob.* A.D. 270), Prudentius (*Psychomachia*, A.D. 375), St. Augustine, Boethius and Dracontius (*Laudes Dei*, A.D. 500). In religion it was revealed through the ubiquity of the Roman State; in law through the universality of Roman jurisprudence. It is manifested most strikingly in the architecture which we have inherited from the Middle Ages and which is associated by an accident of history with the name of the Goths. This "Gothic" architecture, an incarnation of modern idealism, really had its origin under the Roman Empire and may be traced down to our own times, step by step, from the basilica of Trajan and the palace of Diocletian.

Thus Rome, supported by her Church, became the teacher of idealism. The Renaissance, rediscovering this doctrine, contributed to its propagation, particularly in Italy, Spain, France, Germany and England. As a result, great writers like Dante, Cervantes and Shakespeare learned the better to see life whole. Great scholars and critics like Muratori furthered the fruition of Romanticism. The German Romanticists recognized and described the Romantic Principle, made men fully conscious of its historical development, and tried to adapt its teachings to the conditions of German life and thought in their own day. They were, however, not merely a community of writers with a formal program, but a philosophical school striving to revamp men's forms of life and conduct, on the basis of a new knowledge of the meaning of life.

The literary Romanticism of Germany had many forerunners, among them Heinse, Jacobi, Moritz, and Jean Paul. Finding its soil east of the Elbe, where irrationalism was at home, it developed in two stages, first in the preparatory stage of the Schlegels, Tieck, Wackenroder and Novalis, then in the more practical stage of Brentano, Arnim, Hoffmann, Fouqué, Eichendorff and many others. The Schlegels, especially Friedrich, were the theorists, *par excellence*, in whose writings (foremost among them the *Fragmente* of the latter) all the underlying principles may be found, among them the apotheosis of Homer, Dante, Shakespeare, and Cervantes as the great "naïve" or subjective poets, whose caprice was slave to no law; the universality and coextension of the arts; close cooperation between artist and thinker; the broadest possible definition of poetry; the blending of the various literary genres; harmoniousness as an ideal in education; strong emphasis upon the infinite and upon the world of dreams and fancies; subordination of reason to emotion, mysticism and demonic force, whose roots were found in the subconscious; the analysis of feeling in the contemplation of art and in the comprehension of religion; the conception of nature and art as a single living organism; appreciation of the art and literature of all nations; reverence for German medievalism; exaltation of the novel of culture, especially Goethe's *Wilhelm Meister*; and the glorification of sociability and "Romantic Irony." A modern dictum has fittingly caught the distinction between the Classicism of Winckelmann, Goethe and Schiller, and the Romanticism of the Schlegels and their followers: the former is Apolline, the latter Dionysiac.

Tieck was looked upon as a practical exponent of Romanticism. In the words of A. W. Schlegel, who "discovered" him, he was "ein dichtender Dichter,"[2] a poetizing poet, that is a poet's poet, a sublimated artist or archetype—one who produces a concentrate of poetry and is a law unto himself. Novalis and Wackenroder, endowed with more delicate souls and nobler faculties, were the real poet-prophets of the movement.

But the endeavors of the Romanticists could be successful only where the preliminary conditions necessary for a favorable reception of their philosophy existed. These conditions required a freedom from pressing economic problems of the struggle for existence, and the presence of a stratum of highly developed culture and sociability ready to receive the new doctrines.

In the small towns of central Germany, principally Jena and Weimar, where the Romanticists spent the preparatory years in more or less close communion, such conditions were found, in part, to a remarkably high degree. These towns harbored no sore economic misery, while culture and refinement throve aplenty. But Weimar had a population of only six thousand, and the area of the entire duchy was but half that of Rhode Island or of the English county of Cornwall. Jena, the seat of an old rural university, was no larger and socially less glamorous. Hence the young Romanticists, among them the Schlegel brothers and Tieck, soon realized that so parochial an environment could never become the soil for ideas as cosmopolitan in scope as theirs. Moreover, they were too individualistic to remain harmonious.

They turned to the larger urban communities, and their first haven was the Prussian capital. In choosing this city they were well guided, for Berlin, then next to Vienna the largest German city, was enjoying a rapid growth. In the period from 1800 to 1850 its population rose from about one hundred and fifty thousand to over four hundred thousand, an increase of almost two hundred per cent, while the total population of Germany, rising from eighteen to thirty-six million, increased only one hundred per cent. The chief reason for this accelerated expansion is found in that exodus from the rural sections to the cities brought about by the progress of industrialization.

Moreover, a polite society was bidding fair to develop in Berlin for the first time in Germany. It was crystallized in an upper social class based upon no historical foundations and held together by no ordinary common interests. Its impelling motive was social intercourse and enjoyment, unhampered by artificial barriers or accidental differences of birth.

The meeting place of these circles was in the salons, where recent works of literature and the theater, music and art were enjoyed and discussed, where friendships were formed over the teacups, and where the latest gossip was at a premium. Whoever was fitted by endowment and polite training to assert a place in this society was admitted, without heed to origin and station. And so we find the hitherto exclusive nobility rubbing elbows in Berlin, as in no other German city, with the burghers and even with such "questionable" figures as actors, musicians and Jews.

Among the leaders of this heterogeneous society were the young noblemen Wilhelm von Burgsdorff and Count Karl von Finckenstein; the Swedish councillor of legation von Brinkman; the orchestral conductor and composer Reichardt; the philologist, critic and teacher Bernhardi; the theologian Schleiermacher; the publisher and author Nicolai; the actors Fleck and Iffland; the composer Zelter; the sculptor Schadow; the Jewish physician Herz with his brilliant wife Henriette; Dorothea Mendelssohn-Veit, who later married Friedrich von Schlegel; and Rahel Levin, who became the wife of Varnhagen von Ense.

CHAPTER ONE

CHILDHOOD AND SCHOOL DAYS

IN a dingy little structure, Ross-Strasse No. 1 (the old street by that name, not the Neue Ross-Strasse), situated only a stone's throw from the Spree River and thoroughly characteristic of Old Berlin a century and a half ago, Ludwig Tieck was born on Monday, May 31, 1773, at eleven o'clock in the morning. On the ground floor facing the street his father, Johann Ludwig, plied the trade of a rope-maker; behind the shop were the modest living quarters of his family. The house, long a landmark, was torn down early in the twentieth century to make way for a modern business building.[1]

This rope-maker, plain though he seemed, was a man of unusual qualities. On extensive journeys to other lands, which took him as far as the Turkish frontier, he, the son of an artisan, had broadened his vision before establishing a menage of his own in his native Berlin. By dint of industry, excellent common sense and a healthy frugality he had attained a measure of affluence and could later afford a good education for his unusually gifted children.

Nor was he wrapped up entirely in the struggle for a livelihood, although he enjoyed leadership in his guild and on important occasions was designated as its mouthpiece. Once he even appeared before the king as the intercessor of his fellow-guildsmen, being a stanch believer in their ancient rights and privileges. He read widely, discreetly and with independent judgment. The Bible had an honored place upon his bookshelf, also a German edition of Guthrie's and Gray's *History of the World*. Ludwig later inherited this work, which had appeared at Leipzig in 1765. It remained in his library until his death. On the fly-leaf he wrote a long note commenting upon the importance which it and other works in his father's library had in his early development.[2] Goethe's works, too (the Himburg edition, as well as the two editions of *Götz von Berlichingen*), enjoyed a place of distinction in the household at a time when their author was still a passionate advocate of Storm and Stress. Old Tieck was quick to realize the superiority of Goethe's writings to the works of the popular moralizing fabulist, Christian Fürchtegott Gellert, or to those of the poet of nature and war, Ewald von Kleist, or to those of the author of a Prussian grenadier's martial lays, Ludwig Gleim. "The others may do what they will, they

can never produce anything like *Werther* or *Götz*," was his rejoinder to
the defenders of the literature of his day. Besides the works of Goethe
his bookshelf contained the dramas of that eccentric genius J. M. R.
Lenz, who like Goethe belonged to the class of young literary hotspurs,
as well as the three-volume translation of Abbé Marigny's *Histoire des
Arabes* (Berlin, 1753),[2] a book by a disgraced clergyman named Kindle-
ben and the current numbers of a few weeklies and of the *Rheinischer
Most*, a "radical" organ of the devotees of a new ferment in German
letters.

Most of these writings were hardly to the liking of the Rationalist
taste prevalent in the best literary circles of Berlin. For the adherents
of the Enlightenment frowned upon any flight of the imagination. If it
was to soar at all above the realities of everyday life, they preferred to
have it fly no higher than the crow flies. Imitation of nature was the
artist's loftiest goal. Thus the teacher of Enlightenment, Johann Georg
Sulzer, in his *Allgemeine Theorie der schönen Künste*: "Considered
as an active cause, nature is the guide and teacher of the artist; in her
effect she is the general storehouse from which he draws the objects
necessary for his purposes. The more closely the artist adheres to nature
in his mode of working or in his choice of materials, the more perfect
will his work be. The process of nature is the real school of the artist,
wherein he may learn every rule of art. Hence the theory of art can be
nothing else but the system of rules deducted by careful observation
from the processes of nature."[3]

Standing flat-footedly upon the firm ground of experience and traditional morality, the Rationalists loudly proclaimed their unswerving
allegiance to the god of Reason. To quote Sulzer again: "But poetic
genius is important only when reinforced by a keen intellect. . . . In the
soul of the artist reason must always maintain complete control over
the liveliest activity of the imagination."[4]

To win the recognition of these arbiters of light and leading, poetry,
a mere ancillary art, had to do the bidding of her masters, morality and
education. She was merely the "teacher and guide of mankind," in the
words of Sulzer. She could prove her legitimacy only by giving evidence
of her practical utility and innocuousness. Whatever smacked of the
fantastic and miraculous became a sure target for the dry, biting wit
and withering ridicule of the Berlin wags. Such an "enlightened" taste
in literary matters would brook no supernaturalism. The actual worka-
day world seemed sufficient and satisfactory. In spite of oppressive,
omnipresent taxes and in the face of flagrant mistreatment of the common soldiery, the people were generally convinced that their idolized

king, Frederick the Great, had put the state in excellent order. Indeed, down to the humblest trooper and scullion, they were all patrioteers, sincerely proud of the world-wide fame which the Great King and his generals had brought to Prussia.

With all his literary interests the rope-maker Tieck, though not an out-and-out Rationalist, was a child of the Enlightenment. This was manifested particularly in his aversion to the hymns which his wife liked to read in her hours of devotion. He could see no good in them. Why, they were not even truthful, they were superfluous and pernicious. What nonsense, to call Christ the bridegroom of one's soul! One evening the good housewife happened to be intoning the popular hymn of the seventeenth century poet Paul Gerhardt which runs:

> The forests now are resting,
> And all the world's asleep.*

"How can anyone make such silly claims!" interrupted Father Tieck, probably with a twinkle in his eye. "All the world is not asleep. Why in America the sun is shining. There the people are awake."

Yet this show of sobriety on the part of the bluff paterfamilias was but skin-deep. Beneath it lay a wealth of inward feeling, which the stern, reticent man took pains to conceal from his family and sought to gratify in the quiet enjoyment of the nobler things in life. Thus a secret yearning often drew him to a musty house in the courtyard behind Behrenstrasse No. 55, where an actors' troupe headed by director Doebbelin used to stage German plays in an unpretentious way. Old Tieck did not hesitate to associate with the "comedians" in one of the beer-gardens or bowling alleys skirting the city, and even invited some of them to his home, although realizing that they were beneath him and could not be trusted. Still, something about their free-and-easy manner appealed to him and made them good companions for a few idle hours. To cultivate such associations, however, was a bold venture in those days, when the righteous still viewed theatergoing as a cardinal sin and every actor as a depraved, lost soul. No doubt his wife, too, had her misgivings about these guests and received them with an ill-concealed reluctance.

The full facts about the lineage of the elder Tieck's wife have never been revealed. She is said to have been the daughter of a smith named Schale, who leased a manorial smithy from a Herr von Rechow in Jeserig, a village near Brandenburg, some thirty miles west of Berlin. Schale's wife was a Berduschin, or Berukin. Besides this daughter, Anna

---

* Nun ruhen alle Wälder,
Es schläft die ganze Welt.

Sophie, they are reported to have had two sons. After both Schale and his wife died at an early age, the sons moved to the nearby town of Golzow, where they later operated a smithy; Anna Sophie made her home with the family of Prediger Latzke, who was parson in Jeserig from 1747 to 1781. She married Johann Tieck in 1772.

Now in the records of St. Peter's Church in Berlin, where her oldest son, Ludwig, was baptized, her maiden name is recorded not as Schale but as Beneckin (a copyist's error, it seems, for Berukin). This discrepancy led Tieck's biographer, Köpke, to make inquiries of Prediger Hoffmann in Jeserig, Latzke's successor, the Jeserig church records having been destroyed by fire in 1812. A reply from that clergyman, dated February 8, 1855, and based upon reports of older inhabitants of the town, gives the explanation.[2] She bore her mother's maiden name because she was either illegitimate or a pre-nuptial child whom Schale later neglected to legitimize. Köpke suppressed this fact, no doubt because in his day some members of the immediate family were still living.

A kind and gentle soul, she was in her plain, straightforward manner deeply attached to the Lutheran faith of her fathers. She never remonstrated with her husband, who was somewhat of a martinet and lorded over the household like a feudal baron.

The poet was the first offspring of these dissimilar parents. On Sunday, June 6, 1773, he was baptized in St. Peter's Church, receiving the surnames of his father, Johann Ludwig. He had three godfathers and five godmothers, two of them members of the bourgeoisie, the rest of noble lineage. Among them was a chief forester von Kroseck with two daughters, a Fräulein von Holtzmann, and a Captain von Jounck with his wife. This is one of several instances showing that Tieck's parents were anxious to have him transcend the limits of their own social attainment.

The oldest son was followed on February 28, 1775, by the only daughter, Anna Sophie, also endowed with rich imaginative and literary faculties, and on August 14, 1776, by another son, Christian Friedrich, destined to become one of the reputable sculptors of the nineteenth century. If Ludwig was fated to be a Romantic par excellence, it was written in the stars that his brother Friedrich would become a perpetuator of the classical tradition. The parents, however, seem to have had more modest ambitions for their two younger children than for Ludwig—if their choice of godparents is any criterion. For unlike Ludwig, Sophie and Friedrich had only bourgeois godparents.[2]

The relations of the three children cannot be reconstructed in detail. It is clear, though, from Ludwig's early letters to Sophie, from his long and fierce struggle to break away from her influence later, and from Friedrich's lifelong attitude of abject submissiveness to her that she dominated her brothers to a surprising degree. Yet her personality was anything but pleasing, a fact which they both realized; besides, neither brother was sentimental as regards family ties.

At a very tender age the peculiar sensitiveness which Ludwig inherited from his mother was asserted in the pleasure he derived from bright, gleaming colors. Once a friend of the family brought a curio—a fancy little box with a cover which revealed an array of colors mounted in glass. The child was attracted with irresistible force to this wealth of variegated hues, and when the box was taken away from him, he was overcome by a sadness which, as he recalled it seventy years later, seemed the miniature embodiment of that sorrow which falls to the lot of mankind.

No less was young Tieck enthralled by the lights of the outdoor Christmas market, of which he has left a description in the "novelle" *Weihnachtabend*, written in 1834, at the age of sixty-one. "But the evening hours," he relates, "are the most refulgent, when this broad street is illuminated by many thousands of lights from the booths on either side, so that a brightness almost as of daylight is cast over the scene, which seems obscured only here and there by the throngs of people. . . . Thus thousands stroll past the manifold sweet-smelling dainties of sugar and marchpane, joking, with plans for purchases, chatting, laughing, ejaculating, where fruits in charming imitations, figures of every kind, of beasts and of men, everything beaming in bright colors, beckon merrily to those who would fain possess them."[5] To the end of his days Tieck's feeling for colors remained highly sensitive.

To impressions, joyful as well as sorrowful, the child reacted in the liveliest fashion. The deepest of these mental stimuli remained with him, and at the end of his long life he related to his biographer, Köpke, many not incorporated in any of his numerous "novellen" containing frequent autobiographical references. The most disturbing of his earliest experiences came one day when a day-nurse to whose care he was entrusted (they were commonly employed by families of the middle class) set him down upon the steps before the so-called "Stechbahn," a square facing the royal palace. With childish glee he gazed over the square to the bridge and to the statue of the Great Elector. But suddenly he became aware that the nurse was gone. Wishing to play a prank on him, she had hidden behind a pillar. The child was seized by that overwhelming sensation of terror which would grip any youngster in such a predicament. But this lad, endowed with a livelier imagination than the average, suffered greater horrors, for the many statues suddenly took on weird, eerie shapes. When the nurse appeared again, her reassuring words could hardly assuage his dismay, and it was long before he shook off that dark, terrible feeling, the prototype of sensations which later he often sought to convey through his writings.

More pleasantly terrifying memories were left by the hours spent at dusk upon his mother's lap, when she would recall the experiences of her own youth. To the boy even her simplest and most natural narratives became tales of fairies and of miracles, which were impressed indelibly upon his mind. She liked to tell of an uncanny old woman in her native village, whom the young folk looked upon with horror. Ugly and morose, this hag sat in lonely silence in her hut by the spinning wheel. Her only companion was a small dog. When on rare occasions she was accosted, she would answer sullenly and in half-understood accents, which to the children seemed like incantations of evil. She appeared most forbidding when her sole companion, the dog, ran away. Then she stood at the threshold, explored the village with piercing eyes, or ran through the streets with strange gestures, calling the dog, "Strameh! Strameh!" in a shrill voice. Out of such early memories of Tieck grew his delight in the awesome, his "sweet emotions" of horror which pervade the tale *Der blonde Eckbert*. Such curious mixture of pleasure and displeasure, joy and sadness, horror and sensual gratification was an outgrowth of his dual nature, which led to demonism.

Very soon the unusual perceptive powers of young Tieck attracted attention. On his mother's lap he learned the letters of the alphabet; their very forms thrilled his imagination before he could distinguish them. At the age of four he was able to read not only his primer but the historical and poetic portions of the Bible. They held him spellbound, even though he did not always understand, for he read with his imagination more than by dint of reason. The touchingly simple stories of the patriarchs were a source of unending delight. Soon he had read the whole Bible and his mother's precious, beautifully bound and illustrated hymn-books, particularly the Porst edition,[2] several times; also the oriental travel tales of Olearius and Mandelsloh, as well as the Arabian Nights. The neighbors shook their heads gravely over so much precociousness, or thought that it was only apparent—the manifestation of imitative childish pretence.

Among the books which prophetically aroused his first primitive human emotions, taking a powerful hold upon them and leaving an impression strong enough to endure a lifetime, was Goethe's *Götz von Berlichingen*. In the evening old Tieck would often get down one of his copies and read aloud from it to his wife, while young Ludwig squatted in a corner unobserved and listened. The boy was carried away by the majestic sweep of this youthfully ingenuous play. He believed in it, as he did in the Bible, and read in it himself whenever he had an opportunity. It gave him his first taste of life and first impression of the mysterious magic of poesy. Through its pages the world of imagination became sensuously and tactually real. Just as the patriarchs, heroes and kings of the Old Testament stood before him in their living presence, so Götz and his associates were conceived as realities. They were men and women of flesh and blood, like his parents, his sister and brother. It was a keen disappointment when his elders informed him condescendingly that neither this doughty Götz nor any of his comrades was real, that the play was a fable, and that the man who had written it, Goethe, lived in Weimar, only a hundred fifty miles away. *Götz von Berlichingen* had been a sort of revelation to the boy; he was reluctant to see this wonderful world of fancy thus shattered. But while the spell lasted he was under its influence day and night, sleeping and waking.

The figures and conceits of the realm of poetry were revivified more intensively in the boy's mind when he saw these forms stalking awkwardly before his very eyes in the puppet theater and, not long after, more majestically in actual lifelike form. For it was in the puppet theater that he, like Goethe a generation earlier, gained his first all-powerful impressions of the world of make-believe. And at the age of six he was taken by his father for the first time to the real theater of flesh and blood. If we would trust a catalog of literary and theatrical events between 1778 and 1787,[2] apparently copied from Tieck's own notes and reposing among his posthumous papers, the first performance which he witnessed on the stage was that of a French melodrama, *The Fair Arsène*, by Charles Simon Favart (*ob.* 1792). The date of this important event was August 5, 1779. Unfortunately, however, the catalog is incomplete, because the copyist, working many years later, could decipher only partially the puerile scrawl.

At any rate we know that his imitative faculties, which were later to develop to an extraordinary degree, were awakened by these experiences. The result was the impromptu conception of original playlets for a toy puppet show which his artistic brother Friedrich helped him decorate. And soon we find him, and under his guidance little Sophie and Friedrich, testing their own acting skill in the gloaming of the sombre living-room or in their father's workshop.

A few years later these performances and the young showman's repertory became more pretentious. He put on such difficult plays as

Götz von Berlichingen and *Die Räuber*. A version of the latter, which Tieck arranged and which is partly extant, was probably used as his own prompt-book.[6] Ludwig's acting ability was almost matched by Friedrich's, who developed a remarkable facility in imitating the voices of others.[7]

It is no wonder, then, that the imaginative impulse gained the upper hand in the boy, whose mind was essentially of the Romantic type from the outset. It drove him evermore away from the realities and tended to make him introvert. It helped to bring about a duality in his soul. For while, innately, he had strong egocentric, centripetal leanings, he consciously rebelled against this subjective trend and strove for objectivity. He was an introvert who tried to play the extravert. His entire career may be described as an attempt to flee from his subjectiveness and strong self-consciousness. Consequently Tieck was rarely himself, and very changeable. He was always playing a part, always imagining things not in terms of reality, but with the eyes of a showman.

His strong imaginative penchant made him incredibly absent-minded and was a factor in aggravating his violence and passionate temper, which caused him sorrow and humiliation, until he succeeded in overcoming them through rigid self-discipline. But for a while they found rich food in those literary works—Goethe's *Götz von Berlichingen* and *Werther*, as well as Schiller's "glorious and divine"[8] revolutionary *Die Räuber*—which to him always remained supreme achievements of their authors. As late as 1851 Felix Theodor von Bernhardi, after an interview with Tieck, reported that his aged uncle still adhered to this judgment and was willing to add to the list of worthwhile contributions by these masters only the earliest scenes from *Faust*, in particular Faust's colloquy with the Earth Spirit.[9]

He was a voracious reader. With avidity he devoured books, regardless of their subject and literary importance. After exhausting the treasures of his father's shelf, including a copy of Fontenelle's *Entretiens sur la pluralité des mondes* (1686) in the translation of Bode, he took recourse to the lending library. Here tales of horror, stories of notorious robberies, novels of high knightly emprise, and other works of a trashy, subliterary nature, were his steady companions. His zest for reading was so keen that he overtaxed his imagination and undermined his health.

Old Tieck, we have found, had imperious ways, which overawed both wife and children. Ludwig, even as a student of twenty, wrote him letters which are models of filial respect and submissiveness. The stern parent never revealed to anyone the slightest emotion or affection. Years later Ludwig, as a young man, was astonished to learn from the lips of the old man that he had always been his favorite child. The attitude of son to father wavered between absolute respect and secret rebellion against the parent's professed Rationalism.

The routine tasks of his parents made it hard for them to continue supervising his education. Not long after passing his fifth birthday he was entered in a nearby nursery school, operated by a kindly old couple. On rainy mornings he was often carried there in his mother's arms. Presently he exchanged this for a so-called French school, which was badly taught by a tailor's apprentice who had spent some time in Paris. The fact that such a school, inferior and with a tuition fee of but one taler per month, could be maintained, reveals the popularity of French even among the poorer classes of Huguenot Berlin during the reign of francophile Frederick II.

In 1782, at the age of nine, Ludwig was entered in the Quinta class of the Friedrich-Werder-Gymnasium. Here was further proof of his parents' desire to give him opportunity to rise above his rank. It showed, too, that his father recognized his unusual ability. The director of the school, Friedrich Gedike, was one of the foremost educators of the Enlightenment and a helper of Nicolai. He introduced many innovations, the final comprehensive examination (Abiturientenexamen), the term examination and semester grades, and applied the theories of the educacational reformers Basedow and Campe. Here Ludwig surprised his teachers with his memory and precociousness, although he was not rated a model pupil and never received a satisfactory grade in mathematics. Languages were an important part of the curriculum. He continued French and took up Latin and Greek.

Young Tieck made several intimate friends in the Gymnasium. Most important of these, Wilhelm Heinrich Wackenroder, the son of a high Berlin official, was endowed with finer gifts and a more subtle, lovable poetic nature than Tieck. They were the proverbial Damon and Pythias, until Wackenroder succumbed to a nervous disease in 1798. Another friendship, also cordial but less intense and of slighter consequence, was formed with Wilhelm von Burgsdorff, the son of a Brandenburg nobleman. Though he was clever and even brilliant, his frivolity and pride kept him at arm's length from Tieck. Friedrich Toll, the son of an official in the Berlin porcelain factory and an earnest, ambitious and gifted boy, might have become one of Tieck's lifelong friends, had he not died suddenly in 1790 at the age of seventeen. Deeply was the shock of his passing engraved upon Tieck's mind. It brought him one of the chief experiences of his youth: that man is the victim of cruel, blind chance. As late as 1837 he wrote to Friedrich von Raumer that it seemed as though Toll had died but yesterday. A strange infatuation which he felt for another schoolmate, Friedrich Heinrich Bothe, soon disappeared when not requited. But it left the useful lesson that friendship cannot be forced. Later Tieck could scarcely account for this ardent passion; he met Bothe again in 1825 as a pedantic publicist and teacher of the ancient languages. Of less consequence was his friendship for Piesker and Johann Georg Schmohl, a prosaic, practical-minded soul. Each of these friends came from families of much higher rank in the social scale than the Tiecks, for it had not become customary for artisans to send their sons to a humanistic school.

In 1792 Tieck finished the nine years' course of the Gymnasium. In the annual program Principal Gedike published a short paragraph on the qualities of each graduate. His remarks about Tieck, though recognizing his unusual abilities, are reserved in comparison with his estimate of Wackenroder. Perhaps Gedike had not forgotten Tieck's many irregularities. He wrote: "Johann Ludwig Tieck of Berlin, nineteen years old, for nine years a pupil in the Gymnasium and for four years a member of the first class. He has good endowments, and through his industry, which is unmistakable despite all his one-sidedness, he has acquired a very good fund of knowledge; in particular he has developed his taste well. His conduct was praiseworthy. He will study theology in Halle."[10]

In reality it had never been Tieck's intention to take up theology. Even during his last years in school he had struck out along paths which led into the domain of poetry. There had already risen before his eyes the guiding star which was to light his way through life.

His opinions on literature were very definite even as a tyro. Surely Gedike had this fact, too, in mind when he spoke of his one-sidedness.

He studied Greek and Latin diligently, taking lessons in Greek from an unsuccessful old student of theology. His early writings, as well as his letters to Wackenroder, contain numerous classical allusions. At an early date he read the *Odyssey*, preferring the original to a German translation which his father presented to him, and memorizing much of it. Among his earliest posthumous papers we find a translation of the first eclogue of Vergil[11] and a Jason and Medea tragedy.[12] We know, too, that he began a play on Agamemnon (a fragment of it existed in Köpke's day) and planned a comedy *Justinus* based upon Plautus.[13] His unfinished essay *Über das Erhabene* (1792)[14] reveals close study of Longinus and a keen realization of Homer's superiority to Vergil. Indeed, Sophie, the chief character of the unedited comedy *Ich war doch am Ende betrogen*,[6] one of his oldest works, mentions Homer, with Shakespeare and Schiller, among her favorite authors. But Aeschylos and Sophocles do not please her. "Their dialog is too unnatural, and the strokes which they use are too strong and heavy." (Ihr Dialog ist zu wenig natürlich, und alle Züge sind zu stark und plump aufgetragen.) Surely these were Tieck's own views at the time.

Except for his admiration of Homer—the *Odyssey* always remained his favorite Greek classic—, we never find young Tieck waxing enthusiastic over the ancient writers. Not until 1801 did they reveal a great lesson to him—the timelessness of art and the continuity of mythology and history.[15] Looking back upon his readings in this field, he told his nephew Gustav Waagen in 1815: "It was my experience in observing myself and my fellow-pupils during early youth that those young people who had a real understanding for poetry were a long time cultivating a taste for the ancients. If, as is natural, we meet favorites among the moderns and become fond of some great poet of recent times, the beauties of antiquity are readily obscured to a certain degree, so that our appreciation of them is not revived until later. Hence the simple, touching greatness of antiquity comes home to us only after we have won many a battle with ourselves and have lived through a great deal and recognized and discarded many errors."[16] And to Solger he expressed the opinion that antiquity has been overemphasized and modernity neglected;[17] he came to understand ancient Greek literature, he said, through the medium of the modern literatures.[18]

In this respect he differed from his Romantic confrères, the Schlegels, who began their careers suffused in classical lore and traditions. He was attracted only by literature of a character akin to his own and whose purport was perfectly clear and self-evident. Most strongly was he, the natural actor, drawn toward works in the modern dramatic form which afforded him the sensation that he himself might be one of the protagonists.

For medieval German literature he had just as little enthusiasm at this stage as for the writings of Greece and Rome. "So far as I know the minnesingers," he reported in a letter to Wackenroder in 1792, "a surprising monotony pervades all their ideas; it is, anyway, no recommendation for the poetic spirit of their age that it contained only this type of poem, only this circle of feelings."[19]

At an early age he learned Italian and soon read Gherardi's *Théâtre italien*. Next to Dante, whom he rated as one of the four greatest writers of the last thousand years, his favorite Italian authors became Gozzi and Goldoni.

Besides Homer, his first heroes in literature, as we have seen, were Goethe and Schiller in their earliest works. He alluded to them frequently in letters to Wackenroder, speaking highly of their early revolutionary dramas and commending *Torquato Tasso,* published in 1790, but condemning *Der Grosskophta* as bereft of genius. Once he called Goethe "a god."[20] In his pretentious commentary on the dramas of Shakespeare, written about 1794, he interspersed numerous references to these two authors, among many others, always revealing a keen critical faculty.

His reaction to French literature, on the other hand, was less spontaneous and marked. More acute was his interest in the French people and their revolution. In one of his earliest unpublished plays, *Der letzte Betrug ist ärger als der erste,*[21] an old nobleman, speaking of the French Revolution, remarks: "Deposing a king! Why that requires three times as much sense as crowning one. We have many examples." And in the unedited lyric drama *Der Gefangene*[22] of 1790 the longing for universal brotherhood is expressed in the words:

> O will the season never come, I pray,
> When man, embracing man, will call him brother ?*

Later in the same play the chief character has a vision of the Revolution. He sees a band of frenzied citizens bearing banners dripping with oppressors' blood:

> Their watchword's liberty! Ha, they approach,
> Upon their shoulders hovers now the fate of France,
> Before their feet is towered, quivering on the ground,
> Base despotism, while proud freedom weaves
> Herself of stars an everlasting wreath.†

To Wackenroder he exclaimed late in 1792: "Oh, if I were now a Frenchman! Then I would not be sitting here, then—. But unluckily I was born in a monarchy which has fought against liberty, among men who are still barbarian enough to despise the French."[23]

The early writings of Goethe and Schiller naturally took him to their great teacher and model, Shakespeare. His first acquaintance with the bard of Stratford, dating from about 1788, was derived from the inadequate German prose renderings of Eschenburg (1775-1782). But almost simultaneously he chanced upon copies of German acting versions of *Julius Caesar, Hamlet, King Lear, The Taming of the Shrew* and *The*

---

*O wird denn nimmer sich der Zeitpunkt nahn,
 Wo Mensch den Mensch umarmt, ihn Bruder nennt?

†Ihr Losungswort ist Freiheit! Ha, sie nahn,
 Auf ihren Schultern wiegt das Schicksal Frankreichs sich,
 Es türmt zu ihren Füssen sich am Boden zuckend
 Der Despotismus, und die Freiheit flicht
 Aus Sternen sich hier einen ew'gen Kranz.

Merchant of Venice, which appeared in Hamburg, Augsburg, Munich and Prague between 1777 and 1786. These copies were still to be found in his library in 1849.[24] No sooner had he read the first dozen pages of Shakespeare, even in this wretched surrogate-form, when he was transfixed by the wonderful genius of the author. Shakespeare became the experience of a lifetime, an overwhelming revelation. The young enthusiast could live, breathe and dream only Shakespeare. His first model in the study of English was Eschenburg's *Macbeth*. In 1791 he reread most of the plays with Wackenroder, explaining every point to his friend as they went along. In 1792 he tried, with less success, to do the same thing for more humdrum Schmohl. Shakespeare became Tieck's "favorite author"; he was "divine."[25]

In 1786 Holberg's racy dramatic satire, *The Political Tinker*, and at the same time, or even earlier, the compelling humor of Cervantes in *Don Quixote* were revealed to him.

Meanwhile his delight in the stage did not diminish; it became an obsession, a passion. As he related in *Phantasus*: "It cannot be described, and only one who in his youth has experienced a similar enthusiasm for the magic of the stage can understand the delight which flowed in to me from the most insignificant, yes often the most repulsive things. Every lamp-cleaner was sacred to me."[26] To satisfy this craving, he became an ever more frequent visitor to Doebbelin's theater in the Behrenstrasse and to other Berlin playhouses. Whenever he failed to cajole his parents into giving him the few pennies necessary for admission, he knew no greater joy than to steal away early in the morning, slip into the theater with a group of employees or actors and wait for hours in the dark auditorium for the performance to begin.

Turning once more to his catalog of literary and theatrical events, incomplete though it is, we find the following plays marked as having been attended: On August 4, 1783, *Schneider und sein Sohn*, in the Reuss-Garten, with the actor Karl Unzelmann; on December 5, 1785, Beaumarchais' *Figaro*, with the famous Ferdinand Fleck in the title rôle; on January 18, 1786, *Tancred*; on March 6 Holberg's *The Political Tinker;* on April 7 a ballet *Horia und Glocka;* on October 1 of the same year an unmentioned play in a newly opened theater; on December 5, *Verstand und Leichtsinn*, with Doebbelin, and soon after *Die neue Emma*. If most of these plays were poor stuff, this was due to theatrical conditions in Berlin at the time. Tieck was too young to attend performances of *Macbeth* and *King Lear* listed under 1778, and of *Hamlet* and *Romeo and Juliet* under 1779. But it is surprising that according to the catalog he missed *Minna von Barnhelm* in 1787.

Soon after, the musician and composer Reichardt, whom he befriended and in whose house he was a frequent guest, gave him a free pass for the national theater. Here he had the advantage of a much broader repertory. Plays like Goethe's *Götz von Berlichingen*, Schiller's *Die Räuber*, Gerstenberg's *Ugolino* and other "Ritterdramen" were driven home to him with all their awe-inspiring realism. Looking back in 1828 upon his first experiences with the theater, he wrote: "In my early youth there were frequently seen in Berlin, in addition to some weak and unimportant German literary efforts, many French dramas and comedies, the early tragedies of Schiller, and just as many works of Shakespeare, which, though deformed by adaptation, had retained the stamp of greatness. Other English tragedies, like *Athelstane*, *Ethelwulf* and similar works, were performed with approbation, also the mitigated comedies of Farquhar and Congreve. *Emilia Galotti* and *Minna von Barnhelm* held their admirers, as well as Gotter's well executed adaptations. Merry farces cheered us by contrast, and, though it left much to be desired, the theater expressed a sturdy, bright and grandiose character."[27]

With the help of Wackenroder and Burgsdorff he also acted out many of these plays secretly in his father's workshop or in the Tiergarten. One Sunday he came near disrupting the devotional services in St. Peter's Church with his declamation of scenes from *Die Räuber*.[28]

He felt a specially strong attraction for the acting of Fleck, who from 1783 to his early death in 1801 appeared in Berlin. The overwhelming power of the "mighty, genial and bold"[29] Fleck was evident above all in his interpretation of Franz Moor in *Die Räuber*, of Othello, and of King Lear. Tieck saw him at an early date in these rôles, perhaps in 1789, for we find allusions thereto in some of his oldest works and letters. In the eyes of young Tieck Fleck's realism became the supreme and only valid type of good acting. His exaggerated admiration for this actor explains why he later felt repelled by the delicately detailed portraitures of Iffland and by the noble rhetorical style of the Weimar school. For the same reason he disliked the acting of John Kemble and Charles Young in London.

CHAPTER TWO

EARLY WRITINGS. 1788-1792

TIECK, the critical playgoer and child of Rationalism, was remarkably prolific from the start of his career. Between 1788 and 1792 he wrote over thirty works, not to mention numerous shorter poems and translations. The majority have been preserved, though very few are accessible in published form.

The bulk of at least six, however, has been lost. In notes, preserved in the Tieck "Nachlass," Köpke spoke of these as partially extant in 1855.[1] A drama *Agamemnon* was in fragmentary form; an unnamed "Ritterstück" existed in a copy by Tieck's friend Piesker; a six-act "Schauspiel" was called *Rudolf von Felseck*; a five-act comedy, *Der schlechte Ratgeber*, was missing even in Köpke's day; a one-act farce bore the title *Der Querschnitt*; and an adaptation of Schiller's *Die Räuber*, of which only the fifth act is now preserved, was then complete in five acts.[2]

Besides, Tieck planned but did not execute about a dozen additional plays and novels. A small memorandum book dating from his early youth and preserved among his Berlin papers,[3] mentions among numerous projects a pastoral, *Der erste Dichter*,[4] dramas on Orestes and Pylades, Kaiser Ludwig, and King Frederick II and Katt, a comedy *Justin* based upon Plautus, a comic opera and a novel.

The version of Schiller's *Die Räuber* was perhaps his first literary endeavor. Though dated 1789, it may be older and was perhaps written as a school exercise or as an acting version for himself and his friends. Köpke described the first four acts, now lost, as covering 213 pages and being "partially a revision of Schiller's work and partially a copy of the Mannheim stage version." The fifth act, extant in the "Nachlass,"[5] is a workmanlike fusion of Schiller's two versions (*Schauspiel* and *Trauerspiel*) and the wretched Plümicke stage text, with a few original touches. It was apparently Tieck's purpose to raise the level and tone of Plümicke with the help, especially, of Schiller's first version (*Schauspiel*), which he always considered unattainable.[6] But Tieck deviated from the latter in avoiding a meeting of the brothers Karl and Franz, and in following Plümicke faithfully at the end, where Karl suffers voluntary death at Schweizer's hand.

LUDWIG TIECK, THE GERMAN ROMANTICIST

Tieck's other youthful writings will be considered according to categories. They are all found more or less unfinished among his papers in the Prussian State Library, where his "Nachlass" is preserved. Many of them are characterized by cant and ranting. Almost without exception they lack striking literary merit, and little or no attention has been paid to them. Yet they throw valuable light upon his beginnings as a writer and deserve comment. It is noteworthy that most of them are dramas, for young Tieck had a distinctly dramatic flair.

We turn first to eight prose comedies, three of which are definitely ascribable to 1789, while the rest probably date from about the same time. Some were written for a company of amateur actors with whom he was closely associated. The main interest in these conventional works, which in plot usually revert to Schröder's adaptations of French and English plays, is centered in disguises, stern parents who would thwart the plans of their children, mistaken identity, and rivals in love.

The humor of *Der doppelte Vater* (1789),[7] in four acts, depends upon the hoary device of a disguise, managed with a modicum of skill. A nameless five-act comedy—let us call it *Die Nebenbuhler*[8]—, in which the Berlin dialect figures, is just as immature and more slapstick. Its conclusion is missing. Incidentally Tieck satirizes the popular blood-and-thunder dramas of the day by introducing a starving poet who has written a tragedy in thirteen acts and eighty-five scenes, with two-hundred characters, ten battles, thirty-six duels and sixty ghosts. A one-act farce, *Die Heirat*,[9] is extant in two versions, one in twenty-two, the other in thirty-seven scenes, which are in reality different plays on the same theme. Coarse humor and dialect prevail in the shorter play. In the other there is no dialect, but broad humor and, when one of the characters dies, an apparent misunderstanding of the limitations of comedy.

Der letzte Betrug ist ärger als der erste, oder der betrogene Bräutigam, extant in two copies,[10] is a two-act farce. There is much bantering with proverbs, the play serving as a dramatic illustration of the aptness of its proverbial title. When one character says at the end of Act 1: "O, the comedy shall certainly have a second act, and in it I will surely play the leading part," (O, die Komödie soll gewiss noch einen zweiten Akt haben, und darin will ich ganz gewiss die Hauptperson spielen), we have a clear anticipation of Tieck's "Romantic Irony." The plots of the above five plays are briefly summarized in the notes.

Die Entführung (1789), in five acts, is extant in two copies.[11] The protagonists are a proud aristocratic lady who boasts of twenty-five generations of peerage, her weak but sensible husband, and a daughter with a wealthy lover whose family has recently been raised to the nobility. The plot affords opportunity to ridicule aristocratic snobbishness when the husband remarks to his wife: "There may be rabble, too, with fifty generations of ancestors." (Es kann auch Pöbel mit fünfzig Ahnen geben.) It is noteworthy that in the "novelle" *Die Ahnenprobe*, written over forty years later, Tieck dealt with the same theme. Horseplay is supplied by two servants who love the same maid.

An unnamed comedy which we shall call *Hans und Ludwig*[12] and another entitled *Ich war doch am Ende betrogen* (1789)[13] reveal knowledge of Shakespeare. *Hans und Ludwig*, manifestly under the influence of *A Comedy of Errors*, is written partly in the Berlin dialect. The two heroes, twin brothers who are distinguished by the fact that one wears a hat while the other goes bareheaded, meet in a strange town. They are constantly confused by their servants and even by the sweetheart of the one, until the complications are solved.

In *Ich war doch am Ende betrogen* a Jew Moses, like Lessing's Nathan, has adopted a girl. She is Sophie, a beggar's daughter. Moses gives her a liberal education. She writes poetry and discourses more glibly than naturally on literature. While lacking appreciation of Aeschylus and Sophocles, she admires Homer, Shakespeare and Schiller and calls Goethe's *Werther* a unique work. She also enjoys reading Milton and Dryden and believes that Göckingk, Weisse, Kleist, Wieland and Gleim "do our nation honor" (unsrer Nation Ehre machen). But unlike his prototype, Moses is coarse and speaks the dialect of the ghetto. He offers his foster-daughter to two suitors, to one for 10,000, to the other for 20,000 talers. Finally the older of these proves to be the girl's father, while the younger wins her hand.

A five-act prose tragedy, *Gotthold*,[13] is a conventional sub-literary drama of knighthood, a type made popular by Storm and Stress. Tournaments, single combats, dungeons, unhappy lovers, a cruel father, abductions, assaults, violent invectives against murderers and cowards, thirst for avenging grievous wrongs, a mysterious "Knight of Death"—Totenritter—(in reality Gotthold himself in disguise) feature the work. Unhappy Gotthold, who reminds of Trusty Eckart, has lost sister, son and father at the hands of his enemy Wildung. Seeking vengeance, he meets Wildung's daughter, who is just eloping. Though falling in love with her himself, Gotthold slays her and is in turn killed by her lover. The end is missing. A typical product of Storm and Stress, this immature play contains no suggestion of any Shakespearean influence. We date its conception 1788. The manuscript is of 1789.

LUDWIG TIECK, THE GERMAN ROMANTICIST

A similar prose tragedy in five acts, *Siward* (1789)[14], was written after he had made the acquaintance of Shakespeare, for side by side with the trappings of Storm and Stress it contains obvious echoes of Eschenburg's translations of *Hamlet, Macbeth* and *Othello.* Its theme is ingratitude and impatient lust for power. Siward, at first a faithful servant and the favorite of his king, fears the rivalry of a bosom friend, turns traitor, even regicide from sheer ambition and distrust, and is himself killed in the end. A mysterious, demonic power seems to control his actions.

A three-act tragedy of middle-class life, which bears no title, may be called *Der alte Meiners, oder die Liebhaber.*[15] It is of interest as a well motivated psychological study and as an effort to instil deeper passion and more profound tragic import into a bourgeois tragedy. We can detect the impress of the drama *Blunt, oder der Gast* (1780) by Karl Philipp Moritz, a friend of Goethe whom Tieck met about this time at the home of the musician Reichardt. Though tender and soft-hearted, Meiners is a testy and gruff old tyrant, a counterpart of Tieck's own father. Meiners has become soured on life by the death of his wife and all his children but one son, Carl. He loves Carl but rules him with an iron hand and has selected a bride for him. But the latter loves another girl, Sophie, about whom Meiners knows nothing. Hearing that Sophie is in trouble, Carl steals money from his father's safe for her. After a stormy scene between father and son, in which the former remains unaware of the theft, Carl promises to marry the girl of his father's choice, then hurries off secretly to bid Sophie a last adieu. Meiners now learns from a servant of the theft and of his son's whereabouts. Posthaste he follows him to Sophie's house, where he finds the two lovers. Thinking that they are about to elope, he heaps abuse upon them and kicks Sophie as she is on her knees before him. Aroused to frenzy by this shameful conduct, Carl pushes his father down the stairs. Meiners dies, not without a word of forgiveness, but Carl, crushed by his guilt as a patricide, stabs himself. The plan and motivation show how deeply Toll's sad lot had impressed Tieck with the cruelty of man's fate.

A historical tragedy in prose, on Anne Boleyn, of which two acts and about five scenes of the third are preserved in the "Nachlass,"[16] was planned in collaboration with Schmohl. Upon a visit in 1790 to the castle of Fredersdorf with Piesker, Tieck found a copy of the *History of England* by Rapin de Thoyras. The story of unhappy Anne, recounted there at length, appealed to him as excellent subject matter for a historical tragedy in the grand style. He and Schmohl set to work immediately, and tradition reports that Tieck undertook the emotional scenes and the more prosaic Schmohl those characterized by cool calculation. It seems more likely that Tieck did all the actual composition, while Schmohl acted as copyist.

The play, a lengthy exposé of intrigue and injustice against Anne, reveals gaps and inconsistencies, although it is superior to his other early unpublished plays and was executed later than most of them. Gardiner, bishop of Winchester, assisted by Anne's sister-in-law, is plotting against Anne. He writes anonymous, denunciatory letters to the already jealous king and to her uncle, the Duke of Norfolk, accusing her of secret love for a courtier named Norris. The latter really conceives a passion for Anne, which is, however, not requited by her. Gardiner does everything in his power to encourage Norris in his sinful love and make Anne appear guilty in the king's eyes. The play breaks off just before the climax, when the king is about to surprise Anne and Norris at a meeting shrewdly arranged by Gardiner, and when Anne is on the point of fleeing from her cruel husband, who considers her a burden. Among the minor characters are Jane Seymour, the king's sweetheart, and Archbishop Cranmer, Anne's defender.

Fired with enthusiasm for Anne's cause and clearly pro-Protestant in its sympathies, the play is devoid of real life and power, despite Wackenroder's remark that he could find nothing in it to criticize. The influence of Schiller's *Don Carlos* is easy to detect.

Among the lost plays we noted an *Agamemnon*, and in the previous chapter the early translation of Vergil's first eclogue was mentioned. We found that Tieck also wrote a rhetorical Jason and Medea tragedy in prose. It ends with the flight of the heroine and the suicide of the faithless weakling Jason. Learning of Jason's new marriage, Medea confronts him: "Where is that fiery youth, that brave Jason, that loving husband? He is gone and you are his shadow. O Jason, awaken your slumbering love, awaken it!" (Wo ist jener feurige Jüngling, jener tapfere Jason, jener liebevolle Gatte, er ist dahin und du bist sein Schatte. O Jason, erwecke deine entschlafene Liebe, erwecke sie!) When he curses and threatens her with a dagger after she has murdered his children, she tauntingly calls him an impotent wretch. Finally she bids his dagger release him from "this desert of life" (aus dieser Einöde des Lebens). The play is under the influence of Klinger's Storm and Stress tragedy *Medea in Korinth*. It contains images pointing to familiarity with Shakespeare, for instance Medea's apostrophe to Revenge, ending: "Let but revenge be my business" (Nur Rache sei mein Geschäft).

The verse-drama *Niobe* (1790)[17] has a classical setting, too, but with its choruses of youths and maidens—the sons and daughters of Niobe—is more lyrical than *Jason und Medea*. Its metrical form is free but crude. One of its lyrics has been published in the *Nachgelassene Schriften*.[18]

A fragmentary monolog of 122 lines from a projected drama *Der Schwärmer* (1790)[19] is in classical trimeters, with many iambic pentameters among them. It discloses the hero Johnson on the fresh grave of his beloved. The other mourners leave the scene, but he remains to give vent to his grief in mournful accents and philosophical musings on the meaning of life. The work, apparently written after Toll's death, shows the unassimilated influence of Klopstock's odes, Schiller's songs to Laura and the sombre moods of Shakespeare in *Hamlet* and *Macbeth*. The following reminds of Hamlet's soliloquy:

> How, or is perhaps our life itself a dream?
> And death the finish of this dream, awakening
> From heavy slumber. . . . ?*

Several other dramatic poems, among them a phantasy *Der 30. August* and a dirge entitled *Anton*, are also preserved among the Berlin papers.[19]

In a trochaic poem of 285 lines, *Gesang des Barden Longal* (1790),[20] copious explanatory notes, the images, names and general atmosphere show the earliest influence of Ossian upon Tieck. An "Ossianic sketch" *Iwona*, written in an iambic measure and also preserved in the "Nachlass,"[21] is probably the work of his schoolmate Schmohl.

A descriptive play in iambics, with lyric interludes—a sort of "Singspiel"—, bears the title *Der Gefangene* (1790)[22] and reveals Tieck's early liberalism in religious and political questions. It was written after he had read Linguet's *Memoirs of the Bastille*. The scene is laid during the reign of Louis XIV in a dungeon of the Bastille, where a youth, Waller, and a temporarily deranged old man are being held prisoners because they profess the Protestant faith. Waller yearns for the brotherhood of man and exclaims:

> O mortals, mortals, why did ye reject your brother
> So harshly? . . .
> Because I did not pray as ye would have me pray?

*Wie, oder ist vielleicht das Leben selbst ein Traum?
Der Tod das Ende dieses Traums, Erwachen
Von einem bangen Schlummer . . . . ?

Nor sprinkled holy water on myself?
Nor dreamed the dreams that ye have always loved?*

To the accompaniment of a lute the old man intones a ballad prophesying the French Revolution. At the end of the first act the prisoners recognize one another as father and son; at the close they are unexpectedly released from captivity. Waller's wife and two boys call for them, and they depart to live in rural simplicity. Three poems from this lyrical play have been published in the *Nachgelassene Schriften.*[23]

The setting of another two-act verse-drama with lyric interludes, *Die Friedensfeyer* (1790),[24] is medieval Germany "nach einem Kriege im Mittelzeitalter." The young men of the village are returning from war, but Hedwig fails to find her lover, Ludwig, in their ranks. She is told that he has fallen in battle. As she is lamenting his death at the home of his parents, he returns. The manuscript shows pencil corrections of many crudities.

A two-act pastoral, *Das Lamm,*[24] was planned in collaboration with Wackenroder but probably executed by Tieck alone. The pet lamb of the shepherdess Lila has been stolen. She accuses her lover Ludwig, who is innocent. On the point of taking his life in sheer despair, he meets Fernando. The latter, who had stolen the lamb for his own sweetheart, pities Ludwig and returns the lamb. Ludwig is forgiven and a merry song and dance conclude the play. Seven lyrics from *Das Lamm* appear in the *Nachgelassene Schriften.*[25]

Köpke has published only samples of the early lyrics in the *Nachgelassene Schriften.* Others occur in the verse-dramas just considered and in an unedited collection of *Gedichte.*[19] *Elisa,*[26] a love poem of twenty strophes in a trochaic measure, is preserved separately. Without exception they are descriptive in character and contain all the traits of Tieck's later lyricism, rich alliterations and jingling rimes, a profusion of short lines and sacrifice of content to form. The following untranslatable strophe from *Die Friedensfeyer* is typical:

> Frühlingslüfte,
> Blumendüfte
> Schweben über Tal und Feld,

* O Menschen! Menschen! Warum stiesset ihr den Bruder
So grausam von euch? . . .
Dass ich nicht betete, wie ihr mich beten hiesst?
Nicht mit dem heilgen Wasser mich besprängte?
Nicht Träumereien so wie ihr geträumt?

Regenbogen,
Purpurwogen
Malen sich am Himmelszelt.

Foremost among his early writings, and indeed one of his loveliest works, is a romantic verse-playlet *Die Sommernacht* (1789) in one act. Here he pays graceful tribute to Shakespeare and shows the nature of his strongest attraction to the dramas of the bard of Stratford. He was drawn to them first by his gloomy, sombre moods,[27] but most potently by his free sway of imagination, faculty of conjuring up delightful pictures, winsome poetic caprice, and power of breathing life into nature—traits exemplified vividly in *A Midsummer Night's Dream* and *The Tempest*.

Die Sommernacht, whose chief appeal is that of a lyrical ballad, is, like *Niobe*, written in a variety of meters adapted to different moods. Occasional lyric passages interrupt the prevailing iambic pentameters or classical trimeters. The boy Shakespeare, asleep in a forest, is discovered by Titania and Oberon as they are celebrating their reconciliation. Their first impulse is to punish the mortal intruder, but better counsel prevails. Titania speaks:

It was but yesternight we joyful held
Our feast of reconcilement—shall it be
That our first act, united, is revenge?
Is not this Boy as beauteous as a Child
Of Fairyland?*

They decide to shower blessings upon him. Titania decrees that he shall

Sing as none before thee ever sung,
As never after thee shall sing.
. . . A Poet thou shalt be,
The greatest earth has known, whose altitude
No after spirit shall have power to reach.†

Oberon ordains that his genius shall search out the very secrets of the earth's bowels,

*Erst gestern ward gefeiert das Versöhnungsfest;
Soll Strafe denn das erste Werk der Eintracht sein?
O, dieser Knabe gleicht den holden Feenknaben.

†O singe, wie vor dir noch keiner sang,
Wie nach dir nimmer einer singen wird!
. . . O sei
Der grösste Sänger, den die Vorwelt sah,
Zu dessen Höhe nach dir keiner sich
Erschwingen wird.

> . . . then rebound aloft
> And take its flight to heaven. . . .‡

The only meed of thanks expected of him is that he shall sing some day "in sweetest numbers" of the happy reconciliation of the royal pair. Then Puck steps forth and endows the child with

> . . . a merry humor . . . to drive away
> Black melancholy from each human breast.§

And after the great poet's death, exclaims Puck,

> . . . what a strife I'll raise
> Among a hundred little carping souls,
> Who will misjudge with endless blunderings
> Thy noble works. . . .¶

At the end the boy awakens and, though dazed, feels the new powers at work in his soul.

Until 1847 this little gem lay tucked away among Tieck's papers. In that year he chanced to read it to a group of friends, among them Eduard von Bülow and Albert Cohn. Bülow begged Tieck's permission to publish it, and it appeared in the *Rheinisches Taschenbuch* for 1852. In 1853 it was reprinted by J. D. Walter,[28] and again in 1855 by Köpke in the *Nachgelassene Schriften*.[29] At Cohn's suggestion it was translated into English in 1854 by Mary C. Rumsey.[30] Recently (1925) it has been paraphrased by E. Topp and published in the Schatzgräber-Bühne series in Munich.

One cannot help feel the superiority of *Die Sommernacht* to all the other early writings, except perhaps the little play *Das Reh* of 1790. If we did not possess, in the "Nachlass,"[31] a manuscript of the work clearly dating from Tieck's youth and agreeing textually in almost every detail with the published version, we would be tempted to surmise that before exhuming *Die Sommernacht* in 1847 he subjected it to a revision.

‡ Dein Geist belausche in der Erde Schlünden
Der Zauberei Geheimnis, hebe sich
Zum Himmel auf!

§ Ich schenke eine heitre Laune dir;
Die Macht, so oft du willst, aus jeder Brust
Den schwarzen Kummer zu entfernen.

¶ Nach deinem Tode will ich grossen Zwist erregen,
Von hundert kleinen Geistern lauten Zank.
Die Missgunst wird an deinen Liedern nagen,
Doch desto heller wird dein Ruhm dann glänzen.

A prose drama, *Roxane*,[32] in three acts, is based upon Christian Felix Weisse's *Mustapha und Zeangir* (1763). Tieck's immature work, full of corrections in Wackenroder's hand, deals with a conspiracy by Roxane, the second wife of Sultan Soliman, to do away with Mustapha, her stepson, and thus make room for her own child, Zeangir, as heir to the throne. This scheme, which involves a false oracle, is foiled by the appearance of the ghost of the prophet, who has been murdered by Roxane's messenger because he refused to assist in the fraud. In the end Roxane takes poison.

The five-act "Schauspiel" which we may call *König Braddeck*[8] is a fairy play and betrays the influence of Shakespeare and of the fiabe of the Italian dramatist Carlo Gozzi. It is the first work showing Tieck's acquaintance with Gozzi.[33] Braddeck's lovely daughter Lidie is wooed by many suitors. Among them are the noble knight Arthur and the wicked, tyrannical Orosman, who hopes for the early death of his present wife. Orosman finally kills her to make room for Lidie, but Braddeck rejects his suit. With the help of evil demons he wages war against Braddeck and wins a temporary victory, causing the exile of Braddeck and the death of Lidie. Meanwhile Arthur suffers many trials in his search for a golden bough, which he must find to win Lidie's hand. Aided by a kindly goddess, he is successful. Braddeck, who once remarks "The life of man is a dream" (Das Leben des Menschen ist ein Traum), is restored to his kingdom but renounces it in favor of Arthur. In the end the good goddess restores Lidie to life and to the arms of her lover. As in the comedies, the common citizens speak the Berlin dialect.

Das Reh (1790), a poetical fairy play in four acts, published in the *Nachgelassene Schriften*,[34] resembles *Roxane* in plot and *König Braddeck* in Gozzian fairy-tale atmosphere. Strong external evidence suggests that his schoolmate Schmohl wrote the play, but more convincing proof, both of an external and an internal nature, leaves little doubt that Tieck was the author after all.[35]

Printane, the second wife of King Prospero, hates Fernando, the latter's son by a first marriage. With the help of a sorceress she plots his death. She poisons the arrows with which he is to go hunting; when he eats the game he has shot he will himself be poisoned. By accident Fernando shoots the favorite stag of the queen of the elves. It turns into a horrible monster, which has the power of blighting flowers, trees and even crops. Thus partially foiled, wicked Printane now commissions two servants to bring a false oracle, which is to demand that Fernando shall engage in single combat with the monster. The fair Amanda, his betrothed, who is the daughter of the sorceress, secretly dips his arrows into an antidote which will turn the monster once more into a stag. Fernando goes forth to battle the monster, expecting certain death. Meanwhile one of the faithless servants betrays Printane to Prospero, who dashes away to rescue his son. But the latter has meanwhile shot the monster and thus transmuted it again into an innocent stag. The blight disappears and the sun shines. Though Fernando and his father are willing to pardon Printane, she is turned by the fairies into a poisonous tree. The humor is furnished in true Shakespearean style by two roguish servants, Tartaglia and Truffaldin, who are at the same time first cousins of Trinculo and Stephano in *The Tempest* and children of Gozzi. In other respects, too, the play is markedly under the influence of the Shakespearean comedy.

Das Reh, inferior only to *Die Sommernacht* among Tieck's earliest poetical works, shows Tieck for the first time applying his nature demonism to that elfish Romanticism which he had learned from Shakespeare and copied in *Die Sommernacht*. A mysterious relationship seems to exist between man and supernatural beings, such as elves or fairies, and nature. The moods of nature are attuned to those of man. Wrongdoing by the latter has a strange, deleterious effect not only upon the miscreant himself, but upon the elfin world and nature. Later, especially in the tales *Der blonde Eckbert*, *Der getreue Eckart und der Tannenhäuser*, *Der Runenberg* and *Die Elfen*, such demonism was further developed. It is not merely a literary device, but an innate feature of Tieck's psychic trend. Growing out of his duality, it may be called a secularized form of mysticism. From the beginning of his career Tieck, tortured by religious doubts, sought solace in nature. But (here his duality is felt) nature often assumed evil or demonic forms in his eyes.

The "musical fairy tale" in four acts, *Das Ungeheuer und der verzauberte Wald* (written in 1798 and published in 1800), is a revision and adaptation of *Das Reh* in the spirit of the Viennese folk plays. It was intended to serve as a libretto for an opera.[36]

Some twenty-five works from young Tieck's facile pen between 1788 and 1790, only two of which are published, have now been considered. One wonders to which of them he referred when he wrote to his publisher Reimer in 1846[37] that he planned to incorporate "the works of early childhood" (die kindlichen Jugendarbeiten) in a volume of the *Schriften*.

The three-act drama *Allamoddin* and the idyl *Almansur*[38] (both in prose), also conceived and begun in 1790, were published eight years later, the former with two other works of Tieck, by Wackenroder, the latter as an episode in Bernhardi's novel *Nesseln*, which was gotten out under the pseudonym Falkenhayn.

Allamoddin is an exotic play, based upon a story Tieck had found in the *Deutsches Museum*;[39] the scene is laid in Manila. We find Allamoddin, a noble barbarian, king of the Zulu Islands, in prison. The Spanish governor of the Philippines, the tool of a wicked Jesuit, is detaining him, his wife and child because he refuses to turn Christian and believes that his plain, untutored Zulus are better folk than the perfidious Europeans. Through the influence of Allamoddin's friends, the governor is deposed and the Jesuit order expelled. Allamoddin returns home happily with his family and a true friend, who seems a spiritual kinsman of Schiller's Marquis Posa. Excessive sentimentality, close application to the plays of Kotzebue and a mixture of Rousellian and Schilleresque idealism in pasteboard reproduction characterize the work.

Almansur has a tinselled Oriental setting and is not without Ossianic influence. Its hero, disappointed with life and troubled by doubts, adopts a morbid form of Rousellian philosophy when he flees the world and, renouncing all knowledge, seeks comfort with an old hermit at nature's bosom. The scenery amid which the stagy characters move is a patchwork of nature descriptions. We detect the yearning of the young city-bred poet for that solitude of the forest which later becomes one of his chief Romantic motifs. Perhaps his unrequited infatuation for Bothe and Toll's sudden death prompted him to write the gloomy tale, which never rings true.

Eight so-called *Paramythien*, or parable myths, of 1790, five of which are published in the *Nachgelassene Schriften*,[40] are imitations of a form introduced by Herder. Six are in prose, two in verse. The best of them represents Phantasy and Reason before the throne of Jupiter. Reason laments his dull, joyless life. Phantasy is bored by her own glittering trumpery, for "constant play can never make one happy" (ewiges Spiel kann nie erfreuen). So Jupiter marries her to Reason, the "gloomy sage" (der finstere Weise), and henceforth they walk hand in hand, or jointly guide the reins of their chariot. Reason directs the steeds, but when he sleeps Phantasy wields the goad of inspiration. Then the horses dash forward and the chariot shoots through space until, swept by the icy breeze of Saturn or gaped at by the yawning emptiness of Chaos, Reason awakens with a start and, seizing the reins, guides the chariot back home.

This myth would indicate that Tieck still saw in uncontrolled phantasy a menace to poetry and life. Later, for a while at least, he strove to make her his sole mistress in the realm of art. But the dualism of reason and phantasy was also his dualism.

In contrast to 1790, Tieck does not seem to have been happily fruitful in 1791. Needing money, he sold his services to unscrupulous potboilers. *Allamoddin* and *Almansur*, with their subliterary characteristics, have given us grounds for suspicion that he was prone to abuse his gifts by pandering to a depraved taste. Strangely enough, two of his younger teachers at the "Gymnasium" were responsible in encouraging him to continue on this dangerous course. One was the scribbler Friedrich Eberhard Rambach, the author of numerous novels and dramas offering a gullible public entertainment of the cheapest sort—tales of robbers and ghosts, blood-curdling adventures of bold knights, and murder stories which pretended to present psychological analyses of their villains. Rambach, who became a teacher in the Friedrich-Werder-Gymnasium in 1791, first used Tieck as a copyist, then as a junior collaborator. For a collection with the alluring title *Taten und Feinheiten renommierter Kraft- und Kniffgenies* (1791), which opened with an "Appeal to Lucifer," Rambach adopted a story of the notorious eighteenth century highwayman Matthias Klostermeyer, called "der bayrische Hiesel," whom he tried to depict as a sort of Karl Moor. Tieck was commissioned to supply the gruesome ending. He concluded with the confession that he had found it difficult to observe the best traditions of biography and paint his subject as a hero, "because he was no more and no less than a rogue" (weil er nicht mehr und nicht weniger war als—ein Spitzbube). This is the only personal note in Tieck's contribution.

For a second hair-raising novel of Rambach, *Die eiserne Maske, eine schottische Geschichte* (1792), on the theme of two hostile brothers, Tieck also supplied an ending, which he called *Ryno*[41]—a telescoping of the dreams of Richard III, the somnambulism of Lady Macbeth and the death-scene of Franz Moor—, as well as two typically Ossianic poems, "Ullins Gesang" and "Ullins und Linufs Gesang,"[42] reprinted in the *Nachgelassene Schriften*. These show how strongly the Ossianic fad had gripped him.

The tale *Adalbert und Emma* (1792) was also done under Rambach's eye. Much of it is written in dialog, with even an occasional stage direction. A typical tale of knighthood, it abounds in theatrical claptrap and fatalistic views. Mannstein, a valiant knight, has a beautiful daughter named Emma. Secretly she loves Adalbert, her father's squire, who has proved a doughty fighter and his master's rescuer. But their love is frustrated by her father. Wilhelm, another knight, who befriends Adalbert, promises to win Emma for him but falls in love with her himself and thus proves untrue to his friend. Emma, forgetful of Adalbert, is betrothed to Wilhelm. Adalbert kills her and is in turn slain by

Wilhelm. The story shows that after his experience with Bothe Tieck ruminated much on the nature of true friendship. It was published in Rambach's collection *Ritter, Pfaffen und Geister in Erzählungen* (1793) and later reprinted in Tieck's works under a new title, *Das grüne Band*.[43] We note a studied effort to achieve lurid external effects and to give the reader as many thrills as possible. His bosom friend Wackenroder had a poor opinion of the work. Tieck admitted that it was done in haste and should never have 'been written.[44] The sentimentality, which is overdone, derives from the pastoral novel *Estelle* (1787) of the French writer Florian, a weak imitator of Rousseau. In a letter to Wackenroder Tieck called *Estelle* a "masterpiece," which moved him to tears.

He never thought highly of Rambach, his first taskmaster. The following epigram, "An Rambach," preserved among his papers,[45] makes this clear:

> A proverb says the poorest play
> Is most successful ev'n today.
> That's true of this mean cur, I swear,
> He's locked in darkest dungeons, where
> He gnaws his way to freedom's light,
> Remaining frowzy, base and trite.[*]

For another teacher, G. K. F. Seidel, who gave him his first lessons in English and soon realized his linguistic talent and usefulness as an assistant hack, he completed a German translation of Conyers Middleton's *Life of Cicero* (1791-1793). Tieck did the latter half. His rendering is surprisingly good and shows that he had, as early as 1791, acquired a fair knowledge of English and resourcefulness as a translator.

In this potboiling there lurked a danger. It tempted him to exploit his unusual but fatal facility for hasty, meretricious writing. No wonder the work of his early years inoculated him with superficiality, which long remained his gravest fault, until in maturity his better, sounder nature overcame this vice. But he always retained a tendency to improvise.

Except for his excessive skepticism, another teacher, August Ferdinand Bernhardi, exercised a more salutary influence. He was only four years Tieck's senior. In Halle he had studied under the famous philolo-

---

[*] Das Sprichwort sagt, das schlechtste Stück
Hat immer noch das beste Glück.
So widerfährt's dem Lumpenhund,
Er wird in Kellern eingespunnt,
Er frisst sich wieder an die Luft,
Und ist und bleibt ein armer Schuft.

gist, Friedrich August Wolf, and had become an admirer of Goethe and Fichte. Always a cool and deliberate doubter and endowed with a keen sense of irony, he proved in some respects a valuable mentor. He held Tieck's fantasticalness in bounds and turned him more toward realism and observation of the petty events of everyday life. Many of the opinions he inculcated in his pupil later became part of the Romantic doctrine.

The last year of Tieck's literary production to be considered here, 1792 (most of which he spent as a student in Halle and Göttingen, respectively), gave rise to three unpublished works. The epic *Das Märchen vom Rosstrapp, der Gesang eines Minnesingers*,[46] recounts an old legend of the Harz Mountains, which he saw that summer. It was later retold by Grimm. The fierce destructive giant Sandal is enraged because a lovely girl, Buda, wears a diadem which renders him powerless against her. In a rage he pursues her and her beloved Korni and succeeds in shooting the precious ornament from her head. It falls into the Bode river, and evil Sandal reigns supreme until some other noble girl may salvage and wear it. Tieck's work is interminable and tiresome, not at all in the spirit of a minnesong, and gains momentum and interest only toward the end. A prose introduction of six pages is followed by hundreds of riming couplets, mostly in an iambic measure, with lines of varying length. Wackenroder criticized the work as poor in invention, trivial and lifeless. It is also full of vapid lyricism.

An unfinished essay *Über das Erhabene*,[47] probably meant to be read before some society in Halle or Göttingen, reveals study of Longinus, expresses a preference for Homer as against Vergil, and refers to a host of writers, among them Sophocles, Ariosto, Shakespeare, Milton, Kleist and Haller. There can be no question that its author was a voracious reader. Another paper, *Soll der Maler seine Gegenstände lieber aus dem erzählenden oder dramatischen Dichter nehmen?*,[47] is also unfinished. As would be expected of young Tieck, he gave preference to drama, entirely overlooking nature as a subject, perhaps because he had only historical painting in mind.

Of three works which were produced in 1792 and later published, we have already considered the tale *Adalbert und Emma*. The others are the two-act prose play *Der Abschied* and the tale *Abdallah*.

Der Abschied,[48] like his earlier comedies, owes its inception to an external circumstance, comparable to that which gave rise to Goethe's *Clavigo*. It illustrates the truism that an actable play must be composed for the stage, not for the closet, and must grow from the exigencies of a given company of actors and their audiences. He wrote it at the request of Bernhardi for a group of amateur actors who used to meet in various homes and had once acted before the King of Prussia and his court in the home of Baroness Rietz.[49] Until he left Berlin in 1791, as a victim of his outspoken revolutionary ideas and of intrigue, the royal concert master Johann Friedrich Reichardt was the patron of this group. Tieck had met him through his schoolmate Wilhelm Hensler, Reichardt's stepson and a son of Johanna (née Alberti), a sister of Tieck's future wife.

Although Tieck confessed to Wackenroder that *Der Abschied* was the work of two evenings, from the point of view of construction it is probably the best play he ever wrote. Here he succeeded, as scarcely ever again, in so casting a significant action in a small, clear-cut mold that every detail evolves from the emotional state in which the characters are conceived. The play is in direct line with the development of the German bourgeois tragedy inauspiciously begun with Lessing's *Miss Sara Sampson* and carried to greater heights by *Emilia Galotti*, Goethe's *Clavigo* and *Stella* and Schiller's *Kabale und Liebe*. The tenderness of *Werther* and *Stella* is enhanced by a singularly tense, sombre atmosphere. A high-strung woman, Luise, believes that she has been deserted by her lover, Ferdinand Waller. So she weds another, who is noble-minded but impetuous. Their happiness is clouded only by her memories. But Waller, who had been reported dead, returns, and the old love awakens in both. They are determined to withstand it resolutely; the distrusting husband, however, proves the cause of their undoing and death.

Tieck did himself and this capital play injustice when he mentioned it, many years later, in the same breath with the so-called fate tragedies, which became a fad with Zacharias Werner's *Der 24. Februar* (1809).[50] With these it shares only its well knit construction and melancholy mood. Though Tieck's fatalistic views find their reflex, the play does not indicate belief in the blind working of a mechanical fate. Predestination arbitrarily linked to some external object plays no decisive part, as in Werner. An apple, which figures to some extent, has no bearing upon the development of the plot; it merely motivates the presence of the fatal knife. A picture on the wall, too, is only incidental in revealing to the husband the true relation of the lovers. Nor is *Der Abschied* under the influence of Lillo's *The Fatal Curiosity*.[51]

The chief characters, Ferdinand and Luise, are namesakes of Schiller's protagonists in *Kabale und Liebe*. The name Waller, occurring also in *Der Gefangene*, was a favorite type with writers of middle-class tragedies.[52]

Wackenroder, though criticizing Tieck for occasionally letting his characters speak of their emotions instead of acting them (a weakness which Tieck never quite overcame), had high regard for this drama. "O, give up your riming!" he admonished. "Here is your sphere of activity in the field of tragedy, and of gloomy melancholy."[53] In 1798 Wackenroder secretly published it together with *Allamoddin* and Tieck's adaptation of Ben Jonson's *Volpone*.

It is regrettable that Tieck never followed up his two experiments with the modern psychological drama, *Der alte Meiners* and *Der Abschied*, for the latter, at least, proved that he was in advance of Iffland and Kotzebue, then the most popular writers of middle-class dramas. Unfortunately the nervous haste with which he usually improvised, combined with his constitutional lack of concentration, made this impossible. At any rate, compared with his other works of 1791 and 1792, *Der Abschied* stands out as a stroke of genius. Theodor Körner's play *Sühne* is merely a briefer versified version of the work.[54]

The oriental novel *Abdallah*[55] is marked by despair, gloomy fatalism and even more horrors and theatricalness than we find in *Allamoddin*, *Almansur* and the fiction written for Rambach. Though not ordered by the latter, this work, too, owes its inception to a suggestion from him and shows the influence of Schiller's *Die Räuber*. It was published by Nicolai in 1795. A basically noble youth, Abdallah, has become the slave of a devil in human form, who undertakes to ruin him. Abdallah is in love with Zulma, whose father, an oriental despot, is consumed by hatred for Abdallah's father. If Abdallah will kill his own loving parent, decrees the despot, he may have his daughter. Egged on by his fiendish mentor, Abdallah commits the deed. But at the end he is cheated out of his prize. Zulma learns of the patricide and turns away from him in horror. He suffers an agonized death.

No doubt the father-son motif, which was developed also in *Der alte Meiners*, was a heritage of Storm and Stress. In Tieck, as in his models, it is more a fashionable literary device than a living demonstration of the Oedipus complex. We detect only an occasional suggestion of the Expressionist idea of 1920—the protest of the rising generation against a supposed paternal tyranny and oppression. Tieck, always an obedient son, never revolted against his own father's authority. His only revolt was of a literary character—directed against the Rationalism of his parent.

For a while Schmohl asserted a false claim to the authorship of this work. Originally composed as a school exercise, it was later revised and expanded by Tieck. Like his other "dime novels" of this period, it bears testimony to his sadly morbid psychosis and lack of balance during adolescence. What Goethe revealed at the same age in the Weltschmerz of *Werther* and in grim thoughts of suicide, Tieck expressed in penny-a-line "thrillers." But while Goethe's "Weltschmerz" was genuine and possessed universal appeal, his was theatrical, unreal or applicable only to his own case. Later he admitted some of the weaknesses of this type of work. "The young author," he wrote, "to whom his subject seemed very important, wanted to present every single circumstance in its minutest detail. He had not yet learned to be sparing in the use of light and shade and did not know that some things should barely be suggested if the intended effect is to be achieved. Wild, spooky elements, though developed to a gradual climax, prove tiresome in the long run."[56]

We have noted that the great bulk of his early output, which reveals considerable mechanical skill, is cast in dramatic form, while almost all the rest was suggested or assigned by Rambach. This bent for the dramatic type of composition was inborn, no doubt; Tieck, the ingrained actor, always preferred to contemplate life from the point of view of the stage, rather than from that of direct reality. But his flair for the dramatic was strengthened by the circle in which he moved at the time—the artistic social group which had assembled about Reichardt. In it we see the focus of the first Goethe cult in Berlin and one of the cradles of Romanticism. Young Tieck, with his pleasing external appearance and winning way, was the cynosure of all eyes in this company.

He took a prominent part as a playwright and actor in the theatrical performances of the group. As an actor he showed so pronounced a talent for serious as well as comic rôles, and such a flexibility of facial expression and voice, that he seemed destined for the stage. Vehement protests by his father caused him to abandon this plan. This was, no doubt, a tremendous loss for the stage. Possibly he would have become one of the foremost actors of all times—a more distinguished actor than he proved a poet. And yet his histrionic ability never failed to assert itself. He always remained one of the greatest players off the stage.

But he showed no particular talent for music, an important art in Reichardt's home. Later, in the "novelle" *Musikalische Leiden und Freuden* (1822), he humorously described his futile efforts to satisfy his father's desire for him to master the violin, confessing that he acquired only an astonishing facility in cutting grimaces. If he emphasized the musical element so strongly in much of his poetry, it merely shows that he sensed the charm of music and its effect on man's moods, and had a native feeling for melody and harmony.

His passive appreciation of good music, especially Mozart's, was quite sincere. In this connection Köpke relates the following anecdote. In 1789, when Mozart was in Berlin, Tieck attended a performance of *Die Entführung aus dem Serail*. The lad entered the theater some time before the opera was due to begin and saw a strange man in the orchestral pit. He was short, quick, restless and weak-eyed—an insignificant figure in a grey overcoat. He went from one desk to another, and seemed to be hurriedly reading through the music placed upon them. Tieck entered into conversation with him and declared his enthusiastic admiration of Mozart's operas. "Do you really hear Mozart's works often and love them?" asked the stranger. "That is very good of you, young sir." The theater began to fill, and the stranger was called away. His talk had produced a singular effect on Tieck, who made inquiries and learned that it was Mozart himself who had conversed with him.

Tieck also realized the fact, later expressed by Aldous Huxley, that music of all the arts has the least connection with reality. The plays *Die Sommernacht, Das Reh, Die Friedensfeyer*, his early lyrics and the legend *Das Märchen vom Rosstrapp* reveal this belief and the nature of his lyricism, which too often degenerates into riming purely for the sake of melody.

With Reichardt lived his sisters-in-law Marie and Amalie, daughters of the Hamburg pastor Julius Gustav Alberti, who had been a friend of Lessing. They were two of thirteen children. Tieck fell in love with the younger Amalie, who was almost four years his senior, and after a long engagement married her in 1798. But between 1791, when Amalie returned to Hamburg, and 1798 Tieck saw her only at long intervals. In the former year, as indicated, Reichardt left Berlin because he had become *persona non grata* in the court circles. He secured three years' leave of absence with full pay because of the king's personal affection for him. These he spent on his estate at Giebichenstein near Halle and in Italy, France and England. But in 1794 he was discharged from the Prussian service, due to his open sympathy for the French Revolution and to the continual intrigues against him.[57] In 1796 he became inspector in the salt mines at Giebichenstein.

Tieck's strong attachment to his sister Sophie and his love for Amalie are no living factors in his juvenile poetry. Except for the frequent occurrence of the name Sophie, these sentiments play no important part in his early writings. How different is Tieck from Goethe in this respect! Like Goethe he was a subjectivist; but realizing the terrible isolation in which the egoistic ages of Reason and Storm and Stress had left the individual, he struggled toward objectiveness. His whole life and poetic endeavor were devoted to finding a solution to this problem. Consumed by a longing for faith in something besides the ego, he cultivated altruism and sought to overcome his restlessness and skepsis. In the early stages he attempted to fulfil this longing, not by expatiating upon his own love, but by depicting an all-pervading love of mankind, in the conviction that he is happiest who serves his neighbor in anonymity and unselfishness. This lesson is taught with terrible reality in *Siward, Almansur, Abdallah, Das grüne Band* and *Der Abschied*. It occurs again and again in the works of the next ten years.

His lyric poetry, too, is a deliberate excursion into a different sphere, which has no connection with his real world. In its earliest forms it is characterized by imitative, worthless riming. Now he apes the ode of Klopstock, now the dawdling Anacreontic, now the misty world of Ossian, now the minnesong, as revived by Gessner and such poets of the Göttingen "Hain" as Hölty. Tender sentiments and lovely pictures of nature—not his own sufferings—are depicted in melodious rimes, which tease the ear more than the imagination or the mind. With true "Romantic Irony" he himself has poked fun at such jingles in *Hanswurst als Emigrant* (1795).[58]

But despite his striving for objectivity he never quite succeeded in escaping from his corporeal fetters. For his demonism[59] demanded expression and found it in the gruesome horrors and nocturnal moods of *Allamoddin* and of the five narrative works beginning with *Almansur* and ending with *Abdallah*. In *Das Reh* we saw him going a step farther; he spiritualized or demonized nature itself and used it as a sounding board for his imaginative caprices. This is the traditional trend of the young Romantic, which came out more strongly in his subsequent works. It represents a contribution, the importance of which can only be appreciated when we consider what an insignificant, lifeless rôle nature had played in the writings of his predecessors, Goethe alone excepted.

During adolescence Tieck tarried often in the gloomy domain of fear and despair. Though his environment was pleasant and cheerful, though youth and love beckoned alluringly to him, his spirit, dissatisfied with the teachings of books and schools, surrendered to sad broodings and oppressive misgivings. What appealed to him first in Shakespeare, we have found, was "the terrible, horrible, fear-inspiring" (das Fürchterliche, Schauerliche, Angsterregende).[27] Irritability and vague fears made matters worse. It proved fortunate for him that he was attached with a tender affection to a pair of friends psychically better balanced than he—noble Wackenroder and genial Burgsdorff. The former taught him the close relation of architecture, music, poetry and painting, and an unbounded reverence for art and German medievalism. This teaching was destined to become the most important factor in his own creative work and indeed in the development of the arts during the decades immediately following. Eventually Wackenroder also cured him partially of his melancholia. To Burgsdorff Tieck later owed the place of refuge which he and his family called home for almost two decades. He became indebted to him also for the opportunities offered by two extensive journeys through Germany and several foreign lands.

Shall we call young Tieck of 1789-1792 a Rationalist, as most writers have done?[60] His sentimentalism; a love for rhetoric; the differentiation of characters by dialect in the early comedies; the influence of Ossian, Gerstenberg, Klinger, young Schiller and the dramas of knighthood; a preference for modern literature as against the Greek and Latin classics, and an aversion to book-learning in general; an enthusiasm for the French Revolution; a dogged didacticism, which tempted him to dominate such inferior companions as Schmohl; and the use of conventional eighteenth century plots—certainly all these pointed to a rationalistic and Storm and Stress influence. But young Tieck possessed a dual nature. While one side of his soul paid homage to Rationalism and to his inherited Protestant religion, the other sought expression in "Singspiele," "Stimmungslyrik" and the ethereal fairyland of *Die Sommernacht*, *Braddeck*, *Roxane* and *Das Reh*. This phase of his makeup was controlled by a predilection for the exotic, morbid and horrible, by demonism, the imaginative world of Shakespeare's *The Tempest* and the whimsical fabrications of Gozzi, and by an irrationalism which proceeds, contrary to the Rationalist course, from feeling to thought.

Wendriner, in his work *Das romantische Drama*, claims that the influx of fatalistic ideas into Tieck's plays was due to the influence of Goethe, who in *Wilhelm Meister* called for the treatment of fate in drama. It seems clear, though, that Tieck had fatalistic beliefs at least five years before Goethe's novel appeared, for his characteristic fatalism is apparent in his earliest work. Siward seems entirely a victim of some higher power; the action of *Braddeck*, the apotheosis of Shakespeare in *Die Sommernacht*, and the downfall of Abdallah are clearly directed by a force beyond their control. Life is but a dream to Johnson in *Der Schwärmer* and to King Braddeck. *Der Abschied* reflects fatalistic views, though not of a mechanical sort. As yet Tieck's fatalism is not based upon belief in a kind, equitable fate, as in the later works.

His later ironic vein is only hinted at, as in *Der Nebenbuhler*, with its incidental satire against the dramas of Storm and Stress.

LUDWIG TIECK, THE GERMAN ROMANTICIST

To be sure, by 1792 he had not attained any semblance of balance or independence. His works of this period are of historical and psychological, not of esthetic interest. Though they grew partially from his experiences, they are more the result of his readings; they stand in juxtaposition and do not follow in logical, unified sequence. Hardly a single literary type was overlooked by the precocious yet immature young author in his groping. He improvised realistic as well as fantastic plays in the light and serious vein, melodramas, tragedies of knighthood and of the middle class, historical dramas, gruesome novels, pastorals, fables, nature myths, epics and lightsome lyrics. They are constructed not without skill. Their characteristic lesson is altruism. If they may be said to contain a central theme, it is one equally characteristic of him and his cleft personality—a psychic disturbance developed to a gradual climax. This remained one of his favorite motifs.

To agree with Gundolf[61] that all these works, indeed all he wrote before *William Lovell*, are mere trash, would be an unjust, unhistorical and *a posteriori* judgment. In the light of their time at least three possess literary importance or poetic merit, *Die Sommernacht* as a genuine confession, *Das Reh* as the expression of a novel imaginative attitude toward nature, and *Der Abschied* as a skilful bit of dramatic creation.

By and large two main trends of development are discernible. One we may call the Allamoddin-Abdallah line, the second the Sommernacht-Reh course. Only the negligible early comedies, the *Anna Boleyn* experiment, and the two middle-class dramas, *Der alte Meiners* and *Der Abschied*, do not fit into this scheme, but represent intermediary experiments. We are of the opinion that the second trend, with its fairy Romanticism, coupled with certain irrational tendencies and a Romanticism of horror even in the first, shows that from the very start he was settling the issue between Rationalism and Romanticism in favor of the latter. For he was endowed with a distinctly Romantic mind.

CHAPTER THREE

STUDENT DAYS IN HALLE, ERLANGEN AND GÖTTINGEN

WE HAVE considered Tieck's writings through 1792 but must turn back to the early part of that year to trace his physical movements. After Easter he left Berlin to matriculate at the Prussian university of Halle, Bernhardi's alma mater, as a student of theology. Parting from his parents seemed easier than bidding adieu to his beloved Wackenroder. The short trip to Halle was long drawn out. En route he made stops, and even some detours. He tarried in Bülzig with the Schmohls and with his mother's brothers in rustic Coswig. He also stopped in Leipzig, arriving in Halle toward the middle of May. In letters home, some to his father and others to sister Sophie, but all written chiefly for Sophie, he pretended to be happy in Halle and to suffer no want. But to Wackenroder he wrote differently, indicating that neither his studies nor life in Halle appealed to him. But he did not require much money, for through Reichardt's influence he was exempt from the usual fees (Kollegiengelder) and received a municipal stipend.

A typical day in Halle was described in letters to Wackenroder and Sophie.[1] He lived "in a rather narrow street, three flights up, but not very high up, at that." He rose "after four, often not until after five." From six to seven he had empirical psychology with Ludwig Heinrich von Jakob, a Kantian, from seven to eight biblical exegesis with Georg Christian Knapp, a pietist and supernaturalist, from nine to ten logic with Jakob, and from two to three Roman antiquities with Friedrich August Wolf.[2] All these scholars enjoyed good reputations. To be sure, Jakob's publications in the field of economics and finance and his later work as a legislative commissioner in St. Petersburg (1809-) are better known than his philosophical works. His daughter Therese, who married the New York theologian Edward Robinson, is known under her pseudonym Talvj. Knapp is remembered more as the director of the Francke-Stiftung than for his theological writings. Wolf is renowned as a founder of classical philology. His edition of Homer came out in 1784-1785, and the first volume of his famous *Prolegomena ad Homerum* in 1795. That these scholars could offer Tieck no inspiration was his own fault. He was always impatient of the academic pontifications of others, and his interests were too definitely concentrated. More than his studies, the various literary projects which he had brought along, among them *Anna Boleyn*, interested him.

Nowhere do we get a deeper insight into his mind than in the interesting letters he exchanged with Wackenroder. Their affection for each other was all-pervading and surpassed such awakening love for the other sex as would be expected in normal youths of nineteen. As for Tieck, at least part of the reason lies in the tyranny which his sister Sophie exercised over him. Her letters reveal how she struggled to keep his affections. Secretly she sent him money from her own pocket. She was jealous when Bernhardi, not she, received a letter from him. She assured him that he was her only confidante, and spoke constantly of her love for him and of the tears she shed over their separation. She did all she could to nip in the bud any affection for a girl which he might develop. A passing interest in a certain Fräulein Weller of Dahme near Potsdam was promptly quashed by her. She went so far as to open one of the girl's letters to Ludwig and to write her a mendacious note stating that he had enlisted in the army and could not be reached. She tried just as hard to break up his love affair with Amalie Alberti, whom she disliked.

In explaining the relations of Sophie to Ludwig, and incidentally also to Friedrich, it may be helpful to study the sexual inhibitions and abnormalities—the libido—which characterized the three. This takes us into the heart of Freudian psychoanalysis. As often in a family of two boys and a girl of practically equal ages and of abnormal endowment, especially in the case of a girl so self-willed and domineering as Sophie, their infantile sexuality may well have turned very early to the other sex. To psychoanalysts the kernel of the central conflict over infantile sexuality is its incestuous nature, particularly in the girl. But we do not wish to suggest that Sophie developed a "complex" in this direction, nor that through her strong will-power she transmitted it to her brothers. Nor is there firm basis for the belief that this impulse subsequently came to a head, as Varnhagen von Ense in a letter to Bernhardi of February 6, 1807, and Mundt, one of Tieck's Young German foes, later intimated. Because of external inhibitions and internal resistance it remained platonic and subconscious, if indeed it was a factor at all. But many traits in Ludwig's later character—particularly his constant advocacy of morality and his adherence to the religious attitude—may have had their origin in his repudiation of such impulses. Such jealousy as Sophie showed toward Ludwig, of which we shall later see many manifestations, is often a symptom of the same attitude.

But however ardent Sophie's love for Ludwig seemed, all records indicate that no girl could hope to claim the tender attachment to him which he and Wackenroder shared for each other. Friedrich Schlegel's espousal of friendship among men as a part of his doctrine of Romanticism found an adherent in Tieck before he met Schlegel.

To Wackenroder he wrote: "I shall surely never find another who understands me as completely as you, who can overhear my every thought, who are the interpreter of all my sensations, who have so tender and delicate a feeling, whose imagination is so ethereal and chastened."[3] Wackenroder wrote to him: "Were I Alexander, I should feel toward your room as he did toward Pindar's house. It would have to remain an eternal relic, though all Berlin should perish. I shall never regard that room except with emotion, never without being overcome by wistful recollections."[4] And again: "It will soon be twelve o'clock at night. I lay me down to sleep now. I perceive that it is true rapture to write to you. Blessed, blessed is the day which I conclude with the thought of you. It will not leave me even in my sleep. Do you dream of me, too! Are you thinking of me now? Or are you dreaming of me? A most delightful, meltingly soft elegy of Voss begins:

Does my girl think of me?

There is a highly natural, beautiful sentiment in that. Now it has just struck twelve. Good night. Tieck, fly to me, and I shall press the most fiery kiss on your lips. Good night, may heaven be with you! Good night!"[5]

Of course the age of garish sentimentalism, which Germany was just overcoming, is felt in these words. But they convey more than that. They show that the two had a consuming affection for each other, which on Wackenroder's side at least seems almost homosexual and hermaphroditic. Ricarda Huch and others[6] have demonstrated that this was a marked characteristic of the early German Romanticists.

In Halle the terrible realization dawned upon Tieck, as it had upon Goethe in Leipzig, that learning and scholarship held no solution to the riddle of life. Before entering the university he had hoped that such dejection as gave rise to *Almansur* would be dispelled in the bright light of academic knowledge and associations. Now all knowledge seemed futile and irrelevant, while his associations left him lonely and unhappy. His fellow-students were shallow and bent on pleasure alone.

He wrote to Wackenroder: "When I reflect how many hundreds of thousands of things there are, and how many thousands more are daily invented, to pass our time away, it seems to me sometimes as if the whole human race consisted of nothing but children, who know not what to do for boredom. Most of them become scarcely fifty years old, thirty pass with sleeping, eating and drinking, the rest are victims of boredom and worthless occupations; to be sure, I should not, but the feeling often comes irresistibly over me that I must despise such people; yet this contempt soon yields to pity."[7]

And in another place: "That I have no one here with whom and in whom I really live, you will believe. I have already described Schmohl [his room-mate] to you, he always remains the same—petty, pedantic and cold; withal he is not free from affectation, under given conditions he wishes to play the bel-esprit, the sentimentalist, the politician and a hundred other rôles, all of which are equally unbecoming to him. He goes so far as to make himself ridiculous, yet—and for me this is the most intolerable—he is vainer than a girl, at least vainer than we could forgive our sweethearts for being. A pimple in his face can occupy him over an hour, he is apt to make a complete change of garb three to four times a day. He is never happier than when he can be dressing up.—And Bothe!—You haven't the faintest idea, you can and will not believe me, you will take it as an eruption of my bad temper, but Bothe is still more vain than Schmohl."[8]

Another Berlin friend in Halle, whom he admired more than he did the others because he was wealthy, influential and daring, but who led too fast a life for him, was Burgsdorff. With reckless abandon the latter had plunged into the gayest student activities, seduced by another strong-willed epicurean comrade named Wiesel. Wiesel's philosophy taught him that divine power is best manifested on earth by reeling through life in a round of sensual pleasures. Tieck later pictured him as the devilish seducer in the novel *William Lovell*.

Annoyed by loneliness and trivial vexations, unnerved by excessive and ill-advised reading, plagued by melancholia and frequent physical indisposition, Tieck often approached a state of insanity. Moments of unconsciousness alternated with fits of terror and dream-visions, such as had befallen him at home. The Kantian philosophy prevailing in Halle offered him no solace, and the society at the home of Reichardt, who now lived on his country estate at Giebichenstein near Halle, where even the professors were occasional guests, no longer satisfied his craving for companionship.

To Wackenroder he described a memorable night in Halle. On June 3, the birthday of Reichardt's wife, he attended a ball at their house. At eleven he started for home with Bothe, Schmohl and another friend, bored and dejected by the affectation and vanity of the guests, no less than by the small talk of his companions. "It was a divine evening, the moon shone so brightly, the air was so clear and the sky so blue. I accompanied my companions mechanically to the city gate and then turned back, without being observed by them and without speaking a word. I sought from nature requital for the lost hours and received it, I was really happy for once. I walked alongside gardens, where the balsamic fragrance of a thousand flowers greeted me. One by one the lights went out in the houses, the dogs barked behind me everywhere. I passed a water mill whose foaming falls swelled like flames in the light of the moon, everything was so beautiful, so full of adventure. I often sat down to scan the lovely region. The Saale glistened before me like a big lake, a thousand tiny stars quivered on her unsteady surface, a gentle golden haze hovered over everything, the billows of the Saale echoed in the lovely night like the steps of a wanderer, now like the notes of a harp, now like the rowing of a skiff. O, how often did I think of you, how often did I wish you at my side. At last I ascended the cliffs, the most charming place in Giebichenstein. How romantic everything lay before me, it seemed as though I were living in the most distant past; the ruins of the knightly castle looked over to me so solemnly; the cliffs opposite, the cliffs above me, the swaying trees, the barking of the dogs—everything was so awe-inspiring, everything attuned my phantasy to so pure and high a pitch. Often I sat half in dreams, half awake, limning sweet dreams with one eye, gazing into the beautiful region with the other. The setting of the moon is always touching to me, he sinks so calmly, so unpretentiously, to make room for one greater than himself. . . . The breaking of day is always so fearful to me, so full of expectation, all nature seems on edge. . . . The morning red glowed over the whole horizon,—in short this night belongs to the most delightful hours of my life, it will be unforgettable; I have here learned much and felt much that I did not know and had never felt before."[9]

More than sentimentalism and emotionalism, young Tieck's Romantic mold of mind is clearly outlined in this passage. His fondness for the moon, the desire to find compensation in nature for pleasures otherwise denied, the picture of the mill, the lonely night, the stars, the simile of the waves and the wanderer's steps, the longing for a true friend, the use of the word "romantic," the wish to be transported into a distant past, the nocturnal picture of the castle ruins, the awe-inspiring atmosphere, the fluctuation between a dream-state and a state of consciousness, and finally the subconscious fear of daybreak—these are elements which give the passage a truly Romantic stamp.[10]

He also gratified his delight in the gruesome and horrible by voracious reading of cheap, bloodcurdling novels. Once the two-volume "thriller" of Grosse, *Der Genius*, fell into his hands, and he decided to read the whole work aloud, at one sitting, to Schmohl and another friend. He started at four in the afternoon. By nine he had finished volume one. Though the two listeners began nodding at twelve, he continued with ever growing frenzy. It was after two in the morning when he finally finished. He sank back, physically and mentally exhausted. Then the scenes of the novel began to reenact themselves before his mind's eye, and, still crouched in his chair, he fell into a trance. Arising he had delightful visions—rose-colored pictures and blue butterflies—, and heard sweet notes and snatches of song. Then something dreadful seemed to happen. An earthquake shattered all this beauty and hurled him into an endless blackness of flitting shadows. He was wafted through space in an ethereal chariot, felt his hair standing on end, and screamed for help. Dashing into the little bedchamber, where the two friends were now sleeping, he found that it had suddenly become a huge hall. A wild impulse prompted him to strike his comrades down with a sword.

"For a few seconds I was actually insane," he wrote to Wackenroder. "Now a fugitive idea returned, I rushed on to seize the rein again. The chariot stopped. 'For God's sake, I am losing my mind!' I cried and slumped down half unconscious. After a little struggle everything reassumed its natural outlines and I found myself again. I was exhausted. My pulse beats were audible. My imagination was still at work . . . the sight of anything white seemed particularly horrible to me. . . . All tired out I lay on the bed at last. . . . Over an hour I spent in a state bordering on physical helplessness, while all my imaginative powers were feverishly at work. When I shut my eyes I felt as though I were swimming in a stream, as though my head were dropping off and floating backwards, my body forward—a sensation I had never had before. When I opened my eyes I seemed to be lying in a spacious vault, three caskets side by side. Clearly I discerned the white, shimmering bones, everything expanded into fearful length, all my limbs had grown alien to me, and I shuddered when I felt for my face. . . . Several times I fell asleep, but with such convulsive twitching that I was dreadfully tossed upward. At last sleep came, and when I awoke I was quite exhausted. The next day I could not go out and was scarcely able to move from one chair to another."[11]

Such were the youthful excesses of this introvert, which took the place of the average boy's wild oats. Wackenroder was horrified by them. His letters are full of tender admonitions and entreaties.

In such a mood the first draft of *William Lovell* was conceived and the oriental story *Abdallah* completed. Gloomy despair and grievous excesses mark them both. In such a mood, too, the poem "Melancholie"[12] of 1793 was written, with its despairing fatalistic outlook:

> Then Sorrow spoke when came the witching hour:
> Thou art devoted to distress,
> A dupe of fate's hard-heartedness,
> The bows are bent and every single hour
> New bloody wounds on thee will cruelly shower.*

All his life he was subject to hallucinations. One day in 1798, as he was walking from Berlin toward Tegel, he suddenly spied an inn along the roadside, only to find that it was a vision. So, too, tarrying in a house in which a man whom he had never met had recently died, he was confronted by his ghost. Describing the specter to friends of the deceased, he was surprised that its appearance resembled the latter in the minutest detail.

On a walking tour through the Harz in June and July, 1792, the young student found temporary surcease from his morbid broodings. He has not left us such a classical account of the journey as Heine wrote of his own Harz tour thirty years later, but the grand spectacle of the sunrise rent asunder both the physical haze on the hills and the veil of fog which beclouded his mind. A feeling of the certain proximity of God and the consciousness of supreme bliss pervaded him. As an old man he declared that never again did he experience such a revelation.[13]

By autumn he had grown tired of Halle, and upon the advice and example of Burgsdorff decided to abandon the Friedrichs-Universität in favor of Georgia Augusta at Göttingen in the province of Hanover, for almost eighty years allied with the English crown in a personal union. On November 5 he arrived by stagecoach, after almost yielding to the invitation of an English fellow-passenger, who wanted Tieck to accompany him to England.[14] At Göttingen, where he stayed, with only brief interruptions, until the spring of 1794, he was much happier because he felt freer to follow his favorite pursuits, the study of literature, especially English literature, and creative writing. He attended only courses in literature, philosophy and art and, though matriculated as a student of theology, dropped theology altogether.

---

*Da sprach der Gram in banger Geisterstunde:
Du bist zu Qualen eingeweiht,
Ein Ziel des Schicksals Grausamkeit,
Die Bogen sind gespannt, und jede Stunde
Schlägt grausam dir stets neue blut'ge Wunde.

LUDWIG TIECK, THE GERMAN ROMANTICIST

With his hack work he had earned some money and, as he wrote his sister, now dined "only with counts and gentlemen" (lauter Grafen und Herren), enjoyed his Rhenish wine and replenished his sparse wardrobe. Yet this comparatively high living served merely to strengthen his democratic convictions; the time would come, he prophesied to Sophie, when empty compliments must be abolished and only merit esteemed, and every fool or villain, though he grace a throne, despised.

His creed, he wrote to Sophie, in the autumn of 1793, was "to be plain but not simple-minded, to develop all my powers for the common good, and to become nobler and better every day." To be sure, though happy in Göttingen and proud of his social standing as a university student, he lived in comparative solitude there, as he had in Halle. He relates in *Phantasus* that he felt fortunate when he could go off somewhere by himself, on foot or on horseback, since he counted himself "just as little a member of the guild of students as an ally of the trades of bourgeois life."[15]

His professors at Göttingen were the noted classical philologist Christian Gottlob Heyne, whose lectures on Horace first seemed to him inspired; the poet Gottfried August Bürger, famed for his ballad *Lenore* (Tieck met him in February, 1793), who had also been the teacher of A. W. Schlegel; and the Italo-German art-historian Johann Dominik Fiorillo. Here, too, Tieck had the advantage of meeting Georg Christoph Lichtenberg, satirist and physicist in one, who had been twice in England and was now at work upon his *Ausführliche Erklärung der Hogarthschen Kupferstiche*.

The rich Göttingen library afforded Tieck opportunity to satisfy his enormous craving as a reader. The stacks were particularly rich in Elizabethan literature—his favorite field—, and so he set to work reading all of Shakespeare in English for the first time. As we have seen, he had before studied his plays diligently in German and had committed much of them to memory. Now he found a chance to study the commentators, too, among them Johnson, Steevens, Hanmer, Warburton, Home, Malone and William Richardson. He found them "blind" and unappreciative of Shakespeare's greatest virtues.[16] This supercilious attitude was never abandoned. "I now live and breathe Shakespeare," he wrote to Wackenroder in November 1792. "I have never studied him as zealously as now, in a week I copied the whole *Tempest* and am now bringing together a quantity of variant readings and notes; I am working my way deeper into his language, too, and have not yet abandoned my crotchets about him. Recently I also read *Romeo, Hamlet* and

Othello in English, the translation really gives one no true conception of Shakespeare at all."[17]

His love for Shakespeare soon led him also to other Elizabethans, especially Ben Jonson, Beaumont and Fletcher, Massinger and Chapman, and to English writers of the seventeenth and eighteenth centuries.

At this early date he conceived the plan of a great life-work on Shakespeare, with emphasis upon the historical predications of his development. He realized that his own contemporaries, in England as well as in Germany, were wrong in holding that Shakespeare, uninfluenced by any external force, had drawn directly from the wellsprings of nature and genius. In the richly developed intellectual life of the Elizabethan age and in the antecedent perfection of dramatic form and of the art of acting in England, he was the first German to see the prerequisites for Shakespeare's craft. To him the great master did not occupy his lofty pinnacle alone. While he was securely ensconced upon the summit of the British Parnassus, others, among them Ben Jonson, were firmly enough stationed not quite at the top, but at considerable elevations. Tieck deserves credit for being the first German critic to propagate these views. The knowledge of Elizabethan literature was indeed meagre in Germany before his time. In the seventeenth and eighteenth centuries the anthologies of Morhof, Zedler, Jöcher, Bodmer, J. H. Schlegel and Schmid had appeared, to be sure. Lessing, we know, was familiar with Beaumont and Fletcher, as well as with Jonson. But since Herder and Storm and Stress, attention had been centered upon the "God-sent genius" Shakespeare. Even Goethe showed little appreciation for the other Elizabethans, and when Tieck entered the lists the only acceptable translation of a pre-Shakespearean play was Gerstenberg's version of *The Maid's Tragedy*.[18]

Probably in 1794 the first draft of Tieck's never completed *Buch über Shakespeare* was written, consisting of notes on twenty-one plays, in addition to casual comments. This earliest draft comprises over three-fourths of the whole as posthumously published by Henry Lüdeke in 1920.[19] Five other fragments dating between 1796 and 1821, and two brief excursuses combined therewith, constitute all that remains of Tieck's great life project. Incidentally the first draft indicates not only that at the time of writing he was familiar with the English commentators; it also shows that superior air to most of their work which has been mentioned. Later applied also to more recent British critics, for instance Drake and Dyce, it became marked as he grew older and did not fail to draw caustic rejoinders. In his imaginative writings he usually sought to overcome his egocentric bent; in his critical writings he was always an irrepressible subjectivist.[20]

The numerous references to English authors in this first draft serve to show the breadth of his early interest and reading in English literature. There are allusions to writers from Chaucer down to Richardson. As for his criticism here, it is that of the Rationalist school and reveals more interest in practical stage craftsmanship than in theory.

We have noted his interest in Ben Jonson. While he saw in Shakespeare a child of his time but withal a mighty genius everywhere blazing his own trail to achieve the highest effects, he found a cool, observing but classically schooled intellect at work in the satirical comedies of Ben Jonson. In many respects Tieck was akin to Jonson. They had both been reared in a metropolis and had early developed a zest for the theater. With solid force, fulness and power, and with grand acidity, Jonson, a second cousin of that master scoffer Aristophanes, pictured the world in cosmic satires, thus overcoming the melancholia which had once all but driven him, as it was now driving Tieck, to distraction.

In 1793 he adapted the fable of one of Jonson's satires, *Volpone*, and wrote a more or less original play around it. He compressed the five acts of the original into three, eliminated all episodic material, established unity of place, and toned down the pitch so that it would blend better with the decorous and morally more pusillanimous spirit of his time. Where Jonson indulged in political satire, he, who heartily shared the slight interest of his educated contemporaries in public affairs, introduced literary satire. Though the stage direction speaks of a "foreign seaport town," he transplanted the scene to Germany in 1793. Tieck's friends offered the play to the actor Schröder in Hamburg, who rejected it. Under the title *Ein Schurke über den andern, oder die Fuchsprelle*[21] the play was published in 1798 by Wackenroder, together with *Allamoddin* and *Der Abschied*. A revised edition, called *Herr von Fuchs*, appeared in Volume XII of Tieck's *Schriften* (1829). The work is significant as the first of his satires on his own times. In the figure of a traveloguist we see his earliest takeoff on the publisher Nicolai. The play is quite as characteristic of its age and its adapter as is Stefan Zweig's recent adaptation. Possibly Zola knew Tieck's work when he wrote *Les Héritiers Rabourdin*.[22]

With *Herr von Fuchs* Tieck by no means wrote *finis* to his interest in Jonson. In 1800 his literal translation of *Epicoene*[23] appeared, and a year later he started an *Anti-Faust*, which was to bear the impress of *The Devil is an Ass*. Moreover, in practically all his satirical writings during the last years of the century, *Die Teegesellschaft* and *Ein Prolog* (1796),

Der gestiefelte Kater and *Die verkehrte Welt* (1797), *Prinz Zerbino* (1798) and *Der Autor* (1800), he borrowed technical peculiarities from Jonson. *Ein Prolog* reminds of the prolog in *Every Man in his Humour*.[24] Not until after he had been fully exposed to the influence of the Schlegels did he veer away from Jonson. As a scholar and critic, too, he was attracted to the English realist. At an early age he transcribed all the notes of the seven-volume Whalley edition; later made a critical abstract of Gifford's *Memoirs of Ben Jonson*; copied almost all of Gifford's notes, with many sagacious comments of his own, into his personal copy of the folio edition; and finally transferred a part of these notes into the copy of the Gifford edition which he purchased in 1817.[25] Full credit is due him as the earliest German student and popularizer of Jonson.

Simultaneously with *Das Buch über Shakespeare* he planned a work on the earlier English drama and translations or adaptations of numerous Elizabethan plays. Besides, from 1794 on he lectured to his friends on Shakespeare.

Through his reading of Massinger he was inspired to take up again the torso of his tragedy on *Anna Boleyn*, without finishing it, however. John Webster's play *The White Devil* (1612) first brought to his attention the subject matter of *Vittoria Accorombona*, which shaped itself half a century later into his most grandiose novel. In Göttingen he also began *William Lovell* and completed *Abdallah*, *Adalbert und Emma* and *Der Abschied*.

During his first year as a student Wackenroder was his confidant and adviser, doing all he could by letter to keep his friend on the path of moderation. He had not been permitted to accompany Tieck to Halle or Göttingen. At the request of his father, a privy councillor and the chief city solicitor of Berlin, he spent the twelvemonth after graduation from the "Gymnasium" at home taking private instruction in early German literature from Erduin Julius Koch, a noted authority, who published the first complete history of German literature in 1791-1795. Koch instilled in his pupil love for the spirit of medieval German literature, for which the Rationalists had felt only contempt. And Wackenroder implanted his enthusiasm in Tieck.

After Easter, 1793, Wackenroder was finally permitted to enter the university to study law. His father sent him not to Göttingen, however, but to Erlangen in Central Franconia. This was a logical step for a good Prussian official to take, for in 1791 the city of Erlangen had come into the possession of Prussia. Early in May Tieck returned to Berlin to join his friend and to accompany him for a while to Erlangen. He stayed at home for two weeks, spending much of his time with Sophie, who was now more jealous of her brother's affection than ever before and who had herself seriously begun to take up writing. On May 17 he and Wackenroder set out, travelling by way of Jena and Weimar, where they missed Schiller, Goethe and Herder.[26] But they met the Kantian philosopher Reinhold and gifted, liberal-minded Sophie Mereau, who later married Clemens Brentano. Slowly they continued their journey through Franconia, the classical home of ancient knighthood and of "bustling, lively Franconians in their romantic, diversified environment,"[27] as Tieck described them in *Phantasus*. They traversed it in every direction, Wackenroder proving an inspiring companion and *cicerone*. The experiences of this excursion remained as pleasant memories for the rest of Tieck's life. His record of the journey is found in two long letters to Bernhardi and Sophie.[28] Wackenroder has left an even fuller account in two lengthy letters to his parents.[29]

The old city of Nürnberg made a particularly deep impression upon Tieck. In the words of his later admirer, Count Schack:

> Da tat das alte Nürnberg seine Tore
> Ihm auf, und das Entzücken, o! wer nennt's,
> Als vor ihm mit des Bildwerks Blütenflore
> Emporstieg das Portal von St. Lorenz.[30]

In its old houses and churches the atmosphere of the early sixteenth century—the age of Dürer and Sachs—seemed still to live on. As the young student Goethe saw the glory of medieval Germany reflected in the Gothic cathedral of Strassburg, so Tieck found manifold signs of an illustrious past in the architecture of Nürnberg. Five years after, in *Sternbald*, he revelled in the beauties of the old city. In *Phantasus* a generation later he exclaimed: "How I enjoyed strolling through the crooked little streets, across the bridges and squares, where artificial fountains, forms of every kind reminded me of a delightful period of Germany; yes, when the houses were still adorned on the outside with portraits of giants and old German heroes."[31] And into *Der junge Tischlermeister*, finished a generation after *Phantasus*, he again wove tender recollections of Nürnberg.

The conviction of the Rationalists that the German works of art of the thirteenth to sixteenth century were merely manifestations of a limited, coarse mentality found no echo in Tieck and Wackenroder. With intelligent enthusiasm and fervent, sensitive penetration, Wackenroder got at the very heart of those artistic products of naïve faith, simplicity and deep feeling. A mysterious foreboding revealed to him the transcen-

dental nature of the old monuments. His eye feasted upon the splendor
of the Catholic service which they witnessed in Bamberg. He was en-
raptured by the portrait of the Madonna in Pommersfelden, which at
that time was still mistaken for the work of Raphael.

The experiences of the two young students upon this tour should
not be underestimated. The impressions they gained, coupled with what
Wackenroder had learned from Koch and quickly communicated to Tieck,
led directly to that interest in the German Middle Ages, in painting and
even in music which later became a part of Romanticism. Franconia
taught them to feel old German art as a personal experience worthy of
being opposed to classical art. Nürnberg established and fortified their
Romanticism.

In *Der Gefangene, Anna Boleyn* and *Allamoddin* Tieck had not taken
a friendly attitude toward Catholicism. But on the trip to Erlangen he
saw his first monks and wrote to Sophie: "The monasteries should not
by any means be stamped out; here he who rejects the world or whom
the world rejects, finds a safe, holy place of refuge."[32] This parallels
what he expressed to one of his Berlin teachers several years before: "It
was after all a fine custom of the Middle Ages that one could flee from
the confusing noise of the world. One entered a monastery and was free
of all the world's cares. What profound peace it must afford to be able
to devote one's whole life to a single great thought, and to sink into it
all other thoughts which trouble men a thousandfold. I wish we had our
monasteries, too."[33]

This partiality for life behind cloistered walls did not mean, however,
that he subscribed wholly to the activities and customs of the Roman
Catholic Church in his time. He wrote to his sister about a Catholic
service which he attended: "It aroused strange feelings to see a multitude
of wretched folk, who from force of custom or opinion (words fail me,
even blind instinct is really too strong in this connection) moved their
bodies and limbs mechanically in empty ceremonies as if they were
puppets on strings. And yet it seems to me very hard to draw the line
exactly between a meaningless and a significant ceremony—the Catholic ceremony really has much that is beautiful and soul-inspiring—it
might exercise a powerful effect even upon educated minds—, but now
(like all our religion) it suppresses all the forces of the soul and all
sublimity, accustoms men to servitude and is the hateful handmaid to
the despotism of our constitutions."[32]

These words throw light upon his real attitude toward Catholicism.
He admired the opportunities of refuge which its cloisters afforded—to
an introvert and ascetic like him they seemed particularly alluring—,

he appreciated the esthetic appeal of its medieval forms of legend, miracle and art, but he cared nothing for its contemporary theological, moral and political aspects. If we conceive religion as a quadrilateral pyramid, one side of which is cult, the second theology, the third ethics and the fourth mystic emotion, we may say that he was interested in the esthetic forms of the first side and in the sensual appeal of the fourth. He looked at religion, as he did at everything else, from the point of view of a poet.

To Wackenroder faith now loomed as the great force which had kindled the spark of life in the glorious medieval works of art. Appreciation for art blended with pious devotion, and warm-hearted saintly women like Mary, Cecilia and Ottilia began to assume more importance than the cold marmoreal Aphrodites and Dianas of the Greeks. Dürer's representations of Christ and Raphael's madonnas stood out as the pinnacle of all art.

Soon Tieck began to see with Wackenroder's eyes. For he, too, was consumed by an unnamed yearning, which grew out of dissatisfaction with his jejune environment in Berlin. Thus far this discontent had found expression only in the guise of satire; now at last he was slowly developing a set of positive opinions which filled a vacant place in his soul and tended to dispel despair and melancholy.

But with his contemplative enjoyment of the glories of the Middle Ages young Tieck, who later became more of an ascetic, retained at least a bookish interest in the present. His craving for deeds of grand emprise and for new ideals surcharged with ardent emotion found gratification in the early revolutionary developments in France. We have noted his confession of democratic faith and of sympathy with the Revolution. Liberty, brotherhood and equality were catchwords that appealed particularly to his youthful imagination. But soon the bloody outrages of the French devotees of liberty opened his eyes, and he realized that they were only a tribe of pygmies. Thereafter he remained, except in some of his satires, a defender of monarchy and moderate liberalism. The older he grew, the more conservative did he become.

The martial preparations of the imperial army against the French revolutionary hosts cast their shadows over Franconia, too. As he journeyed across the country he chanced to discover a large encampment of imperial troops near Fürth. With much humor he recalled in *Phantasus*[34] how a company of itinerant actors tried to stage an open-air performance of a military play against this background, how the rabble interrupted the undertaking, and how he himself was almost court-martialled for his part in the ensuing free-for-all encounter.

The sight of one of the gloomy castle ruins near Berneck in the Fichtelgebirge had a powerful effect upon him—

> Berneck, die Burg, wo halbvermorschte Särge
> Von Mord noch künden, stieg wie ein Gespenst
> Durchs Dunkel auf. . . .[30]

Count Schack sings in his elegy on Tieck. The natural scenery, Tieck later confessed, made "an almost tragic impression" (einen fast tragischen Eindruck)[35] upon him. The cliffs and dark valleys reminded him of the days when knighthood was in flower. In this mood he sketched a five-act tragedy, *Karl von Berneck*, around an idea which he had previously conceived. It was to be a pendant to *Abdallah*. He completed and rewrote it in 1795. The theme is that of the murder of a mother and a brother, a variation of the story of the house of Atreus as related by the ancient Greek dramatists. Tieck's modern *Orestes* (Wackenroder once referred to the play as "Orest in Ritterzeiten")[36] is Karl von Berneck, a gloomy, melancholy youth (also akin to Hamlet), who slays his unchaste Clytemnestra-like mother, Mathilde, and her lover. Karl has a brother, Reinhard, and both love the same girl, Adelheid. Maddened by jealousy, Reinhard is on the point of murdering Karl, when a sudden change of heart, brought about by fraternal affection, prompts him to renounce the girl in favor of his brother. But unhappily an ancient curse hovers over the Bernecks. One of their ancestors had been a fratricide, who is doomed to stalk as a restless death-bringing ghost until some descendant, inflamed with love, shall kill his own loving brother. To bring about this terrible consummation, the ghost thwarts the union of Adelheid and Karl. The latter, confronted by his mother's ghost and tortured by the consciousness of his guilt as a matricide, begs Reinhard to kill him. Reinhard, embracing him, stabs him to death with the ancestral sword, and to atone for his crime turns monk.

The artificiality of *Karl von Berneck* produces an almost comic effect. Clearly the "morning mist"[37] has not yet lifted from the young writer's mind. Later he confessed that "the unique idea of the ending does not take full possession of one's soul because the passion is too feeble" (der originelle Gedanke des Schlusses bemächtigt sich nicht der Seele ganz, weil das Leidenschaftliche zu schwach ist).[35] Like the tale *Abdallah*, the play is little more than a deliberate endeavor to pander to popular delight in the horrible. As an attempt to grip the reader and mirror his own sufferings, it is a failure. Tieck also stated, some thirty-six years later, that it represented the first attempt in Germany to introduce fate in this manner. The family curse which wreaks vengeance on innocent

descendants for an ancient crime; a blind force which nullifies all freedom of action and will; and the fatal weapon which must serve a second
time as the instrument of death were used for the first time as the trappings of a tragic drama which, superficially considered, seems to resemble
the tragedy of the ancients. But the heart of the latter is missing here,
for the action is not inevitable and leaves no awe-inspiring impression.
It is an outgrowth of morose superstition, not of a clarified philosophy
of life. In this sense *Karl von Berneck*, much more than *Der Abschied*,
became one of the forerunners of the German "fate tragedy" of Zacharias Werner and Adolf Müllner, though we have no evidence that it
influenced them. Indeed, like Grillparzer's *Die Ahnfrau* it represents
an advanced type of "fate tragedy" because it personifies fate.[88]

In his subsequent discussion of the work Tieck said that his chief idea
was love as a mediating power; fate proves mightier, none the less the
brothers are in the end reconciled in love. Tieck claimed, too, that he
realized from the start the difference between this fate and that of Greek
tragedy. He purposely set about to substitute spookiness for spirituality.

Besides anticipating the technique of the "fate tragedy," the play
develops his typical motif of a psychic disturbance and the Tieckean
idea of self-negating love. It is significant, too, in introducing old popular beliefs and elements from the world of the German folk legends.
The first draft, extant in part in Tieck's Berlin "Nachlass,"[39] corresponds
roughly in content to Act IV of the finished play. But it is inferior to the
latter. All the events constituting the tragedy have occurred before the
curtain rises, and the talk which ensues does not leave a clear picture.

Soon after its completion a company of actors came near producing
it; only his own apathy and failure to push the plan frustrated the
performance.[85] We have already indicated that *Karl von Berneck* (published in 1797 in the *Volksmährchen*) is far inferior to *Der Abschied*.
The strictures of Tieck against the latter, noted in the previous chapter,
are more applicable to the former.

Little need be said about Tieck's studies in Erlangen. He found no
congenial professors or interesting lectures. According to the *Register
zur Matrikel der Universität Erlangen* published by Karl Wagner in
1918, Tieck and Wackenroder matriculated on May 2, the former in
theology, the latter in jurisprudence. This date, several weeks before
their actual arrival in Erlangen, is probably explained by the fact that
they had been previously registered.

In October Tieck went back to Göttingen with Wackenroder and
Burgsdorff, who had joined the pair. Their plan to return by way of
the Rhine could not be carried out because Burgsdorff, careless as he

was, gambled away their joint travelling funds. Nor did Tieck go home to Berlin for another visit, despite the urging of his sister. He now resumed his studies of Shakespeare and the Elizabethan age. The immediate result of these lucubrations was a complete German prose version of *The Tempest*, done in two days[40] and adapted for the contemporary stage. In it the incipient young Romanticist tried to go Shakespeare one better by elaborating the lyric and musical elements in the play, which at this point in his development was his favorite. Nicolai published the adaptation in 1796, with the creditable essay *Shakespeares Behandlung des Wunderbaren* as a preface. On the title page Tieck's name was mentioned for the first time as an author.

It is interesting to note the similarity, even in title, of his introductory paper on the marvellous and Bodmer's treatise on Milton of 1740. Tieck discusses very illuminatingly the problem how a dramatist should treat the supernatural. Writing in Lessing's manner, he shows a clear recognition of the distinction between Shakespeare's technique in tragedy and that which he employs in comedy. He deals first with comedy and finds that Shakespeare creates an illusion of supernaturalism by restricting the action in such cases to a supernatural milieu, excluding the world of realities; by presenting a variety of characters and interests and never allowing the emotional tension to grow extreme, and by creating diversion through humor and music. In tragedy, on the other hand, the world of spirits is introduced only incidentally as a climax to a tragic effect. In comedy as well as tragedy, the introduction of supernatural elements must be well prepared. Finally, a natural symbolic explanation for these elements should always be possible.

On February 23, 1794, Tieck had submitted this essay to the Leipzig publisher G. J. Göschen for the *Thalia*,[41] which was edited by Schiller. Since the latter rejected it, Tieck was free to use it as an introduction to the Nicolai edition of his version of *The Tempest*.

About the same time he wrote an essay on the Boydell Shakespeare gallery, *Über die Kupferstiche nach der Shakespeare-Galerie in London*. The views of his Göttingen professors Fiorillo and Heyne are reflected in its pages. Through the good offices of Heyne it was published in Nicolai's *Bibliothek der schönen Wissenschaften* in 1795. Borne by the conviction that the best scenes were missed or bungled by the illustrators, it shows Tieck's intuitive appreciation of Shakespeare's native power, an ability to sense the most dramatic situations in his plays, and his characteristic supercilious attitude toward latter-day British criticism of Shakespeare.[42]

He also started a poetic translation of *The Tempest* in 1794.[43] It was his first attempt at verse translation but, so far as it goes, can hardly be called a success. He is inexact in his rendering of the content and only approximates the form of the original. His verse is not much more than a sort of rhythmic prose.

Meanwhile Wackenroder was in the Göttingen library making notes and abstracts for Koch on old German manuscripts. Thus he and through him Tieck became better acquainted with and more appreciative of the German minnesingers, for whom Tieck had expressed his contempt some time before. But Tieck's interest in this field was destined to remain dormant for almost a decade. Other occupations engaged his attention.

THE YOUNG PROFESSIONAL WRITER

THE last letter which Tieck wrote to Sophie from Göttingen is dated May 6, 1794.[1] It is full of promises to return home soon. But like similar promises, this one was broken. Instead of heading for Berlin, he made his way with Wackenroder to Hamburg to visit the Albertis, particularly Amalie, whom he had not seen for several years. He also paid his respects to Klopstock, whose personal appearance and old-fashioned opinions were a disappointment, and to the revered actor and playwright F. L. Schröder. His visit to the latter disturbed Wackenroder, for he feared that his friend was once more planning to embark upon a stage career.

On the way to Hamburg the friends stopped to inspect the libraries at Braunschweig and Wolfenbüttel. In the former city Tieck looked up the aged poet and translator Johann Arnold Ebert, friend of Klopstock, contributor to the *Bremer Beyträge* and translator of Young's *Night Thoughts*. He also met the literary historian Johann Joachim Eschenburg, famed for his prose translation and commentary of Shakespeare's plays (1775-1782), a work which had afforded Tieck not only a gateway to the English poet but even his means of learning English. Both Ebert and Eschenburg were professors at the Carolinum and ranked among the foremost German expositors of English literature.

They were much impressed by Tieck's enthusiasm for Shakespeare and Elizabethan literature, and by his extensive first-hand knowledge in this field. His adaptation of *The Tempest* and the tone of his essay on the Boydell gallery also pleased them. Through Eschenburg he secured a copy of the fourth Shakespeare folio of 1685. Presently Ebert and Eschenburg recommended him to the veteran Berlin publisher, Christoph Friedrich Nicolai. This man, one of the most maligned figures in German literature, was born in Berlin in 1733 and had taken up the publishing business early in life. But his interest in books extended beyond their printing, binding and sale. A voracious reader, he soon acquired an estimable fund of information and some very positive opinions, especially about English literature. He defended Milton and attacked Gottsched for depreciating the British writers. Joining forces with Lessing and Moses Mendelssohn, he published the important *Bibliothek der schönen Wissenschaften* (in which one of Tieck's Shakespeare articles appeared) and the epoch-making *Briefe, die neueste Litteratur betreffend*. Later he got out the *Allgemeine Deutsche Bibliothek*. Through his reviews in the latter, which took on more and more the Rationalistic tone of the Enlightenment and hammered away at mysticism and Jesuitism, finally turning also against Storm and Stress, Goethe and Schiller and Kant's philosophy, Nicolai incurred the undying hostility of very influential circles. His novels and other publications served only to strengthen this antagonism. Growing out of his Rationalism and literalism, it overlooked the fact that he was a man of principles and a courageous fighter against odds; that he stands out as one of the first Germans to recognize the advantages of English literature; and that he successfully combated superstition, bigotry, sham mysticism and excessive sentimentality.[2]

When Tieck met Nicolai at Berlin in 1794, the latter was sixty-one and enjoyed a reputation as the all-powerful leader of the forces of Enlightenment in Germany. But, though Nicolai had grown too old to realize it, these forces were now moribund, even in Berlin; in 1796 Goethe and Schiller attacked him severely in their *Xenien*. He, too, was impressed by Tieck and volunteered not only to take him into his employ as a hack writer but to publish *Abdallah* and other works. Since Tieck had not prepared for any practical occupation at the university and since his family would not hear of his becoming a thespian, he gladly accepted the offer of Nicolai, who even advanced him money. It now became his ambition to enter that calling which was not yet recognized as one of the professions, but occupied the borderland between them and mere avocations. He wanted to become a professional writer.

When Frederick William II ascended the Prussian throne after the death of Frederick the Great (1786), it was expected that militarism would make way for the cultivation of the humanities, the arts and the amenities of life. But the new king soon showed that he was bent chiefly on pleasure and self-satisfaction. Little wonder that morality, already undermined in the reign of francophile Old Fritz, suffered still more by the example of the new ruler. While the former had at least inculcated in his subjects a sense of duty and of justice, the latter set a bad example with his host of favorites and mistresses. The popular philosophy of the Enlightenment represented by Mendelssohn, Garve, Engel and Nicolai could neither create new ideals nor stem the tide of materialism, licentiousness and frivolity. At the same time the secret society of the Rosicrucians and many spurious forms of free masonry gave an impetus to mystification, hypocrisy and superstition.

The popular literature reflected the social evils of the day. Cheap novels of crime still had the strongest appeal, but they were being hard pressed by the tales of contemporary high society, with their sentimentality, immorality and wanton humor.

When Tieck sold his services to Nicolai he, too, was expected to conform to this style of writing. It seems like irony that the young author of *Die Sommernacht*, who was immersed in Shakespeare, admired Goethe and had dipped into Cervantes, and who realized the shortcomings of the trashy literary products of the time (though he himself had written an *Allamoddin* and an *Abdallah*), should now be forced to turn out hasty sketches destitute of morality and idealism but abounding in materialism and Rationalism.

Ever since 1786 Nicolai had been publishing, as a purely financial venture, a series of tales under the ironical title of *Straussfedern* (Ostrich Plumes). They were written mostly in a humorous vein and leaned upon various collections of old, long-forgotten French anecdotes, such as the *Amusemens des eaux de Spa* and the *Bibliothèque de Campagne*. Their lack of originality—the fact that they were borrowed plumes—is indicated by the far-fetched title. The editor of volume 1 of the *Straussfedern* was Johann Karl August Musäus, famed for his satire on Richardson, *Der deutsche Grandison*, and for his satirical and jovial *Volksmärchen der Deutschen*. After his death (1787) the project was continued by Johann Gottwerth Müller, the author of the popular novel *Siegfried von Lindenberg* and other novellistic burlesques. He got out volumes 2 and 3.

Tieck might have felt flattered by Nicolai's invitation to continue a project begun by such renowned writers, but in reality he took up the work with reluctance. The humdrum tone of the French tales and the "smart" Rationalism which he was expected to read into them palled upon him from the outset. On the other hand, here was a chance not only to earn money but also to assume many different rôles and to play the objectivist. Nicolai sent him the French material in washbaskets; he had to wade through it and select the most suitable stories, though he would have preferred to use English models or, better still, to write original tales.[3]

In his first three stories, *Schicksal, Die männliche Mutter* and *Die Rechtsgelehrten*, written in 1795, he followed instructions faithfully. They ridiculed sentimentalism and Tieck's own belief in fate.[4] But in *Die Brüder* of the same year, and in the eight contributions of 1796 (seven tales: *Der Fremde, Die beiden merkwürdigsten Tage aus Siegmunds Leben, Ulrich der Empfindsame, Fermer der Geniale, Der Naturfreund, Die gelehrte Gesellschaft, Der Psycholog*, and one playlet, *Die Teegesellschaft*), Tieck threw his models as well as discretion to the winds and struck off original compositions, which, however, preserved the atmosphere and cynical tone of their supposed models. He succeeded so well that even Nicolai was deceived.

In *Die beiden merkwürdigsten Tage aus Siegmunds Leben* he related to Nicolai's delight how a young man, provided with the best of recommendations, applies for a position, but is on the point of being rejected because he lacks the necessary protective influence. About to despair, he enlists the help of an evil woman, whose authority over the hiring official is so great that he secures the job. Pressed by Nicolai to show him the model for this story, Tieck confessed that it was original. Nicolai did not believe him and peevishly remarked: "I should not have thought you so vain, young man."[3] In *Ulrich der Empfindsame* and *Fermer der Geniale* he pleased his employer by attacking the opponents of Rationalism. *Ulrich*, full of satire against the educational theorists, suggests practical activity and Rationalist philosophy as panaceas for Wertherian daydreaming, while *Fermer* shows a true child of the fantastic Storm and Stress era finding satisfaction in the narrow confines of everyday life, but not until after he has sowed his wild oats. The other tales reflect the same cocksure but shallow philosophy of life.

Tieck had been forced to publish volumes 4 to 6 anonymously; not even the stories bore titles. His only compensation was five talers per sheet. In volume 7, appearing in 1797, and containing besides the one-act skit *Die Teegesellschaft* the tales *Der Roman in Briefen* and *Die Freunde*, Nicolai finally deigned to apprise the public that a new editor was in charge. In *Die Teegesellschaft*, which shows the influence of Ben Jonson, the author, disgusted by the sentimental mannerisms of the theater, tried to "carry out a flippant joke perhaps too flippantly, without resorting to misery, lamentation and love."[5] At the risk of seeming paradoxical, we may today claim more value and interest for the play than it had when it was written, for it gives a faithful portrait of Berlin society at the end of the century. We hear the waggish but witless talk over the teacups, we witness the lively but unintelligent interest in political and literary questions, the superior outward contempt but secret attraction for superstitious beliefs, and the false sentimentalism and excessive sobriety characteristic of the best circles in the Prussian capital. Tieck had moved in this set before going to Halle; now he enjoyed enough opportunities to renew his acquaintance with it.

Of the two tales of volume 7, *Der Roman in Briefen* does not add to our picture of Tieck's work in the *Straussfedern*. The other, *Die Freunde*, clearly a preliminary study for the *Volksmährchen* which were to follow, is significant. It is a genuine phantasy piece, a soulful, pulsating bit of poetry, consisting in the main of an eerie dream. So out of harmony was it with the general spirit of the *Straussfedern* that he prefaced it with one apology and followed it up with another. It will be discussed in the next chapter. In 1933 a French translation by Albert Béguin appeared in Paris in a collection entitled *La coupe d'or*.

With volume 8, published in 1798, for which he wrote only *Merkwürdige Lebensgeschichte Seiner Majestät Abraham Tonelli*[6] and *Ein Tagebuch*, the *Straussfedern* came to an end. The former, he himself stated, is based upon an early eighteenth century chapbook. The original has never been found, and some writers have expressed doubt as to its existence. But a letter from Varnhagen von Ense to Rahel of October 13, 1808, definitely proves the accuracy of Tieck's statement. Varnhagen writes that he has just discovered in the Dresden library the story of the tailor's apprentice Tonelli. He has compared it with Tieck's version and found that the latter has added only a jest here and there but followed the source faithfully.[7] Recent research in Dresden has not brought the original to light.

At any rate, Tieck's *Tonelli*, written in the style of the *Volksmährchen*, is marked by humorous situations, which have a strong human appeal and remind of Keller's "novelle" *Kleider machen Leute*. It tells of a stupid, unromantic artisan who, like Gottfried in *Der gestiefelte Kater*, stumbles into all sorts of romantic experiences and finally ascends a throne. Unfortunately Tieck did not take advantage of the opportunities which the plot afforded and which were worthy of the talents of a Jean Paul. A continuation which E. T. A. Hoffmann later planned was not carried out. *La coupe d'or* (1933), mentioned above, contains a translation.

Ein Tagebuch is based upon incidents from two novels of the seventeenth century, *Philanders von Sittewald Gesichte* by Moscherosch and *Simplicius Simplicissimus* by Grimmelshausen.

Almost without exception these compositions are marked by a presumptuous and blasé irony. Some contain mockery of his earlier ethical and esthetic views and are parodies of his older works. Only rarely do we detect an interest in gloom or horror and a leaning toward the world of the fairy tale. As a rule the plot deals with everyday life and with people who have a philistine aversion to unusual adventures, yet are devoid of a sense of that poetry inherent even in a humdrum existence. The stories are all typical of Berlin. Most of them revolve around a single problem, of paramount interest to Tieck at this time: How can one best make one's way in the world? Unfortunately they are written in a careless, hasty style and are the work of an artificer, not a poet. In lack of ideals and triviality they remind of Kotzebue. Their chief significance lies in the opportunity they gave Tieck to develop his ability as an extemporaneous narrator, to play the chameleon, and to practise that satiric, parodistic vein which soon came to the fore in *Der gestiefelte Kater* and *Prinz Zerbino*. In a sense, too, they were an antidote to the corrosion of those moods in which he had written *Almansur* and *Abdallah*. By laughing at himself, as it were, he manifested that sanative "Romantic Irony" for which he later became famous. The author himself called his *Straussfedern* stories trifles, the only purpose of which was entertainment.[8] Yet he was tempted, about fifteen years later, to incorporate some of them in *Phantasus*. To judge by a letter of October 22, 1818, to Collin, editor of the *Jahrbücher der Literatur*, he planned to insert *Tonelli* and *Ein Tagebuch* (he calls them "Jugendsünden") in volume 4 of that work, which did not appear. Anonymously Sophie and Bernhardi also contributed to the *Straussfedern*.

The unfinished humorous novel in two volumes, *Peter Lebrecht, eine Geschichte ohne Abenteuerlichkeiten*, was begun in 1795, simultaneously with the *Straussfedern*. The second part was written as an afterthought. The work came out anonymously. As the phrase "ohne Abenteuerlichkeiten"—without adventures—in the subtitle indicates, the book is done in the same vein as the *Straussfedern*. It abounds in irony and in persiflage of the sentimental novels, as well as of prevalent educational theories. The thin plot relates the story of Peter, whose parents after their marriage took monastic orders and, heedless of their vows, begot twins, a boy and a girl. The children are reared in ignorance of each other. Peter becomes a private tutor and is engaged to his sister without knowing her identity. On the eve of their wedding day she is abducted by a rival. Peter, a mediocre fellow, to whom the limitations of a monotonous existence are not irksome, marries the daughter of a tenant farmer. In attenuated form the humor of Laurence Sterne, manifest in the subtitle, pervades the novel, concerning which Tieck wrote many years later: "One of the little French books attracted me so much more that I ventured upon a freer form, divided it into chapters and planned to have it appear as a small novel. I had given the hero of the story the trivial name of Friedrich Lebrecht, and when my publisher [*sc.* Nicolai] looked these sheets over he liked the farcical work so well that he read it to his family. His son [Karl], who himself became a publisher, took possession of the little book with the intention of sending it forth into the world himself; his father yielded it to him, and I had to change the first name of my hero from Friedrich to Peter, so as to make the title more piquant, in the opinion of my patrons. Thus the little work was published [Berlin and Leipzig, 1795-1796], and made its fortune in some circles and was praised in many journals and criticisms of those days as something excellent and promising [especially in the *Neue Allgemeine Deutsche Bibliothek,* 32, 155]. To be sure, it voiced the mediocre education of many people, the superficial enlightenment, the moderate humor and the gentle satire which were understood and approved. Even some of my friends were of the opinion that to write in this manner was my true calling and that other tasks which I had set for myself were too far removed from truth and naturalness."[9] The style is much like Thümmel's and shows acquaintance with Jean Paul.

Today the humor of *Peter Lebrecht* seems forced, while the moralizing, as well as the satirical attacks against the foibles of the age are mere balderdash. But some of the *obiter dicta,* among them a fine tribute to Goethe, are sagacious. Why did he embody the work in his *Schriften* thirty years later? He was surely not prompted by pride, but by the desire to let the work stand as a biographical record. Another more practical reason was the wish to defeat the purposes of Nicolai's pirated edition of his works (1799), in which it was included.

Several works undertaken between 1795 and 1798 originated independently of Nicolai. In 1795 Tieck's old teacher Rambach launched a monthly magazine, which he called *Archiv der Zeit und ihres Geschmackes.* It was to cover a wide field, including politics, literature and criticism, and was to be a neutral mouthpiece for important writers of Berlin and other German centers. Men with divergent views, among them Nicolai, Gedike, Ramler, Bernhardi, Zschokke and Veit Weber, agreed to contribute. Tieck published a trifling little tale, *Die Sühne, eine Scene aus dem Mittelalter,* in the first volume, without getting credit for it. He later confessed that he purposely concealed his identity and wrote it in the name of another.[10] Like *Die Freunde* and *Abraham Tonelli* in the *Straussfedern,* it is a preliminary study for the *Volksmährchen,* which he was soon to write for Nicolai. Later, in volume 14 of the *Schriften* (1829), the title was changed to *Die Versöhnung.* In 1842 a French translation by M. E. de La Bedollierre appeared. And in 1845 J. C. Hare and J. A. Froude published an English translation in their *Tales from the Phantasus.* These two renderings help to show Tieck's extreme popularity in France and England during the fifth decade of the nineteenth century.

A review by Tieck of some recent Almanacs of the Muses and pocket calendars appeared anonymously in the *Archiv* early in 1796; it was continued in 1798. Here he gave his frank opinion of the almanacs of Schmidt, Voss, Becker, Falk and Schiller. The criticism was not always favorable and displeased Rambach, who, with his ramified literary connections, could ill afford to step on anyone's toes. Of Schiller's famous poem *Würde der Frauen* he writes, for instance, that it "is without doubt extraordinarily beautiful in certain spots, but I confess that, try as hard as I might, I have not been able to find a real plan in it. There are thoughts which are contrasted in mostly very well chosen images, but which do not connect with one another and still less elucidate one another. In a word, I miss a unified lyric and poetic course and find only a prosaic, rational connection, a sort of controversy or colloquy on the dignity of women and the weaknesses of men." Expressions like "what is the sense of this trifling, unpoetic idea?", "the contributions of —— are not good, anyway," "neither the Muses nor the Graces smiled over the cradle of this ballad," and "if only this poet had not ground out such happy prospects in his repugnant rimes" can be found on every page of Tieck's two reviews. Since this quarrelsome tone pervades the notices, they would have made Tieck enemies had they been signed. They are marked by that unbridled subjectivism which we have already noticed in Tieck's critical work. The very adjectives he uses to qualify the lyrics which he approves—"sanft," "zart," "melodisch," "lieblich"—, as well as those which he applies to reprehensible products—"hart," "rauh," "prosaisch"—, throw an interesting light upon the character of his own lyricism. The continuation of 1798, under the influence of the Schlegels, is more trenchant.[11]

For another work of 1795, a three-act puppet-play mostly in verse entitled *Hanswurst als Emigrant*, we must refer to the *Nachgelassene Schriften*. In form it is an imitation of the old German marionette plays which were still popular in Tieck's childhood, in content a satire at the expense of Gottsched and the other purists who had banished the clown —a relic of the English "comedies" imported into Germany early in the seventeenth century—from the German stage. It was his conviction, later reiterated in *Der gestiefelte Kater*, that the clown is permissible and that if Germany is to have an indigenous theater, this figure, introduced successfully on the stage by Shakespeare, the greatest dramatic genius and most illustrious model for Germans, must have a place in it. And so he put the following words into the mouth of Hanswurst at the end of the play: "You know, Gottsched expelled me because he alone wished to play my part. The scholars made common cause with him because I stood in their way. Lessing and a few other good people sided with me, to be sure, but it was of no avail. The majority of votes were against me. Sadly I left my fatherland, roamed about all over the world, and was a soldier, a scholar and a writer. . . . Now it has pleased a brand new poet to summon me back. . . . But, alas, I am no longer

THE YOUNG PROFESSIONAL WRITER

the regular clown. Head and limbs are of wood, my colleagues are even of leather!"[12]

This sketch is significant, too, because it introduced for the first time Tieck's ironic confusion of the two worlds of reality and make-believe. It presents the technique of a play within a play and is a preliminary study for *Der gestiefelte Kater*.

Tieck's chameleonism, a result of his dualism, is illustrated by the multifariousness of the works which engaged his attention in the middle of the 'nineties. Cynical writings like the *Straussfedern* stories and *Peter Lebrecht* ridicule the very mood in which a fate drama like *Karl Berneck* is written. Between these lie studies in, and translations from, the English and such a skit as *Hanswurst*. And then, in turn, a novel, *William Lovell*, dispels the Rationalist philosophy of the *Straussfedern*.

Die Geschichte des Herrn William Lovell[13] is an epistolary novel in three volumes and nine books. The younger Nicolai, who also published *Abdallah* and *Lebrecht*, got it out in 1795 and 1796. The work, which is an outgrowth of Tieck's early emotions and passionate strivings—a reflex of the gloomy moods which beset him during his student days—, was written desultorily between 1793 and 1796. It reveals the true nature of the poet more accurately than any of the works hitherto discussed and is a genuine confession.

The plot is as follows. Lovell, an innocent but morally weak young man endowed with deep feeling—a sort of modern Abdallah—, falls prey to a Parisian siren and thus becomes untrue to his sweetheart at home, who is a namesake of Tieck's sweetheart Amalie. Yet during this escapade at Paris he continues writing his Amalie letters full of platonic affection. His sensualism gets the best of him, and he reels through the whole gamut of physical pleasures. In Rome he falls in with Balder, a hardened libertine, who has but to look forward to insanity in his mad quest for sensual thrills. Moral invertebrate that he is, Lovell goes from bad to worse. At times his pensive nature still crops out, and apparently under the influence of Fichte's philosophy, he tries to fight his way to a rational explanation of his conduct. It is, to be sure, an egotistic philosophy, which he, the true introvert, voices. He writes: "Thus my external mind controls the physical, my inner mind the moral world. . . . I myself am the only law in all nature, everything obeys this law."[14] This thought is expressed also in the verses:

> Since we conceived them, creatures thrive,
> To distant clouds the earth is lashed,
> In her dark shafts there doth arrive

A ray from us, bright and alive.
Why is not earth in scattered ruins dashed?
We are the fate that props it unabashed.

I meet myself, no other mate,
In empty, barren desert land.
I suffer worlds to gravitate
Elements to be ordinate,
And change occurs when I do but command,
Rendering old things new again and grand.

From fearful chains now happily fled
I go through life audaciously
'T is but a prize of duties dread,
The figment of a coward's head,
Virtue exists, but thanks alone to me,
An echo of my mind it fain would be.

What reck I forms whose sickish light
Doth only from myself derive?
Let vice and virtue now unite,
They are but fog and misty night,
My light alone into the darkness strives,
Since I conceived it, virtue thrives.*

* Die Wesen sind, weil wir sie dachten,
   In trüber Ferne liegt die Welt,
   Es fällt in ihre dunkeln Schachten
   Ein Schimmer, den wir mit uns brachten:
   Warum sie nicht in wilde Trümmer fällt?
   Wir sind das Schicksal, das sie aufrecht hält!

   Ich komme mir nur selbst entgegen
   In einer leeren Wüstenei.
   Ich lasse Welten sich bewegen,
   Die Element' in Ordnung legen,
   Der Wechsel kommt auf meinen Ruf herbei
   Und wandelt stets die alten Dinge neu.

   Den bangen Ketten froh entronnen,
   Geh' ich nun kühn durchs Leben hin,
   Den harten Pflichten abgewonnen,
   Von feigen Toren nur ersonnen.
   Die Tugend ist nur, weil ich selber bin,
   Ein Widerschein in meinem innern Sinn.

(Continued on bottom of next page)

His crass solipsism is fortified by Lovell's fervent conviction that he is in harmony with nature. But at the same time we see his brooding intellect trying to analyze this belief—a typical case of Romantic dualism, bound to lead to nature mysticism.

Such philosophizing does not lift Lovell out of the morass, and soon he pictures life again as nought but a mad orgy. His finer sensibilities waste away. He seduces a poor, innocent girl, Rosaline, who ends her life in the Tiber. Returning home to England, he finds that his father is dead and that his patrimony has fallen into the hands of a false friend. Lovell tries to poison him, but failing he seduces his sister. He becomes a murderer, a gambler, a robber. Then he goes back to Rome, but meets only ridicule at the hands of his former companion. The latter wills him his autobiography, from which it appears that he ruined Lovell so as to wreak vengeance upon the latter's father for some supposed wrong. Finally, like Almansur, Abdallah and Goethe's Werther, Lovell seeks comfort in solitary communion with nature. He would atone for his sins through loving care of the flowers and trees. Before he can realize his intention he is shot in a duel by the brother of the girl he has deserted.

We have indicated that *William Lovell* is a confession. To what extent this is true we learn from a note by Varnhagen von Ense among his Berlin papers which seems to contain a basis of truth. Varnhagen relates that the story of Rosaline's seduction in the novel conceals an instance of true Goethean atonement on Tieck's part. Tieck, this indefatigable gossip-monger goes on to say, had seduced his future sister-in-law, Marie Alberti. Her resulting mental anguish but undying admiration for him caused him terrible qualms, which he could scarcely overcome. This incident and the subsequent vicissitudes of Marie will be discussed later.

With good reason Lovell describes his life as a dream. And indeed, the appalling and tiresome pictures of debauchery, revealing no struggle against fate and no striving for a noble goal, had best be regarded as figments of an overheated imagination—"dim phantoms," as A. W. Schlegel said.[15] Only the hero's despairing search for tangible ends, his continual self-analysis, which fails to bring true comprehension but leads to pessimistic resignation, and Tieck's own veiled confession of wrongdoing should be considered real. The scanty action, the puppet-

> Was kümmern mich Gestalten, deren matten
> Lichtglanz ich selbst hervorgebracht?
> Mag Tugend sich und Laster gatten!
> Sie sind nur Dunst und Nebelschatten!
> Das Licht aus mir fällt in die finstre Nacht,
> Die Tugend ist nur, weil ich sie gedacht.[14]

like characters and the silly, awkward invention, which imitate Richardson and Goethe but remind more of Schiller's *Geisterseher*, are negligible.

And yet *William Lovell*, which unlike his other works of 1790-1795 and many of later date, is not an improvisation, shows that Tieck has at last gained artistic mastery over his subject matter. The character of the hero, however bad it may be, is at least unified, logical and psychologically correct. Moreover, *William Lovell* furnishes an excellent illustration of its author's demonism growing out of his dual nature. As usual in Tieck there is a continual reversal from pleasure to displeasure, from happiness to melancholia, from horror to voluptuous delight in the gruesome. "An evil demon pursues me in the shape of an angel," writes the self-styled chameleon, Lovell, laying bare his (and Tieck's) irrational psychic trend. In addition, the important motif which pervades most of his writings except his hack work—that of a psychic disturbance gradually developed to a climax—is here clearly apparent.[16]

Later Tieck described the work as a warning against megalomania and hypocritical virtuousness. He wished to show the necessity of self-limitation and of resignation, without which man cannot live.[17] He himself gradually learned this lesson in the school of hard knocks, as he told Solger in 1815.[18] His novel is the "mausoleum" of his sufferings and mistakes. For had not his own life been a struggle against, and, in his affair with Marie, an exemplification of, the vices which he ascribed to Lovell? Was he not continually fighting with himself to conquer his egoism? Did he not hold that objectivity can best be attained through some form of self-negating love? Lovell is consumed by yearning for such a saving affection. The character Emilie Burton once writes that everything is sacred so long as it is an outgrowth of love, the divine pledge. Throughout the novel love is regarded as a mystic or demonic means of knowledge.

The basic idea of this literary-philosophical lecture on hedonism, then, is salutary, although Tieck is opposed to cool reason or mediocrity and stands on the side of that very "Phantasie" and "Genialität" which he knows are so dangerous and which help to spell the hero's ruin. But the eulogy of Arnim, who found in it "a wealth of novelty and poetry" (Fülle an Neuheit und Poesie) and called it "divine grain on the barren old Richardsonian field" (himmlische Saat auf dem dürren alten Richardsonschen Felde),[19] and the statement of Karl Rosenkranz (1839)[20] that the novel is his most profound and characteristic work, would hardly find a supporter today. Jean Paul's *Titan* is now accepted as more successful in this genre.

The name of the hero was not original. In 1792 he had read Ben Jonson's comedy *The New Inn* and found there the "melancholy guest" Lovell. He discovered the same name in Richardson's *Clarissa Harlowe* and in Shakespeare's *Richard III* and *Henry VIII*. Perhaps, too, he mispronounced Richardson's Lovelace (Lovel-ace). Especially in Jonson's work he could see a reflection of his own endeavor to delve into the depths of the human soul and to expose hypocrisy, effeminacy and mendacity in all their manifestations. In such a temper he was prone to despise life itself and to arraign human nature in its totality.

The chief external source of *William Lovell* is the French novel *Le paysan perverti* of Nicholas Restif de la Bretonne (1734-1806), an indefatigable scribbler of inferior rank, who has been dubbed "the Rousseau of the gutter." Tieck was attracted to his work, which depicts immoral life in Paris under Louis XIV, by the motif of an innocent man sinking into the morass of sin through temptation and natural inclination. He wished to emulate this model and to depict in a similar manner the deleterious effect of temperament and wicked associations. But whereas voluptuous action and lascivious scenes were ends in themselves for Restif, Tieck was interested in them insofar as they made it possible to portray the contacts of a passionately self-indulgent youth with the world.

In this respect *William Lovell* is a psychological novel and resembles Goethe's *Werther*. It occupies the same place in Tieck's life as the latter does in Goethe's. And, with its wavering between the narrowness of the Enlightenment and Tieck's own genial but uncertain striving for a freer, deeper philosophy, it has an even more pronounced autobiographical character than Goethe's novel. But where Goethe offers authentic art, he gives us claptrap and exaggeration.

In its psychological dissection of character and in the detailed descriptions of the psychic states of the hero, which form the bulk of *William Lovell*, it goes back also to Richardson, especially *Clarissa Harlowe*. It derives its English locale and other externalities from Richardson, too. Though they are no unusual features for that period and strike us as unreal, they seemed so genuine to one contemporary of Tieck that he accused the author of having translated the novel from the English.[21]

Not only are Richardson and his character Grandison mentioned, but there is a positive influence to be noted. Tieck himself spoke of his "observance of the costumes and manners of the English" (Beobachtung des Kostüms, der Art und Weise der Engländer).[22] Lovell's letters to Rosa at the time of the seduction of Rosaline remind of those from Lovelace to Belford. Just as Lovell vows that he will marry Rosaline after her seduction, so Lovelace has similar intentions toward Clarissa, even after the violence. In neither case does the girl continue to love the man after the deception. Lovell causes Mortimer's house to be set on fire so that he may see Amalie once more; similarly Lovelace takes advantage of a fire to be near Clarissa. The relation of Amalie and Mortimer is like that of Anne Howe and Hickman. Clarissa's maid Lisa is as naïve and awkward as the old servant Willy in Tieck's novel. Lovelace and a friend stop in disguise at an inn to be near Clarissa unnoticed; similarly Lovell and Willy live as peasants to associate more easily with Rosaline. The conclusion of the two novels is similar. Both Lovell and Lovelace are shot in a duel, and Emilie Burton like Clarissa dies of a broken heart.

While noting the dependence of *William Lovell* upon *Le paysan perverti* we saw, too, that the former is on a much higher plane. There are also differences between Tieck's novel and Richardson's. In *William Lovell* we are taken to a realm beyond good and evil; we are only given an insight into the depths of a soul. Tieck has no use for the complacency, reflection and cocksure rationalism of a Richardson. Indeed, *William Lovell* is a broadside against cool moral preaching, written with warmth of feeling and presenting characters who seek to penetrate the mystery of life.

With Restif de la Bretonne, Jonson and Richardson we have not exhausted the literary models for the content and spirit of *William Lovell*. Its Bohemianism may be traced to Heinse's *Ardinghello*[23] and to Restif, and ultimately to Fielding and Smollett in England, Abbé Prevost, Louvet de Couvray and Choderlos de la Clos in France, who in a somewhat sadistic age had made the Lovell type of "hero" a commonplace. The distinction lies in the fact that these authors wrote novels of manners, while Tieck's work is the picture of a soul. With all his rakishness, Lovell is a philosopher.

Tieck's attitude toward materialism and toward the ethics of power finds its models in Wieland's *Agathon*, as well as in Restif; his determinism is traceable to Schiller's *Geisterseher*; the reaction to conventional morality to Nicolai's *Sebaldus Nothanker*, as well as to Jonson and Richardson; the sentimentalism to Wieland, Jean Paul and Richardson; the feeling for nature to Rousseau and Goethe; the doctrine that "Gefühl" is a moral instinct to Klinger and Schiller; the consciousness of the limitations of knowledge to Goethe's *Werther* and *Faust*, also to Moritz's *Anton Reiser*;[24] and finally the general theory of knowledge to Kant and Jacobi.

THE YOUNG PROFESSIONAL WRITER

What is the place of *William Lovell* in the series of autobiographic-psychological novels opened by Goethe's *Werther*, continued by Jacobi's *Woldemar* and Moritz's *Anton Reiser*, and concluded by Tieck's novel? They are without exception psychopathic studies representing, in the order named, a progressive aggravation of morbidity, with *William Lovell* at the peak. Its hero inhabits an altogether supersensual, supernatural world. Of the leading characters in the four novels he has overcome Storm and Stress most completely and is unquestionably the best type of the Romantic.[24]

The epistolary form, consistently observed by Tieck, was suggested by Richardson and Goethe's *Werther*. But even this extremely subjective manner of narration did not satisfy him in his eagerness to give complete expression to the emotions of his inmost soul. And so he resorted to the device of interspersing lyric poems in the prose narrative. In these he poured forth his deepest feelings, just as Goethe did in *Wilhelm Meisters Lehrjahre*, published almost simultaneously.

The use of interlarded verse, found in Germany in *Frauendienst* of Ulrich von Lichtenstein in the thirteenth century, became popular in prose works of the eighteenth century during the age of Richardson and sentimentalism. It led to a sort of mixed genre, half verse, half prose— the latter often rhythmic. To such prose Goethe resorted in the Ossianic passages of *Werther*. In *Wilhelm Meister* he conformed to the prevailing style in using interpolated verse. But with his sure touch of genius he placed the device upon a higher level. His interludes grew not merely out of the situation, but out of the emotional world of his characters, in which he lived for the time being. Hence they are more varied and more dramatic than ever before, and always akin to Goethe's personality as a poet. Tieck had used verse promiscuously even in his earliest prose works—in imitation and for stylistic reasons. In *Abdallah*, for instance, verse intensifies the prevailing mood and contrasts variant moods. But in *William Lovell* the verse becomes part and parcel of the work itself. How this practice was further developed will be seen in *Die schöne Magelone*, *Der blonde Eckbert* and *Der Runenberg*. At any rate, the style which he introduces in *William Lovell* foreshadows the blending of the various literary genres which became so characteristic a token of German Romanticism.[25]

A further parallelism with *Wilhelm Meister* seems to exist. Like Goethe's novel, *William Lovell* was not cast in its final form until after the poet had been cured of the psychic disturbances described so vividly in the novel. Both Goethe and Tieck would show how a highly gifted contemporary youth gropes his way through life. Each lets his hero be guided by a mysterious force over which he has no control. The essential difference is that Wilhelm Meister stands the test, while Lovell's entelechy brings up in the deepest abyss of vice and despair.

There are three editions, all prepared by Tieck. The first (1795-1796) is in nine books; the second (1813) in seven; the third (*Schriften* 6 and 7, 1828) in ten. The second is a drastic revision of the first, omitting sixty-nine letters and abbreviating others, especially those containing off-color, unduly sentimental or immature passages. It reveals much stylistic improvement, too, and bears the imprint of the author's visit to Italy in 1805-1806. In this revision Tieck tries, without success, to alter the motif of the novel, making it a defense of the golden mean and of resignation. The third redaction restores twenty-five letters but otherwise leaves the second edition virtually intact.

The experiences of Tieck's two years away from home, his friendship for Wackenroder and his renewed association with Sophie, Friedrich, Wackenroder and Bernhardi after his return to Berlin soon brought him more balance. For the summers of 1795 and 1796 he and Sophie rented a little cottage in the Mollard (later called Wollank) vineyard at the Rosenthal gate at the north end of town. This was a rural section in those days. Here sister and brother devoted much time to each other and were happy. They had numerous and frequent guests: brother Friedrich, who with Schadow represented the plastic arts; Wackenroder; Bernhardi, who played the critic; Wesseley, a musician who set Tieck's version of *The Tempest* to music; also the composer Zelter, the actor Fleck and the poet Ramler. In this environment Tieck, temporarily delivered from the influence of Nicolai, became a changed, though not yet a mature, man.

CHAPTER FIVE

BLAZING NEW TRAILS

IN 1796 the average educated German looked with contempt upon the old folk songs and the cheap, popular books which could still be bought from the chapmen in the public markets of the cities. The *Reliques of Ancient English Poetry* published by Bishop Thomas Percy in 1765 and the recreated popular ballads of Bürger, whose *Lenore* appeared in 1773, caused surprise and consternation in many circles. And when Herder collected folk songs of the Germans and of other nations and a few years later (1778-1779) published them for the edification of his fellow countrymen, he was ridiculed by such men as Nicolai. Goethe's interest in Nürnberg's naïve cobbler-poet Hans Sachs, arising simultaneously with his interest in *Götz von Berlichingen* in 1771 and culminating with the sincere poetical tribute, *Hans Sachsens poetische Sendung* (1776), can hardly be described as contagious. The venerable fairy tales were disdained by most people as immoderately adventurous, illogical creations of irresponsible minds and hence pernicious and damnable. Little wonder, then, that the *Volksmärchen der Deutschen* of Musäus (1782-1786), with all his partiality for the stories, reveal their author's satirical attitude and feeling of superiority on every page. And in 1790, when Bertuch got out in *Blaue Bibliothek aller Nationen*, a new German edition of the *Contes de ma mère l'Oye* by the seventeenth century French writer Charles Perrault, containing his ingenuous versions of Sleeping Beauty, Little Red Riding Hood, Bluebeard, Puss in Boots, Cinderella and Tom Thumb, the *Allgemeine Deutsche Bibliothek* could see no reason for publishing such "trash" and condemned it without qualification.

Writing the *Straussfedern* with their Rationalist views of life and of art, and storming out *William Lovell* brought Tieck a meed of mental clarification. He attained a greater balance of mind and felt the gradual dawning, in his soul, of a new world of fantasy and primitive feeling. And it was that much despised reservoir of folk poetry, preserved from the Middle Ages, and pointed out to Tieck by Wackenroder, which gradually transfused new blood into his poetic veins.

In part 2, chapter 1, of his otherwise cynical *Peter Lebrecht* he had proclaimed that the popular and fashionable "Mordgeschichten" and "Ritterromane" of the day were nonsense and rubbish. And not content with this negative animadversion, he proceeded to break a lance for the time-worn popular literature which had fallen into such ill repute. It required no mean courage on his part to surprise his taskmasters, the Nicolais, and the general reading public with such a broadside as the following: "The ordinary readers should by no means scoff at those popular novels which are sold by old women on the streets for a penny or twopence, for Horned Siegfried, the Children of Haimon, Duke Ernst and Genevieve contain more real invention and are written in an immeasurably purer and better style than those beloved modish books. If the reader is unwilling to take me at my word, let him read those poorly printed and despised stories for himself, and if his taste is not yet completely ruined, he will prefer the latter to the former."[1]

In thus praising the old folk tales, he showed a natural reaction against the literary slavery in which the Nicolais held him, and perhaps the direct impress of Musäus. There is more of the real Tieck in the spirit of the passage just quoted than in that of the *Straussfedern.* How did this interest in Siegfried, Duke Ernst and Genevieve develop in him? The Storm and Stress writer H. A. O. Reichard had already imitated the tone of the chapbooks. No doubt Wackenroder's influence was also marked. Besides, it is likely that the words of the Duke in Act II, Scene 4, of *Twelfth Night* had left a deep impression on his mind:

> that piece of song,
> That old and antique song we heard last night:
> Methought it did relieve my passion much,
> More than light airs and recollected terms
> Of these most brisk and giddy-paced times.

For during this time Shakespeare was again engaging much of his attention; about 1797 he wrote the second draft (some thirty pages) of his *Buch über Shakespeare.* Moreover, he was casting about subconsciously for a native mythology which would be on a par with that of antiquity. In the folk tales he must have felt he had found such a body of indigenous popular traditions—the outgrowth of the poetic spirit inherent in the German race itself.

And so it is not surprising to find the following passage in the same chapter of *Peter Lebrecht*: "As a matter of fact, I have a manuscript lying here which will presently appear in print under the title: *Volksmährchen,* and which contains naught but wonderful and adventuresome stories. The reader must not take this as a joke, for I mean it quite seriously, and the book will be published presently by the publisher of this story. . . . Whoever does not like the present book, may try the forthcoming one."[2] Tieck kept his promise. In 1797 the *Volksmährchen herausgegeben von Peter Leberecht* were published by the younger Nicolai in three volumes.

In the preface to volume 11 of his *Schriften* Tieck explained that for the *Volksmährchen* he again used the name Peter Lebrecht (here Leberecht) at the behest of Karl Nicolai.[3] The latter, whose principles were less admirable than those of his father, was interested chiefly in speed and output, not in type or quality of work. But naturally even *his* Rationalist soul rebelled against any such "wonderful and adventuresome" fabrications as these tales. The caption "herausgegeben von Peter Leberecht," he felt, would excuse the collection and brand it as the product of a mind narrow enough to take delight in such absurd, irrational literature. Furthermore, though Tieck had been paid five talers per sheet for the *Straussfedern*, which were supposed to be adaptations, he received only four talers for the much more original *Volksmährchen.*[4] This is indication enough of his publisher's attitude, and it led Tieck to complain bitterly in his letters to the older Nicolai.

The purpose of the demonic poet was not that of his publisher. He was intent upon putting an end to the proud reign of Reason, and did not hesitate to make this clear throughout the *Volksmährchen*, which he provided with a serious as well as a humorous preface, the former of which is meant humorously and vice versa. Here reason was held up to ridicule, and miraculous happenings with all their winsome iridescence came into their own.

The elements of wonder and of horror, which to the Elizabethans were the chief characteristics of "High Dutch" literature,[5] had dropped out of the life of the German people by the end of the eighteenth century. Hence Tieck was forced to seek them in the distant past and in foreign climes. He found such elements in the old fairy tales, as they had been naïvely retold by Basile and Perrault, and in the fiabe of the Italian folk poet Gozzi, who had already been his teacher in *König Braddeck* and *Das Reh*. He discovered them also in the old German chapbooks and in the foremost native writers of the seventeenth century, Moscherosch, Grimmelshausen and Christian Weise, whose works had attracted him in Göttingen.[6] These ready-made sources were ideal for him, with his more reproductive than creative imagination. They were much more tractable than historical sources and took him into a far-off, colorful land of poesy, miracles, dreams.

In one of the *Straussfedern, Die Freunde*, written in 1797, he has left an autobiographic record of the bewitching experiences which caused him to center his attention upon the world of the *Märchen*. Not without reason the hero of the tale is named Ludwig. " 'Am I enchanted?' he cried, 'or have my dreams and phantasies deranged me? Is it the wonderful effect of solitude that I do not recognize myself, or are spirits and genii hovering about me, who hold my senses enthralled?' . . . Now there was a ringing and a sounding everywhere, a thousand lovely voices spoke in confusion, and in the settling red of evening countless blue butterflies were cradling themselves, the reflection glistening on their outspread wings. . . . In the midst a palace gleamed with thousands and thousands of colors. . . . All his cares, all his erstwhile recollections were shaken off; his soul reechoed the singing which surrounded him externally; all yearning was stilled; all known and unknown wishes within him appeased."[7] Ludwig was among the fairies, who greeted and treated him pleasantly. Only now and then the crowing of a cock came to his ears or a post-horn resounded in the distance to remind him that he was only a mortal, or to bring fleeting, wistful recollections of the cold but beloved earth.

Of course this is a dream, but it grew so potent in Tieck that for a span of years it captured him completely and took the place of concrete reality. At the end Ludwig awakes from his dream, only to learn that the fairies are figments of our sickish imagination, calculated to instil "supernatural craving for supernatural goods, so that in our subsequent fit of melancholy intoxication we would fain despise the lovely earth with its glorious gifts."[8] Not so Tieck, who became more enamored of the allurement of fairyland.

This tergiversation, more apparent than real, did not take place suddenly, but by degrees. At first it was the unmatched charm of the ageless chapbook tales which captured his fancy. Their medieval setting in itself could not be objectionable even to Nicolai, for the action of the most popular novels of the day was also supposed to take place in the Middle Ages. Tieck preserved that setting in the earliest of his *Volksmährchen*, entitled *Die Geschichte von den Heymons Kindern, in zwanzig altfränkischen Bildern*,[9] from which he had related an incident in *Karl von Berneck*. His version of the tale was written in 1796. He imitated also the goodnaturedly candid and entertaining tone, as well as the artless simplicity of the "Volksbuch," which had been translated from the original French and appeared at Simmern in 1535 and at Cologne in 1604. Whether he also used Ariosto's *Orlando Furioso* as a source is doubtful. Certain it is, however, that he did not realize the French provenience of this chapbook and others. He thought he had discovered a typically German mine of poetry, just as Goethe a generation before had mistaken Gothic architecture as German in origin.

The story concerns the four children of Count Haimon (Aymon) of Dordogne, the hero of one of the best known legends of the Carolingian cycle. Tieck succeeded in making a virtue even of the obscurities and difficulties of the corrupted original. For since these qualities were diametrically opposed to the Rationalist demands for absolute clarity and perspicuity, Tieck purposely emphasized them. He refrained from applying ordinary equine psychology to the actions of the wondrous and recalcitrant steed Bayart, which once subdued is wont to sink in its knees whenever its master Reinold would mount it, until it finds a watery grave. Tieck also avoided any subjective indication of his own attitude toward the story. His sole desire was to afford others the same delight which he had derived from the homely narrative. To be sure, he omitted all the cant and affected piety of the original, as well as many superfluous characters and incidents. He also made slight additions and changes for the sake of better coherence. A. W. Schlegel happily referred to Tieck's version as "a woodcut in poetry."[10]

Internal evidence would indicate that the second chapbook which he adapted was the so-called *Schildbürgerbuch* of 1598, a revision of the *Lalenbuch* of the year before. It tells of the stupid pranks attributed to the citizens of Schilda (now Schildau) in central Germany. He called his version *Denkwürdige Geschichtschronik der Schildbürger in zwanzig lesenswürdigen Kapiteln.*[11] Our reason for surmising that this was undertaken later than the story of the Children of Haimon is that his treatment of the Schildbürger shows considerably more freedom. His purpose was also different. While in the former he told a story for the sake of the story alone and eschewed parody, he tried in the latter to deal with the old German extravaganzas in the same manner in which Wieland a generation before had treated his Greek source in *Die Abderiten*. In other words, Tieck applied the generalized satire of his source to the specific conditions of his own day and age. Here the second leading characteristic of the *Volksmährchen*,—their biting satire—entered. An example from the first chapter will illustrate. He relates that, having decided to recount the history of the Schildbürger for the edification of his own contemporaries, who could learn many lessons from history, he purchased a copy of the tales from an old huckster. The latter, with tears in his eyes, expressed his astonishment that a man like Tieck, who made the impression of being "enlightened," should buy such perversive literature. "Why, in the interest of the Enlightenment and of mankind," exclaimed the huckster, "they are now trying to displace Till Eulenspiegel, the Children of Haimon, Horned Siegfried and such books by others which are more recent and much more insipid."[12] The poor old man feared that he would soon be expelled from the land as a corrupter of the public morals. Surely the satire inherent in this passage is answer enough to the charge of the *Allgemeine Deutsche Bibliothek* that Tieck was trying to revive "die Bänkelsängereien des 16. Säkuli."

Other instances of such satire, which is freer, more poetic and more goodnatured than that in the *Straussfedern*, abound. In chapter 6, when the Schildbürger try to carry light rays in kettles, sacks and pails into their town hall, which they have forgotten to provide with windows, one of them argues that this is just as feasible as sending light and enlightenment between the covers of books to regions in intellectual darkness.

In another place a false Diogenes, forgetting the rôle he is to play, asks the king for a thousand talers instead of his place in the sun.[13] Similarly, self-consciousness and vanity; imaginary freethinking, which is in reality superstition; bigotry and intellectual servitude; utilitarian abuse of the theater; proud contempt of the old puppet-plays and folk tales; and gross misconception of the functions of tragedy come in for their share of scorn, too. But the humor, while amusing, does not yet suggest Aristophanes; it reminds more of *Peter Lebrecht* in singling out minor evils of the time and presupposes a knowledge of contemporary conditions.

In discussing this work in the *Athenäum* in 1798, A. W. Schlegel compared Tieck with a pirate, who nonchalantly enters the ports of the powerful nation of Schildbürger and their no less formidable allies, the ubiquitous Philistines, and launches a withering attack.[14] It seems anomalous that Karl Nicolai should have aided and abetted the author by serving as the publisher of such an incursion against the stronghold of Rationalism. For it was clear that Tieck had in mind Nicolai's good friends, the popular playwrights Iffland and Kotzebue, when in chapter 8 he described Augustus and Hans Knopfmacher, the foremost poets of the land of the Schildbürger. There could be still less doubt about the identity of "der Märkische Herr Schmidt" in chapter 1. He was the Rationalist parson Schmidt of Werneuchen, whose naturalistic songs, to be sung while milking cows, had aroused Tieck's sense of humor in his review of the Almanacs of the Muses. Schmidt is the same poetaster whose *cacoethes scribendi* was aptly ridiculed by Goethe in the poem *Musen und Grazien in der Mark*.[15] And in *Zerbino* Tieck styled him "der Sandpoet."[16] Nor could there be any question but that the archaic flavor of Tieck's style was meant to banter contemporary writers who preened themselves upon their use of language.

The third folk tale, which he published under the title *Wundersame Liebesgeschichte der schönen Magelone und des Grafen Peter aus der Provence*,[17] was treated in still different fashion. While he feigned faithfulness and naïveté in the story of the Children of Haimon, and introduced contemporary satire in his *Schildbürger*, he was less the actor of a part and more the creative poet in his version of *Magelone*. He deviated markedly from the earliest Provençal and French sources, as well as from the German chapbook of 1527 and its progeny. The pages of his tale are filled with fancy and sweet sentimentalism. Miracles are accepted as natural occurrences, and numerous interspersed lyrics express or suggest in dulcet tones the feeling of the bygone but devout times of our forefathers.

This rococo pastoral, in which feeling is more important than action, seems to establish a mysterious bond between man and nature. The sensations of the former are reflected in the latter. Peter, the hero, is a romantic dreamer, whose yearnings are as vague as those of Tieck. He wanders about as a minstrel and a sort of quixotic knight. A cousin of Ludwig in *Die Freunde*, he hears music everywhere, which seems to reflect his undefined emotions. The interlarded lyrics play a more important part than in *William Lovell*. They become a lyric accompaniment of the epic substance and prove so infectious that even the prose is lyricized. The whole story is written in a lyrical frame of mind, in a style which reminded A. W. Schlegel of Goethe[18] and which was fast becoming typically Romantic. Mood is more important than content. The charm of the prevailing word-melodies is more essential than the meaning of the words themselves. These melodies have been enhanced by the music which Johannes Brahms, has composed for them. Even foreigners have been attracted by the rhythmic flow of his words. Thus the noted American composer, Harvey Worthington Loomis, as late as 1902, set the *Magelone* song "Geliebter, wo zaudert dein irrender Fuss" to music accompanied by a fair rendering of the text.[19]

It is no accident that at this time Tieck wrote his most characteristic, and at the same time some of his best, lyrics. Prominent among them are "Auf der Reise," "Nacht," and "Herbstlied," probably all written in 1796, and "Zuversicht" and "Kunst und Liebe" of 1797.[20] Despite their vacuity, the rich vowels and rimes, pictorial coloring, frequent alliteration and assonance, and pronounced rhythm give these lyrics a high musical potency. They show his predilection for soft, particularly dark, neutral colors, for the light of early morning and evening, and for the silvery moon.[21] Many composers besides Brahms have been attracted to them, among these Mendelssohn, Reichardt, Otto Nicolai, Friedrich

Wollank and August Bergt. Romantic poetry and music always go hand in hand. Tieck's Romantic writings in particular—his narratives and dramas as well as his lyrics—fairly cry out for musical settings.

For the sake of his lyrical interpretation of *Die schöne Magelone* he went so far as to do violence to the old story itself. In his version the dramatic meeting of the lovers in the hospital at the end of the tale becomes a saccharine and sentimental pastoral idyl. "After two days Peter had quite regained his strength. He sat with Magelone, without recognizing her, before the door of the shepherd's hut. Bees and butterflies swarmed about them, and Peter acquired confidence in his nurse, so that he told her his story and his whole misfortune. Magelone suddenly arose and went to her chamber, there she released her golden locks and freed them of the bands which had held them. Then she donned her costly clothing, which she had kept locked up, and so suddenly returned before Peter's eyes. He was beside himself with astonishment, he embraced the loved one he had found again, then they repeated to each other their stories, and wept and kissed, so that one might have been uncertain whether they sobbed thus heart-rendingly for grief or excessive joy. So the day passed for them."[22]

As in the story of the Children of Haimon, the religious element is discarded. An attempt to blend and merge the various arts is plainly apparent. Tieck himself later became aware that he had done violence to the old story. In *Phantasus* he has Friedrich speak as follows about his version: "When an old tale has so hearty a core, which gives the story a great and touching character, it is nought but a sign of our pampered, narrow times if we quite mistake this beauty and seek to improve it by arbitrary modification, whereby the product as a whole loses its central idea and its purpose."[23] And Clara rightly adds: "The old poem is a glorification of love and devout humility, the new story a sweet manifestation of free thought and disbelief."[24] In 1803 he undertook another *Magelone*; it was to be a dramatic paean on love and would have left the early Christian flavor of the chapbook intact. Only the *Prolog*, written in a variety of meters and leaving a distinctly lyrical impression, was completed.

The drama *Ritter Blaubart*, *Ein Ammenmärchen*, written in one evening, was originally in four acts, and appeared in the *Volksmährchen* and at the same time as a separate work.[25] A generation later he rewrote it in five acts and published it again in *Phantasus*. With it he meant to produce a practical play for the stage, but there is record of only one successful performance—that of May 3, 1835, by Immermann in Düsseldorf. An earlier performance in Berlin by Wolff and Devrient was planned but not given. Tieck's own Berlin presentation of February 1, 1846, and a later one in Dresden proved failures.

Tieck found the fable of Bluebeard, the cruel murderer of many wives, in Perrault. The idea of dramatizing it in a half ironical way, which smacks of Rationalism, came from Gozzi (perhaps also from Colman), though he himself rightly expressed the opinion in *Phantasus* that his work is not an imitation of Gozzi's manner.[26] In the introduction to the first section of his works in 1828, he reiterated that this combination of the humorous and the bizarre in dramatic form was made independently of Gozzi; pure pleasure in the fiabe of the Venetian writer and, we may add, interest in the puppet plays, caused him to adapt, in a different style, and in German fashion, a fantastic fairy tale for the German stage.[27] As a psychological reproduction of a fairy tale it belongs to the same type as *Die schöne Magelone*, though cast in dramatic form.

The fairylike unreality of the landscape, the uncanny color of Peter Berner's beard, the weird environment of his castle, his haggish housekeeper Mechtilde, and the intimate medley of spectacular and emotional elements point to Gozzi. On the other hand, the pathos and melodrama of Agnes' life in Bluebeard's house, especially her overpowering curiosity and her experiences in the forbidden chamber of horrors, are relics of German Storm and Stress. All these elements are excellently done. The atmosphere of horror is capital and reveals such outstanding dramatic ability that Hebbel later called it one of the finest works in all literature.[28]

By investing the old story in a garb of satire, Tieck, then, carried out in his own way the ideas of Gozzi; but he made the work a bit incongruous thereby. For the plain narrative of the gruesome, even tragic, action does not always harmonize with his ironic sallies against "prim poets," shallow popular philosophy and Fichtean idealism. Perhaps the satirical woof is too slender to balance that stark realism of the original story which gives the drama its unusually strong moving interest. The alternation of tragic and comic scenes, especially the entertaining conversations of Claus, the Fool, and the Councillor, who constantly fluctuate between the two worlds of the real and the imaginary, smack of Shakespeare. Yet Tieck stresses the diverting episodes more than Shakespeare does.

In *Blaubart*, as in his later plays of this kind, plain logic is supplemented by more profound psychological motivation. The play is full of effective contrasts. The three brothers, Anton, Simon and Leopold, represent geniality, pedantry and melancholy dreaming, respectively.

One of the two sisters is jovial, the other sad; one of the fools is genuine, the other affects idiocy. Simon, the hypochondriac, is given "second sense," true to the author's fatalistic beliefs. Among other things, this character divines the outcome of the play—his murder of Bluebeard— in a dream. The action moves slowly. Each successive mood is dwelt upon with care. The ironical tone, which comes out strongest in the two fools, proves so infectious that it is communicated to the more serious characters.

We have suggested that *Blaubart* owes something to the puppet shows. Indeed, all his works of this genre resemble these plays in their creation of childlike illusions and in the display of an irony which looks down from above and leaves the ultimate control of the situation in the hand of him who guides the strings. No wonder that Tieck's first attempt along these lines, *Hanswurst als Emigrant*, had actually been a marionette play.

The satirical fairy drama of the Bluebeard type was destined to become popular with Tieck. And with good reason, for it fits his nature like a glove. Here he found an excellent opportunity for giving free play to fancy and reason alike. Here was a vehicle for his perplexing dual nature. The dramatization of simple fairy tales served him as a welcome means of introducing elements and designs quite alien to the fairy tales themselves.

As we have indicated, the most characteristic trait of the work, and indeed of all the similar dramas which he was still to write, is the incongruousness and duality of the two chief ingredients. On the one hand we have the fairy-tale element and on the other the mordant humor which, though hardly more than plain irony *sans phrase*, is usually referred to by the technical term "Romantic Irony." Like the marionette play, all the works of this type contain some parody of the dramatic form. Irony and satire always lurk in the background. If we bear this in mind and read them in the serio-comic spirit in which they are written, they retain a certain artistic value and authenticity. But few would agree with Hebbel's opinion, mentioned above, or with Solger, who called *Blaubart* a "truly classical work" (das wahrhaft klassische Werk).[29]

Tieck's "Romantic Irony,"[30] a term much used and frequently misinterpreted, is found in essence even earlier than *William Lovell*, but is best seen in his dramatized fairy tales of a satirical vein. It was natural to a man endowed with such intellectual mobility, and was early emphasized by his teacher Bernhardi. But its technique was not original with Tieck. Beaumont and Fletcher had used it in *The Knight of the Burning*

Pestle, when they introduced two characters who appear as spectators and, unable to distinguish the real from the make-believe, criticize the acting of one of their apprentices. Ben Jonson had employed it constantly. In the clown scenes of *A Midsummer Night's Dream* we find it suggested by Shakespeare; Holberg applied it in *Ulysses of Ithaca* at the expense of the Aristotelian unities, when he has a young man make his exit, only to return immediately as an old graybeard. We find it frequently in Aristophanes, Cervantes, Fielding and Foote, also in Gozzi, Sterne, Swift and Jean Paul.

To Tieck "Romantic Irony" meant toying with his art and amounted in practice to the arbitrary destruction of his own poetical illusion. It served him as an expression of his strong native subjectivism and as a means of purging himself thereof.[31] He used it as a mediating force between his critical reason and his unbridled poetic fancy. Born actor, he continually felt constrained to play a. part. His "Romantic Irony" facilitated this. Hence, while other writers, particularly Shakespeare and Cervantes, employed it as a creative, cosmic force—a means of deliberately stressing their independence with respect to their environment—, he used it as a sop to his histrionic nature. Unfortunately he overdid the device, which he once described, in its highest form,[32] as "that ultimate perfection of a work of art, the guarantee and highest proof of true enthusiasm, that ethereal spirit which . . . hovers contented and naïve over the whole."[33] In ridiculing even his characters and plots—a thing which would never have occurred to Shakespeare—he impaired the effect of his writings. He was the first noted ironist without a single definite point of view, who satirized anything and anyone, even himself. Indeed, he seemed to aim less at satire for its own sake than at toying with confusion.

Friedrich Schlegel's "Romantic Irony," as defined none too clearly in the *Athenäum*, is different from Tieck's. It is derived chiefly from Shakespeare, despite Schlegel's denial of this source. Schlegel would use it as a means of contemplating individual objects of our relative and conditional environment in the light of cosmic absoluteness. Tieck's later friend, the philosopher Solger, devoted much acumen to the analysis of "Romantic Irony." Other writers, among them Brentano, Eichendorff, Grabbe and Heine, employed it after Tieck. But it redounds to his credit that in his hands it never became as cynical and nihilistic as in Heine's.

Blaubart must have pleased Karl Nicolai and his friends beyond all expectation, for prompted by the suggestion of a "clever, worthy woman,"[34] Elisa von der Recke, he presently urged Tieck to write another work on the same subject, showing as piquantly as possible how each of

Bluebeard's seven wives falls prey to him. Thus arose the "psychological" prose tale *Die sieben Weiber des Blaubart* (1797), which, however, does not exactly carry out the original intention. In effect it is a satirization of the popular novels of knighthood, ultimately becoming a satirization of this satirization. Gotten out anonymously by Nicolai as a separate work, not as a part of the *Volksmährchen*, it professes to be published in Turkey. Tieck himself had a poor opinion of the composition and rightly so, for it lacks all piquancy and is a disconnected medley of sense and nonsense, gruesomeness and fun. In 1828 he described it as a sort of repudiation of the "moral tendency"[34] in the literature of the later Enlightenment and as a "playground for roguery, fun, curious happenings, and, indeed, bizarre critique and self-persiflage of the action."[35] One of the features, borrowed from Gozzi, is the introduction of a leaden head, a gift to the hero from his fairy godmother. This head, when properly questioned, gives him excellent advice. He consults it whenever he is about to marry, but, since it steadfastly counsels him against matrimony, he invariably disregards its advice. After it is finally buried with due ceremony, its gravestone is marked with the following satirical epitaph: "Stay, wanderer! Hereunder lies a great soul, which gave itself up entirely to the pursuit of wisdom, and developed only the head as the noblest part of the body." Incidentally this work involved Tieck in an altercation with the censor, who objected so strongly to the tone of the first chapter on "Moralität"—a persiflage of traditional morality—that he was compelled to rewrite it.[36]

Of the eight works which Tieck incorporated in his *Volksmährchen*, the unpretentious little tale *Der blonde Eckbert*, which in a general way belongs to the same type as *Blaubart* and *Die schöne Magelone*, is by far the best. It alone offers a modern reader quite the same enjoyment and pleasure which his contemporaries must have derived from it. Its genesis is interesting. Pressed by insatiable Karl Nicolai to supply more grist for his publishing mill, he responded that he was working on a story to be entitled *Der blonde Eckbert*. As a matter of fact, he had neither begun the tale nor even planned the plot; the title came to him on the spur of the moment.[37] This is characteristic of so improvisatory a writer.

It is a weird story of sin, belated remorse and retribution, which, if a lesson is to be read into it, teaches that a wrong once committed can never be effaced. On a misty evening in autumn, by the fitful light of the moon and the fireplace, Eckbert's wife, Bertha, tells his friend Walther the story of her youth—how she left home and wandered off to live with a strange old hag, who owned a dog and a bird. The bird laid a precious egg—a jewel—every day and sang a quaint and happy but untranslatable song:

> Waldeinsamkeit,
> Die mich erfreut,
> So morgen wie heut
> In ewger Zeit,
> O wie mich freut
> Waldeinsamkeit.

One day Bertha stole the bird in the old woman's absence and fled; its song grew plaintive:

> Waldeinsamkeit,
> Wie liegst du weit!
> O dich gereut
> Einst mit der Zeit.—
> Ach einzge Freud,
> Waldeinsamkeit.

Finally it died. Then she enjoyed life with the proceeds of the precious eggs she had taken, and eventually married Eckbert.

Walther seems to have had previous knowledge of Bertha's story, for he mentions the name of the hag's dog. His friendship for Eckbert now cools markedly. Bertha, tortured by remorse and disturbed by Walther's strange demeanor, dies. Eckbert, distrusting Walther, kills him.

A new friend, Hugo, also proves untrue to Eckbert, who seems to recognize Walther in him. To his horror Eckbert, now a morose hermit, chances upon the old woman with her dog and bird. They have both been restored to life, it seems. The bird now sings:

> Waldeinsamkeit
> Mich wieder freut,
> Mir geschieht kein Leid.
> Hier wohnt kein Neid,
> Von neuem mich freut
> Waldeinsamkeit.

The hag reveals to him that both Walther and Hugo were in reality she; that Bertha was actually Eckbert's sister; that Bertha failed to stand the mysterious test to which she was put when entrusted with the bird (which is perhaps the embodiment of poesy), and that her evil deed led to a chain of sins, as well as to her own and Eckbert's undoing.

The principal motif and the atmosphere of horror have a mysterious fascination. They are derived from stories which Tieck heard as a child on his mother's lap. An old hag and her dog Strameh or Strohmian, in particular, stood out in his mind as subjects of his mother's narratives. Intermingled with such recollections are echoes of fairly-tale motifs (the oppressive secret, the rewarding and punishing witch) and of one of Musäus's tales, *Ulrich mit dem Bühel*, where the golden eggs are laid by a hen, which is also stolen by an ungrateful refugee. Finally there is the mystic charm of "Waldeinsamkeit"—sylvan solitude—as expressed in the variated song of the miraculous bird.

A veil of poetry is cast about the whole story, and not even an echo of the actual world penetrates it. The real and the unreal become organic units. The miraculous is treated as if it were the most natural thing. Our power of reasoning avails us naught in analyzing it. If the hag assumes several forms, is this a dream? If Eckbert sees Walther, Hugo and the hag as different manifestations of one and the same being, is it madness? Yet Eckbert is not described as psychopathic. The only explanation can be that Tieck has erased all borderlines. His method fuses the mythical specter (such as Banquo, seen only by Macbeth) with the psychic ghost (Hamlet's father, seen by all) and creates a "magic idealism." The only minor flaw of the story is the obtrusiveness of the motivation. The theme of unwitting incest at the end (compare *Peter Lebrecht*) might well have been dispensed with. But this, like the "moral lesson," is secondary. What counts here is not so much Bertha's guilt as the fastening of the mood of horror upon helpless human beings.

The word "Waldeinsamkeit" was coined by Tieck for this story. It has come to acquire a broad connotation, suggesting the green of the forest; a clear, bright twilight; the hallowed rustling of the treetops; the singing of the birds; the detachment of the individual from the world in some cool forest glen. When Tieck read the tale to a group of friends, Wackenroder objected to the term, calling it unheard-of and un-German and suggesting "Waldeseinsamkeit" in its place.[37] Despite his magisterial strictures it has found acceptance as an expression of those strangely mixed emotions which pervade the story. In the first volume of the *Athenäum*, and again orally in 1800, A. W. Schlegel fittingly described the verses on "Waldeinsamkeit" as the quintessence of Tieck's poetry.

Der blonde Eckbert is a product of dreams and fancies, which spin a web of varicolored moods and atmospheres. Like the fairy tale *Nadir* in *Almansur*, and the *Straussfedern* story *Der Fremde*, it delves into the depths of the subconscious. It combines the "sweet shudderings" of his early youth and the alluring music of *Magelone*. He quite succeeds in giving poetic form to his mystic feeling for nature (a secularized type of mysticism) and in making of nature a sort of allegory for the vague strivings and imaginings of mankind. The awe-inspiring potency of Romantic writing is here seen at its best. True to his fatalism, which told him that man is at the mercy of higher powers and of his own impulses, the horrible or demonic is conceived as residing in nature itself and as controlling and overpowering man. Though dreadful and all-pervading, it has an irresistible fascination for mortals.

This active element of fear, so different from the naïveté and light-heartedness of the average German fairy tale, contrasts strongly with the passive, calm, dignified tone in which he relates his narrative. His language is a beautiful poetized prose, much like Goethe's at its best and quite dissimilar from that of young Schiller, who had frequently been his model. But it is far from mere imitation of Goethe (though inspired by his *Märchen* in the *Unterhaltungen deutscher Ausgewan-derten*) and reveals a new, typically Romantic style, which appears more or less markedly in all of Tieck's later works.

With *Der blonde Eckbert* he also inaugurated a new development of the technique of interpolating verse in a prose work. He had always individualized such verse through the medium of a character or a situation, so that it either served as an incident in the plot or added lyric flavor. But here he uses as an interspersion the single strophic poem quoted above, which recurs as a *leitmotif* attuned to each prevailing mood. It expresses the inmost spirit of the whole work and grows out of the prose and back into it again.[38]

There is complete harmony between content and form. The tale is told as in a dream. Even the tempo of the narrative, at first measured and slow but growing faster and faster as the climax approaches, is adapted to the changing mood.

Three categories of Romantic fairy tales may be distinguished: 1. in which supernatural characters associate with ordinary men (Musäus, Fouqué), 2. in which the characters and atmosphere are exclusively supernatural (Goethe's *Märchen*), and 3. in which the supernatural characters are mere hallucinations of the hero. *Der blonde Eckbert* blends all three categories but tends to stress the third.

Tieck's contemporaries were enthralled by the work. Schiller's friend Huber and later Hebbel called it one of the best tales in literature; Steffens related that without its salutary lesson, its effect upon him would have been annihilating.[39] Nor is it any wonder that, with its matchless imagery, it has remained a favorite in Germany and has contributed to keeping the spark of Romanticism alive there. The musician Ernst Rudorff was inspired by it to compose an overture. The popularity of *Der blonde Eckbert* in England is more surprising. Between 1823 and 1845 four different English renderings appeared; the best is by Thomas Carlyle.[40] W. Fischer has published an Esperanto translation (Magdeburg, 1909). In 1933 a French translation by Albert Béguin appeared in Paris in the collection *La coupe d'or*. Recently, too, an Italian text edition by Mondini appeared in Florence.

We have completed our consideration of volumes 1 and 3 of the *Volksmährchen*. The former contains *Der blonde Eckbert*, *Blaubart* and *Die Heymons Kinder*; the latter *Die Schildbürger* and the drama *Karl von Berneck*. The second volume offers two other works besides *Magelone*. The one, *Ein Prolog*,[41] written in iambic pentameters and stylistically dependent upon Jonson's prolog to *Every Man in his Humour*, as well as on Goethe's early satirical Shrovetide plays, anticipates the other, *Der gestiefelte Kater*, in form as well as content. The scene is the auditorium of a theater and the characters are the spectators awaiting the rise of the curtain. The wit and satire—not yet as pungent as in *Der gestiefelte Kater*—are directed against the popular contemporary plays and the audiences who enjoy them. A transient Englishman, disgusted by the coarseness of the rest of the spectators, leaves the theater before the performance begins, preferring to sacrifice his admission fee rather than "wait among stupid fools for something stupid to happen." Tieck also takes the opportunity to ridicule Fichte's idealism when he has one of the spectators deny the real existence of aught but himself.

If *Blaubart* is a dramatized fairy tale with an appendage of incidental literary satire, *Der gestiefelte Kater*,[42] again written in a single evening, is a dramatized literary satire with an incidentally appended fairy tale. It brings to the fore a new type of fairy-tale treatment—the ironic-satiric travesty. Whereas the other three types which we have considered, well exemplified in *Die Heymons Kinder*, *Die Schildbürger* and *Blaubart*, respectively, all took at least their own poetic form seriously, the new type toys even with the poet's creative function. Out of the simple contrast between archaic form and modern meaning there has developed a three-cornered contrast between subject matter, form and the process of writing itself. Thus the demand of the Schlegels for "Universalpoesie" was met with a satiric "Universalpoem."

The play appeared in two separate editions (one claiming to be an Italian translation), as well as in the *Volksmährchen*. Once again Perrault (and to some extent also the Italians Straparola and Basile) furnished the tale—the famous story of Puss in Boots who wins a kingdom for its master—, and Gozzi the spirit of the work, the plan of attack against literary adversaries, and numerous inventions of character and motive. Tieck was familiar, too, with the works of the Irish-French writer Anthony Hamilton, particularly with *Le Belier*, a parody of Perrault, and *Contes des Fées*, satires on the Romantic tales. But his purpose was diametrically opposed to Hamilton's. Numerous other models were also used. Besides Gozzi, he mentioned *Melampe* and *Ulysses* of the Danish Holberg, the Elizabethans Fletcher and Jonson, Swift and above all Aristophanes.[32] He might have referred also to the Viennese burlesques, a popular type. In each of these models he could see the stage used as a means for ridiculing itself.

In Tieck's play the literary lampoonery, of which he proves a master, is aimed chiefly against that Rationalism once described by him as a deliberate attempt to cut man off from heavenly and eternal things[43] and another time as "vapidity which, devoid of understanding for depth and mystery, dragged everything it could not and would not understand before the bar of so-called human reason."[44] It is also aimed at the fickleness and stupidity of the unimaginative audiences of the day. "Enlightened," as they were, they demanded absolute verisimilitude and crass illusions instead of giving free rein to their fancy. Incidentally the satire is directed against sentimentalism, the vapid plays of Iffland and Kotzebue, exaggerated admiration of Mozart's music (as Tieck, otherwise an admirer of Mozart, thought) and of stage settings, and the banishment of the clown from the German stage.

In part the shafts of ridicule are turned against the archeologist Karl August Böttiger, too, who had just published what to Tieck seemed a puerile book in praise of the acting of Iffland, for whom he never had much use. When he wrote *Der gestiefelte Kater*, he had not made the personal acquaintance of Böttiger, who was the director of the "Gymnasium" in Weimar. But soon after they had an embarrassing meeting at Herder's house.

In 1828 Tieck wrote of his *Kater*: "All my recollections—what I had heard at different times in the pit, in the loges or the salons—awoke, and so this Kater arose and was written in a few happy hours. It was not my avowed purpose to depreciate anyone through bitterness, or to insist stubbornly on some tenet, or even to praise up better things; whatever seemed to me silly or stupid was represented as such with all its contradictions and ridiculous presumptions, and clearly illustrated by just as stupid but jolly a nursery tale."[45]

Tieck's "Romantic Irony" is here self-evident. It is not only characterized by abrupt transitions from the serious to the comic vein, but the serious passages are written in a mood of sly humor, and vice versa. The author constantly remains master of the situation; his characters are mere puppets. The spectators rail at the actors, thus becoming actors themselves, while the actors ridicule the spectators, thus taking their place. The play itself is criticized. A discussion as to whether the audience is well depicted leads to resentment on the part of members of the audience. So he gleefully perplexes his "enlightened" contemporaries. Above this motley array lingers Tieck, who laughs the whole throng to scorn. The total impression, as was noted, is one of a three-sided contrast and of infinite Aristophanic wit—as if we were regarding a droll figure reflected in a maze of mirrors—, the real blending with the phenomenal in bewildering confusion and both being ridiculed. No doubt this is what A. W. Schlegel had in mind when he termed the play "das Schauspiel eines Schauspiels."[46]

Though Tieck denied it, his work probably contains some political satire, too. The Bugbear is said to be a reference to the French Revolution, the king is supposed to remind of Frederick William II of Prussia, the princess of Countess Lichtenau, Nathanael von Malsinki of the Tsar, and Leander of Aloys Hirt, the tutor of Prince Henry of Prussia.[47] However, these political allusions should not be taken seriously, for Tieck always kept aloof from the important questions of the day.

Later, in volume 2 of *Phantasus*, he published a revised and inferior version of the play. The satire at Iffland's expense was broadened, the figure of Böttiger made more ludicrous, and a new character, the Mystic, introduced. He represented Zacharias Werner, the father of the Fate Drama, whose religious play, *Das Kreuz an der Ostsee* (1806), aroused Tieck's ridicule.

Whoever would read the bold, sardonic play nowadays should read it in its original form. It is not difficult to catch its general spirit, for philistinism and literalness are ever with us, but fully to appreciate its satire is another matter. The elder Nicolai wrote to Tieck on December 19, 1797: "When you allude to anecdotes of the local stage in *Der gestiefelte Kater*, it is perhaps not even interesting for local readers, who regard unimportant anecdotes of the theater and the pit as despicable. But what, then, are readers in other places to think, if they do not know what they are reading about?"[48] Perhaps Friedrich Schlegel was thinking of this when he wrote to his brother that the play is not "rich, insolent and poetic enough" (nicht reich, frech und nicht poetisch genug).[49]

In extenuation we may say that literary satire is as legitimate as political satire and that Tieck's allusions are no more obscure than those in Goethe's Walpurgis-Night scenes. Moreover, works in this vein are exhibits of the literary foibles of their day. In a deeper sense they ridicule life itself and smile over the whole breadth of the earth.[50] In his letter to Goethe of April 10, 1798, Schiller referred to "unser würdiger gestiefelter Kater."

As for the fairy tale, the figures remind of wood carvings or marionettes and can be enjoyed even by children. Much has become proverbial, thus the king who dotes on roast rabbit and the princess who writes poetry but is weak in grammar. It has usually been called a poor stage play, though Tieck meant it for the stage.[51] To be sure, its performance in Berlin at the command of Frederick William IV (1844) was not a success. But a revision by Jürgen Fehling for the Berlin Volksbühne in 1921 enjoyed popularity. In book-form Tieck's burlesque, which inspired A. W. Schlegel, Eichendorff, Oehlenschläger, Platen, Brentano and Immermann in a like direction, had immediate success. As late as 1921 E. Maddalena published an Italian translation in Florence. The popularity of the work actuated Tieck to write similar plays. This was a mistake; one such venture was sufficient.

Die verkehrte Welt, ein historisches Schauspiel in fünf Aufzügen, written in a few days, was planned as a counterpart. Its source was an idea in a play by the same name in the *Zittauisches Theater* (1683) of Christian Weise. In spirit it is indebted to Cervantes' *Viage del Parnaso*. Again literary satire prevails; the execution reminds of the Viennese burlesque parody. Skaramuz and Pierrot, mask-like figures and stock comic characters, resemble Gozzi's masks. The parody of a naval battle in Act IV can be traced to Gozzi.

In a prolog (called epilog, while the prolog is at the end) an orchestra and a symphony express their opinions. The plot concerns the stupid clown Skaramuz, who has usurped Apollo's place. He feeds Pegasus and the rest of his live stock in the stables and makes a spa of the Castalian spring. To the Muses he issues quarterly leases on Parnassus, at the foot of which a baker and a brewer are established. He claims to be the prime mover of the arts and boasts that he has at last made Parnassus arable. But war arises between Skaramuz and Apollo. The spectators scramble upon the stage to take sides with Skaramuz. Apollo is victorious.

The technique of *Der gestiefelte Kater* has been carried to extremes, for the barrier between stage and audience disappears entirely. In Tieck's opinion, as expressed in a sort of Aristophanic parabasis, good confusion is better than bad order.

Originally *Die verkehrte Welt* was intended for the *Straussfedern* (not the *Volksmährchen*, as Tieck later said),[52] but in a sharply critical, though not unfair letter[48] Nicolai turned it down, calling it eccentric, unnatural, obscure and misleading in its allusions. In view of the many perversions, it is no wonder that, according to Tieck's own statement of 1828,[53] the publisher mistook Acts I-III and Acts IV-V, respectively, for two different plays. Unger also rejected it. Finally it was published in Bernhardi's *Bambocciaden* (1799), with a preface stating that the work is partly Bernhardi's. The latter had made this misstatement the condition for accepting it. It is wellnigh impossible of production. One feels sure that the projected performance of which Eduard Mörike spoke in his novel *Maler Nolten* would have been unfeasible. The version in volume 2 of *Phantasus* is a revision. Schleiermacher found it very witty and mirth-provoking, adding that "Tieck is in a class by himself" (einzigartig).[54] Wilhelm Grimm later deemed it his brightest and best work.[55]

Another play of similar character, in six acts, written with "true youthful enthusiasm" (aus wahrer Begeisterung der Jugend),[56] is entitled *Zerbino, oder die Reise nach dem guten Geschmack, gewissermassen eine Fortsetzung des gestiefelten Katers*. The name Zerbino may have been suggested by a play of Lenz, now lost, called *Zerbin, oder die neuere Philosophie*.[57] Tieck's work was published at Leipzig and Jena in 1799, and in the same year also in the *Romantische Dichtungen*. Here the influence of A. W. Schlegel, who in a letter of December 11, 1797, suggested a drama of this very kind, is already apparent.[58] In 1828, when revising it for his *Schriften*, Tieck deemed it necessary to write a twenty-page commentary.[59] And indeed, this was imperative, for *Zerbino* teems with obscure literary references. It is also a *locus classicus* for "Romantic Irony."

Zerbino is the son and heir of Gottlieb, the owner of Puss in Boots. He suffers from sentimentality. Turned into a "promising young man" by the magician Polykomikus, he sets out in search of good taste. He meets with the various literary tendencies of the day, which appear in allegorical form. This affords opportunity for attacking Nicolai, Kotzebue, Iffland, Falk and others. (Tieck's denial of this intention cannot be credited.)[60] Nicolai, as Nestor, runs across Dante and Ariosto in the garden of poetry, quarrels with them and gives vent to his anger at failing to find Bodmer, Gellert and Gessner. Gozzi, Petrarch, Tasso, Hans Sachs and G. A. Bürger also appear. Dante, Shakespeare, Cervantes and Goethe are celebrated as the "Sacred Four" of modern art, and those who disagree with Tieck's interpretation of any or all of them (as Soltau, the Rationalist translator of Cervantes, had misconceived the "Romanticism" of the Spanish satirist) are berated. High tribute is paid to Goethe,

With whose name art in Germany awakes,[61]
Who still will sing you many noble songs
To light your hearts with rays of poesy,
That henceforth ye may understand it well.*

Failing to discover good taste, because the language of nature and of
the great poets can no longer be understood, Zerbino decides to seek it in
Zerbino itself, or, in its absence, to destroy the play and with it himself.
With the aid of Nestor he reverses the drama, and the previous scenes
reoccur. Finally Tieck must enlist the aid of his compositors, readers and
critics to set the play aright and make the continuation of the performance possible. Returning finally to his court, Zerbino discovers that his
derelict dog Stallmeister (Burgsdorff owned a dog by that name) has
become court pedagog. He calls him a dog, is pronounced crazy and
imprisoned. Only after he has solemnly declared that poetry is folly
and the Enlightenment admirable is he released.

This rollicking hodgepodge of irony and nonsense, in which trees,
flowers, bushes, birds and even the blue of heaven become articulate,
defies description. In deference to the wishes of A. W. Schlegel, its plan
and purpose are more ambitious than those of *Der gestiefelte Kater*.
Tieck does not merely wish to cast floodlights upon the two opposing
domains of imaginative poetry and sober prose. He aims to give an
exhaustive description of their character. The result is a surfeit of lyric
interludes and extravaganzas. In the end these, though often admirable
in themselves, destroy the unity and coherence, which are throughout
menaced by the poet's sovran play of wit. As Hebbel later remarked in
his diary (I, 323), the purpose of the work—to advocate true poetry by
showing up the false—is defeated by its wretched form. A suggestion
of Goethe, that Tieck let him have the idyllic section of the drama for
the Weimar stage, was happily disregarded. Tieck never seriously
thought of *Zerbino* as a stage play. But the Austrian writer Collin rated
this as Tieck's best work.[62]

Zerbino is not without traces of fatalism; thus the old king is clearly
a fatalist. The leading motif—a prince suffering from a baffling disease
—is borrowed from Gozzi's *L'amore delle tre melarance*, a fiaba which
Goethe had used in *Der Triumph der Empfindsamkeit*.[63] As always,

---

* Mit dessen Namen Deutschlands Kunst erwacht,
  Der euch noch viele edle Lieder singt,
  Um euch ins Herz den Glanz der Poesie
  Zu strahlen, dass ihr künftig sie versteht.

LUDWIG TIECK, THE GERMAN ROMANTICIST

Tieck made free use of many sources. In discussing his fairy-tale dramas from *Blaubart* to *Zerbino* we have mentioned his chief literary models; they extend from Aristophanes to Christian Weise. We may now add the pseudo-Shakespearean *Pericles*. It so enthralled him with its fusion of epic and dramatic elements that he modelled a whole series of plays, *Zerbino*, *Genoveva* and *Octavian*, upon it.[64] Finally we mention the early burlesques of Henry Fielding (*Tom Thumb* and *Pasquin*) and the satirical middle-class comedies of Samuel Foote (*The Minor*, *The Orators* and *The Devil upon Two Sticks*).[65] It is not without significance that between 1796 and 1798 Nicolai, perhaps at Tieck's suggestion, published a translation of the *Dramatic Works* of Foote under the editorship of F. H. Bothe.

We have pursued Tieck's career between 1795 and 1799 far enough to realize that during these years he blazed new trails. He revived the old chapbooks and fairy tales, or at least their spirit, in narrative or dramatic form. *Die Heymons Kinder* he reproduced in an archaizing, consciously naïve style (type 1); *Die Schildbürger* (and before it *Abraham Tonelli*) in a satirical spirit (type 2). Two old tales he treated in a more artful, artificial manner (type 3), the one (*Die schöne Magelone*) in a lyricizing narrative reproduction, the other (*Blaubart*) in a psychological dramatic style. The tale *Der blonde Eckbert*, though original in plot, belongs to the same general category. A fourth type was introduced by the ironic-satiric travesties of fairy-tale material, *Der gestiefelte Kater*, *Die verkehrte Welt* and *Zerbino*. All these types, with the addition of a fifth in *Genoveva* and *Octavian*, were destined to be used for many years more, as we shall see. Type 3, especially, won his favor. A whole series of stories, among them *Der Runenberg*, *Liebeszauber*, *Die Elfen* and *Der Pokal*, resemble *Der blonde Eckbert* in being independent works which breathe the spirit of the "Volksbücher." In German they are called "Kunstmärchen."[66]

Thus Tieck, in tapping the springs of popular poetry, paved the way for a wealth of poetic creations and quickened his own pulse beat as a poet. He envisaged Shakespeare and Goethe with new eyes. Poetry and art were set upon a loftier pinnacle. He began to see life whole. He who had been more or less an artificer now became a poet. Moreover, the old folk poetry cured his imagination of morbidity. By and large, no other single influence in his life proved as potent or as happy. We may call him the first poet of urban and urbane life. In the writings of the *Volks-*

mährchen class, praised by Savigny as a storehouse of serious and humorous writings, superior to Jean Paul and not inferior to Goethe,[67] he has earned that title by making the popular literature of the Middle Ages palatable to the city-bred of his day through a seasoning of satire, urbane wit and Romanticism.

CHAPTER SIX

COLLABORATION WITH WACKENRODER AND
NEW ASSOCIATIONS

WE HAVE pointed out that Tieck combated egoism with the theme of altruistic love and by the use of irony. Another weapon in this constant struggle now came to his attention. He had always been interested in art. The fondness and talent for art evinced by his brother Friedrich formed an important factor from the start. His earliest impressions were secured at Reichardt's home in Berlin; he was imbued with a more profound love for every phase of art by Wackenroder. Journeys with the latter in 1793, 1794 and 1796, when he caught glimpses of the collections at Pommersfelden, Braunschweig, Wolfenbüttel, Nürnberg and Dresden were of importance and led to certain writings which mark a definite stage in his search for an objective outlook.

While the works of the *Volksmährchen* class, characterized by childlike feeling, unrestrained imagination and satire against the Enlightenment, were appearing, these new writings, in which a novel view of art was expressed, were taking shape in his mind. If the *Volksmährchen* were an indirect reflection of Wackenroder's enthusiasm for the literature of medieval Germany, the new books revealed the direct inspiration of Wackenroder and his sincere love for the days of yore, in particular for their art. They contain more the thoughts and emotions of Wackenroder than of Tieck. The latter merely added some lucubrations of his own along the general lines pursued by his friend. These works are three in number. In two, *Herzensergiessungen eines kunstliebenden Klosterbruders* (1797) and *Phantasien über die Kunst, für Freunde der Kunst* (1799), Tieck and Wackenroder collaborated throughout. The third, *Franz Sternbalds Wanderungen. Eine altdeutsche Geschichte* (1798), was composed entirely by Tieck but inspired in its colloquies by Wackenroder.[1]

The *Herzensergiessungen*, conceived and in part written by Wackenroder without Tieck's knowledge, derive their name from the fiction with which their authors surrounded the work. The supposed writer is a lay brother (a favorite figure since Lessing's *Nathan der Weise*) who "pours out his heart" on the subject of art. This notion was suggested by Reichardt, who at Tieck's request brought out one of the papers (Wackenroder's panegyric of Dürer) in 1796 as a sample in his periodical

Deutschland. Reichardt feared that in the absence of such a fiction his contemporaries would not understand the warm enthusiasm for the much despised art of the Middle Ages here manifested. The sober Protestantism of the late eighteenth century was worlds removed from the realm of the Renaissance.

To a large extent the anonymously published *Herzensergiessungen*, over three-fourths of which is Wackenroder's work, are short narratives dealing with medieval painters and their paintings. Much of the material is derived from a noted work of Giorgio Vasari (1511-1574), the Italian Renaissance painter, architect and writer. Vasari's book is entitled *Le vite de' più eccelente pittori, scultori ed architetti* (1550). Other works which influenced Wackenroder are Malvasia's *Felsina pittrice* (1678), Bellori's *Le vite de' pittori, scultori ed architetti moderni* (1728), German works of J. G. Bohm and J. von Sandrart, and Felibien's *Entretiens*.

Interested at first only in the art of medieval Germany, Tieck and Wackenroder had broadened their perspective upon a visit to the Dresden gallery in 1796 and had come to realize that the Italian painters of the Renaissance were easily the peers of Dürer, Cranach and Krafft. And so we find in the *Herzensergiessungen*, side by side with a paper "In Honor of the Memory of our Venerable Sire Albrecht Dürer" (Ehrengedächtnis unseres ehrwürdigen Ahnherrn Albrecht Dürers), tributes to Raphael, Francesco Francia, Leonardo da Vinci, Pietro di Cosimo and Michael Angelo.

We hear Raphael saying to a disciple: "The world singles out many special qualities in my pictures; and when my attention is called to this or that good point, I must sometimes regard my own work with a smile because I have succeeded so well with it. But it was all achieved as in a delightful dream, and while I worked I always gave more thought to the subject than to the mode of representing it."[2] The tone of the papers is well struck by this flagrantly anachronistic interpretation of Raphael's method. There is nowhere a word of criticism, comparison or analysis. Enthusiasm, reverence and belief are everything.

Of Leonardo we read: "In him the disciples of art who are eager to learn may see that it is not enough to pledge allegiance to a flag, and to practise their hand in skilful wielding of the brush, and, armed with a slight and volatile pseudo-enthusiasm, to campaign against pensive study based upon a true foundation. Such an example will teach them that the genius of art is not unwillingly mated with austere Minerva; and that in a great and open soul, when it is directed toward a single major endeavor, the entire multifariously complex image of human knowledge is mirrored in lovely and perfect harmony."[3]

LUDWIG TIECK, THE GERMAN ROMANTICIST

We find also apostrophes to faith as the concomitant of true art. In a paper by Tieck, *Brief eines jungen deutschen Malers in Rom*, this idea is carried to extremes. A Catholic service which the young German painter attends in Rome makes so deep an impression upon him that he embraces the Catholic faith, like Schiller's Mortimer in *Maria Stuart*, written three years later.

But the most significant of these diaphanous, almost timid confessions of faith in art (they may be called the tenets of a religion of art) are the profoundly inspired essays wherein nature and art are lauded as divine languages, and the enjoyment of art is conceived as tantamount to prayer. "Art represents for us the pinnacle of human perfection. Nature, as much as the mortal eye can see of it, resembles interrupted oracles from the mouth of the godhead. But if it be permitted to speak thus of such things, we may perhaps say that God contemplates the whole of nature or the whole world as we regard a work of art."[4] And great works of art "do not exist so that the eye may see them, but that man may enter into them with his heart, which comes to meet them, and that he may live and breathe for them."[5] Thus nature, art and religion are enlisted to complement each other, in preparation for the Christian mythology of Hölderlin and Schelling.[6]

We have sought to point out in the Introduction that Romanticism is really a philosophical school striving to revamp our forms of life on the basis of a new knowledge of the meaning of life. To the Romanticists, and to Wackenroder in particular, the creative faculty is only one phase of their striving for this new consciousness. Hence they were always at pains to understand and interpret, philosophically, the nature and problems of art. Hence their study of art is not empty estheticism, but an attempt better to grasp and explain life and the world. Naturally, then, in their eyes the activity of the artist partakes of religion. In this sense Wackenroder was a hierophant of art.

In the *Herzensergiessungen*, Wackenroder also gave splendid though vague and emotional utterance to his love for music. Two papers which he calls "The Remarkable Musical Life of the Tone Artist Joseph Berglinger" (Das merkwürdige musikalische Leben des Tonkünstlers Joseph Berglinger) are devoted to this subject. Joseph is transfigured whenever he hears music in a church or at a concert. "It seemed as if his soul were disembodied and hovered freely in space, or as if his body, too, had turned soul."[7] In the fate of the gentle youth who is too ethereal for this world and who, after pouring forth his very soul in an impassioned oratorio, dies in the flower of his years, Wackenroder unwittingly depicted his own sad lot. He died of a nervous fever on February 13, 1798, at the age of twenty-five.

After Wackenroder's death Tieck got out a series of his friend's papers which he entitled *Phantasien für die Kunst, für Freunde der Kunst* (published by Perthes, with whom he remained in touch for over thirty years).[8] Here he interpolated original essays written under Wackenroder's inspiration. About three-fifths of the work is Tieck's. In the *Phantasien* the spirit of the two Berglinger letters is further dwelt upon, and music is given precedence over painting. We find apostrophes upon "the miracles of the art of tones" (die Wunder der Tonkunst), on "various species of each art, particularly the different types of church music" (Von den verschiedenen Gattungen in jeder Kunst und insbesondere von verschiedenen Arten der Kirchenmusik), on "the peculiar inner nature of the art of music" (das eigentümliche innere Wesen der Tonkunst), and on "the psychology of present-day instrumental music" (Seelenlehre der heutigen Instrumentalmusik). Music is styled the richer language, which contemns words because it can better give expression to deep, pious faith and mysterious emotion. The beautiful, naïve admiration for music, especially instrumental music, expressed in these papers is almost unparalleled in literature. One must go to some of the finer examples of Luther's Table Talks to find their equal in German letters. The great composer whom Tieck seeks in the essay *Symphonien* to write a symphony of victory for the last act of Goethe's *Egmont* arose soon after in the person of Beethoven.

To be sure, Tieck became guilty of overemphasis. He explicitly tried to transform poetry into music, as he had implicitly attempted in *Die schöne Magelone*, and sang:

> Love doth think in music rare,[9]
> Thoughts are all too far away;
> When sweet music holdeth sway
> Love spreads beauty everywhere.*

His predilection for this musical type of poetry and for a love which thinks in terms of music, is easily explained. He did not possess Goethe's power of giving vivid form to his inmost feelings. Too often his lyrics, though singable, lack tangibility, and their images are nebulous and unsteady.[10]

> *Liebe denkt in süssen Tönen,
> Denn Gedanken stehn zu fern;
> Nur in Tönen mag sie gern
> Alles, was sie will, verschönen.

LUDWIG TIECK, THE GERMAN ROMANTICIST

In the papers *Die Farben* and *Die Töne* Tieck argues in favor of blending the optic and acoustic elements, an idea with which he had toyed in *William Lovell* (VI, 351) and in *Die verkehrte Welt*. It produces a peculiarity of his style which modern psychology describes as synaesthesia : the curious faculty of harmony between the senses, whereby a given strong impulse not only causes the sense actually stimulated to respond, but compels other senses to vibrate simultaneously. This universality of sensation, expressed by Schelling in the dictum "architecture is frozen music," and by such expressions as "red is a loud color," is characteristic of German Romanticism. Long before the French symbolists coined the term *audition colorée*, Jean Paul and after him the Romanticists had predicated a relationship between colors and tones.[11] A. W. Schlegel, for instance, associated the vowel "a" with the color red, "o" with purple, and "u" with black. E. T. A. Hoffmann went so far as to ally odor with color and sound. In Tieck the feeling for color is strong.

His contributions to the *Herzensergiessungen* and the *Phantasien* are sometimes distinguished from Wackenroder's in that they are not original, but mere reflections of Wackenroder's views. Tieck's discourses also lack the intimacy and fervor of Wackenroder's. Where Wackenroder speaks his mind in plain, unalloyed but impressive language, he indulges in extravagant, rhetorical exaggeration and seeks to dazzle his reader with ornamental image or bold paradox. In Wackenroder we have a sincere confession of faith, in Tieck pyrotechnics and striking invention. He subscribes heartily to Wackenroder's religion of art, yet reveals an interest in worldly Watteau. The differences between the work of the two men lay in disposition. Wackenroder had a more delicately and more finely attuned nature, Tieck greater powers of visualization and exposition. Moreover, while Wackenroder approached these subjects from the point of view of art, he considered them (as he considered everything) from the standpoint of poetry.

We compare the difference between Tieck's apostrophe to Raphael and Wackenroder's homely tribute. Tieck writes : "Often have I accosted thee in thoughts and aloud, thou precious countenance, all my cares, my sorrow have I lamented to thee in lovely, superstitious hours, and then thou didst regard me as if thou knewest me, as though thou didst understand me better than my friends who are about me. Even from my childhood the sound of thy name hath gladdened me heartily. What is it that draws my soul to thee Unknown, who art so friendly to me ? Ever do I speak to thee as though thou wert present. I am intimate with thee when thou art near; whatever I think and whatever I chance upon,

I tell to thee; like from a dear friend of my heart I take leave of thee in the evening and lay me down to rest."[12]

How much less affected and stilted are Wackenroder's words, in which he tells of "that time when the admiring world still saw Raphael living in its midst,—whose name does not readily pass over my lips without my calling him involuntarily the Divine One—that time—oh, how gladly would I sacrifice all the shrewdness and wisdom of the later centuries for the privilege of having lived then!"[13] In the *Phantasien*, to be sure, Tieck strikes a much more sincere note than in the *Herzensergiessungen*. These later contributions seem to take their inspiration more directly from the heart.

Wackenroder was not creative, and anything but critical. His appreciations are couched in vague generalities applicable to any work of art. They reveal more piety than power of visualization. But he uttered his thoughts and convictions with more warmth and childlike naïveté than did any other Romanticist, and with a strong feeling for artistic form. His works are milestones along the road to a true appreciation of art. Perhaps that is why his few modest writings have exercised a more profound influence than works of authors more grandiose and ingenious. Much has been said against the unfortunate effect which his Catholicizing, Nazarenism and Pre-Raphaelitism have had on art in the nineteenth century. Although he may be called a precursor of Ruskin, it should be considered that the conscious preference for the Nazarenes and for the primitivism of the Pre-Raphaelites is not yet present in Wackenroder. His knowledge of the older masters was too incomplete for that. What characterizes him best is his genuine feeling for the glory of the Middle Ages.

Tieck, whose instinct for friendship was highly developed, felt conscious of his debt to Wackenroder. He owed him not only a better comprehension of the simplicity and devoutness of old German poetry and art; through his association with Wackenroder his soul was enriched, ennobled and refined. But Tieck also gave. He improved Wackenroder's taste and style and helped mature his judgment. They grew and developed together.

If we compare Tieck's and Wackenroder's views on art with those of such Storm and Stress writers of a generation before, as Hamann, Herder and young Goethe, we find marked agreement in their tendency to comprehend art intuitively. But the Romanticists have a broader perspective in that they also take non-German art into account. Moreover, they link genius and religious faith much more closely and write in a more fervent, elegiac tone. On the other hand, they are more interested in painting and music and in the Christian Middle Ages than was Winckelmann.

In 1795-1796 Goethe published *Wilhelm Meisters Lehrjahre*, which exercised an immeasurable influence upon all the German Romanticists. In the *Athenäum*, launched by the Schlegels in 1798, Friedrich Schlegel averred that this "Bildungsroman" represented Goethe's poetry at its best and should be considered with Fichte's philosophy and the French Revolution as one of the three "greatest tendencies of the century." He described the book as "absolutely new and unique," because in it "everything was thought and expressed as might be expected from one who was at once a divine poet and a perfect artist." He declared it to be an all-in-one, the perfection of "Romanpoesie," which was synonymous with universal poetry. Naturally, then, the Romanticists considered it their duty to write similar novels, going Goethe one better if possible. Tieck's *Wilhelm Meister* novel is entitled *Franz Sternbalds Wanderungen, eine altdeutsche Geschichte.*[14] Like the stage version of *The Tempest*, the title page bears his name. Influenced by Florian's preface to *Estelle* and conceived under the spell of the new art-cult inspired by Wackenroder, the work was executed in a mood of poignant grief over the friend's serious illness and unexpected death. "Jeder fühlende Leser wird mit mir die schöne Hoffnung beklagen, die die deutsche Literatur durch seinen frühen Tod verloren hat,"[15] he wrote of Wackenroder in the preface to the *Phantasien*. But *Sternbald*, though revised for the *Schriften* forty-five years later, was never finished. According to an unedited letter from Varnhagen von Ense to Bernhardi of February 6, 1807, Tieck was thinking of a continuation at that time.

Franz Sternbald, the hero, seems a kinsman of that young German painter in the *Herzensergiessungen* who is so deeply impressed by the Catholic service in Rome. He is a young Nürnberg painter of the sixteenth century, who studies first at home under Dürer, then journeys to the Netherlands to become a disciple of Lucas van Leyden, and finally goes to Italy in search of his ideal as an artist. He receives the highest consecration of art from divine Raphael, and is incidentally rewarded by the hand of the girl he loves, but whom he had once magnanimously renounced. Tieck succeeds in limning many charming pictures of German medieval life and gives us historically reliable descriptions of Dürer, Lucas and Messys. But the simple glorification of medieval art and the straightforward account of Sternbald's progress on the road to education and culture (manifestly stimulated by *Wilhelm Meister*) are unduly interrupted or disturbed by longwinded speeches on art, ecstatic pseudo-Catholic utterances on the great painters of the time, a parade of lifeless characters, and occasional lyric effusions, sometimes four pages in length, expressing Tieck's own feelings. There is a wealth of sparkling imagery and pictorial adornment; echoes of Cervantes' *novelas* and particularly of his *Persiles* are heard.

In the latter, much weaker, part of the novel, which takes place in Rome, the author, without deserting his Goethean model, leans on Heinse's lascivious novel *Ardinghello*, too,[16] and to some extent upon the same author's *Hildegard von Hohenthal*. The result is unfortunate, for Tieck, though perhaps consciously opposing Heinse, catches only his frivolous tone, without the rich glow of color. The wanton scenes in the bath and in the painter's garden are to be deplored, particularly since this style of writing was not natural to Tieck. We may subscribe to the view which Coleridge expressed to J. H. Green in 1817 after reading the novel: "I do not *very much* like the Sternbald of our friend; it is too like an imitation of Heinse's Ardinghello, and if the scene in the Painter's Garden at Rome is less licentious than the corresponding abomination in the former work, it is likewise duller."[17] Nor are the characters in this part of the story real human beings.

Starting out to write a plain, objective artist's tale in the style of the *Vite* of Vasari and in the tone of the *Herzensergiessungen*, which may be called the earliest stratum, he became ever more enamored of the plan to deepen and broaden the work, so that it would conform better to the *Wilhelm Meister* scheme of a "Bildungsroman." An impracticable youth, guided by feeling and emotion, must be brought into contact with the world. During the first part, the relation of Franz and Sebastian is similar to that of Tieck and Wackenroder. But in the later portion it may be compared with the relationship of Wilhelm Meister and Werner. This introduces a second stratum—too much "Meisterhaftes (Wilhelm Meisterhaftes)," as Hebbel punningly remarked (Diary I, 255)—, which rifts the unity of the novel and introduces a fatal dualism. Nor does the homely Christian piety of the lay brother, which suggests the sixteenth century, blend with the eighteenth century philosophy inspired by Goethe. There are many anachronisms in Sternbald's speeches, for the hero is not as much a child of his age as is Wilhelm Meister. Sternbald is also a less active figure than Meister. He seems to reach his goal without the *élan vital* and the Goethean spirit of striving. In the latter half his passivity is overdone for the sake of the atmosphere—a typically Romantic "Wanderstimmung."

A third stratum, finally,—the imaginative element—is the cream of the work. It consists of imponderables, such as changing moods and impressionistic glimpses of nature caught in the light of emotions or psychic states. Here Tieck takes his rank beside Goethe and Jean Paul as a great "Landschafter der Seele,"[18] a pioneer in discovering the psychic values of the German forest, hill and dale. Here he delights for the first time in lyric contemplation of his favorite landscape—the lovely, mysteriously charming countryside of central Germany with a babbling stream or waterfall and the sound of a French horn in the distance. Now he sees it in the winsome colors of springtime, now in black nocturnal spookiness, and now in the awesome light of the moon.

The last part of *Sternbald* is surcharged with sweeping polemics. But it is not only the Enlightenment against which he now turns his shafts. Here his subtle preaching is designed to cast contumely upon the spirit of Protestantism, which he thought had been engendering a blight of sobriety over literature and art ever since the sixteenth century, giving birth to such an excrescence as Rationalism. Carried away by this thought, he exclaims that Protestantism has seduced men from the straight, lovely highway because, as Ludoviko remarks in book 4, chapter 1, it has "attacked the divinity of our religion, which lies before us like a wonderful poem, and is not comprehensible to any but him who understands it." Instead of a "fulness of divine religion" Luther has created a "dry emptiness of reason, which leaves all hearts pining; the eternal stream of great images and colossal light-forms is drying out; the parched, indifferent world remains behind, and bit by bit, with impotent struggles, what is lost must gradually be reconquered; the realm of the spirits has vanished, and only a few individual angels return."[19]

Sternbald is deeply moved by such indictments. In the effect which they have upon him we may see an autobiographic touch: "Franz dried his tears, he suppressed his sobs. It seemed to him as though an unseen power were urging him to arise, to seize the hand of the Unknown, to rush into his arms and to cry: Accept me as thy brother! He felt the loneliness, the emptiness in his own heart; Ludoviko had expressed those wishes which had so often secretly disturbed him; he desired to give free sway to his lamentation, to his sorrow."[20] Surely this was also Tieck's own attitude toward Catholicism in 1798. When we consider that in such *Volksmährchen* as *Die schöne Magelone* he had still omitted the religious element purposely, we must realize that his reaction toward religion suffered a radical change within a short time.

Undoubtedly *Sternbald*, which like *William Lovell* is not an improvisation, has enjoyed the widest influence of any work by the early German Romanticists. Compared with *William Lovell*, it shows considerable development under the influence of Goethe and Wackenroder. In a sense it gave birth to Romanticism because it was the first practical realization of the theories of the Schlegels. Both in content and form it is typically Romantic.

Less specialized than the *Herzensergiessungen* or the *Phantasien* and a sincere glorification of the lives of the saints, of nature, history, mythology and mankind, it was in content the most potent factor in calling attention to the medieval art of Germany and the Netherlands, and in furthering a religion of art which places creative work in a category with divine services. It taught that the highest achievement in art is an allegorical Christian landscape, which in and through nature best reveals the ideology of the Christian religion. By virtue of the influence of the novel, the Pre-Raphaelites—van Eyck, Hemmling, Lucas van Leyden— came to be preferred (through Ruskin, even in England) to the great Renaissance masters who followed them. The doctrine of art which reverted to antiquity for its standards was now eclipsed. Instead of finding perfection in clear-cut plasticity and well rounded beauty of form, men began to seek the expression of infinity in art and to associate it with fervent feeling and religious ecstasy.

Stylistically, too, it did more than any other work to fix the *Eigenart* of Romantic writing, which was Tieck's peculiar contribution. Friedrich Schlegel called the style of *Sternbald* typically Romantic.[21] What, in a word, are the characteristics of this style? The most striking are rhythmic musical prose, which really requires instrumental accompaniment; interspersed lyric poetry (warmly praised by A. W. Schlegel),[22] which adds lyric flavor or even becomes an episode in the plot; similes taken from the psychic world (thus when forms are described in *Sternbald* as "hovering like thoughts," 16, 241); the preference for such subjective senses as hearing as against the more objective senses; frequent synaesthesia; use of archaisms; and the employment of vague, mystic language to express equally vague thoughts (thus in *Der blonde Eckbert*, where the singing of the mysterious bird is compared with "the music of French horns and shalms mingling in the far distance.")[23]

The Romanticists, especially Friedrich Schlegel, were loud in their praise of the novel and its implications, though Friedrich's brother August Wilhelm found "too many pretty sunrises" in it. Only Caroline, the latter's wife, took a thoroughly critical attitude.[24] On June 10, 1798, Tieck sent Goethe a copy of the first volume, assuring him that "it is a great boon to be the contemporary of a great man" and hoping to meet him soon, "so that I can hear from your mouth whether and how I should continue on the course which I have undertaken perhaps too frivolously and rashly."[25] Goethe wrote a reply but did not send it. Then he met Tieck on July 21, 1799, and saw him repeatedly during the next year. But though Goethe's attitude toward him constantly remained cordial—he always blamed the Schlegels, not Tieck, for the excesses of Romanticism—, he compared the novel with a charming but empty vase, felt that the musical element was too strong[24] and later made it clear, in his *Schriften zur Kunst*, that he deplored "das klosterbrudrisierende, sternbaldisierende Unwesen"—perversions in the manner of the *Herzensergiessungen* and of *Sternbald*.[26] And though he refrained, in the essay *Neu-deutsche religios-patriotische Kunst* (1817)—written by J. H. Meyer but a record of Goethe's convictions—, from criticizing the Romantic element of *Sternbald*, he felt that the sections on art lack the most essential prerequisite—natural understanding of art. In short, Goethe thought that the philosophy of art suggested by Wackenroder and Tieck and carried to extremes by their successors—especially the belief that art is rooted in blind inspiration and religion rather than in rules and hard work—was based upon a fallacy. Nor did he indulge Tieck's typically Romantic delusion that during the Middle Ages Germany had a form of "patriotism" which revelled in art.

Nevertheless Tieck's views on art remained in vogue for more than a generation. Jakob Grimm, the father of Germanic philology, was stirred to enthusiasm by his descriptions of Nürnberg and sixteenth century life in Germany. Leading painters like Johann Friedrich Overbeck, Philipp Veit and Peter von Cornelius subscribed to them heartily. Not until the spirit of the times had changed did the classical school come again into its own. Not until then did the ideas expressed in the *Herzensergiessungen* and in *Sternbald* finally lose their general appeal. But the admiration for Nürnberg and its pristine glory, so nobly documented in these works, has remained a living factor to this day, while the brave attempt to recreate a better, more patriotic, more religious age will always stand as a milestone in German literature.

Sternbald is not the only work planned by Tieck while he was spellbound by *Wilhelm Meister*. He conceived a second novel of culture, *Der junge Tischlermeister*, on the pattern of Goethe's great work—as though one were not enough! In it he wished to utilize the experiences of his own youth and to sketch around them "clear and definite cross-sections of genuine German life, its conditions and prospects."[27] Originally the novel was to show the cabinet maker Leonhard, a typical German youth of the time, transplanted from an average bourgeois environment to high society, only to find true happiness eventually in the limitations of plain, everyday living. Until 1811 this work remained a mere idea in Tieck's mind. Then he began to set it on paper. But interruptions and difficulties interfered. In 1819 his publisher began printing it, in the hope that this would speed the author. In vain, for he did not finish its composition until 1836.

Like *Wilhelm Meister*, the early sections are rich in autobiographic elements, but not as winsome and human. The design of the finished work is quite different from what must have been in Tieck's mind at first.

In his preface to volume 2 (1836) Tieck, strangely enough, mentions only the "novelas" of Cervantes, not *Wilhelm Meister*, as having influenced the work, and dates its conception in the spring of 1795, before the appearance of Goethe's novel. This was probably done with a purpose—to suppress the existence of the Goethean influence. The correct date of conception is doubtless 1796. In its bearing upon his later development *Der junge Tischlermeister* will be discussed later.

We have had occasion to note Tieck's sensitiveness to external influences. One such influence, also noticeable in *Zerbino*, makes itself felt in the natural philosophy of *Sternbald*. It is that of Jacob Böhme.[28] Böhme (1575-1624), born of peasant stock near Görlitz in Lausatia between Dresden and Breslau, became a cobbler like Hans Sachs, but through a series of mystic revelations and visions, which he described in that quaintly curious work, *Aurora, oder die Morgenröte im Aufgang* (1612), was converted to mysticism and theosophy. Discovering this work in a Berlin bookstall and learning that its author was ridiculed by the Rationalists as an untutored religious fanatic, Tieck read it attentively. At first he was attracted by its wit and humor, but soon its philosophy, so closely akin to poetry, began to weave its spell. He was seduced by the fervent, glowing life in Böhme's writing, the richness of his apperception, his profound meaning, the fresh light he cast upon all the riddles of the human mind, and the idea that religion, philosophy and poetry are all rooted in intuitive cognition and inspiration.

The instinctive longing of Tieck, the poet, for religion and his yearning for a confirmation of his own philosophical views found support in Böhme's mysticism. His later friend Solger once stated that intuitive penetration into the nature of things was closely allied with poetic inspiration and religious devotion. In *Aurora* these three activities of the mind are simultaneously at work, just as fairy-tale poetry, nature animation, naïveté, allegorization, simple piety and free sway of the imagination in the domain of the infinite stand out as early characteristics of Tieck's writings. Böhme's theosophic concept of the spirit of God, of the forces of nature and of the kingdom of Christ was quite in harmony with Tieck's views and to his liking.

In the Shrovetide farce *Der neue Herkules am Scheidewege* (1800), later renamed *Der Autor*, Tieck has the Old-Fashioned Man—der Alt-frank—indulge in a warm encomium of Böhme. If you wish to cast your eye into the depths, he says to the Author, if you would edify your mind, quaff the wine of life and feel at home in springtime, the time of blossoms, nightingales, songs of birds and manifold spirits—then read Goethe and

> Aurora, that famed Morning Red,[29]
> Writ by the prophet whom they chide,
> To whom all worlds are open wide,
> Whose sacred, undefilèd tongue
> Of God's profundity hath sung.
> 'T is Jacob Böhme, German sage,
> Let him thy mournfulness assuage,
> His every word gives thee delight,
> Surrounded with a splendor bright,
> He's spun around his head divine
> A halo glorious and fine.*

It is clear, then, that Böhme helped him in temporarily overcoming the despair of his adolescence, in toying for a while with a more cheerful philosophy and in enriching the imagery of his poetry. Böhme brought him passing cheer by offering a religious interpretation for his pantheistic leanings. Reared in the soil of Rationalism, he could not have achieved this of his own accord. It was in Böhme's sense that he now approached Christianity. The poetry inherent in Böhme attracted him, too, for to him mysticism like every other phenomenon was merely a manifestation of poetry. Did he not write to Friedrich von Raumer on December 21, 1817, that he "looks at everything from the point of view of poetry" (aus der Poesie heraus die Dinge anzusehen)?[30]

In yet another way Böhme had a less beneficial effect upon his development. Böhme's symbolic view of nature aided him in overcoming that antipathy toward symbolic and allegorical poetry which he mentioned to

---

*Auroram, jene Morgenröte,
Von dem Propheten, den sie schelten,
Dem aufgeschlossen alle Welten,
Des heil'ger unentweihter Mund
Der Gottheit Tiefe hat verkundt,
Den grossen deutschen Jacob Böhme,
Dass er von dir die Schwermut nähme,
Jedwedes Wort in ihm dir lacht,
Und all umzogen mit Glanz und Pracht,
Er hat durchaus sich gesponnen ein
In eitel Glori und Heiligenschein.

Wackenroder as early as 1792.[31] Böhme taught him that all poetry should be symbolic. Henceforth he could better understand, appreciate and imitate the allegories in the poetry of Dante, Calderon, Camoens, Jonson and Spenser.

Böhme's habit of comparing men with flowers and of revelling in auditory and visual delights, as well as his love of the stars and of precious stones were soon Tieck's habit and love, too. Coupled with Schelling's natural philosophy and Friedrich Schlegel's mystic interpretation of nature, Böhme's mysticism and theosophy, which he did not tire of expounding to his friends, became an important factor in Tieck's mental conditioning. No wonder Novalis, who himself studied Böhme diligently and took many elements from him, and who called Goethe "der Böhme von Weimar," styled Tieck "der Verkündiger der Morgenröte"—the herald of Böhme's *Aurora*.

We have indicated that much of what he found in Böhme was merely a reflex and fortification of views which he already possessed. But these views had not only the bright, happy aspect which has been discussed; there was also a gloomy side. Long before reading Böhme, he had seen in nature a puissant, invisible something, which stirred him, but against which he was powerless. So he had endowed even nature with life, but with a life which terrified him because it was alien to him. The same sort of mystic pantheism, which rendered man a prisoner to nature, greeted him in Böhme's pages. From this point of view the study of Böhme proved very deleterious. Böhme led him to Tauler, Suso and Bruno. Bit by bit they effected a psychic revolution within him, which cast him into a slough of despond, stressed the demonic side of nature, which he knew all too well, and taught him the omnipresence of evil. This undermined his poetic vein. Mysticism supplanted religion in his soul. The cure for this bane—a more realistic outlook on life—, he admitted in 1817,[32] was very slow, being achieved by Homer, Sophocles, the *Nibelungenlied*, Shakespeare and, most important, by Solger.

Naturally such new interests served to estrange Tieck from the Nicolais. The farther he veered from Rationalism, the stronger became their protests. In volume 3 of the *Volksmährchen* the younger Nicolai had gone so far as to insert a signed statement that he was not responsible for the contents and had become aware of their nature only after they had been printed. And still Tieck continued to work for them, despite their criticism of his style and point of view. The reason is patent. He had married Amalie Alberti in the spring of 1798 and, dependent upon his pen for a living, needed money more than ever.

His chief work for the Nicolais, after the discontinuance of the *Straussfedern* and the *Volksmährchen*, was probably of an editorial nature. As was suggested in the previous chapter, he may be responsible for Nicolai's edition of Foote. At the same time Nicolai got out an edition of the plays of Tate Wilkinson. We know, too, that Tieck was doing other translations from the English for Nicolai and keeping up a correspondence which on Tieck's side was deferential, on Nicolai's admonitory and censorious. This continued, not until 1798, as we are usually told, but until May 3, 1799, when the publisher peremptorily withdrew his support. The writer possesses a letter by Tieck of that date, wherein he states to Nicolai: "It is in many respects welcome to me that you take work away from me which really tires me and is unsuited to me, but it surprises me that you do so without having my consent."

Later in the same year the Nicolais, or at least the son Karl, took another step without Tieck's consent. He got out a twelve-volume edition of *Johann Ludwig Tiecks sämmtliche Schriften*. It excludes the *Herzensergiessungen*, the *Phantasien* and *Sternbald* but includes *Abdallah, Peter Lebrecht, William Lovell*, the *Volksmährchen, Die sieben Weiber des Blaubart*, the adaptation of *The Tempest*, and three inferior English novels which Tieck had not translated, but which had been turned into German by Wackenroder, Sophie Tieck and the musician Wesseley. Most of the genuine writings had not appeared before under his name. He brought suit against Karl Nicolai, proved by his correspondence that the pirated edition ascribed works to him for which he was not responsible, and won his case. This closes the chapter of Tieck's relations with the younger Nicolai. He corresponded with Friedrich, the father, in a friendly though superficial way as late as 1803.

The *Neue Allgemeine Bibliothek*, an important organ of the Nicolais, now treated Tieck with open contempt. In 1801 he was scolded as "a very boring fellow" (ein gar langweiliger Geselle) ;[33] his works were ridiculed as "mediocre prattle" and "insipid stuff" (mittelmässiges Geschwätz—fades Zeug).[34]

The unauthorized edition did him serious injury, despite the favorable judicial decree. It was reprinted and sold by other publishers. As late as 1829 he deemed it necessary to warn readers against it. Another pirated edition of his works in thirty volumes, published by Grund of Vienna in 1817-1824, was also a thorn in his flesh. The reason for such flagrant injustice, from which all writers suffered, was the absence of adequate protection by copyright. In the eighteenth century a German author's rights were guaranteed only by limited state privileges. In 1794 Prussia finally adopted a defective copyright law. Not until 1837 were the

Prussian laws on the subject modified. Countrywide protection was not vouchsafed until the diet of the German Confederation passed a series of copyright laws between 1837 and 1857.

But even without these disputes he could not have maintained his relations with the Nicolais. His views of art had changed so radically that no impecuniousness could hold him down to this bondage. The Nicolais represented the ideals of Old Berlin. He knew that these were ossified, and he fought them with acerbity.

This explains why the two Schlegel brothers, who were about to form a new literary party, now discovered a kindred soul in Tieck.[35] For some time Friedrich Schlegel had known Reichardt, Tieck's old patron. In 1797 he published in Reichardt's *Lyceum der schönen Künste* the first series of those important fragments, the *Kritische Fragmente*, in which he proclaimed the new doctrine of Romantic poesy. The basic ideas bear a striking similarity to the thoughts which Wackenroder and Tieck had evolved independently. They revealed also a marked resemblance to the notions expressed in Tieck's first review of the recent Almanacs of the Muses (1796). Moreover, it was not difficult to detect their close spiritual kinship to the *Volksmährchen*. Obviously Romanticism was in the air. Its theory developed in the Schlegels while Tieck was independently evolving its practice. Since the Schlegels were themselves not productive poets, they were happy to welcome Tieck as a practical exponent of their ideas.

At least eight factors drew Friedrich to Tieck: their mutual admiration of Goethe's poetry, their aversion to Rationalism, the novel *William Lovell*, Shakespeare, Spanish literature, Dante, Jean Paul Richter (to whose works Tieck introduced Friedrich) and Tieck's practical Romanticism, especially as it had been expounded in the *Volksmährchen*. August Wilhelm was chiefly attracted to Tieck by his interest in Shakespeare, whom the former had begun to translate into German.

Toward the end of July 1797, Friedrich came to Berlin, arriving while Tieck was absent upon a visit to Amalie in Hamburg. As soon as Tieck returned home, Friedrich made his acquaintance at the home of the banker Veit, who was then still the husband of Dorothea Mendelssohn; by September they were on fairly friendly terms. Meanwhile August Wilhelm had discussed Tieck's adaptation of *The Tempest*, the *Herzensergiessungen*, *Blaubart* and *Der gestiefelte Kater* in the *Allgemeine Literatur-Zeitung*, a highly respected literary journal, and found much to praise in the young Berlin writer, whom he had not yet met personally. Though he was generally not given to lavish eulogy, he called Tieck "einen Dichter im eigentlichen Sinne, einen dichtenden Dichter,"[36] a term which we have tried to define in the introduction. He was even more enthusiastic about *Der blonde Eckbert*, *Die schöne Magelone* and Tieck's lyric vein and, as we have noted, mentioned him in the same breath with Goethe.

And now Friedrich began to write letters to his elder brother, with long reports of his direct contacts with Tieck and of his personal impressions of him. These letters, while showing circumspection and fastidious taste, reveal at times a repulsive, oracular tone. He wrote that Tieck came to see him frequently and expressed much confidence in his, Friedrich's, judgment.[37] But "he is quite childishly awkward and ignorant in the mercantile aspect of the literary vocation." Friedrich wished to secure a new publisher for him but found the Berlin publishers unresponsive. "In society and especially in the circles which I know," wrote Friedrich, "he is a welcome figure. The fact that he is often whimsical and at times a bore, is counterbalanced by the circumstance that he is always modest and not infrequently very humorous. But he has withdrawn from society and lives almost entirely in the little group which he has gathered about himself." Moreover he is "lean in spirit and body," still "a mere boy," not a genius like Wackenroder, an "ordinary and coarse individual" in comparison with Schleiermacher, and devoid of philological ability. And finally Friedrich felt that an author who could conceive such contradictory works as the *Straussfedern* and *Die sieben Weiber des Blaubart*, on the one hand, and the *Herzensergiessungen* and the *Volksmährchen*, on the other, must be a moral invertebrate. He wrote to his brother: "Of character there is not even a little crumb visible in him, and I fear, I fear, with his total lack of skill, cleverness and wisdom, he will quickly sink into the class of the young scoundrels in German literature, the Woltmanns and so forth. He has a slight instinct for 'gentlemanity' and honesty, but how rapidly can that be lost in the shuffle in the case of a man devoid of character."

There is, no doubt, some truth in these snap judgments of twenty-five-year-old Friedrich, yet they must be taken with a grain of salt. We find in Friedrich's words not only a certain antipathy to Tieck, which increased in direct proportion to the growth of August Wilhelm's admiration for him; we ascertain also exaggerated self-assertion and the desire to belittle Tieck in August Wilhelm's eyes, to Friedrich's own advantage. If we turn to Tieck's earliest judgment of Friedrich, we discover evidence of a similarly unfavorable reaction. Tieck found him ridiculously vain and self-centered. Later he confessed to Solger that Friedrich was taciturn and shy and demanded blind confidence. He told Raumer that Friedrich never understood or tried to understand him, being too much wrapt up in himself: "He looked down upon me with kindly condescension and honored my talent with almost exclusive love. But he did not deem it worth while to understand me, and whenever I made an effort to understand him, Spinozism, Fichteanism, Platonism and whatever else he called it turned into affected mysteriousness, and I was ironically waved aside."[38] And to August Wilhelm he wrote thirty years later, after Friedrich's death, that the latter had never taken him fully into his confidence; at first Friedrich's philosophy, later his religious fanaticism, estranged them.[39]

Although the first impressions of these two men hardly formed the basis for a true friendship, they revealed at least the possibility of fruitful cooperation. For Tieck discerned in Friedrich a helpful and suggestive counsellor and critic, while Friedrich felt constrained to acknowledge and admire his talents as a productive poet.

It is to be noted, too, that from the outset the Schlegels, especially Friedrich, wanted to take this new "find" under their wings. Tieck never availed himself fully of their patronage—to Friedrich's disgust. However, there is no doubt but that the Schlegels enlisted him in their Romantic cause and made a conscious partisan of him. Before meeting them he was a poet of clearly Romantic tendencies. After making their acquaintance he came to be looked at more and more as the official exponent of Romantic poetry.

Early in 1798 an important event caused Friedrich radically to revise his appraisal of Tieck. *Sternbald* appeared. As was noted above, Friedrich immediately became enamored of the work, though at first he tried to conceal his admiration from Tieck. He felt that this novel was the incarnation of poetry itself, a "divine book," "the first novel since Cervantes which is Romantic." He went so far as to rate it higher than *Wilhelm Meister*. From this time on Friedrich's attitude toward Tieck became more cordial and sincere. The backbiting ceased. If this was due in great measure to *Sternbald* (of which August Wilhelm's opinion was, as we have noted, much less favorable), it is ascribable in smaller degree to Friedrich's realization that his disparagement of Tieck to August Wilhelm was useless and could only harm him, Friedrich, in his brother's eyes.

Yet it cannot be maintained that the egoist Friedrich, despite a certain affection for Tieck, ever came to rate him very high. Even after they had spent the winter of 1799-1800 together in Jena, he confessed to Rahel Levin that "with Tieck one exhausts the possibilities of conversation in a single winter."[40] Tieck always remained "hopeless" and devoid of character in his eyes.[41] He seemed to him to lack the ability "in einen anderen Geist einzudringen."[42] He always respected his poetry, however, and on occasion deemed even works like *William Lovell* and *Zerbino* superior to anything Goethe had written. In his lectures in Cologne during the winter of 1803-1804 he placed *Zerbino* on a plane with the comedies of Aristophanes. A few years later he began a poetic eulogy of Tieck.[43]

Meanwhile, in May 1798, August Wilhelm, much colder and less impulsive than Friedrich, had also come to Berlin and met Tieck. Not at all affected by Friedrich's belittlement of Tieck, he immediately entered into amicable relations with the young author of the *Volksmährchen* and adapter of *The Tempest*—much more amicable than Friedrich had ventured to establish. But although the friendship between Tieck and the older Schlegel ran a somewhat more even course, it never became as close as that of Tieck and Friedrich.

August Wilhelm, the detached critic, soon realized that his own interests and aversions were also those of Tieck, the poet. In his subsequent critical writings the latter clearly showed how much he had learned from his new mentor and friend. His judgment became keener and his feeling for the nuances of language and verse grew more secure. What had been vague, intuitive feeling now became conscious conviction.

For the furtherance of their doctrines the Schlegels now founded their own periodical, the *Athenäum*, to which Tieck, however, did not contribute. In the first number August Wilhelm, reviewing certain books, published a glowing critique of the *Volksmährchen*. He lauded the work as signifying the birth of a new literary school, which took its light and leading from Shakespeare and Goethe. In conclusion he wrote the following words of theoretical admonition to Tieck, the wisest words which were ever uttered to the poet. "Let him not forget," wrote August Wilhelm, "that every effect of art resembles a focus, and that without focalization no flame can be kindled; let him always keep the highest aim of art in mind and have sufficient respect for his fine talents so as not to be tempted to achieve less than his level best. Let him collect himself and practise compression, and let him also prefer those external forms which constrain him thereto of their own accord."[44]

In the course of the next few years Tieck and the Schlegels saw their community of interests growing constantly stronger and more comprehensive. The letters of 1799-1801 testify to numerous joint projects.

No doubt the relationship bore some advantages for all concerned. In part the Schlegels derived their very theories from Tieck's writings, perhaps to a greater extent than has been recognized. Starting out as a classical philologist and a cosmopolite, Friedrich transferred his chief attention to modern, particularly German, literature under the impress of Tieck's practical espousal of that literature. Tieck also increased the antipathy of the Schlegels for Wieland and weaned them from Iffland. At any rate he (and with him Wackenroder and Novalis) may be called the spiritual instigators and practical expositors of Friedrich's theoretical Romanticism. As for August Wilhelm, he was the first fully to recognize his merits as a poet, to encourage and instruct the young writer in developing them, and to make him more self-confident. As Tieck confessed to August Wilhelm in December, 1797, even before meeting him, he had formerly looked down too much upon his own works and cared too little about his literary reputation.[45] He also aided Tieck in improving his literary form, particularly his metrics. He supported him in his interest in Cervantes and Shakespeare. Tieck, on the other hand, developed Schlegel's interest in the Spanish drama; he also published a very favorable (hitherto overlooked) review of Schlegel's *Gedichte* in the *Allgemeine Zeitung* (Beilage 9, 1800). And it was Tieck who, moved by "Pietät," eventually took up Schlegel's unfinished translation of Shakespeare, which he had as early as 1799 vainly promised to review, and pressed it to completion. The continuation, carried out more than a generation later under his supervision, is imperfect, to be sure, but it finished a work which would otherwise have remained a torso.

The Schlegels had also a deleterious influence upon his development. Although in theory August Wilhelm preached unity and coherence, of which Tieck was sorely in need, in practice he encouraged his inclination toward laxity of form and led him to believe that multifariousness was a virtue instead of a vice. Hence we find him, under the sway of the Schlegels, constantly trying to outdo himself. His tendency toward multiformity in *Der gestiefelte Kater* becomes an accomplished fact in *Zerbino*. His dramatic structure, still close-grained in *Blaubart*, is dissolved in lyricism, melody and Romantic atmosphere in the later plays, *Genoveva* and *Octavian*. As a result of his association with the Schlegels he also gained notoriety as the high priest of their doctrines and soon became a butt for ridicule. By 1803 he realized that he had been duped and was stirred "by indignation when he thought how the Schlegels had taken possession of him by force and how through their accursed trumpeting the quiet, modest course of his art had been disturbed by a miserable rumor."[46] But it was too late; the damage had been done. He had too definitely linked himself with them, whose critical powers were great but whose lack of creative poetic talent proved a prenatal curse on their new literary school.

CHAPTER SEVEN

THE ROMANTIC FREE-LANCE

BY 1799 Tieck had acquired a fair knowledge of Spanish, a language whose literature was frowned upon with deep suspicion by the Rationalists. His studies in Spanish, perhaps prompted by Bouterwek, dated back to his student days in Göttingen early in 1793. Three waves of interest may be distinguished in these preoccupations. Up to about 1799 Cervantes attracted him chiefly; then for a generation Calderon monopolized his attention; in 1818, under the influence of Solger, the beauties of more realistic Lope de Vega dawned upon him, and thereafter Lope remained the chief object of his admiration and affection.

As years went on, he became an ever more diligent student of Spanish. His treatise on Spanish literature, like that on Shakespeare, remained a mere project, though he promised it to Cotta as early as 1800, even giving him a partial account of its contents,[1] and offered it to the Königsberg publisher Nicolovius in 1802.[2] In 1832 he assured the publisher Perthes that he had not yet abandoned the plan, saying that he proposed to introduce the work with a free translation of the *Viaje entretenido* of 1616 (a description of contemporary actors and their mode of life), followed by the development of the Spanish theater and those characteristics which distinguish it from the stage in other parts of Europe. Finally, there was to be a treatment of Lope, Montalvan, Tirso Molina, Calderon and of Spanish literature in general up to the beginning of the French influence.[3] The "Nachlass" in Berlin contains a whole sheaf of notes which would undoubtedly have been incorporated in this work. They discuss critically over a dozen of Calderon's plays, also works of Montalvan, Lope and Cervantes. Among "Spanier nach Calderon" they speak of dramas of Salazar, Moreto y Cabañas, Figueroa, Solis, Zamora and others, but mostly without enthusiasm. When Tieck's library of thirty thousand volumes was sold at auction in 1849, Spanish literature was represented therein more adequately than any other, even better than German and English.[4] In 1887 an unbiased American critic, E. P. Whipple, rated his work as a Hispanist higher in some respects than George Ticknor's.[5]

Tieck's early prepossession for Cervantes, whose *Don Quixote*, in German translation, he read with avid interest as a boy, was quite in harmony with the views of the Romanticists in general. They raised the

Spanish satirist to a high pinnacle and, as was their wont, tried to naturalize him and to read Romantic theories into him. In *Don Quixote* Friedrich Schlegel saw one of the most typically Romantic novels in world literature. He derived not a little from the work for his own theories. August Wilhelm wrote a penetrating characterization of Cervantes and experimented for a while in translating him.

The first German translation of *Don Quixote* worthy of any comment had been made a generation before by Friedrich Justin Bertuch.[6] It appeared at Leipzig in 1775-1777 and proved popular enough to warrant two authorized and two unauthorized editions. About 1798, encouraged and aided by August Wilhelm, Tieck set out to make a new and more nearly perfect rendering. He felt that *Don Quixote*, which in his eyes, too, was more suffused than any other work with the spirit of Romanticism, deserved the best possible interpretation at the hands of those who were seeking to propagate that spirit.

Of course the desire to graft Schlegelian Romanticism upon a Spanish satiro-philosophical poem of the early seventeenth century was futile. While Cervantes painted his hero as a ridiculous dreamer and fanatic—a general laughing stock—, Tieck would represent him as a martyr of knighthood. That such an interpretation of Cervantes was based upon a misconception goes without saying. As Grillparzer, his avowed enemy, correctly stated: "What Cervantes, with an artist's wisdom, merely suggests in the background—the originally noble nature and lucid moments of his hero—, Tieck would like to bring into the foreground."[7]

There was a special reason for his unusual attitude toward Cervantes' masterpiece. He regarded it as perfectly mysterious. The author had, he thought, secreted a deeper meaning into the poem, hidden in it a defense of the noblest qualities of chivalry and knighthood—an apology for what was best in the idealism of the Middle Ages. Perhaps Tieck came to think of himself as Don Quixote and of Nicolai as Sancho Panza. Thus his own idealism was aroused from a state of lethargy; he better realized the grandeur of the human imagination and its power in combating the ills of life. This helped him in his psychic struggle against pessimism.[8]

Tieck's translation (published by Unger, who had also done *Sternbald*) was made with care. His statement to Solger in 1815, that he had only a poor edition of the original, a wretched dictionary and a hazy knowledge of Spanish at his disposal, cannot be taken too literally.[9] We know that he used several early editions of Cervantes, which he zealously collated. According to a newspaper clipping among Varnhagen von Ense's Berlin papers, the Spanish minister in Berlin, Count Casa-Valencia, lent him aid. His model was Bertuch, upon whom he improved, in accordance with the Romantic theory of translation, by better catching the changing moods and spirit, in particular the humor and the lyric element. Yet even Tieck's rendering is not flawless; his knowledge of Spanish, though passable, was still too imperfect for that. His language seems less virile than that of the original. But the translation proved popular and instrumental in making Cervantes, who had been considered exotic and hard to understand, much better known in Germany. Praised highly even by Heine in his *Romantische Schule*, it is still a standard translation and deserves a place near A. W. Schlegel's Shakespeare as an important literary achievement. The fourth edition came out as late as 1852-1853. A rival translation by the Rationalist D. W. Soltau (1800), though perhaps revealing a better knowledge of Spanish, is not nearly as close to the spirit of Cervantes.[10]

His occupation with *Don Quixote* aroused Tieck's interest in other works of its author, especially in the early pastoral novel *Galatea*, the tragedy *Numancia* and the *Novelas*, which he planned to translate in collaboration with A. W. Schlegel. In 1801 he spoke of a veritable "craving" (Wut) to translate *Galatea*.[11] And Cervantes led him to Calderon, whose German discoverer and advocate he became together with A. W. Schlegel. Between 1803 and 1809 the latter translated five dramas of Calderon under the title *Spanisches Theater*. It caused Tieck to drop a similar project, which he mentioned to Cotta in 1800 and which was to include works of Cervantes, Calderon and Lope. In an anonymous article in the *Zeitung für die elegante Welt* (June 7, 1803), marked "T," he reviewed Schlegel's *Theater*, styling the plays "even more important than Shakespeare's."

Calderon, with his miracle comedies like *La devocion del cruz* and *El magico prodigioso* and romantic dramas in the style of *La vida es sueño*, seemed to Tieck, who as a lad of sixteen had called life a dream,[12] to possess spiritual kinship with Böhme. Their earliest influence is felt in *Genoveva* and becomes more marked in *Octavian*, as we shall see. In time (by 1818) his admiration for the Spanish writer had become so great that Solger felt constrained to counsel moderation, showing in his critique of the lectures of A. W. Schlegel on dramatic art and literature, that after all the mythology of Calderon is abstract, even cut and dried, and unlike Shakespeare devoid of psychological depth. Tieck at once adopted these views, as will be noted. Still, as late as his Dresden period, he frequently selected Calderon's plays for his public recitations.

THE ROMANTIC FREE-LANCE

From about 1800 on he was undergoing the religious crisis mentioned in chapter 6. As he confessed to Solger almost a generation later, he had become so enamored of mysticism that it threatened to take the place of religion in his heart.[13] But his devoutly religious, though not orthodox, nature rebelled against this tyranny, as a letter to Friedrich Schlegel of 1803 testifies.[14] Here Tieck, assuaging his own qualms, exclaims that, despite all false temptations, the core of things and the secret of true understanding of the human soul lie alone in revealed Christianity.

No wonder, then, that he found the chief attraction of Calderon in his unique blending of the sensual and the hypersensual, as well as in the interfusion of miracles of poetical fancy and religious faith. He discovered in Calderon transcendental problems considered from the point of view of life, ideal aspirations, a struggle against human passions, the dream of faith, the triumph of the Cross, luminous and yet mystic poetry, music and artistry, and visual splendors clothed in formal richness.

He was delighted to witness Calderon's dramatic form frequently expanding far beyond the narrow limitations of the eighteenth century German stage. In multifarious lyric patterns the poet's feelings found rich expression, and instead of a closely confined series of happenings, Calderon unfolded a kaleidoscopic picture, deepened by pious devotion and enhanced by glowing southern imagination. It seemed to him as though all the genres of poetry were most effectively synthetized by Calderon. But above the charm of his fantasy and his warm sympathy with human suffering there loomed something even greater—the magnetism of religious ecstasy. To his eyes Calderon's belief in miracles, his veneration of the saints and his sensual Catholicism unfolded a new and grandiose world of poetry. The realm of wonder, which he with the help of the fairy tale and of vague, foreboding legendary figures had always striven to conjure up, was found ready made and perfect in the *teatro* of Calderon.

It occurred to him to combine the lessons derived from the great Spanish poets with other teachings and enthusiasms which held sway in his domain of poetry. Why not associate the manner of Calderon's legends with the spirit of medievalism, which he had so often exalted? Why not, in a great poetical work patterned on the style of Calderon, glorify the heyday of German feudalism, which Goethe's *Götz von Berlichingen* had endeared to his heart as a child? Why not adhere at the same time to the personal outlook on religion, as expressed by Schleiermacher in his *Reden über die Religion*? Why not glorify the spirit of an all-embracing Christendom, as Novalis did in *Die Christenheit oder Europa*? Why not shape a new German medieval mythology in the sense of Friedrich Schlegel, and introduce the "magic (dynamic) idealism" of Novalis? And finally, why not fuse into this unique scheme the grand nature philosophy of Jacob Böhme, with its portents and natural miracles, its astrology, its emphasis upon the principle of evil, and its human moods attuned to the seasons? These must have been his thoughts when he cast about for a subject for his next ambitious work. And soon he found the raw material which seemed well suited to the purpose.

This material, casually referred to in *Sternbald*, was the medieval legend of Genevieve. During his stay at Hamburg in 1797 the unpublished Storm and Stress drama *Golo und Genoveva* of Friedrich (Maler) Müller, who meanwhile had left Germany to live in Italy, was loaned him by his future brother-in-law Christian Waagen. Müller, whose chief source was a puppet play, had finished his creditable work, marked by freshness, deep feeling and individualism, in 1781. But Tieck read it very hastily and later, when unjustly accused of plagiarizing Müller, candidly confessed that only its melancholy mood and Golo's song "Mein Grab sei unter Weiden" remained in his memory. Certainly Müller's straightforward imitation of *Götz von Berlichingen* has as little in common with Tieck's epic-lyric glorification of the Middle Ages, as Tieck's work, in turn, has with Hebbel's psychological *Genoveva* of 1841. Hebbel (Diary II, 65, 81) wrote his play in conscious opposition to Tieck's. Moreover, Tieck's principal source is not the puppet play but the Kochern chapbook, which he read in 1798.

In the summer of 1799 Tieck, with his young wife, visited his brother-in-law Reichardt in Giebichenstein. There the tragedy with the undramatic title *Leben und Tod der heiligen Genoveva*[15] flowed lightly from his pen. By November the 6,500-line play was completed in Jena; it appeared in volume 2 of Tieck's *Romantische Dichtungen* (1800). Inspired by the Spanish poets, Shakespeare, Jacob Böhme and the other influences suggested above, and growing out of his enthusiasm for the chapbooks and the Middle Ages and for the art and religion of bygone times, this work combined all the qualities which constitute Romanticism. *Genoveva* is the fountainhead of the Romantic drama, a focus, as it were, for the multiple rays emitted from innumerable sources. Converging in this Romantic document par excellence, they cast a new but after all only fitful light upon the whole realm of German poetry. *Genoveva* introduces Tieck's fifth (and last) type of fairy-tale reproduction— "universal poetry" of atmosphere and mood.*

*For the other four types see above, chapter 5, p. 92.

He adhered faithfully enough to the old legend, though he introduced witchery, magic and extraneous episodes. The legend tells the following story. Genevieve, who lived in the eighth century as the daughter of a duke of Brabant, is wedded to Count Palatine Siegfried of Hohensimmern near Trèves. During her husband's absence she is falsely accused by his steward Golo of infidelity. Condemned to die, she is spared by a softhearted squire, yet deserted by him in the forest and apparently doomed to suffer certain death. But for six years she manages to subsist in a cave in the Ardennes, nourishing herself and a son Schmerzenreich, who is meanwhile born to her, with herbs and the milk of a doe. Finally her husband ascertains her innocence, finds her while on a hunt and returns her to his castle.

Tieck's primary purpose was not to dramatize this plain tale. True to a Romantic tenet, he would create a "picture of the times" by conjuring up musical moods and atmosphere and reproducing the heartiness, courtly love and piety of Genevieve's day. To achieve this he summoned up all the poetic powers at his command. The age he presents is one surcharged with religion. Crusades, religious speeches, visions, dreams, prophecies and miracles figure prominently. And yet we find the characters descanting upon the godlessness of their time—a sly reference, of course, to his own age. This peculiarity—it might be called a manifestation of "Romantic Irony"—gives the work an undeniable stamp of spuriousness. Tieck, lacking the deep positive religiousness of Genevieve, fails to make the religious atmosphere in which she moves seem authentic. As usual, he is much more successful in the description of the moods of nature.[16]

Concreteness and reason are subordinated to atmosphere, to the mysticism of incense and medieval Catholicism. Strong emotions are eschewed, even in Golo. Tieck depicts him not as a villain but as a languid, melancholy dreamer—a winsome, longing youth impelled by the Jacob Böhmean principle of evil, who engages in a hopeless struggle against that principle. His fatalism seems to make him personally irresponsible:

> It is the stars that shape our destiny,[17]
> Our every virtue, every vice,*

he says to a pilgrim. His melancholy song, "Dicht von Felsen eingeschlossen," serves as his leitmotif. The seasonal element, too, plays an important part. Golo's love, awakening in spring, is attuned to the changing seasons, until it dies in winter. The pictures of strife and battle

---

*Die Sterne sind's, die unser Schicksal machen,
Und unsre Tugend, unsre Laster.

against the Saracens appear unreal and more like old tapestries than frescoes. They do not take us into the midst of combat, but merely evoke vague memories of deeds long ago performed. Karl Martell's heroism, Genevieve's piety and Siegfried's love seem just as shadowy as Golo's passion.

Elizabethan influence is felt. Like *Pericles*, Tieck's play is built upon a solid epic groundwork. An interlocutor, Saint Boniface, serves the same purpose as the pseudo-Shakespearean Gower and as the chasseur in *Zerbino*. By means of transitional reports, which have a marked archaic flavor, he supplements the fragmentary action and knits it more closely together. While the dramatic element is subordinate, the lyric passages are designed to play upon the emotions and to win the reader's heart. They are adorned with a wealth of strophes of the most intricate pattern, teeming with a dazzling array of interlaced rimes and assonances. Tieck's form is arbitrary in every sense. The use of the *redondilla*, the *octave* and the sonnet reveal the influence of Calderon.

To be sure, the serious and emphatic tone of the play commands respect. Moreover, he introduced psychology with telling effect when he invented a secret though slight inclination of Genevieve for Golo, yet painted her strong enough to withstand it and remain a saint in our eyes. But, we may ask, since her stanch Christian faith is triumphant over his fatalism, was it good dramatic logic to make her suffer so grievously in the wilderness? The fact that the answer to this important question is brought out so vaguely in the drama, only serves to show up its weakness. Genevieve, it seems, had been destined to become a nun, but broke faith with her Savior by once harboring a passing thought of love for Golo and then by marrying Siegfried. Now, since God is mightier than Nature (here we have the basic, truly humanistic idea of the play), she must suffer and atone for her sin.

Frequent changes of scene, pseudo-naïve and marrowless talk *about* religion, diffuse epic descriptions and long interlocutory scenes, which amplify but do not deepen the source, help to convince us that Tieck lacks the style and formative power of the true, positively religious dramatist which his mode of treatment demanded. The musical element, which Brentano believed was his forte, though it made his poetry one-sided,[18] prevails.

When Iffland suggested that the play be revised for the stage, Tieck curtly refused to make any concessions, in reality on account of his dislike for Iffland and not, as he stated thirty years later, because he had never intended the drama for the stage.[19] Later he related that Kotzebue also wished to revise it.[20] As the basis for the libretto of an inferior "three-act romantic drama with ballet" by Görner, with music by Huth, it was twice performed in Berlin in 1841 with little success. Occasionally the play, which is more operatic than dramatic, more subjective than objective, reminds of Wagner's *Tannhäuser*. In two letters to the publisher Frommann of January and December 1801, respectively, Tieck actually called it "my opera, the fairy tale."[21] It seems a pity that no first-rate composer was attracted to it.

We have mentioned Müller's *Golo und Genoveva* of 1781 and Hebbel's *Genoveva* of 1841 and drawn certain comparisons. Perhaps now a few more words on this subject will not be amiss. Whereas both Müller and Tieck have enriched the story and animated its actors—the former with more dramatic instinct than the latter—, Hebbel expertly dramatized the legend. He emphasized Golo, who is an *active* character as compared with *passive* Genevieve, and deepened the Christian and mythical elements so as to fuse them into a tragedy of human solitude. Finally Otto Ludwig's *Genoveva* fragments, while indicating opposition to Tieck's conception, resemble his drama in suggesting Genevieve's secret passion and in making her husband an elderly man.[22]

Friedrich Schlegel was delighted with *Genoveva*, calling it gentle and tender, and penned a sonnet in praise of the work and its author. At first August Wilhelm also praised it highly. Schleiermacher found much beauty in it and felt that it merited repeated reading and careful study.[23] Bernhardi reviewed it excellently in the *Archiv der Zeit* (I, 457). Brentano referred to it in his novel *Godwi* as "ein wunderheiliges Gedicht." The greatest living German poet, Goethe, who had meanwhile met Tieck personally through A. W. Schlegel's mediation, received it with friendly approval, though not with boisterous acclaim. On December 5 and 6, 1799, Tieck read the play to Goethe in Weimar. He took two evenings to complete it. Goethe followed with manifest attention and approbation. Then he turned to his nine-year-old son, August, who had heard the latter part of the drama, and stroking his hair said: "Well, my son, what do you think of all the colors, flowers, mirrors and magic arts about which our friend has read to us? Is that not quite wonderful?" (Nun, mein Söhnchen, was meinst du zu allen den Farben, Blumen, Spiegeln und Zauberkünsten, von denen unser Freund uns vorgelesen hat? Ist das nicht recht wunderbar?) In his *Tag- und Jahreshefte* for 1799 Goethe reported that Tieck's "truly poetic treatment" gave him "very much pleasure" and won his "most cordial approval."[24] To be sure, some contemporaries, who admired Goethe more than they did Tieck, for instance Jean Paul, were not a little irritated by Goethe's approval.

Schiller's reaction was not as consistent as Goethe's. He, who had published a few of Tieck's lyrics in his *Musenalmanach auf das Jahr 1799*, had also met him (in July) and expressed his opinion to him of Goethe. He found that while he lacked forcefulness, he was delicate, sensible and significant, and seemed to possess an agreeable nature and pleasant talent, without coquettishness and immodesty.[25] When his friend Christian Körner descried a mine of true poetic talent in *Genoveva*, Schiller agreed and praised Tieck's personal modesty and interesting manner, as well as his "pleasant Romantic tone," his poetic talent and invention. But he found that under the Schlegelian influence he was hollow and jejune. Tieck, he felt, had taken up the Romantic manner "with much success" (mit vielem Glück). "His is a very graceful, imaginative and tender nature; only he lacks power and depth and will always lack them. Unfortunately the school of the Schlegels has already spoiled a great deal in him; he will never quite recover from this. His taste is still immature, he does not maintain the same level in his works, and there is even much vacuity in them."[26] A fact which Tieck later stressed repeatedly, that *Genoveva* exercised an influence upon *Maria Stuart*, with its Catholicizing element, and *Die Jungfrau von Orleans*, with its echoes of a wondrous fairy world, was not mentioned by Schiller.[27] Today this influence is no longer disputed. The whole scheme of *Die Jungfrau* clearly goes back to Tieck. In the use of miracles Schiller even outdoes him.

Presently Schiller's ill humor toward the Romanticists grew. One of the chief reasons was his increasing antipathy toward Caroline, the wife of A. W. Schlegel. He also despised August Wilhelm himself, who did not tire of ridiculing his idealism. In consequence Schiller's opinion of Tieck also become less favorable. He gave up hope that the young Romanticist would undergo any further poetic development at all and relegated *Genoveva* to the limbo of uncultured prattle.[28] This conviction he later confirmed, writing to Körner that the manner of the Schlegels and Tieck was quite obnoxious to him (ganz und gar zuwider), and to Wilhelm von Humboldt that their doctrine impressed him more and more as empty caricature (immer hohler und fratzenhafter).[29]

Though severe in tone, this criticism touches a sore spot not only in Tieck's work but in the entire output of the Romanticists. The new poetic life which they strove to create was fashioned of tenuous stuff— of ethereal fabric—, presentiments, yearnings and subtle emotions raised to the nth power. Tieck would have us believe that such a phenomenal life represents a far loftier existence than our real existence can ever hope to achieve. But in practice it does not attain poetic reality even for the poet himself. He merely longs for its fulfilment. Like a will-o'-the-wisp it is flashed before his eyes from out of the supposed desolation of the sober here and now, indistinct in its outlines, translucent and incorporeal.

Tieck's own bosom friend of later years, Solger, did not hesitate to judge *Genoveva* almost as adversely though not as severely as Schiller.[30] While expressing his admiration for the work, he called it too purposeful and arbitrary. It does not express "a frame of mind, as much as a yearning therefor." The scenes and characters seemed to him remote, the form too epic and reflective. He found a surfeit of far-fetched costume and portraiture, a lack of compelling reality and too great a variety of shading in the speeches. In other words, he missed "den eigentlichen dramatischen Nerv, die wahre praktische Kraft." Tieck argued these points with him at length during the winter of 1816-1817, and after Solger had advised him to reread the work himself as though it were the product of another's pen, he made the following candid admission on January 30, 1817: "It is one of my peculiarities that for years I held Shakespeare's *Pericles* in perhaps exaggerated veneration. Without it *Zerbino* would never have been written, and much less *Genoveva* and *Octavian*. I had, as it were, fallen in love with this form, which so marvellously fuses epic and drama; it seemed feasible to me to inject even lyric poetry, and it is with veritable rapture that I look back upon those hours in which *Genoveva* and later *Octavian* arose in my mind's eye. Perhaps I set about to incorporate this rapture too physically, too literally, and the result was mannerism."[31]

Doubtless he has overemphasized the influence of *Pericles* to the prejudice of other equally important impulses. But the passage shows his state of mind during the *Genoveva* period and his willingness to admit some of the defects of the curious work.

We have noted the strong Catholicizing tendency in *Genoveva*, which is emphasized at the end by the retirement of Count Siegfried and his hopelessly precocious son into solitude to do penance. In 1829 he inserted in the preface to volume 11 of his *Schriften* a warm retrospective defense of his right as a young poet to glorify the admirable traits which he found in medieval Catholicism.[32] A poet, he averred, is free to seek his inspiration where he will, and need not be embarrassed by any contemporaneous disputes of a theological or political nature. Why, he asked, should he not have been at liberty to glorify the Catholic form of Christianity from the point of view of cult, legend, miracle and general artistic appeal? If Goethe in his Roman Elegies could revive the spirit of pagan Rome with impunity, and Schiller could likewise apotheosize the philosophy of ancient Greece in *Die Götter Griechenlands*, who might be so bold as to deny him to speak out what was in his heart? His attraction to Catholicism, he went on to say, was all the more natural since that religion was in his youth on the defensive against "disbelief, shallow enlightenment, pseudo-philosophy, hatred of all that is holy, mysterious and traditional"—qualities which "passed for Protestantism."

Naturally the spirit of *Genoveva* soon exposed him to the charge that he, though born Protestant, had followed the example of numerous contemporaries and secretly embraced the Catholic faith. These rumors, first cropping up soon after 1800, persisted for over two generations, until his Boswell, Köpke, definitely refuted them in 1855.[33] In 1803 the Norwegian philosopher J. N. Möller, who had read *Genoveva* and other works of Tieck, wrote him a letter formally inviting him to turn Catholic. Möller, who married a sister-in-law of Tieck, himself became Catholic in 1804. While in Munich in 1804 Tieck associated with the Catholic philosopher Franz von Baader and the convert Karl von Rumohr. During and immediately after his stay in Italy (1805-1806) it was frequently stated that he had been converted. Dorothea Veit-Schlegel, herself a proselyte, reported the rumor on December 1, 1805.[34] In an unedited letter of Varnhagen von Ense to Bernhardi of January 12, 1807, the Danish poet Oehlenschläger is said to have asked Tieck point-blank whether he had been converted and to have received a negative reply. The same correspondent, however, wrote to Bernhardi about a month later that Schleiermacher refused to believe the denial, suggesting that Tieck is a secret agent of the Church.

In 1809 Arnim and Caroline Schlegel-Schelling heard similar gossip to the effect that when in Rome he had offered to become a professional proselytizer, volunteering to convert prominent Germans for an annual consideration of six hundred talers![35] In 1814 A. W. Schlegel told H. C. Robinson in Paris that Tieck had gone over to Catholicism.[36] The poet Johann Heinrich Voss, a bitter foe of the Romanticists, published a pamphlet in 1820 publicly denouncing him as a religious renegade. Tieck never replied formally to Voss, but to the publisher Perthes he wrote in 1821: "The gossip of old Voss is quite contemptible, and if one replies he will gossip all the more in his despicable way." (Die Klätschereien des alten Voss sind mir ganz verächtlich, und antwortet man, so klatscht er nur von neuem auf ganz gemeine Weise.) In 1825 he commented to the same correspondent concerning the "lies" of Voss and added that some day he might issue an open statement about them.[37] In 1829 Schelling expressed to Robinson his belief in the report that Tieck had turned Catholic.[38] The Young Germans, among them Laube, did all in

their power to noise the rumor about.[39] In England the truth of the statement seems to have been accepted, as the *Foreign Quarterly Review* of
1837 and James A. Froude in *Tales from the Phantasus* (1845) testify.
The fact that Tieck's wife, his daughter Dorothea, his sisters-in-law
Marie and Charlotte, as well as countless Romantic writers, like Friedrich Schlegel and Zacharias Werner, were actually converted (Amalie
and Dorothea became Catholic some time before the summer of 1805),
helped to strengthen these assertions.

It is hardly necessary to repeat that such statements are based on
serious misunderstanding of Tieck's nature. Not interest in Catholicism,
but the yearning, love and emotion of the modern poet with respect to
the naïve age of Genevieve, characterize his attitude. In the *Phantasien*
a young painter writes from Rome that in order fully to understand and
reverence a great Catholic painting, he must believe in it and in what it
depicts; hence art has converted him to Catholicism. In the same way
and for the same purpose the poet of *Genoveva* embraced the faith of
Genevieve's age, but only figuratively. His watchword and touchstone,
we have found, were always poetry, and in the light of poetry he regarded religion, too. The poet Eichendorff, a stanch Catholic, always
considered Tieck a Protestant, as his satirical dramas, containing many
digs at Tieck, show. No doubt there is something in Eichendorff's charge
that to Tieck Catholicism was naught but an esthetic toy. In that sense
Brentano called him "närrisch katholisch."[40] Caroline concurred when
she styled his Catholicism a poetic mannerism.[41]

It is regrettable that Tieck did not write a treatise on the relation of
the various creeds to Christianity, as he planned in 1802. This work
would undoubtedly have made his position on matters of religion clear
once and for all. Some of his ideas, however, were later utilized in *Der
Aufruhr in den Cevennen* and in *Eine Sommerreise*.

At any rate, it required a more marked poetic genius and a more pronounced creative individuality to breathe life into such nebulous forms
as hovered in his imagination when he wrote *Genoveva*. The poet who
was endowed with these gifts and could mold such stuff as dreams are
made of into visible shapes, and give them consistency, and feel at
home among them, was Friedrich von Hardenberg, who called himself
Novalis. The religious faith and sincere attachment to things transcendental which Tieck craved with infinite longing were the birthright of
Novalis. His rich soul-life exuded the most exhilarating wine to fill the
bottles of Romanticism which Tieck, the sober visionary, could not fill.

We have noted that Tieck with his wife and infant daughter Dorothea spent the summer of 1799 in Giebichenstein. From there it was not

far to Jena, where the Tiecks were anyway considering making their home. On a visit to Jena, he was introduced by A. W. Schlegel to Novalis, who frequently came over from Weissenfels to see Schlegel. He found that he had much in common with the young poet-prophet, whom he soon learned to admire and respect and saw frequently during the next year. Here, he felt, was a man who might take the place of the lamented Wackenroder, here was a man whose deeply religious soul attracted him irresistibly and turned his own thoughts more directly to religion. And Novalis realized that Tieck, the experienced, facile writer, who was himself somewhat of a genius, could teach him the routine of writing as none other could. For was he not the author of *Sternbald*, a work which served as an inspiration to Novalis? Enthusiastically Novalis wrote to him from Weissenfels: "Your acquaintance opens a new book in my life."[42] The letters of Dorothea Veit-Schlegel, also one of Friedrich Schlegel to Schleiermacher, indicate that Novalis fairly fell in love with Tieck and in moments of ecstasy rated him a greater poet than Goethe.[43]

The friendship proved fruitful. It was Tieck who led Novalis to set his thoughts on paper in imaginative form. And without his influence it is doubtful whether we would possess as much as we do of Novalis' all too grandiosely planned novel *Heinrich von Ofterdingen.*

In Tieck's allegorical poem "Der Traum" at the end of the *Phantasien über die Kunst* we clearly discern the prototype of Novalis' "blaue Blume," the symbol of Romantic poesy. The poet, accompanied by his friend, is walking through a dark, forbidding rocky valley surrounded by menacing crags. There is fear in his heart; his tears flow freely. No star shines to light their way, and they can comfort each other only with their true friendship. Suddenly they discover a tiny blue star lying at their feet. Out of it grows a beautiful miraculous flower, which gladdens their hearts and makes their "spirit penetrate e'en to infinity."

But Tieck's attitude toward dreams is, as usual, not identical with that of Novalis. In theory dreams, with their reality for the inner spiritual ego, are in the eyes of the Romanticists tantamount to life, while life, with its unreality for the external ego, is like a dream (as in *Braddeck*, where Tieck called life a dream); dreams appealed to the fatalism of the Romanticist because they were interpreted as the vehicles of fate. But in practice the more sober Tieck always remains cognizant of the line which separates them, while Novalis merges dream and life.[44]

Novalis' essay *Die Christenheit oder Europa* bears the impress of Tieck's predilection for the Middle Ages, as it does the stamp of Schleiermacher's *Reden*. Other works, among them an edition of hymns and sermons, were planned by Novalis and Tieck in collaboration.

THE ROMANTIC FREE-LANCE

As the prophet of Jacob Böhme, Tieck attracted also Novalis to the humble seventeenth century philosopher. In gratitude Novalis wrote the poem "An Tieck," wherein he celebrated him as the "Verkündiger der Morgenröte." The child in the poem—

> A child so sad and ever loyal
> Expelled into a foreign land,

is, of course, Tieck himself.

But unfortunately Novalis' span of life was destined to be almost as brief as Wackenroder's. He died of consumption in 1801, some five weeks before his twenty-ninth birthday. The passing of Novalis was an inestimable loss to Tieck. He wrote to Friedrich Schlegel that a part of his soul, a part of his life-giving element, a part of his love had been taken away from him: "If I like to believe in the influence and effect of the stars upon myself and my life, if I sense the friendship of the plants, the sky and the water for me, I must feel more strongly the direct, necessary influence and afflatus of befriended souls upon me."[45]

In memory of his friend he joined with Friedrich Schlegel in editing *Novalis Schriften* (1802). This two-volume collection, of which five editions appeared, idealizes Novalis at every turn, much more so than the later editions of Heilborn and Bölsche do. Yet it is an important work, since practically everything Novalis ever wrote, in particular his unfinished novel *Heinrich von Ofterdingen*, was published therein for the first time. The author himself had got out only some fragments, *Blütenstaub*, in the *Athenäum*; the essay *Die Christenheit oder Europa*; and, posthumously, a sheaf of poems in the Schlegel-Tieck *Musenalmanach* (1802). Tieck's outstanding contributions to the edition were the introduction and a characterization of Novalis' plans for the second part of *Heinrich von Ofterdingen*. To be sure, this characterization, based upon notes of Novalis which are partially preserved in Berlin, is not always quite reliable. As late as 1846 Tieck published a third volume with the help of Eduard von Bülow. It contains Novalis' diary, additional poems, letters and fragments. Since then very few new writings of the author have come to light—only several poems and an essay on Schiller's *Die Götter Griechenlands*.

In Jena the Schlegels and their gifted wives, Caroline and Dorothea (now Friedrich's common-law wife), who both possessed literary talents, kept an open house. Novalis and Brentano, the translator Gries, the artist Bury and the architect Hans Christian Genelli were frequent guests. But their most intimate associates were Schleiermacher and the two philosophers Fichte and Schelling.

Fichte,[46] one of the keenest thinkers and strongest characters of all time, was the oldest of this group. Five years the senior of August Wilhelm and ten years older than Friedrich, he had become professor of philosophy at Jena in 1794, where he remained until 1799. The theories of Romanticism are largely based upon his transcendental idealism. He extended the philosophy of Kant into the realm of the idealistic and developed a definite epistemology, a codification of the body of scientific knowledge, based upon a theory predicating a mutual interdependence of ego and non-ego. Fichte transformed the cosmos into a mirror of the ego; he found the center of gravity in man himself. Out of his and Schelling's thought, moreover, the philosophy of history and of art arises.

Schelling, thirteen years his junior, was the youngest of the group. He had come to Jena in 1798 as a teacher. His was a philosophy of activism. "It is impossible," he asserted, "to philosophize on any subject which cannot be set into activity." Schelling's nature philosophy is tantamount to "creating" nature, to freeing it from its lifeless mechanistic process; to him nature is human reason in a germinal state. His ultimate goal is a philosophy of art. With his synthesis of Greek and Christian ideals he developed a Hellenic-German view of the world. Like Fichte he was a thorough idealist, deducing the entire fund of conscious knowledge in the three successive spheres of art, religion and philosophy from the absolute as a creative idealistic principle. He believed in development and in the unity and reasonableness of the universe. If Fichte's motto may be said to have been "I am," Schelling's was "I become."

In impassioned discussions the Schlegels, Fichte and Schelling sought to solve the problems of art, philosophy and natural science, each to his own satisfaction. They were concerned with transforming life on the basis of an idealistic culture, destroying Rationalism and establishing a new poesy and science in its stead. In October 1799, Tieck and his little family also came to live in Jena, remaining there until about the end of June 1800. They stayed in the house of A. W. Schlegel, where this circle met almost daily. Here that spiritually animated sociability (born in the Berlin salons), which Friedrich Schlegel postulated in his *Athenäum* fragments and which became a hallmark of Romanticism, was fully developed along cosmopolitan lines. Later, when the Romanticists scattered in every direction, they took this doctrine with them.

It was a rich period in Tieck's life, full of intellectual feasts, for, as we know, he had much in common with the two Schlegels, but even more with Novalis. As late as 1827 A. W. Schlegel wrote retrospectively of those Jena days: "I have since lived in the most spirited and cultured circles and have met many of the most notable contemporaries in Germany and abroad. And yet my memory often harks back with yearning to that free and fruitful communion of spirits at an age when we were all drunk with hope."[47]

But prior to his friendship for Solger, Tieck's mind was not receptive to systematic philosophy, only to mysticism. He did not like to read books on philosophy and grasped abstract reasoning with difficulty. In once reporting to Schleiermacher that he is full of "Philophysik" (an allusion to his predilection for Böhme), Friedrich Schlegel added aptly that the "philo" preponderates in his case.[48] Though trying to play the prophet and seer, the rôle of a funmaker was more congenial to him.[49]

Furthermore the unity and concord of this circle were continually threatened because every member of it, in deference to the prevailing subjectivism, insisted upon the full assertion of his own individuality, regardless of the claims of the others. As Dorothea Veit-Schlegel wrote to Schleiermacher,[50] it was questionable whether they understood each other, nay whether they knew exactly what they themselves were driving at. Nor were they all quite agreed as to Fichte's transmutation of the cosmos into an ego. By implication Tieck had opposed the doctrine in *William Lovell* and indeed shunned subjectivism (which he knew was his weakness) wherever he could. Moreover, he was too much in love with nature to accept Fichte's dictum. Novalis, on the other hand, subscribed to Fichte's theories but wished to develop them further and to put them into practice. As a matter of fact, it seems that the Romanticists were striving for an amalgamation of Fichte's "Ich-Philosophie" and Schelling's activistic "Naturphilosophie," deciding that the development of nature is a process of growing conscious, which reaches its climax in man.

We have noted what the two Schlegels thought of Tieck. Caroline, August Wilhelm's wife, was always prejudiced against him. Her carping critical remarks about him in letters must be taken with a grain of salt. In 1801 she wrote to her husband that he is "foggy and fantastic" (ein Nebler und Schwebler—a phrase borrowed from Goethe)[51] and full of crotchets and trickery (Nücken und Tücken).[52] Friedrich's mistress Dorothea, on the other hand, usually expressed respect and even a liking for him, but at first joined Caroline in ridiculing his wife for her awkwardness and lack of esprit. Caroline scoffed at Amalie's plain manner and clothing, her lack of intellectual interests, of vivaciousness and grace. Dorothea found that Amalie cut a sorry figure. Tieck's own sister hated her. But Novalis thought highly of her, while the Schlegel brothers defended her.[53]

LUDWIG TIECK, THE GERMAN ROMANTICIST

Schleiermacher had a cordial feeling for Tieck and, though fearing his inability to comprehend the Schlegelian ideology, was convinced that he could utilize and reproduce it to advantage.[54] Fichte, while not taken in by his personality,[55] and without sharing his enthusiasm for Böhme,[56] cherished him as a friend[57] and grossly overrated him as a poet, believing that with the exception of a few of Goethe's works, *Genoveva* was the finest poem in the German language.[58] Schelling, though disliking Novalis, admired Tieck for his *Volksmährchen* even before he met him; after they became acquainted, Tieck found Schelling quite receptive to Böhme's philosophy,[56] and thought he had discovered in him a true admiring friend.[59] But in the long run he displayed almost as little faith in Schelling (whom he soon deemed awkward in speech and not firm in his views) as he did in Schleiermacher.[60]

In a confidential letter to his sister Sophie and her husband Bernhardi of early December 1799, Tieck expressed himself very sharply concerning all the Schlegels except August Wilhelm.[61] Of Dorothea he wrote: "It gives me a devilishly sick feeling, if I may be permitted to say so, to see how the beast acts . . . the others seem enthralled because the whole business is swinishness. . . . Schelling pays his addresses to Mrs. Schlegel [i.e. Caroline, who later married Schelling], so that the whole town is agog with gossip; Mrs. Veit [i.e. Dorothea] flirts with Wilhelm Schlegel, and thus everything is topsy-turvy. The women would be happy if we took a part in these doings. Friedrich is a general laughingstock on account of *Lucinde*. Such people ought to take pains to observe all the proprieties because they want to look down on morality and because their doctrine falls with their conduct, and is considered false. . . . It is lamentable that these persons with their divine gifts are turned into veritable monkeys by absurd women. Be convinced that Caroline is really the cause of all the quarrels in which they are involved. But they do not notice this because in the end she always plays the woman and wants to mitigate what has happened. They are almost universally hated here, only that means precious little because most of the people are of the rabble. . . . Wilhelm improves with acquaintance, he is goodnaturedness itself and would not harm a soul. But he plays a part which they have really learned from me and to which Wilhelm is not at all equal. . . . Friedrich was much more cordial in Berlin, we are drifting farther apart. Mrs. Veit is indescribably brutal, a connoisseur of music, confidante of the Schlegels, a Lucinde to a disgusting degree, a true emetic, ready for anything. And Mrs. Schlegel has more shrewdness than intelligence and more intelligence than nobility, and more nobility than womanliness. She is like

. . . a hermaphrodite. One never thinks of them as women. . . . One could wax Juvenalian over these absurd whores."

These criminations and recriminations furnish eloquent testimony that Rudolf Haym's "Romantic School" was not a well knit body of writers and thinkers. Certainly Tieck was a dissenting member in essential points. He had much more in common with the later Romanticists, the Heidelberg group, to which Arnim, Brentano and the Grimms belonged. For while the Schlegels and their circle harked back to antiquity, he, like the Heidelberg devotees of Romanticism, was more rooted in the soil of medieval Germany and Böhmean mysticism and had been strongly under the influence of Storm and Stress. And while the Romantic philosophers wanted to infuse the light of the soul into nature, Tieck, the author of *Der blonde Eckbert*, tried to show the restraining influence of nature upon human existence.

The Jena Romanticists concurred only in their approbation of the great masters of literature—the Sacred Four whom Tieck glorified—, Dante, Shakespeare, Cervantes and Goethe. And Goethe, who lived but a few miles away in Weimar and seemed not ill disposed to the group, was esteemed by them all as the high priest of poetry on earth. During his stay in Jena Tieck visited him several times. Goethe now described him to Schiller as "a very tolerable nature."[62]

In their opinions of Schiller they disagreed. While the Schlegels and their wives, blinded by personal animosity, did not conceal their bitter and vindictive enmity toward him, Tieck never forgot his youthful admiration for Schiller's early dramas, especially *Die Räuber*. But no doubt the Schlegels influenced him, too, against Schiller. As early as October 20, 1799, Savigny reported that Tieck denied Schiller a claim to genius.[63] As regards Schiller's later plays, however, Tieck's criticism was a mixture of approval and disapproval.[64] But since his opinions concerning these works were expressed much later, we shall reserve our discussion of them for a subsequent chapter.

During his stay in Jena, as we have seen, and then in 1801 at Dresden, Tieck came into personal contact with Schiller, but only in a superficial way. We have noted Schiller's statement to Goethe concerning his sensibleness and significance. But they had no mutual spheres of interest or of ideals; they were so different that they seemed to live in two separate worlds. Not even Shakespeare could bring them together, for while Schiller paid most attention to the tragedies and historical dramas, Tieck was still enamored of the fairy plays and spurious works like *Pericles*. Similarly, in Spanish literature Lope attracted Schiller, while Tieck was in love with Calderon. Schiller's low opinion of Tieck's poetry is attested by the fact that he went so far as to advise him to confine his literary activity to an intensive study of Spanish.[65] On the merits of the plastic arts, too, they failed to agree; thus Schiller could not share Tieck's admiration for such a master-colorist as Correggio.

Schiller strove with Goethe to flee the confines of reality and to seek refuge in a realm of perspicuous plastic beauty and of classical perfection founded on the basis of Grecian esthetics and in the spirit of ethical idealism. The Romantics, on the other hand, wished to delve into the tenebrous recesses of modern feeling and to discover new poetic treasures. While Goethe and Schiller pleaded for symmetry, harmony, clearness and perfection, Tieck and his confrères advocated formlessness, discordance, vagueness and endlessness. It need not surprise us, then, that soon anything miraculous or inexplicable, be it pleasant or horrible in form, came to be regarded as Romantic. In view of these marked dissimilarities it is astonishing that he, for his part, did not realize the important difference between the Classicists and himself until after the appearance of Goethe's *Italienische Reise*.[66]

CHAPTER EIGHT

ROMANTIC POETRY AND POLEMICS

DURING the first twenty-five years of his life Tieck's health had been good. He indulged freely in outdoor exercise, especially in horseback riding, and was considered healthy and robust. Henrik Steffens, who made his acquaintance at the end of the century, described his appearance as stunning.[1] But beginning late in 1799 his physical condition deteriorated.[2] In part at least this trouble was due to dissipation. We have it on the authority of the Swedish diplomat Brinkman in a letter to Rahel Levin of July 30, 1795 (preserved among Varnhagen von Ense's Berlin papers), that he kept very late, irregular hours and did much carousing.

He became subject to attacks of gout, which grew more serious and painful. Rheumatism of the joints, particularly of the knees and sometimes of the hands, soon set in, too, and for long periods he was totally debilitated. To make matters worse, he twice contracted a rheumatic fever when in Munich (1804 and 1808-1810), each time being long confined to his bed. During the winter of 1813 at Ziebingen, at the age of forty, he had scarlet fever. On the trip to England and France in 1817 his rheumatism became worse. A. W. Schlegel reported to Tieck's brother at the time that he was quite wry, distorted by pain and very morose. This ailment, which later took him to the baths in Baden-Baden or Teplitz almost every year, permanently disfigured him. His head was oddly tilted to the right side, and his limbs became stiff. Of course these sufferings aggravated his natural penchant for melancholia and self-pity. Like Coleridge he often "roamed the black heath of distress." One wonders how he could subsist for eighty years and be as prolific as he was.

Often the associations with his new friends in Jena were disturbed by Tieck's physical indisposition, which tended to make him testy and disagreeable. But, as we have seen, differences of opinion also cropped up. By July 1800, the Romanticists had reached the parting of the ways, despite the efforts of the Schlegels to keep the circle together.[3] Though they met occasionally thereafter, they never lived together again. A. W. Schlegel went to Berlin and during the next three winters delivered public lectures on his theories of art and on ancient and modern literatures. Yet in these public pronouncements he never tired of referring to Tieck's works as the practical fulfilment of the Romantic program. Later, too, he always cherished an affection for Tieck. Tieck himself regretted that he had to leave Jena.[4] Indeed, he and the Schlegels never quite abandoned their relations. We have thirty-nine letters from August Wilhelm to Tieck between 1797 and 1841, thirty-four from Tieck to August Wilhelm between 1797 and 1837, sixteen from Friedrich to Tieck between 1797 and 1828, and nine from Tieck to Friedrich between 1801 and 1822.[5] Tieck's letters to the Schlegels, particularly those to Friedrich, are among the finest which he, a negligent correspondent, ever wrote. He was pained, no doubt, as he confessed to Friedrich von Raumer in 1824, to Brinkman in 1835 and to Count Yorck von Wartenburg as late as 1853, that Friedrich later abandoned poetry and scholarship to become a religious fanatic and mystic.[6] He was stung to the quick when August Wilhelm later obstructed and censured his continuation of the German Shakespeare. Yet he did not hesitate in 1828 to dedicate the second volume of his *Schriften* to Friedrich, recalling "the beautiful days which we spent together when we were still young" (der schönen Tage, die wir beide, noch jugendlich, mit einander verlebt haben) ; and the fifth volume to August Wilhelm, assuring him that "remembrance and love have never perished in me" (Andenken und Liebe sind aber bei mir niemals erloschen), and that the days of their earliest friendship were "one of the most splendid and happy periods of my life" (eine der glänzendsten und heitersten Perioden meines Lebens). As late as 1827 A. W. Schlegel was proud to have been the discoverer of "that rare poetic genius"[7] which was Tieck's. Shortly after Friedrich's death in 1829 Tieck thought of writing his biography,[8] a task which was still unaccomplished one hundred years later.

Tieck always had many acquaintances and admirers, still his close friends were few in number. But the short list, in which Wackenroder, Novalis, Solger and Raumer play an important part, would not be complete without the name of the two Schlegels.

The next important work which he undertook bears the imprint of the Schlegelian influence and shows improvement over the *Volksmährchen*, of which it was to be a continuation. It is the two-volume collection which appeared in 1799-1800 under the characteristic title *Romantische Dichtungen*, at first to be called *Romantische Darstellungen*. Imbued by August Wilhelm with a new confidence in his own work, he now abandoned his anonymity. The intelligent and thoroughly reliable Frommann in Jena, a true friend, published the work. The part played by the *Romantische Dichtungen* in disseminating and popularizing the term "romantisch" can hardly be overemphasized. Here the word, first used by Friedrich

Schlegel in the *Athenäum* as a *terminus technicus*, was applied for the first time to a product of the German Romanticists themselves. Probably Tieck did not realize, when he selected this title, that it would soon attain general significance as the designation for a new literary program and a new "school" of writing. He stated later that he selected it without any ulterior motive, not meaning to suggest a novel or higher type of poetry and merely wishing to indicate that his collection aimed to introduce the reader to most divergent and multifarious regions of feeling, emotion and imagination in rapid, ever-changing succession.[9]

The *Romantische Dichtungen* contained two ambitious dramatic works —*Zerbino*, which had already been published separately, and *Genoveva,* here printed for the first time. Of the three other works, two, *Der getreue Eckart und der Tannenhäuser* and *Sehr wunderbare Historie von der Melusina,* are prose tales with interspersed lyrics, continuing the style of some of the *Volksmährchen* and of *Genoveva;* the other is a satirical play, *Leben und Tod des kleinen Rotkäppchens,* written somewhat in the manner of *Der gestiefelte Kater* and *Zerbino.* Certainly the motley array of subjects, moods and styles offered the reader a good picture not only of the author but also of his conception of what "romantisch" means. The work is marked by manifestations of every type and peculiarity of writing for which he stood during the first half of his life— interest in the old folk literature, naïveté alternating with a high degree of city-bred sophistication and parody, occasional sensualism and frequent irrationalism, the lyric mood, sudden transition from one atmosphere and form to another, an artist's predilection for medievalism and Catholicism, hostility toward Rationalism, striving of an introvert for objectivity, "Romantic Irony," and interest in various phases of psychic disturbance or aberration developed to a gradual climax.

In *Der getreue Eckart und der Tannenhäuser,* written one night under the spell of the new friendship with Novalis, he was a pioneer; he utilized the legend of the Venusberg—the subterranean love court of Venus in the Hörselberg in Thuringia—for the first time in modern literature.[10] In joining this legend to that of Trusty Eckart, the faithful liegeman and admonisher, he followed tradition and the *Heldenbuch,* for Eckart was supposed to guard the approach to the Venusberg and warn mortals against entering. Yet in introducing also the story of the Pied Piper of Hamlin—he makes him a minstrel who lures men to Venus —, which had hitherto had no connection with the Tannhäuser and Eckart legends, he was again an innovator. But of one of the chief sources for the story of the Venusberg, namely the old Tannhäuser ballad, which Heine and Wagner later used, he seems to have had no knowledge. He was, however, familiar with the Eckart narrative in the *Heldenbuch*.

The story of *Der getreue Eckart und der Tannenhäuser* is as follows. The Duke of Burgundy, formerly a friend of Trusty Eckart, who had once saved his life, now hates him because Eckart is too good and faithful. He has already killed two of Eckart's sons. Eckart's third and last son, Conrad, goes to the duke to intercede for his father. Meanwhile an old man accosts Eckart and tells him his own story—how his sons were lured away by a minstrel to the hellish court of Venus. Eckart, now hearing that Conrad has also been killed by the duke, himself confronts the latter but is scorned. Later the duke, in distress, is rescued by Eckart, who unrecognized carries him to safety on his shoulders. The duke, finally learning the identity of his rescuer, begs his forgiveness for the murder of his children and, making Eckart the guardian of his own children and regent of the duchy, dies. Soon the fiendish minstrel of the old man's story appears and lures the orphans of the duke to the court of Venus. Eckart, too, is attracted but withstands the temptation and gives battle to the minions of hell. He succeeds in saving the children but must himself die. His spirit guards the entrance to the court of Venus ever after, warning all mortals to stay away.

Thus far the first part of the tale, which contains numerous verse interludes in ballad form. These ballads take up and continue the prose narrative until the prose begins again, thus constituting an integral component of the story.

The second part takes place over four centuries later. Young Tannenhäuser has mysteriously disappeared. His friend Friedrich von Wolfgang longs for him. One day he finally returns. But he seems quite changed and says that he is bound for Rome. Reluctantly he tells his story.

In a fit of jealousy he had killed his rival in love, thus causing the death of his sweetheart Emma, too. Smitten by pangs of conscience, he hastened home, only to find his mother dead of grief over his misdeed. His father died while telling Tannenhäuser of her death. Half insane, Tannenhäuser threw himself into a life of ribaldry in a vain effort to forget his sorrow. Finally he summoned the devil, who directed him to the Venusberg. There Trusty Eckart warned him, but Tannenhäuser dashed past the faithful old admonisher and entered wholeheartedly into the profligate life at the court of Venus. Now, he says, concluding his story, he is on the way to Rome to do penance and secure the Pope's forgiveness.

Friedrich is astounded by this narrative, because he knows that it is merely a figment of Tannenhäuser's feverish imagination. For he, Friedrich, has married Emma. But Tannenhäuser refuses to believe him even when confronted with Emma. He insists that Friedrich's story is nothing but a design of the devil to prevent him from going to Rome for absolution. So he remains deaf to Friedrich's entreaties and goes. Returning from Rome, he kisses Friedrich and tells him that the Pope has refused to condone his sins. With this he disappears. To his horror Friedrich finds that on his brief second visit Tannenhäuser had murdered Emma. And Friedrich too is doomed, for whosoever has been kissed by a denizen of the Venusberg must himself become one. Friedrich departs in search of Tannenhäuser and the Venusberg.

While the first part is related in the naïve, childlike language of the fairy tale (the *Heymons Kinder* type of reproduction, which we have called type 1), with interspersed ballads, the second part is told in a thoroughly artful and artificial style (type 3 according to our classification at the end of chapter 5), without verse interludes.

Two brief passages will illustrate the difference in manner. The following from part I, describes the scene when Eckart confronts the duke. " 'Are you the duke of Burgundy?' he addressed him. Whereupon the duke answered with 'Yes.' 'And you have had my son Dietrich executed?' The duke said 'Yes.' 'And my youngest son Conrad, too,' cried Eckart in grief, 'was not too good for you, and you have had him killed?' Whereupon the duke again answered with 'yes.' "[11]

The following, from part 2, deals with Tannenhäuser's last meeting with his father. " 'I am keeping watch,' spoke the old man, 'for my wife still sits beside me.' My senses vanished, I fixed my eyes on a corner, and after a short while something like a mist seemed to be stirring; there was an undulation and a surging, and the well known form of my mother was visibly shaped out of it, looking at me with earnest mien. I wanted to leave, I could not, for my mother's form beckoned and my father held me fast in his arms, whispering softly to me: 'She died of grief for you.' "[12]

The character of Eckart in part 1 seems related to that of Gotthold in the early drama by that name, and is weakly sentimental; the Romantic yearning of Tannenhäuser, a kinsman of Lovell, in part 2 is much more effectively portrayed. But the latter section is marked by sultry sensualism and uncanny hallucinations, leaving the reader to wonder what is real and what imaginary. This peculiarity, as well as the attribution of demonic qualities to nature, are traits common to this tale and to *Der blonde Eckbert*.

An interesting mixture of nature "Märchen" and saga, this story, like *Der blonde Eckbert*, would offer a psychological explanation for the rise of the old legends of wonder. Just as Tannenhäuser's experience turns out to be a fiction of his imagination, so, Tieck would suggest, all the medieval narratives of this type are products of great emotional stress. And Tannenhäuser's yearning for the Venusberg is his evil yearning for nature (again a humanistic idea!). A decade later, as we shall see, when he gradually turned to more realistic subjects, such vague conglomeration of irrationalism and realism was refined by building upon a more realistic foundation and by transplanting the miracles into a historical or psychological atmosphere.

Unfortunately *Der getreue Eckart und der Tannenhäuser* is not an organic unit. The two separate parts, so different in style, are in reality two distinct stories, connected only by the main motifs which they have in common. The first part is a glorification of fidelity which resists all temptations, the second a warning against the mysterious allurement of the senses. It redounds to Tieck's credit, however, that in this story, as in *Der blonde Eckbert* and in the stories which were to follow, the ethical lessons are of enduring significance. In his conception of the important part which evil plays in the world—also a significant feature of *Der blonde Eckbert*—he was again influenced by Böhme.

Der getreue Eckart und der Tannenhäuser proved popular. Schiller's friend Huber deemed it a rare masterpiece.[13] In 1816 it was translated into Danish by Johan Krag. In England it appeared thrice, first in 1826, translated by Thomas Roscoe, again in 1827 by Carlyle, and then in 1845 in *Tales from the Phantasus* (the last-mentioned being a revision of Roscoe's translation). Roscoe deemed it necessary to "warn the English reader, unacquainted with the wild and daring cast of this author's productions, that he must not be too much startled at meeting with a few of those more supernatural exhibitions which Tieck so much delights in conjuring up." The curious dualistic tale, which wavers disturbingly between the ingenuous tone of the fairy tale and the conscious mannerism of "Stimmungspoesie," has also left its imprint upon later German literature. Not only Brentano in his *Romanzen vom Rosenkranz*, E. T. A. Hoffmann and Heine, but also Wagner in his opera *Tannhäuser* were influenced by Tieck's studied attempt to create an atmosphere of awe.[14]

As appears from Wagner's *Mitteilung an meine Freunde*, he owed to Tieck his first acquaintance with the legend of Tannhäuser, but was not inspired by him to deal with the subject. In fact, it would seem that the anti-papistic tendency of Wagner's opera was in part prompted by direct opposition to what Wagner called Tieck's "katholisch frivole Tendenz."

The figure of Wolfram in Wagner's work may well reflect Tieck's Eckart.

Quite the same style prevails in *Sehr wunderbare Historie von der Melusina*.[15] Verse is here even more plentiful, constituting one-fourth of the entire tale. The work rates as the most inferior of all of his attempts to revive an old chapbook. As a tale retold it is not in a class with his *Heymons Kinder* (though belonging to the same type of fairy-tale reproduction), and as a poetic recreation it fails to measure up to his *Magelone*. In no sense has he created a great literary work of art comparable to the pictorial representation by Moritz von Schwind. The overtures of Konradin Kreutzer and Mendelssohn were inspired by Tieck's tale.

The original German version, based upon a French novel of Jean d'Arras, was by Thüring von Ringoltingen. It was printed in 1474. Melusina, a water sprite, half woman, half fish, appears to Count Reymund of Poitiers. He takes her home, together with her treasures, and as his wife she builds the castle of Lusignan. One day Reymund surprises her in the bath and discovers her dual form and nature. She vanishes and thereafter appears only in mourning weeds on a high turret of the castle whenever one of the family dies. Tieck spins this story out at length, without giving it new depth, and dwells upon the motif of the forbidden question. He introduces extraneous elements, much picturization, and indulges in verbose discussion of the mysteries of nature. In 1807 he set out to dramatize the subject but finished only two scenes. This dramatization would have been a great improvement, for whereas the earlier version fails to make the most of the mythological germ in the tale (the endowment of a water sprite with a human soul), the drama would probably have stressed it.

In the last work of *Romantische Dichtungen*, the "tragedy" *Leben und Tod des kleinen Rotkäppchens*, his ironical vein came once more to the fore. Again he took an old fairy tale, that of Red Riding Hood, and used it as a peg on which to hang his cynical observations on contemporary conditions. The play belongs to the *Schildbürger* class (type 2) of fairy-tale reproduction. But an element of tragedy was also introduced. Instead of the German version with its happy ending, he used the French story, in which Red Riding Hood suffers death at the hands of the wolf. To justify such an outcome, Tieck, satirizing tragic justice, painted her in dark colors. Her mother is a Rationalist, her father a tippler who looks forward to the death of his mother-in-law. No wonder Red Riding Hood is overbearing and sophisticated as well as frivolous. Paying no heed to the warnings of her grandmother and other friends, she walks calmly into the jaws of fate as represented by the wolf. He, too, is a product of his environment, like Karl Moor an erstwhile idealist who through disillusionment has turned atheist, materialist and misanthrope.

The dog, on the other hand, represents the point of view of the average burgher, being sturdy and pious but pecksniffian. Ridicule of such sentiment as the dog utters constitutes the very heart of this tragicomedy, which reveals but few traces of the childlike qualities inherent in genuine fairy tales. Tieck allowed keen observation and clever wit to prevail. The dog's admonishing words, for instance, "Bau, bau nicht zu sehr auf Sicherheit. . . . Bau, bau auf deinen Mut nicht zu sehr," are very droll, the word "bau" being at the same time the canine bark and the imperative of "bauen."[16] With this work he concluded for the time being his series of satirical fairy-tale plays. As late as 1851 the Englishman J. B. Smith considered the little skit worthy of an adaptation. In 1862 Feodor Wehl arranged it as a German Christmas play. Since then it has been frequently staged. An interesting and successful performance was given on the Schwabing shadow stage in Munich during the winter of 1907.

At the end of *Romantische Dichtungen* Tieck published an important advertisement, wherein he announced a new periodical, *Das poetische Journal*. He wrote: "Whereas so many prosaic subjects, like politics, economics and even acacia trees, have found their own journals, it is perhaps not unjust to announce poetry for once, too, at the head of a journal—poetry which is so often sheltered as a stop-gap in the corners of such journals, where it does not belong. It will be my chief purpose to develop my thoughts on art and poesy more in a descriptive than in an argumentative way. They will, therefore, adhere primarily to the works of the greatest acknowledged poets of modern times, who are always the starting point and conclusion of my observations. Thus, for instance, Letters on Shakespeare will form a regular article in each number; in these I shall communicate the results of my study of his dramatic art and pursue historical and critical investigations which will throw light upon the works of this inexhaustible and still insufficiently understood mind. Similar articles on older English and German and the splendid periods of Spanish and Italian literatures shall be joined therewith, gradually achieving a picture of true modern poetry (not of that which is usually represented as such). I shall seek to make this picture as clear as possible by poetic imitations and reproductions of foreign, especially Spanish and English products."[17] He promised also original poetry in a light vein and continuations of the *Herzensergiessungen* and *Phantasien*.

But only one volume, in two fascicles, appeared. The reasons for the discontinuance are stated by Tieck himself in a letter to Frommann of April 1802.[18] They were lack of subscribers, waning interest on Tieck's part, and his realization that the *Briefe über Shakespeare*, if continued in this form, would transgress too much upon a more scientific *Buch über Shakespeare* which was to follow. "You will do me a great favor," he wrote to his publisher, "if you will discontinue the undertaking now" (Sie erzeigen mir einen rechten Gefallen, wenn Sie es hiermit aufhören lassen).

With the exception of one article by F. Majer and a madrigal by Friedrich Schlegel, all the contributions are from his pen. There is a preface marked by the same enthusiasm which we have found in the advertisement, and by sharp satire against the "carping dissectors of beauty" (knaupelnde Schönheitszergliederer). It is followed by a poem in *terce rime*, "Die neue Zeit," proclaiming the program of the Romanticists. The Old Era, the mother of Rationalism, has been impregnated by Enthusiasm, who has freed himself from long captivity. A child is born whom even its enemies must serve, and the light of springtime is again seen on earth. The "atmosphere becomes a sea of fragrance" and Rationalist poets are forgotten, while Hans Sachs comes into his own again. New gods and old superstitions are enthroned; man and the godhead are joined in eternal union. The great Pan stalks once more through the forests. And for the poet it is glorious to proclaim the sun after long rains and storms. Poesy is triumphant and joyfully "announces her future colorful splendor."[19]

There are two instalments of *Briefe über Shakespeare*.[20] Of particular note is their warm defense of A. W. Schlegel's translation of Shakespeare. As compared with the first draft of *Das Buch über Shakespeare* (1794), his criticism is now less Rationalistic and more Romantic and ethereal. His conception of Shakespeare's artistic forms has broadened under the influence of the Schlegels. He now devotes more attention to Shakespeare's contemporaries, above all Jonson and, in a slighter degree, to Massinger, Kyd, Beaumont and Fletcher, Marlowe, Greene, Peele, Lodge, Heywood and Rowley. Besides, he is now less the practical stage craftsman and more the theorist. The same applies to the second and third drafts of *Das Buch über Shakespeare*, which date from about 1797 and 1800. Of special interest is the belief, first expressed in the *Briefe*, that the Shakespearean theater had an upper stage, with a stairway, and over it a third tier for musicians.

Two literary satires are the best works in *Das poetische Journal*. The first is the verse parody *Der neue Herkules am Scheidewege*, later renamed *Der Autor, ein Fastnachtsschwank*.[21] In the tone of the early poetic confessions of Goethe, such as the first *Faust* scene, he here tried to draw a picture of his own individuality and nature, seeking to defend himself against the misconceptions of his detractors and against unintelligent imitators. The technique is a combination of that of Jonson and of the style of the old Shrovetide revues. Various types of persons, among them Lessing, an Admirer, a Man of the World and an Old-Fashioned Man, appear in succession in the Author's study and converse with him. This affords opportunity for a wealth of satire. The moral of the work is: Remain true to yourself and travel your own road despite the critics. If you dislike the new age, revert to the old. Indeed, if you will, retire to the forest chapels, where pristine glory and faith still live.

Many of the jibes are at the expense of Brentano, a talented poet but very emotional and demonstrative, who adored Tieck and learned a great deal from him, especially the technique of musical effect. Tieck had met him through A. W. Schlegel in Jena, where Brentano was a student, and they had become good friends. But in his reckless and extravagant play *Gustav Wasa*, Brentano had parodied the manner of *Der gestiefelte Kater*;[22] Tieck now retaliated good-humoredly by depicting Brentano as the young Admirer. This did not affect Brentano. In his novel *Godwi* he paid Tieck a fine tribute, calling him unassuming, kind, witty, rich in feeling—in short a poet and artist who was a source of inspiration to all his friends. Nor was he piqued by Tieck's advice to subdue his ebullience and work more systematically, nor by his friend's conviction that he lacked a feeling for nature and naturalness. In 1801 Brentano vainly endeavored to enlist Goethe's help in getting Tieck appointed director of the Frankfurt theater.[23] Between 1803 and 1805 he tried hard to secure a professorship for him in Heidelberg. These efforts were heartily supported by the other Heidelberg Romanticists, especially Savigny.[24] About the same time he suggested that Tieck collaborate with Arnim and himself in the *Wunderhorn* collection of folk songs.[25] In 1804 Tieck saw him again at Ziebingen and at Weimar, and in 1806 in Frankfurt and Heidelberg. In 1808 Brentano had various plans for delivering Tieck from his rustic solitude in Ziebingen.[26] In 1813 they met again in Prague, and late in 1817 at Berlin.

The second squib, in prose, bears the title *Das jüngste Gericht, eine Vision*,[27] and is also done in a happy vein. Like many of Tieck's humorous works, it is aimed against the Rationalists, particularly Johannes Daniel Falk, whose satire in his *Taschenbuch für Freunde des Scherzes und der Satire* irritated the Romanticists because of its vagueness and harmlessness; against Nicolai, who is condemned to listen to the jests of the devils for two thousand years without being permitted to reply; and against the *Allgemeine Literaturzeitung*, which the devil deprives of the syllable "All," thus making it a "Gemeine" (i.e. mean, vulgar) *Literaturzeitung*. Tieck's dislike of this journal was prompted by A. W. Schlegel, who, once a regular contributor, had turned against it. At the end Judgment Day comes for Tieck, too. The judge takes him to task for *Zerbino*. He replies that it was only a jest. The judge is half willing to let this excuse pass, but his parting shot is too much even for Tieck. How can I condone you, though, he asks, for ridiculing even the Day of Judgment in this, your latest squib!

We have seen that in the *Briefe* he manifested once more his lively interest in Jonson. The same interest came to the fore in his translation of Jonson's *Epicoene*, also published in *Das poetische Journal*.[28] Unlike *Ein Schurke über den anderen* of 1793, a free adaptation of Jonson's *Volpone*, his version of *Epicoene* aims to be a literal translation. It cannot be called an unqualified success. We find errors, misunderstandings of the original and evidences of carelessness. Moreover, where Jonson's language is pregnant, racy and fresh, Tieck is too often sterile, insipid and trite. As a pioneer in introducing Jonson in Germany he deserves full credit none the less.[29]

Finally, under the title "Erinnerung und Ermunterung" *Das poetische Journal* contains a garland of twenty sonnets, most of them in honor of various friends old and new.[30] Among those here celebrated are Tieck's schoolmate Toll, who had died in 1790; Wackenroder (four sonnets); the Schlegels (a particularly fine, penetrating sonnet on Friedrich); Novalis; Wilhelm Schütz, a schoolmate and himself a Romantic poet (two sonnets merely inscribed "An—" and "An einen jüngeren Dichter"); Tieck's brother Friedrich; and his sister Sophie. Tieck's sonnets are imitative of Shakespeare's and merit serious consideration. A. W. Schlegel called them "divine."[31] At least one in this collection, entitled "Leben," deserves quotation.

> How often life is death but in disguise!
> Many will waken only when they die!
> How few can fan a flame to rise on high!
> How seldom life bears courage as a prize!
>
> They think they live, but far away do steal
> From harsh, cruel life, and in their hopes forlorn
> They fain would see a heavenly glory born.
> Decomposition is their aim and zeal.

> They stumble and unknowingly progress,
> Ill, sick at heart, and in a motley mass,
> Nor dead nor living, free of joy and pain.
>
> On starry nights I ask in happiness:
> Through what desert of thine it came to pass
> That pleasure from this radiance thou canst gain.*

On the whole, the sonnet form, with its rigid metrical requirements and the necessity for clear-cut treatment of a single subject, appealed more strongly to him than any other type of lyric. We find, too, that he was more successful with it than with other forms, except the poems in free verse written in Italy. Perhaps an organic defect in him, already hinted at, may be cited as a reason for this circumstance. He was deficient in original plastic talent and needed, for his own creative powers, materials which had already received definite shape and outline at the hands of predecessors. No doubt Gundolf had this peculiarity of Tieck in mind when in his book on Shakespeare he applied to him the ingenious aphorism "Nur am Geformten wird er produktiv." It applies as well to his preference for chapbook and other ready-made material in his choice of subjects.

Tieck's preoccupation with the sonnets of Shakespeare, which also goes far to explain his eminence in that form, may be traced back to 1801. It led to his translation of the eighteenth in 1807, thirteen years before the first complete renderings by Lachmann. His version of this sonnet is preserved among his unpublished papers in Berlin.[32] It compares very favorably with many more recent attempts, being more exact than Friedrich Bodenstedt's, not as free as Max Wolff's and closer than Ludwig Fulda's, though inferior to Stefan George's. His interest in this phase of Shakespeare's work culminated in the article *Über Shakespeares Sonette einige Worte*, in *Taschenbuch Penelope* (1826), with samples of translations by his daughter Dorothea. Her renderings of the entire sonnets have not been published.[33]

*Wie vieles Leben ist verhülltes Sterben!
Wie mancher wird im Sterben erst erwachen!
Wie wen'ge nur die Gluth zur Flamme fachen!
Wie seltne Lebensmut mit Leben erben!

Sie dünken sich zu sein, entfliehn dem herben
Gefühl des Seins und in verworfnen Sachen
Soll ihnen Himmels-Glanz entgegenlachen,
Auf die Verwesung geht ihr eifernd Werben.

Nur taumelnd, unbewusst schreiten sie weiter,
Krank, tiefbetrübt in buntgemengten Horden,
Nicht sterbend, lebend nicht, ohn' Leid und Wonnen.

(*Continued on bottom of next page*)

ROMANTIC POETRY AND POLEMICS

Literary small fry were the subject of a pamphlet which was begun almost simultaneously with the *Journal*, and, though announced in the *Archiv der Zeit* in December, 1800,[34] was never finished because of inertia.[35] Under the title *Bemerkungen über Parteilichkeit, Dummheit und Bosheit, bei Gelegenheit der Herren Falk, Merkel und des Lustspiels Camäleon* (1800) it was published by Köpke in the *Nachgelassene Schriften* (1855). Tieck turns to those "who he believes occupy the same cultural level as he does"[36] and invites them to join him in opposing the mean, vulgar attacks which were being launched against the noble-minded proponents of new roads in literature and threatened to stifle the inchoate Romantic art. In the enemy's camp he found humdrum Falk, who was also made the butt of ridicule in *Das jüngste Gericht*, and Garlieb Merkel, a friend of Kotzebue and resident of Weimar from 1797 to 1799. From 1800 on Merkel published *Briefe an ein Frauenzimmer*, being reports on recent developments in German literature and containing bitter attacks against Goethe, as well as the Romanticists. Against Merkel Tieck, jointly with A. W. Schlegel, wrote also a sonnet (published as a pamphlet in 1799), wherein the rime "Merkel—Ferkel" (young pig) occurred.[37] In his satirical poem "Der neue Alkinous" (1802 or 1803) Goethe used the same rime.

Nowhere has Tieck expressed his creed as effectively and earnestly as in the fragmentary *Bemerkungen*, a veritable *pro domo*, which earned the high praise of Schleiermacher. He clearly states the aims of his numerous satires, above all his dramatized fairy tales, because he has noted that they had been misunderstood. He deplores the ignorance of the mass of readers and the unfairness of critics like Falk and Merkel, and launches an attack against his rival D. W. Soltau, the Rationalist translator of *Don Quixote*, whose supporters had assailed Tieck's rendering. Finally, in a seething section he pays his respects to the noted Berlin theatrical director and actor Iffland. That Iffland was gifted Tieck never denied, but he recognized his talents only in comic rôles. By and large he felt that in imitating the French school, Iffland had contributed not a little to the degeneration of the art of acting in Germany.

But the underlying reason for his hostility toward Iffland is to be found in their personal relations. At first Iffland felt kindly toward Tieck and late in 1799 requested him to translate one of Cumberland's comedies.[38] At the same time he invited him, as we have seen, to revise *Genoveva* for the stage—an invitation which Tieck foolishly ignored.

> Schau ich zur Sternen-Nacht, so frag' ich heiter:
> Durch welch Verdienst ist dir die Gnade worden,
> Dass dich die Freud' anlacht aus diesen Sonnen?

But unpleasant incidents also occurred. Thus Iffland had promised in 1798 to stage *Das Ungeheuer und der verzauberte Wald* (for which Reichardt had agreed to write music), but then went back on his word.[39] Soon after something more serious happened. Iffland produced in Berlin a comedy by the actor Beck entitled *Das Camäleon*, which was clearly an insulting travesty on the Romanticists. Under a thin veil Tieck was depicted as a cheap, ridiculous poetaster devoid of all character. Tieck thereupon opened a brief but angry correspondence with Iffland, demanding that the work be suppressed. Iffland replied evasively that Tieck had misunderstood Beck's intention, and that the play was not aimed at any individuals. "Your literary and physical existence," he wrote, "perhaps even your name, are entirely unknown to the author of *The Chameleon*. I now reside in the same town with you and have read nothing by you except your *Sternbald* and your two letters to me. I should gladly have dispensed with the latter."[40]

We have it on the best contemporary authority, however, that Tieck harbored a real grievance. He replied heatedly to Iffland's lame explanation.[41] To be sure, the printed text of the play was considerably toned down, but the stage version as produced at Berlin in 1800 was a flagrant libel of Tieck and the Schlegels.[42] On the strength of Tieck's complaint the play was ultimately forbidden by the Berlin police.[43] It is with this incident that the tirade against Iffland in the *Bemerkungen* chiefly concerns itself.

In 1801 he began a last settling of accounts with all his adversaries— in a comedy which he called *Anti-Faust, oder Geschichte eines dummen Teufels*.[44] But he finished only the prolog and the first of five projected acts. The extant portions remind of the Charon prelude and of the deliberations of the devils in the old Faust plays. Among others Wieland, whom Tieck had attacked in *Zerbino*, and whom the Schlegels, instigated by Tieck, had berated in the *Athenäum*, came in for his share of criticism as a Rationalist. The uncompleted portion was to be done in the style of Jonson's *The Devil is an Ass*. He took the fragment along to Italy in 1805, meaning to expand it into a satire at the expense of literature as a whole.[45] We have reason to regret that he dropped the work, for the fragment is full of wit and jovial humor.

As has been noted, he had left Jena with his family at the beginning of summer, 1800. From there he went for a four months' visit to his wife's home in Hamburg. In Hamburg, where the subject matter of *Genoveva* had chanced to fall into his hands not long before, he now discovered, again by sheer accident, the old chapbook of Emperor Octavianus. He studied it, and in the course of two years of creative transmutation (spent in Berlin and Dresden amid endless financial worries), expanded it, but did not deepen it, into the grandiose "comedy" *Kaiser Octavianus*.[46] It represents the sum total and conclusion of his poetic and programmatic endeavors during the first half of his life and is his most remarkable, but not his best work. It was printed by Frommann in 1802 and 1803 and published in 1804.

In subject and content *Kaiser Octavianus* is closely related to *Genoveva*, both being poetry of atmosphere and mood. But while *Genoveva* was the work of a religionist, *Kaiser Octavianus*, practically bare of religion, is the product of an esthete. Echoes of *Cymbeline* and *A Winter's Tale* abound. Its form and dramatic structure remind of *Zerbino*. It is extremely multifarious and colorful, a typical Romantic all-in-one, with a jumble of pathetic and comic, fantastic and realistic elements. Three main strata may be distinguished, fanciful and sentimental scenes of courtly life, humorous and burlesque sections, and passages which convey the atmosphere of "Waldeinsamkeit." In characterization it is an improvement over *Genoveva*, while the latter is superior in unity of action and style. The basic motif, as in *Genoveva*, is the calumniation of a virtuous woman, her repudiation by her husband, her steadfast faith and love, and her eventual victory. In both plays the struggle between paganism and Christianity is stressed. But in *Kaiser Octavianus* this is done in a much more shallow way, purely for the sake of creating atmosphere.

The Empress Felicitas, a more lifelike figure than Genoveva, is accused of adultery. Though she is condemned to die, her sentence is commuted to lifelong exile. Her two sons, who remind one of Cymbeline's sons, are kidnaped, one by an ape and the other by a lion. Her fate and that of the children, one of whom, accompanied by the lion, grows up with her in Palestine, the other becoming the ward of a good but comically naïve Parisian burgher, form the subject of the main plot. We have scenes in a Franconian city and at a great annual fair, see pictures of an oriental harem, catch glimpses of battle and of deeds of high emprise. Small but valiant corps of Christians fight hordes of heathens (Mohammedans), and brave knights face powerful giants in single combat. Several conversions to Christianity take place. Momentous affairs of state are unfolded before our eyes.

Traces of fatalism are found. Like Genoveva, Felicitas is a passive character, whose fate is sealed by her fellow men; like Genoveva again, she is saved by a higher justice. Those who ridicule fate suffer destruction, as always in Tieck. Octavian himself, an astrologist, resembles his wife in possessing "second sense."

The work consists of a prolog and two parts, the first in fifteen scenes, the second, which is less dramatic, in five acts. The play covers over four hundred pages. The last act of part 2 effects the reconciliation of the parents and the two sons, who bring their brides along.

While the keynote of *Genoveva* was still melancholy and reminiscent of the *William Lovell* mood, Tieck, consciously struggling against a melancholia born of mysticism, now drowns his sorrow in poetry of cheerful, devout confidence. Faith overcomes every obstacle, and the world of make-believe in which *Kaiser Octavianus* moves makes sport of all tragic happenings. On the other hand, *Genoveva* is richer in real poetry. *Kaiser Octavianus*, more strikingly under the influence of Calderon and of Böhme's allegorical interpretation of nature than *Genoveva*, is encased in a slough of allegory.

In *Sternbald* he had written: "All art is allegorical; we seek to attach a general meaning to the particular, and thus allegory arises. The word designates nothing else but true poesy, which seeks what is lofty and noble and can find it only by this means." True to this questionable observation, he has in *Kaiser Octavianus* relegated substance to a subordinate position. The poetic subject matter serves merely as a symbol, or more frequently as an allegory, for the idealistic content.

In *Sternbald*, again, we find him voicing the hope that he might some time "express in a peculiar handiwork what now moves my mind and heart, this fullness of charm, this calm, jovial cheerfulness which surrounds me." He would like to produce a great, wondrous poem, "full of fluttering splendor and vagrant tones, full of will-o'-the-wisps and moonbeams." Obviously *Kaiser Octavianus* is the consummation of these dreams.

The prolog is called "Der Aufzug der Romanze." Here he was clearly prompted once more by a yearning for a new poetical mythology. Allegory fairly runs riot, and we have in effect a Calderonian *auto* celebrating the mystery of poetry. Love, the daughter of Greece and of Christianity, marries Faith. Their child is Romance, who appears on a white horse. Their trusted servants are Valor and Jest. Over the forest rises the "moon-illumined magic night":

> Moon-illumined magic night,[47]
> Holding every mind enthralled,
> Lovely, wondrous fairy world,
> Rise, in ancient splendor dight.*

> *Mondbeglänzte Zaubernacht,
> Die den Sinn gefangen hält,
> *(Continued on bottom of next page)*

These verses, which have become famous as the watchword of Romanticism and the fluid in which Romanticism has floated through the nineteenth century, constitute the theme of the entire prolog. In truly Romantic fashion he plays upon this motif in multifarious variations. The prolog may be called the *pièce de résistance* of all of his early works and of Romanticism in general. When his friends in Berlin did him honor on May 31, 1833, to commemorate the sixtieth anniversary of his birthday, they fittingly arranged a public performance of this prolog, with a musical setting by Franz Gläser. The four allegorical motifs of Love, Faith, Valor and Jest introduced in the prolog recur frequently in the body of the play. But only Love is presented convincingly. His Faith seems more poetic than real, his Valor too feeble, and his Jest too frigid.

Romance also makes her appearance in the course of the drama, serving as prolog and interlocutor. Here he followed the technique of the Elizabethan *Pericles*, as he had done before. To the casual observer it seems surprising that a play of such vast bulk but with so thin a plot should require so much prolocutory and interlocutory matter. The reason is that here, as in his *Märchendramen*, he did not wish to write a drama in the ordinary sense. He desired to express his views of Romantic poesy "allegorically, lyrically and dramatically,"[48] no doubt to the prejudice of dramatic form. Romance, like Felicitas and the fair Turkish Girl of the second part, serves to embody and express not only her own vicissitudes, but the very essence of Tieck's poetry and love.

Side by side with the glory of knighthood, love in all its various moods plays a very important part, as it does in all of his major works during the first half of his life. Once again he saw in self-sacrificing and ever confident love of one's fellow men the best means of overcoming hated subjectivism. Here this trend becomes particularly clear, for Love is wedded to Faith, and, as Romance says:

Love can never doubt and waver.[49]*

Unluckily, though, the play has no consistency. It melts away in varicolored individual pictures of epic diffuseness and lyric melody. On each page we perceive an abundance of musical effects in every imaginable strophic form,—a veritable symphony of meters—borrowed primarily from Spanish or Italian literatures but very expertly constructed. Calderon's *vers de romance*, the *redondilla*, *octave*, madrigal and sonnet are introduced as no German dramatist before or after has dreamed

Wundervolle Märchenwelt,
Steig' auf in der alten Pracht!

*Niemals kann die Liebe zweifeln.

of introducing them.[50] An empress descants in *terce rime*, the common people converse in sonnets, the rulers of various countries are distinguished by their use of different metrical forms. No artificial patterns are too ornate to be enlisted. Assonance side by side with rime leaves a peculiarly haunting effect. In the lyric love passages one is reminded of the manner of Gottfried von Strassburg; the Nibelungen line is also used. Moreover, the meter of Hans Sachs,[51] plain prose, and the coarse, punning humor of Shakespeare are freely employed. If versatility of form, mood and effect be the criterion—an empty criterion it would be—, this is certainly "universal poetry" with a vengeance. But metrically the only significant and fruitful feature which Tieck, the learned metrist, has introduced is the use of the Spanish trochee.

In a sense the external form of *Kaiser Octavianus* is a fitting frame for the world picture which it graces. But what sort of a world did he have in mind, what world is it which harbors the Emperor of Byzantium, King Dagobert of France and his major-domo, King Balduin of Jerusalem? It is a pasteboard composite, a Romantic fantasmagoria of the Middle Ages. Yet even this wide scope did not give the poet leeway enough. So he jettisoned the whole realm of historical concepts, as it were, and conjured up a new Romantic world, which has never existed and could nowhere exist, giving it some of the color and a little of the substance of early Christian chivalry. This explains why the tenuous historical background does not carry conviction and why the outlines, except in some comic scenes, are dim and vague. Even the humor of the purely comic figures—Pasquin in the first, and the peasant Hornvilla (a cousin of Autolycus) in both parts—is forced and bookish. The actions of shrewd Hornvilla, who deceives everyone by appearing now as a Christian and now as a Turk, and who makes a business of religion, show how subordinate a rôle is assigned to religion. Individual lyric and narrative passages, a few highly dramatic scenes, and some pithy prose passages stand out. The scenes in which the love of Mirabella for one of Octavian's two sons is unfolded are rich in southern color and oriental beauty.

But in his studied objectivity Tieck did not even offer poetic symbols for his own soul-experience. He remained passive.[52] He shied away from his ego and from the here and now, preferring to deal in unreal abstractions and in lofty generalities of whose beauty he has dreamed a poet's dream. Not only reason but even personal feeling was eschewed and phantasy proclaimed as queen and high priestess in the domain of poesy. He once wrote to Friedrich Schlegel that Romanticism is chaos out of which certainty or positiveness (Gewissheit) must develop.[53] But this "certainty" is woefully lacking in his *chef-d'oeuvre*.

He believed that the essence of his art was nowhere revealed so clearly as in this work. Even while writing he felt that it would be superior to *Genoveva* in some respects.[54] In a sense, though, *Kaiser Octavianus*, despite all its "Romanticism," shows him breaking away from that trend. The Romantic problems which had interested him in *Genoveva* are now all ignored, with the exception of estheticism. The whole province of Romantic feeling is dissolved, so to speak, in a sea of esthetics. That alone now seems to hold his attention.

To Frommann he emphasized that it was a *comedy* (in the medieval sense), adding: "I must confess that I have a certain predilection for this work; it is possible that I deceive myself, but I am conscious of having constantly labored with love, and I have not written hastily."[55] Hence in 1828 he set it at the head of his collected *Schriften*, awarding it first prize, so to speak, among all his writings. But only if read in the spirit in which one reads Calderon or a fairy tale can this carefully written (not improvised) literary curio still be enjoyed today. Like most of his Romantic writings, it fairly clamors for a musical framework.

To the rising generation it represented a glorious achievement.[56] The Romanticists acclaimed it a great masterpiece. In a letter to Goethe, A. W. Schlegel described it as "an incomparable work, quite the opposite of *Genoveva*, only in its way perhaps still more perfect and energetic."[57] The esthetician Friedrich Ast, who in general preferred Tieck even to Goethe, called it "the perfect example of modern poetry."[58] Tieck's daughter Dorothea saw in it the incarnation of his amiability and the whole depth and glory of his art and love.[59] It strongly influenced Uhland's early writings. Little wonder, though, that Goethe, the steadfast apostle of noble simplicity, calm greatness and clear-cut plasticity, could never stomach it. He complained to A. W. Schlegel on May 3, 1802, of its diffusiveness, although praising Tieck's talent in individual points, and even preferred Friedrich Schlegel's consanguineous but poetically worthless drama *Alarkos* because it was at least more closely knit and therefore plastically more effective.[57] Arnim found more prolixity than "ancient splendor" in it.[60] The judgment of Brentano as expressed to Arnim in August 1803 was even more telling. He wrote: "It is anyway very audacious and imprudent to cast such quite finished nature poems [*sc.* as the chapbooks] into rime, to mix in a few nature-view recipes à la Jacob Böhme, and to make a hubbub about spring and the forest. The assonances and the affected archaic German, too, are hitched up together like steer and ass. With a few vulgar characters, however, he is eminently successful, but all the principal figures, and *another* court jester, are very tedious."[61]

Between *Genoveva* and *Kaiser Octavianus* Tieck planned to insert the dramatic *Magelone*, begun in 1803. Here natural philosophy was to be shaped into a mythology of love. But only the prolog was finished.[62]

CHAPTER NINE

THE END OF EARLY ROMANTICISM

THE first era of German Romanticism had wellnigh come to a close with *Kaiser Octavianus*. The theorists had had their day in court; in support of their arguments Tieck and Novalis had presented many practical exhibits of Romantic poesy. Novalis was now dead, while Tieck had reached an impasse. After *Kaiser Octavianus* he found no new contributions to that particular brand of Romanticism, which may be described as poetry of moods, caprices, atmosphere. The Romantic "Stimmungsdichter" had exhausted his Romantic "Stimmungen." The burden of carrying on was now to be left to a younger group who were spiritually akin to Tieck, among them Fouqué, Chamisso, Eichendorff, Brentano and Arnim.

Only the pure lyric form, the lyric for its own sake, not as one mode amid a wealth of multifarious forms, had been neglected by the early Romanticists. To make good this deficiency, Tieck, in collaboration with A. W. Schlegel, got out the *Musenalmanach für das Jahr 1802*—a sort of afterthought. It was published by Cotta. We find it mentioned for the first time on December 21, 1800, in a letter from Schlegel to the publisher, and again five days later by Cotta to Schiller. Cotta, it seems, had made its publication contingent upon the discontinuance of Schiller's similar undertaking. On March 31 of the next year we find Schlegel reporting that the manuscript is practically ready.[1]

The list of contributors to this three-hundred-page almanac reads like a catalog of early Romanticists. Among them were, beside Tieck and the elder Schlegel, the former's sister Sophie, Friedrich Schlegel, Novalis, Schütze and Schelling. Yet the almanac proved that there was but one truly lyric poet in their ranks—Novalis. He, who died before the *Musenalmanach* could appear, published his "Lob des Weins" and seven "Geistliche Lieder" in it and thereby established his claim to distinction as a lyricist.

Tieck was well represented. By far his longest and most ambitious effort was a *Romanze* entitled "Die Zeichen im Walde." It consists of one hundred fourteen four-line stanzas in the trochaic *vers de romance*. Alliteration is plentiful, and each second and fourth line has assonance (occasionally rime) in "u", which, expressing his synaesthesia, is meant to suggest an atmosphere of horror. We quote two typical stanzas, without, however, quite preserving Tieck's assonance in our translation:

> Storms again are roaring, howling,
> Rattling from that ancient tower,
> And the ravens shriek the louder,
> And the croak of frogs resoundeth.
>
> . . .   .
>
> With a whine the old man writheth,
> Satan strikes and wounds him often,
> In his bed he lieth lifeless
> When the morning dawneth darkly.[2]*

Words like "dunkel," "Turm," "Unke," "Grund," and "Sturm" are favorites. The obscure plot, which deals with portents, murders and midnight horrors, is designed to make one shudder but, after the novelty wears off, evokes only boredom and ridicule. Archaic words like "begunnte" and "Nachtgevögel" seem absurd. It is surprising that Friedrich Schlegel called it "divine and perfect."[3] Probably this poem was uppermost in Schiller's mind when he called the almanac clever yet deleterious in its influence.

A cycle of eight poems, entitled "Lebens-Elemente,"[4] deals with the earth, the subterranean realm, water, air, fire, light, work and the Sabbath. Only the poem "Das Unterirdische," foreshadowing the theme of the tale *Der Runenberg*—the enticing power of subterranean rocks and metals—is significant. He did not deem four poems superscribed "Der Besuch" worthy of republication, incorporating them neither in the Dresden edition of *Gedichte* (1821-1823) nor in the Berlin collection of 1841. Three others, "Einsamkeit," "Der Zornige" and "Sanftmut," despite their perfection of form, have the typical vagueness and intangibility of Tieck's lyricism of which Hebbel was thinking when he wrote (Diary I, 214) that it lacked "das Medium des vermittelnden Menschengefühls." For a moment in "Der Zornige," when he exclaims

> To arms, to arms,
> Whoe'er takes joy in battles![†]

---

* Wieder braust der Sturm und heulet
Rasselnd her vom alten Turme,
Und die Raben krächzen lauter,
Und es dröhnt der Ton der Unken.

. . .   .

Winselnd windet sich der Alte,
Und der Satan schlägt ihm Wunden,
Tot liegt er in seinem Bette,
Als der Morgen aufgedunkelt.

† Zu den Waffen! zu den Waffen!
Wer sich je der Kämpfe freute!

we expect a surprise, but the hope for an objectivized, realistic content soon fades when we read:

> For the light I fight and battle,
> And I struggle for the open.*

In "Sanftmut," with its revealing last line: "Und in Gott entfleusst der Geist" (Into God the spirit floweth), his typical attitude toward nature is disclosed. It is an expression of religious feeling turned toward worldly things. God is conceived as the essence of all possible experiences of reality. Yet this demonic Pan-like state of mind toward nature achieves nought but Romantic dissolution, for unlike Goethe's feeling for nature, it is occupied with sensual phenomena rather than with the essence of things.[5] Tieck has the yearning of a city-bred man for the open country; he does not commune with nature itself. Instead of being envisaged in realistic scenes, nature is nought but a reflex of his psychic state.

Generally speaking, Tieck's attitude toward nature may be summarized as follows. He shows no interest in the lowlands and centers his attention upon the hills of Central Germany, which he vests with demonic qualities. He emphasizes the linear element; colors play a minor rôle here. But he has a predilection for virgin nature and sylvan solitude. Here he stresses light and color, particularly green, but he also speaks frequently of twilight, the night and the wind. The acoustic and musical element—the rustling trees, the babbling water, the singing birds and the plaintive French horn—is as strong as the optical element is in Goethe. Often he personifies the flowers. He shows much interest in the moon and clouds, symbolizing, idealizing and stylizing to a high degree. Red, gold and silver are his favorite colors here. Yet, although his feeling for nature points the way from Romanticism to Realism, it is scarcely marked by great individuality or originality.

The three poems "Einsamkeit," "Der Zornige" and "Sanftmut" were reprinted in *Kaiser Octavianus*.

Of the eighteen poems which he contributed to the *Musenalmanach* only two sonnets to the memory of Novalis have true lyric value. As usual, he achieves his best work as a lyricist when confronted by the rigid restrictions of the sonnet form. The value of these two poems is further enhanced by the fact that they reflect genuine feeling and emotion, whereas most of his lyrics are cold, musical descriptions devoid of any residuum of personal experience. In the first he expresses the idea that Novalis' tender, ethereal nature was in itself a token of his early death:

* Nach dem Lichte geht mein Kämpfen,
  Nach der Freie will mein Streiten.

LUDWIG TIECK, THE GERMAN ROMANTICIST

> Since thee I saw, I trusted in the feeling
> That thou wouldst have to leave us and this planet.
> Thou'rt gone, farewell, we are not separated.[6]*

In the second Novalis is compared with a flower which dies at night in contemplation of the stars:

> Thus wert thou drawn aloft and into heaven,
> Midst music and embraces came thy parting.
> Springtime has passed, let us lament, poor mortals.[7]†

About the same time he planned another novel, *Alma, ein Buch der Liebe*, but only thirty-two sonnets, destined for it and written in 1803,[8] as well as two other lyrics, "Briefe der Minne" and "Epistel an Alma," dated 1806,[9] have been preserved. The work was to be a glorification of love and a counterpart to *Sternbald*, with little external action—a characterization of love in all its phases and moods.[10] Eros was here to be exalted in the spirit of his published writings of this period, especially *Genoveva* and *Kaiser Octavianus*, and in the spirit of the projected *Magelone* drama. No obstacle was to be so great, no calumny so severe but that love could not overcome it. This constantly recurring motif of love as a panacea against egoism, which is one of the most redeeming features of his world picture, does not die away until after the appearance of *Phantasus* (1812-1816).[11]

From August to November 1800 Tieck had remained in Hamburg, then returned to Berlin. But he tarried there only half a year. By April 1801 the literary feuds in which he became embroiled, quite against his will, proved too much for his mental and physical well-being. Repulsed by this logomachy and allured by the art treasures and lovely surroundings of the Saxon capital, which harbored only pleasant memories, he migrated to Dresden. There he sought surcease from annoyance, deciding to occupy his mind with the study of art and with literary production. On the whole, though, it was an era of dark melancholia. But the political problems of the day found no marked echo in his soul.

About Easter 1802, bitter grief came into his life. His mother died and the shock of her death killed his father a week later. In old age the latter had been subject to fits of melancholia. Ludwig and his sister arranged the obsequies. Their brother Friedrich, who under the tutelage of Bett-

---

*Seit ich dich sah, vertraut' ich dem Gefühle,
Du musstest von uns gehn und dieser Erde.
Du gingst: fahr wohl; wir sind ja nicht geschieden.

†So wurdest du zum Himmel hingezogen,
Sanft in Musik schiedst du in Freundesarmen,
Der Frühling wich, und Klagen ziemt uns Armen.

kober and Schadow in Germany and David d'Angers in France had developed into a sculptor of note, could not be present.

In 1799 Tieck's former teacher, Bernhardi, had married Sophie. As the latter grew up, she hounded her brother more and more with her love and jealousy, extracting from him a promise never to leave her. Varnhagen von Ense, in his unpublished Berlin papers, states that Tieck inveigled Bernhardi into marrying his sister, so as to be rid of her himself. But Tieck and Bernhardi quarrelled as early as 1796. Bernhardi's satirical tale *Sechs Stunden aus Finks Leben* is said to be a take-off on Tieck. Some of the correspondence of Tieck and Bernhardi was published by the latter's son Wilhelm in 1867.

By 1802 Tieck's health had become bad, and his condition was aggravated by worry over his sister. For she was becoming estranged from her husband and complained to her brother about his tippling, his infidelity and cruelty. Wilhelm, her first child, was born in 1800. According to her letter of March 1, 1803, to her brother Ludwig, her second child, Ludwig, born in 1801, died on February 28, 1803. The third, Felix Theodor, was born in November 1802. Later, when these nephews grew to manhood, they became a source of vexation to Tieck.[12]

Sophie's health, too, broke down after the birth of Felix, and so she decided to cast the imagined cause of all her misery—her husband—out of her life. With the children she deserted him, going to live for a while with Friedrich and later heading south to seek recovery in Italy. Of a haughty, overbearing nature, she refused to heed Ludwig's advice and make a compromise with Bernhardi.

The full facts about Sophie and Bernhardi have never come to light, and it is very difficult, now that over a century and a quarter have elapsed, to probe them to the bottom. Certainly neither she nor her husband appear to have been blameless; his life as well as hers was marked by excesses. If we would believe the story told not only by Bernhardi, his relatives, descendants and friends, but also by other antagonists of the Tiecks, Sophie was mendacious, untrustworthy, cruel and spiteful to a high degree.[13] According to this version, she, not Bernhardi (an honest, faithful school teacher of modest tastes, who because of a diabetic condition used practically no alcohol),[14] was to blame for their marital difficulties. And indeed, there is abundant evidence to support this allegation. For not only did she squander his money; she deceived him for years in a shameless manner. Her principal lover was A. W. Schlegel, with whom she secretly exchanged long piquant love letters, using cool, formal notes as a blind; and whom she persuaded that Felix Theodor was begotten by him, hoping thus to attach him more closely to herself.[15]

In Schlegel's letters to her she is called "meine geliebte Freundin und Schwester" and the children "die beiden Engel." He frequently sends her money, implores her to guard her health and come to Madame de Staël's estate at Coppet. She was also passionate and violent and did not shrink from intrigues and lies in her craving to lord it over the men with whom she came into contact. All of Tieck's friends, even noble Fichte, were at some time under her baleful influence.[16]

The other side of the story, told by Sophie and A. W. Schlegel, accuses Bernhardi of cruelty, non-support, laziness and loose living. He is said to have had clandestine love affairs with Tieck's sister-in-law, Marie Alberti, and with several household servants, one of whom bore a child as a result.

In chapter 6 we noted the poet's early interest in art. Acquaintance with the able connoisseuse Rahel Levin and the sculptor Schadow helped to fortify his views. Conversations on the subject with the Schlegels were mutually beneficial, too. There can be little doubt that Tieck's opinions on old German art are reflected by Friedrich Schlegel in *Europa* (1803). In Jena Tieck met the painter Bury and perhaps discussed art with Goethe.

Although art usually remained of subordinate interest, yet he made the most of his opportunities in the field. With Wackenroder he left Romanticism its two standard breviaries (and its novel) on art, and called attention to the neglected German, Dutch and Flemish schools, as well as to the artistic side of the German Middle Ages. Moreover, he possessed a good knowledge of the English, French and Spanish schools of painting. It was he, no doubt, who with the Schlegels guided and inspired the Rheno-Frankish painters headed by Peter von Cornelius. Later, as we shall see, he wrote a long critical treatise on art.

In Dresden he found an opportunity to converse with several artists, Hartmann, Kaspar Friedrich, Bury and a young painter four years his junior. This was the Pomeranian Philipp Otto Runge, a mediocre artist, to be sure, but who under his tutelage developed into one of the most characteristic representatives of Romanticism in the field of the plastic arts. When he met Tieck he was merely an average epigoniad of the neo-classical tendencies of the latter half of the eighteenth century. Tieck influenced him strongly, drawing him away from his unpromising moorings and making him acquainted with Böhme and the Romantic program. He taught him to look at Dürer with the eyes of a Sternbald (a novel which Runge knew and admired) and filled him with a mystic religious symbolism and a longing for the sylvan solitude which Tieck had never tired of celebrating.[17]

THE END OF EARLY ROMANTICISM

Runge and Tieck were soon in agreement on their attitude toward the Weimarian classicism of Goethe. They admired and longed to assist Goethe's effort to recreate moribund German art but, disillusioned, resolved that the new art must take a different course from the formalism demanded by Goethe. Landscape dependent not on form but on inspiration must be the channel for their views, they decided. Along this path Tieck urged Runge.

To Runge's newly awakened love for Dürer there was now joined a lively interest in the Dutch school exalted in *Sternbald*. The mystic hart and the oak began to appear in his work, also musical instruments and cherubs making music. Thus the synaesthetic views of the lamented Wackenroder, who had advocated the linking of music and painting, came into their own once more. In 1803 Runge made five vignettes for Tieck's collection of *Minnelieder*, and in 1804-1805 two drawings for the *Heymons Kinder*. He took up chromatic studies and formulated a favorite theory of Tieck regarding the mystic and symbolic forces of the primary colors and of light and darkness. Tieck introduced him to Correggio, a master of color, and taught him to associate color with feeling, inspiration and music. It is significant, too, that under his influence Runge, who produced over fifty paintings between 1802 and his death in 1810, projected his four *Tageszeiten* (a cycle of decorations), which sought to epitomize their common views on landscape and color and to mark the cornerstone of the new art which Runge and Tieck deemed inevitable. The depth of Tieck's influence is all the more surprising since their intimate friendship lasted but two years. After 1803 they communicated only by letter.

Tieck's interest in mysticism had taken him from Jacob Böhme to the earlier mystics, especially Tauler, and finally to the church father, St. Augustine. This preoccupation was shared by the young Norwegian Henrik Steffens, who was of the same age and had an interest in philosophy, natural science and literature. Steffens had delivered lectures at Kiel in 1796, gone to Jena to study under Schelling, and finally to Freiberg in Saxony to work with the geologist Werner. Tieck made his acquaintance in 1799 at Reichardt's house in Berlin. In 1801 they met again in Dresden. The ebullient, ever active Norwegian who never learned good German, served as Tieck's chief link with Scandinavia. By marrying a daughter of Reichardt and a niece of Tieck's wife, he became a distant relative of Tieck. It was the latter who induced him to give up a professorship in Denmark and settle in Germany, whereupon he taught for a while at Halle, from 1811 to 1832 at Breslau and later at Berlin. In his bulky autobiography, *Was ich erlebte* (1840-1844), he has left a vivid account of his good relations with Tieck, which were marred, however, by divergent views on politics and religion.

In Dresden Tieck and Steffens saw much of each other. They engaged in long conversations on natural philosophy and geology. Steffens expressed his belief in the existence of a mysterious relationship between nature and the life of the human soul. He related how on a journey undertaken in 1794 he had gained a fantastic impression of the rocky coast of Norway and linked it with the mysteries of nature. He also explained his interest in the tales of various nations, how they reveal the character of their locale, and in the relation of saga to climate, topography and other conditions. Of course this subject was not new to Tieck. As early as 1790 he had demonized nature; Böhme merely confirmed his views; Novalis had put them into practice in *Heinrich von Ofterdingen*. Schelling, the pantheist, had given many hints in *Ideen zu einer Philosophie der Natur* (1797) and *Von der Weltseele* (1798). In the *Phantasien* Tieck had already suggested as a literary motif the thought of Böhme that "another sun rules in the bowels of the earth" and that plants and stones are intimately connected with the earth.[18] And in the poem *Der Unterirdische*, published in the *Musenalmanach für das Jahr 1802*, he had clearly expressed the underlying idea which was now put into practice in *Der Runenberg*. Steffens' views merely possessed the novelty of being more daring and far reaching.

As was his wont with all experience concrete or abstract, he combined the ideas of Steffens and his own notions and interpreted them in terms of improvised poetry. In a single night of 1802 he wrote the tale *Der Runenberg*, sending it off immediately to a Cologne publisher, who got it out late in 1803 in an almanac. The story is as follows. Christian, a young hunter, is resting high up in the mountains, sad and discouraged. Whenever he pulls a root, a curious plaintive tone seems to issue from it. A stranger accosts him, to whom Christian relates his story. His father, a gardener in the distant lowlands, had often told him tales of the mountains, cliffs and subterranean mines. Christian had presently conceived a strong yearning for these parts, and heedless of his father's advice to stay at home and be a gardener, had left his native heath and taken service as a hunter among the forbidding crags. The stranger confesses that he, too, loves the rugged highlands and points out the Runenberg, about which Christian only vaguely remembers his father telling a gruesome narrative. The stranger disappears, but Christian ascends the Runenberg as though possessed.

Reaching the end of the dizzy course, he finds a wall which seems to extend into the clouds. He peers through a window and discovers a mysterious hall rich in stones and crystals. A stately woman of super-natural beauty is pacing to and fro with a torch. She sings, then disrobes and appears before him in all her entrancing loveliness. Taking a tablet, she seems to read it. Christian is strangely moved. Finally she hands it to him, and with that the whole picture vanishes from his sight. When he awakens on a hilltop he searches in vain for the hall, the supernatural woman and the tablet.

In a daze he descends and discovers a pleasant village. He takes part in the church service and learns that the harvest festival is just being observed. Now he meets a charming girl, Elizabeth, whose father, a wealthy farmer, makes him his gardener. In six months he marries her; they have a daughter whom they name Leonora. Happy though he is, he longs to see his parents once more and to tell them of his bliss. Setting out on this mission, he meets an old man gazing intently at an unusual flower. The man turns out to be his father, and the flower possesses the mysterious power of foretelling coming events. It had prophesied the father's reunion with his son. Christian's parent now tells him of his mother's death and consents to accompany him to his new family and home.

Again a happy time ensues, and Elizabeth is blessed with several more children. One day a stranger, whom Christian seems somehow to remem-ber, stops at his house. He tarries for three months and then goes, enticed by a "magic image" in the mountains. But he leaves his great store of gold in Christian's care. Christian conceives a lust for this gold, but in deference to his father's warnings tries to overcome it. Even after the money has been invested, because of its owner's failure to return, he craves it, recalling now that the stranger was in reality the supernatural woman of the mountain. He becomes wanton and frivolous, fears flowers and plants and hears a mysterious groan whenever he uproots one. His father diagnoses his disease, saying that his heart has turned to cold metal and that he is drawn to wild crags instead of lovely gardens. Plants are to him naught but symbols of decay.

Again the harvest festival is at hand, but Christian wends his way to the forest instead of to the church. There he finds the stranger who had left the gold. But suddenly the man's form turns into that of a loath-some old hag. She introduces herself as "das Waldweib," but in departing leaves in Christian's mind a fleeting recollection of the beautiful super-woman. In the grass where she had stood he discovers the magic tablet. He takes it to his father, who warns him to cast it away. Madly Christian dashes off to find "das Waldweib." He fails to return, and meanwhile affairs at home go from bad to worse. Elizabeth remarries. One day a dishevelled man with a heavy load accosts her, saying that he has returned from the most forbidding mountains with rich treasures. He reveals them; to Elizabeth's horror they are ordinary field stones of flint and quartz. Obviously he is Christian, now out of his mind. She tells him that she is married again, and he, unconcerned, is content to return to his "Waldweib." Kissing her and his oldest daughter, Leonora, farewell, he disappears forever.

Arnim accused Tieck (and Novalis) of plagiarizing the *Volkssagen* of Otmar (the pen name for Johann Karl Christoph Nachtigal), which appeared in 1800.[19] Of plagiarism there can be no question in *Der Runenberg*. But it seems very likely that Tieck knew Otmar, who also stresses the horrible yet enticing power of the mountains over men (then no uncommon idea), and greed for the gold which reposes within the mountains. The motif of the miraculous flower, too, is found in Otmar, as is the notion that nature is jealous of her independence and resents being conquered by man.

Believe as we may about the influence of Otmar, it is patent that the gloomy horror and demonization of nature which beckon to us at every turn in *Eckbert*, without having taken definite shape there, assume real form in *Der Runenberg*, reflected in the alluring power of subterranean rocks and metals. All who succumb to their lure are enticed from the lightsome joys of the earth's surface to their mysterious underground realm, and there they remain enthralled. Mere stones appear to them as costly treasures, and their souls fall prey to the ghastly "Waldweib," who is both an illusion of the hero and a metaphorical incarnation and demonization of the mountain. The mountain symbolizes brute, unconscious force petrified and banished to dark depths. And the root which

> shrieks like mandrakes torn out of the earth,
> That living mortals, hearing them, run mad . . .

is a clear reference to a widespread medieval superstition. Withal the tale, one of Tieck's masterpieces in this style, offers an eerie admixture of the nocturnal side of the natural sciences and of the world of fairy tales. It is one of the best examples in literature of the third category of Romantic fairy tale, as described above in our discussion of *Der blonde Eckbert*. The story is a metaphorical structure, with an interplay of the human soul and animated nature.

The language of *Der Runenberg* shows Tieck, a master of German prose, at his best. Interlarded verse, though less frequent than in *Die schöne Magelone* and not used for a *leitmotif* as in *Der blonde Eckbert*, creeps even into the dialog and attempts onomatopoeic suggestion of metals, flowers and other natural phenomena.

THE END OF EARLY ROMANTICISM

The sound ethical core of *Der blonde Eckbert* and *Der getreue Eckart und der Tannenhäuser*, and the author's humanistic opposition to naturalism, are also present here. James A. Froude in 1845 classed these three tales in one category as "different exhibitions of very similar ideas; a single sin unrepented of and unatoned for becomes a destiny; a seed from which, however diminutive and trifling it may look, a whole life of crime and wickedness shoots up as a matter of course, perhaps inevitable."[20] The "single sin" in these three tales is inordinate desire, or, to state it differently, lack of continence. This leads to the psychic aberration, which is in each case carried to its terrible climax. But to labor this idea would be to misinterpret Tieck's underlying intention. He did not mean to place any moral lesson in the foreground. His chief purpose was to create atmosphere and moods, which flit like shadows over nature and the souls of men.

A resemblance in the theme of the Nibelungen saga and that of *Der Runenberg* is apparent. Is it possible that Wagner was influenced by the tale in his conception of the curse inherent in the Nibelungen treasure? Tieck's little work, which he later regretted having sent off too hastily to the Cologne publisher, became very popular after its republication in part 1 of *Phantasus* (1812) and has remained a favorite short story to this day. Hoffmann's *Bergwerke von Falun* is congeneric. It has been twice translated into English, first by Carlyle (1827), whose rendering is superb, and again for the *Tales from the Phantasus* of Hare and Froude (1845). The previously mentioned recent French collection, *La coupe d'or* (1933), contains a translation by Béguin.

Nine years passed before Tieck wrote anything comparable to this little story. For the time being his productiveness waned. How shall we explain this long blight in a poet otherwise so prolific? Why had he exhausted his Romantic moods? His physical sufferings and ill humor over the attacks of his opponents robbed him of pleasure in bright, cheerful poetry which hovers in the ethereal realm of dreams. He told Brentano in 1803 that "the ingratitude of the public with respect to his art" dejected him and deprived him of joy in his work.[21] He also began to realize that through the Schlegels he had been made the dupe of official Romanticism.[22] Moreover, a constitutional change was gradually taking place within him between 1804 and 1820, brought about by the fact that he had matured at last. He had come to perceive more and more the rift in his own personality, which was a source of constant suffering and caused unproductive silence. With herculean effort he had striven to overcome it by depicting its dire effects, as in *William Lovell;* by the study of art and the early literature of Germany, England and Spain; by irony; and by self-discipline. The better he succeeded (though his success was never more than partial), the farther he turned away from giddy Romanticism to balanced realism. Moreover, we know that mysticism, in which he had once taken an extravagant interest, blasted his poetry in the long run; his cure from this ill, through the medium of the ancients, the *Nibelungenlied*, Shakespeare's historical dramas and Solger's philosophy, was very slow, as we have seen.[23] Homer, he wrote to Friedrich Schlegel, now taught him the continuity of mythology and history, showed him that the whole historical world is a unit and that realism (that is, history) offers as rich a mine of poetry as does pure imagination: "alles, was Geschichte gibt und Poesie, so wie alle Natur, und alles in mir, sieht mich aus einem einzigen tiefen Auge an, voller Liebe, aber schreckvoller Bedeutung."[24] The *Nibelungenlied* and Shakespeare, not in his fairy plays but in his great tragedies and histories, were soon to bear the same lesson in realism for him. Solger's influence will be discussed later.

The themes of love and art, which had served him as bulwarks against his dual nature and egoism, now dissatisfied him as too subtle. Poetic faith and comprehension of life through the power of imagination seemed insufficient. Nor did irony alone suffice. So he was casting about for something to take their place in his poetry. Not until he found it in the cultivation of sociability, in simple, practical faith and in naïve belief in the miracles of daily existence,[25] could he engage in productive work. The first indication of his discovery of these new tenets is in a very important letter of 1803 to Friedrich Schlegel, wherein he writes that revealed Christianity now serves him as the key for understanding mankind; this makes all miracles clear and renders everyday life miraculous. "Without this simple faith . . . everything entices me into a vast abyss of insanity."[26] Beginning in 1821 this belief in the omnipresence of miracles became the basis of his philosophy in the "novellen." His internal change to a more realistic attitude toward life was revealed also in his gradual shift from nature demonism to the demonization of everyday life, exemplified in his "new manner" from 1811 on.[27]

Then, too, the political condition of the fatherland was such as to silence a poet of Tieck's type. As has been suggested, he never concerned himself seriously with political questions of the day because he had an ascetic horror of them. He wrote to Friedrich Schlegel in 1803 that he lived in the past, better still in a timeless realm, "fast in der schönen Einsamkeit eines Klosters."[28] In a letter to Solger of 1816 he spoke of the spiritual anarchy and brutalization of the age. And the more agitated the times became, tending to monopolize public attention, the more did he turn his back on them. It is no coincidence, therefore, that he enjoyed his greatest fame and richest productivity before 1806 and again between 1820 and 1830, when his German compatriots were politically most apathetic and their literature was most aloof from politics. On the other hand, the turbulent years from 1806 to 1820 and those beginning with 1830, were not among his happiest. Indeed, during these periods he definitely relinquished his right to the title of a representative German. Like Nicolai two generations before, he was eclipsed.

Under these circumstances it is no accident that *Fortunat*, which was to serve as a counterpart to *Kaiser Octavianus*, was delayed for almost a generation; not until 1816 did it see the light of day.

Early Romanticism had died an easy death. With its yearning for a lovelier world it had succeeded, by a system of cabalistic sorcery, in conjuring up a wealth of new forms sparkling with a golden sheen. But much of this splendor proved naught but dross because it lacked the support of a firm connection with things mundane and the impetus of true, deep feeling. The ultimate goal of early Romanticism, so far as the human mind is concerned, had been mysticism and inscrutability. It need not be explained that this vague objective deterred, rather than attracted, readers. Such devices as comparison of the human soul with the flowers of the fields—a favorite thought appropriated by the Romanticists from Böhme—tended to create "Stimmungspoesie" but left no concrete images. Feeling had been everything to the young Romantics, just as it is to Goethe's Faust, who exclaims passionately:

Wenn ihr's nicht fühlt, ihr werdet's nicht erjagen.

Tieck's words in *Sternbald*: "Wer es nicht mitfühlt, dem ist es auch nicht zu beweisen," sound strangely familiar. But he went even farther than this when he expostulated in the same work: "Wozu Worte? Wer versteht die Rede des andern?" And as for expressing the noblest human emotions, particularly love, words and thoughts seemed quite inadequate to him:

Words have evermore deceived thee,
Thoughts have cheated, snared and grieved thee.[29]*

More fatalistic expression, finally, was given to his Romantic view of life in the words of *Blaubart*: "Das Leben von uns allen ist wohl nur ein albernes Puppenspiel,"[30] which remind of his words in the juvenile play *Braddeck*: "Das Leben des Menschen ist ein Traum."

In the long run, then, his clear intellect, now at last mature, could not be content with the dissolution of all solid components of life and art.

*Sprache hat dich nur belogen,
Der Gedanke dich betrogen.

LUDWIG TIECK, THE GERMAN ROMANTICIST

He had not succeeded in conducting men into such a new land of poesy. On the other hand, mindful of his obligation to those "who occupy the same cultural level" as himself, he was reluctant to yield the higher ground which he felt he had won for the free play of the poet's imagination. Here was a dilemma, no doubt, made more serious by the politically agitated, critical days upon which Germany had fallen, but in which we saw that he was not interested. The temporary solution which he sought and found lay in the scientific study and better comprehension of bygone ages.

For ten years he had been concerned with the era of medievalism and the early modern epoch. But his occupation with them could hardly be called more than desultory. Besides, he had read into them much that they did not contain. So now, spurning other temptations and remaining the free-lance writer he always was, he began a more systematic investigation of those times and those poets who he believed had made the Romantic ideal their life's goal and had breathed its spirit.

His interest in literature had never been bounded by national frontiers. As early as 1793 he had taken up the study of Cervantes, followed some years later by a serious preoccupation with Calderon. It has been noted that a history of the Spanish theater was long one of his favorite plans. His systematic study of Shakespeare and the Elizabethans dated even farther back. A *Buch über Shakespeare*, of which three drafts have been considered in previous chapters, occupied his mind incessantly. To be sure, these works were never completed. The chief reason is that they were too grandiosely planned. Their great literary heroes were to be set in relief against too ambitious a background, which was to embrace a history of the human race up through the seventeenth century. Indeed, everything which he ever wrote about English and Spanish literatures was part of a series of building materials for the unfinished structure of a magnificent history—a dream-history—of Romantic poesy.

More recently, under Wackenroder's inspiration, his enthusiasm for medieval art had paved the way for a better understanding of medieval German literature. Laying aside his English and Spanish studies for a while, he now devoted himself almost exclusively to the task of expounding German literature of the twelfth to fourteenth centuries. Such an interest was not only natural, it was timely, too. Napoleon was just setting about to conquer and denationalize Germany. This led to a growing popular pride in the glory of the German past, in the era when the country could still boast of mighty emperors, and in the literature of that era.

THE END OF EARLY ROMANTICISM

Tieck's interest in Middle High German literature may perhaps be traced as far back as his Jena period. It was first aroused by the *Helden-buch*. After the death of Novalis it was intensified and turned him to a study of the minnesongs and the *Nibelungenlied*. Foremost among his plans was a recreation of the latter supplemented by Old Norse sources. But he found this project too ambitious and arduous for the time being. Hence he centered his attention upon the minnesongs. In 1801 the edition of the Paris (Manesse) codex of *Minnelieder* by Bodmer (1758-1759) chanced to fall into his hands. This codex, which he had not yet seen, remained in Paris until 1888, when it was taken to Heidelberg, there to be known as the "grosse Heidelberger Liederhandschrift." But the contemplation and study of Bodmer's work afforded him much pleasure, and he devoted more than two years to a redaction of his own.

His edition of two hundred twenty modernized German minnesongs, entitled *Minnelieder aus dem schwäbischen Zeitalter*, appeared in 1803; the publisher was Georg Andreas Reimer in Berlin, who had got out Friedrich Schlegel's and Tieck's edition of Novalis. As the sponsor of Schleiermacher, the Schlegels, Fichte, Fouqué, the Grimm brothers and Lachmann, he was the Romantic publisher *par excellence*, destined to publish numerous later works of Tieck.

A judicious and able introduction of thirty pages, *Die altdeutschen Minnelieder*,[31] precedes the poems. It is a compendium of the history of Romantic poetry as he saw it and an illustration of his expository style at its best. He proved here his birthright as an accomplished student of comparative literature. The period of minnesong is described as one of the golden ages of Romanticism, worthy of a place beside the era of Cervantes or Shakespeare. He lauds the multifariousness of the minnesingers, their independence of authority, their winsomeness, their success in uniting substance and form, their perfect handling of rime and of other devices. Always believing that music had priority over words, he now made the questionable discovery that the minnesingers shared this conviction. No less dubious is his theory, which he converted into practice, that the Middle High German writer may ignore quantity and add or omit vowels at will.

"Poetry," he wrote of that age, "was a common necessity of life and unsevered from the latter, hence it appears so sound and free, and however much art and stern schooling some of the poems of the time may reveal, yet one would not like to call this poetry art. It is learned, but not in order to appear learned; its mastery is concealed in innocence and love, the poet is unconcerned about interest, and hence he remains so simple and naïve in all his artistry."[32]

This paean, which is in marked contrast to the antipathy for the "Minnelieder" expressed to Wackenroder ten years before, was of inestimable potency in calling attention to Middle High German poetry. While the work of Opitz in the seventeenth century, of Bodmer and of other scholars in the eighteenth, had been instrumental in arousing the scholarly world to a realization of the importance of German literature between 1100 and 1300, Tieck's essay, more than his modernized minnesongs, helped to make this period widely and genuinely popular.

Tieck's strophes and songs are more skilfully divided off than were Bodmer's. But his arrangement of the poems is curious. He does not give the center of the stage to the overshadowing figure of Walther von der Vogelweide. Apparently he was more enamored of his precursors, in particular Heinrich von Veldecke, and of his successors, among them the sugary dandy Ulrich von Lichtenstein and the decadent formalist Hadlaub. His adaptations, too, which A. W. Schlegel criticized adversely when they were still in press,[33] are awkward. Though they consciously strive for an archaic flavor, they do not preserve content and form with much care. Finally many curious neologisms, which he coined for the sake of the rime but tried to pass off as legitimate Middle High German vocables, proved deleterious in their influence upon future generations. But the age for which he wrote was not a scholarly one, and in its existing form his work exerted a stronger popular influence than a more expertly executed edition could have hoped for. It will always stand out as the first independent work of the Romanticists on old German literature.

With all its shortcomings Tieck's *Minnelieder* had a great effect upon the future of literature and scholarship, too. The work served Uhland as an introduction to the minnesong and in subject matter, image and diction deeply influenced his own poetry, as well as that of countless other German lyricists and balladists of the nineteenth century.[34] It also served as a model for the scientifically much more accurate *Des Minnesangs Frühling* of Lachmann and Haupt and was one of the most important factors in arousing Jakob Grimm's enthusiasm for early German literature.[34] He described Tieck's introduction as "hinreissend"—compelling. Inspired by it, he set to work studying the Bodmer collection in Savigny's library and then, in 1805, the Paris codex. No finer example could be found of the influence wielded by a poetic dilettante upon a great scholarly mind destined to father a new science. What Grimm might have done without this initial impulse must remain a matter of speculation. The fact stands, however, that his inspiration came from Tieck. Tieck, on the other hand, as his hostile nephew Felix Theodor

Bernhardi reported many years later, never acquired either understanding or appreciation for the work of the Grimms. He disapproved what he construed as their attempt to delve into the meaning of art, and called them pedants.

But Tieck's opponents, above all Kotzebue and Merkel, who had just founded a new periodical, *Der Freimütige*, were not amenable even to this manifestation of Romantic enthusiasm. They could only find in it food for the most pusillanimous readers. "Whoever," was their Cassandra-like prophecy, "has the nature of an ant and can laboriously pick a few seeds of grain from a great mass of rubbish, well, he will perhaps, with many sighs and yawns, work his way through this whining and constant stammering about Wunne, Meye, Minne, and Vögelein. All others will certainly toss this dear, stout, juiceless and feeble book impatiently aside after a few pages." Similarly, Schiller compared Tieck's adaptations to the chirping of sparrows and ridiculed their limited mental horizon.[35]

According to a letter of December 24, 1807, to Reimer (in the writer's possession), Tieck would have liked to get out a second improved edition.

CHAPTER TEN

THE EARLY YEARS IN ZIEBINGEN (1802-1810)

WHEN he settled with his family in Dresden in the spring of 1801, Tieck was almost thirty. He had a wife and one child (Agnes, his second daughter, was born in 1802) but no source of income except his literary work—then a more precarious means of livelihood than today. The position at the theater in Frankfurt which Brentano tried to secure for him, and for which Tieck solicited Goethe's support late in 1801,[1] slipped through his fingers. Accustomed to life on a larger scale in Berlin, the cramped provincialism which he soon noticed in Dresden palled upon him. He therefore welcomed an invitation from his old schoolmate and university chum von Burgsdorff, a dapper, dashing young Lothario, who delighted in playing the rôle of a Maecenas, to settle with his family upon the Burgsdorff ancestral estate at Ziebingen, not far from Frankfurt on the Oder. Burgsdorff was a likeable chap, generous and well-meaning, but his easy-going manner made him somewhat of a reprobate. Tieck had not seen him since leaving Göttingen in 1794. Meanwhile Burgsdorff, a born globe-trotter, had travelled constantly for four years and been in Vienna, Paris, Madrid and London. He had lived for almost a year in England.[2]

Late in 1802 Tieck moved with his family to Ziebingen. To be sure, in 1807 the Burgsdorff estate passed into the possession of the young adventurer's relative, Count Finck von Finckenstein, an educated gentleman and a patron of the arts, who had lived on a neighboring estate in Madlitz. But the count, who immediately won Tieck's friendship and often invited him to Madlitz, was happy to continue the offer of hospitality when he became the owner of the Ziebingen manor.

Count Finck von Finckenstein[3] was born in Berlin in 1745 as the son of the well known minister of Frederick the Great. Having chosen law as his vocation, he passed through the various stages customary for a man of his rank, becoming in 1775 second president of the Stettin "Regierung" and in 1777 president of the Neumark "Regierung" at Cüstrin. In 1797 the king relieved him of his duties on account of his decision in a certain litigation. Although later fully exonerated, the count did not take public office again, but remained in the bosom of his family. He showed not only a passive interest in literature but also published a critical edition of Ewald von Kleist's *Frühling* and translations of Greek and Roman bucolics.

ZIEBINGEN (1802-1810)

Through Tieck the count was soon converted to Shakespeare and to medieval German and English letters. The poet also found a cultured circle in the count's home. The latter was the father of thirteen children, three of whom had died in infancy. With the exception of the oldest son, Karl Friedrich Albrecht, a friend of Rahel Levin, who had entered upon a diplomatic career, all the rest, six daughters and three sons, lived at home or upon one of the neighboring estates. Tieck grew particularly intimate with the oldest daughter, Henriette Amalie Dorothea (born in 1774), who became his lifelong friend.

Literature and music, in particular old Italian chorals, were favorite topics of conversation. Here Tieck was inspired to write his formally excellent but extravagant *Gedichte auf die Musik*.[4] He also put the finishing touches upon his *Minnelieder*, discussed in the previous chapter. Moreover, he collaborated with Reichardt in a quarrelsome review of Goethe's translation of the autobiography of Benvenuto Cellini.[5] In 1809 a schoolboy friend, Wilhelm Schütz, also joined the circle. He purchased a patent of nobility to marry one of the Finckenstein daughters. The architect and writer on art Genelli, a close friend of one of the other Finckenstein girls ("einer Gräfin von Finckenstein innig verbunden," as Varnhagen von Ense puts it), lived on the estates, too; Tieck, to whom he was hostile, had met him in 1799 in Jena. In this environment Tieck remained, with certain interruptions, until 1819.

It is the irony of fate that he, the city-bred man and first metropolitan poet of Germany, was banished for so many years to this solitary, rustic retreat. Materially it was fortunate for the family, who had more than once tasted the bitterness of gipsy life, but spiritually it proved a calamity for the poet. This, added to the factors mentioned in the previous chapter, helps to explain why, aside from the three little tales *Liebeszauber*, *Die Elfen* and *Der Pokal* (1811) and the three prose interludes of *Phantasus* (1812), he, who had been so prolific in the city, did practically no creative work now that he had been taken out of his element. It shows why, for sheer boredom, he toyed with so fantastic an idea as becoming a clergyman.[6] On September 11, 1817, A. W. Schlegel wrote to Tieck's brother not without basis: "In that prolonged solitude, surrounded by people who swear by his every word, he has probably become a queer bird."[7]

In addition to the *Minnelieder*, the *Nibelungenlied* occupied much of his time in Ziebingen. At an auction in 1802 he had acquired a copy of *Der Nibelungen Liet, ein Rittergedicht aus dem XIII. oder XIV. Jahrhundert* by Christoph Heinrich Müller (called Myller), published at Berlin in 1782. This imperfect edition afforded him his first thorough

acquaintance with the Middle High German classic. Influenced by it and
by A. W. Schlegel's Berlin lectures, he seriously took up the task of preparing a modernized version, which was at first to be supplemented by
Old Norse elements. He corresponded with both the Schlegels about the
plan, which by 1804 was a matter of fairly common knowledge. In
November 1804 he read parts to Arnim and Brentano at Ziebingen. In
1805 his work was announced in the "Messkatalog" of the Göttingen
publisher Dieterich and by A. W. Schlegel in the *Jenaische Zeitung*. As
preserved in the "Nachlass," this version presents the first half of the
lay, telling the story in five "Gesänge" as far as the transfer of the
treasure to Worms. It leans upon Müller but adds many original touches.
The rimed couplet, not the strophe, serves as the basis.

In the summer of 1803 Tieck interrupted his residence in Ziebingen
for the first time. He accepted the invitation of Burgsdorff to accompany
him upon a journey to the south.[8] In June they set out for Dresden,
where they met Fouqué, then twenty-six, who was destined eight years
later to enrich world literature with his tale *Undine*. From there they
turned to Bohemia, visiting the baths at Teplitz and at Karlsbad. Then
they turned westward to the Fichtelgebirge and Franconia, which called
up in Tieck's mind memories of Wackenroder. They revisited the ruins
of Berneck and renewed their acquaintance with Erlangen, Pommersfelden and Nürnberg. Also Bamberg, Würzburg and Heidelberg were
touched. At Heidelberg, Brentano, Savigny and Creuzer tried to secure
a professorship for Tieck. But before Tieck and Burgsdorff could complete their itinerary, the latter became involved in a game of faro and
lost almost all his funds. With difficulty they managed to return to
Dresden, and after two months' absence Tieck rejoined his family in their
Ziebingen home. The trip, marred by too much haste and the abrupt
conclusion, increased his love for Germany and German history.[9] In
Eine Sommerreise, written in 1833, he has left a poet's account of this
vacation, which he so sorely needed. This "novelle" is full of ardent love
for his fatherland and of true appreciation of the rich and varied beauty
of its landscape.

In the autumn of 1804 his wanderlust was perforce aroused again.
His ailing and thoroughly unhappy sister, who we found had fled with
her children from her husband, had been advised by physicians to go to
Italy. Since she was too frail to travel alone, Tieck, under her thumb,
decided to accompany her, leaving his wife (whom Sophie despised)[10]
and children behind in Ziebingen.[11] In a letter from Brentano to Arnim
of December 26, 1804 (preserved among the Varnhagen von Ense papers
in Berlin), Tieck is reported as having said that he purposely kept his

wife in ignorance of his whereabouts and was glad to be away from the sandy desert of Ziebingen.

Tieck and Sophie reached Munich, where they tarried because Sophie seemed on the verge of a breakdown. Then Tieck himself became desperately ill. A malignant attack of rheumatism confined him to bed for many months. At first the noted connoisseur of art, Karl Friedrich von Rumohr, an early convert to Catholicism, and later his own brother Friedrich nursed him. Despite excruciating pain his mind remained active. A girl who used to sit at a window of the house opposite his room left an indelible impression upon his mind. She seemed to him a mysterious, fascinating figure. Seven years later she became the inspiration for the weird "novelle" *Liebeszauber*. The long weary hours in the sick-bed were spent, whenever possible, dictating parts of his modernized version of the *Nibelungenlied* or playing with illustrations of the lay which his brother had prepared.

When his health permitted, he availed himself of the treasures of the Munich library in further preparation for his resuscitation of the great Middle High German epic. He found there the Munich codex, which he compared with Müller's text. This collation led him to undertake a second version of the famous classic, which unlike his first is divided into strophes. Moreover, it shows more faithful adherence to the original. But the more deeply he delved into Middle High German literature, the stronger became his desire to go to Italy. For in the library of the Vatican, he knew, a rich abundance of medieval German manuscripts was stored.

Some time before, Sophie had met a wealthy young nobleman from the Baltic provinces, Karl Gregor von Knorring. He had soon become A. W. Schlegel's successor as her lover; in unpublished notes among his papers that indefatigable gossipmonger, Varnhagen von Ense, relates how she was in the habit of feigning convulsions and then, while her husband sought medical aid, would make amorous advances to Knorring. The same source claims that Felix Theodor was begotten by him. With Knorring, who had followed her to Munich, Sophie proceeded to Italy during the autumn. Although the contrary has been claimed, she did not become Catholic there.[12] But according to a letter from A. W. Schlegel to her of July 7, 1805, she was planning to be converted so as to insure her children better protection against deportation to Germany after Bernhardi had ascertained that she was in Rome.

In the summer of 1805 Tieck, accompanied by his brother, Rumohr and two copper engravers, Franz and Johann Riepenhausen, who are responsible for some etchings for *Genoveva*, finally set out for Italy, too. At last that yearning for Italy which stirs every German breast and had long made itself felt in Tieck was to be realized. In the poem "Sehnen nach Italien," written as early as 1796, he had given it expression in the lines:

> Shall I pine and ever languish,
> And in loving waste away?
> Will not fate give heed to me,
> All my brooding, all my anguish
> Are of no avail, I pray?*

Now his guardian spirits finally deigned to fulfil the poet's dream, of which he had sung:

> They lead the tired trav'ler
> To sweet, sweet peace,
> To joy and to rest,
> To the cradle of art.[13]†

The itinerary of the travellers can be traced in detail through two letters which Franz Riepenhausen wrote to his father from Rome in August and September 1805.[14] It appears that Friedrich Tieck proved a disagreeable companion, while Ludwig, still in extremely poor health, was ultracritical, testy and unapproachable. But with improving health, his better nature appeared and he turned out to be "a jewel of a friend" (die glänzendste Perle von allen).

Rumohr and Tieck became fast friends on the trip, despite some trouble alleged to have been caused between them by the Riepenhausens. In the poem "Abschied von Rom" Tieck spoke of him as:

> Noble Rumohr,
> Whose friendship gave me cheer and consolation
> In many an hour of illness.[15]‡

They met again in Munich in 1808 and, despite a temporary estrangement in 1809, carried on a desultory correspondence for a generation.[16]

* Soll ich in mir selbst verschmachten,
Und in Liebe ganz vergehn?
Wird das Schicksal mein nicht achten,
Dieses Sinnen, dieses Trachten
Immer unerhörend sehn?

† Sie führen den Müden
Dem süssen Frieden,
Den Freuden, der Ruh,
Der Kunstheimat zu.

‡ Der edle Rumohr,
Dess Freundschaft ich in mancher kranken Stunde
Trost und Erheitrung danke.

ZIEBINGEN (1802-1810)

By way of Florence, which furnished the background for the "novelle" *Der Pokal* of 1811, the five men went to Rome. But the vestiges of an illustrious antiquity appealed to Tieck less than to Goethe a generation before, though in his poems on Italy he often speaks of the glory of ancient days. He could not understand Goethe's viewpoint, for he was much more attracted by St. Peter's, the great monuments of medieval art, the works of divine Raphael and overtowering Michael Angelo. Music, poetry and painting interested him (who was "modern" in Spengler's sense) more than statuary. And in the pomp of the Church he saw the reflection of the radiant, mystic splendor of the Middle Ages as it had been preserved to his own day.[17]

In prose he wrote his impressions most succinctly and clearly in a letter to Friedrich von Raumer of June 16, 1816,[18] although a querulous book by Raumer on a trip to Venice angered him. The higher circles, Tieck found, were difficult of access but graced by a pleasing ceremoniousness. The common people, the middle class, the coffee houses, gambling establishments and carnivals proved most interesting. He found little public spirit but much provincial municipal consciousness, sometimes fanatical yet often keen and noble. In this respect Italy seemed a caricature of Germany. However, he discovered that the Italian cosmopolites were usually stupid atheists, struggling for a chimerical political liberty. The Italian theater, especially its comedy, pleased him, and he saw some excellent actors. As for objects of art, he recommended works of Correggio in Parma; of Francesco Francia, one of his "favorite painters," in Bologna; and Avanzini's copy of Raphael's Madonna in Piacenza.

His keen sense of art thrilled to the splendor of the Italian church festivals. The esthetic side of Catholicism appealed to him mightily. No wonder the rumors of his conversion began to grow more numerous. But to him Catholicism as a creed was just as imperfect as any other religion. As he said to Robinson in London twelve years later, its existence requires the existence of Protestantism as a counterbalance.[19]

In Rome he associated less with Italians than with foreigners. He met Coleridge, who at the time remained unaware of Tieck's "eminence as a poet," and discussed with him the spurious plays of Shakespeare.[20] He was a frequent visitor in the German colony, which had its focus in the home of Wilhelm von Humboldt, resident Prussian minister in the Eternal City. No less frequently was he seen in the circles which gathered about the prince of Sachsen-Gotha and to which Kotzebue belonged. He associated also with the poet Tiedge. A favorite form of entertainment was afforded by amateur theatricals. Once he directed a performance of

Kotzebue's *Der Wirrwarr*. In a poem bearing the title of the play he discussed the event and rebuked the vapid playwright. A reflection of his carefree life in this carefree Italo-German environment is to be found in the "novelle" *Der junge Tischlermeister* of 1836.

The guide of most Germans in Rome was Friedrich (Maler) Müller, the erstwhile Storm and Stress poet, who, having settled in Italy in 1778, eked out a miserable existence as a painter.[21] We have noted how Tieck became acquainted with his drama *Golo und Genoveva* at Hamburg in 1797. Meanwhile he had read other works of Müller, also unpublished. Now the two men became acquainted, Tieck finding that Müller had lost practically all his interest in literature. Partly because he admired Müller and his early writings, of which their author had no critical opinion whatever, and partly because he wished to put an end to the rumors that his own *Genoveva* was a plagiarization of Müller's play, he decided to get out an edition of this writer's chief works and secured his permission therefor. It will be discussed in the next chapter.

A travel book about Italy, planned in 1807, was not written. Artistically the finest fruit of his journey are two sheaves of poems entitled *Reisegedichte eines Kranken* and *Rückkehr eines Genesenden*.[22] They are unmatched by anything in his lyric output and indeed by any German lyrics of those years. Even Friedrich Schlegel, who was critical of Tieck's later writings, lauded them.[23] One fails to find aught comparable to them before the *Nordseebilder* of Heine, which began to appear in 1826 and were perhaps influenced by Tieck.[24]

In their earlier stages the Romanticists, and Tieck in particular, had striven to volatilize everything concrete and to create only floating clouds of mood and emotion, which were borne aloft by melodious strophe and sonorous rime. Now, without overcoming his dualistic nature or his demonism, he was breaking away from the trammels of this tradition and beginning to realize its corrosive influence. This is clear not only from his subsequent practise as a poet but also from his opinion as expressed in a letter of April 9, 1818, to his brother. He was then able to make light of "that vacuous ideal which draws many friends of art after it like a will-o'-the-wisp, so that they believe they can hover and live without time, creed and peculiarity in a region of beauty, a veritable Beyond, cutting off behind them all ties and threads, memories and feelings which bind them to their world and age."[25]

In the poems which he wrote in Italy free verse, previously employed only in exceptional cases by Klopstock and young Goethe to give expression to ecstatic feeling, was used for the first time in its full effectiveness and adaptability to many moods. He jotted them down hastily in his diary during 1805 and 1806. In 1823, when he published them in the third volume of his *Gedichte*, he planned to rewrite them in a more regular metrical form and to introduce rime.[26] Fortunately he was diverted from doing so.

The experiences described in this poetry and the enthusiasms which they engender stand out sharply. We find esthetic enjoyment of art and nature, and on occasion do not miss wit and irony. His eye saw clearly. He visualized each image distinctly, allowing it to take possession of his poor invalid soul, or later of his happier mind cheered by the hope of convalescence. And what he saw was presented with realistic truth yet with subjective coloring. Only an occasional deficiency in rhythm or too prosaic a cataloguing of events shows that he was not only improvising but tilling virgin soil.

The reason for his high attainment in these seventy-five or more poems, with their wealth of rhythmic patterns, is the same which applies to his sonnets. Each poem deals with a definite clear-cut subject. No vague thoughts and feelings are indicated. Verona, Bologna, the Vatican, Florence, Pisa, Lucca and dozens of other points are dealt with singly. Each description has the effect of a beautiful cameo. What he offers is tangible and concrete. His subject matter lay ready before him, and he had merely to mold it into shape. Whenever this was the case his chances for success were always auspicious.

Here a new art is practised for the first time. It shows no trace of the wild intoxication of his adolescence and of the vague yearnings of his early manhood years. Reality has now become the objective of his endeavors; but he does not strive for a purely naturalistic reproduction, which would ignore the ideas behind the objects and their careful esthetic evaluation. For he has learned that while we should not constantly seek a meaning in life, intellect is needed if life is to have a deeper significance. In this spirit he now became the disciple of Goethe, to whom he did sincere homage in the gardens of Villa Borghese:

> Here thou too didst walk,
> Noblest genius,
> Our fatherland's ornament and joy,
> Goethe, German glorious singer.
> Here, so announces legend,
> Thy song of Tasso was written;
> And every whispering leaf
> Of the laurel rustles thy name,
> The fountains speak of thee,

And a ghostly shudder
Flies over me and on,
Still whispering solemnly in the distant stone-pines.[27]*

In Verona he wrote a poetic account of a play based upon Goethe's *Werther* and performed in the arena, a structure which interested him less than did Julia's grave.[28] In Rome he told of being chided by a compatriot for preferring Goethe's *Faust* to that of a certain Schink.[29]

He eternalized his work at the Vatican library,[30] but later lamented that he had become so engrossed in studying the old German manuscripts that he begrudged every moment lost for this task. He sang:

And I had to go to Rome
To become thoroughly German.[31]†

This thought was repeated to Solger in 1816.[32] Indeed, sometimes overpowering homesickness for Germany seized him. What displeased him most in Italy was "the hated three-colored banner of the world conquerors."[33]

After the warm sun of Italy had relieved him of physical suffering, he devoted most of his time (a solid half year) to transcribing the manuscripts of Middle High German poems in the Vatican library.[34] He paid special attention to the epics found in the *Heldenbuch*. In the introduction to the *Minnelieder* he had explained his interest in them, saying that they preserve "much of the tone of an epic age," and have "a greatness and sublimity" which only occasionally yields to coarse, barbaric descriptions.[35] Much in the *Heldenbuch* reminded him of the *Nibelungenlied* and appeared to him to be derived from it. In 1807 he planned to have Zimmer, the publisher of the younger Romanticists in Heidelberg, get out an edition of the lays of the *Heldenbuch;* he even sent him the begin-

* Hier auch bist du gewandelt,
Edelster Genius,
Unsers Vaterlands Zier und Lust,
Goethe, deutscher herrlicher Sänger.
Hier, so verkündet die Sage,
Ward dein Lied vom Tasso gedichtet,
Und jedes lispelnde Blatt
Des Lorbeers rauscht deinen Namen,
Die Springquellen reden von dir
Und ein Geisterschauer
Fliegt über mir hinweg
Und säuselt noch heilig in den fernen Pinien.

† Und ich musste nach Rom gehn,
Um erst recht stockdeutsch zu werden.

ning of the manuscript. This plan remained unexecuted, though resumed in 1816.

He also made a complete copy of the Vatican (now Heidelberg) manuscript of *König Rother*, a minstrel's epic dating from approximately 1140. He deciphered it much more successfully than did Amelung, his predecessor.

For his modernized edition of the *Nibelungenlied*, which he planned on a large scale—it was now (in a second version which he began) to include five books ending with the *Klage*—, he collected a mass of new material; on his return from Italy he stopped at St. Gall for the purpose of collating the excellent manuscript there (now known as B). It had not been used by Müller for his edition of 1782, and in fact did not receive attention before Friedrich Heinrich von der Hagen's edition of 1816. As we shall see, von der Hagen owed his knowledge of it to Tieck.

Although Tieck did not finish his *Nibelungenlied*, his poetical version of *König Rother* is found in completed form among his papers in Berlin.[36] With the exception of a fragment entitled "König Rother zieht einer Jungfrau die Schuhe an" and published by Arnim in his *Zeitung für Einsiedler* (1808),[37] this adaptation has remained unedited. Tieck's work with *König Rother*, done at a time when even the name of this old lay had fallen into oblivion, is epoch-making.

In the summer of 1806, just a year after he had set out for Italy, he travelled home by slow stages, stopping among other places at St. Gall, at Heidelberg, where he saw Brentano, at Frankfurt to visit Goethe's mother and Bettina (with whom he had a sort of love affair, although he said later that she was always repulsive to him),[38] and at Weimar to pay his respects to Goethe.

Bernhardi heard nothing from his wife after she had left with their two sons in the autumn of 1804. But between then and 1806 she corresponded eagerly with A. W. Schlegel. He did all he could to incite her against her husband. When Bernhardi got wind of her whereabouts in Rome and wrote her a letter, Schlegel advised her not to reply but to employ dilatory tactics. He deemed it expedient for her to secure a false passport and thus evade Bernhardi.

Then, in September or October 1806, Sophie, anxious for a divorce, so that she could marry Knorring, brought formal charges against Bernhardi. She charged him with adultery and insufficient support and alleged that he had made false, slanderous statements about her. These accusations are reiterated in a letter (now in the Preussische Staatsbibliothek) which she wrote from Rome on October 29 to her brother Ludwig. Bernhardi retaliated with countercharges against her, to which she in turn replied. Early in 1807, it seems, the formal trial began before the Berlin Stadtgericht and proved very embarrassing to all concerned—so embarrassing to Tieck that as late as 1829 he asked Menzel whether the court records could not be destroyed. Bernhardi used as much of the above-described damaging evidence against her as he had been able to ascertain. Fichte, who with Wilhelm Schütz and Fouqué was on his side, appeared as an eyewitness of illicit relations between her and A. W. Schlegel. Schleiermacher, among others, sided with Sophie. Tieck played a despicable part in the proceedings. He turned completely against his old friend Bernhardi and gave testimony about him which, the latter subsequently remarked, was the best piece of fiction ever produced by his imagination. If we would trust Varnhagen, Tieck also tried to malign Bernhardi in the eyes of the latter's aged father.[39] A letter of the elder Bernhardi to Tieck of January 13, 1807, is preserved.

Interesting sidelights are cast upon the trial by the correspondence of Bernhardi and Varnhagen, found among the latter's papers. On December 14, 1806, Varnhagen warned Bernhardi that Sophie was slandering him in public and agreed that it would be prudent to try to persuade Tieck to effect a quiet settlement. At the same time, however, he confessed that neither he nor Tieck's intimate friends knew the whereabouts of Sophie and Ludwig, though suspecting that they were in Rome. (She was in Rome, he still in Munich). On December 28 Bernhardi informed Varnhagen that he had written to Tieck but received no reply; now he has sent another letter in care of Tieck's wife in Ziebingen. On January 12, 1807, Varnhagen, though regretting to lose Tieck as a friend, assured Bernhardi of his wholehearted support but was still unable to say where Sophie was hiding; he surmised that she might be in Coppet with A. W. Schlegel. Then, on February 2, Bernhardi reported that his case had been called but postponed because a voluminous affidavit, presented by Tieck in his sister's favor, required a new respite for its thorough study. It is a vile document, he added, which accuses him of issuing threats and a challenge to a duel against Knorring. In the light of all the facts, exclaimed Bernhardi, one cannot refrain from the solemn public declaration that the Tiecks, as well as Knorring and A. W. Schlegel who sided with them, are scoundrels (Schufte) devoid of honor (ehrlos). And on February 13 he wrote to Varnhagen that he was still waiting for "des ehrlosen Tiecks Antwort" to his conciliatory letter.[39]

Although Sophie was granted a divorce, the outcome of the suit constituted a victory for Bernhardi. Since she was now living with Knorring, Bernhardi was awarded the custody of the two children. In 1810, it seems, she married Knorring (by some this second marriage is dated earlier).

From 1807 on, after Tieck's return from Italy, his close collaborator in his Germanistic studies was von der Hagen.[40] Tieck prepared a clean copy of *König Rother* and sent it in instalments to von der Hagen. But in the end von der Hagen published his own modernized version, the original text of which he owed entirely to Tieck, in volume 1 of his *Deutsche Gedichte des Mittelalters* (1808), without even acknowledging Tieck's assistance. And yet Tieck's unpublished version of the poem, with all its weird errors, is superior to von der Hagen's cumbersome modernization, though Wilhelm Grimm and Brentano felt that he would have been more successful with a prosaic, instead of a poetical, reproduction.[41]

In the same way Tieck assisted von der Hagen with other medieval German poems. He helped prepare parts of the *Heldenbuch*, among them *Laurin* (*Kleiner Rosengarten*) and sections of the Dietrich saga, for the later volumes of von der Hagen's *Gedichte des Mittelalters*. Fragments of Tieck's versions of these and other poems are in the "Nachlass."

In his letters to von der Hagen he proved an acute critic of the old lays. He detected the identity of Rother and Osantrix and of Hake and Eckart; he held definite ideas about the age of *Iwein* and *König Rother*, calling them the oldest manuscripts he knew, and expressed his dislike for the *Wolfdietrich* lay because it is primarily a compilation. As an intuitive philologian Tieck, who as early as September 1802 wrote A. W. Schlegel a learned letter on the courtly Tristan poems,[42] was certainly far ahead of von der Hagen and his predecessors.

His treatment of Tieck in regard to *König Rother* was duplicated by von der Hagen in the case of the *Nibelungenlied*. Though Tieck gave him aid and called his attention to the St. Gall manuscript, he published samples of his version in 1805 and his complete edition in 1807 (which was materially a great success) without any reference to Tieck. The latter's friends, among them Rumohr and the Heidelberg Romanticists Brentano and Arnim, were quite angry over such seeming rudeness, but Tieck, though disappointed that von der Hagen had stolen his thunder and convinced that his own version, so far as finished, was better, bore him no grudge.

In fact, Tieck continued working upon his own edition even for a while after the appearance of von der Hagen's. About 1807 he started a third version. The "I. Buch in 5 Gesängen" and the first two cantos of a second book, carrying the story as far as the deliberations concerning Siegfried's death, are complete in the "Nachlass." In 1808 Arnim begged

Tieck for a sample of it for his *Zeitung für Einsiedler*, but in vain. Finally, in 1853, shortly after Tieck's death, von der Hagen honored the memory of his coworker by publishing one hundred nine strophes of his rendering in the *Neues Jahrbuch der Berlinischen Gesellschaft für deutsche Sprache*.

Tieck's work surpasses not only von der Hagen's stilted modernization, but also the version of Simrock, which has remained popular to this day. Tieck's superiority over Simrock is all the more surprising since the latter had the advantage of Lachmann's textual researches, while Tieck was forced to construct his own text. We have cause for regret that he did not find a worthy collaborator[43] and that his dilatoriness[44] as well as the excessive magnitude of his plan made it impossible for him to complete the work.[45] According to the draft in the "Nachlass,"[46] it was to consist of five books, each containing five cantos. Data in the "Nachlass" show, too, that in 1853, before von der Hagen published the fragment of Tieck's rendering, Köpke planned to insert it, together with a draft of the entire translation, in the *Nachgelassene Schriften*.[47]

When it became clear that Tieck would not enter into public competition with von der Hagen, his initiated contemporaries, at least, did not fail to give him due credit for his work. Arnim regretted that he abandoned his own version in favor of von der Hagen's,[48] and Wilhelm Grimm, in his review of the latter's work in the *Heidelberger Jahrbücher* (1809), made honorable mention of him,[49] writing to Arnim soon after: "The credit for having made the poem known again, I could not possibly ascribe to von der Hagen, since it belongs to Tieck, a fact which I have acknowledged."[50]

Tieck's views concerning the *Nibelungenlied*, best expressed in the preface to his *Minnelieder*, are interesting and reveal the influence of A. W. Schlegel's Berlin lectures. He dated its earliest parts "several hundred years" before the beginning of the fourteenth century and thought it would be "just as futile to inquire about a single author as it is in the case of the *Iliad* or *Odyssey*." This statement, written in 1803, sounds like Lachmann's findings thirteen years later in his important paper *Über die ursprüngliche Gestalt des Gedichtes von der Nibelunge Not*. Obviously Tieck anticipated Lachmann's theory of the individual lays. Perhaps this is explained by the fact that he, like Lachmann, had been a student of F. A. Wolf, who was the originator of this theory with respect to the Homeric poems. Tieck called the work a "true epic, a great phenomenon . . . a perfected poem of the greatest comprehensiveness." It is characterized by "pure sublimity."[51] Biographically his occupation with the great German epic is important as marking a step in his gradual deliverance from the crippling effect of mysticism upon his poetic vein.[52]

Nor did Tieck carry out his plan to publish *Parzival* and *Titurel* and to write a history of medieval German poetry against the broad historical background of the Middle Ages. The latter was really the ultimate objective of his painstaking Germanistic studies in Rome and during the decade which followed.[53] Notes for this work are preserved in the "Nachlass."[54]

As was often the case in his life, his Germanistic studies were profitable to Tieck in helping to win him back to poetry, and to others as well. But they were not carried to their natural fruition. He devoted years to the work, became in a sense a connoisseur (always remaining a dilettante, to be sure), but brought out only fragments and an occasional production. This phenomenon, illustrated also by the fate of his studies in Spanish and Elizabethan literatures, is to be explained in part by von der Hagen's untrustworthiness, but chiefly by Tieck's inability to concentrate. Despite this tragic futility, however, he must be rated both in his old German and Elizabethan studies as a forerunner of modern critical scholarship and as one of the pioneer appreciators of the perennial charm and beauty of these literatures.

Besides the *Reisegedichte eines Kranken* and *Rückkehr eines Genesenden*, the following original poetical works date from this period: a three-act farce, *Der neue Don Carlos* (1807), preserved among the posthumous papers;[55] an epilog to Holberg's *The Busy Man* (written in 1807 and published among the poems);[56] and a fragment of a play *Das Donauweib* (written in 1808 and published in Förster's *Sängerfahrt* in 1818).[57]

Das Donauweib was to be a reworking of the Viennese folk play *Das Donauweibchen*, or *Die Donau-Nixe*, which he had seen in 1801 in the Dresden summer theater.[58] The farce *Der neue Don Carlos* would be worth publishing because of its bright humor, clever situations and satire against the disparagement of the clown, the ignorance of audiences and officials, and the futile efforts of theatrical directors to educate them. Like his earliest comedies, it contains a measure of horseplay. A troup of actors comes to town, but the mayor refuses to permit them to practise their art, despite the manager's eloquent defense of the moral values inherent in the theater. When *Wilhelm Tell* is suggested, the stupid official replies that the play holds a brief for insubordination and rebellion. His strictures against other famous dramas are equally asinine. Finally the manager's coquettish wife prevails upon him to sanction a performance of *Don Carlos*. The result is an amusing improvised parody of Schiller, continually interrupted by the remarks of the inept audience and the replies of the actors. In the targets of its ridicule *Der neue Don*

Carlos has much in common with *Der gestiefelte Kater*. But it shows Tieck at a transitional stage. His setting and background are no longer those of the fairy tale; they are realistic. In this respect the work reveals his self-styled "new manner" (neue Manier),[59] which we shall see plainly manifested in later writings.

Tieck was not a so-called patriotic poet, who with lyre in hand aroused his compatriots to fierce savagery and fine frenzy. In 1804 he was not nearly as "patriotic" as Arnim.[60] A series of patriotic historical plays which he planned, according to a letter to Cotta of 1800[61] and one of 1813 to Solger,[62] remained a project, chiefly because of his *idée fixe* that the stage was degenerate since 1790 and not fit to write for. And yet he was proud to be a German and a descendant of those noble Teutons whose exploits are recounted in hero lore. Had he not spoken lovingly of the German Middle Ages, he exclaimed to Solger,[62] long before most Germans gave the fatherland a thought? Had he not told Solger that a poet must have a fatherland?[63] To Friedrich Schlegel he expressed the hope in March 1813 that Germany would soon be free.[64]

He disliked the French for their militarism.[65] But he realized that the Germans were not a nation and that they lacked national interests; they strove for particularism when they needed nationalism; never having enjoyed it, they had no appreciation of liberty. On the whole he tried to be optimistic even in the darkest Napoleonic days, believing that they might lead to an awakening of genuine patriotism. In the "novelle" *Der Geheimnisvolle*, written in 1821, he has the musician exclaim: "If a fresh spirit goes through all countries and destroys and unites what has never yet been united and has long not been separated, they may be roused from their sleep and deliberately do homage to a new force which seems destined to rule over Europe. Yes, they will be forced to rear in themselves a sublime European spirit in place of their small-town provincial stubbornness. How much will they gain, then, in return for the seeming loss of wretched shadows!"[66]

The Finckenstein family and their friends in Ziebingen shared his convictions. They aided the fatherland as best they could. Victims of Napoleonic persecution, like Reichardt, who with the aid of Count Schlabrendorf had published a pamphlet against the Corsican in 1804, were sheltered from the enemy.

Occasional trips from Ziebingen to Dresden or Berlin served to keep Tieck slightly in touch with the literary world and brought him new friends. In Dresden in 1806 he met the Danish poet Oehlenschläger, who became his admirer and later visited him three times. At Sandow, Burgsdorff's estate, he spent a day in 1807 with Arnim. He had met him in

1792 at Giebichenstein, seen him again in Dresden in 1801, and become intimate with him when Arnim and Brentano paid a long visit to Ziebingen in 1804.

In 1807 he also made the acquaintance of the Swiss historian Johannes von Müller; somewhat earlier he renewed that of the painter and critic of art Hartmann. The latter, who had settled in Dresden in 1803, was a friend of the great but unhappy and as yet unknown poet Heinrich von Kleist. Tieck himself met Kleist at Dresden in 1808 through Hartmann, and it was Hartmann who later gave him some of the manuscript material and also information utilized in Tieck's introduction to the *Hinterlassene Schriften* (1821) and the *Gesammelte Schriften* (1826) of Kleist. A letter from Tieck to Hartmann of 1816, in the possession of the present writer, indicates this.

Kleist impressed Tieck by his eccentricities and peculiarly abnormal mentality, but also by his geniality and affability. He did not fully realize his greatness, however. Kleist had just entered into collaboration with Adam Müller for the publication of the periodical *Phöbus*. In it he got out many of his prose works and fragments of *Penthesilea, Der zerbrochene Krug* and *Robert Guiscard*. He was working upon *Kätchen von Heilbronn*. During its composition Tieck gave Kleist advice and assistance with a view to rendering it more suitable for the stage. But Tieck's suggestions were not of a happy nature. Kleist had introduced a poetical scene, in which a malevolent water sprite at the behest of Kunigunde tries to entice Kätchen, who is walking along a cliff, into the water. Kätchen almost succumbs but is saved by her escort Eleonore. Tieck called Kleist's attention to the difficulties of presenting such a scene upon the stage, and Kleist, though usually impervious to suggestions, rashly destroyed the scene. This is to be regretted, for it would have helped to preserve more uniformly the naïve atmosphere of the fairy-tale setting. Kleist was soon sorry that he had made the concession to Tieck and admitted that he had paid too much attention to the advice of others. Tieck also realized his mistake when he subsequently read the play without the scene.[67]

Most important among Tieck's new associates was the Berlin philosopher and esthetician Karl W. F. Solger. He became his most intimate friend and remained so until his premature death in 1819. They met in 1808 at von der Hagen's house in Berlin; late in 1810 and early in 1811 they exchanged visits in Frankfurt and Ziebingen, respectively. They became closely associated in 1811 after a stay in Warmbrunn in Silesia.

In 1808 Tieck's sister and Knorring stopped at Vienna, where the latter had relatives. In a letter from there of May 31 (Preussische Staatsbibliothek) Sophie implored her brother to come and live with them for a while, so as to prevent the gossips from spreading rumors of a complete break between brother and sister. Though disgusted by his sister's conduct, Tieck reluctantly complied. He spent the summer in the Austrian capital. Here he found Friedrich Schlegel, now a convert of the Mother Church, who was much disappointed to discover that he had not changed his point of view.[68] In Vienna it was planned to make Tieck one of the directors of the famous Burgtheater. But he, who had failed to secure a similar position at Frankfurt in 1801, when he might have accepted it, remained skeptical, and with good reason. No definite offer was tendered to him, due to Iffland's apathy. In October he repaired to Munich, where similar negotiations were started, without his taking the initiative. They also led to no practical results. In Munich he found Caroline, August Wilhelm's former wife, now married to Schelling. They were of the opinion that Tieck had become more dignified. Schelling found him pleasant and lovable and enjoyed his readings.[69] Caroline hoped he would stay in Munich; she was also delighted with his readings.[70] But irretrievably prejudiced against him, she still maintained, as she had ten years before, that he was "a pleasant and worthy scamp," and a "stowaway on life's journey."[71]

In Munich, where he had been ill in 1804-1805, he was now attacked a second time by his old ailment, but even more viciously than before. He became practically paralyzed. In 1809 his condition grew worse, and for months it seemed as though he would never be able to walk again without crutches.[72] Not until late in 1810 could he return to Ziebingen, stopping en route at Heidelberg in September. As a result, his erect, elastic figure was bent and distorted for life, and only his noble, attractive head still showed signs of stateliness.

Later he attributed his trouble in Munich to the climate. To some extent, no doubt, he was correct. But contributory factors may have been his poor physical condition, dissipation and overindulgence.

His fame as a poet caused a circle of distinguished and beautiful women to pay visits to his bedside. One of his nurses was spry, vivacious Bettina Brentano. In a letter to Goethe of January 1809, she reported that "der arme reiche Tieck," despite unbearable pain, was wont to exercise his palsied hand by writing poems, especially songs of springtime. One of these, "An Fanny," is published among his *Gedichte*.[73] Bettina's letters to Arnim contain a detailed account of his unhappy plight.

His physical ailment was aggravated by mental sufferings. He was estranged from his wife (a Catholic convert since 1805), whom he had left in Ziebingen and did not even inform of his illness; for a while he contemplated divorce and eventually a second marriage with a Munich girl.[74] There is no proof, however, for the rumor noised about by Caroline and later repeated by Hebbel and Wilhelm von Chézy, that Amalie was unfaithful to her husband and in his absence lived with Burgsdorff.[75]

Knorring, who practically supported Tieck and his sister, was kept in Vienna, chiefly by financial difficulties. Sophie, who was with Ludwig in Munich, where she was described by Caroline as faithless and vicious,[76] caused Ludwig much concern. Contrary to the terms of the divorce decree, she had retained the custody of her two sons. According to her letter to Ludwig of May 31, 1808, Bernhardi had made an effort to wrest them from her early that year in Vienna. Now, in 1809, her former husband appeared one day in Munich with the police to take them away by force. Tieck, who secretly sympathized with Bernhardi but was forced to side with Sophie, had difficulty in smoothing matters over and in persuading Bernhardi to allow her to keep Felix Theodor, the younger boy.[77] The latter, who bore a striking resemblance to his mother, was brought up in practical ignorance of Bernhardi's existence.[78]

Tieck's ever-present financial difficulties were acute in Munich. He lived in an almost criminally careless manner, borrowing freely but rarely squaring an account.[79] Finally he was compelled to take up a loan of one thousand florins on Savigny's signature. He never repaid the debt —a sin of omission which Savigny, who had been his friend and admirer, could not forgive him.[80] He who had once praised the *Volksmährchen*, now found that Tieck's writings were too refined and that he had "etwas erstaunlich Totes in sich, persönlich wie in seinen Schriften."[81]

One important acquaintance of his second stay in Munich should not be overlooked. Friedrich Heinrich Jacobi, an able man of affairs, philosopher and creative writer, who had enjoyed the friendship of Wieland and Goethe, had become professor of philosophy in the Munich Academy of Sciences in 1804, and in 1807 was made president of that body. Tieck met him in 1808 and discovered in him a kindred soul and a perfect exemplar of "purest humanity."[82] Bettina reported that Tieck spent whole days at his home.[83] Jacobi attempted to communicate the spirit of his own philosophy to him and introduced him to the thought of Hamann. The pleasant impressions left by their associations were never blotted from Tieck's mind. On October 28, 1818, he wrote to the publisher Perthes: "When I lay ill at Munich in 1809-1810 I saw a great deal of your friend, glorious Jacobi, to me one of the most delightful and perhaps the purest and noblest phenomenon of mankind; his acquaintance, especially through his existence as a man . . . has really been epochal in my life."[82]

As these lines indicate, his enthusiasm for Jacobi was due more to the latter's personal charm than to his philosophy, although we surmise that he was more amenable to the mystic "Gefühlsphilosophie" of a Hamann and a Jacobi than to the transcendental idealism of the Romantic philosophers. As he later confessed, his conversations with Jacobi reminded him of two men speaking from opposite sides of a chasm, where the speakers hear an echo rather than their own words.[84] The reason must be that Tieck was not yet ready for systematic philosophy in any form. Only Solger's esthetics, which were soon to dawn upon him, made philosophical thinking more palatable to him.

CHAPTER ELEVEN

1811 TO 1817

DESPITE handicaps which confronted him, Tieck's appetite for literary work, though not for creative production, continued unappeased. After his trying experiences in Munich he went to Baden-Baden, where he found the baths beneficial. Then he returned to Ziebingen, and soon after, in 1811, his *Alt-Englisches Theater oder Supplemente zum Shakespeare* appeared in two volumes.

A. W. Schlegel had published seventeen genuine Shakespearean plays in his famous translation between 1797 and 1809. Tieck supported this undertaking in every way; indeed, the first two acts of *Love's Labour's Lost*, done about 1800, were based upon the work of Tieck himself.[1] In 1801, when Schlegel had a dispute with his publisher Unger, Tieck tried to help him find a new publisher. And in 1806, after Schlegel had apparently abandoned the project, he proposed to Unger's wife a continuation of his own.[2]

We know that Schlegel planned to include the so-called spurious plays, missing in the original folio editions. As early as January 7, 1800, he wrote to Goethe: "*Cromwell* and *Oldcastle* are indisputably from his maturest period and belong, it seems to me, among Shakespeare's most excellent plays. When you get to read them you will be surprised at the English blindness."[3] Tieck shared this opinion, and at the same time regarded these older dramas of paramount importance because they throw light upon the author's development. In 1802 Friedrich Schlegel recommended that Tieck translate *Pericles* and *The Pinner of Wakefield*.[4] Since A. W. Schlegel had meanwhile lost interest not only in the spurious plays but in his translation of Shakespeare generally, Tieck now decided to take a more active hand.

Volume 1 of *Alt-Englisches Theater* contains, in German translation, *King John*, *The Pinner of Wakefield* and *Pericles*; volume 2, *Locrine*, *The Merry Devil of Edmonton* and the old *King Leir*. Most of the translating was performed by himself, a part of *Locrine*, however, by some unidentified friend. On the whole the renderings are very good for one who lacked Herder's uncanny power of sensing the spirit of another language and A. W. Schlegel's taste and scholarship. We may say that they are the best poetical translations from the English which he had made up to that time, better than his unfinished rendering of *The Tempest* of 1793. Indeed, they are the best he ever did. Here he is usually faithful to the original and often reveals resourcefulness and skill. Errors are not frequent.

In a long letter Jakob Grimm sent Tieck considerable material for his two prefaces.[5] These have been reprinted in *Kritische Schriften I* and are significant because they openly express his favorite theory of Shakespeare's protean versatility, and his consequent belief in the Shakespearean authorship of the doubtful plays. Every one of them, he averred, is by Shakespeare himself. He always adhered to this fatuous notion. In a letter to Raumer of 1821[6] he incorporated a chronological catalog of Shakespeare's plays; it includes no less than sixty-two titles!

The real value of *Alt-Englisches Theater*, on the other hand, lies in the fact that it afforded German readers their first introduction to pre-Shakespearean drama. Although of course he impaired its effect, and revealed an astounding ignorance of Shakespeare's poetic personality, by blindly assigning these six inferior plays to him, yet it enabled more level-headed Germans not only to judge their nature, but also, by comparison, to form conclusions on Shakespeare's preeminent position as an Elizabethan. Two later collections, *Shakespeares Vorschule* (1823 and 1829) and *Vier Schauspiele von Shakespeare* (1836), are continuations of *Alt-Englisches Theater* and will be discussed in a subsequent chapter.

Another draft of *Das Buch über Shakespeare*, the fourth, was written about the same time. It covers only three pages and is superscribed "Plan des Ganzen." A perusal of it reveals how comprehensive he planned to make the work. In chapter 9 we have mentioned this as a reason why it was never finished. He conceived three gigantic sections, each of which might have comprised several volumes and would have amounted to a general history of western Europe, as well as a history of comparative literature from about 1300 to Shakespeare's death. A few sentences will make this clear: "In the first section, as an introduction, there is to be a discussion of the spirit of the Middle Ages, of the great phenomena of their literature and poetry, of the decay of those times and its causes. What a turn history and with it art then took. Boccaccio in Italy, Chaucer and Gower in England at the borderline of the greatest epoch. In England at this time a newly flowering hero-age and chivalry, but without particular influence upon poetry, an Indian summer, as it were. The flaring up of an heroic spirit under Henry V; then the preparation for the civil wars, while the Reformation is being prepared in Germany. Influence of this transformation, which in some countries directly penetrates every phase of life. Destruction of almost all poetry."[7]

The fifth and last draft of *Das Buch über Shakespeare* (1815), which presents two introductory chapters, regards Shakespeare as marking

the consummation and turning point of poesy in its historical development, and in attempting to study the unfolding of Shakespeare's peculiar
genius.

References to *Das Buch über Shakespeare* pervade his works almost to
the end of his life, but after 1820 the prospects of its completion dwindled.
He does not seem to have written a line of it after 1815. As a result he
and his project became the butt of ridicule. He went to England in 1817
to gather material in the British Museum for the completion of the work.
He read and studied numerous Elizabethan plays and had many copied.
But instead of using the new material for the given purpose, he allowed
himself to be diverted, publishing the two volumes of the *Vorschule* and
wasting much of his thunder in the two introductions. Then, far from
realizing the seriousness of this blunder, he took up a score of other still
more extraneous projects and duties. The external reason for this fiasco
was his constant and desperate need of funds. The internal reasons have
been previously suggested: lack of concentration and excessive magnitude of his plans. Yet it is misleading to say that the gist of what would
have become the *Buch über Shakespeare* has been lost. With the help of
the material published by Lüdeke from the "Nachlass," the *Briefe über
Shakespeare*, the prefaces to *Alt-Englisches Theater* and (later) *Shakespeares Vorschule*, his notes to the Schlegel-Tieck translations, the
"novelle" *Dichterleben* and occasional remarks, we can form a pretty
clear picture of his *magnum opus*. In fact, he himself, alluding to his
Buch über Shakespeare, stated in the preface to volume 1 of *Shakespeares
Vorschule* (1823) that many of the views to be expressed in that place
have become common property because he never concealed them in conversation.[8]

The probable significance of his contribution is discussed by Lüdeke:
"Tieck's work, had it appeared, would doubtless have been epoch-making.
To be sure, very much of Tieck's learned work would not have withstood
the onslaught of advancing research. His pet ideas would too readily have
fallen prey to criticism. But the grandiose conception of the whole, the
assignment of Shakespeare to his place in the proud history of European
thought, the combination of rich knowledge and lively imagination which
Tieck commanded for the revivification of Shakespeare's world, the
delicate feeling for the psychic impulses of another, which is the poet's
endowment, and his actor's blood, which he shared with Shakespeare,
might have given the work a peculiar charm and value which no
biography of Shakespeare has ever attained. Even though unsatisfactory
from a scholarly point of view, it would have been a great achievement

by virtue of its intention, and as such would not have failed to accomplish its purpose."[9]

His principal weakness as a student of Shakespeare was his uncritical predilection for the doubtful plays. This led him to fantastic conjectures, which have often been the subject of caustic comment. The American scholar George Ticknor, who met him late in 1835, writes: "Many of his notions are very bold; as for instance that the 'Fair Em' is by Shakespeare. He told me today that he thinks Milton superintended the edition of Shakespeare to which his sonnet is prefixed, because the changes and emendations made in it, upon the first folio, are poetical and plainly made by a poet.* It would be a beautiful circumstance if it could be proved true."[10] On the other hand, his greatest strength lay in his method, which considered Shakespeare in the light of evolutionary history.

We have called attention to his failure to concentrate, which led to project after project and torso after torso. Improviser that he was, he could work best at top speed. But he was not lazy even when the muses failed to smile upon him. A fragment of a diary written in 1815—not a creative period in his life—, which is preserved in the "Nachlass,"[11] gives evidence of this. Though it reveals expressions like "not in the mood" and "ill and out of sorts," and once, on his birthday, "I was melancholy, as always on this day," it contains a series of working schedules which map out tasks beginning at five or six in the morning and ending at ten or eleven at night.

In the previous chapter we noted how he made the acquaintance of "Maler" Müller in Rome and became interested in his works. During the summer of 1803 he had met in Erlangen J. P. Le Pique, a Protestant clergyman, who was proud of Müller as a compatriot of the Palatinate.[12] Soon after Tieck's return from Italy Le Pique and he decided to act as coeditors of Müller's writings. In Mannheim they sorted the Müller papers and negotiated with a publisher. Tieck then dismissed the matter from his mind, leaving it to Le Pique and to a certain Friedrich Batt. But Le Pique encountered difficulties with both Müller and the publisher, so that the project was deferred. Finally, in 1811, he induced another publisher to get out the edition, in three volumes, but without mention of Tieck as one of the editors.

This edition is comparable in importance to the Schlegel-Tieck edition of Novalis. Prior to it only fragments of Müller's *Genoveva* drama had been published in the *Zeitung für Einsiedler* (1808), and many of his poems were totally unknown. To be sure, the Tieck-Le Pique collection

---

*Tieck reiterated this theory in a note on the title page of his copy of the 1632 folio, now in the British Museum.

is not complete, and, besides, Müller was then still living and writing. Therefore Hans Graf Yorck could call his edition of Müller's *Gedichte* (1873) "eine Nachlese." But even today no definitive edition of Müller exists; the eclectic collection of *Lyrische Gedichte* by O. Kohl (1905) and K. Freye's selections in *Sturm und Drang* (1911) have only the advantage of modernity over the work of their predecessors.

A position midway between esthetic contemplation and untrammelled poetic creation must be assigned to a work which Tieck conceived in 1800, but which did not begin to appear until 1812. He called it *Phantasus* (a title already used for a poem in *Sternbald*), *eine Sammlung von Mährchen, Erzählungen, Schauspielen und Novellen* (in three volumes, 1812-1816). It has probably brought him more fame than any other single work. As early as 1800 he spoke of it as having been begun, and in 1802 Friedrich Schlegel mentioned an undertaking of this sort.[13] *Phantasus* was originally to be named *Volksmärchen* or *Die Gartenwochen* (the latter designation according to an unfinished work of Cervantes). Anticipated by Arnim's *Wintergarten* (1809), it is a series of stories within a story, like the Catalonian animal epic, the heroic epic of Firdusi and above all the novels of three Italian writers, Straparola, Basile and Boccaccio. From the two last-mentioned he borrowed the literary device of stringing a series of works, some new, some old, like beads upon a necklace, thus forming an artistic unity of an otherwise incongruous conglomeration. Just as the *Pentamerone* of Basile contains fifty tales, so Tieck originally planned to have the same number.[14]

As in the *Decameron* a group of cultured men and women are pictured gathering for the sake of informal intellectual intercourse and exchange of stories, experiences and opinions. They are seven in number and, as he later wrote,[14] were meant to represent different moods of the author. Manfred was to be the humorist, Friedrich the enthusiast, Lothar the lover of the theater, and so on. Each was to take the floor seven times. Tieck was Germany's first cosmopolitan poet and advocate of polite society. Here his ideal of social culture, enriched by what he had learned in the best circles of Berlin, Jena and Dresden, and fortified by his association with the refined Finckensteins[15] and their coterie in Ziebingen, found its embodiment. The artistic enjoyment afforded by the interlarded poetical works and by the long conversations in which they are enframed becomes a new comprehensive form of *savoir vivre*. In his desire to hide his subjectivism behind a veil of objectiveness, the German poet of urbanity devised this mold for his own peculiar requirements. While Boccaccio has only brief transitional passages between his tales, Tieck wrote lengthy conversations, some of fifty pages and more.

The result is that the string is oftentimes more important and occasionally more valuable than the beads themselves. All the characters talk like professors of literature or of history; sometimes they prove skilled orators. They speak discursively and with a prolixity which too often grows tiresome. Through these conversations a sort of thin plot runs, although action is lacking. For a while he planned to place more emphasis upon this plot.[14] Because the characters are brought into various relations to each other, more than on account of their colloquies and readings, they become mildly interesting. Yet the chief activity of the seven men and women besides talk, is to take an occasional meal.

Various factors show that we are here dealing with Tieck's later "novellen" style, his "new manner." The conversational atmosphere predominates; the characters are all members of the higher class; and the interest is centered upon discussion of a multitude of problems. Referring to the multifariousness of the work, Wilhelm Grimm compared it with a well furnished house, praising its graceful sociability but wondering whether its excessive cleverness might not have a bad effect.[16] Tieck's earlier nature demonism and supernaturalism bid fair to give way to an interest in real problems of history and of the here and now. The favorite subjects for discussion are Elizabethan and Spanish literatures, especially Shakespeare and Calderon, early German poetry, the natural scenic beauties of Germany and problems of histrionics. Much of the material is of an autobiographic nature; as he wrote to his brother, he inserted many jests and anecdotes with which he had often entertained him and Sophie.[17] Although a great deal of the talk is gossipy, it is sagaciously put. Moreover, his histrionic nature, his delight in imagining himself in the rôle of another, comes out very markedly.

His method of introducing new topics of conversation and of making the transition from conversation to the interspersed poetical works is simple enough. For example, some one chances to mention Gozzi. Another speaker wants to know whether any German has ever imitated him. "I have," says Lothar, whereupon he reads *Blaubart*. A debate on the work follows. From this develops a discussion of why dramas are customarily divided into five acts. Shakespeare offers illustrations, and so on seemingly *ad infinitum*. A certain "Romantic Irony," here manifested as aloofness on the part of the poet toward his own work, to which many of the inserted writings are subjected, is apparent in the critical discussion. His attitude is always critical, sometimes even censorious. He wanted to indicate thereby that he had outgrown his works of from ten to fifteen years ago, which were, in part, here republished.

His predilection for this type of presentation was natural. In Ziebingen, where *Phantasus* was written, he cultivated the habit of reading aloud to an assembled audience from his own or others' works, a habit which he had formed in Jena and was to continue for the rest of his life.

The language of some of the conversations in *Phantasus* is unmatched for nobility of diction and beauty of style. As Jean Paul rightly said, Tieck's prose is more poetic than his poetry. Several of the passages would deserve quotation at length. But it must suffice to call attention to a few of the finest. We refer to the passage in which Germany is described as seen by a poet (*Schriften* 4, 14-16); the one which compares dinner to a dramatic poem (4, 58-71); and the one in which Goethe, Schiller, Shakespeare and other great poets are toasted (4, 87-89). Some of these apostrophes became famous in their day. In her *Fragments from German Prose Writers* (1841) Mrs. Sarah Austin presented seven of the best to English readers. They have not lost their appeal and still deserve to be read.

The long but charming poem which introduces *Phantasus* and bears the identical title (Arnim unjustly called it a jingle of words)[18] is important because it reveals his frame of mind from about 1802 until he executed the work. It represents a poet who is sick, dejected and moodily meditative. Suddenly a miraculous youth bedecked with flowers appears to him and urges him to cease brooding and come out to enjoy the glorious springtime. The poet asks him who he is and why he appears in such outlandish, old-fashioned trappings. He introduces himself as the poet's erstwhile friend, Phantasus. The poet confesses that he has drifted far away from his old moorings, has toyed with stern reason, history and philosophy, and has tried to understand plants, rocks and metals. But all these lucubrations, he sadly confesses, were in vain; they have served only to bring melancholy; perhaps the absence of his old crony Phantasus was to blame. Now the youth takes him out among the trees and flowers, and soon the poet is once more under nature's spell. In a grotto he discovers Horror (der Schreck) entertaining Simplicity (die Albernheit) with delightfully terrifying tales of fairyland. He sees also Jest (der Scherz),[19] who at first sports about as a gnome and then suddenly waxes large and forbidding. He meets Love and is finally enthralled by the great god Pan, the demonic incarnation of nature, in whom Tieck has pictured the essence of his living natural philosophy and demonization of nature.

We can, then, descry the intention of forty-year-old Tieck. He regretted that the trials and tribulations of life had all but robbed him of his poetic vein. Now (under the influence of Solger) he would live his youth, and all its predilections and literary associations, over again, but with more wisdom, moderation and concentration. Now that he had achieved mastery over them, he would delight reminiscently in the joys which had been his when he was twenty-five. For this reason, probably, Friedrich Schlegel applauded the work,[20] although his views on literature had meanwhile drifted far away from Tieck's.

The beads which we find on the conversational string are of varying splendor and size. All in all thirteen works are scattered throughout the three volumes of the original edition. Eight of these are old acquaintances, only changed here and there. These are the three tales *Der blonde Eckbert*, *Der getreue Eckart und der Tannenhäuser*, and *Der Runenberg;* Tieck's version of the chapbook *Wundersame Liebesgeschichte der schönen Magelone;* and the four dramatized fairy-tale satires *Ritter Blaubart*, *Der gestiefelte Kater*, *Die verkehrte Welt* and *Leben und Tod des kleinen Rotkäppchens*. Upon their appearance in this form the Grimms felt that they were already outmoded and devoid of live interest.[21] Of the five new works two are dramas and three tales. The tales, which are all products of 1811, possess intrinsic value. They are original stories and belong to the Eckbert type.

In *Die Elfen*, characterized by unusually rich, delicate and independent invention, we see the brighter, lovelier aspects of that popular belief in natural philosophy which had taken on a gruesome mask in *Der blonde Eckbert* and *Der Runenberg*. The child Marie lives with her parents in a lovely village unusually blessed by bounteous nature. But nearby is a dark, forbidding fir forest, in which a poor tribe seems to exist in abject misery. No one dares approach the place. One day Marie, running a race with Andres, a neighbor's boy, enters the forbidden forest and to her surprise finds herself in a beautiful, supernatural world. A lovely radiant girl, Zerina, accosts her and invites her to stay; this invitation is repeated by a stately woman dressed all in gold, who adds, however, that Marie may remain only for a while. Marie and Zerina play with gleaming pollen, which makes vegetation blossom forth more luxuriantly; they rise aloft into the clouds and alight gently; they admire the beauteous palace; meet a gruff dwarf who is prince of metals; explore a wonderful pond which irrigates the lands of men; and inspect the hall of fire. Marie, who never tires amid all the wonders of this timeless realm, finally learns that she is among the elves. But when their king comes to pay them a long visit, she is told that she must return to her mortal abode, being forbidden, however, to reveal to any mortal where she has been.

Sadly she goes, thinking she has been absent from home but a brief time. But to her surprise she discovers much at home changed, for she has been away for seven years. Everyone finds her bewitchingly beautiful and decorous, though she refuses to divulge her whereabouts and experiences during her absence. Meanwhile vegetation in the village grows richer than ever. After some months Marie marries her old playmate Andres. Their daughter, whom she names Elfriede in memory of her secretly beloved elves, proves remarkably precocious. One day Marie discovers that Elfriede communes secretly with Zerina, who has given her an elfin's coin and a miraculous rose, which blooms until winter. Zerina notices to her discomfort that Marie is aware of her association with Elfriede, but she continues it, having taken a fancy to the child. Then Marie has a quarrel with her husband about the dwellers in the fir woods, whom he calls ragamuffins and thieves. Carried away by her zeal to prove that they are not unworthy, she takes him to Zerina's and Elfriede's secret tryst. Zerina immediately bids the little mortal playmate a sad farewell and flies off as an ugly crow. She has been defiled, for Andres, an uninitiated mortal, has laid eyes upon her. Terrible portents are witnessed in the village. Though the sun shines, there is darkness. Trees and plants perish and misery prevails. In the night the elves migrate from their forest abode; with their departure all the mortals of the village are enveloped in inexplicable gloom. Elfriede, and soon after her Marie, waste away and die.

This simple, ethereal tale, woven of a poet's dreams and of the purest gossamer, is as fine and mature a piece of work as Tieck ever did. It belongs to the first category of Romantic fairy tale, as described above in our discussion of *Der blonde Eckbert*, and is on the same level as the *Volksmärchen* of Musäus. But dissecting it seems like brushing the dust from the wings of a butterfly. He has here enriched the mythology of elementary spirits, gnomes and sylphs, as developed by Herder, Wieland, Zachariä, Goethe and Matthisson, with ideas of Böhme and with Otmar's popular tales of dwarfs and nixes. Old legends of the association of delicate supernatural beings, dwarfs and goblins with innocent mortals, the mysterious blessing which these spirits radiate on human beings and nature alike, the ingratitude of men and their consequent punishment, attended by the migration of the elfish creatures, have been combined into an harmonious work of art irresistible in its charm. From it seems to emanate the expression of a practical natural philosophy, of a mystic attitude toward nature.[22] We are reminded of the introductory poem *Phantasus*, where in the end Pan is discovered to be the incarnation of grotto, woods, field and valley. Nature is again demonized, much more tangibly than in his earlier tales; we may say that it has been "elfinized." And the moods of men are finely attuned to those of nature. But horror has yielded to sad resignation. The magic nature-atmosphere of *Der blonde Eckbert* has disappeared. Nature is no longer a chaos, an invisible foe of man, but an allegorical miracle. Uhland's *Traum* and Hoffmann's *Das fremde Kind* seem under the influence of Tieck's story. No less than four renderings of *Die Elfen* have been made; that of Carlyle (1827) is excellent.[23]

The second tale, *Der Pokal*, grew out of a trivial experience which Tieck had in Florence, when he helped a girl up who had stumbled on the steps of a church, and out of an unhappy love affair of "Maler" Müller which had become a source of gossip. It tells of Ferdinand, who spies a lovely girl ascending the church steps to attend mass. She sees him, too, and stumbles and is helped to her feet by him. They conceive a secret love for one another; he resolves to remain in the town, though only a visitor. But while she is rich and a native and betrothed to another, he is poor and a stranger. One day Albert, an old friend, agrees to tell Ferdinand's fortune with a marvellous golden goblet. Out of it the image of the girl he loves is conjured up, but Ferdinand impetuously breaks the spell by kissing her and thus ruins his happiness, as it turns out. Soon after she leaves for a visit to distant friends. He waves her a stealthy farewell, while she drops him a rose.

Then years pass. A wedding is being celebrated. At the last moment the bridegroom announces another guest, an old recluse. The latter is deeply moved at the sight of the bride, and remembers every nook and corner of the house, which he says once belonged to a friend named Albert, now dead. Of course the recluse is Ferdinand. He is surprised also to find Albert's wonderful goblet there. It turns out that the bride is a daughter of Ferdinand's erstwhile sweetheart. Her mother, now a matron of sixty and a widow, whose husband had bought the house from Albert, recognizes Ferdinand. They exchange experiences and soon realize that they have been kept apart by an inexorable fate, a sort of curse brought down upon them by Ferdinand's impetuous conduct and lack of self-control at the time Albert conjured up her spirit in the goblet.

With its strange blending of real and fantastic elements, this tale bears a close resemblance to the spook stories of Tieck's later years, *Pietro von Abano* (1824), *Die Klausenburg* (1836) and *Der Schutzgeist* (1839). A prepossession for the divine service of the Catholic Church is also apparent, as is that fatalism which we have had frequent occasion to notice in Tieck. Crystal-gazing, too, plays an important part.[24] The narrative is well handled. Only now and then the motivation, even of the realistic portions, seems a bit awkward, improbable and artificial. Carlyle translated the work into English in 1827, Hare and Froude in 1845. Both

Die Elfen and *Der Pokal* are translated by Albert Béguin in the recent French collection *La coupe d'or* (1933).

The third new tale in *Phantasus* is *Liebeszauber*. As an attempt to present an utterly weird, horrible action in a modern, realistic setting, it is a bold venture. Emil is quiet, melancholy and pensive, while his friend Roderich is boisterous, fickle and bent upon enjoyment. Though they are continually at odds (much like Tieck and Burgsdorff), yet the friendship of these opposite types is steadfast. Roderich hurries off to a masquerade; Emil follows later but stays only a short while. On the way he sees an exceedingly ugly hag clad in a bright red bodice with gold fringes, a yellow hood and a green dress, receiving two candles from some suspicious-looking men. In the house opposite Emil's and Roderich's rooms there lives a beautiful girl with whom Emil is secretly in love. Though he has greeted her on occasion and she has shown no disinclination toward him, he has never ventured to cultivate her closer acquaintance. She lives with an adopted orphan girl. Upon returning to his room Emil is surprised to see the hag and the two candles at the window of the girl's apartment. The girl, too, appears at the window; she seizes the orphan by the hair and despite the child's entreaties allows the hag to cut its throat. Behind them a dragon thrusts forth its tongue and laps up the child's blood. Its fiendish green eyes glance over to Emil and he collapses.

Just as in *Der Pokal*, there is a break at this high point. Then to our surprise we find Emil and the same girl celebrating their wedding. But we learn that meanwhile Emil has passed through a terrible ordeal. At first he had been completely deranged; now his memory is still deficient, for he can recall only his childhood and early youth. The very first time he was able to go out after his dreadful experience, he spied the girl of his love. Dashing out of the carriage to accost her, he wooed and won her. Wealthy as he was, he bought a beautiful house, in which the wedding feast is now to take place. Yet he is far from happy; he seems tired of life and tortured by a feeling of his own unworthiness. The fact that the bride appears pale and serious is explained by Roderich to another guest in the following way. He says that an orphan child whom she had adopted had been kidnaped some time ago. Emil's moroseness is meanwhile heightened by his discovery among the servants of a very ugly hag, who seems vaguely familiar to him. While the bride retires to her room to dress for the dance, Roderich and the other guests mask in very fantastic fashion. Roderich himself has procured a hag's costume —a bright red bodice with gold fringes, a yellow hood and a green dress, with an appropriate mask. Donning the costume in jest, he enters the room in which bride and groom are preparing for the dance. Emil sees him, and the identity of Roderich's costume with that worn by the hag on the night of the murder awakens his power of memory. He becomes a veritable madman, attacks his bride with a dagger to avenge her murderous deed, and kills her. A tussle with the hag ensues, and both she and Emil fall over the railing of the stairway, fatally wounded. Dying, the hag confesses her part in the murder of the orphan.

Both *Der Pokal* and *Liebeszauber* (criticized by Arnim as too artificial)[25] are spooky and morbid, but the former ranks as a superior work of art. Although the blending of dreams and of magic with events of daily life strikes the reader as curious even in *Der Pokal*, yet the miraculous element is there depicted so delicately, enveloped in so poetic a haze, and combined so well with human sentiments that we are not unwilling to let the poet transport us for a while into this eerie realm. In *Liebeszauber*, on the other hand, with which E. T. A. Hoffmann's *Sandmann* (1817) seems to have kinship, the effects are far too crass to leave a favorable impression. There is no attempt to motivate the murder of the orphan. Real events and hallucinations (such as the dragon) are not distinguished. Improbable coincidences (we recall Roderich's possession of the hag's costume) are treated, in truly fatalistic fashion, as natural. Partial loss of memory and similar curious quirks of the mind become essential factors in motivation. In the earlier tales, as *Der blonde Eckbert* and particularly the second part of *Der getreue Eckart und der Tannenhäuser*, similar peculiarities were noted. There, as in most of the dramatized fairy tales, it was also impossible to distinguish between the real world and the realm of make-believe. But the real world was so subdued and vague that the dualism did not disturb us. In *Liebeszauber*, however, with its contemporaneous and earthly setting, such dualistic treatment cannot but be disconcerting. The total absence of supernatural characters in these two new tales is an additional indication of Tieck's turn toward realism. We may call it poetic realism, a fantastic mélange of everyday happenings and fairy-like events.

We have referred to Tieck's "Romantic Irony" in the conversations. An excellent illustration is given when he has Clara, one of the conversational characters, remark in the talk which ensues after *Liebeszauber*: "These stories penetrate one's marrow and bone too incisively, and in sheer horror I vainly seek refuge in my thoughts. It is positively abominable to invent such things. I tremble and fear and surmise that from every bush, every arbor a monster may accost me and that the dearest, most familiar forms may suddenly be transmuted into strange ghastly creatures."[26] But to his brother Tieck expressed his satisfaction with these three stories. He was particularly fond of *Der Pokal* and *Liebes-*

zauber, feeling that he had here accomplished an important feat—"viel in unsrer Sprache geleistet."[17]

It is clear, then, that in 1811 Tieck did not quite relinquish the attainments of Romanticism. He upheld his close relationship to transcendentalism and reiterated the poet's right to let his imagination roam in the realm of dreams and miracles. This was natural, since magnetism (particularly such animal magnetism as he was thinking of in *Liebeszauber*), visions and specters had gained extreme popular interest. Favorite writers like E. T. A. Hoffmann, who in the preface to the *Serapionsbrüder,* 1819-1821, called Tieck "the accomplished master," delighted in introducing these elements in the midst of a realistic setting.

But Tieck claimed that his three tales, particularly the last two, are written in a "new manner." It combines the narrative form adopted by Goethe from the great Italian novelists and the content of the philosophical and artistic views held by the Romantics. In his new style as in his old, Tieck is an irrationalist usually interested in some form of psychic disturbance, which is developed to a climax. But while the old manner practically banished realism and emphasized the demonic forces of nature, the "new manner" deals with the realistic world but introduces diablerie and demonic elements into it.

The three-act fairy-tale drama on the theme of Tom Thumb, *Leben und Tod des kleinen Thomas, genannt Däumchen*[27] (again based upon Perrault), 1811, approaches *Der gestiefelte Kater* and its progeny in form but belongs in content and spirit to the *Rotkäppchen* type of fairy-tale reproduction. While the earlier plays ridiculed the Enlightenment, which was dead, even in Berlin, and glorified the naïve poetry of fairyland, *Däumchen* has a different, though equally satiric purpose. It is written in a style suggesting that of an ancient Greek drama and means to make sport of those who would transplant the spirit and the fatalistic ideas of Greek tragedy to the contemporary German stage. The humor of the scenes between the sentimental Hofrat Semmelziege and his gentle but practical wife Ida is bold. They and the mushroom-gathering philosopher Alfred serve to introduce various realistic touches. Tieck's wit wins the day when he throws the mantle of antiquity over all the well known paraphernalia of the German fairy-tale world. The effect is ludicrous when Tom steals Leidgast's Seven League Boots and the latter descants in iambic trimeters on his loss.

What justification he had for such badinage was presently shown when the so-called fate tragedy, a decadent offspring of Romanticism, bade fair to monopolize the German stage. Later he admitted to his brother[17] that of all his works of this type this is the only one which was done "rather hastily" (etwas übereilt). To Solger he confessed that it has "too much symmetry and too little harmony."[28] Solger, too, was dissatisfied with it.[29] Wilhelm Grimm called it Tieck's poorest work.[30] More enjoyable are the three *Romanzen vom kleinen Däumchen. Nach altenglischem*, 1811.[31]

By far the longest work in *Phantasus* is the dramatized fairy tale *Fortunat* in a prolog and two parts, each of the latter consisting of five acts. Not an improvization, it was planned in 1800 (as a treatment of educational problems), written in 1815 and 1816, and published in volume 3 of the work under consideration. Like *Däumchen* it is directed against the fatalistic ideas of Werner and Müllner. Tieck admitted composing it with "apparent carelessness" (scheinbare Nachlässigkeit), but claimed in a letter to his brother than this was intentional.[17] Like *Genoveva* and *Octavian*, it is a dramatization of an old chapbook—the story of Fortunatus, who owns and later bequeathes to his sons a marvellous bag containing a never-ending supply of gold, as well as a wishing-cap which takes one forthwith wherever one desires to go. The first edition of the *Volksbuch* appeared at Augsburg in 1509 and proved a popular source for later writers. Tieck was familiar with the dramatization of Hans Sachs (1553), as well as with Thomas Dekker's far superior English version of 1600. We may classify Tieck's work as a fairy-tale reproduction of the Blaubart-Eckbert type.

In his treatment the theme is the curse of a fortune too easily won. Fortunatus in part 1 learns through experience that wealth must go hand in hand with virtue and continence, but in part 2 his rich heirs, Ampedo and Andalosia, abuse their trust, one through laziness and supineness, the other through insolence and vanity, and lose everything. The lesson is that neither "fate" nor "luck," but industry, perseverance and common sense win life's battles.

Although the harsh mixture of comic and tragic motifs reminds of *Blaubart* and, as in *Octavian*, the length of the play is out of proportion to the importance of the subject matter, yet marked differences are to be noted between Tieck's manner in *Fortunat* and that of his earlier dramatizations. Even if the characters are still types, they seem more real here. The language, too, is firmer and the plot more closely knit. The style of the chronicle plays is followed more faithfully. Traces of beneficial Shakespearean influence are commoner. The background, particularly in the prolog, is realistic and hence indicative of his "new manner." A perusal of the letters which Solger wrote to him while *Fortunat* was being composed leaves no doubt but that these characteristics are due in great measure to his influence.

On the other hand, *Fortunat* is marked by a noticeable lack of melody, of rich rhythmic swing, color, Romantic glamor, and above all by an absence of mysticism under Böhme's influence. No doubt A. W. Schlegel had this in mind when he wrote to Tieck's brother that as a piece of poetical writing *Fortunat* is not on a higher plane than Tieck's earlier works.[32]

In 1828 Tieck voiced the questionable opinion that it would be suitable for the stage if the latter were only "freer"—a reference to his crotchet that the modern, as opposed to the Elizabethan, stage is a handicap to the dramatist. He preferred the second part to the first.[33]

The author thought highly of *Phantasus* and wrote to his brother on April 9, 1818,[17] that he would find no sign of illness or slackening power in the work. But in its present form it is only a torso. As noted, he had originally planned that each of the seven characters should recite seven works, which with the introductory poem would have made fifty. But the third volume, which appeared in 1816 and contained *Fortunat*, the thirteenth piece, brought the collection to a premature conclusion. A letter to Collin of October 22, 1818, owned by the present writer, shows Tieck at work preparing copy for the fourth volume. It was to include a revision of *Die Schildbürger, Die sieben Weiber des Blaubart* and revisions of two *Straussfedern* stories, *Abraham Tonelli* and *Ein Tagebuch*. After 1820 he still hoped to complete *Phantasus*, but in vain. Other writings which were to be fitted into it, among them the three dramatic sketches *Magelone, Melusine* and *Das Donauweib*, remained unfinished. In the edition of *Phantasus* appearing in the *Schriften* (volumes 4 and 5, 1828) two works, namely *Rotkäppchen* and *Fortunat*, were eliminated. In the second separate edition (1844-1845) *Rotkäppchen* but not *Fortunat* was restored.

The name *Phantasus* has become a fixture in German literature since Tieck, as not only the "novellen" *Der neue Phantasus* (1887) of Utis (a pseudonym for the Germanist Max Rieger), but also the better known cycle of poems by Arno Holz show. The form, adopted by Hoffmann, Hauff and many others, has become very popular.

In the previous chapter we noted the treatment which von der Hagen had accorded Tieck in his *Deutsche Gedichte des Mittelalters* and his *Nibelungenlied*. But in 1811 we find them still eagerly collaborating. Tieck prepared a rendering of the lay *Die Ravennenschlacht* and sent it to von der Hagen, the latter in turn sent the *Rosengarten* lays to Tieck. Tieck also gave von der Hagen a portion of the *Sängerkrieg* in the version of the Vienna manuscript.

LUDWIG TIECK, THE GERMAN ROMANTICIST

In 1812 Tieck finally got out, under Cotta's imprint, his second and last consequential publication in the field of old German literature, his version (according to the sole existing manuscript in Munich, which he used in 1808) of *Frauendienst, oder Geschichte und Liebe des Sängers Ulrich von Lichtenstein*, a work dating from about 1250. The narrative sections, which in the original are strophes of four rimed couplets, were turned into prose. As a modernization the work has its faults. While there is good reason for Tieck's drastic abbreviations and for his leaving neuter plurals like "Weib" and "Lied" uninflected, it was unwise to use such obscure vocables as "Bejag" (Preis), "die Preise" (das Getose), "die Schlaue" (misprint for "Schaue," der Anblick) and "viel nah" (beinah). Nor are such awkward violations of New High German usage as "Würde ich gewährt" (p. 189) and "ihr Mut nun nicht ist wie einst so gut" (p. 198) defensible. Misprints abound. There is only an eleven-line "Beschluss des Herausgebers," no introduction, although a year later he planned one as an afterthought.[34]

In 1813 von der Hagen still had in his possession Tieck's manuscript of *Dietrich*, which the latter wished to adapt, also his *Nibelungen*.[35] As late as 1816 Tieck wrote to his unreliable, ungrateful collaborator that he was still interested in Germanics and would himself like to get out an edition of the *Heldenbuch*. As a matter of fact, on September 28, 1816, he sent to the Heidelberg publisher Mohr[36] part of the manuscript of a proposed collection of *Alt-deutsche Gedichte*. It was to consist of several volumes, to contain a lengthy preface and, among other poems, his version of *König Rother*. The title which we find written over his manuscript of *König Rother* in the "Nachlass," namely "Alt-deutsche epische Gedichte grossentheils zum erstenmal aus Handschriften bekannt gemacht und bearbeitet,"[37] is evidence of his serious intention. The delay in completing the work, he explained to Mohr, was due to von der Hagen's vacillation. But by 1818 his interest has waned and made way for studies in Elizabethan literature. The relations of Tieck and von der Hagen, however, always continued to be friendly; they can be traced in letters as far as 1841. In that year von der Hagen, speaking before the Gesellschaft für deutsche Sprache und Altertumskunde, called Tieck Goethe's successor.

In chapter 9 we found that by 1803 art, as Wackenroder taught it, had become too subtle as a weapon in Tieck's struggle for greater mental balance. Since that time he had developed. A "new manner," with more realism, had crept into his style. This trend, coupled with his stay in Italy, made it possible to revert to his interest in art, particularly painting, from a new angle, much more sober and matter-of-fact. The result of this study is a manuscript of six hundred quarto pages (seventy thousand words), now in the National Library of Vienna, bearing the title *Geschichte und Theorie der bildenden Künste* (Cod. Vindob. 12821). Nowhere does Tieck's development between 1797 and 1817 come out more clearly than in a comparison of this manuscript with the earlier writings on art inspired by Wackenroder. The work is not dated, but in a discussion of the theory of color on sheet 33 a reference to Goethe's *Farbenlehre* (1811) shows that this date is the *terminus a quo*. Probably it was produced desultorily between 1811 and 1817. The manuscript, written in a very careless hand and difficult to decipher, has received no notice by Tieck specialists; indeed, they seem unaware of its existence. Yet it is a remarkable document and places Tieck in the foremost ranks of early nineteenth century critics of art.

The first main subdivision, on ancient architecture, covers only thirty-four pages. Five orders are discussed, the Locrian (*sic!*), Doric, Ionic, Corinthian and composite. Brief sections on temples, basilica, aqueducts, roads, theaters, arches and baths follow. More modern architecture is not considered.

The second subdivision, on painting, is over twelve times as long and comprises more than two-thirds of the manuscript. It is limited to the period from 1400 to 1700, and, after discussing the early painters from Cimabue and Giotto to Raphael, establishes these schools: 1. Roman (Raphael, Giulio Romano, Zucchero, Feti, Sarti and Mengs), 2. Florentine (chiefly Leonardo, Michael Angelo and del Sarto), 3. Venetian (Titian, Veronese and Tiepolo), 4. Lombardian (Francesco Francia, Correggio, Caravaggio and the Carraccis), 5. Neapolitan (chiefly Ribera, Rosa and Solimena), 6. Genoese (Cambiaso, Castelli and Bacciccio), 7. French (Freminet, Poussin, Blanchard, Mignard, Le Sueur, Le Brun, Watteau and David), 8. Spanish (Greco, Velasquez, Murillo), 9. Flemish (de Vriendt, Rubens, Jordaens, van Dyck and Teniers), 10. Dutch (Lucas van Leyden, Rembrandt, van Laar, Wouverman), 11. German (Dürer, Holbein, Heinz, Elzheimer, Dietrich), and 12. English (Richardson, Hogarth, West and Reynolds). Over one hundred fifty artists are mentioned; the more or less extensive appraisal of the work and style of each is usually preceded by a biographical sketch. Sixty pages on "Praktische Mahlerey," discussing such topics as weaving, tempera, fresco, miniatures, pastel and pottery, conclude the lengthy chapter.

The section on sculpture (eighty pages) which follows discusses the development of that art between 1300 and 1700 in Italy, France, the Netherlands, Germany, Spain and England. The ancient sculptors are barely mentioned. A final chapter takes up, largely from the practical side, a variety of minor arts, among them gem-cutting, engraving, wood-cutting and marquetry.

Tieck's work is not literary in style and reads more like a set of full notes. His division cannot be called very happy. For the sake of local classification he jumbles the Renaissance and Rococo periods and confuses portraiture and landscape painting. Moreover, his neglect of the glory that was Greece, intentional though it is, goes too far. Conversely architecture since Roman times and the contemporary artists, with the notable exception of the French painter David, are practically passed over in silence.

But Tieck's critical opinions are both expert and independent. We can quote only a few in this place. Raphael's strength, he finds, lies chiefly in his expression, composition and ability to depict supernal beauty; but he overdoes his lights and shadows. Giulio Romano is a mannerist, though a good one; but his coloring is deficient and his outlines seem too hard. Moreover, he overloads his canvas. Leonardo is outstanding in expression and imitation of nature, while Michael Angelo is characterized by a plain, straightforward manner. Titian stands forth as the greatest colorist and portraitist. Francesco Francia is distinguished by correct drawing, faithful imitation of nature, good coloring and great industry. Correggio is a master at blending lights and shadows; his chief aim was to please the eye. Blanchard is a French Titian, Le Sueur a second Raphael, Mignard a Correggio. Velasquez, an artist who in Tieck's day had not been fully recognized, is assigned a place beside the great masters because of his ability as a colorist and his fidelity to nature. Rubens is too much addicted to showiness and exaggeration. Van Dyck rates second only to Titian as a portraitist. Rembrandt, one of the most curious geniuses of all times, has never been surpassed in originality. Dürer, while intelligent, original and inventive, is characterized by "dryness." Richardson did uniformly good work, while Reynolds was instrumental in improving the taste of his countrymen.

We have considered Tieck's judgments in his great work on the plastic arts sufficiently to realize that he indulges neither in fine rhetoric and panegyrics nor in a jejune classification of artists and their works. Like the *Reisegedichte*, it is a noteworthy realistic work, unsurpassed by any similar production of its day and age. As in 1797, Tieck still found the two cradles of modern art in Italy and the Lowlands; as then, his interest in medieval times far surpassed his appreciation for antiquity. But his point of view has become saner and more mature; no longer does he overemphasize the Pre-Raphaelites; now art seems to him not so much religion as hard work buttressed by inspiration and talent.

Among his numerous sources, which he frequently criticizes, are Vasari, Baglione, Crespi and Pascoli; Falconet, d'Argenville and Felibien; Palomino; Mengs and Sandrart; Richardson and Walpole.

We have seen how Tieck met Solger. Upon making his closer acquaintance during the summer of 1811, Tieck was immediately won over by his learning and modest, yet accessible and communicative ways, and by his deeply religious nature. Solger believed that Tieck was the one and only great poet in a "counterfeit age" (gefälschten Zeitalter).[38] Their conversations and eminently worthwhile letters between 1811 and 1819 were beneficial to both, but especially to Tieck, who learned and profited not a little. "Certainly there is no greater delight," he once wrote to Solger, "than association with a true friend who agrees with us in our most important views of life and art."[39]

Solger was interested in translating Sophocles, but he had also an understanding and love for Romantic poesy. In his *Erwin* may be found a trenchant exposition of the esthetic basis of Romanticism, particularly of "Romantic Irony." He considered this irony to be the child of a union between mysticism (which he interpreted in the broadest sense as including poetry and religion, in a word insight into things) and reality.[40] The impress of Solger's esthetics, which advocated concreteness, was first felt in the change of style in *Fortunat* and then in the style and subject matter of the "novellen" of the twenties. Solger helped him with his editions of Kleist and of the *Deutsches Theater*, and with his Shakespearean studies. They planned a journal. His association with Solger, too, completed his recovery from the baleful influence of mysticism, which had brought him despair and all but ruined him as a poet; for he learned from Solger that mysticism cannot take the place of religion and that the mystics, above all Böhme, lay too much emphasis upon the reality of evil.[41] Solger showed him the advantages of Lope's realism over Calderon's mysticism. He helped to restore Tieck's self-confidence and to turn his mind more toward systematic philosophy, theoretical problems and criticism. Tieck became less the naïve, instinctive poet, who wrote when and as the spirit moved him, and more the reflective thinker and teacher who ponders and expounds fundamental principles and standards.

Matenko (p. 63) sums up Solger's influence upon Tieck as follows: "Solger's theory of irony gave to art an objective validity in the ultimate; his theory of "reales Nichts" [the negation of evil as positive nothingness] eliminated the ultimate possibility of evil in the universe; that of the identity of religion, philosophy and art, justified art and religion, as well as philosophy, as aspects of divine revelation. By means of these ideas Tieck found a rational solution for the problem, ever present in his mind, of harmonizing the whole of experience, a solution which corresponded to what Tieck had felt intuitively all his life and which was of particular importance to him after his intellectual débâcle following upon his contact with Jacob Böhme."

To his own brother Tieck wrote on November 22, 1819, soon after Solger's death, that Solger was to him "in a certain sense everything, my teacher and guide, my oldest friend, a loving heart" (in gewissem Sinne alles, mein Lehrer und Führer, mein ältester Freund, ein liebevolles Herz).[36] Tieck, in turn, gave Solger's *Erwin* and *Philosophische Gespräche* the benefit of advice and criticism.

The dark days of 1813, when Germany was at the mercy of the martial Corsican, forced Tieck and his family to flee to Prague. He vainly tried to borrow money for the trip from Friedrich Schlegel.[42] In Prague he spent a happy third of a year—from June 2 until about October 3[43]—with Brentano, the minor poet and Fichtean Ludwig Robert (a younger brother of Rahel Levin), and their respective sisters Bettina and Rahel. He had frequented the latter's house in Berlin as early as 1794. But Tieck's and Rahel's friendship never ripened because of radical differences in temperament. On November 17, 1835, he wrote to the Swedish councillor Brinkman of their associations in Prague: "I saw her daily and talked a great deal with her, often until far into the night. I always sought to make clear to her the unbridled arbitrariness of her nature and mode of thought."[44] They disagreed particularly on Goethe. Tieck felt that she was devoid of artistic and poetic appreciation, unreliable and untrue to herself.

Tieck also met Beethoven in Prague, but no intimacy developed because Tieck, reared amid a Mozartean atmosphere, failed to grasp the deeper significance of the new leonine genius. Later, in the "novelle" *Musikalische Leiden und Freuden*, Tieck accused him of "far-fetched originality." In the Prague theater he enjoyed the acting of Liebich.

After the besom of war had swept past Ziebingen, he returned and rusticated there for five more quiet years. We have discussed his attitude toward his country's plight during the Napoleonic days. Additional incidents show that he was not apathetic. In April 1814, eight months after Theodor Körner's death on the field of battle, Tieck wrote to his father Christian: "Of few dead can one say with such certainty that they have not wholly died, as of your noble son, who has sacrificed his life to the most sacred cause."[45] In 1815 Tieck helped raise subscriptions for Helmina von Chézy's *Neue auserlesene Schriften der Enkelin der Karschin*, which was sold by subscription for the benefit of wounded German soldiers.[46] Germany's national awakening aroused his warm enthusiasm.[47]

His statement to von der Hagen on June 16, 1816, that he was still interested in German literary studies, was proved not only by *Fortunat* but also by the appearance of *Deutsches Theater* in 1817. It is a two-volume collection of German plays from the fifteenth to the seventeenth century, each volume prefaced by a splendid critical preface. The development of the German drama from the Shrovetide plays of Hans Rosenplüth and Hans Sachs through Jacob Ayrer and the "English Comedians" to Opitz, Gryphius and Lohenstein was illustrated by a series of well chosen sample plays. Among the twenty dramas included are an *Octavian* by Sachs, a *Fortunat* of the "English Comedians," the *Dafne* of Opitz, *Cardenio und Celinde* and *Peter Squentz* by Gryphius, and *Ibrahim Bassa* by Lohenstein. His interest in these works was of a twofold nature. As a Romanticist he wished to rescue them from oblivion; as a student of the theater he wanted to show their significance in the development of the German drama.

His prefatory critical discussion[48] was long considered standard. Even so recent a work as Arnold's *Geschichte des deutschen Dramas* still leans upon him at crucial points. Interesting from the dramaturgic point of view is the idea, first expressed here, that the old English stage may be related, through the stage of the medieval mystery drama, to the ancient Greek theater. During his last years in Berlin he reverted to this mistaken notion. Of interest is also the idea that the English stage is diametrically opposed to the Spanish.

The manuscripts of the two Rosenplüth and five Ayrer plays which he used are still preserved in the Dresden library, whence he drew them. A copy of the second printing (1624) of *Englische Comedien und Tragedien* (1620)—a very rare book—he borrowed from Brentano.[36] Unfortunately his *Deutsches Theater*, too, was to remain a fragment. Four additional volumes, carrying the work into the eighteenth century, were planned. But his preface to Eduard von Bülow's edition of Schröder's dramatic works (1831), reprinted in the *Kritische Schriften II*, compensates us in a measure for this loss.

The mass of material which he had collected on the "English Comedians" could not be used in its entirety for his prefaces. Later he placed it at the disposal of the scholar Albert Cohn, who catalogued his library in 1849 for Asher. Cohn used it as the basis of further research for his *Shakespeare in Germany in the Sixteenth and Seventeenth Centuries; an Account of English Actors in Germany and the Netherlands and of the Plays Performed by them during the same Period* (London and Berlin, 1865).

CHAPTER TWELVE

THE JOURNEY TO ENGLAND AND FRANCE

W E HAVE noted that after 1810 Tieck's interest in old German poetry waned, while he paid more attention to Elizabethan literature. But the deeper he delved into this subject, the more he felt the lack of materials. Having exhausted the stores of the German libraries, he found it impossible to procure books from England. He was facing an impasse in his labors. What, then, could have been more welcome than an invitation from Burgsdorff to accompany him upon a visit to England? The first allusions to the plan are found in letters of January and February 1817, to Solger,[1] the publishers Cotta[2] and Reimer,[3] and Helmina von Chézy.[4] Incidentally the preparations for this journey were vainly used as a lever by friends of penurious Tieck, especially Steffens, to secure him a position or pension from the Prussian government.[5] Tieck also approached the publisher Reimer for a loan of twenty Friedrichd'or for purchasing books in England.[3]

On May 3 the two adventurers left Berlin in Burgsdorff's coach and travelled leisurely, stopping at many points. In Cassel they made the acquaintance of the Grimm brothers, who found Tieck bent with gout but with the air of a man of the world.[6] They arrived at Calais on the twenty-eighth. Early the next morning they crossed the Channel in foggy, dreary weather. Tieck had reached the land of his desire.

On that day the travellers made Canterbury, where they inspected the cathedral and spent the night. The following morning they continued to London by way of Faversham. Immediately after arriving at the capital they learned that the theaters were still open and that John Kemble, then almost sixty, was appearing for the last time in his famous Shakespearean rôles. That same evening they went to Covent Garden and saw Kemble as Posthumus in *Cymbeline*. The performance was a disappointment to both. Tieck felt that Kemble did too much declaiming, and some of that poorly. The acting seemed prosaic and the text garbled. The German actors Fleck and Schröder, whom he had admired in his youth, were superior, he felt.

Kemble's Brutus, which Tieck witnessed the next night, left a better impression, but he was particularly struck by the inappropriateness of the high, deep stage for Shakespeare's stage. Yet he found the acoustics better than in the average German theater; the only similarity between the English stage of his own day and the Elizabethan stage, as he imagined it, was in the proscenium. On the following day, a Sunday, he inspected Westminster Abbey and London Bridge. On Monday, June 2, he saw Kemble as Cardinal Wolsey in *Henry VIII*. Having become accustomed to this actor's "slow plaintive delivery,"[7] he was impressed by the performance.

The other theatrical performances which he attended during his stay in England follow in chronological order. On June 5 he saw Kemble as Hotspur in *Henry IV, Part I*; on the sixth, in Drury Lane, *Rugantino*, an adaptation of Zschokke's *Aballino*, preceded by an entertainment for the benefit of the actors Knight and Wallack; on one of the following evenings (Burgsdorff's date, June 9, is incorrect, according to the testimony of the *Times*) Kemble in *Hamlet*; on the eleventh, in Drury Lane, Kean in *Macbeth*; on the eighteenth, in Covent Garden, Miss O'Neill and W. C. Macready in Sheil's *Apostate*; on the twenty-first Kean in *Richard III*; on the twenty-third Kemble in *Coriolanus* (Burgsdorff incorrectly assigned to this day *King John*, which Tieck missed); on July 13 two plays in the Haymarket Theater, one of them probably Sheridan's *Critic*; the next night *The Merchant of Venice* in the same theater (Burgsdorff mentioned this play, Tieck not; perhaps he missed it). He witnessed the following plays on days which have not been determined: *Othello* in Covent Garden, with Young in the leading rôle; *Richard III* at the same theater, with Booth; *Hamlet* with Kean; Cumberland's *West Indian* at Drury Lane, and on the same evening *Doctor and Apothecary* as well as Patrick's *The Return*; three plays, *A Trip to Scarborough*, *The Devil to Pay* and *The Wedding Day*, with Miss Alsop at Drury Lane; *Don Juan*, a melodrama; and finally Foote's *Mayor of Garratt*, at Covent Garden. In addition he attended Astley's Theater, a well known circus near Westminster Bridge, on June 3 and again on June 12.

In *Henry IV, Part I*, the text of which was rudely cut, Tieck missed much of Hotspur's humor. Kemble's Hamlet gave him a few new suggestions as to the reading of the part but betrayed signs of the actor's advanced years. In the same rôle he saw also Edmund Kean, who, he was told, resembled Garrick. While Kemble's manner seemed to him too slow and deliberate, Kean, a young man of thirty, spoke too rapidly and seemed affected. The remark of Coleridge that "seeing him act was like reading Shakespeare by flashes of lightning" seems to describe Tieck's impression, too.

The last rôle of Kemble that he saw was Coriolanus, in which the veteran actor bade his final adieu to the stage on June 23. In many scenes Kemble proved his greatness, despite mutilation of the play and numerous excisions. The impressive spectacle of Kemble taking leave for ever of the scenes of his many triumphs, and the disgraceful actions of the rabble after the play were described in some detail by Tieck.[8]

Three rôles of Kemble he missed: Addison's *Cato* because of an aversion to the play; *King John* on account of another engagement; and *Macbeth*, for which Tieck, a newcomer in London at the time, could not secure admission. He regretted missing the last play because it afforded him his only opportunity of seeing the famous Mrs. Siddons, Kemble's sister.

Tieck summed up his impressions of Kemble as follows. Though his acting was interesting, instructive and expert, yet his mannerisms were so pronounced that one had to get accustomed to them. He was first of all a declaimer and then an actor, who gave the Shakespearean characters an interpretation diverging from that intended by the author (according to Tieck). His speech was too slow, he lacked the necessary humor, and failed to give his rôles the stamp of authenticity and naturalness. His creations suffered also from want of individuality.

Besides seeing Kean in Hamlet, he witnessed the young idol of Drury Lane as Macbeth and as Richard III. In the former rôle he seemed to Tieck weaker than in *Hamlet*. In *Richard III* the eccentricities of Kean which struck Tieck in *Hamlet*, came to the fore again.

The rendering of the same part by Booth, which he also witnessed, was a poor imitation of Kean's inferior interpretation. Tieck regretted that the English still use Cibber's "wretched revision of this powerful drama."[9]

The Othello of Young, whom Washington Irving called "the best actor now on the English stage,"[10] also displeased sensitive Tieck, but Miss O'Neill as Desdemona delighted him. Her acting and that of W. C. Macready impressed him more strongly than that of any actor he saw in England.

Since Tieck had the conviction that the modern drama should not be played in large theaters upon huge stages, he was attracted several times to the Haymarket Theater because of its smaller size and hence intimate character. The performances which he witnessed there were excellent, precise, unforced and graceful, without being superficial. It was there that he saw Sheridan's *Critic*, which with its satire against Cumberland was already obsolescent, though still popular. Only the first act, in which the satire is sharp and the wit pungent, could hold his undivided attention. *The School for Scandal*, which he would have liked to see, was not offered during his stay in London.

Of Cumberland's *West Indian* he saw a satisfactory performance in Drury Lane, but not as good, he thought, as that which Fleck and his troupe used to give in Berlin. He agreed with the German actor in conceiving the hero O'Flaherty, as a gruffer, coarser soldier than the English actor Johnston conceived him. Moreover he objected to the popular songs which Johnston interpolated. Tieck, who never mastered spoken English, had difficulty understanding the text of these ditties.

At least twice he attended Astley's Theater, a popular circus near Westminster Bridge. He enjoyed this form of entertainment and confessed that in Germany he had never seen anything comparable to it. It was advantageous, he felt, to have a special place for such spectacles, rather than to house them in "legitimate" theaters.

Tieck summed up his impressions of the theaters. His chief interest lay in Shakespeare. But he missed the lighter plays like *Twelfth Night* and *As You Like It*, as well as the Julia of O'Neill. On the whole he detected a similarity between French and English methods of producing tragedies; they resembled one another in their striking misconceptions. Nor were the Germans, by and large, superior in this respect, he felt. If a choice was to be made, the French style struck him as preferable to either of the others because it was more mature and finished. At the same time he remembered that the English theater is the oldest of the three and that the art of acting reached a high stage of excellence during the reign of Elizabeth. He called it true to nature, simple, more or less colored by caprice and irony and the opposite of the false pathos and declamatory fervor introduced by the French. While the interpretation of Shakespeare was in the hands of a Burbage, an Alleyn, a Betterton and a Garrick, with their vivacious and natural style, he felt it was secure. But now that the French manner, with its monotonous, inflated style, has crept in everywhere—in Germany through Iffland—, it is no wonder to him that Shakespeare often fails to impress audiences.

Tieck is not fair in his scathing criticism of the English stage. The strictures against English acting, found in *Phantasus*,[11] which was written some years before the visit to England, show that he had preconceived notions; the remarks just considered show that during his eight weeks' stay in England he did not modify these prejudices. Granting the weaknesses of the English theater at the time, its unnaturalness, the deficiencies of the aging John Kemble, who even at the height of his career hardly measured up to his sister Mrs. Siddons, the shortcomings of Charles Kemble, whom Macready once styled a first-rate actor of second-rate parts, the youth and comparative inexperience of Kean, and the bad taste of the lower classes, we still realize that Tieck's complaints are often unjust. Before coming to England he had witnessed most of Shakespeare's plays only in the flat German prose renderings of Eschenburg. It seems like effrontery to compare the effect of such performances by a Fleck or a

Schröder, who were alien to the world of Shakespeare, with productions by a Kemble or a Kean, who with all their flaws were at least reared amid the traditions of English Shakespearean acting and used a text which, though curtailed or rearranged, was at any rate the poet's original language. It seems like hardihood, too, for him to hold up Fleck's interpretation of the Irish major in Cumberland's *West Indian* as preferable to that generally given upon the English stage. In these matters, Tieck, despite his own remarkable ability as an expert in theatrical questions and a declaimer, assumed the same supercilious position that he took toward the English critics of Shakespeare.

Later he did not change his opinion. In a letter to Winkler, probably of 1838, he wrote: "After all it may be that the English theater is even worse off than ours. . . . Who attends the theater in London? Not the connoisseurs."[12]

Besides the theater he found other attractions in London. On June 3 he attended an exhibition at the Art Academy and was struck by the work of the sculptor Chantrey, whom he later met. Not until the ninth—ten days after his arrival in London, where he spent forty days in all—did he begin going to the British Museum to pursue the work which had brought him to England. The delay was due in all likelihood to the difficulty of securing access to the rare books and manuscripts which he wished to consult. Shakespeare and his immediate successors under Elizabeth and James I, also Drayton, Daniel and others, had proved more or less available in German libraries. Dodsley's collection and its continuation, as well as the works of Fletcher, Jonson and Massinger, were accessible there, too. But many of the older plays had not even been printed, and most of the quarto editions he thought he could find only in the Museum or at Cambridge. His knowledge of them prior to this time was confined to brief and, as he thought, uncritical notes of British commentators.

Hence it was his ardent wish, he wrote in the preface to volume 1 of *Shakespeares Vorschule* (1823), to secure access to the treasures of the British Museum. He acknowledged the cooperation of its officials, especially that of the young Bavarian architect Nathanael von Schlichtegroll, who was employed there and whose father, Adolf, Tieck had met in Munich. With the assistance of young Schlichtegroll, he had careful copies made of the most important dramas, beginning with *The Birth of Merlin*. To Reimer he wrote on December 8, 1817,[13] that he agreed to pay £2 for each play copied; for this purpose he secured an advance of £25 from the Prussian minister in London. One of the dramas, *The Second Maid's Tragedy*, Schlichtegroll himself transcribed from the unpublished manuscript, doing the work so carefully, according to Tieck, that his copy was more accurate than the first English edition of 1824. In all Tieck had fourteen plays copied completely and eleven others partially. But since the clerical labor of making the transcripts could not be completed during his brief stay in London and because of financial difficulties, the manuscripts did not reach him until after his return.

Tieck himself stated that he attached most importance to those dramas which he could assume were enjoying the greatest success when Shakespeare arrived in London. It was these efforts, he thought, which influenced the populace and the playwrights; they were imitated by Shakespeare and proved instrumental in shaping and developing the English dramatic school for the two hundred years which followed. First of all he turned his attention to those dramas which at some time have been attributed as early works to Shakespeare himself, or in which he may have collaborated.

All these volumes he had copied, as well as a few by younger contemporaries of Shakespeare. In that age, he was now convinced, poetry and dramatic art matured and reached a higher stage of perfection than anywhere else in modern Europe.

The upshot of Tieck's work in the British Museum was that he gained a better first-hand knowledge of the literature of the Elizabethan period; that he secured enough grist for four volumes, namely the two published parts of *Shakespeares Vorschule* (1823 and 1829), the third posthumously published part,[14] and the *Vier Schauspiele von Shakespeare* of 1836,—that is, everything of any consequence which he still published in this field; and that he became more confident of his own ability as a critic of Elizabethan drama. Consequently he took a still greater interest in the doubtful plays and lowered his already poor estimate of the work of the English critics, so that it became an obsession with him to cast stones at them. But so far as his projected *Buch über Shakespeare* is concerned, his researches in England led to no practical results.

As a bibliophile he also utilized his time in England by purchasing numerous rare books. He bought *Friar Bacon and Friar Bungay* and Middleton's *The Witch* at a high price, a copy of Thomas Hawkins' *Origin of the English Drama*, six volumes of old plays, the works of Daniel and of Marston, and numerous travellers' guides. He imported the first copies of Scott's *Waverly* and *Tales of my Landlord* into Germany and took along the memoirs of Cumberland, some works of Byron, and Steevens' *Twenty Plays of Shakespeare*. He later confessed to Reimer in a letter[13] that the trip cost him 700 talers, although Burgsdorff bore all the necessary expenses.

LUDWIG TIECK, THE GERMAN ROMANTICIST

The visits to the British Museum were important from yet another point of view. Soon after his introduction there he met the young anatomist and surgeon Joseph Henry Green, an intimate friend of Coleridge and a serious student of philosophy. And on June 13 he was invited to dinner at Green's house in No. 22 Lincoln's Inn Fields. In the party was also Coleridge, who had met Tieck eleven years before, when they discussed the spurious plays of Shakespeare. But Coleridge confessed that at the time of the first meeting he was unaware of Tieck's "eminence as a poet."[15] Henry Crabb Robinson, the journalist and diarist, who had spent some time in Germany, was also present at Green's. Robinson assures us that it was "an afternoon and evening of very high pleasure indeed."[16] Though he found Tieck's exterior unprepossessing, he considered his face shrewd and clever. Tieck's air resembled that of an able man of the world, rather than that of a poet. Tieck did not take a leading part in the conversation, due partly at least to his deficient knowledge of spoken English. The course of the conversation led the others to give him information. But what he did say, Robinson generously adds, "was sensible and judicious." Coleridge was not entirely in his element either, for "his German was not good and his English was not free. He feared he should not be understood if he talked his best. His eloquence was therefore constrained." One of the principal topics of discussion seems to have been Elizabethan literature, of which Tieck expressed a more favorable opinion than Robinson expected.

The next few days Tieck probably spent in the Museum, but on the fifteenth, when there was an improvement in the weather, he took time for an excursion to Richmond. And on the eighteenth he was present at the dedication of Waterloo Bridge. The following day he went sightseeing with the Prussian consul general.

Meanwhile Coleridge had written to Robinson, suggesting another meeting with Tieck, but received no reply. On the twentieth he repeated the suggestion, proposing a "dies attico-germanico" at Highgate.[17] He added that it would "grieve" him "sadly" not to see Tieck again, and he appended some questions for him about Tauler, Böhme, Spanish divines of mystic theology, and Giordano Bruno.

On June 24 Robinson, Green and Tieck accepted an invitation from Coleridge to pay him a visit at Highgate. Most of the day was spent in "chatting miscellaneously."[18] They discussed Tieck's own writings, the works of Fichte, G. H. von Schubert, Solger, Wolf, Böckh, Böhme and the mystics, and also a plan of Tieck to publish an English edition of Elizabethan plays. Coleridge read several of his own poems, and he and Tieck philosophized, Coleridge doing most of the talking. Tieck proved "a good listener" and "an unobtrusive man." But this was probably due in large part to his insufficient command of English.

They also touched upon the subject of religion. Far from proving a zealot, as Robinson, familiar with the rumors about his conversion to Catholicism, expected him to be, Tieck said that with intolerant persons of either party he always took the opposite side. Yet when Robinson ventured to suggest the incompatibility of the Catholic religion with any great improvement, Tieck sidestepped with the remark that it was difficult to decide on questions of national character, and that without the Catholic religion the people in Catholic countries would be worse off. The Spaniards, he thought, owed their deliverance from the French to their religion. But at the same time he admitted that England owes all her greatness and excellence to the Reformation and that the existence of the Catholic system as such requires the existence of Protestantism. "This," concluded Robinson in judging Tieck's views, "is a very harmless Catholicism."

When the conversation turned to literature, Tieck "spoke with great love" of Goethe yet censured "the impious Prolog to *Faust*" and wished that an English translation might be made from the Fragment of 1790. Perhaps it was on this occasion that Robinson read to Tieck the two sonnets of Wordsworth, *On Twilight* and *On Sir George Beaumont's Picture*, eliciting from him the remark: "Das ist ein englischer Goethe."[19]

During the following days Tieck and Robinson saw more of each other. On the twenty-sixth Robinson called and chatted about Tieck's projected tour through England. The last recorded meeting with Robinson upon English soil took place on June 29. Robinson summarized their conversation as follows: "He is well read in the English dramatic literature, having read all the English plays which were accessible in Germany; and he has a decision of opinion which one wonders at in a foreigner. He has no high opinion of Coleridge's critique, but he says he has learned a great deal from Coleridge, who has glorious conceptions about Shakespeare. Coleridge's conversation he very much admires, and thinks it superior to any of his writings. . . . Of Ben Jonson he thinks highly. The pieces he distinguished were Bartholomew Fair (perhaps his best piece), The Devil is an Ass, The Alchymist, The Fox, The Silent Woman, etc. He says his work on Shakespeare will be minute as to the language,[20] which he thinks underwent changes. Of German literature he does not speak promisingly. The popular writers (such as Fouqué) he despises, and he says that unhappily there have sprung up a number of imitators of himself. He praises Solger's work very much, and he is the only recent writer whom he mentioned. Of Goethe he spoke with less enthusiasm than

I expected. . . . The want of religion in Goethe is a great scandal to Tieck, I have no doubt."[21]

On the same day Robinson (not Coleridge, as Köpke writes)[22] introduced Tieck to the mild-mannered philosopher William Godwin, who had little time for speculation or discussion, however.[23]

It is interesting to note Tieck's disparaging remarks about Coleridge as a critic of Shakespeare, despite a similarity in their views, also his low estimate of Coleridge's writings. Yet Coleridge later remained friendly toward him and corresponded with him. When Tieck left England for France on July 21 he bore a letter of introduction from Coleridge to Southey. Robinson later visited Tieck three times, in 1829, 1834 and 1851 and had stimulating conversations with him.

Upon Green Tieck had a direct influence, persuading him to go to Germany to continue his studies and commending him to the attention of Solger.[24]

On June 30 Tieck left London with Burgsdorff and another German for a ten days' tour of a part of the island. Following the Thames, they travelled by way of Windsor to Oxford. Here on July 1 they inspected the colleges, also the Bodleian library. The next day they proceeded to Woodstock, where the Chapel House attracted their attention, and to Stratford and Shakespeare's house. Here, we may say, Tieck had reached the real goal of his journey.

In his "novelle" *Der Mondsüchtige* (1831) he gave a retrospective medley of fiction and truth concerning his visit to Stratford. The account is in the form of a letter from an uncle to his nephew. The former, touring in England with a German compatriot, writes that he has had a serious dispute with his fellow traveller because the latter wished to skip altogether Stratford, "which beckoned to me like a gleaming shrine because of Shakespeare."[25] They parted company there, "for he wanted to have everything over with in one hour." It should be noted, incidentally, that while the first half of this statement is fiction, the rest is truth. Tieck could never have afforded to desert Burgsdorff; but the latter, the very prototype of a modern tourist, hurried him along during the entire trip. Tieck wrote to Solger from Paris that they travelled in great haste,[26] and later, on September 17, when they passed through Heidelberg, Creuzer complained to Görres: "Tieck was very much rushed by Burgsdorff."[27] To his brother Tieck wrote of the journey on April 9, 1818, that "it went too fast even for a person in good health."[28] There is evidence that Burgsdorff was by nature nervous and highstrung. Shortly after his premature death Tieck wrote to Friedrich on October 24,

1822: "I call him unhappy because the poor man did not enjoy his life in any way."[29]

The uncle in *Der Mondsüchtige* continues: "But I had made up my mind to be at home in the birthplace of my favorite, and before I realized it I was living next to the house in which he had spent his boyhood days and the years of his early youth. How often was I in the low rooms; the entire house has still essentially the same furnishings as it had three hundred years ago. It is surprising that the frail building has been preserved so long, since that larger one in which he lived later is no longer standing. It was destroyed at the desire of a later owner, a clergyman, who wished to erect a new edifice, and such a one has actually been built. This misfortune, as I must designate it, occurred as late as 1750. The owner must have known the poet but little and loved and revered him still less." Except for the fiction of a longer residence at Stratford, this statement is true. Tieck was there on July 3, but not longer than half a day.

The church in Stratford, writes the uncle, was more beautiful than he had imagined it. He broke a linden branch along the shady walk leading to the sanctuary. The bust of Shakespeare seemed excellent and worthy of being copied by some great master sculptor, who might produce a replica for all eternity. What pleased him most about this "speaking likeness" of the great poet was its freedom from idealization and its simplicity, which reflected the spirit of Shakespeare's time and of his fellow Stratfordians. Then he proceeds to relate how the bust was once colored, with brown eyes, thin brown hair and a gold-embroidered doublet, but how to his surprise he found that it had now been whitewashed. The blame for this he attributes to the Shakespearean editor Malone, "who has painted over and whitewashed so many beautiful passages of Shakespeare without clearing them up."[30] Despite this blunder the bust is found praiseworthy.

Another "novelle" of Tieck, *Eine Sommerreise* (1833), indicates the impression gained by treading the meadows along the Avon near Stratford and picturing Shakespeare as a youth and man. "Here," he exclaims, "nature lets us poetize freely."[31] It was at Stratford, in all likelihood, that Tieck conceived the idea of writing his "novelle" *Dichterleben*.

From Stratford the tourists hurried north to Warwick and were delighted with the castle, the view, the lovely region, the church, the churchyard and the bridge. Burgsdorff liked Warwick and its environment more than anything on the entire trip. Tieck in *Das alte Buch* (1834) recollected the "solitude of Warwickshire"[32] and its beautiful forests. In *Eine Sommerreise* he remarks that the castle of Warwick is a great and inspiring work of art.[33]

From Warwick they continued northward to Kenilworth and inspected the ruins of the castle. Then they turned westward to Kidderminster (we correct Burgsdorff's sequence here) and southward to the town of Gloucester and to the historical fields of Gloucestershire. Gloucester itself seemed ugly, but its cathedral was interesting. Crossing over to Hereford, they saw Ross and Monmouth and travelled on the River Wye as far as Chepstow. Thence they ferried across the Severn, reached Bristol and were soon in Bath, which impressed them as a splendid town. On the ninth they continued to Stonehenge and Salisbury, where they saw the cathedral, and thence to Southampton. From there Tieck returned to London on the tenth. Burgsdorff went on to the Isle of Wight, reaching the city two days later.

According to Köpke, Tieck's stay in England ended with this "swing around the circle."[34] But Köpke is in error, for he now remained in London twelve days longer. Rejoined by Burgsdorff on the twelfth, he continued his visits to the theater, inspected the Alien Office on the sixteenth, dined at the Prince of Wales Coffee House on the seventeenth with Burgsdorff, Schlichtegroll and others, and went to Lakington on the eighteenth. The nineteenth was the "unpleasant final day" in London. En route to Dover on the twentieth, they inspected the cathedral in Canterbury once more, and on the twenty-first crossed over to Calais. Tieck's journey to England was at an end.

But the two travellers did not return home directly; over six weeks elapsed before they were back. By way of Boulogne, Abbeville and Beauvais they proceeded to Paris, arriving there on the twenty-fourth, if we would believe Burgsdorff, but according to a letter from Tieck to Solger, on the twenty-fifth;[35] at any rate certainly not "during the first days of July," as Köpke stated.[34] This error, which would cut down the stay in England to four weeks, when in reality it lasted almost eight, has been generally copied.

For about sixteen days they stayed in Paris, visiting the theaters, the Palais Royal and Tuileries, the museums and galleries, and the Bibliothèque Nationale, which Tieck frequented during the last ten days. Here he inspected the Manesse codex of minnesongs, which remained in Paris until 1888, also the manuscripts of the *Heldensage* and a more complete version of the *Heymonskinder* than he had ever read. Among several plays he saw *Macbeth*, with Franconi in the leading rôle. We have noted that he bore a letter from Coleridge to Southey. But whether it ever reached Southey through Tieck is doubtful. Once Tieck was mistaken for Napoleon, but as he disliked him and called him the tyrannical oppressor of Germany,[36] he was not flattered.

On August 9 Burgsdorff and Tieck left Paris and travelled by way of Chalons, Verdun and Metz. There they boarded the diligence for Luxemburg but had to leave it before Thionville because Tieck felt ill. Continuing by water, they reached Trèves on the fourteenth and Coblenz on the fifteenth. Then by slow stages they proceeded, Tieck stopping with Goethe in Weimar for about a week. On September 4, after an absence of four months, the voyage ended in Berlin.

We have referred to the stress under which he labored throughout the journey. Restless Burgsdorff was continually straining at the leash, brooking delay only with extreme reluctance. It is no wonder that Tieck's health, none too good at the start, almost broke down under the pressure. A. W. Schlegel, who just before Tieck's arrival had left Paris for Coppet, where Madame de Staël was to be buried on her country estate (she had died in the metropolis on July 14), reported to Tieck's brother of having heard that Tieck had grown "quite wry" (ganz schief), distorted by gout and rheumatism, and critical of everything.[37] And Friedrich Schlegel, who saw him in Frankfurt, wrote to his brother that Tieck's physical condition was sad; that he revealed signs of his former self only when engaged in lively conversation.[38] He also seemed very "materialistic."[39] Only after he was settled once more in Ziebingen could Burgsdorff report to Solger that on the whole Tieck had stood the trip well.

Tieck himself has recorded some of the impressions gained during his sojourn in England. We have already quoted from them. To Solger he wrote on July 26: "England pleased me in some respects, in others not, and I thoroughly disliked London. How fortunate we are, my friend, that we were born as Germans and live in Germany. The true spirit, liberty and soulfulness, are to be found only with us, and though one does not often discover superlative values among us, yet the possibilities therefor are present. In this we are uniquely fortunate—a circumstance which most people completely overlook."[40] The provincialism of these remarks is striking.

England, it seemed to him, had unlearned the joy of living since Elizabethan times. The joviality of those days, he felt, had given way to an exaggerated Puritanism and a pedantry which killed all individualism. In the preface to volume 1 of *Shakespeares Vorschule* he remarked: "Aside from all poetic love for older periods, it is certain that Old England at the time of Elizabeth reared a far jollier people, inclined to wit and jest, than we now find there. With the Puritan Revolution these customs disappeared and made room for a misunderstood pietism. Nor did the old spirit return after royalty was restored, and if the island gained power and wealth, yet these have brought with them a certain pedantry of living which threatens gradually to dissolve all individualism in dry uniformity."[41]

In justice to Tieck it must be said that he was the first German fully to appreciate the frank, naïve animalism of Elizabethan England, so coarse yet so unsullied by blighting vice. He was the first to realize that the saving grace of the Elizabethan, with all his laxness of living, was his freedom from a banal philosophy of cant. In later life he did not revise his judgments, as harsh as they are in part.

The significance of his visit to England may be summed up under several headings. He found material for two important collections of Elizabethan plays, comprising thirteen dramas. He purchased numerous English books, among them rare and valuable editions. His frequent visits to the London theaters convinced him of the inability of contemporary British actors and audiences to do full justice to his idol, Shakespeare. Moreover, he came into personal touch with a group of important Englishmen. His visit to Oxford, Stratford and other points made no deep impression upon Tieck's later work. Significant references to England which reveal first-hand knowledge are rare in his writings. The great Shakespeare "novelle" *Dichterleben*, in a prolog and two parts, which we should expect to be a repository of such independent observations as he might have made, is devoid of real local color. In fact, it seems as though Tieck, with his exaggerated notion of the differences between the England of Shakespeare and that of 1817, purposely avoided the latter as a model when he wrote *Dichterleben*, and relied upon his own preconceived ideas. In this strengthened consciousness of the discrepancy between the England of 1600 and that of 1800 is to be found the keynote of Tieck's impressions of England.

A series of travel letters on England was begun but left unfinished.[42] But in the essay *Über das englische Theater*, first published in the *Dramaturgische Blätter* (1825-1826), at least one phase of his impressions of England is recorded. Other more ambitious works were planned but not executed. One, an anthology, was to contain 1) Greene's *Friar Bacon and Friar Bungay*, 2) *The Birth of Merlin* "by Rowley and Shakespeare," 3) Middleton's *The Witch*, 4) *Edward III* "by Shakespeare," 5) the "older version of Shakespeare's *The Taming of the Shrew*,"

6) scenes from Kyd's *Spanish Tragedy*, 7) extracts from the *Canterbury Tales*, and 8) samples from Lyly's prose. Items 1) and 2) later appeared in *Shakespeares Vorschule* and 4) in *Vier Schauspiele von Shakespeare*. Tieck also planned a translation of Cumberland's memoirs and of Scott's *Waverley* and *Tales of my Landlord*.[43]

CHAPTER THIRTEEN

A NEW HOME IN DRESDEN

TIECK did not remain in Berlin very long. His poor health, more than homesickness for his family, made it imperative to go back to Ziebingen. Once there again amid the scenes which in fifteen years had become homelike to his eyes, he felt easier, although his physical condition did not improve.

He now began mapping out plans for the continuation of his publications in English literature, a very desirable step toward relieving his hopeless financial situation. To be sure, he was handicapped by the delayed arrival of the books which he had purchased and the manuscripts of Elizabethan plays of which he had ordered copies in London. His inability to pay promptly was the chief reason for the delay. On February 3, 1818, he complained to von der Hagen[1] that he had received only eight manuscripts. The rest did not reach him until spring, it seems. His books apparently did not come before February, as a letter of the eighth to Reimer indicates.[2] When they finally arrived, he began work at once on the projects described at the end of the previous chapter.

But his days in Ziebingen were numbered. Hardly had he settled down to serious work, when his old patron, the count, died on April 18 on the nearby estate in Madlitz. He had suffered a stroke a week before. With his death Tieck lost a friend who had always preserved his love for literature and a youthful spirit. "Had he not become the owner of an estate, or been a jurist before," Tieck wrote after his death, "he would surely have become one of the most cultured and noblest of men."[3] Of the seven children who survived the count, six—three sons and three daughters—lived upon his estates. Every passing day made it clearer to Tieck, now forty-seven years of age, that their home could not continue to shelter him, his wife and two daughters.

He had never planned to remain in Ziebingen permanently. Without his realizing it the years had rolled by. He did not live very happily with his wife. Though a loving, self-sacrificing soul, she was a plain housewife who showed little interest in her husband's poetry and no sympathy with his unstable mode of living.

The older daughter Dorothea, a serious-minded girl and her father's pride and joy,[4] was almost twenty. Talented and soulful, she seemed of a calm, almost severe simplicity and sternness, but in association with

dear friends, like Raumer or the poet Friedrich von Üchtritz, she could
be heartiness itself. Unfortunately she was cursed with the same wavering, problematic soul as her father, but lacked his preciously carefree
levity. Hence the difficult situation of the family weighed heavily upon
her mind. During the Dresden period she became her father's valued but
silent collaborator in his numerous projects of translation. Fearing that
their prestige would suffer if it became known that she, devoid of any
systematic linguistic or critical training, had a hand in them, he never
let her collaboration become publicly known.

Agnes, the younger daughter, born shortly before the family's arrival
on the estate, was seventeen. She had inherited more of the simple, house-
wifely ways of her mother. The gossipmongers have done much to
blacken her name. Wilhelm von Chézy in his *Erinnerungen* (I, 196)
calls her the illegitimate daughter of Burgsdorff. In an unpublished note
among his Berlin papers, Varnhagen von Ense also tells this story, adding
that the deception occurred while Tieck was absent in Italy and that upon
his return Burgsdorff persuaded him to recognize Agnes as his rightful
daughter by paying him an annuity. But this cannot be true, for Agnes
was born over two years before Tieck's departure to Italy. Hebbel in his
diary (IV, 13) reports illicit relations between Agnes and Count Wolf
Baudissin, one of Tieck's Dresden disciples.

The further education of his daughters, Tieck must have felt, required a less parochial environment. And so he decided to move to
Dresden, a city which had always appealed to him as pleasant, urbane
and healthful, and where he hoped, moreover, that he would be less
subject to his old ailment.[5] In July 1819, the Tiecks, accompanied by
Henriette, the oldest daughter of Count Finckenstein, who was a year
younger than Tieck, left Ziebingen and established a new home in the
Saxon capital. En route in Berlin they met August and Ottilie von Goethe.

Henriette, who had an absorbing admiration for Tieck, which was
heartily reciprocated by him, remained a fixture in the household, becoming a more important member of the family than Amalie. Since he had
no income whatever, she supported him and his family. And as he could
scarcely have afforded even the most modest living quarters, she leased
for him a pretentious second-story apartment in a dark gray house at
the Altmarkt, which in the course of the next generation was to become
famous as "the castle of the old Romanticist."

Ever since 1802, when he came to Ziebingen, Henriette had been his
true friend and admirer. In Dresden she became his *alter ego*. It was she
who nursed his gout, accompanied him to the theater and did the honors
at his social functions. She sacrificed her fortune in catering to his

bibliophilism. Thousands of times she presided at his readings, always listening with rapture and visible enthusiasm. His wife and daughters took all this graciously. They deemed it inevitable in so Romantic an age. Others, however, did not tire of gossiping and snickering about the peculiar relations of this "Count Gleichen" and his "women." In her letters to A. W. Schlegel, Charlotte Ernst went so far as to speak of bigamy.

To Solger he wrote soon after his arrival in Dresden: "I had an incredible yearning for Dresden. I could not wait until I got here; in a quiet morbid way, which is usually not peculiar to me, so that I often feared the tension might be a sign of some serious, dangerous illness. Since I am here I feel more cheerful than in many years. Everything seems bright and clothed in a new garment, and, what surprises me most, the same things delight me which oppressed and made me melancholy when I lived here in 1801 and 1802, young and healthy, but buried under melancholy and despair which I can now barely imagine. Thus all my plans are rising with new force and fresh colors before my mind's eye."[6]

In the memoirs of Wilhelm von Chézy we find a description of his personal appearance when he arrived in Dresden. His head, particularly his forehead and eyes, seemed like those of a healthy, robust youth. But his body, deformed and shrivelled by his ailment, made him appear a feeble old man.[7]

On October 25, hardly three months after coming to Dresden, he was shocked to receive news from Berlin of the death of Solger, his dearest friend during the last ten years. Fortunately another friend, Friedrich von Raumer, was ready to take Solger's place in his affections. He was also an academician, having been professor of history at Breslau up to this time. Simultaneously with Tieck's removal from Ziebingen to Dresden, he answered a call to Berlin, where he occupied the chair of political science until his retirement in 1853. The correspondence of Tieck and Raumer is the most important in the latter part of Tieck's life and contains a wealth of opinions on prominent contemporaries, on literature, history and music.[8] That they encouraged, assisted and influenced each other in their work is apparent. Raumer aroused Tieck's dormant interest in history, politics and current events and aided him in developing into a historical novelist. Tieck inspired Raumer with a love for literature and the theater, especially Shakespeare. He awakened in him a penchant for literary finesse and Romantic adornment, which helped to keep the Romantic attitude toward history alive in Germany throughout the first half of the nineteenth century.

A NEW HOME IN DRESDEN

Despite his fondness for Dresden Tieck was not certain during the early years of his sojourn whether to stay there, writing to his brother on November 22 that he would prefer Berlin. Before going to the Saxon capital, he carried on negotiations through Solger with Chancellor Hardenberg (whom Tieck knew personally) for a position in the Prussian Academy of Arts. And in 1820 the possibility of an academic post at Berlin loomed, as the correspondence with his brother shows. But he decided that he was too old to see the "academic jocosities" (die akademischen Spässe) through, and that as a too lately converted professor he would prove a bungler and lout. Probably through Steffens he had received the honorary doctorate from the University of Breslau in 1816.

In those days Dresden could claim the same qualities and offer the identical charms which render it so attractive today. Its situation in the lovely broad valley of the Elbe; the nearby Lössnitz; the many eminences overlooking the city; the readily accessible "Alpine" resorts of "Saxon Switzerland" along the river, clustered around Schandau; the pleasing valley of the Gottleuba are perennial sources of delight to a modest lover of nature. The city itself, the creation of such lavish and in their way distinguished rulers as John George II, who laid out the "Grosser Garten" in the seventeenth century; Augustus I and II, who made modern improvements, erected many beautiful buildings and collected precious art treasures in the eighteenth century; and King Anthony, an active builder and collector in the nineteenth century, was already then famed for its striking beauty and advantages as a center of art and culture. Buildings such as the "Hofkirche" and the "Frauenkirche," the "Georgenschloss" and the "Prinzenpalais," the Brühl palace with its stately terrace, the "Zwinger" and the Japanese Palace; the prospect of cupolas, towers, spires and copper-green roofs unfolding before the eyes of the approaching traveller; the priceless art objects and magnificent paintings in the "Zwinger" and, more recently, in the adjoining museum—all these and many other attractions have given Dresden just claim to the distinction of being a "German Florence."

But the city which could point to such natural advantages, unmatched buildings and unique treasures of art had remained small, and the souls of its good citizens were petty and timorous. The men of letters who were born or had made their home there expressed the same pusillanimity in their writings. They were wholesale purveyors of honeyed pocket-almanac tales, novels of lovesick knights and lovesome ladies, and gruesome ghost-stories for which readers were clamoring.

LUDWIG TIECK, THE GERMAN ROMANTICIST

For Romanticism had become popular and widely accepted by the mass of middle-class readers after the Wars of Liberation. As usual after a war fought for some seemingly idealistic cause, the bourgeoisie, disappointed by the futility of the profuse bloodshed in the name of liberty, suffered a reaction after the herculean struggle. And the rulers, unmindful of their solemn pledges, strove with chicanery to reestablish the ancient feudal state. To achieve this purpose more fully, they gave their subjects to understand that all liberal and democratic ideas would be regarded as evidence of subversive, revolutionary sentiment. They suited the action to the word, introducing a relentless system of espionage which kept track of every vestige of independent thought, exercising a rigid censorship and landing those in prison whose orthodoxy was clouded by the slightest shadow of suspicion. Medieval knighthood, the glory of pristine customs and beliefs, old-fashioned Germanism, fanciful day-dreaming, in short all the fashions and foibles which may be re-garded as excrescences of Romanticism, were now proclaimed by princes and princelings as the fittest themes for literature because they were the most innocuous. Of course the loyal poetasters and all the other literary small fry took these hints from above and carried them out with alacrity. There was no other course, even for a gifted independent mind, so long as the path of discretion was preferred.

Hence it came about that that very attitude and style of writing which had been ridiculed by educated readers and critics twenty years before, and had served a small coterie of independent thinkers, to which Tieck belonged, as an ideal for their artistic striving, now degenerated into a tool of the worst political and ecclesiastic reaction. At the same time this literary fad became the toy of a new reading public which had sprung up and consisted of the self-sufficient, sentimental, yet critical and well read intelligentsia.

Tieck had earned his reputation as the poet of early Romanticism par excellence. Practically all the problems which had agitated him a generation before had been solved. Rationalism had been defeated by Romanticism, transcendental philosophy was now the basis of thought, Goethe had been accepted, and science, literature and art were matters of common knowledge, interest and appreciation. But cured of mysticism by Homer, Shakespeare's realism and Solger's philosophy, and over-coming much of the cleavage in his personality, he had drifted from his original moorings, to which his noble, independent mind could adhere only so long as Romanticism measured up to his fondest dreams of poetry. Though not without his fault, it was surely against his will that Romanticism had become trivial stuff instead of genuine poesy, and practical dawdling instead of theoretical reverie. Under these circumstances it seems the irony of fate that he should now be proclaimed by a host of lesser lights as arbiter and master of the fashionable movement.

Soon he found himself surrounded by a throng of buzzing admirers, whose blind admiration made it hard for him, susceptible to flattery as he was, to withstand their lionizing. The first to approach him were Count Otto Heinrich von Loeben, who under the pseudonym of Isidorus Orientalis wrote extravagant novels such as *Guido*, decadently sentimental tales and emotional lyrics, and who succeeded in winning Tieck's friendship while retaining that of his enemies, Winkler, Kind and the other members of the Dresden "Liederkreis," whom we shall consider below; Count Friedrich von Kalckreuth, son of a well known general and author of tawdry Romantic writings; Ernst Otto von der Malsburg, who was Hessian chargé in Dresden but in private life an admirer and translator of Calderon (after his sudden death in 1824 at the age of thirty-eight Tieck inherited his Spanish library);[9] and Wilhelm von Schütz, the schoolmate of Tieck who out of admiration for Friedrich Schlegel had become a Romantic poetaster.

Tieck came into contact also with Karl Förster, the able translator of Petrarch and Tasso, whom he later saw frequently in the Dante circle of Prince John (Philalethes); Karl Maria von Weber, the composer, who was royal musical director in Dresden; the Berlin historian Johann Wilhelm Loebell; the Hellenist Karl Otfried Müller; the lyric poet Wilhelm Müller (whom he met through Kalckreuth and Loeben in 1820, urging him to publish his *Waldhornistenlieder*, the second edition of which is dedicated to Tieck);[10] the physician, painter and psychologist Karl Gustav Carus (whose practice as a painter influenced Tieck's feeling for colors);[11] Karl Christian Vogel von Vogelstein, professor at the art academy in Dresden, who later painted a splendid portrait of Tieck and a group painting featuring Tieck and the French sculptor David d'Angers; and Karl von Holtei, who starting out as an actor became theatrical secretary and author after he had suffered an accident which maimed him.

In 1822 Tieck was delighted by a visit of Jean Paul, whom he had met at Weimar in 1799. He worshiped Jean Paul's works in 1798, and was influenced by them in his poetry of atmosphere, though not always approving their style and bizarre humor.[11]

It should be noted that the majority of these new friends, of whom a complete list would form a lengthy catalog, were members of the nobility; the rest belonged to the higher circles of the bourgeois intelligentsia. The wags and gossips in Dresden and elsewhere, who were ill-disposed to Tieck, soon felt they had discovered a shrewd ulterior motive in his preference for men of rank or position, such as Malsburg.[12] According to them he was canvassing the field for two worthy sons-in-law! However, a less ridiculous and quite natural explanation is not difficult to detect. We find it in the fact that it was precisely the aristocracy and the upper middle class who condemned independent liberalism most strongly and considered themselves the appointed harbingers of light and leading for the untutored masses.

A glance at their correspondence shows how these men in the higher walks of life were attached to Tieck. Count Loeben wrote to him in 1821 that he occupied an "unattainable place in the firmament of poets" and that "those whose eyes are turned upwards can behold Tieck."[13] Malsburg addressed him the same year as "you dear, good, glorious man, of whom I do not know whether I should love or admire you more, but to be loved by you is bliss to me,"[14] and called him the saint of Dresden.[15] In 1822 Loebell felt "more strongly attracted" to him "than to any other poet now living."[16] And Count Baudissin, whom Tieck met several years later —in 1827[17]—and who became his collaborator in the translation of Shakespeare, wrote to him in 1830 that while Goethe's prose seemed to him incorrect and angular, and Schiller's stilted, Tieck's carried him away and filled him with rapture.[18]

The rising generation of writers, among them Grabbe, and later Friedrich Hebbel and Gustav Freytag, looked up to him as to a demigod for a cheering word. While Goethe in his old age often took an attitude of aloofness toward the younger poets, Tieck showed a warm interest in them, so far as they seemed to him promising. In time his reputation as a counsellor of literary novices became so great that more than one hundred manuscripts were sent to him annually by unknown authors.[19] Shortly before his death he said that he possessed "more than thirty volumes" of correspondence. Much of this has been lost or scattered. But in the letters to him which have been preserved—they number over seven hundred[20]—practically every name of any importance in German literature between 1820 and 1850 is represented.

Foreign writers also vied with each other in paying homage to him. H. C. Robinson, Coleridge and Carlyle from England;[21] Ticknor, Irving and Cooper from America;[22] Ampère, Marmier and Montalembert from France; Schukowski, Uwaroff and Stackelberg[23] from Russia were among them. His relations to Scandinavia were particularly cordial, due chiefly to the mediation of the Norwegian expatriate Henrik Steffens, a distant relative of Tieck by marriage. His closest friends from the northern countries were the Swedish poet Bernhard von Beskow, whom he met in

1819 and with whom he kept up a correspondence for many years; the Swedish diplomat Brinkman; and the Danish poet Oehlenschläger. The latter never failed to visit him when he came to Germany—he was there in 1806, 1817, 1831 and 1844. His grudge against Tieck for an unfavorable review of his drama *Correggio*[24] and for a poor reception of his German translation of Holberg quickly wore off. Oehlenschläger's plays, above all *Alladdin*, are clearly under the influence of Tieck's, in particular *Octavian*. Among numerous other Scandinavians whom Tieck counted among his friends, occasional guests and correspondents during a period in which they and their literature went in strongly for Romanticism, were the Swede Atterbom and the Danes Hans Christian Andersen, Heiberg and Molbech.

We have had occasion to refer to Tieck's readings. With his natural histrionic talent, he had begun early in life reading and acting out plays before groups of friends. During the winter of 1799-1800 in Jena he often entertained the Schlegels in this way. In the autumn of 1808, when he lived in Munich, Caroline, otherwise hostile to him, derived "altogether unique enjoyment"[25] from his readings and Schelling found "royal pleasure" in them. In Ziebingen he cultivated the habit of setting aside certain evenings, on which he read to the Finckenstein family and other friends.

And when he settled in Dresden he continued this practice, but made the occasions more pretentious and memorable by introducing an air of formality and admitting not only distant acquaintances but even total strangers. Often his readings occurred twice a week. Thousands of listeners from every corner of the globe attended these functions between 1820 and 1840; no tourist could say that he had "done" Dresden without having been present. Countless Germans, among them Carus, Steffens, Alfred Meissner, Niebuhr, and the actress Karoline Bauer, and scores of foreigners, among them the Englishman H. C. Robinson and the American George Ticknor, have left vivid accounts of his "Leseabende."[27] They agree that he would have become the greatest actor of the period if he had chosen that career, and that he possessed one of the strongest, one of the most charming and winning personalities of all time. Brentano called him the finest mimic talent off the stage; Menzel referred to him as "ein inwendiger Schauspieler."

Tieck's closer acquaintances were rarely absent from a "Leseabend"; others received invitations by word of mouth or note. In the morning the orderlies from the hotels would stop in, ask the old servant of the family what was to be read, and announce the number of prospective listeners. Before the reading, which began promptly at seven, tea would be served. The spacious salon was well lighted; many paintings hung on the wall, and under them canapes and divans were lined. Tieck, a short but very distinguished looking man with wonderfully deep-brown, sparkling eyes, played the condescending but gracious grand seigneur. When in good humor he would allow the guests to select the program. At the tea table the tall, slim, frail countess—anything but good-looking— presided, clad rather showily in a frilled, ruffled gown. Tieck's two daughters assisted her in doing the honors.

At seven he sat down at a small table under a candelabrum and, announcing the title of the work which he was to read, began in a re- markably euphonious, distinct voice. He read with few gestures but some mimicry, changing his voice only in comedies to indicate the different characters. Sometimes it seemed as though he could reproduce several voices at the same time. Often he read for three, sometimes four hours without a pause. All witnesses agree that he read well, recreating rather than merely reproducing.

Yet to some, who were forced by social convention to attend frequently, the readings proved a bore. Knitting and smoking were prohibited. Usually it became very warm in the room, because Tieck abhorred fresh air, even in summer. Yet no one dared budge or, worse still, show signs of inattention or drowsiness, because the austere countess, who could listen attentively to plays which she had heard him declaim scores of times, watched every member of the audience like a hawk. The better to achieve her purpose, she wore a green visor and sat at a favorable point of vantage. To the initiated it was a source of relief when he read a comedy, not only because that required less patience on the part of the audience, but also because he seems to have excelled in this genre. After finishing, he usually gave a brief extemporaneous critique of the work.

When he read one of his own productions—*Blaubart* was his favorite —it was a gala dress event, to which formal invitations went out. Shakespeare was his favorite author. It was an impressive experience to hear him read one of Shakespeare's tragedies. When the sculptor Rietschel started work on a statue of Tieck, his colleague Rauch wrote to him: Immortalize Tieck and make him as heroic as he seems when reading Shakespeare. Goethe, Goldoni, Holberg and Euripides were also fre- quently heard. He often read Calderon, too, but with less success than other authors. Aristophanes he read only to men. He never presented a work merely because it was modern or popular or lent itself particularly to his style of treatment. He always required that it should possess literary significance and merit and be worthy of his energies and of his listeners' attention.

No one enjoyed his readings more than Tieck himself. He considered them his ideal form of exercise and of devotional service. In the course of time he developed a methodology, his chief rules being to breathe only through the nose and to retain a critical attitude toward his own reading.[28]

On rare occasions he was wont to prepare a special treat for a select gathering of friends. He would make his appearance on a platform or makeshift stage and improvise an entire play without any assistance whatever. Once on his wife's birthday he staged an intricate, highly amusing improvisation, in which an amorous orang-utan was supposed to be the protagonist.[29] This is altogether characteristic for an author who was so strongly dualistic, so markedly a player of parts and so incorrigibly an improviser. Of interest in this connection is also the anecdote related by Köpke, and repeated by Varnhagen von Ense in an unpublished note, that Tieck once quite deceived an acquaintance as to his identity by suddenly changing his voice and posture and distorting his face so as to make himself unrecognizable.

Varnhagen held the opinion that his habit of reading and his mismanagement of his personal affairs, coupled with unconscionable, almost criminal irresponsibility in money matters, were Tieck's outstanding vices.[30] No doubt he carried his readings to excess, deprived himself thereby of valuable time for literary work, exposed himself to adulation and consequently to self-sufficiency, and, by admitting listeners who belonged in a circus or variety show, but not in this environment, became a butt for the ridicule of the half-educated or ignorant. On the other hand, by virtue of his highly expert reading, his "Leseabende" proved an educational force and a source of esthetic enjoyment, which made him a formidable rival of the royal theater. On no other basis can the attendance of such men as Grillparzer, Hegel, Herbart, Ranke, Thorwaldsen, Jean Paul, Immermann and Eduard Devrient be understood. In no other way can it be explained why even so critical an observer as Grillparzer admitted in his diary (VIII, 231) that Tieck's reading had the same effect as an excellent stage performance. His readings did more to promote a knowledge of Shakespeare and Jonson, Calderon and Lope, Gozzi and Goldoni than any German theater or institution of learning in their day. Finally they developed into an instrumentality of international significance, an excellent means of bringing the German world of letters in closer touch and greater esteem with other countries, especially England. Through them he became an important mediator, so important that had it been the custom for the German land of poets and thinkers to maintain an ambassador of letters abroad, he would have been the logical candidate.

As a group, the members of the so-called Dresden "Liederkreis," or "Vespertiner,"[31] were least enthusiastic about his settling in Dresden. Originally known as the "Dichtertee," this coterie of shallow, saccharine would-be poets did more to trivialize and negate the nobler aspects of Romanticism and to perpetuate the once fashionable writings of Gellert and Rabener than any other body. Their leader, Friedrich Kind, co-editor of the *Morgenzeitung*, was a self-styled poet and wrote unoriginal clap-trap idyls and imitations of that form of Romanticism which deals with specters and ghosts. His best work is the libretto of *Der Freischütz*, which thanks alone to Weber's charming music—an important factor in undermining Rossini's popularity in Germany—has remained alive to this day, more so than anything Tieck ever wrote. Theodor Winkler, known as Theodor Hell, who felt very proud of his "Hofrat" title, was manager, then secretary of the royal theater, edited the *Abendzeitung*, and turned out facile translations or adaptations of French vaudevilles and unctuous lyrics. Eduard Gehe penned historical tragedies, which in their awkward simulation of Schiller's rhetorical style were tragic make-weights. Friedrich Kuhn perpetrated insipid occasional verse. Other ad-herents were Loeben and Kalckreuth, Arthur von Nordstern, Roos, Nostitz and a number of women, including Helmina von Chézy, Therese an der Winkel and Fanny Tarnow. The minor poet Tiedge was friendly to the "Liederkreis."

Their pettiness was aggravated by the faint-hearted and malicious gossip K. A. Böttiger, now curator of the Dresden museum, whose previous relations with Tieck were mentioned in chapter 5. Not realizing that there are disparate grades of poetry, Böttiger increased the superiority complex of this mutual admiration society by assuring the members that they were the equals of any and all competitors. Tieck and Böttiger exchanged cordial letters until 1829, though in 1826 Tieck admitted that he could never trust the soft-spoken pedant.

In books, newspapers, but particularly in pocket almanacs, which were then beginning to gain unprecedented popularity, these writers had domi-nated the literary scene in Dresden ever since the removal of Christian G. Körner and his family to Berlin in 1815. Only a few adherents beside Loeben and Kalckreuth were palatable to Tieck, chiefly the genial musician Weber, the scholarly translator Förster and the thoroughly likable Friedrich August Schulze (known as Laun), with whom Tieck once even thought of collaborating and who as late as 1841 defended him in the *Allgemeine Literaturzeitung*.[32] The rest envied, feared and hated him, feeling instinctively that he was their master.

His attitude toward the group can best be traced in his letters to Winkler, which cover the period from 1821 to 1838.[33] Forced by the director of the theater, Herr von Könneritz, to accept in his *Abendzeitung* the dramatic critiques of Tieck, whose reputation as an expert on these matters had become formidable through his utterances and public readings, Winkler remained outwardly civil but recalcitrant enough. He was particularly annoyed by Tieck's eulogies of Shakespeare, Goethe and Schiller and by his vicious attack on Gehe. By February 1825 the relations were quite strained, although an external rift never took place. They will be considered further in conjunction with Tieck's work as a dramatic critic.

But against another group, which developed some years later and played a much more important rôle in literature, his onslaughts were of an altogether more vicious and serious nature. We refer to the Young Germans, among whom he numbered Heine, Börne, Gutzkow and Laube. These writers, who wanted to destroy Romanticism and replace it with a new, timely poetry, despised and persecuted him as one of their worst foes. They berated him as passé and decadent, as a secret Catholic apostate, as a reactionary and foe of that political and social progress which they meant to import from France in the form of republicanism and improvement of the social order according to the theories of St. Simon.

His abhorrence of strong sensualism, his noble refined style seemed to the young hotspurs who craved for "emancipation of the flesh" and for bold assertion of their individuality, nothing short of spinelessness and impotence. They looked at him askance and denied him practically all talent and character. They charged that he was responsible for that slavery, delicate but effeminate toying with mood and atmosphere, glorification of the Middle Ages and affected piety which had settled like a blight upon literature and robbed it of all life and direct appeal.

Numerous "novellen" of Tieck constitute serious attacks, direct or indirect, against his new rivals, whom in *Das alte Buch* (1834) he called "yelping, worthless dogs" (kläffende, nichtswürdige Hunde). In private utterances he expressed himself even more bitterly against them. "What do these ignorant youths take me for?" he wrote to Brockhaus. "Do I aim perchance at being a stupid Tory? Am I against liberalism? Or against genuine liberty? Nonsense! . . . To be sure, I am opposed to these miserable deputies of German liberty, against this tribe who are neither freemen nor Germans. You have no idea how many of this evil sect have foisted themselves upon me. . . . These Gutzkows and so forth—how devoid of ideals, talent and knowledge, yea devoid of education, not to mention culture."[34] And in the preface of *Der junge Tischlermeister* he scornfully exclaimed that their theories had been commonplaces to him even before they were born. He was particularly sharp against Heine, whom he began reading in 1834. To Immermann he called him a gipsy[35] and in *Das alte Buch* painted him as the disciple of a "subterranean, hunchbacked, crooked-legged, stuttering gnome" (unterirdischer, bucklichter, krummbeinichter, stotternder Gnom).

The Young Germans for their part, particularly Heine, were at first only mildly bitter, or apathetic, or even lukewarm toward him. Heine attacked him perfunctorily as early as 1827 in the *Reisebilder*. In his work on the Romantic School (1835) he continued this attack, although in passing he called him "a great poet," a "true son of Phoebus Apollo" and (in a deleted passage) a sensible man whose head has been turned by the Schlegels. But when the effect of Tieck's sallies in *Das alte Buch* became more marked, Heine's antipathy against him grew. In *Tannhäuser*, written in 1836, he inserted the following offensive lines on him:

> In Dresden sah ich einen Hund,
> Der einst gehört' zu den Bessern,
> Doch fallen ihm jetzt die Zähne aus,
> Er kann nur bellen und wässern.

A variant of this strophe is found in *Elementargeister* (1837). Then, in the preface to the second edition of *Das Buch der Lieder* (1837), he called him the erstwhile Romantic wonder-dog, who has now turned into a miserable old whelp (dem ehemaligen romantischen Strohmian, der jetzt ein alter räudiger Muntsche geworden). Finally, in *Shakespeares Mädchen und Frauen* (1838), he wrote: "Ah, this Tieck, who was once a poet and rated among the ambitious, if not among the highest, how has he degenerated since! How wretched the stint that he now reels off annually, in comparison with the free products of his muse during his earlier moon-illumined fairy-world time. As fond as we once were of him, we abhor him now, the impotent envier, who defames the passionate sufferings of German youth in his gossipy 'novellen.' "[36] A caustic article on Tieck by Gutzkow and Wienbarg has appeared posthumously.[37]

While he was being thus attacked, Tieck wrote retrospectively of Romanticism in 1828: "The attempt was made arbitrarily to recreate olden times in art, poetry and history; and a Middle Age as it never existed was described and recommended as a model; novels of chivalry, more puerile than the old ones, pushed their way forward with candid haste, delivered sweet sermons of a falsely poetic Christendom, and with stiff-necked gravity taught chivalrous virtue and the duties of servitude, submission to rulers and dukes, love and fidelity; in tone and sentiment so beneath all the jollity of Don Quixote that for this very reason wit and satire found no lever in them to cast them off the table of the goddess of fashion. Pristine art, at first misunderstood and scorned, now rated as the only art, and its fortuitous and awkward characteristics were regarded as the highest perfection. Religious sentiment, now revived, soon degenerated into sectarianism and persecution, and even scholars believed they could best show their devoutness by seeking to destroy scholarship, while there were artists who summoned up enthusiasm only when they turned away with holy terror from the beauty and statuary of the Greeks."[38]

In his declining years Tieck spoke in the same tenor to his Boswell, Rudolf Köpke: "An attempt was made to establish me as the head of a so-called Romantic School. Nothing was more remote to me than that, and, indeed, I have kept aloof from partizanship all my life. Yet I was continually attacked on this score, in writing as in speech, but only because people did not know me. If I were asked for a definition of Romantic, I could not give one. Indeed, I am unable to distinguish at all between 'poetic' and 'Romantic.' "[39]

His attitude toward Calderon, whom the Schlegels continued to revere, also shows a marked change. Under Solger's influence he now declared without hesitation that those who ventured to place Calderon on a par with, or even above, Shakespeare were literary inebriates. Naught but misguided enthusiasm, he felt, could induce anyone to foist such polemic, dogmatic views upon poetry and the theater. To Solger he was constrained to write late in 1818 that Calderon contains "scarcely a trace of that grand reason which makes Shakespeare so divine and genuinely human, nothing more of that noble naïveté which I must always admire in Lope."[40] A few weeks later he reported to the same correspondent that "Calderon is a perfect mannerist, and in his manner great and incorrigible; but it seems to me uncertain as yet whether Lope is not the greater poet, although he has perhaps completed but little or nothing. Yet Calderon, too, has his great weaknesses."[41] In 1824, when Friedrich Schlegel visited Tieck at Dresden, the latter informed Raumer that Schlegel "now reveres only the drunken poetry of Calderon and the Orientals, which with all its intoxicated bombast is none the less so infinitely matter-of-fact. He reproaches me with having lost my understanding for Calderon. He has lost his for Shakespeare, which is certainly worse."[42]

LUDWIG TIECK, THE GERMAN ROMANTICIST

Considering the transformation which Tieck had undergone, it is a pity for German literature that he and the Young Germans could not come to terms. His letters to his publisher Brockhaus[48] are not without indications that he had something in common with them. His various travel "novellen," *Die Reisenden* (1822), *Der Mondsüchtige* (1831) and *Eine Sommerreise* (1833), reflect the preference of the Young Germans for the epistolary travelog. His love for fairy tales, his irony and his genialty were shared by Heine. Nor was Tieck very far removed from their cosmopolitanism. We have already noticed his own statement, in *Der junge Tischlermeister*, concerning the relationship of his ideas to theirs. And *Vittoria Accorombona* (1840) depicts a "modern" woman quite of the type indorsed by them. He opposed the pragmatic nature of their writings without realizing that his "novellen" usually had the same character. They for their part underrated the vital importance of his "novellen" in their influence upon the development of that genre.

The fact is that no contemporary of Tieck comprehended those underlying causes for his chameleonism nor the changes in him which we have discussed. They did not know that he had overcome much of his problematic nature. They failed to realize that while, during the last decade of the eighteenth century, the world of Shakespeare's *The Tempest*, and, in 1800, Cervantes and Calderon seemed to him to offer a radical cure for the excessive sobriety which still prevailed in the world of letters, the realism of Shakespeare's histories and of Lope now loomed before his eyes as a proper antidote for the fantasticalness and effeminacy which he himself had unwittingly helped rear with his Romantic poetizing. His critical reason, now mature, recognized the dangers of vague toying with presentiments and moods. The flood of fate tragedies which was sweeping over Germany demonstrated to him that the demand for tragedy in the grand style could not be filled with the Romantic formula. The new narrative literature, on the other hand, which found its setting in the realm of the fairy tale or against a false historical background, was too intangible and incorporeal and failed to carry conviction.

Only in the field of lyric poetry could the state of semi-consciousness, could timelessness, the dusk of twilight and the prophetic demonization of nature still assert their rights. It is, therefore, no coincidence that Tieck's first literary undertaking after settling in Dresden was to publish his collected poems. They appeared at Dresden in three volumes between 1821 and 1823, and represent the first comprehensive collection of his shorter lyrics. Including the seventy-odd poems in free verse which originated in Italy and some thirty sonnets meant for the unfinished novel *Alma*, the three volumes contain over three hundred titles.

Lyrically his best years, as we have seen, were 1797 with about thirty, and 1798 with some forty poems. But the years 1803 with forty-five and 1805 with sixty were even more prolific. It is significant that the otherwise very unproductive decade from 1812 to 1822 was just as sterile from the point of view of lyric output, being represented by but ten poems. Many of them had been published before, in almanacs or as parts of such works as *William Lovell*, *Sternbald* and *Octavian*. Others, particularly those in the third volume, were new to his readers.

His chief purpose in thus bringing out his lyrics, he stated in his brief preface to the first volume, was to comply with a wish frequently expressed by many friends, especially those of a musical bent—"besonders der musikalischen." They show characteristics which we have previously described. On the whole they are indeed musical and singable, but too sublime, thin, ethereal and bodiless. With their lack of tangibility and of content and their frequent playing on words, a typically Schlegelian phrase is applicable to them. They represent the "poetry of poetry," that is an extract which has gone through a process of disembodiment in the distillery of Romanticism. They reveal a wealth of lyricism, but it is a lyricism raised to the second degree.

In 1841 he published a new edition. It came out at Berlin in one volume and, while omitting about forty items (not always the most inferior) of the earlier edition, contained about the same number of new poems.[44]

The fact that he saw fit to publish a collection like the *Gedichte*, as well as the circumstance that as late as 1828 he could still say that *Octavian* "is the clearest expression of my purpose in poetry,"[45] shows that, although he had turned away from Romanticism, he still adhered with warm feeling to the poetry of his youth. We may even say that at heart he had remained what he had always been, an exemplar of the Romantic type. As will appear from the discussion of his later works, his mind retained its Romantic mold. His demonism, though shifting its objective, remained with him, as we have seen, also his fatalism and that egocentric trend, which he now sought to conquer by the cultivation of sociability, as well as by a belief in revealed Christianity and in the miraculous nature of scores of relatively trivial events which occur in everyday life anywhere, anytime. In the light of such a philosophy his Romanticism expanded into a belief in the omnipresence of the supernatural element. "Nature, our knowledge thereof, art and science, the plain noble life of innocent children, the charm of spring, understanding for poetry and the ability to perceive Him, the Eternal God, everywhere

—here the true disciple finds miracles and the key to their comprehension," he exclaimed in 1829 in *Die Wundersüchtigen*.

But in addition to the change in viewpoint, he now developed new ideals, the "new manner," and a new purpose. If he had once been essentially a poet of moods and atmosphere, now, in an age of pamphleteering, he became a poet of culture and education. While many of his old motifs recurred—the magic of forest and mountain, the world of knighthood, the land of elves, goblins and witches, astrology, the ironical treatment of miracles and the fantastic treatment of modern questions—, he now abandoned the fiction of poetically reproducing a superhistorical or transcendental realm. Instead of using materials as tokens of his various psychic moods, he recreated forgotten times, espoused causes close to his heart or explained curious, exotic or mysterious phenomena. No longer did he attempt to convey his own volatile caprices to the reader; he wished merely to reveal and interpret events and their actors. And in place of the flowery lyric language of *Die schöne Magelone* he cultivated the dignified, leisurely prose of his "new manner," refined yet melodious, pure yet simple.

In the main this expositor of culture and education set himself two tasks during his Dresden period. In the drama, which could now boast of many monuments, and in literature generally, he strove to be the critic, as he had frequently been before, calling attention again and again through his readings, critical writings and work as "Dramaturg," to the great prototypes and traditions, and battling sham, vacuity and folly. In this field, Savigny felt, Tieck had more talent than as a poet.[46]

In narrative literature he aimed to combine his powers as poet and critic. First he developed a form, the "novelle," suited to the needs of the time (with its popular pocket almanacs) and calculated to offer instructive entertainment to the enlightened, blasé readers among the upper classes. Then he illustrated that form with examples.

His health did not take a definite turn for the better in Dresden. Partly for this reason he rejected the offer of a professorship in Munich tendered to him in 1826 through Eduard von Schenk.[47] The official letter of appointment, dated October 25, 1826, is preserved in the Bavarian "Kultusministerium."[48] Tieck purposely made his conditions so exorbitant that the matter fell through. A letter to him from Count Armansperg of October 26, wherein he was informed that the king could not modify the offer to include a free dwelling, would indicate this.[49]

As already noted, he often spent his summers at the baths in Teplitz; several times he went as far as Baden-Baden. In 1828 he made the longest journey of his later years, visiting Justinus Kerner in Swabia, A. W. Schlegel in Bonn, and Goethe in Weimar.

By 1820 we find the character of Tieck definitely enough crystallized to enable us to see it as a whole. Its main lines of development have been indicated, and frequent reference has been made to individual aspects of it. The period of adolescence, for instance, is well documented by his correspondence with Wackenroder, examined in chapter 3.

While a man's character may emerge from his works and from utterances of contemporaries, his own letters usually bring us much nearer to his "Eigenart." Despite strong subjectivism, however, Tieck, the introvert, rarely divulged his inmost self even to his friends. Most of the intimate letters which he may have written were destroyed by his daughter Agnes after his death.[50] We are fortunate, therefore, in possessing at least a few letters by him which are remarkably revealing.

His fundamental trait, duality or chameleonism, is well described in a letter of 1832 to Raumer. "Is it not the bliss of true friendship," he asks, "that we are loved by each true friend in a quite peculiar, different way, just as we approach every one of them with a specific kind of love?" Continuing: "How could A. W. Schlegel have profited by that affection which I showed for Novalis? Wackenroder would have been at a loss to understand my spiritual outpourings in the style of Solger, and Solger would surely have withdrawn if I had offered him the kind of friendship I gave Wackenroder. You and Solger are kindred souls, yet I consort in a different way with each. . . . This necessary, almost artificial diversity of conduct is too often overlooked. The more true friends a man has, the more richly does he shape himself and develop."[51] He once expressed the same sentiment to Solger when he wrote that the most acute letter-writers always assume the character of those to whom they are writing.[52] These thoughts, characteristically Romantic as they are, and expressed in very similar words in the first part of *Phantasus* (*Schriften* 4, 22 ff.), depict his typical attitude of adaptability in life and literature and explain his histrionic ability. In the case of such a man it is very difficult to be certain when he is wearing a mask and when not.

He was also aware of his quixotism, writing to Friedrich Schlegel in 1803: "Es geht mir wie dem Don Quixote, welcher überhaupt nicht so gar unrecht hatte."[53] He was no less conscious of his easily disturbed dynamic temper. It was well-nigh impossible for him to concentrate. To Raumer he wrote in 1817: "If I could only acquire your and Solger's calm industriousness. Since my early youth this has been one of my greatest sufferings, that I can but rarely master my mood and that I devote myself to dreams, plans, wishes and often unfruitful studies, then suddenly working as in a storm, producing too much and too rapidly. If you have a son teach him orderliness. But even that does not always help. In my case elders and superiors did all they could, and yet it is the lack of this ability which has so often caused me most sorrow in life."[54] He admitted to Friedrich Schlegel his "impetuousness in every thought, in every feeling, in every development, even to the border of insanity."[55] Invariably he was in a hurry; the phrase "in Eil" is found in scores of his letters. Hand in hand with this vice went negligence, which he frankly conceded,[56] and procrastination, of which he wrote that it had taken root in him so deeply that he could not overcome it, hard as he might try.[57] Naturally one with these faults is a poor correspondent. In addition his "letters always have the peculiarity of possessing no content,"[58] to quote his own words again.

The nature of his creative process as a poet was conditioned by his character. Writing was to him a matter of facility. He could work only in a spirit of haste and levity: "Mit Leichtsinn muss die Entwicklung des poetischen Triebes anfangen, und in schönem Leichtsinn muss sich auch das Talent wieder ausbilden, in Sicherheit und Leichtigkeit, sonst ist die Poesie ebenso sehr eine Qual als eine Ergötzung des Gemütes."[59] Thus the born improviser. As soon as he took a subject too seriously or deemed it too important, he became "timid and fearful" and lost his productivity.[59] This explains why works produced on the spur of the moment, like *Der blonde Eckbert*, are among his best, and why those to which he applied himself for years, like *Octavian* and the work on Shakespeare, were partial failures or remained fragments. The novel *Vittoria Accorombona* (1840) is an exception and represents the ultimate consummation of a desire, expressed in 1801, to become "more careful" with his works.[60]

His creative process explains, too, why mere conception of a work was in his mind tantamount to having completed it (he frequently wrote to publishers of having practically concluded works which we know were not even begun). As soon as he had conceived it, it stood vividly before his mind's eye as a finished product.

Such an impulsive writer naturally suffered long periods of unproductivity. To Raumer he wrote in 1822: "And why have I failed to carry out so many plans, and perhaps the best? If the reason were to be found in great blows of fate, I might be less disturbed. No, the causes were moods, pamperings, procrastination, laziness, delight in reading, revelling in imagination, exuberant projects, toying with life, and above all that contemptible pusillanimity of which you have no idea, which again and again causes me and my life to fall so flat."[61] To A. W. Schlegel, too, he confessed that he read "far too much."[62] This accounts for the bookishness of his works, particularly after 1820. His unproductiveness never degenerated into mental idleness, however. In chapter 11 we noted his energetic plan of work in 1815. In 1801 he wrote to the elder Schlegel that his soul was always occupied: "ich bin nie müssig, es ist mir von Gott verliehen, immer im Gemüt beschäftigt zu sein."[63]

Tieck was also an inveterate hypochondriac. He complained constantly about his health, his mood, his shortcomings. To Raumer he mentioned his "petty hypochondria."[61] Sensitive to a fault, as he confessed to Friedrich Schlegel in 1813,[64] he was tortured by fanatical melancholia. "It has always been natural for me to regard life as an oppressive burden, even in the absence of pain, misfortune, or external cause," he told the younger Schlegel.[65] At times everything within his ken seemed evil, sinful and necromantic[66]—an idea branded deeply into his soul by the mystics. "Pain and suffering have really been my career," he lamented in 1825.[67] And in 1822: "Since 1805 my health has been such that I have almost always had cause for complaint."[68]

Asceticism was also a hallmark of his character—a characteristic which he consciously sought to overcome by means of his soirées. Even in childhood we saw him yearning for life behind cloistered walls. At thirty he felt that he lived in the past, "I would almost rather say in a timeless condition . . . almost in the lovely solitude of a monastery."[69] Every fit of melancholy aroused in him this yearning for monasticism.[70] He found life with its vicissitudes hard to comprehend; it seemed like a fairy tale,[71] or a dream,[72] or a puppet play.[73] Often he and his own possessions appeared alien to himself; reality deadened his poetry.[74]

He always maintained a naïve, artless outlook upon life. Indeed, in his later years he was more childlike, though less sportive and unrestrained, than in youth.[75] He wrote to Friedrich Schlegel in 1803: "je älter ich werde, je mehr tritt meine Kindheit entwickelt wieder in mir hervor."[74]

This may have been an advantage for his poetry, but it proved calamitous economically. Soon after meeting him in 1797 Friedrich Schlegel wrote to his brother that Tieck was a mere child in mercantile affairs. He always remained so. His debts constantly mounted, even in Dresden, when he had not only a salary but an income from his "novellen," so high that it exceeded that of any other German author, as he himself once confessed to a friend. His household in Dresden proved expensive. During the later years he spent over three thousand talers per annum, then a staggering sum. Entertainment connected with the soirées required considerable funds; still more money went to gratify his bibliophilism, which became a passion. Whoever offered him a rare edition of Shakespeare, or Calderon, or Lope could be sure that he would pay even the most exorbitant price. To make both ends meet, he accepted gratuities from Countess Henriette until her fortune ebbed away. From others he borrowed without discrimination, rarely repaying a debt. Burgsdorff, Wackenroder, Bernhardi, the Schlegels, Savigny and others were thus duped by him. His fault, however, was not dishonesty, but abysmal carelessness, ignorance of the value of money and a loathing of everything that suggested business. "If we could only abolish money!" he exclaimed to A. W. Schlegel in 1800. "It oppresses me continually to think that I work for it."[76] Only in the light of this attitude can we understand his frequent maneuvers to violate his contracts with the publishers Max, Reimer and Brockhaus; the sale of his thirty-thousand-volume library to Asher in 1849, after he had mortgaged it to Brockhaus in 1840;[77] and the feeling toward him which gave rise to Varnhagen von Ense's ugly story that he never completed the novel *Der Aufruhr in den Cevennen* because Reimer had paid him in advance for the entire work.[78]

His was a nature which needed friends. He told Friedrich Schlegel that each deceased or distant friend was like a vital organ torn from his body.[79] To his real friends he remained true and chided those who "discard theirs like an old coat."[80] About fifty years after the death of his schoolmate Toll (as we have seen) and forty years after Wackenroder's death he wrote of them to Raumer as though they had but recently died. And seventeen years after Solger's death he still engaged in imaginary conversations with him.[81] That Tieck had a likable and winning way is attested by all who stood close to him.

There was malicious gossip concerning Tieck's philandering. His relations to his sister need not be rehearsed here. Varnhagen, as noted in chapter 4, told about illicit relations with Marie Alberti, ascribing her conversion to Catholicism to her resulting unhappiness and adding that when he had tired of her, Tieck passed her on to Bernhardi.[78] But whoever is familiar with the Rosaline episode in *William Lovell* and with the life and character of Marie, an older sister of Amalie and a noble and gifted woman, must feel that this incident was richly atoned. She became a painter and later the head of the so-called Klemens-Schwestern in Münster, where she died an early death as a victim of her work nursing the ill. A recent account of her by Heinz Jansen (who has, however, remained in ignorance of the Varnhagen story) does not leave the shadow of a doubt that her life was otherwise beyond reproach. Her conversion (probably not earlier than 1803), though due in the main to Tieck's and Bernhardi's treatment of her, is in small part at least ascribable to the enthusiasm for the Catholic faith prevalent in the Romantic circles of the time. We have noted that, independently of her, two of her sisters, Amalie and Charlotte, as well as the latter's husband, the Norwegian philosopher Möller, also turned Catholic.[82]

Many contemporaries, among them Charlotte Ernst in her letters and the actress Karoline Bauer in her memoirs, related rumors of a secret affair between Tieck and Countess Henriette. Hebbel gives credence to these rumors in his diary (IV, 13). Malicious Caroline Schlegel reported that he had amours with several of the Finckenstein daughters in Ziebingen.[83] But it must be remembered that these charges are unproved. In discounting them, Wilhelm von Chézy recalls that Tieck was practically paralyzed most of his life.[84]

To be sure, his relations to his wife, who was intellectually inferior to him, were not always good. He left her for long periods and is said to have contemplated divorce after ten years of marriage. It was during his absence in Munich and Italy that she and her older daughter became Catholic. In showering ostentatious attentions upon her more cultured rival, who was five years younger than she, he was inconsiderate of Amalie's feelings and unfair to her. A revealing letter of Dorothea to Üchtritz, written in 1839, two years after her mother's death, gives insight into the misery of his domestic life. The marriage of her parents, this introspective daughter writes, was an unnatural union, a calamity for Tieck, which impeded his career and ruined his finest poetic talent. Of domestic happiness there was no trace, she adds, concluding that if he had not made the mistake of marrying Amalie, he would have earned for himself a higher place in literary history. The impression which this letter gives is, however, relieved by another of the same correspondent to Luise Hensel, in which she writes that her mother always cherished a self-sacrificing love for her husband and children, possessed a bright, youthful nature and took interest and pleasure in every phase of life.[85] The root of the trouble between Tieck and his wife, it seems, was incompatibility.

Nevertheless he wrote a tender love letter to Amalie in 1806, after his return from Italy;[86] some affectionate notes in 1825, when absent on an inspection tour of the German theaters; and grieved sincerely over her death in 1837.

Undoubtedly Tieck, the experienced man of the world, was vain in his later years. He proved susceptible to flattery and, if we would believe Karoline Bauer and the actor Pauli, played favorites while "Dramaturg" in Dresden. His conceit goes far in explaining the pomp with which he conducted his frequent soirées, and his liberality in welcoming almost all auditors. Surely Varnhagen von Ense had this vaingloriousness in mind when, as we have noted, he referred to the readings as one of Tieck's vices.

He had a deeply religious nature, though never subscribing to any orthodox faith. As we have seen, he harbored sympathy and understanding for the Catholic faith but never embraced it; from 1798 on, when he became steeped in the writings of Böhme, Tauler, Suso and Bruno, mysticism practically supplanted religion in his heart.[87] But by December 1803 he again regarded the revelations of Christianity as the key to an understanding of the human soul and of the supernatural element.[88] He therefore opposed atheism, but was even more antagonistic to cool, destructive skepticism, which denied the existence of supernaturalism while offering no constructive suggestion as to a substitute. "Nothing has ever been more incomprehensible to me than the indifference of those who, encompassed by miracles and surrounded by spirits and apparitions, feel the eternal existence of all magic powers, yet wrap themselves in doubts, without, however, surrendering entirely to these doubts. They sacrifice the mystery but do not acquire its opposite, a non-mystery."[89]

His attitude toward philosophy was simple enough, once he had been cured of mysticism. Though unable to grasp abstract thought with ease, he gradually developed, under Solger's influence, an unshakable faith in a totality of experience. Such faith explains his mature attitude toward philosophy. As Matenko concludes (p. 74), it "made it impossible for him to find satisfaction in a single formula or dogma and hence alienated him from most systematic philosophers."

Finally, he was less concerned about his fame and about the effect of his work upon posterity than about his influence upon his contemporaries. He was moved by a sense of gratitude on his sixtieth birthday, he wrote to Raumer, because his writings had not been without influence upon his age and upon noble souls.[90] And the letters to Reimer from 1846 to 1853[91] contain references to his desire for a definitive edition of his collected works, in the hope that he may thus exercise his "authority and greatest possible influence" upon his age. Clearly Tieck had the same modest outlook on posthumous fame as Schiller ascribes to the actor in the prolog of *Wallenstein*.

CHAPTER FOURTEEN

IN THE SERVICE OF LITERATURE AND THE THEATER

THE first task which Tieck set for himself as a champion of culture and education was of a critical nature and envisaged two of his favorite fields, literature and the theater. Linked together, they appealed strongly to related sides of his character, bookishness, and predilection for the world of make-believe. Roughly speaking, his critical activities as a writer, declaimer and theatrical expert during his generation in Dresden may be divided into four categories. He strove to rescue from oblivion, or to promote a more accurate knowledge of, nine German writers of the past fifty years, Lenz, Goethe, Schiller, Üchtritz, F. L. Schröder, Kleist, Solger, Adelheid Reinbold and his own sister Sophie. He furthered the understanding, and improved the condition, of the modern theater and drama. He aimed at a new interpretation of Shakespeare and did much to make his name almost a household word in Germany. Finally, he carried the comparative method farther than it had ever been carried in the study of letters and called attention anew to English, Spanish, Italian and French literatures.

His service in the interest of the nine German authors whom we have mentioned was important in the light of historical development. Kleist was the first of these to whom he turned. After Kleist's greatest, then still unpublished play, *Der Prinz von Homburg*, had been staged with some success in Vienna, Breslau and Frankfurt earlier in 1821, Tieck became desirous for Dresden, the city of his new choice, to do similar honor to the memory of the man whom he had known and learned to admire thirteen years before in that very city. He took up the matter with Hans von Könneritz, who was director of the royal theater. Since his readings, with their high-class repertory, were offering redoubtable competition to that playhouse, which presented a rather steady fare of vapid French and native farces and melodramas, Könneritz was more than willing to conciliate and oblige Tieck in every possible way. So he gladly consented to assume the risk of putting on the unknown play of the quite obscure author, at the same time arranging an opportunity for Tieck to prepare the audience for the unusual drama, especially for the odd climax, the hero's humiliation in the third act, by means of an article in the Dresden *Abendzeitung*.[1]

LUDWIG TIECK, THE GERMAN ROMANTICIST

The Dresden performance took place on December 6, 1821, and although it is probable that no one in the audience shared Tieck's deep appreciation and understanding of Kleist's masterpiece, yet the evening was a success. This was probably due in no small measure to his article. Tieck expressed his gratitude to Könneritz and the actors, as well as to the audience, in a second essay in the *Abendzeitung*.[2] Here he called the performance "as correct and precise a one as I have ever witnessed."

In the same year he posthumously published *Der Prinz von Homburg* for the first time, together with another complete hitherto unedited play of Kleist, *Die Hermannsschlacht*, and all that has survived of a third, *Robert Guiscard*. He called the collection *H. von Kleists hinterlassene Schriften*. Upon this publication he had begun working as early as 1816. In that year he wrote that Kleist's relatives were helping him collect the dramas of the "noble and unhappy" poet, who stands out (der vorzüglichste) among all the younger poets and will some day perhaps be recognized.[3] Two years later he wrote von der Hagen that he would derive no material profit from the edition, since Kleist had left debts which were to be paid from its proceeds.[3]

This work was followed five years later by a fuller edition, *Heinrich von Kleists gesammelte Schriften*, in three volumes, prefaced by a fifty-page introduction.[4] The latter was destined to remain the most important contribution to Kleist scholarship for many years.

Some of the factual information and material, as we have seen, he owed to the painter Hartmann, a friend of Kleist, whom Tieck had met in 1806. He also benefited by Solger's aid and by information which Schütz obtained for him from a cousin of Kleist and from the poet's friend Pfuel. His favorable critical reaction to Kleist's work, however, was original with Tieck and represents a clear-cut, acute and sane point of view. If this introduction, as well as the essay on Goethe and his times prefacing the edition of Lenz's works, were his only extant critical writings, they would suffice to assign him an important place in the annals of German literary criticism. Although he did not appraise Kleist quite correctly (he considered him more from the dramaturgic point of view than as a great poet and, in regarding him chiefly as an unhappy, eccentric genius, he hardly rated him higher than Lenz), yet modern Kleist criticism is built upon the solid foundation which he supplied.

Tieck's contemporaries did not accept his high evaluation of the poet. Their position is illustrated by the echo it found abroad. In 1829 the Scottish critic Robert P. Gillies, writing in his *Foreign Review and Continental Miscellany*, severely chided him for "overrating" Kleist, whose plays "never will pass muster along with those of Müllner, Houwald,

Raupach and other living authors."[5] It took at least two generations before Kleist came fully into his own, but when he did, Tieck's preface played its part in fixing his fame.

Textually, Tieck's edition is not reliable. Misguided by poetic intuition and caprice, he has taken unwarranted liberties with Kleist's language. His text of *Die Hermannsschlacht*, in particular, based upon an abandoned old manuscript, is unsatisfactory. Moreover, his compilation of *Gesammelte Schriften* is not complete. He has omitted several of Kleist's contributions to *Phöbus*; also his political articles in the *Berliner Abendblätter* (published by Köpke with other addenda in 1862). Since Tieck's time a number of poems, too, have come to light. In 1859 Julian Schmidt published a revised and supplemented redaction of the Tieck edition.

In the same year in which *Kleists gesammelte Schriften* came out, Tieck, in collaboration with Friedrich von Raumer, published *Solgers nachgelassene Schriften und Briefwechsel*, which he had in preparation ever since Solger's death in 1819.[6] It includes minor writings of his friend, most of them unimportant, and numerous letters from and to Solger. The most valuable of these were exchanged with Tieck. A comparison of their text with the original letters, preserved in the State Library in Berlin, shows that Tieck worked with only moderate care and made arbitrary omissions and changes. Introduction and epilog, by Tieck, are brief. The modern edition of the Tieck-Solger correspondence, by Matenko, offers textual improvements and adds over thirty letters.

In 1828 he got out a more important edition, *Gesammelte Schriften von J. M. R. Lenz*, in three volumes. The significance of this eccentric writer, who had been a friend of Goethe in Strassburg and Weimar, lies in the fact that he was one of the leaders of the Storm and Stress movement and a forerunner of Romanticism. Like most of the young revolutionary poets of the 'seventies, he had fallen into oblivion. The long introduction, running well over one hundred pages and reprinted in the *Kritische Schriften* under the title "Goethe und seine Zeit," is one of the weightiest pieces of critical work Tieck ever did, despite its fragmentary nature. "Der ganze Tieck steckt in dieser Vorrede," Immermann wrote to Michael Beer.[7] It was a mistake, however, to publish the essay as a preface to the edition of Lenz, for it deals with him only incidentally. The real topic of the paper is the age of young Goethe in the light of its historical significance. Tieck's friend Professor Loebell had good reason to complain that, hidden among the resuscitated writings of an author who would be read as little as Lenz, this brilliant critique would not enjoy the amount of dissemination it deserved.[8]

LUDWIG TIECK, THE GERMAN ROMANTICIST

In many respects Tieck's opinions on Lenz have remained standard. If he is still regarded as an unhappy genius; a curious, strangely touching figure; and the same sort of precursor of Goethe as Greene and Marlowe were forerunners of Shakespeare, this is due to Tieck. The technics of modern scholarship have expanded the conception of his problematic character and failure in life, as well as contributed to the more exact delimitation of his striking relationship to the Romanticists. All the more credit is due Tieck if we consider that his preoccupation with Lenz was a work of friendship and love more than of criticism.

He secured many of the facts of Lenz's life from Dr. G. F. Dumpf, a physician in Livonia with whom he corresponded in 1812, 1820 and 1821.[9] Dumpf, who possessed numerous papers of Lenz, had published the poet's drama *Pandaemonium Germanicum* in 1819.

As we have indicated, the most important part of this prefatory paper is not the sketchy account of Lenz, but the fuller treatment of the significant era in which he lived, in particular of young Goethe. Although Goethe had himself said to Eckermann on March 30, 1824, that he (Goethe) was by far the greater poet and that his own relations to Tieck were not as good as they should be because the Schlegels had deliberately patronized Tieck and tried to establish him as his rival, yet Tieck's remarks on Goethe are not dictated by envy. To be sure, the discussion, most of which is in dialog form, reveals two souls in Tieck struggling for supremacy. One would bestow unqualified admiration upon Goethe, the other is doubtful and skeptical.

The underlying reason for this duality is that he contemplated Goethe purely as a poet, not as an exemplar of noble humanity. And as a poet Goethe seemed to him admirable only during the first half of his life. But in the light of what was known about Goethe's life in 1828, we may ask, was not this attitude defensible? What is it that we today admire most in the *senex mirabilis* of Weimar? Surely the universality of his interests, his many-sidedness, the manner in which he rounded out his life and his human qualities. But Tieck knew little about these matters and pondered less about them. We are aware how truly he had written to Raumer in 1817 that he considered everything from the vantage of poetry.[10] Hence he was justified in preferring the genial, ingenuous and straightforward poesy which Goethe wrote as a young man to the less spontaneous and more classical works of the aging poet. He also held that Goethe's later cosmopolitanism, his reversion to ancient Greek models and his disregard of the exigencies of the stage were inimical to his (Tieck's) highest ideal, the development of a truly national German art. He never abandoned this viewpoint. Unfortunately, however, it developed into an obsession and a crotchet, as when he said to Köpke (and among others to Theodor Bernhardi and Varnhagen von Ense) not long before his death, that Goethe's life at the Weimar court prejudiced and arrested his poetic development, and that only *Götz von Berlichingen* and the "oldest fragments" of *Faust* are great poetry.[11]

As in the case of Kleist, Tieck's text of Lenz's works is not trustworthy. Moreover, the drama *Das leidende Weib* in volume 1 is by Klinger, not by Lenz, and the essay *Über Herders älteste Urkunde* in volume 3 is from the pen of Häfeli. *Der Waldbruder* by Lenz, published in *Die Horen*, was overlooked. Tieck knew about the existence of Lenz's drama *Catharina von Siena* and made a conscientious but futile search for it. On January 8, 1825, he wrote about it to Johann Heinrich Friedrich Schlosser,[12] a nephew of Goethe's brother-in-law, with whom Lenz had had contacts, but Schlosser, too, failed to give him any clue as to the whereabouts of the manuscript. The incident shows at least that he exercised some care in performing his labors as a redactor.[13] After Tieck's day a rich second harvest of Lenz's dramas was published by Karl Weinhold in 1884 as *Dramatischer Nachlass* (about a dozen additional plays and dramatic fragments). In 1891 the same editor, in *Gedichte von J. M. R. Lenz*, brought out a number of hitherto unknown poems by Lenz.

Nowhere does the nature of Tieck's literary criticism stand out more clearly than in his utterances on Schiller, which are scattered in several papers of 1823 and 1827[14] and anticipate the critique of Otto Ludwig. Nowhere is native admiration so carefully tempered with studied appraisal. Nowhere does he show so clearly that his ideals as a critic were much higher than his achievement as a poet. Here, too, we detect that duality which is manifest in his every movement.

Die Räuber strikes him as a weak beginning on Schiller's part, full of exaggeration, false pathos and arbitrariness. Franz Moor is a "mere caricature" (Fratze). And yet true theatrical instinct and dramatic talent cannot be denied the young author[15] of this play, which in his boyhood Tieck had reverenced and imitated as an inspiring masterpiece. Although *Don Carlos* was the first play of Schiller to "take" with audiences, it contains more philosophy, politics and history than poetry,[16] and no lyric element.[17] There is too much intrigue; the action, deficient in itself, is retarded by Marquis Posa, an "impossible" figure.[18]

The drama of *Wallenstein* is a "great monument" and a source of pride for all Germans. The subject is happily chosen because it has historical significance. But according to Tieck Schiller errs in adducing too many motives for the downfall of the hero.[19] Here lyric strains are introduced by Schiller for the first time.[20] Yet the romantic element supplied by the love episode is thin, unreal and out of place. The ending is weak because it offers no clear prospect for the future.[21] The weaknesses of Schiller's earliest plays are still apparent in *Wallenstein*. There are improbabilities, the characters at times contradict themselves, the motivation is occasionally poor, and there is a surplus of reflection.[22] But it is a pity, Tieck found, that Schiller did not continue along the lines of this play and, emulating Shakespeare's example, write a series of national historical dramas.

Maria Stuart, which shares with *Wallenstein* the distinction of being one of Schiller's "best plays," also contains lyric atmosphere.[23] The titular character is the most ably delineated woman in Schiller's works.[24]

Die Jungfrau von Orleans is consciously "Romantic" as opposed to the two foregoing dramas. Though "an excellent play," it has been misunderstood. But Schiller erred in introducing too great a number of miracles.[25] Here and in his two subsequent plays Schiller "dissolved his action into speech, sentiment and situation."[26]

Die Braut von Messina, an unhappy example of "cold splendor," represents good theory but poor practice.[27] It is the "weakest play in literature" on the theme of two hostile brothers, a veritable bane for the stage, which has led to countless imitations, all as undramatic, impossible and devoid of inner necessity as Schiller's "quite undramatic work." If the "stage is out of joint," it is chiefly the fault of *Die Braut von Messina* and its unfortunate and inconsistent linking of the idea of fate with that of man's moral freedom.[26]

Wilhelm Tell, on the other hand, is a "glorious" work, full of the spirit of liberty and righteousness. It is a piece of splendid virtuosity, in which the poet sets himself the most difficult problems and solves at least some, for instance the apple scene, with great brilliance. However, *Wilhelm Tell* is not Schiller's best play because of the numerous obstacles inherent in the subject. The plot is too loosely knit, wherefore form and coherence suffer.[28]

In summing up his appraisal of Schiller, Tieck criticizes his failure to find a convincing ending, his preference for cosmopolitan idealism, as opposed to German nationalism, his usual failure in portraying women and his employment of rhetoric and lyricism for their own sake. The last-mentioned fault, he found, has been imitated and has proved nothing short of a calamity for the German drama.[29] Schiller's manner has spoiled actors and pampered the public, he thought. The former have become accustomed to treating every rôle with the elevated pathos and rhetoric characteristic of Schiller. The latter heed the rhetorical pyrotechnics and ignore the drama as a whole. Besides, later writers, under the spell of

Schiller, have imitated him slavishly instead of developing their art. He felt, too, that Schiller's later plays show too little regard for the stage and that their authority and influence have prejudiced the development of the best stage traditions. In the philosophy upon which these works are grounded he could see only an artist's aberration.

And yet Schiller is the "poet of the nation,"[30] whom Tieck proudly joins his compatriots in admiring. "That it is not my intention," he exclaims,[31] "to abuse the poet whom I, too, venerate, I need scarcely add. Whoever can misinterpret me and my endeavor to the extent of thinking otherwise, should, if he be fair, pay no heed at all to my remarks. Sensible persons have long recognized and asserted that the idolatry which has been carried on with Schiller's works has (like any idolatry) wrought great harm to our literature."

On the other hand, his reaction to Schiller also shows his subjectiveness as a critic and the failure of his own poetry to live up to his critical standards. Criticism, intuitive in its nature, was one thing, his own poetry another; they seemed to have no logical nexus. In discussing *Die Braut von Messina*, for instance, it does not appear to have occurred to him that his own *Karl von Berneck*, too, introduced fate on the stage. With far less artistic instinct than Schiller he portrayed fate in the form of blind, capricious chance. As for his severe criticism of the lyric and rhetorical elements in Schiller, he forgot that he carried these same devices to much greater extremes in *Genoveva* and *Octavian*. Indeed, all of his animadversions, especially against Schiller's reflectiveness, sententiousness and weakness of characterization, apply much more to Tieck and to the imitators of Schiller than to Schiller himself.

The personal relations of Schiller and Tieck, we know, had never been good. Schiller detected his weakness and disliked him because of his friendship for the Schlegels and Reichardt. Tieck developed a secret jealousy of Schiller because of his ability and his intimacy with Goethe. To Raumer he wrote very querulously in 1829 of the correspondence between Goethe and Schiller, claiming that in it they were both unmasked as petty schemers.[32]

But it should not be overlooked that he ungrudgingly recognized Schiller's true greatness. Even his adverse criticisms, which we have purposely emphasized, redound in part to his credit. In them he bravely sought to stem the tide of blind admiration which bade fair to submerge the more solid merits of the author of *Wallenstein* and *Wilhelm Tell*. Moreover, he was the first writer to sound a warning against the danger which undiscerning admiration and slavish imitation of Schiller's later plays held in store for the future development of the German drama.

LUDWIG TIECK, THE GERMAN ROMANTICIST

Toward the end of his life Tieck modified some of his ideas concerning Schiller and added others. He came to believe that *Die Räuber* (particularly the earlier version), with its "titanic force," is Schiller's finest work, that *Die Braut von Messina* contains "beautiful passages," and that the *Demetrius* fragment is the outstanding achievement of Schiller's later years. He spoke unfavorably of Schiller's ballads, despised such a poem as *Das Ideal und das Leben*,[32] and held the original opinion that Schiller and Goethe did not profit by their mutual friendship.[33]

Of comparatively less consequence, though also important in revealing his uniformly high ideals, were Tieck's critical efforts in evaluating the work of the young dramatist Friedrich von Üchtritz, the acting and playwriting of Friedrich Ludwig Schröder, and the fiction of Adelheid Reinbold and of his own sister Sophie. Üchtritz, a talented young author, befriended Tieck through his writings, as six extant letters from Tieck to him and four from him to Tieck show.[34] He became a favored member of the author's inner circle and carried on an extremely interesting correspondence with Dorothea between 1831 and her death.[35] Through Tieck's efforts his noble but unactable tragedy *Alexander und Darius* was published in Berlin in 1827 with a preface by Tieck, wherein the latter, though candidly admitting weaknesses in construction, language and versification, pointed to young Üchtritz as a truly gifted author.[36] He thought it was the best play since Kleist's *Prinz von Homburg*.[37] Unfortunately this *macte nova virtute* could not bear fruit; Üchtritz and his lifeless plays have since been forgotten.

Schröder was one of the foremost actors in Tieck's youth, and the latter never tired of descanting upon his virtues. In 1831 he prevailed upon the young scholar Eduard von Bülow, who had settled in Dresden in 1828 and had become his eager disciple, to make a collection of the numerous plays and adaptations which Schröder had prepared for the stage. This was in itself a laudable and worthwhile endeavor, for Schröder had been one of the German pioneers in introducing numerous foreign plays, among them acting versions of Shakespearean and English Restoration dramas, to the German stage. Tieck enhanced the value of the four-volume edition by prefacing it with a sixty-page introduction,[38] which has distinct independent value as a succinct account of the development of the stage in England and throughout the European continent from its beginnings until 1800. His ideal in this discussion is one which forms the unifying principle, so to speak, of all his numerous dramaturgic papers, namely the establishment of a national theater and a "bürgerliches Drama" for Germany. The section which deals more specifically with Schröder retains only historical value. It gives a survey of the development of the middle-class tragedy in France and England and its spread to Germany. It offers an account of Schröder's imitations and adaptations based upon a score of foreign writers, among them Diderot, Gozzi, Moreto, Fletcher, Farquhar, Goldsmith and Colman, some of which later served as models for Iffland and Kotzebue. Finally it emphasizes Tieck's standards of natural, unaffected acting as practised so gloriously, he thought, by Schröder and his "old school" and abused so flagrantly by "the more recent sophistic school of Iffland."[39]

In 1833 Tieck's eccentric sister Sophie died. Although her later relations to her brother (to be considered in a subsequent chapter) were not pleasant, yet he decided to pay a final fraternal tribute to her memory by recalling the days of her youth when she still loved him and guarded his affections jealously. In those days she had been an author, too, and had written a considerable number of poems, stories and novels,[40] some of which had appeared in Nicolai's *Straussfedern* and Bernhardi's *Bambocciaden* about two generations ago. Tieck had always thought highly of her works, praising them warmly to her in a letter of 1802. Now in 1836 he published her chief novel, *Evremont*, in three volumes, prefacing it with a few remarks, which he signed, without however revealing her authorship. This decadently Romantic work hardly merited being exhumed. Tieck's statement to Brockhaus that it is the "loveliest and maturest work which has appeared for a long time"[41] is just as exaggerated as is his conviction, expressed to his publisher Josef Max in November 1836,[42] that it contains "soul, love, sentiment, noble humanitarianism, benevolence, purity, profundity, keen observation and subdued sorrow." More accurate is his guess that if published "twelve years sooner" (when trivial Romanticism was in its heyday) it "would have made a very deep impression." The reviewers attacked it as a lifeless dilution.[43]

Another young woman author, Adelheid Reinbold, who with her three younger brothers depended upon the support of the Viennese banker von Pereira, attracted his attention by a charming little "novelle" *Irrwisch-Fritze*, published in the 1830 issue of the almanac *Urania*. He admitted her to his inner circle, showered her with kindness and made her his protégée and pupil. She reciprocated by showing him unbounded admiration. In an unpublished essay addressed to him she calls him and Goethe the greatest literary figures, the former being the poet of "reason and fantasy," the latter the poet of "human volition."[44] Through Tieck's good offices she published her *Novellen und Erzählungen* under the pseudonym Franz Berthold in 1836. He supplied a brief preface to the work, which enjoyed considerable success.

LUDWIG TIECK, THE GERMAN ROMANTICIST

Early in 1839 Adelheid Reinbold died suddenly. Tieck honored her memory by writing a noble letter to Frau von Pereira, begging her to continue her financial support in favor of Adelheid's three younger brothers,[45] and by publishing her novel *König Sebastian* in the same year. To be sure, the latter was already in press when she died. He introduced it with a few heartfelt prefatory remarks in which he revealed her identity.[46] Three years later he got out, "with greater confidence,"[47] two volumes of her *Gesammelte Novellen*. Like Sophie Tieck, Adelheid Reinbold has been forgotten by posterity. And yet her works deserve a better fate than those of Sophie. Their lively action, plastic characters and human touch make them seem modern and not unenjoyable even today.[48]

We have weighed Tieck's services in the interest of nine compatriotic writers. Save in the cases of Goethe and Schiller, his was more a work of friendship, love or "Pietät" than of criticism. But in his constant striving to promote what seemed to him noble in literature and art and to combat baseness, triviality and vileness; to regard every work of art in its larger aspects rather than in its details; to further a healthy national growth in matters of the spirit; to tolerate no blind idolatry; and, in studying literature historically, to approach it from the international point of view—in pursuing these aims he was animated not by quixotism or petty self-interest but by high standards of genuine criticism. Indeed, he never took up the cudgels for any writer except for the purest motives. He never indulged in immoderate praise and fulsome flattery, nor in undue condemnation. If he seems to laud Üchtritz, Sophie and Adelheid Reinbold beyond their true merit and criticizes Goethe and Schiller more severely than they are criticized today, it is because our sense of values has shifted during the past one hundred years, not because Tieck had a special axe to grind.

When asked to review some work by a friend for which he did not care, he usually preferred to risk the loss of that friend by recording his frank opinion (as in the case of Oehlenschläger's *Correggio*[49]), or he maintained a judicious silence (as his letters to Winkler of 1823[50] concerning Malsburg's *Das ledige Ehepaar* prove). Looking back at the end of his career over his critical activity, he could say that "only once in my life did friendship for an author and his amiability seduce me to pronounce too favorable an opinion concerning him."[51] This author was Eduard von Schenk, the work in question his tragedy *Belisar*. Consequently Tieck suppressed his review of Schenk's play, refraining from publishing it in his *Kritische Schriften*—a highly characteristic step. The manuscript of the paper, covering seventeen quarto pages, is extant[52] and seems not nearly as favorable to Schenk as would be expected. His drama is called "good, though not of the best, and not perfect;" much more space is devoted to unfavorable criticism of Grillparzer, whom Tieck despised, rating him below scribblers like Zedlitz and Hornbostel.

We come to his second great task as a critic, his attempt to further the understanding, and improve the condition, of the modern theater and drama. Upon arriving in Dresden in 1819, he found the local theater in quite as bad a state as most of the theaters throughout Germany. Frivolous French comedies and vaudevilles furnished the bulk of the theatrical fare. Kotzebue and Iffland were the most popular German authors. The plays of Lessing, Goethe and Schiller were practically unknown. Before 1821 only two Shakespearean plays had been produced in Dresden, *Macbeth* in 1819 and *Hamlet* in 1820.[53] But Könneritz, the director of the theater, was very friendly to Tieck,[54] more so than his secretary, Hofrat Winkler, who derived a handsome income from his adaptations of the French vaudevilles.

As soon as Tieck had shown his mettle as a dramatic expert through his readings and, perhaps, his utterances in private conversations, Könneritz invited him, without Winkler's support, to contribute dramatic critiques to the *Abendzeitung*, of which Winkler was the editor. But Tieck, sensing the attitude of Winkler and his friends, did not respond with alacrity. His first papers were the Kleist articles late in 1821; regular contributions did not follow until early 1823. Once begun, however, they appeared with fair regularity for over a year. The more important number about thirty; some of them are very lengthy and came out in instalments.

His papers are distinguished by sharp, constructive criticism and freedom from flattery. Their high critical standards, dignified tone and clarity of style remind of Lessing. If they err in dealing too lengthily with unworthy plays, it must be remembered that they were written for his contemporaries, not for posterity, and had a didactic purpose. Moreover, he possessed the ability of writing so interestingly even about the dullest, most ephemeral play that to this day almost every line of these three hundred pages[55] makes entertaining and instructive reading for a casual reader who has never heard of the works under review. He was also strikingly successful in recreating, by mere description, the acting of individual players.

The tragedy of *Anna Boleyn* by Eduard Gehe, a friend of Winkler and a member of the "Liederkreis," was slashed so mercilessly that Winkler complained. Unabashed Tieck replied: "You say it will shock him. My dear man, so much the better, if he will once look into himself with a critically doubting eye. Either he will abandon the utterly thankless work, or he will study, learn, take pains, rack himself—and not shake tragedies out of his sleeve. Let him remember that Schiller labored for seven years at *Wallenstein*. Let him reflect that poor Kleist rewrote many scenes ten times." Perhaps these few sentences from his own pen throw more light upon his ideals as a dramatic critic than pages of description could.

No less scathing are his reviews of two comedies of Clauren (a pseudonym for Heun), whose mean triviality struck Tieck as nothing short of immoral. The keynote of both papers is found in the sentence: "Criticism would be wasted on such products."[56] In the discussion of the works of other comic writers, such as Töpfer and Frau von Weissenthurn, we can often read Tieck's supreme contempt between the lines. A longer paper on Houwald's fate tragedy, *Der Leuchtturm*, is written in dialog form and pours forth his whole abhorrence of this type, in which fate plays a dull, mechanical part. It ends with the Horatian "Quodcumque·ostendis mihi sic, incredulus odi."

Favorable papers are that on *Wallenstein*, discussed above, one on Kleist's *Kätchen von Heilbronn*, and another on Holberg's *Political Tinker*. A criticism of Körner's *Toni* develops into a classical discussion of the basic differences between epic and dramatic poetry. In the case of plays by Shakespeare and Goethe, he is content with a critique of the performance. A long discussion of the actor Esslair is excellent in recapitulating his favorite histrionic principles. But the finest papers are those on Shakespeare, which will be discussed below.

As noted in the case of Kleist's *Prinz von Homburg*, he soon made his influence felt upon the Dresden theater through his suggestions. Thus by virtue of his urging *The Merchant of Venice* was performed in Dresden for the first time in 1821, according to a three-act arrangement which he made; *Romeo and Juliet* in 1823; *King Lear* in 1824. Goldoni, Holberg and Schröder, too, owed him a place in the repertory. It is not surprising, then, that despite the machinations of Winkler and the "Liederkreis," who disliked him for his truculent idealism and constant references to Shakespeare and Goethe, and hated him for his attacks on members of their cohort, he was invited in September 1824, upon the retirement of Könneritz and the installation of a new director, Wolf Adolf von Lüttichau, to become "Dramaturg." His duties were defined as: 1. giving the director advice and aid in his literary tasks (selection of plays), 2. training the younger and less experienced actors. His salary was to be six hundred talers (which was increased to eight hundred in 1838), and he was to have the title of "Hofrat."

Tieck, almost fifty-two years old, gladly accepted the position, his first since leaving Nicolai's employ in 1799. His duties began with the new year. Now at last he was paid to do what he had been punished for trying to do in his youth, he jokingly remarked to the actress Karoline Bauer.

One of his first assignments was to accompany his new chief, Lüttichau, on an inspection tour of the theaters in a number of German cities. They left early in May and returned toward the end of June, stopping among other places at Prague, Vienna, Munich, Stuttgart, Strassburg, Frankfurt and Braunschweig and averaging one play, ballet or opera a day. In Vienna and Munich he was received with great cordiality. The impressions of theatrical conditions in the German-speaking countries which he gained on this journey[57] were not favorable. Usually the play was inferior and the acting worse. But a performance of *King Lear* in Vienna and the acting of Mlle. George in Strassburg compensated him for many disappointments. During his absence from home he wrote two lively letters to his wife and daughters in Dresden, showing greater devotion to his family than he had manifested in years. Nine letters which Amalie, Dorothea and Agnes wrote to him during the same time are among the most sprightly, chatty and human in the entire Tieck correspondence.[58]

Upon his return home it soon developed that his strong opposition to the prevailing low standards of taste would make his position very difficult. It also became apparent that the nature of his official activities had been so vaguely circumscribed that his efforts to influence the management of the theater were severely handicapped. Lüttichau, a pleasant, sociable man who welcomed advice but rarely took it, was far too lenient with the actors.[59] The bureaucrats in the theater were deaf to his suggestions. The public resented the "despotic" manner in which he foisted his taste upon them. The actors, to whom he gave his time without stint, drilling each one individually for hours at a time, grumbled about the unabbreviated performances of Shakespeare's plays and were indignant over his plain-spoken criticism of their work. An unpublished letter of the actor Pauli to the actress Julie Gley of December 10, 1830, voices bitter complaint about Tieck's tyranny. And the Dresden playwrights could not forgive him his severe judgment of their feeble efforts.

A good illustration of his awkward position is given by the American visitor George Ticknor, who sojourned in Dresden in 1835-1836. At that time Princess Amalie of Saxony, a prolific author of trifling comedies under the pseudonym of Amalie Heiter, had written a new play, *Der Oheim*. Not without malice it was submitted to him anonymously with a mass of other inferior dramas, all of which were promptly rejected. Later he did not even remember seeing it. Thereupon it was sent to Berlin and performed with success. Ticknor adds: "Tieck was the responsible person in this case, as he is in all similar ones, and suffered accordingly for his mistake."[60] Retrospectively Tieck wrote to the critic H. T. Rötscher on May 2, 1847, that his relations to Princess Amalie always remained cordial none the less, although he told her frankly that he deemed her plays "schwächere Iffländische."[61]

It is clear, then, that Tieck was not spared the indignities and intrigues which have always been the lot of men with exquisite literary taste who venture to oppose, with their own artistic standards, the indolence and commercialism of the existing stage, the public's witless love of pleasure, and the venal criticism of the day.

And yet he succeeded in having at least some justice done to the great works of the past and to the best achievements of living dramatists. Shakespeare, in particular, was produced more frequently and completely during his incumbency than ever before on a German stage. After 1825 he arranged performances of *King Henry IV* and *Much Ado about Nothing*, among others. He also put on Lope's *Star of Seville*, Calderon's *Dame Cobold* (which was, however, hissed by the audience),[62] Goethe's *Tasso*, Kleist's *Der zerbrochene Krug* and Grillparzer's *Ein treuer Diener seines Herrn*. To celebrate Goethe's eightieth birthday in August 1829, he produced *Faust I* with an elucidating prolog. The performance was novel in some respects. Due partly to the whim of Tieck, who in 1817 had censured the Prolog in Heaven as impious, and partly to the Dresden prudes and the orthodox Catholic court, everything which seemed objectionable from the point of view of religion or morality was omitted.[63] H. H. Houben in *Der polizeiwidrige Goethe* (1932) gives an amusing account of the extreme cuts in this version of *Faust* and in a second even more prudish revision by Winkler. And yet Tieck's emasculated redaction, as well as a less "moral" version which he prepared for Leipzig, were promptly forbidden by the Saxon censor.

Other occasions, like the centenary of Lessing's birth in the same year, were commemorated with fitting reverence, and no opportunity was missed to impress the public with Tieck's concept of lasting greatness. He was also anxious to better the physical condition of the theater building and corresponded in December, 1825, with the architect Schinkel on improvements.[64] Lack of funds, however, prevented definite action before 1841.

But the period of his fruitful activity as "Dramaturg" came to an end about 1830. With the growing realization that his efforts were in vain, he became less energetic and more perfunctory in the performance of his duties. He retained his official position, however, up to the time of his removal from Dresden. Looking back upon this phase of his work in Dresden, he wrote to Eduard Devrient in 1838 that, despite his high hopes in 1825, he had been able to accomplish but little, and that only reticently and apologetically.[65] In theatrical circles, which have usually taken a hostile attitude toward his dramaturgic efforts, his failures in Dresden have been exaggerated and considered proverbial for the fate of the man of letters who rashly interferes in the business of the theater. He was vanquished in this long, hopeless struggle; the victor was Winkler.

A number of additional papers also served the interests of the stage and the drama. The articles *Costüm* and *Dekorationen* (1825)[66] oppose showiness and realism in costume and scenery. He was against the historical accuracy of costumes advocated by the Berlin "Intendant" Count Brühl. *Über das Tempo, in welchem auf der Bühne gesprochen werden soll* and *Soll der Schauspieler während der Darstellung empfinden, soll er kalt bleiben?* (1825)[67] contain valuable instructions for any actor. A long paper entitled *Das Dresdener Hoftheater im Januar 1827*[68] offers a critique and appraisal of the work of each actor on the roster of the theater, about thirty in number, with special attention to such outstanding artists as Carl Devrient and Julius. To this catalog he appends a frank statement of the chief virtues and vices of the troupe. *Über die neueren französischen Stücke auf dem deutschen Theater*[69] is a candid attempt to wean German directors, particularly the Dresden management, of their preference for modern French comedies and vaudevilles, which, he felt, would sooner or later spell the ruin of serious dramatic art. Incidentally he chides writers like Winkler, "who waste their time translating such superficial works and later have them printed under their own name." A glance at Wolff's *Almanach für Freunde der Schauspielkunst*, which proves that from 1817 on such plays actually dominated the German repertory, shows the timeliness of his warning.

One of his finest critical papers, the seventy-five-page article *Das deutsche Theater*,[70] deals once more with the whole question of the terrible plight in which he saw the German stage. He traces its development through the eighteenth century, with due attention to Lessing's merits and demerits, studies the good and bad influence of Schiller and Goethe and finds the brightest epochs about 1760 and between 1780 and 1800. But where is there a trace of those times now? he asks. In conclusion he writes: "Unless we can use Shakespeare as the cornerstone for our stage, adding Goethe, Schröder, Schiller and even some of the blameworthy writers [he probably has Grillparzer among others in mind], and enlist English, Italians, French and even Spaniards, but with discrimination and critical care, the confusion will grow worse and increase rapidly, and every one will realize that although our literature may be remarkable, we Germans have no use for a genuine theater."

The last article to be considered here is a set of sixteen reviews of as many plays performed in Dresden in 1827.[71] Like the three foregoing essays, it was published in the Dresden *Morgenzeitung* in 1827. Among the dramas considered are Shakespeare's *Julius Caesar* and *Othello*, Goethe's *Tasso*, Schiller's *Kabale und Liebe* and *Wilhelm Tell*—indication enough of Tieck's sanative influence upon the repertory. Here as always we find no gratuitous praise. Where commendation is deserved, he gives it, as in the case of Oehlenschläger's *Correggio*. The result is invariably honest criticism.

In looking back over his industrious dramaturgic activity we are unfavorably impressed, though not surprised, by only one fact. It is the strong dualism between his theories in that realm and his own previous practice while he was still a "Stimmungsdichter" and not yet a writer of culture and education. To say the least, his own poetic output does not always measure up to what he said and did between 1820 and 1830. He could criticize dramas, not write them; he had no idea of the sequence of dramatic events.

Outstanding among his theories are no doubt his belief in the need for a strong "Nationalbühne;" his idea that an era of great literature must also be an era of a strong theater; his opposition to cosmopolitanism and modern French influence (even to the French ballet as against classical dancing); his advocacy of the Shakespearean tradition; his belief in staging dramas as they were written, unpruned and altogether intact; his cry for good realistic middle-class dramas; his defense of careful speech on the stage and of natural acting, as opposed to the stiff, artificial classical and Gallic influences of Weimar and Iffland; and his desire to compromise between the Elizabethan and the modern stages, with a preference for the smaller theater and the graduated, flat stage, with a superstructure and a stairway, curtainless for all but certain modern dramas. The practical, concrete nature of his criticism made it all the more valuable for actors. Inasmuch as he points the way from the priority of poetry over the theater to the independent sway of the latter, his position in the field of dramaturgy is midway between that of Goethe and Laube.

In 1826 he collected his *Abendzeitung* articles of 1821, 1823 and 1824 and published them, together with his remarks of 1817 on the London theaters, as *Dramaturgische Blätter*. This collection was reviewed with high praise by Goethe, who wrote: "Tieck's judgment is based upon esthetic enjoyment, and his enjoyment upon knowledge." On the strength of the work the *Foreign Review and Continental Miscellany* in 1828 treated him as the leader in German literary criticism.[72] Heine called it his most original work; later Hebbel lauded it, and more recently Hermann Hettner. No doubt it is a milestone in the history of German dramaturgy. An amplification of the *Dramaturgische Blätter*, with the articles of 1825, 1827 and later papers, appeared in 1852 as volumes 3 and 4 of the *Kritische Schriften*, edited by the actor Eduard Devrient.

The unifying principle, positive goal and criterion of Tieck's criticism always remained constant and may be summed up in one word: Shakespeare. His interest in this single author seems to refute the charge of his enemies that he could never devote himslf unqualifiedly to any ideal for any length of time. As a young Romantic poet he had discovered in him the supreme conscious, inscrutably purposeful artist, whose cultivated genius, far from blindly obeying nature and instinct alone, was predicated by rules and artifice. At that time he paid most attention to *The Tempest*, rating it even higher than *A Midsummer Night's Dream*, until A. W. Schlegel set him right. His interest was then centered in the dramatic theory of Shakespeare, particularly in his comedies. But after 1820 he naturally cast his eye more on questions of practical stage craftsmanship and, under the influence of Solger's philosophy and Raumer's historicism, began to turn to the historical plays and to the immortal tragedies *King Lear*, *Romeo and Juliet*, *Hamlet* and *Macbeth*. Shakespeare, he told Solger,[73] was one of the forces which cured him of the baleful influence of mysticism. Despite his lifelong study of Shakespeare, however, Tieck never learned from him to be a dramatist. But he now used Shakespeare as his great "talking point" and teacher in showing the way to the establishment of a national theater, also as the key to the understanding of his own time.[74]

Two projects conceived in London in 1817, aimed to introduce to German readers a number of the spurious plays, some of which he considered genuinely Shakespearean. One of these is the collection edited in German translation under the title *Shakespeares Vorschule*. Part 1, published in 1823, contains Greene's *Friar Bacon and Friar Bungay*, *Arden of Feversham* and Heywood's *Lancashire Witches*. The first two were translated by Dorothea Tieck; we do not know who did the last. Tieck himself merely revised and edited. Part 2, containing *Fair Em*, *Second Maid's Tragedy* (ascribed to Massinger) and the *Birth of Merlin* (ascribed to Shakespeare and Rowley jointly) came out in 1829. The translators were Dorothea and Count Baudissin. The two long and important prefaces, by Tieck, were reprinted in the *Kritische Schriften*.[75] Here he considered not only the plays in question, but the entire development of English dramatic literature between 1580 and 1620. Of greatest importance he deemed those dramas which were in vogue in London when Shakespeare arrived there as a tyro: "because it is these attempts which determined the populace and the succeeding writers, to whom the great poet attached himself by imitating them, and which, despite many assertions to the contrary and much subsequent deterioration, have in the course of the past two hundred years given rise and shape to what we must call the English school of dramatic art; a school and a form which, as I have frequently asserted, is also the most suitable and natural for us Germans in contrast to the more restricted French and Spanish theaters which developed later."[76] A third volume, to contain *Mucedorus*, *Nobody and Somebody* and *The Fair Maid of Bristol*, did not appear. But the translations had been completed and were published in our own times from the "Nachlass."[77] An edition of the same plays in the original English text was also planned by Tieck. A fourth volume, to contain four plays, was contemplated, too.[78] Possibly they were later used for the second project.

As early as 1816 he began corresponding with Cotta about the publication of translations of three plays which he ascribed to Shakespeare, namely *Edward III*, *The Life and Death of Thomas Lord Cromwell* and *Sir John Oldcastle*.[79] In May 1819 he wrote to Cotta that he would send the manuscript before Michaelmas. There was more correspondence with the publisher between 1822 and 1830 regarding the project. An introduction was also planned, but not written. As a letter of 1829 to Menzel shows,[80] Tieck actually sent the manuscript of his three renderings to Cotta in that year. But seven years elapsed before they were finally published, together with Baudissin's rendering of *The London Prodigal*, as *Vier Schauspiele von Shakespeare, übersetzt von Ludwig Tieck*. The title is a misnomer, not only because none of these plays may claim Shakespearean authorship, but also because Tieck, though the responsible editor of all four, translated only three. But like

Baudissin's *Ben Jonson und seine Schule* (1836), his translation of *The London Prodigal* bears the impress of Tieck's inspiration.

The translating in both projects reveals a fluent art crystallizing into routinary technique. While form and language are good, the sense of the original is often violated and even the metrical pattern not always observed.

In his numerous dramaturgic articles of the period he often "puts on his Shakespeare spectacles," to use an expression of his adversary Grillparzer.[81] Four papers, all published in the Dresden *Abendzeitung* in 1823 and 1824, deal specifically with Shakespeare, one on *Romeo and Juliet*, another on *King Lear*, a third on the characters in *Hamlet* and the last on Hamlet's monolog.[82] In his writings on *Hamlet* one can feel his opposition to Goethe's ideas as expressed in *Wilhelm Meister*. Many of his views were novel and striking at the time, for instance that Falstaff, modelled on Oldcastle, constitutes an attack on the Puritans; or the theory that Hamlet in his famous monolog does not contemplate self-destruction; or again the notion that Hamlet and Ophelia have had a serious love affair and illicit relations; finally the belief that critics and actors have underrated the importance of the other characters in the play, in particular the king. Almost as unwonted was his theory, best expressed in a paper in the "Nachlass,"[83] that Lady Macbeth, far from being a fiend, was basically a kind, gentle woman. In his day he was considered an outstanding authority on Shakespeare, even by some British writers. Payne Collier, for instance, turned to him for evidence concerning a possible visit by Shakespeare to the continent and used Tieck's reply as the basis for his own opinion on the subject.

As early as 1807 Tieck undertook the task of translating Shakespeare's sonnets. Evidences of his efforts are found in the "Nachlass."[84] He left the work unfinished, after toying with it for some four years, and finally assigned it to his daughter, whose pedestrian renderings, made in the 'twenties, have been preserved.[85] As a letter to the publisher Max of 1825 shows, he planned to have him publish these renderings.[86] But only samples were given in Winkler's *Taschenbuch Penelope 1826*, in an effort to enlist public interest in this phase of Shakespeare's work.

One of Tieck's most important Shakespeare projects was the completion of the translation of Shakespeare's works, which A. W. Schlegel had begun late in the eighteenth century and had discontinued in 1811 after translating seventeen plays. We have seen that as early as 1793 Tieck had begun a poetic translation of *The Tempest* and that in 1800 he did two acts of *Love's Labour's Lost*. He had also tried his hand at *Macbeth* in 1819. His share in Schlegel's undertaking, the unpleasant incidents with Schlegel and the publisher Reimer to which it led, and the storm of controversy concerning its merits, which has lasted well into the twentieth century—all these matters have been detailed in another place.[87] Suffice it to state here that the nine-volume edition, containing revisions of the seventeen Schlegel translations and nineteen new translations, came out between 1825 and 1833; and that Tieck did not mention himself because he did not do any of the translating personally. His contribution consisted only of training his two translators, Dorothea and Count Baudissin, for the tremendous task, constantly supervising their work, and providing brief introductions and a scanty commentary. It is a strange coincidence, unique in literary history, that Tieck's name is today familiar to the masses only in connection with this translation, which in reality is not his work at all. However, he deserves high credit, despite the inferiority of the continuation, for preventing the greatest German product of the art of translation since Luther's Bible from remaining a mere torso.

Although his grandiose work on Shakespeare and his times was not finished, yet its author played an important rôle, through his other writings and efforts, in making a correct historical interpretation of Shakespeare possible in Germany. In his adaptation of *Romeo and Juliet* (1811) Goethe had tampered with Shakespeare's text; in his essay *Shakespeare und kein Ende* (1815) he still revealed the old but false notion that Shakespeare did not write with the stage in mind. Tieck set out not only to refute this, but to show the nature of the Shakespearean stage, upon which the author's plays could be presented without condensation or modification.

He pondered this technical problem of production all his life. In the earliest draft of his work on Shakespeare he conceived the Elizabethan theater with an open rear stage, on each side of which was an interior which could be closed off and decorated at will. We have seen that in the *Briefe über Shakespeare* (1800) he adopted the upper stage (a balcony borne on pillars) and a third tier for musicians. The walls of these tiers were to be hung with curtains, to conceal characters if necessary. On either side a stairway led to the balcony. This plan remained the basis of all his later ideas on the subject. In England he added only the idea of a rear stage which can be shut off and is a few steps higher than the front stage.

In the Dresden performance of *Romeo and Juliet* in 1823, which he helped arrange, he went as far as he was permitted in transforming the modern theater of illusion into a geometric stage (Raumbühne), with a minimum of movable scenery and a maximum of permanent architectonic settings. He had expressed this same ideal in the conversations of the second volume of *Phantasus* (1812).

The first authentic illustrations from Shakespearean times, which came to his attention in the volume *The Old English Drama* (London, 1825), seem to have altered his ideas but little, although they showed no stairway at all.

Sketches found among Goethe's papers, and dating probably from 1828, illustrate Tieck's ideas on the three-tier stage, with a minimum of movable scenery, for *A Midsummer Night's Dream*. The epoch-making performance arranged by Tieck at Potsdam in 1843, to be discussed later, followed these ideas. In the Dresden performance of *Macbeth* of 1836 he mapped out a permanent setting for three acts, with a stairway serving now as a mountain ascent for the witches and now as a stair from the castle yard to the upper living quarters.[88]

A long section of one of his most important "novellen," *Der junge Tischlermeister* (1836), is also devoted to developing his notion on the Elizabethan and the modern stages. A sepia sketch of the reconstruction of the London Fortune Theatre of 1600, which he, together with Baudissin and the architect Gottfried Semper, worked out about 1836, and the illustrations of Elizabethan stages with several tiers in Baudissin's *Ben Jonson und seine Schule* (1836), inspired by Tieck, serve the same intention.[89] Up to recent times his "Shakespearean stage" was generally regarded as correct and valid; today we know that it was constructed from insufficient evidence. Yet he was the first to try to liberate the drama from the straightjacket of the scenic stage—the "Illusionsbühne"—by means of a geometric stage with permanent architectural settings. Thus he paved the way for performances, not only of Shakespeare but also of Goethe and Schiller, which are as complete, as faithful to the author's intentions and as much in keeping with his spirit as possible.

Tieck was a bold pioneer in the study of Shakespeare, who pointed the direction toward the era of the modern critics and through the very misconceptions of his intuitive criticism challenged later scholars. He made no systematic exploration of Shakespeare, but rather a series of useful forays. We may call him the first German to take Shakespeare's contemporaries seriously and to study Shakespeare, the product of careful discipline and application, not the heaven-sent genius, against the background of his times. He early recognized the joyous naïveté of Shakespeare's times as opposed to the Puritanism which followed. Besides, Shakespeare's popularity on the German stage is due mainly to his example. On the other hand, with his supercilious attitude toward the Shakespearean critics and because of his insistence upon the Romantic point of view, his critical studies, though extensive and searching, were largely futile for the purposes of philological research.

The fourth and last characteristic of his critical endeavor, we found at the beginning of this chapter in his far-reaching use of the comparative method and in his emphasis upon the other literatures of western Europe. This is not restricted to any one group of his critical papers. They all have a rich sprinkling of references to English literature from Chaucer to Scott, and many allusions to Cervantes, Lope and Calderon, to Dante, Tasso and Gozzi and, less frequently, to French writers. Few authors before Tieck who addressed themselves as he did not to scholars, but to a wide circle of cultured readers had so large a horizon, so comprehensive a view of the literary scene.

Aside from his essays on Shakespeare, six papers of the Dresden period are distinguished by the fact that they apply this comprehensive comparative treatment to subjects which in themselves partake of the nature of comparative literature. Thus they become comparative in a twofold sense. They are the introduction to a new edition of a German seventeenth century Robinson Crusoe novel, *Die Insel Felsenburg;* the article *Bücherschau* in the *Morgenzeitung* (1827), dealing with the novels of Hegner, a Swiss writer, Steffens, an expatriated Norwegian, and Salvandy, a Spaniard; the introduction to Dorothea's translation of *Obregon* by the Spanish writer Vicente Espinel; the preface to a collection of German classical and popular poetry; the foreword to a collection of one hundred "novellen" from the literatures of all nations made by Eduard von Bülow; and finally the prefatory remarks to Dorothea's translation of Cervantes' *Persiles and Sigismunda* (1837).[90] These papers give him title to the distinction of being the first German critic writing for general readers to introduce the comparative method on a large scale and to deal with subjects pertaining to comparative literature.

CHAPTER FIFTEEN

THE "NOVELLE"—A NEW LITERARY FORM

IN 1821, the same year in which he began to engage in critical activities and to undertake a systematic campaign as a harbinger of culture and education in theatrical and literary questions, Tieck set to solving the second problem. This poet of urbanity, who was also a critic, wanted to give his contemporaries a new type of literature to meet the requirements and help fortify the views of men and women of the highest refinement and breeding. He felt it imperative to combine his poetical and critical gifts in order to combat a host of evil and, he thought, dangerous impulses which had crept into the literature of the "barbaric"[1] times in imitation of his own Romanticism.

One of these emanated from the chivalrous novels of Fouqué, who we remember had sided against the Tiecks in the Sophie-Bernhardi trial. While admitting that Fouqué possessed rich talent and imagination and had produced a masterpiece in *Undine*, Tieck held that his inventiveness was too arbitrary and incongruous. Caricature and adventurousness, he felt, had taken the place of art in Fouqué. Besides, lack of irony robbed him of creative imaginativeness. Instead of recreating the Middle Ages, he seemed merely to toy with them and became the Don Quixote of modern poetry, but one without a Sancho Panza to accompany him. To Tieck Fouqué was chiefly responsible for the thin, decadent Romanticism of knighthood which dominated literature about 1820.[2] He was a "complete mannerist," we read in a letter to Friedrich Schlegel of 1813, and lacked the experience necessary for composing true poetry.[3] His works, added Tieck, were "distortions and misunderstandings of images and understandings of others." That these "others" were Tieck himself and the rest of the early Romanticists becomes clear from the sentence: "Anyway I derive no pleasure from all those trends to which we gave the impetus."

He found another pernicious influence in the fantastic ghost stories of E. T. A. Hoffmann. This "diminutive fidgety man with most mobile facial expression and piercing eyes," who had "something uncanny and in the end was afraid of his own ghosts," seemed to him to have produced only caricatures and literary grimaces.[4] He believed that despite his gifts Hoffmann (who has outdone even Tieck in expressing pure music in words) exercised no salutary influence upon literature.[5] But his real reason for opposing Hoffmann throws light upon his profoundly religious nature during the second half of his life. "All these new-fangled stories are more than despicable," he writes in *Das Zauberschloss* (1829). "A terrible fear seizes us when life and everything which may give it content is exaggerated and driven to a senseless climax. Thus our firmest and most necessary sources of comfort and tranquillity are represented as the most evanescent and ridiculous matters."[6]

No less baneful, he found, was the effect of the immoral tales which Clauren published in the almanacs. They seemed to him bare of cultural value, manufactured merely for those "who wish to kill idle time with a book. And indeed many do not rise higher than to the conviction that the arts exist only for this purpose. To them such an author must be welcome."[7] And the "unnaturalness, coarse contradictions and lack of character and cohesion"[8] which he discovered in Clauren's comedies, he detected also in his narratives. He disapproved no less of the tales of Contessa and Weisflog, of the *Waverley* imitations of Tromlitz and Van der Velde and of the "fate dramas" of Werner and his followers.

These influences, as dissimilar as they seemed, had certain common characteristics which to him were ominous. They all aimed to win the approval of the masses by pandering to the prevailing fashions and shallow inclinations which he thought were based on a misunderstanding of his own Romanticism. They sacrificed standards to success. They were on occasion exceedingly "smart" and sophisticated. And finally they had many imitators, especially in such sentimental groups as the Dresden "Liederkreis."

In order to combat them he undertook to invent his new vehicle, the "novelle." For the sake of achieving a wide influence with it he produced as many specimens as possible—two score in half as many years. With justice to him it may be said that in style, sociability, high moral and intellectual tone, idealism and nobility of purpose they stand head and shoulders above the output of the Claurens, Contessas and Weisflogs. As literature, to be sure, the tales of Hoffmann are superior.

But can it be denied that Tieck had himself played the part of a Clauren or a Weisflog some twenty-five years before, when he wrote his *Straussfedern* tales? The essential difference seems to be that he had cherished at least a sanative satiric purpose. The type of work which he had once performed in the service of Nicolai as a youth of twenty-two, he now took up once more in Dresden as a man of almost fifty. But what was forced labor then became voluntary service now; what had once been done haphazardly and immaturely, against his will and without honest conviction, was now inspired by a lofty artistic purpose and a settled philosophy of life.

This reversion, in his high maturity, to that didactic, educational and cultural form with which he had begun his literary career shows how important a form it was for Tieck, the Romantic poet who had been reared on a Rationalist fare. After coming into early dominance, it was submerged for a generation. Now, blended with the dialog style of the *Phantasus* conversations, it not only emerged into ascendency again in a riper, more human form, but gained absolute and final supremacy in his literary purview.

He himself has left a long definition of the "novelle," which has great authenticity because it was written in 1829, at the height of his "novellen" period.[9] He complains that the term "novelle" has come to be used for any short, often trivial story, and that while the word "novel" has acquired a definite connotation, "novelle" is still vague and uncertain. The Italians, he finds, first used it in the form "novela" for any narrative or event which was novel and unknown. In the hands of Boccaccio (of whose naïve delight in story-telling he hardly shows a trace) the Italian "novela" became characterized by obscenity and wantonness, or by satire against the clergy. He concludes that the Spanish "novela," on the other hand, as developed by Cervantes, assumed a much more moral and modest tone.

The three great masters of the "novelle," he states, have been Boccaccio, Cervantes and Goethe, whose example should teach us that the "novelle" must be distinguished from the event, the story, the narrative, the incident and the anecdote. But apart from saying that "an event should be presented differently from a narrative, and a narrative be differentiated from a story," he does not expatiate upon the distinction between the various types. In discussing the "novelle," however, he becomes more specific. He finds that it should stand out among all the types of compressed narrative in that it "brings into the highest relief an incident great or small, which, plausible as it may be and likely as its occurrence may seem, partakes of the miraculous and perhaps of the unique."

While the terms "incident great or small," "plausible" and "likely" point back to the realistic *Straussfedern*, the words "miraculous" and "unique," on the other hand, show that Tieck was not ready to jettison all the achievements of Romanticism. As indicated, his "novellen" retained many of the fantastic elements for which he had become known. But in his youth he saw miracles in nature, as in *Die Elfen*, where vegetation dies when the inviolability of the elves has been disturbed by mortals. Often his characters had been mere hallucinations—men envisaged in a trance—, as in *Der blonde Eckbert*, where illusion and madness take the place of reality and rational thought. Now his miracles are found in realistic happenings; they are ubiquitous, existing within us and without us and pervading our entire existence. In introducing this motif in a new vehicle, he was conscious of being an innovator. He wrote to his brother Friedrich in 1822: "ich bilde mir ein, eigentlich unter uns diese Dichtkunst erst aufzubringen, indem ich das Wunderbare immer in die sonst alltäglichen Umstände und Verhältnisse lege."[10] And his characters, as queer and whimsical and crazy as they may be, are at least real types and no longer figments of a Romantic dreamer.

The Romantic motifs which he now employed were means to help instruct and improve the minds of cultured readers. In regard to theme there is a relationship between *Der blonde Eckbert*, *Der Runenberg* and *Die Elfen*, on the one side, and *Das alte Buch* on the other. So, too, in the case of *Sternbald* and *Der junge Tischlermeister;* or in the case of *Die sieben Weiber des Blaubart* and *Die Vogelscheuche*. But in his "new manner" he no longer poetizes, he expounds; he no longer conceives fancies or weaves atmosphere, he reconstructs men and events. Conversational in their nature, like the framework of *Phantasus*, the "novellen" aim more at complete discussion of certain phases of life than at connected action.

In *Das alte Buch* his sentiment is conservative and didactic, his purpose to attack Heine and French Romanticism. In *Der junge Tischlermeister* he is a production manager, who from the fulness of experience explains how Shakespeare's *Twelfth Night*, Goethe's *Götz von Berlichingen* and Schiller's *Die Räuber* should be staged. And *Die Vogelscheuche* is the mouthpiece of a literary reformer who would laugh the stodgy pen-pushers of Dresden to scorn. As for his new style, he avoids the flowery lyric language of his youth and writes a serene, simple, pure, and melodious prose, modelled on the style of Goethe's *Wilhelm Meister*, but more archaic and more diversified and with a stronger ironic disposition.

To continue with his definition of the "novelle," he requires that it should have a "turning point," at which it effects a complete but unexpected *volte face*, without disturbing the logical development of the plot. This turning point should make a particularly strong impression upon the reader's imagination by containing an element of surprise and wonder, which in the final analysis, however, is natural and commonplace. In every novel of Cervantes he discovers such a central point; in the "novelle" in Goethe's *Unterhaltungen deutscher Ausgewanderten*

THE "NOVELLE"—A NEW LITERARY FORM

(his foremost model) he also finds one. While the "novelle" may for the rest be "bizarre, capricious, fantastic, gently witty, loquacious, much addicted to description even of details, tragic and comic, pensive and jocose" (bizarr, eigensinnig, phantastisch, leicht witzig, geschwätzig und sich ganz in Darstellung auch von Nebensachen verlierend, tragisch wie komisch, tiefsinnig und neckisch), it should never lack "that curious and striking turning point" (jenen sonderbaren auffallenden Wendepunkt) which distinguishes it from other types.

His theory of the "Wendepunkt" has not only caused discussion but exercised influence upon his successors, particularly Otto Ludwig.[11] Perhaps Hebbel, an admirer of Tieck, may have derived from this idea his notion that great turning points in history furnish suitable settings for historical tragedies.

It is already evident that Tieck's definition involves definite technical requirements and lays down elastic principles regarding subject matter. Part of it, so far as we have considered it, is derived from the great masters of the "novelle," in whose footsteps he was following. To some extent it resembles the Goethean concept as expressed in the interrogation: "What is the 'novelle' other than an unheard-of event which has come to pass?" But Tieck has added a typical ingredient of his own in the turning point or reversal, which grew from the inmost needs of his Romantic subjectivism. He had used the same term prior to 1829, but in the sense of a reaction to previous admiration. In 1818 he wrote to Solger of finding "a turning point in every art," at which his admiration changed to antipathy; in literature Klopstock produced this shift in his soul, in art Rubens[12]—ostensibly because of their lack of ideals and excessive sensualism.

By virtue of the turning point, events and characters which at first seemed real become playthings of the poet's will and of his more far-reaching underlying intentions. Hence the "novelle," as a work of art, serves him not as an end in itself but as a means of projecting himself and his views of art or of life. The power which enables him to do so and holds him suspended over his subject, so to speak, is irony. This new interpretation of the concept introduced into Romantic theory by Friedrich Schlegel in 1798 was derived from Solger. It dominates Tieck's "novellen" and offers him his excuse for making them the vehicle of polemics against the many phenomena of the time which he deemed pernicious.

No wonder, then, that almost without exception the forty narrative works, most of them "novellen," a few of them novels, which he wrote between 1821 and 1840 are "Tendenzdichtung"—program literature.

No wonder that his definition, here leaning upon Cervantes, contains the statement that "all social classes and relations of modern times, their conditions and peculiarities" (alle Stände, alle Verhältnisse der neuen Zeit, ihre Bedingungen und Eigentümlichkeiten) are fit, clear-cut subjects for the "novelle" and possess intrinsic poetic value. Only in the light of these convictions is his intention clear when he writes that in the genuine "novelle" the sentiments and opinions to be expressed and the vocations to be represented must be developed by contrast and by arguments between the characters; that by virtue of debate, decision and conflicting opinions the "novelle" must offer a poetic means of clearly suggesting and proving, within the confined limits of a work of art, what in actual life often repels us as passionate violence and narrow-mindedness because it appears in too vague a form or is given too free a rein.

Tieck (though once criticizing Iffland and Kotzebue for being "too didactic")[13] feels that the "novelle" can be used as a potent medium for reflecting those leading themes and problems of life which have agitated the greatest writers of all times. If the dissonances of life were an effective theme for the tragedy of the ancients, he asks, why cannot the modern writer deal with them from this point of view in the "novelle"? Occurrences which defy the dictates of human intellect and conscience, as well as the laws of morality and justice—in other words the acts of fate—, may also be treated thus on a high plane, he avers. "If tragedy," he exclaims, "strives to exalt us in heavenly intoxication to the summit of Olympus through pity, fear, passion and enthusiasm, so that with lofty pity we may contemplate and comprehend from a clear height the doings of men and the eccentricities of their fate; if the novel of the Elective Affinities [by Goethe], as a tragedy of family life and of modern times, takes us into the labyrinth of the heart; just so the 'novelle' may from its point of view solve the contradictions of life, explain the caprices of fate, ridicule the madness of passion, and weave into its artistic tissue many riddles of the heart and of human folly, so that our eye, thus rendered more acute, can recognize what is human, be it depicted in mirth or in sadness, and detect a higher reconciling truth even in the blameworthy."[14]

Thus far his definition of 1829. We have scrutinized it carefully enough to see that it is ponderous and contains a sprinkling of theoretical vagaries. It need not surprise us, then, to find that in practice he does not always live up to it. To be sure, his earlier "novellen," those he wrote between 1821 and 1829, still fit into his theory, though not always perfectly or even conveniently. An incident, often more wondrous than likely, is projected in relief; a turning point is usually discernible; details are dwelt upon (often to the detriment of the main plot); the underlying intention of the author is clearly stressed; and, as in the *Schildbürger* of 1796, themes and problems of life, though at times of a very secondary nature, are freely aired.

One condition of his definition was scarcely ever observed, however. His "novellen" do not attempt to depict "all social classes and relations of modern times, their conditions and peculiarities." Rarely does he introduce representatives of the lower classes, except in mob scenes.[15] His characters belong almost exclusively to the aristocracy and to the cream of the middle class. Nor does he offer a full, accurate picture of conditions between 1820 and 1840. At best he gives only a view of certain phenomena in the intellectual life of the times. It was the so-called "Biedermeier" age,[16] an era of good-natured candidness, philistine narrowness and severely plain, modest sobriety, when all classes suffered under the pressure of the restoration, and when even art in its various forms revealed signs of the economic pauperization caused by the Napoleonic wars. His "novellen" present a veritable mine of more or less raw materials for the study of this age. Almost every page betrays the era in which it was written, be it through the unnatural, excessively rhetorical speeches; the over-severe fathers and soft-hearted mothers who occur so frequently; the hero's easy tears; the precocious children in the dim background; the tender young swains and lasses, who seem far too good to be true; the slow tempo of life; and his naïve way of putting things, which strikes us as involuntary humor.

Even with the help of his seven-page definition we are at a loss to see why a given "novelle" could not have been styled a story or narrative, or a series of events, incidents or anecdotes bearing a moral in politics, religion or art appreciation, or constituting a lecture on charlatanism in one of its various forms. In other cases again, as in *Der Aufruhr in den Cevennen*, a "novelle" becomes to all intents and purposes a novel. In view of such confusion it is not surprising that in his introduction to Bülow's *Novellenbuch*[17] Tieck discusses more novels than "novellen."

No doubt he was aware of the tendency to expand his "novellen" into the breadth of novels. He admitted it to his publisher Max, saying that he could easily have made novels of most of them by mere amplification and retardation of plot development through additional episodes, and adding: "perhaps it would have been more convenient for me, too."[18] This blending of genres evoked a protest from Hebbel, who condemned "Mischlinge."[19]

On the other hand, the "novellen" do not lack a dramatic element, either. Not only are many of them in dialog, but their structure, too, frequently reminds of that favorite genre, the drama, to which he always gave the highest place in literature. At first he planned some of the early "novellen" as dramas. *Der Geheimnisvolle*, for instance, written in 1821, was originally meant to be a comedy.[20] Others, as *Der Wassermensch* (1834), are partly written in the dramatic form, with actors' directions. It may be said that many of his "novellen" are drafts of unexecuted dramas.

The later "novellen," those written in the 'thirties, deviate much more markedly from the definition of 1829. Some are undistinguishable from stories, narratives or events; others could well be called novels. Often they project not a single incident, but a series of events or merely a set of opinions. The idea that the event should be "likely but miraculous and perhaps unique" is more than once lost sight of, and in vain do we seek a turning point in the majority. Indeed, the only features of the definition which his later "novellen" seem to observe consistently are that they present their author's underlying intentions— his desire to preach to the upper classes the gospel of right living and correct thinking and to raise their standards in esthetics, religion and politics—, and that they depict themes and problems of life which to him seemed of prime importance.

In view of these many deviations from his definition, it is little wonder that near the end of his life he expressed himself much less dogmatically on his conception of the "novelle." He told Köpke about 1848[21] that "it is not easy to say what the 'novelle' really is and how it may be distinguished from the consanguineous types of novel and narrative. . . . It is too much simply to say that the 'novelle' must have a pronounced tendency, yet one expects in it something salient, a point in which one discovers oneself. When I survey my 'novellen' I must say that the majority have such a point, while others again do not. . . . But the sharp epigrammatic point should not be stressed too strongly, otherwise *Wilhelm Meister* might be classed as a 'novelle' and *Die Wahlverwandtschaften*, which has so marked a tendency, would surely be one. . . . It is very hard to find a general definition covering all the phenomena of this type."

In the "novellen" reason, tradition and conservative beliefs have become synonymous to Tieck with moral rightness. He has relinquished the idealistic demands of his youth, which sympathy with the French Revolution had produced in social life and politics, and love for the Middle Ages in religion. Only with regard to the life of the private citizen, to literature, art and culture in general, and to his abhorrence of the trivial, the sordid, the mean did he retain his ideals unaltered. His literary output after 1820, particularly, is evidence of his abiding championship of high humanistic standards in these fields, a championship which in 1825 he once compressed into the words: "Good breeding and refined conduct have always seemed to me the necessary elements for the realization of the fact that I have a soul in my body."[22] Qualities like this prompt so fine a critic as F. Th. Vischer to praise the "novellen" in his letters to Mörike, though feeling that in general their author "lacks caliber."[23]

Tieck's "novellen" are educational guide books for travellers in the realms of history and society. They represent a development of the "Kunstnovelle" along the lines of such Romantic dialog narratives as Schelling's *Clara* and Tieck's own *Phantasus* conversations, and give rise to a new form—the "novelle" of debate. His wide reading in literature and history and his profound knowledge of art, esthetics and dramaturgy are evident on every page. The only indications that he was now well along in middle life, with old age not far ahead, are his opposition to the younger generation, to whom he felt culturally superior, and his more mellow philosophy. He who had striven in 1800 to supplant established customs and beliefs was now a *laudator temporis acti*. But his style has become more like the historian's than the poet's. It blends Romanticism, in its love of remote places and of travel, and modern historical writing, in its predilection for exact reports of recorded happenings. Often these are personal reminiscences or accounts of experiences of others, often historical studies based upon source materials.

Whatever the various themes of his "novellen," the majority of the most characteristic present pictures of life among the upper classes in his day, or give a reflex of what he deemed the best thought on subjects which concerned refined men and women. As indicated before, they discover evidences of demonic force in ordinary experiences, explaining the uniqueness of the incidents in question, so far as it is not merely apparent, by an extraordinarily singular concatenation of events and constellation of characters.

We have found that from his earliest beginnings Tieck was a fatalist, believing that a higher power often controls man's destinies. In his "novellen" period he continued to adhere to this creed, which constitutes one of the unifying principles of his life. But his fatalism has become more mature; he now believes in a kindlier, more reasonable fate. Its quality is best illustrated by the "novelle" *Der 15. November*. No automatic, mechanical fate, he finds, guides us through life. We are controlled by a higher fatalistic principle, which emanates from heaven and is in effect a divine dispensation. No logic or reason will explain it. Godlike in its character, it is perfectly natural and beneficent, but at the same time miraculous and supernatural.

The historical and fantastic "novellen" pursue the same tendencies as the others. This is manifest in the very subjects with which they deal and, more clearly still, in numerous interpolated episodes, as well as in the rich framework of dialog into which the stories are set. These conversations are so elaborate that the plot often fades into insignificance before them. In conscious opposition to Scott's penchant for description, Tieck developed the dialog form, which, however, swelled his "novellen" to an inordinate bulk, interfered with the even course of the narrative and deflected the interest from the principal characters and their fate to gratuitous discussion of a wide variety of topics.

Tieck's characterization in the "novellen" is scarcely an improvement over that which we found in his earlier writings. He did not possess the power of *creating* characters a priori, he could only *describe* them a posteriori by drawing up a catalog of their qualities. Consequently even his best characters are hardly more than types, such as we may remember having met. Often these types are whimsical and distorted; often their unusual behavior, which is now comical, now gruesome, stamps them as bordering upon insanity. But no newly fashioned specimens of humanity, no Falstaffs, Juliets, Egmonts, Gretchens or Fagans arise from his pages. He does not study their psychological basis. His "novellen" are therefore surprisingly deficient in purely human content and interest. They may be compared with a set of marginal notes upon their epoch. It is difficult today to understand the remark in Hebbel's diary (I, 212) that Tieck depicts *developing* characters, and the statement (230) that his "novellen," though lifting the veil too completely from life and nature, are colorful and lively. More comprehensible is the same writer's complaint about Tieck's shallowness and failure to collect himself in the depths of his soul, so that we see the "dancing pen" rather than divine Apollo behind it.[24]

All these remarks apply to the "novellen" and novels as a group. They apply less to *Der Gelehrte, Des Lebens Überfluss,* the fragment *Der Aufruhr in den Cevennen, Der Hexensabbath,* and *Vittoria Accorombona.* The last, particularly, reveals less programmatic or propagandistic intention; the characters are better rooted in the soil of their time and portrayed in action; here and only here does he attempt to delve into the foundations upon which their psychology rests. That he seems to surrender to his sworn enemies, the French Romanticists and

THE "NOVELLE"—A NEW LITERARY FORM

the Young German advocates of emancipation and social radicalism, by depicting a sympathetic emancipated woman, is mildly interesting but hardly surprising in view of his chameleonism. More significant is the circumstance that in this final work he reverts to that psychological analysis of character which he had once applied to such Romantic figures as William Lovell.

Generally speaking, the "novellen" are important in the history of the type as a special variety conditioned chiefly by the personality of their author. They represent a form which enabled him to combine his delight in story-telling and his pleasure in the wonderful and curious with social criticism and art appreciation. Of course so incongruous a mixture did not produce homogeneous or well rounded works. All too frequently invention, composition and delineation of characters—vital elements for any literary masterpiece—were quite relegated to the background and made to serve didactic, disputatious ends.

The framework of his "novellen" is often a dinner party or a social gathering, at which men and women of parts (without distinction of birth!), representing divergent points of view, are assembled. Such a setting afforded him opportunity to ventilate from various angles the problems which were nearest his heart and constituted his real *raison d'écrire*, so to speak. This device has been used by many of his successors in the field of the novel, among them the French realists Zola and the Goncourt brothers.

At times the views of the differing parties are somehow reconciled, but in such a way that Tieck's antagonists in real life suffer discomfiture and humiliation. Sometimes the author refrains from taking sides and merely lets the representatives of opposing views state their opinions. His ability to assume the rôles of different persons, suggesting the atmosphere of spirited intellectual conversation, was evident in the framework of *Phantasus*. In the "novellen" he developed it to a high degree of virtuosity, overemphasizing it to the detriment of his literary art.[25]

Excessive conversationalism, coupled with the fact that its subject matter is today so defunct as to require a commentary for its elucidation, makes many of the "novellen" tiresome. A modern reader, to enter into their spirit, must familiarize himself with the subjects under discussion. When thus approached in the proper state of mind and regarded in correct historical perspective, most of them can still afford a certain degree of pleasure.

Tieck had at least two forerunners in the "novelle" whose work stands higher, Goethe, the originator of the form in German, and Kleist.

LUDWIG TIECK, THE GERMAN ROMANTICIST

The latter, particularly with his masterly *Michael Kohlhaas* (1808), had ushered in a decade which may be termed the classical period of Romantic narrative literature. In 1811 Fouqué's *Undine* and Arnim's stories came out; in 1812 the Grimm collection of fairy tales; from 1814 on Hoffmann's tales; and in 1817 Brentano's remarkable *Geschichte vom braven Kasperl und dem schönen Annerl*. Then the masters of the "novelle" who followed Tieck, not without learning from him and his predecessors, did much to improve the technique of the genre. The productions of Paul Heyse, Theodor Storm and Gottfried Keller are superior, except in style and high moral purpose, to Tieck's efforts. With them the "novelle" has come to assume those qualities which we associate with it today—unity, coherence, brief but telling characterization, purely human interest, and concentration upon a single motif, which is poetically isolated, as in the drama. Only ignorance of their "novellen" or blind prejudice could have prompted Turgenef to write to Julian Schmidt in 1873: "Les Allemands n'ont pas le talent de conter."

Tieck's "novellen" are distinguished from those of his successors by paucity of invention, which is relieved only by diverting episodes and other accessories. His favorite, oft-recurring theme—the union of two lovers who have finally succeeded in overcoming the opposition of their stubborn, whimsical fathers—is too unoriginal and threadbare, the obstacles confronting the lovers are too superficial and the means of surmounting them too improbable, forced and fortuitous. This plot, so typical of the "novellen," reminds of Iffland's middle-class plays, which are usually inferior, however, in execution and ethical design. We noted above that in form the "novellen" revert approximately to the *Straussfedern* stories of 1795-1798. In plot, we may say, they recur to some of his earliest dramas of 1789-1790, namely *Der doppelte Vater*, *Der letzte Betrug ist ärger als der erste*, *Ich war doch am Ende betrogen*, *Die Entführung*, *Der alte Meiners* and *Braddeck*, and to the tale *Adalbert und Emma* of 1792.

His inevitable duality is manifest also in his "novellen." He would create an artistic and characteristic reflex of contemporary life. But lacking sufficient originality and strength to desert those plots which he and other authors of the Enlightenment had cultivated, he retained not only the time-worn subject matter, but also the narrative technique of his youth, using "modern" devices only as an ornamental cloak to cover the stiff lines of his clumsy framework. The shallow psychology of the Enlightenment, which treats all men alike, is applied to the actions of his characters. But in their opinions and speech he is at pains

THE "NOVELLE"—A NEW LITERARY FORM

to differentiate them. This is a token of the impractical age in which he wrote—the "Biedermeier̊zeit"—, when feeling and sensibility were stressed to the prejudice of utilitarianism, and the psychic faculties, though far from understood, were deemed more important than the physical. The reader's esthetic enjoyment is marred by a sense of disproportion and misplaced emphasis.

But Tieck's "novellen," which Hebbel called colorful, crystalline and characterized by logical orderliness, will retain value in the history of manners as exhibits of the reactionary spirit prevailing after the Wars of Liberation, as faithful pictures of better German society during this faint-hearted age, and as products of an exalted, noble-minded criticism of certain aspects of contemporaneous life. He rightly told Brockhaus that there is a grain of truth in every one of them.[26] And to his brother Friedrich he wrote in October 1823: "Is not all writing a return to, and resuscitation of, what is present and true? Only, of course, it must not be done in an insipid manner."[27] The closer the subjects lie to his heart, the more valuable is his criticism. The most potent fillips to his controversial ardor are hypocrisy, pietism and various types of mysticism, be it adherence to religious miracles or to blind fate, or superstitious belief in spirits and ghosts. In addition, he combats unwholesome literary and artistic trends, extreme democracy and aristocracy, untruthfulness and arrogation of fine taste and artistic culture by the half-educated.

The decade from 1820 to 1829 was one of extreme reaction and consequent political calm. Hence the broad, general themes of his "novellen" fitted very well into the spirit of that time and proved widely popular. But after 1829 the political skies, affected by the disturbances in France and the events in Poland, grew dark. Readers began to demand treatment of actualities in literature. Tieck, however, spurned such subjects and berated those who cultivated them. Bit by bit his popularity was thus undermined. The more he ignored the real burning problems of the day, entrenching himself behind such innocuous subjects as we have indicated, the more did he lose contact with his age, justifying Grillparzer's jibe of 1837, which compared his "novellen" with weak tea. Strangely enough, what had happened to him during the Napoleonic era now repeated itself.

Most of the "novellen" first appeared in various annual pocket almanacs, a form of periodical which then enjoyed immense popularity. Among them were *Wendts Taschenbuch, Berlinischer Kalender, Rheinblüten, Dresdener Merkur, Orphea* and *Brockhaus' Urania*. In 1825 Tieck established an almanac of his own under the title *Märchen und*

Zaubergeschichten, of which only one volume appeared. In 1831-1832 and 1834-1835 he got out six of his "novellen" in his own *Novellenkranz*. Four volumes were issued under the imprint of his old associate Reimer. The first collected edition of the "novellen" was published by the Breslau firm of Josef Max in seven volumes (1823-1828). A new revised edition by the same publisher, in fourteen volumes, appeared in 1835-1842; volumes 1-4 had to be reprinted in 1838 and again in 1847.[28] Then in 1844-1846 Tieck let Reimer round out the twenty volumes of his *Schriften*, begun in 1828, by publishing twelve "novellen" in volumes 17-20. In 1852 these were reprinted with the subtitle *Gesammelte Novellen I-IV*. They were supplemented in 1853-1854 by eight additional volumes of "novellen." This twelve-volume edition is the most complete and textually the most reliable.

Max, Brockhaus and Reimer, whom we have mentioned in connection with the "novellen," were Tieck's most important publishers. His relations to Josef Max in Breslau were close and personal. They began inauspiciously in 1818, when Max decided against *Shakespeares Vorschule* and other projects which he had brought along from England. But between 1823 and 1840 he published not only the "novellen" in the editions described, but also the *Dramaturgische Blätter*, Dorothea's translation of *Obregon*, Sophie's *Evremont* and the novel *Vittoria Accorombona*. Max always showed Tieck extreme kindness and fairness. The same can scarcely be said of Tieck's treatment of Max.[29]

After *Shakespeares Vorschule* had been rejected by Max and also by Reimer, Tieck turned with it in 1820 to Brockhaus in Leipzig. Brockhaus accepted it and thus began a relationship which was to continue to the end of Tieck's life. After the death of F. A. Brockhaus in 1823 these relations were carried on by his son Heinrich. Like Max, the Brockhauses were loyal to him and patiently tolerated his many caprices and attempts to prejudice their interests or play off other publishers against them. Besides *Shakespeares Vorschule*, they published *Solgers Nachgelassene Schriften*, ten of the "novellen" in their almanac *Urania*, Bülow's *Novellenbuch*, Dorothea's translations of Cervantes' *Persiles and Sigismunda* and of Sparks' *George Washington*, the *Kritische Schriften* and Köpke's biography of Tieck.[30]

With no publisher did Tieck deal so intimately and over so long a period as with the Reimers. Besides the *Schriften* and the *Gesammelte Novellen*, described above,[31] they published the following works: the edition of Novalis, the *Minnelieder*, *Altenglisches Theater*, *Phantasus*, *Deutsches Theater*, the Schlegel-Tieck Shakespeare, *Der Aufruhr in den Cevennen*, the four volumes of Tieck's *Novellenkranz*, *Der junge Tisch-*

lermeister, a later edition of *Don Quixote* and the editions of Kleist and Lenz. Tieck's letters to them cover fifty-one years, from 1802 to 1853, those up to 1838 being to Georg Andreas and the later ones to his son Georg Ernst. No other letters throw as much light upon his plans and methods of work. Together with his letters to Max and Brockhaus they form an indispensable source for a correct understanding of the author, especially during his "novellen" period.

CHAPTER SIXTEEN

THE EARLY "NOVELLEN"

THE classification of Tieck's "novellen" for purposes of individual discussion presents problems arising not only from their number and bulk but also from the multiplicity of topics. Two attempts have been made to class them according to subject matter. The first was by J. L. Hoffmann in 1856;[1] he discussed three types, fantastic, social and historical—an utterly inadequate classification. The second more important attempt was made in 1884 by Jakob Minor in an enlightening article.[2] He found that apart from *Der junge Tischlermeister* and *Vittoria Accorombona*, which defied systematization, there were eight categories, namely "novellen" dealing with questions of the day, those dealing with great writers, historical "novellen," stories of ghosts and magic, "novellen" of roguery, satires against the Young Germans, mere anecdotes and epic narratives.

The weakness of Minor's mode of procedure is due to several reasons. His compartments are not always mutually exclusive. Not every "novelle" fits into a single group; some belong in two or three. Besides, plot and subject matter are not as essential to Tieck as is his critique of the times. We shall, therefore, avoid every form of classification and observe a purely chronological method of treatment, devoting the present chapter to the "novellen" written before the July revolution of 1830 (an important event in the political and literary history of Germany), and chapter 17 to the later "novellen." This seems desirable not only for practical reasons, but also because each of the two groups thus acquired shows, in a rough way, a unity of purpose. The "novellen" of the first group are generally aimed against some form of ultraconservatism, while those of the latter group usually attack one of the doctrines of the Young Germans.

The first of the "novellen," *Die Gemälde* (1821),[*] is one of the most characteristic. The plot is so simple that Wilhelm Grimm called it trivial and complained that when he reached the end he was still waiting for the beginning.[3] A young man wastes his large patrimony but is saved by some fine pictures which are hidden in the wainscotting. They are accidentally discovered at a drunken revel (the discovery constitutes the turning point) and enable him to marry the girl of his choice and to live to a ripe, respected age.

* In each case the date of writing, not of publication, is given.

THE EARLY "NOVELLEN"

Far more important than the plot is the underlying purpose—a discussion of the conflict of opinions aroused by the opposite tendencies in the prevailing theories of art. These divided the artists of the time into two camps. In the one were the adherents of the old classical tradition, in the other the devotees of the more recent school, which had arisen as the result of Wackenroder's and Tieck's meditations, studies and writings on art. Like literary Romanticism, this Romantic school of esthetics, launched in defense of old German and Nazarene art, had degenerated. It had developed a reactionary form of religionism and an ultramontanism which banished all worldly beauty. Tieck, the well informed critic, realized that he himself was partly responsible for this development and wanted to present a true, unprejudiced picture of the situation. So in *Die Gemälde* he praised the sensual, happy classical beauty of Giulio Romano and overlooked the objections against him in his *Geschichte und Theorie der bildenden Künste*. On the other hand, he did not altogether reject religious painting, although he censured the exaggerated veneration of old German customs (Deutschtümelei) externally manifested even in clothing and coiffure, which had been suggested by himself and Wackenroder but brought distinctly into vogue by A. W. Schlegel's Romantic colloquies on paintings in the *Athenäum* (1799). Tieck's young painter Dietrich represents this fatuous trend. And yet the representatives of academic classicism are also slyly ridiculed.

Tieck writes with calmness and circumspection. He shows more animation, and bitterness, too, when he argues against the self-styled connoisseurs (represented by the prince—is Burgsdorff his prototype?) who claim omniscience but are really ignoramuses. This deceiving nobleman is himself deceived by a tippling forger named Eulenböck, one of the most delightful creations in German "novellen" literature, who of all of Tieck's characters comes closest to being more than merely a typical figure. His is one of the many genial ironists in the "novellen." His remark that a given brand of wine represents the poetry of its native locality has become famous. But the frequently repeated statement that Eulenböck is a counterpart of the architect and writer on art Genelli is refuted by Tieck in a letter.[4] Count Schack's suggestion that he represents Tieck's nephew Gustav Waagen must also be taken with a grain of salt.[5] As for the principal character, he bears many of Tieck's own characteristics. His predilection for humorous speeches in praise of good victuals and drink was also Tieck's. Three English translations appeared between 1825 and 1833.[6]

LUDWIG TIECK, THE GERMAN ROMANTICIST

The interest in art, particularly in old paintings, evinced by Tieck in *Die Gemälde* accompanied him through life. We have had previous occasion to refer to it in discussing his relations with Wackenroder, the Schlegels and Runge, and in commenting upon the unpublished manuscript *Geschichte und Theorie der bildenden Künste* reposing in Vienna. It appears very markedly, too, in his correspondence with the noted art collector Sulpiz Boisserée, whom he met about 1808.[7] Boisserée had an unbounded admiration for Tieck and justly considered him an able connoisseur. Some of Tieck's judgments in his letters to Boisserée are indeed sound, as that on the painting of a Dying Virgin owned by Boisserée (now in the Munich Pinakothek), which, Tieck readily discerned, was the work of a German artist who lived after Dürer and spent some time in Italy.[8] In the course of his Dresden period his preoccupation with painting also earned him the friendship of the noted artist Vogel von Vogelstein, whose portraits of Tieck have been mentioned.

Not long after *Die Gemälde* Tieck wrote *Der Geheimnisvolle* (1821). With it he sounded one of his favorite "novellen" themes, a typical social problem, namely insincerity in political and social life and the perniciousness of lies. The germ of the tale lies in an incident to which allusion has been made. In 1804 his brother-in-law Reichardt, using material furnished him by Count Schlabrendorf, secretly published a pamphlet against Napoleon. Though shielded by the Prussian chancellor, Count Hardenberg, he was forced to flee from the emperor's wrath. Around this nucleus of fact Tieck builds his plot, the locale of which is clearly Ziebingen. Kronenberg, a vain secretmonger and liar, who pharisaically censures others for the same fault of which he is guilty, falsely claims the authorship of a book against Napoleon. His prevarication involves him in serious trouble and almost costs him his life. Most of the other characters in the "novelle" are also untruthful, conspicuous exceptions being noble Cäcilie and young Emmerich. The latter gives expression to Tieck's own patriotic sentiments, his belief in the necessity of German unity, and his disbelief in excessive outspokenness of the public press. Tieck's semi-dramatic treatment has been referred to in the previous chapter.

As *Der Geheimnisvolle* depicts a gallery of prevaricators, so *Die Reisenden*, written in the spring of 1822, pictures an assemblage of fools. A tourist travelling incognito—a fad in Tieck's day—is mistaken for a madman and incarcerated in an asylum. Here most of the happenings, largely of a ludicrous nature, take place. We are introduced to many well drawn types, some really insane, while others are merely eccentric and hover on the borderline separating sanity from lunacy. One of Tieck's best figures is young Raimund. Though sane, he is suspected of being deranged, and every attempt to clear himself of this mistrust makes him more suspicious in the eyes of the "experts." His chief handicap arises from a false belief, which becomes an obsession, that his sweetheart has died. Minutes seem as years to him; this earns him the nickname of Methuselah. In the end the old physician in charge of the asylum loses his own mind and dismisses all the inmates. Tieck's ultimate purpose in composing this modern catalog of fools seems to be to deal in a realistic, satiric way with the typically Romantic question: Where does rational thinking end and madness begin? The "novelle" well illustrates his abiding interest in demonism. But from his nature demonism of 1797 to his new realistic demonism is a far cry. *Die Reisenden* contains many reminiscences of Burgsdorff.[9] A certain similarity to *Los Locos de Valencia* of Lope, from whom he borrowed numerous motifs for the "novellen,"[10] is evident. A French version appeared in 1833.[11]

Die Verlobung (1822) is a polemic against exaggerated and complacent piety and against Tieck's old Romantic theory that art and religion are identical. Orthodoxy, he felt, had been labored to such an extent that it had led to mere lip-service, external religionism and intellectual flaccidity, and had undermined mental and moral discipline. The lesson which he would point seems to be that a cultured man may possess truly religious instincts without being orthodox. This idea is pressed with some insistence and stamps *Die Verlobung* as the first markedly programmatic "novelle."

Apparently the protest it voices was timely. Shortly after its appearance the publisher F. A. Brockhaus noted in his diary that it contains "words spoken in the nick of time, for conditions are now bad, indeed. People care less whether a man does right and fulfils his duty than whether he observes the externalities of religion."[12] Similarly, Goethe felt that Tieck has dispelled gloomy clouds and revealed a clear blue sky of common sense and pure morals.[13]

As usual when Tieck's chief purpose is argumentative and not narrative, the plot is thin and insignificant, serving merely as an illustration of the subject of controversy. A young and beautiful but poor girl consents with reluctance to marry a very pious young baron. She is saved from him by an equally rich but less pious count, who marries her and settles the mortgage on the family mansion. The characters, however, are well portrayed. The principal one bears the name of Tieck's elder daughter Dorothea and mirrors the noblest aspects of her personality. An English translation by Connop Thirlwall came out in 1825.[14]

Musikalische Leiden und Freuden (1822), suggesting in title Hoffmann's *Johannes Kreislers des Kapellmeisters Musikalische Leiden* and written one year after Weber's *Der Freischütz*, is composed in a bright, humorous vein. It is of twofold interest and value as an historical document, showing Tieck's own reaction to music and reflecting conditions in the musical world of his day. The autobiographical element is strong. Early in life he had come to understand and appreciate music at Reichardt's home in Berlin and later in Halle and Giebichenstein. He conceived a boyish admiration for Mozart. But his own attempt to play the violin, delightfully described by the "layman" in the story, was an utter failure. Wackenroder had opened his eyes to the close relationship of music and the rest of the arts, with the result that many of his works possess a strong musicalness and marked synaesthesia, as we have noted.[15] His friend Burgsdorff was very musical. And in the home of Count Finckenstein at Madlitz (he was the model for Baron Fernow in the story) Tieck also heard much music.

The trend of his argument in this "novelle" is against spuriousness in music, particularly against ignorant "lovers" of music, stupid amateur performers and the caprices of audiences and singers, in short against all the various abuses of the art. There is no mistaking the types which he introduces, for instance the dilettante enthusiast Kellermann, who is always ecstatic, generally over some composition which he has never heard; Count Alten, the "concert hound"; the musical director tortured by the whims of the public; and the Italian singing teacher, in whom the soulless virtuosos are attacked. It is in this "novelle" that we find Tieck's charge that Beethoven is guilty of farfetched originality. As often in Tieck, the "novelle" is a story framed within a story, so constructed that in the end framework and narrative proper are blended into a unit.

The setting of *Die Gesellschaft auf dem Lande* (1824) is eighteenth century Brandenburg. The theme, the evil of untruthfulness, is identical with that of *Der Geheimnisvolle*. Though Tieck opposed the "fanaticism for veraciousness" ascribed to the Teutons, and could condone a white lie,[16] he demanded truth and frankness in all matters of importance, making this demand one of his leading motifs.

As usual the plot is simple. Franz has seen Adelheid at a ball and fallen in love with her. By her brother, his friend, he is invited to the family's country estate. There he poses as a painter. But Adelheid, repulsed by his disingenuous mode of courting, conceals her love for him and encourages another suitor, until the latter has a serious quarrel with her father, the baron. The father, a champion of the "good old times," wears a queue and expects all his friends to do likewise. His steward Römer, who poses as a former hussar, has a particularly fine queue, which is cut off half in jest by Zipfmantel, the miller. The resulting ignominy is too much for Römer, and he dies. Thereupon it turns out that he was a base charlatan, who had lied so long and persistently about his past that he had come to believe his own prevarications. Needless to say, Franz wins Adelheid, and a happy ending is achieved. The tale is written in a pleasantly humorous vein. Some of the characters are well portrayed, especially Römer (modelled on a figure Tieck met in Ziebingen), the old baron (a take-off on the ultraconservatives of the time) and the baroness (who, like Tieck's Ziebingen friends, unable to distinguish between "mir" and "mich," always uses the accusative in addressing servants and the dative in social intercourse).

In its day this "novelle" was praised. A. W. Schlegel read it "with unending delight" and felt that nothing since *Don Quixote* could compare with it.[17] Of interest are a fine tribute to Frederick the Great, also the mature fatalism and belief in supernaturalism affirmed in the words: "Do we toy with ourselves, or does a higher hand shuffle the cards? Perhaps in the very important moments of our lives these two possibilities come to the same thing."[18]

Pietro von Abano oder Petrus Apone, Zaubergeschichte (1824) deals with medieval superstitions, spooks and magic and is charged with an atmosphere of fantasticalness. In being more a narrative portrait than a disquisition it is hardly a "novelle" in Tieck's sense, rather a fairy tale in the Romantic style. Like *Dichterleben*, which was to follow, it marks a transition from the "novelle" of contemporary conditions to the historical type. But instead of allowing the magic element to be manifested in nature, as he had done in *Der blonde Eckbert*, he makes the devil and his human underlings its ministers. The hellish medieval magician Apone of Padua, in love with dead Crescentia, calls her back from the grave. Hovering between life and death, she is promised full life by the sorcerer if she will marry him. But her yearning for death is stronger than her will to be resuscitated under such conditions. In the end it turns out that Apone was under the influence of Berecynth, a demon, who restores him to life, only to spirit him away. And Crescentia has a twin sister, who had been kidnaped in infancy and is now rescued and married by Antonio, Crescentia's lover. Of interest is Tieck's belief that childlike faith works greater miracles than sophisticated sorcery.

The source which Tieck used is the *Storia della letteratura italiana* of Girolamo Tiraboschi.[19] Though lacking unity, the difficult subject, which Brentano also used in his *Romanzen vom Rosenkranz*, is handled cleverly (as Niebuhr, too, thought)[20] and with a degree of skill. As in his earlier Romantic tales, Tieck banishes realism and all reference to contemporary everyday life. In later works, when he mixed spiritualism, magic and realism, as in the modern tale *Der Schutzgeist* (1839), he was less successful. A continuation of *Pietro von Abano*, announced in 1824, did not appear. In 1827 the tale was used as the basis for an opera by Spohr (text by Karl Pfeiffer). Two English translations were published in 1831 and 1839, respectively.[21]

Dichterleben (1824), with a prolog *Das Fest zu Kenilworth* (1828) and a second part (1829), is again more narrative than argumentative and rates higher than any of the "novellen" preceding it except *Pietro von Abano*. As early as 1800 he had planned a novel on the early English drama.[22] The three "novellen" comprising *Dichterleben*, together covering three hundred fifty pages in the *Schriften*, are in a sense the consummation of this plan. They deal with that period in the history of English dramatics, the first thirty years of Shakespeare's life, which held the greatest interest for Tieck. On the model of the "Künstlerdrama" made popular by Goethe's *Tasso*, Kind's *Van Dykes Landleben*, Castelli's *Rafael* and Oehlenschläger's *Correggio*, they introduce a new type of "novelle," which deals with the lives of great poets.

Considering the three "novellen" as an entity, we may call them a sort of repository for the unused materials of the book on Shakespeare. We become acquainted first with Shakespeare, the highly precocious child, and with the environment in which Tieck pictured him. The Middle Ages and the heyday of the Catholic Church in England still cast their shadows. The influence of a gloomy, harsh and prosaic father (who is modelled somewhat on the plan of Tieck's own father) is outweighed by the more buoyant, tender and poetic nature of the mother (Tieck's mother). We meet Ann Hathaway, who early calls the boy "meinen kleinen Mann," and with Shakespeare we are participants in the festivities at Kenilworth in 1575. In the first part of the "novelle" we accompany the obscure beginner to London and witness him wresting the poetic laurels from Greene and Marlowe, the leading playwrights of their day, and finding a friend in wealthy Southampton.

Thus far Shakespeare, the harmonious genius, free of all demonic passion, is seen only in the background, while his more experienced but utterly unbalanced rivals play the principal parts. There is irony in the fact that although their ideas seem to impress him, he never puts them into practice. There is fatalism in the prophecy of a soothsayer that he will be a great poet.

At the opening of the second part Shakespeare is seen at the inn of Davenant in Oxford. The time is about 1593, and *Love's Labour's Lost* has been half finished. Two sections constitute this latter portion, Shakespeare's narrative of his own life up to his flight to London, omitted between the prolog and part 1, and his visit to Stratford with Southampton. While he was almost a mythical figure in the first part, without blemish or reproach, he is brought closer to us in the latter part, where we witness him in a struggle with himself. Unfortunately, however, the nearer he is brought, the smaller he seems. His views on poetry are those of Tieck, the nineteenth century critic. His Protestant faith, with its contempt for Puritanism and the Anglican Church but its kindly feeling for Catholicism, is also Tieck's.

From a letter to his publisher Max of 1840 we learn that Tieck planned a continuation in the form of a full-length novel.[23] In another letter to Max of 1842[24] we read that it was to deal with Shakespeare's "later relation to Ben Jonson and the other poets, but particularly with the story of Essex and his private secretary Cuffe." Tieck adds: "The building materials for this work have been ready for many years, and it is quite possible that you, my friend, will publish it in a year or two." This promise was not fulfilled.

Among his works of this type written thus far he considered *Dichterleben* his favorite.[25] At the time of its appearance it created a furore. The critics practically agreed that it was the finest piece which had flowed from his pen in at least a generation, an outstanding literary masterpiece, superior to any of Scott's novels.[26] Wilhelm Grimm thought it showed remarkable insight into the human heart; Immermann and Hebbel had words of high praise for it.[27] As early as 1824 Tieck suggested that Brockhaus publish an English rendering.[28] In 1828 A. W. Schlegel thought that if translated into English it would cause quite a stir.[29] Such a translation (of the first part) appeared at Leipzig in 1830 but passed unnoticed. In 1837 *Blackwood's* brought selections from the prolog and both parts.[30] A Danish version of the first part came out in 1826.[31] In 1832 two French translations, one of the prolog and the two parts, the other of parts 1 and 2, appeared.[32] A three-act drama, *Shakespeare* (1836), by Braun von Braunthal, is based upon the first part. A novel by H. C. König (1839), a drama by Holtei (1840) and Wildenbruch's *Christoph Marlowe* (1884) also owe much to Tieck.

The chief basis of *Dichterleben* is not, as might be expected, historical source material or tradition, but his own intuition as a poet. A recent

English critic, Professor John G. Robertson, has given an interesting appraisal of the work. He calls Tieck's interpretation of Shakespeare thoroughly Romantic and characterizes the novel as mediocre, inanimate and devoid of all English atmosphere.[33] However this may be, it is true that, in comparison with Scott's *Kenilworth* and such modern novels of Elizabethan England as Virginia Woolf's *Orlando* and Eduard Stucken's *Im Schatten Shakespeares*, Tieck's effort seems futile.

Der Aufruhr in den Cevennen, of which four sections were planned but only two appeared, is Tieck's first real historical "novelle," or more properly novel. The historical background is the uprising of the Calvinist Camisards in the Cévennes mountains of southern France in 1703.

He explained his first acquaintance with the subject and the genesis of his work as follows. His attention, he reported, was first attracted to the theme in 1806, upon his return from Italy, through three dramas of J. von Sinclair. Some years later he chanced to read a story by Misson entitled *Le théâtre sacré des Cévennes* (London, 1707), containing the visions and vicissitudes of Camisard refugees in England. This and the fact that the fate of the Camisards had never found objective treatment appealed to him so strongly that he decided to treat the material himself. Now he set to work reading numerous pertinent sources, among them the *Lettres des Protestants des Cévennes aux Réfugiés François-Allemands* (Berlin, 1704), a French *Histoire des Camisards* (London, 1744) and the memoirs of the Catholic Duke of Villars (1734-1736). But one important work, *Histoire des troubles des Cévennes* (1760), he did not discover until after he had practically completed the work, which he began in 1820 and finished in 1826.[33a]

But in the summer of 1829 Brentano told Johann Emmanuel Veith that he was responsible for calling Tieck's attention to the subject, having confidentially communicated to him "eine längere Dichtung" on the theme.[34] The truth of this is borne out by the fact that in October 1806 Brentano recommended Sinclair's dramas to Arnim.[35] Moreover, Brentano started a play on the same subject.[36] It would seem, therefore, that Tieck either met Sinclair, or became acquainted with his works, through Brentano.

Nor is Tieck's catalog of his specific sources for the "novelle" complete, as shown by Lebede's recent research into the records of his loans from the Dresden library. To be sure, Tieck quotes his chief source for purely historical facts, the pro-Protestant and rather subjective *Histoire des Camisards*, which he drew from the library for thirteen months (1822-1823). But he used at least seven other important works, the Catholic and pro-Camisard *Histoire du Fanatisme* of Brueys, the more

THE EARLY "NOVELLEN"

objective *Histoire de France sous le règne de Louis XIV* by Larrey, the *Mémoires* of Guiscard, a *Histoire de l'Edit de Nantes* (1693-1695), a *Histoire générale de Languedoc* (1733-1745), the *Monumens de la Monarchie Françoise* by Montfauçon, and, for geographic orientation, Herbin's *Statistique générale et particulière de la France.*

He adheres with fidelity to the historical facts as he ascertained them from the gloomy account of would-be prophets, cruelties, carnage and pillage which his sources gave. Even the miracles which he reports are in the sources. The Camisard leaders Cavalier, Catinat, Roland, Ravenel and Mazel, like their opponents Basville, Montrevel and Julien, are a poet's recreations of extravagant historical characters. Because he found them ready-made in the sources, they are among his best figures. The masses are also effectively introduced, sometimes to the detriment of plot development.

But the main plot, the story of Edmund and his family, is his own free invention. In development it may be compared roughly with Schiller's *Wilhelm Tell*, Edmund's father being a sort of Attinghausen and Edmund himself a combination of Rudenz and Melchthal. Edmund, at first a fanatical Catholic, is converted by a sort of miracle into an equally zealous Calvinist. The scene in which he is forced to destroy his own house, marked by gloomy fatalism (of which there are many traces in the work), is one of the finest among a wealth of stirring scenes. In the end the hero is cured of all fanaticism, whatever may be its hue, and led to peace and conciliation, by Father Watelet, a wise old priest who has obviously studied Jacob Böhme and like Tieck been influenced by him. His discussions with Edmund on the subject of faith are an important part of this "novelle" and reproduce Tieck's own clarified, unbiased views. While adhering to his inherited creed, Father Watelet opposes belief in supernaturalism and superstition. Miracles, he holds, are to be found not in deviations from the laws of God and nature, but in these laws themselves. And Christianity is to him an elastic religion, which permits every man to make his own code. The character of the unbeliever, Lacoste, may owe traits to Schopenhauer.

It is significant that Tieck here reverts, as he does also in *Der Hexensabbath*, to one of his favorite themes, the gradual development of a psychic disturbance. Such disturbance he now prefers to study under the aspect of religious superstition, which becomes a menace in times of fanaticism. Here, as in *Vittoria Accorombona*, his chief characters are demonic men and women impelled by magic or mysticism, who trespass beyond the bounds set for human beings. In this sense they are akin to William Lovell, Eckbert and Tannenhäuser.

LUDWIG TIECK, THE GERMAN ROMANTICIST

Of course religion plays a weighty rôle. And yet religion is important chiefly as a part of the historical milieu. The latter is paramount. Moreover, the work is significant in giving us a picture of his purpose in writing historical "novellen." He would use them as a means of revealing a relationship between bygone ages and his own times, and of thus discovering a general human significance in history.

Although most contemporary reviewers did not greet the work with great warmth,[37] many notable critics, among them Jacobs, von Hauch, Menzel, Johanna Schopenhauer,[36] A. W. Schlegel,[29] Immermann,[38] Gries,[39] Schleiermacher[40] and Joseph von Hormayr,[41] were loud in their praises and implored Tieck to finish it. Raumer felt that he deserved a theological degree for it.[42] The historical novelist Häring (Wilibald Alexis) credited him with discovering in it the secret of the poetical treatment of history in novellistic form.[43] His failure to complete the "novelle," despite these many encouragements, led to various rumors, the most pernicious being that of Varnhagen von Ense previously referred to. The unedited correspondence with Reimer, the publisher of the work, throws new light on the question.[44] As late as April 1838 Tieck promised him to complete it that summer, but in July 1845 he wrote to the younger Reimer that he never finished it because old Reimer was opposed to a continuation. That this is probably true and that the publisher's opposition was due to external economic reasons, is indicated by the fact that in 1846, twenty years after its appearance, the edition of the extant section was not yet exhausted.[44]

Even today critics do not agree as to its merits. Witkowski feels that it cannot be rated highly as a work of art.[45] But Berend calls it a masterpiece of historical fresco painting[46] and Willoughby gives it the palm among the later works.[47] No doubt it has elements of greatness, but it lacks vitality. This fatal defect, brought about less by such minor flaws as the verbal perversions of Frau Barbe, or the precociousness of little Eveline (a typical Tieckean child), and less by the sentimental ending than by the obtrusiveness of the argument on religion, deprives the work of truly lasting significance. But after all is said and done, it remains one of the most compelling works of the aging poet, and visualizes his ideas of tolerance, as *Nathan der Weise* does Lessing's.

Madame Burette's English translation (1845) is fairly readable. In 1880 A. Langert based an opera upon the "novelle."

In view of the energy devoted by Tieck to the last three works, it is no wonder that his next "novelle," *Glück gibt Verstand* (1826), shows a marked slackening of his powers. Bäring, an old country parson, is a philistine, but also a gruff and stern parent. He has lofty ambitions for his exceedingly modest son Simon, who has studied law. He wants him to apply for a high judicial post. With misgivings Simon departs to the city to submit to the necessary examination, taking a fond leave of Sidonie, his sweetheart, of whom his father disapproves, not because she is older than he, but because she is a poor orphan. Before Simon can present himself to the minister to seek the desired appointment, he falls into the hands of some friendly adventurers, who pose as influential noblemen. One plays the part of the ruling prince and treats Simon with such kindness that he develops enough courage to apply successfully for the position. The real prince takes a fancy to him and at the same time gives his father a promotion in rank. Better still, Simon is permitted to marry Sidonie, who unexpectedly receives a handsome sum of money.

The triviality of this plot is relieved by occasional clever incidents and digs against philistinism. There is an amusing conversation on the joys of pipe-smoking and of wearing a nightcap. As in Tieck's earliest comedies, particularly *Der letzte Betrug ist ärger als der erste*, proverbs play an important part. Not only is the title proverbial, but the actions of the hero throughout are guided by proverbs which he had heard discussed at the beginning. But the critic who wrote of this "novelle" that "few poets make it as clear as Tieck that substance is inconsequential and form or mode of treatment all-important"[48] must have been strongly prejudiced in his favor.

Although *Der funfzehnte November* (1827) is not one of his best "novellen," either, it is significant from one point of view. A program "novelle," the trend of its plot and indeed its very title (a mockery of such titles as *Der 24. Februar*) serve as a disputation against the "fate dramas" and their mechanical conception of fate. But it presents his case not by argument or mere talk, rather through the medium of the story itself. His reasoning is that a higher, divine conception of fate and a nobler fatalism exist than that espoused by such dramatists as Werner and Houwald. The essence of this exalted fatalism is absolute faith in the inscrutable wisdom of God. The tale which illustrates this idea and pictures his mature conception of demonic force is the most soulful and pious of all his "novellen," but the plot is too far-fetched, the motivation too deficient, and the characterization too conventional.

The son of a wealthy Dutch merchant, a gifted young man, is suddenly deprived of part of his reason and power of speech. Though very strong physically, he is now a moron in all his actions. But one aptitude has remained with him—he is very clever at building. Sensing some terrible misfortune, he sets to work constructing a huge boat. This occupies him for two years; on his birthday it is finished. Then the dike breaks. With almost superhuman exertion he saves numerous lives in his craft. Exhausted, he sinks into a long, deep sleep. When he awakens, he is completely cured. He marries the girl who has nursed him through his illness with loving care, and they live a happy, genuinely pious life ever after.

Except for an amusing minor incident, which describes how a Werther enthusiast is hoaxed by some robbers, the unity is well observed. The main idea came to Tieck from a Dutch copperplate representing a flood. Incidentally he takes occasion to defend the Dutch against the then prevalent charge of stolidity. He paints them much more favorably than he does a German swaggerer.

Der Gelehrte (1827) is one of the best "novellen," free of propagandistic purpose and bizarre effect, artistically sound, and rich in harmless humor and excellent characterization. A very bookish professor, who has been an inveterate celibate, suddenly decides to marry. With unerring instinct he selects that one of three eligible daughters who will make him the best wife. She is Helena, the Cinderella of her family. Marriage soon serves to cause an electrifying transformation in the morose ascetic. He becomes quite human, adopts a more mellow outlook upon the world and becomes aware of countless amenities of life to which he had been blind.

Tieck has woven many autobiographic touches into his "novelle." The professor's passion for books, abhorrence of street noises, philanthropic bent and contempt for money were traits of Tieck himself. Helena's charming womanliness, combined with a love for learning, was a characteristic of Dorothea, while her domesticity was a quality of his other daughter Agnes. Among the many apt humorous touches, the episode in which the butler Werner proposes to the housekeeper is prominent.

The little story served Freytag as the model for incidents in his novel *Die verlorene Handschrift*. Freytag's hero, Felix Werner, bears the name of Tieck's butler, while the butler Gabriel in the Freytag novel is patterned on the same model. In Freytag a lost manuscript of Tacitus plays an important part; in Tieck a misplaced slip bearing an emendation of Quintilian.

But the present-day reader, interested in the psychological study of character, seeks in vain a depiction of the various steps in the transformation, which takes place too suddenly in the soul of Tieck's professor. Tieck's successors in the "novelle" would undoubtedly have considered this metamorphosis of the bookworm the most alluring phase of the subject.

Der Alte vom Berge (1828) is characteristic in introducing as its protagonist one of those "queer birds" who are as numerous in the "novellen" as in Jean Paul's novels and in the narratives of such successors as Raabe and Keller. In this case he is a man who, professing theoretical misanthropy and leading the life of a recluse, is in reality a very warm-blooded philanthropist. Blessed with wealth, he gives large sums for factories and human betterment. But he dies before he can make a will to prevent his fortune from coming into the possession of relatives who he thinks are frivolous and wasteful. As frequently in the "novellen," however, God disposes more wisely than man proposes. What was looked upon as a misfortune turns out a blessing in disguise, for, as the sequel proves, the money gets into the right hands after all. While the plot is clever, the motivation, as usual, leaves much to be desired.

On April 3, 1828, Tieck wrote to the publisher Max that no work had caused him more trouble and been so much delayed as *Der Alte vom Berge*.[49] While he had begun it "with pleasure" (mit Freude), he was soon interrupted by illness and other distractions. Max preferred it to *Der Aufruhr in den Cevennen*, Tieck not. An English translation appeared in 1831, a French version in 1833.[50] A new French translation, by Bournac and Hella, appeared in 1931.

One of the brightest, most humorous and most entertaining of the "novellen" is *Das Zauberschloss* (1829), a parody of E. T. A. Hoffmann's spook stories and Müllner's "fate dramas," also a burlesque of contemporary bluestockings and their affected writings. A Herr von Freimund, who wishes to marry his daughter to an elderly "Landrat," resolves to celebrate the betrothal in Schloss Graupenheim, an old castle which he has just purchased and which, as popular tradition has it, is haunted. Two friends of the family precede the rest to make the necessary preparations. On the way they meet a poetess, who has composed verse in honor of the occasion. Only with difficulty is she prevented from reading it and other effusions to them *in extenso*. Arriving at the castle, they find it locked. Then a terrific shower surprises them, and they are quite marooned. To make matters worse, the deaf gardener takes them for burglars. Finally the rest of the party arrive. But the fiancé is missing, and worse, the commissary wagon fails to come. Potatoes are the only available fare. There is but one small lamp, which is accidentally overturned. Mysterious noises, as well as other terrifying circumstances practically convince the frightened assemblage that the castle is really haunted. To cap the climax, the bride's horses shy and run away with her into the black night. Her aged fiancé, a belated arrival, is less perturbed by this than by his hunger. When the bride returns the next day as the happy wife of her real lover, a young army captain, it becomes clear that the runaway was merely part of a scheme devised by the captain's father, an old friend of Herr von Freimund.

To his brother Tieck described *Das Zauberschloss* aptly as "ein Spass, wo ich mir den Spass gemacht, viel Spass aus einem nichts zu entwickeln."[51] Next to *Die Gesellschaft auf dem Lande* it was A. W. Schlegel's favorite.

Into this jovial "novelle" Tieck has woven another little tale, *Die wilde Engländerin*, which is a masterpiece of realistic fiction. It is read by one of the characters to prevent the poetess from presenting her poetry. The plot relates how a coy, prudish girl devotes herself to astronomy and mathematics, but spurns love and a noble, wealthy lover until after he has accidentally seen her partially nude as she dismounted from her horse. This twenty-page story on the theme of a woman's chastity (similar in motif to Hebbel's drama *Gyges und sein Ring*) is done very delicately and has a well managed turning point. The development of the girl is described with psychological finesse, yet with grace and naturalness. It would be prudish to charge Tieck with impropriety in his mode of treatment. A comparison of the egregiously few piquant incidents found in his later writings—such episodes occur in *Däumchen*, *Die Vogelscheuche*, *Der junge Tischlermeister* and *Eigensinn und Laune*—with those in almost any present-day novelist, shows how intent he was to spare his readers' blushes and how closely allied to that spirit which developed into the Victorian tradition.

The feverish search for contacts with the supernatural world, characteristic of Tieck's day, is exposed in *Die Wundersüchtigen* (1829). The career of Cagliostro and the activities of the Rosicruceans and Illuminati at the end of the eighteenth century, attacked by Goethe in *Der Grosskophta*, had furnished crass illustrations of how fanatics, deceivers and deceived, working hand in hand, resorted to cunning means of cheating a gullible public, who craved for some form of supernaturalism which the Age of Reason had tabooed. Tieck looks upon this rage for miracles as though it were a social or moral disease. Animal magnetism and somnambulism are the particular targets of his attack. Two types of "wonder workers" are presented, Feliciano, an unconscionable Cagliostro, and Sangerheim, a more principled imposter. In practice one is as pernicious as the other.

His moral purpose in writing this tale, which we distinguish from such a "novelle" as *Das Zauberschloss* by its stern tone and the absence of humor, is a variation of his favorite doctrine: That miracles *do* exist, but that they are not as crass and tawdry as those spurious ones of the professional mongers. Real miracles, he finds, are marked by divine benevolence and occur in the broad daylight of routinary life. And since they proceed from God, it behooves man neither to construct systems upon them nor to draw conclusions therefrom.

Such a "novelle" as *Die Wundersüchtigen* can have little more than antiquarian interest today. But in its time it was praised as an opportune document and considered superior to Goethe's drama in effectiveness.[52] An English writer in the *Foreign Quarterly Review*, after discussing the "novellen" in general and this one in particular, assures his readers "that with respect to purity of style, moral tendency and philosophic truth, no more estimable works can be found in the whole range of German literature."[53]

Though not published until late in 1830, *Der wiederkehrende griechische Kaiser* was begun in 1829 and finished before July, 1830, as Tieck's letters to Brockhaus show. It is a long historical "novelle," originally planned as a drama, a sort of exposé of the machinations of politicians and statesmen. The scene is laid in Ghent in 1202 during the fourth crusade; the plot, dealing with a pretender, is of the type of Schiller's *Demetrius*. Johanna rules as regent of Flanders while her father, Count Balduin, is absent in the Holy Land. There he acquires the Greek imperial crown but dies soon after. When word of his death reaches Flanders, trouble begins to brew. Most of it is caused by two intriguing grandees, each of whom plots to force Johanna to marry his son. One of the factions, to thwart the other, spreads the rumor that Balduin is still alive and trumps up an imposter who claims to be the emperor. The king of France appears as the *deus ex machina*. Through him the pretender is unmasked and the warring factions are brought to rest. He also effects the recognition of Ferdinand, a hitherto obscure kinsman of Balduin who had himself lived in ignorance of his lineage. Ferdinand loves Johanna, who requites his affection, and all ends well.

Tieck's contemporaries regarded the "novelle" highly. One reviewer praised the masterly portrayal of the historical background, the rich variety of characters, the colorful individual scenes and the genuinely poetic conception.[54] Another deemed his characters incomparable, his scenes very lively and his humor in a class by himself.[55] Laube claimed that the tale converted him definitively to realism. But the present-day reader is disappointed by the work. He finds a mass of irrelevant detail and great prolixity. The background seems vague, the characters untrue to life, the speeches long-winded and tiresome, and the foolery of the jester trite. There are many indications that the subject matter was quite alien to Tieck's talent.

As an historical "novelle," however, *Der wiederkehrende griechische Kaiser* shows certain improvements over *Dichterleben* and *Der Aufruhr in den Cevennen*. Above all, it contains more frequent realistic touches. There is also a noticeable effort on Tieck's part to individualize the characters more sharply and to achieve plastic effects. This applies particularly to the figures of the two grandees, who are well contrasted. No doubt he was gradually learning a useful lesson from Scott.

CHAPTER SEVENTEEN

THE LATER "NOVELLEN"

W ITH *Der Jahrmarkt, Der Hexensabbath* and *Der Mondsüchtige*, all written in 1831, the second series of Tieck's "novellen" begins. We find that it contains a much larger proportion of irrelevant or insignificant works than the first series. Were it not for the little gem *Des Lebens Überfluss*, written in 1837, and the respectable novel *Vittoria Accorombona*, which closes not only the long cycle of his novellistic writings but his literary career, we should be tempted to believe that his talent as a writer was gradually waning. His irony and attitude of Jovian aloofness were disappearing by degrees. As time went on, it became ever clearer that he could no longer master his hatred of his new foes, the Young Germans, sufficiently to effect as just a distribution of light and shade among the parties as the highest standards of his craft demanded.

This becomes manifest in his very first work of the period, *Der Jahrmarkt*. It is the earliest of several humorous "novellen" of roguery which he wrote, a type found in Le Sage's *Gil Blas*, as well as in Spanish literature, and later used by Balzac. His model for the story, it seems, was Lope's *Ferias de Madrid*. The meager plot tells of a company of people who undertake a journey from the country to attend the annual fair in town, where they are mistaken for a band of thieves. But more important than the action, from Tieck's point of view, are the lengthy conversations. Their favorite themes are the "art" of begging and the depredations of the Young Germans in the provinces of literature, politics and society. The latter topic, in particular, which was destined to loom large in his writings of the 'thirties, serves to mar the unity of the "novelle" and to convert what should be a work of art into a doctrinal brochure. As in *Das Zauberschloss* and *Die Wundersüchtigen*, he seeks to rationalize on seemingly mysterious events.

In *Der Hexensabbath* we have a work of quite another type and of much higher quality; like *Der Aufruhr in den Cevennen* it is an historical "novelle" dealing with fanaticism and demonic aberration. But the plot is better developed than in the latter, while the characters are skilfully grouped and contrasted, some representing the enlightened élite, others the dull-witted religionists and still others the hypocritical schemers.

As in *Der Aufruhr in den Cevennen*, Tieck uses a broad political and social background. The time is 1459, the place France under Philip the

Good, the occasion the famous witch trial of Arras, as related in the memoirs of Jacques de Clerq. With power and psychological skill he shows how religious fanaticism is set in motion by a seemingly insignificant impetus and gradually spreads, until it becomes a demonically consuming force, which cruelly destroys not only the lives of noble individuals but the whole texture of a happy social life.

Madame Katharina Denisel, an admirable woman of parts, now thirty-six, has been a widow for twelve years, death having relieved her of her coarse, brutal husband, whom she was forced to marry. Through all her sufferings she has retained her sunny disposition and gracious manner, which combined with her refined sensualism, esthetic culture and nobility of soul make her a typically Tieckean woman. But she is misunderstood and suspected of evil practices because of her insatiable love for literature and the arts, which has attracted to her salon a circle of the most cultured people. Among them is the poet Labitte, a sort of fifteenth century Tieck, who may also owe some traits to the English painter Blake.[1] Like Tieck, Labitte despises superstition and discovers the only valid supernaturalism in the manifestations of divine love. Opposed to her are two fanatics, one, the bishop, a conscientious, basically honest zealot, the other, the dean, a scoundrel. Gertrud, an old madcap, presents herself to the gullible bishop as a witch and thus sets the terrible machinery of persecution in motion. What began as a ripple mounts to a tidal wave, to which Katharina, too, succumbs when the rascally dean denounces her. Poetic justice is done when his own mother and half sister are also swept away by the maelstrom.

This gloomy picture of the seamy side of the Middle Ages, like *Der wiederkehrende griechische Kaiser*, reveals the influence of Scott, particularly in its vivid street scenes, its able treatment of the lower classes as a huge, seething mass, and above all in its subordination of ideas to events. Its superiority to *Der Aufruhr in den Cevennen* is in direct proportion to the increased effect of this influence. There is also a relationship between *Der Hexensabbath* and de Vigny's historical novel *Cinq Mars* (1826), as well as Merimée's *Les Etats de Blois* and *Chronique de Charles IX* (1829). Nor should it be overlooked that the "novelle" was written in the same year as Hugo's *Notre Dame de Paris*. Although Tieck expressed no sympathy for French Romanticism, a perusal of *Der Hexensabbath* and *Vittoria Accorombona* admits no doubt but that it left an imprint upon him. For Merimée (particularly his dramas), on the other hand, he expressed high admiration, writing to Raumer in 1827 that *Les Etats de Blois* made an almost unparalleled

impression upon him, reminded him of Kleist, possessed true Shakespearean spirit and was unmatched by anything in French literature.[2]

The most glaring defect of the "novelle" is in the numerous anachronisms of which Katharina and Labitte are guilty. Still Raumer was
overwhelmed by the work and considered Labitte's speeches "the
grandest and most profound utterances ever made."[3] A French translation appeared in 1833.[4]

Der Mondsüchtige is typical of the later "novellen" period; it combines an insignificant plot possessing some clear Romantic traits with
an argument against the opinions and practices of the younger generation. It had become customary among the latter, who linked poetry
with partizanship, to indulge in irreverent criticism of Goethe and to
play up Schiller against him. Tieck, though accepting Goethe only with
certain reservations, as we have seen, and resenting the cool treatment
which Goethe had always accorded him, respected the master so highly
that he deemed it necessary, less than a year before Goethe's death, to
write this "novelle" in his defense.

In form *Der Mondsüchtige* is a travel "novelle" in letters (a type
popularized by the Young Germans), in tendency a paean on great
authors, particularly Goethe. The correspondents, in whose letters the
plot is developed, are an uncle and his nephew. Years ago the former
had secretly married a girl who shared his love for Goethe's poetry,
but whose father separated the young couple by force. Thereupon she
died. The nephew, like his uncle a dreamer and literary enthusiast, is
now on a journey through Germany, which takes him to many scenes
of Goethe's life and works. He casually meets a girl, with whom he
falls in love, but they are soon separated. A long time he searches for
her in vain, encountering various experiences and fighting a duel with
a contemner of Goethe. In the end he finds his girl in Geneva and
learns that she is his uncle's daughter, her mother having died at her
birth.

Many of the events, among them the uncle's visit to Stratford-on-
Avon, have an autobiographic character. This fact, combined with
Tieck's noble defense of Germany's proudest literary tradition, assures
the work a certain lasting interest, despite the puerile action. Incidentally he here still adheres to the old Schlegelian idea that "Dichter"
is connected with "verdichten," meaning to solidify or knit together.
This explains the uncle's angry remark that the opponents of true
poetry are "Dünner und Dehner"—diluters and expanders. At least
one reviewer took serious offense at his implied exaltation of Goethe at
the expense of Schiller.[5] But Grillparzer was stirred to admit that Tieck

LUDWIG TIECK, THE GERMAN ROMANTICIST

possessed at least a modicum of the Goethean spirit. Zelter reported to Goethe on December 3, 1831, that he read the tale with satisfaction.[5]

In 1832 Tieck produced only a single "novelle," *Die Ahnenprobe*. Here he deals with one of the chief problems which troubled his contemporaries and caused the rift between the old generation and the new, the relation of nobility and bourgeoisie. We found that he had treated the same question in one of his earliest comedies, *Die Entführung*. Throughout his life he remained conscious of its presence, although by virtue of his unusual gifts he had never been embarrassed by his lowly origin. That hatred of the aristocracy which the French Revolution and youthful radicalism tended to implant in him soon passed. Had not the annihilation of differences of blood, at least among the intelligentsia, been one of the best achievements of Romanticism? But the July Revolution once more made this ever thorny problem a burning question. Tieck's mature solution in *Die Ahnenprobe*, so far as it can be read between the lines, is only a compromise. But it met the demands of the period halfway and at the same time showed the Young Germans that Tieck opposed their agitation in favor of a radical social levelling.

A count, who is a virtuous, substantial man, refuses to consent to the union of his daughter and his secretary because the latter is of bourgeois origin. The mother of the secretary, who turns out to be a former sweetheart of the count, spurned for the same reason, supports the latter in his unyielding attitude. Meanwhile the count, who at heart is thoroughly favorable to the young man's match, hopes that his researches among the church records will prove that the secretary is really of noble lineage. It develops, however, that his family have merely been honest, respectable artisans for three centuries. But mindful of his own erstwhile love affair, the count is swayed by sentimentality to give the young couple his blessing. To simplify matters, the secretary is ennobled by royal patent.

Manifestly Tieck, who became ever more conservative with the advancing years, did not wish to abandon differences of rank, yet he wanted to demonstrate that in certain deserving cases these differences are not insurmountable. Four years later he, who surely believed in the existence of a "bourgeois nobility," in which he included his own family, presented the same type of argument in *Der junge Tischlermeister*. Incidentally a Club of Liars is described in *Die Ahnenprobe*; its members espouse the ideas of the Young Germans, and in their smug complacency they remind of such prominent Dresden clubmen as Kind and Böttiger. Once they are the solemn auditors at a learned lecture on kettle soldering. A wealthy nobleman who belongs to the circle has a prodigal son and ultimately loses his entire fortune. Tieck leaves the reader to draw the moral.

The plots of *Der Mondsüchtige* and *Die Ahnenprobe* (the latter reminds of Lope's *Perro del Hortelano*) represent Tieck's favorite type. Each deals with two love affairs, one of the older, the other of the younger generation, so managed that in the end they are linked.

Die Sommerreise (1833) belongs to the same category. Like *Der Mondsüchtige* it is a travel "novelle." Walther travels in search of a man who has eloped with a friend's cousin. The abductor turns out to be his companion Ferdinand. This exceedingly scanty action serves Tieck as the barest excuse for offering a graceful recapitulation of multifarious experiences and views and for motivating a detailed description of a voyage through southern Germany. His reminiscences are related in quite realistic fashion, with mention of definite places and persons. For instance, Ferdinand gives a vivid account of his associations with the Schlegels and Novalis in Jena. Tieck claimed that he used as his source the records of old friends, whose acquaintance he renewed at Prague in 1813. In reality he utilized his own notes on the trip with Burgsdorff during the summer of 1803, seeking to add to their interest by the haphazard insertion of humorous anecdotes and satiric extravaganzas. His promise to show how a stanch Protestant becomes a zealous Catholic and a stout Catholic a confirmed Protestant was not fulfilled.

The propagandistic purpose of the work seems the demonstration that the "good old times" of thirty years ago were happier than the new era of the Young Germans. It is the irony of fate that he selected for this purpose a vehicle—the travel diary—which his opponents had popularized. The reminiscent mood in which the "novelle" is written is characteristic of his old age in general, but more particularly of the year of its composition. For on May 31, 1833, he celebrated his sixtieth birthday. To him it served as an occasion for wistful memories, to his friends in Dresden and Berlin as a day of joyful celebration.[6] Gottfried Keller's fragment *Reisetage* was apparently inspired by Tieck's story.

The other "novelle" of 1833, *Tod des Dichters*, represents a nobler effort. It deals with the Portuguese poet Camoens. In long conversations and circumstantial accounts, whose language reads like that of a jubilee volume, Tieck describes the life of the poet; thereupon his last hours and death are depicted. A friend relates the principal events of his life, his sweetheart tells of his love; an Italian officer describes the *Lusiad*. The poet himself remains in the background until the end, then he comes forth in all his greatness and glory—an incarnation not so much of the sixteenth century Portuguese writer as of Tieck's abstract ideal of the Poet. Like other characters whom we have discussed, his opinions and judgments are those of the aging nineteenth century critic, extremely conservative and royalist withal, who is resigned to the thought that he, too, is soon to die, leaving a precious heritage to a new but unworthy generation which will not hear of him. This note of sad resignation (characteristic of Tieck in 1833) and the beautiful exalted prose in which it is written are the finest traits of a work marked by prolixity and anachronisms. The unhappy military campaign of chivalrous but hasty King Sebastian, which brought misfortune to Portugal, gives the tale a fittingly gloomy background. In 1847 Alfred Baskerville published a passable English translation.[7]

Almost simultaneously with Tieck's "novelle," Camoens' *Lusiad* appeared in a German translation by Donner. But Tieck (who, to be sure, in a letter of December 24, 1807, in the present writer's possession, had told Reimer that he finds Camoens "sehr mittelmässig, wo nicht schlecht") deserves credit for introducing his countrymen to the personality of the Portuguese master. Camoens had already been the subject of poetic treatment by the Portuguese poet Garrett in 1825. After Tieck he was frequently treated thus, in novels, stories and poems, by German, French, Scandinavian and English authors.

In *Die Vogelscheuche* (1834), a "fairy-tale 'novelle' in five acts," Tieck introduced a new form (barely suggested in *Pietro von Abano*), which reverts, externally at least, to the Romanticism of his youth, with its interest in elves and other supernatural beings. The revival of this interest is indicated also by the intentional blending of the dramatic and novellistic genres. The author of the *Phantasus* conversations, who in his introduction to Lenz had called Goethe's dramas "novellen" in dialog and who knew the medieval Spanish dialog novel *Celestina* and Lope's *Dorotea*, as well as Schelling's *Clara*, now wrote a dialog "novelle" himself. Instead of a *dramatis personae*, however, he furnished a parody of the popular but long-winded descriptions of the hero's clothes and the scenery. He also renewed his "Romantic Irony," as in a court scene, where the plaintiff, citing Tieck as an authority, is promptly refuted by the defendant.

But as in the works of the type of *Der gestiefelte Kater*, Tieck's Romanticism is counterbalanced by a liberal amount of satire. It is directed against French Romanticism, especially Hugo and his lurid charnel-house scenes, the German "fate drama," which is here associated with the Romantics of France, the belittlers of Goethe, but above all the poetasters of the Dresden "Liederkreis," to whom this "novelle" signified a veritable bombshell.

To edify his fellow-citizens through the ennobling influence of art, a resident of a small town has made a scarecrow of burnt leather in the form of a hunter and set it up in a pea-patch. His daughter Ophelia, a sentimental lass, falls in love with it. She adores it as her Adonis, her caveman (she calls it her Bavarian Hiesel) and her Robin Hood all in one. But one night the watchman sees it come to life and flee. Simultaneously with this strange occurrence a Herr von Ledebrinna arrives in a neighboring town. He soon ingratiates himself with the pillars of society and helps them found a learned club, which he calls "die Ledernen"—the leathery folk. Each member is given an apt nickname, the critic Ubique (Böttiger is meant) becoming Pliant, the municipal poet Ulf (Kind) Distended, and Ledebrinna himself Impenetrable. The purpose of the club is to encourage its members to act as scarecrows and buffers against the geniuses of literature. Ophelia transfers her affection for her leathery lover to Ledebrinna, who on their wedding night confesses that he is the scarecrow miraculously suffused with life.

Supernatural scenes, too long drawn out to be effective, alternate with realistic scenes in this baroque hodgepodge of horseplay and irony. Incidentally Tieck has interspersed many sagacious comments on various topics. He discourses entertainingly on the Schlegels and indulges in an intelligent discussion and defense of the intellectual rights of women (a favorite topic of his declining years). When he intercalates the papers of a Cousin Martin, he violates the unity of his tale for the sake of slyly parodying Hoffmann.

Today no one not a specialist in German literary conditions during the first half of the nineteenth century can appreciate the negating satire of contemporary scribblers, critical cynics and clannish faddists who waged a futile war against common sense, good taste and noble sentiment. Even the unbiased critics of the time realized that few elements of this esoteric diatribe would live.[8] A British critic, writing in 1835 and certainly no farther removed from the conditions Tieck describes than anyone today, called it "the most absurd and unintelligent attempt at satire that was ever written by a man of genius."[9] His letters to Max, however, show that Tieck himself thought very highly of the work. He wrote it with "great poetic joy" (grosser poetischer Lust); few of his writings gave him "such uninterrupted pleasure" (in so ununterbrochener Freude); he felt that it was altogether unique. It was widely read but, as he himself confessed, not because of its merit as a poetic work.

Of the same type is *Das alte Buch und die Reise ins Blaue hinein* (1834), a veritable symphony of Tieckean inventiveness. It has three plots—a story within a story, which is again set within a story. The narrator, who is the poet, mentions a friend, a modern unpoetic philistine, who has told him a story from an old book. It is a commonplace humorous narrative of small-town life. But into this is woven a fairy tale, a sort of Tannhäuser narrative, which is the *pièce de résistance* of the work.

Here we are introduced to Adelstan, a knightly youth, who in his wanderings through the mountains has met and kissed the fairy Gloriana. She, in love with him, has made him one of her kind, so that he can understand nature, the heart and the "love of love," which is the essence of poetry. Like Oberon and Titania they rule triumphantly over the spirits. Whatever mortal Adelstan regards, or touches, or embraces is turned into a poet. But he has one enemy, the ugly "arsenic prince" or gnome Hannes, who possesses the identical power over mortals. Adelstan kisses Gottfried von Strassburg, Dante, Shakespeare, Chaucer, Cervantes and others. By the time Klopstock is born, Adelstan is an old man and can point only a warning finger at him. But with Schiller he has a confidential tryst, while he warmly clasps Goethe, Byron, Scott and Manzoni in his arms. When he embraces Tieck under a replanted linden, he is very decrepit. Now he has died, and ugly Hannes rules supreme over Hugo and his "roh-mantschende" (coarsely diluting—a pun on "Romantisch") school and over Hoffmann, Börne, Heine and Müllner.

Besides being formally the clearest reversion to Tieck's earliest Romanticism, this "novelle" is significant in representing his first expressly personal attack against his opponents.

Der Wassermensch (1834), also an incursion on the Young Germans, observes the customary "novellen" technique in loosely linking two unrelated plots. As usual one of the plots is very bookish, while the other has a marked propagandistic flavor; both are presented in dialog form. A company of cultured people, returning from an entertainment at which Schiller's ballad *Der Taucher* has been recited, discuss the sources of this poem (which is unfairly criticized), as well as of Goethe's *Der Fischer*, speculating on how the theme could be utilized for various literary genres. One of those present, Florheim, who is betrothed to the daughter of the hostess, is asked to contribute something to the discussion. In a burst of anger he is revealed as a Young

German (the one and only place in his "novellen" in which Tieck used the term *expressis verbis*) of the most radical sort. He attacks the aristocracy, feudalism, patriotism and the monarchical form of government and lauds republicanism, the Jewry, Napoleon and France. The company are horrified and his fiancée sends him packing. When last heard of, he is on his way to Paris to observe his extreme, immature notions in practice. Like the "Wassermensch" in one version of Schiller's plot (Tieck means to suggest), his head has been so long immersed in the water of Young German theories that he has lost his mind.

In *Weihnacht-Abend* (1834) Tieck allowed himself a respite, as it were, from the one-sided controversies in which he had recently engaged. This "novelle" has no ulterior purpose—the first of that kind since the second part of *Dichterleben*. It is unusual, too, in introducing an environment of poverty and suffering. But unluckily the plot is but an insignificant anecdote, which he has failed to adorn with poetic gloss. It concerns an unhappy woman who, once rich, has fallen into wretched poverty through a chain of inevitable circumstances. But on Christmas Eve she finds her long-lost son who, once cast out of the house by his father, has meanwhile become wealthy in foreign lands. Thus the happy ending, for which Tieck always strove, is achieved. Of greater interest are a lively description of the Berlin Christmas market as he knew it during his childhood and an objective depiction of his own father, whom Tieck resembled more and more as he grew older.

Eigensinn und Laune (1835) took up again the logomachy against the Young Germans, aiming its barbs above all at their proposed emancipation of women and at free love. To demonstrate what these objectives would lead to, Tieck has concocted a plot with a sort of female Lovell as its central figure. She is beautiful, charming and wealthy, but in her youth falls in love with a coachman. He goes through a course of training to prepare for his marriage with her. But in Paris she chances upon a swindler, with whom she has a son. Then she marries a sedate banker, who has saved her father's fortune. Bored by this marriage, she elopes with a French officer, who turns out to be the transformed coachman. At the end of her life she is discovered in her native town, under an assumed name as the manager of a brothel, with a daughter whom she has had by the coachman. Her lovely daughter is wooed by a gardener and an alleged foster son of the chief of police, but both lovers desert the girl when they learn of her mother's profession. After a radical uprising of the populace, in which all the characters are involved, the heroine learns that the chief of police is her former lover and his "foster son" (a secret radical leader) her child. The latter and she commit suicide, while the gardener has a change of heart and marries the heroine's daughter.

The work suffers from lifelessness, deficient motivation, obtrusiveness of purpose, and superabundance of repulsive coarseness. Numerous reviewers of 1835 recognized these weaknesses, though others praised Tieck, who was usually averse to so salacious a plot, for his brave exposé of evils which were admittedly crying for mitigation.[10] In the consideration of the author's development, the work is important as a preliminary study for *Vittoria Accorombona*, where he gives a more sympathetic portrayal of an independent modern woman and depicts her in all her greatness and nobility. As in *Peter Lebrecht, Der blonde Eckbert* and other early works, unwitting incest lurks in the background as the terrible wages of sin.

Not much need be said about *Übereilung* (1835), which from the alleged papers of a professor recounts examples of extreme absentmindedness or ignorance. Anecdotes from the lives of Fichte, Madame de Staël, A. W. Schlegel, Steffens and Oehlenschläger are used to illustrate.[11] More serious interest attaches to Tieck's remarks on German influence in recent Danish literature.

Though not his most important, *Der junge Tischlermeister* (1836), in two parts and seven sections, is the longest finished "novelle." We have seen how it was planned, probably in 1796, as a pendant to *Sternbald*, begun in 1811 and almost printed in 1819. But whereas it would originally have become a sort of Romantic "Wanderroman" in the style of *Wilhelm Meister*, a glorification of the German artisan, it turned out quite differently two generations later. For its author was a changed man. It does not give "clear and definite cross-sections of German life," as Tieck promised. Instead it is a curiously uneventful, loquacious "Reisenovelle." The hero, Leonhard, is a bourgeois, who as a cabinetmaker proves a good Greek scholar, an estimable expert in dramatic literature and dramaturgy and a happy-go-lucky wayfarer and philanderer. He leaves his good wife for a while to hobnob with a group of aristocratic ladies and gentlemen given to voluble talk on questions of esthetics and to furtive kissing of their companions of the other sex. Before arriving home again, apparently with as clear a conscience as Tieck himself in 1806 and 1810, he renews the acquaintance of an erstwhile flame of his, which leads to more amours.

The most interesting part of the work is the beginning, which presents a fetching account of Tieck's own early experiences. The most valuable feature, however, is a detailed description of performances of Shakespeare's *Twelfth Night* and *As You Like It*, Goethe's *Götz von Berlichin-gen* and Schiller's *Die Räuber*, which the hero helps his noble hosts arrange. It reminds of a similar disquisition on *Hamlet* in *Wilhelm Meister*. Here Tieck's most mature ideas on the subject of stagecraft are exhibited.

Believing, as we have seen, that the modern stage, in aiming at reality instead of art and at deception instead of poetical illusion, is too literal and realistic, Tieck has Leonhard revert to the Elizabethan stage. He does away with the curtain and proposes changes of scene only in fairy plays. No imperfect deception achieved by perspective satisfied him; he desired real architecture on the stage. The plays mentioned are put on in the great hall of an old castle. *Götz von Berlichingen* is produced along the narrower wall on a stage with the customary scenery. *Twelfth Night* is done against the long wall on a stage without decorations. Two pillars ten feet high bear a balcony, to which a pair of stairways lead. At the foot of these pillars are three broad steps leading to a small platform stage. This, sometimes curtained for slight changes, is used for interiors.

But in producing *Die Räuber* on the same stage, Leonhard soon dis-covered that a modern play requires a certain amount of realism. So he drapes the pillars to represent tree trunks and uses the small platform stage as a grotto and the stairways as mountain paths leading to the heights. The performance of *Die Räuber*, as described in *Der junge Tischlermeister*, is a curious mixture of clever ideas and "Romantic Irony." The play is put on in order to give the stupid neighbors a pre-text for arranging a hunt. But what delights them most, the pitched battle between the robbers and the authorities, occurs offstage in Schiller's version. To remedy this "defect," Tieck stages this fight, making it a battle royal with guns, powder and vicious dogs. Perhaps his amusing idea came from Schikaneder (the author of the book for Mozart's *Zauberflöte*), who had actually tried such an experiment in Regensburg. Possibly he also had in mind the performance of a military play in an army camp at Fürth in 1793, mentioned above in chapter 3. Certainly he did not intend his suggestion to be taken as seriously as Immermann did, who carried it out in Düsseldorf.[12]

A number of mad or half-mad characters, Magister Fülltreu, Daniel and Franke, supply an element of humor in the vein of Jean Paul.

A tendency similar to that of *Die Ahnenprobe* is not wanting. Its drift is that differences of caste are not all-important and that culture and breeding seem quite as essential for the aristocracy as for the bourgeoisie. To be sure, Leonhard is matured by his association with his noble friends, but they, too, profit by association with him. The reviewers of the time tended to agree that Tieck's aloofness in real life from the problems which he pretends to discuss in this "novelle" makes him an inferior advocate and judge of that middle class whose rights he seeks to espouse.[18] And, indeed, Leonhard is a poor representative of the productive class; his forte is talk. It was left to a more able novelist, Freytag, to portray the German bourgeoisie at work.

Wunderlichkeiten (1836), like *Der Jahrmarkt*, is a "novelle" of roguery. Priceless jewelry has been stolen from a family of the high aristocracy, and only after much complication does the thief turn out to be a lady's maid whose fiancé is a swindler posing as a count. The latter travels about with Martin, an innocuous, inexperienced student of theology, whom he exploits. Martin's mother is a fanatical collector of old paintings, all of which prove to be counterfeit, quite as in *Die Gemälde*. Other whimsical characters also occur in this "novelle" of eccentricities, but the greatest oddity is the fact that they are all embroiled in the theft. This is cleared up by the imprudence of the thief herself, who on quitting the service demands a certification of her innocence, thus arousing suspicion and hastening the dénouement. The moral of the tale appears to be that we are all victims of physical deception or mental delusion.

Die Klausenburg (1836) is an eerie "novelle" of somnambulism, animal magnetism, a family curse and a stalking specter, which seems to rival the ghost stories of much despised E. T. A. Hoffmann. Unlike *Das Zauberschloss*, it is not written in a burlesque vein. A gipsy curse pronounced upon an ancestor is being horribly fulfilled with the aid of a terrifying ghost. But, wonder of wonders, the last descendant of the family learns to his joy that this is a benevolent specter, for it transmits valuable papers and information. A Danish translation appeared in 1839, an English rendering in 1844.

In two subsequent stories, *Der Schutzgeist* and *Abendgespräche*, both written in 1839, Tieck introduced supernatural elements in the same palpably realistic manner. The former relates the story of a countess who many years before had seen her guardian spirit in the form of a child in the cathedral of Strassburg, and had met it again at important crises in her life. Now, on the point of death, she yearns to behold this spirit once more. She undertakes the journey at Easter time, rescuing her son from robbers on the way, and actually has a meeting with her "Schutzgeist," who returns to her a prayer-book received from her at their earlier tryst. *Abendgespräche* is just as weird, consisting of several tales of diablerie narrated by various characters. One is fulfilled in the course of the "novelle." Here, too, a happy ending is achieved by means of documents.

Tieck has been severely criticized for writing these three "novellen." Critics have called attention again and again to the inconsistency of attacking Hoffmann's tales and then writing similar ones. They have also criticized his serious artistic blunder of depicting the world of specters in too realistic a fashion. The latter charge is fully justified and can be supported by Tieck's own early essay *Shakespeares Behandlung des Wunderbaren*. By involving a man in a tussle with a ghost and allowing a specter to hand a document to a mortal (*Die Klausenburg*), he oversteps the bounds. Even a psychic ghost (such as that of Hamlet's father, who is seen by more than one person) should never be brought into such close contact with men. If it is to be used at all, it must occur in an exclusively supernatural, or at least unworldly, atmosphere, as in *Der blonde Eckbert*.

The other accusation of inconsistency cannot be maintained. He was not trying to vie with Hoffmann, a fact which no writer seems to have realized. On the contrary, these "novellen" are a link in his chain of anti-Hoffmann propaganda. His chief objection to Hoffmann, as we have seen, was not that he wrote ghost stories, but that he created caricatures, exaggerations of life and its meaning; worse still, that he thereby undermined the comfort and tranquillity which man derives from his best moral and religious instincts. As a counterbalance, Tieck's specter stories are rooted in religious beliefs (*Der Schutzgeist*), or depict benevolent ghosts (*Die Klausenburg* or *Abendgespräche*), or seek to demonstrate by means of hallucinations that genuine faith and superstition are sometimes very closely related (*Abendgespräche*). And yet he is doubtless guilty of other inconsistencies. The most serious is his use of such devices as animal magnetism, which he had spurned only a few years before. His fickleness and lack of stability are sufficient to explain these quirks. With the advancing years he placed ever more credence in the significance of hallucinations and clairvoyance, as his relations to Justinus Kerner and Count Yorck von Wartenburg[14] indicate. Grillparzer's ire was aroused particularly by *Die Klausenburg*. In his diary (X, 175) he called its author "ein innerlich unwahrer Patron."

In August 1837 Tieck finished *Des Lebens Überfluss*. Although not favorably received at the time of its appearance and not as important in design as most of the other "novellen," it has gradually gained recognition as his best tale. Here his peculiar gifts, rare poetic *Eigenart* and Heinesque whimsicality achieve free, unrestrained expression. The result is a work which in ease, joviality and ingenuousness comes closer to the comedies of Shakespeare than any drama he ever wrote.

In illustrating the truism that care-free, heartfelt love can overcome seemingly insurmountable obstacles, the work voices a sort of philosophy of poverty and adversity. Hebbel, who was very fond of the story and praised its freshness and richness, expressed its theme in the following words: "that a pure man can maintain his independence against fate, provided he has enough strength to toy with his burden."[15] This motif, which could readily have been turned into tragic channels, is treated with exquisite irony.

Heinrich Brand, a young bourgeois, has married a girl of noble family. But being somewhat radically inclined and an adherent of St. Simonism, he loses his post at the legation and quarrels with his wife's family. The young couple are thus forced to shift for themselves during the first months of their marriage and to suffer poverty. But they are so happy with each other and so ebullient in spirits that the inclemency of their fate leaves them quite unscathed. Their cheerful philosophizing helps them bear all hardships with equanimity. When the weather turns cold, they begin using the stairway for kindling wood. This leads to amusing incidents and attracts not only wide attention, but also (by the time the stairway is completely gone) the forgiveness and aid of the relenting parents.

The objections that there is a similar situation in Jean Paul's *Blumen-, Frucht- und Dornenstücke*, that the keynote of *Die Ahnenprobe* is again struck, and that the dénouement is brought about arbitrarily do not detract from the charm of the tale nor from the graceful manner in which it is presented. Its technique has since become very popular. The final climactic events are related first, while the narrative which follows serves to explain them. A general similarity to *Die Gemälde* lies in the fact that an exuberance of spirits, which at first threatens to become the undoing of the hero, turns out a blessing in disguise. In other "novellen" similar unexpected favors are showered upon unsuspecting mankind by a kindly Providence. The philosophy upon which Tieck bases these events throws much light upon his mature conception of fatalism and his refined idea of supernaturalism. Ferdinand Kürnberger's charming tale *Heimlicher Reichtum* has much in common with Tieck's plot. An abridged English translation appeared in *Blackwood's* in 1845, the "peak" year of his remarkable popularity in England. In this single year eleven of his works came out in English renderings, one (*Die Elfen*) twice.[16] Recently an Italian text edition by Mondini appeared in Florence.

Liebeswerben (1838), a "novelle" of roguery, is far inferior to *Des Lebens Überfluss*. Two publicists, members of the Young German movement and consequently depraved individuals (according to Tieck's crotchet), deceive wealthy Wallross by telling him of a fair unknown maiden who loves him. As he goes to the rendezvous arranged by them, they administer a beating to him. But in the end they are cheated by a greater swindler than themselves, who indulges in such practices as animal magnetism and clairvoyance. Incidentally the "novelle" voices his strong opposition to the newly developing machine age, in particular to railways and steamships (as a matter of principle he never used the railway in his later years, even on his frequent trips between Berlin and Potsdam). It also argues against ephemeral writing, especially against the newspapers, which were beginning to assert themselves as "bearers of culture."

His letters to Max show that Tieck thought well of the "novelle," despite the bitter attacks to which "the young ignorant Germans" subjected it; he felt that posterity would vindicate the work.

Die Glocke von Arragon (1839), to which he referred in letters to Max as a trifling and luckless work, is scarcely a "novelle" at all, but a conglomeration of prose discussion, a long poem in Spanish romances, and a revised version of Novalis' lovely tale *Hyacinth und Rosenblütchen*. One of the characters of *Der Wassermensch* reappears as the narrator, and there is reference to *Der Tod des Dichters*, where the bell of Vilella, which brings misfortune when it tolls, is mentioned. Tieck relates the story of the bell in verse, according to Lope's *Campana de Aragón*. It involves Ramiro, who leaves the cloister to become king and encounters difficulties with his vassals when he bids them found the bell. At the end of this curiously disjointed "novelle" the radical Florheim of *Der Wassermensch*, now living in Paris as a disillusioned conservative, tells the Novalis tale, which is here entitled *Die Rückkehr*. The theme of the bell of Vilella was not new to Germany. Weisflog had used it for one of his stories, and in 1829 an unknown young author had submitted to Tieck a drama on the subject.[17]

The last tale which Tieck was to finish, *Waldeinsamkeit* (1840), brings the long series of "novellen" to a fitting close, for it is in many respects characteristic of the genre and of the aged author's mature outlook upon the world. The introduction, autobiographic in character, relates the origin of the now famous word "Waldeinsamkeit," which he had introduced in *Der blonde Eckbert* over the protests of his friends. To this preface he has joined, not without sly irony, a plot which tells the following story.

LUDWIG TIECK, THE GERMAN ROMANTICIST

A young man troubled by *Weltschmerz* and constantly dreaming of the bliss of sylvan solitude is given a sleeping potion at a drinking bout and taken to a lonely hut in the woods, to remain there under lock and key until his rival has married his sweetheart. In this environment, with only two "thrillers" for his diversion, he is soon cured of his Romantic enthusiasms. Of course he finds it possible to flee from his involuntary "Waldeinsamkeit" in time to defeat the plot against him and to marry the girl himself.

Tieck's critics, again misunderstanding, have claimed that it was his purpose to indicate that he had turned his back completely upon his own youth. This is hardly the case; he was merely indulging in an ironic smile over certain extravagances to which early Romanticism had led. It was not his intention to ridicule the happiest years of his own development, but to censure the misinterpretation of those years, to reprove the confusion of the poetic and the commonplace, and to check the misapplication of the expression "Waldeinsamkeit" as a platitudinous slogan. The concept was no longer his own private property, but one of those elements assimilated into the very lifeblood of German literature.

Another fairy-tale "novelle," like *Die Vogelscheuche* and *Das alte Buch*, bearing the title *Der Hüttenmeister*, was begun about 1840 but left unfinished.[18] In technique the work resembles *Das alte Buch*. It purports to present a rambling, uneven manuscript from the hand of an odd individual about whom little is known. Between the leaves are remarks and manuscripts of others. In this way biography, fairy tale and "novelle" are hopelessly jumbled. Some parts pretend to be faithful reports of true happenings, others are admittedly invented, others again are the work of a lunatic. "Romantic Irony" of the *Zerbino* type figures prominently. In effect the fragment is a parody of the methods of modern editors as Tieck saw them, particularly those who devoted their attention to Middle High German manuscripts.

Externally his last years in Dresden had not been eventful. His routine was interrupted only by occasional illness and by the summer trips to Teplitz or Baden-Baden. One of the journeys to the latter resort in 1836 almost ended in sudden death as the result of a serious accident to his carriage. But his happiness was more disturbed by the fate which falls to the lot of every aging man, the gradual dying away of those he loves best. To be sure, the death of Friedrich Schlegel in Dresden on January 12, 1829, was not a severe blow, for they had long become estranged. The passing of Goethe, who four years before had received him and his family for the last time, made a deeper impression upon him, according to Dorothea,[19] although his Goethe, the Goethe of 1770-1775, had died long since. And when word reached him in 1833 that his eccentric sister Sophie was no longer among the living, he regarded her passing almost as a deliverance from an unpleasant burden.

We have seen how Sophie had early acquired pernicious influence over her two brothers, which can perhaps be best explained by psychoanalysis. She idolized Ludwig and felt jealous of all who won his attention. He in turn made many sacrifices for her sake, even leaving his family in 1804 to come to her aid in an hour of need. During this period his pretty sonnet to her was written.[20] But when he tried to appeal to her reason at the time of her difficulties with Bernhardi between 1806 and 1809, and to persuade her to effect a compromise in order to save her own face, she used all her tremendous influence upon him, so that he humiliated himself by shamefully turning against Bernhardi at the trial. Then, when he continued preaching reason to her, she turned upon him savagely, just as she had on Bernhardi, and severed their relations completely, spreading the rumor in Germany and abroad that he was a brutal, loveless egoist.

After 1810, it seems, she wrote but a single letter to him (in 1828), not even informing him of her marriage with Knorring or of her departure to Erwita in Esthonia, and saw him casually only once, when she accompanied her husband and son Felix Theodor to Heidelberg in 1820. She became ever more domineering and squandered the estimable fortune of her henpecked second husband. On the journey to Heidelberg she insisted upon travelling in a coach drawn by nine horses and accompanied by a pretentious retinue, being forced, however, by ebbing funds to dispose of most of the equipage before the trip was ended. Her later life was not happy. In a letter to her brother Friedrich of April 23, 1826, preserved among the Varnhagen von Ense papers in Berlin, she wrote from Erwita that she was quite homesick, adding "ich glaube, wenn ich sie [sc. die Sehnsucht] nicht bald befriedige, so werde ich nicht lange mehr leben."[21]

Her younger brother Friedrich never succeeded in ridding himself of her dominance, lived in poverty to help her financially and sacrificed time and energy to pander to her whims. The letters from her to him which have been preserved, full of complaint about her unhappiness, show how insistent she was in conciliating him and binding him closer to herself. Ludwig turned a deaf ear to his attempts at a reconciliation from 1818 on and warned him frequently against her, but in vain.

LUDWIG TIECK, THE GERMAN ROMANTICIST

It is not too much to say that Ludwig's relations to his sister from about 1806 on form one of the saddest chapters in his life. Yet he mentioned her baseness and weaknesses of character only on rare occasions, and even then in a sparing manner. Thus he once poured out his heart to Friedrich Schlegel in a confidential letter of 1813,[22] to his own brother in letters between 1818 and 1823, and, at the very end of his life, in a letter to Count Yorck von Wartenburg.[23] He loathed Sophie's sons, writing to his brother Friedrich that Wilhelm was dissolute and should be a mechanic, not an author, and that Felix Theodor was a superficial fop, braggart and spendthrift. For years the latter used the name of von Knorring, until forbidden by the family to do so. Later he was ennobled by the king of Prussia. To Varnhagen von Ense Tieck confessed in a letter of May 11, 1852, that he supported Wilhelm's wife after Wilhelm had squandered her fortune and deserted her.[24] Four letters of Tieck to Felix Theodor of 1851-1852 reveal a changing and more friendly attitude.

Descendants of the Bernhardi family are still living. Anna Bernhardi of Berlin is a grandchild of Wilhelm. The late General Friedrich von Bernhardi, the author of *Germany and the Next War*, was a son of Felix Theodor.

With the passing of his wife on February 11, 1837 after a long illness—she was afflicted with dropsy—, Tieck suffered the first irremediable blow. A splendid letter to Raumer, written under the impression which her death made upon him, shows how disconsolate he was, despite their utter incompatibility.[25] The sudden death of Adelheid Reinbold in 1839 was also a severe shock.

It is no accident that one of the best works of his declining years, the novel *Vittoria Accorombona* (1840), was written during this unhappy time. None of his writings incubated so long. In a letter to Max of 1840 he confessed that he had borne the subject in mind since 1792 and had it worked out in his imagination as early as 1825.[26] He became acquainted with his principal source, John Webster's play *The White Devil* (1612), at Göttingen in 1792. Some time later he read Nahun Tate's *Injured Love or the Cruel Husband* (1707).

Vittoria Accorombona is not an improvisation. Its composition took most of his time between 1836 and 1840. He told Max that he composed it "with great love and unceasing enthusiasm." To distinguish it from his other writings of the past generation, he called it a novel ("Roman"), though planning to have it appear among the "novellen." The fact that Max got it out as a separate work was a complete surprise to him.

THE LATER "NOVELLEN"

The scene is laid in Italy during the second third of the sixteenth century and presents a gloomy but colorful picture of a degenerate age. This age is characterized by a high but frivolous culture and reveals many relics of medieval barbarism, especially in its desecration of women, who are looked upon as mere chattel. Vittoria, the heroine, is a truly noble, highly cultured girl, far ahead of her times, whose mother conducts a sort of Tieckean salon. Vittoria shudders at the thought of marriage, knowing that it is almost as bad as being sold at the slave mart. But she is swept away in the maelstrom of her age. To save herself from suitors like dissolute Orsini and lustful Cardinal Fernese, and to win for her brother the support of the honorable old Cardinal Montalto (whose model Tieck found in Leti's late seventeenth century *Vita di Sisto V*), she consents to wed his immature, weak and dissolute nephew Peretti. Though she despises him, she cares for him as a dutiful wife. While his recklessness and licentiousness know no bounds, she opens a salon in his home and cultivates good breeding.

Then she meets Duke Bracciano, a man in his forties, who though not unsullied, is a powerful and commanding figure. He conceives a wild passion for her, strangles his wife Isabella, whom he deems guilty of infidelity, and has Vittoria's husband killed. Vittoria, suspected of the latter crime, is imprisoned, but by virtue of her dignified manner and Bracciano's good reputation allays all suspicion. While she is being detained, however, the weak, aged pope dies. Bracciano avails himself of the anarchy which rules supreme during the ensuing conclave to free Vittoria and make her his wife.

The new head of the Church, Sixtus V, who had been none other than the unenergetic scholarly old Cardinal Montalto, proves to be a mighty pope, and sets out to uproot sin and licentiousness with an iron hand. Bracciano and Vittoria flee from his wrath and spend a brief period of idyllic bliss on the shores of Lake Garda. Then Bracciano is imprisoned and Vittoria falls victim to assassins sent by Orsini, her lover whom she had once spurned.

All the characters, high and low, are suffused with the spirit of the degenerate times, not least the heroine, despite her advanced interests and views. This gives the work its tragic note. The only hope which Tieck seems to express lies in the fact that even in times like those such near-greatness can arise as Vittoria embodies. Of all his works this is the most "modern." It is comparatively free of his customary interminable colloquies. It brings into play not only the masses and the leaders as part and parcel of the historical background of their age, which is at the same time their fate, but also noble representatives of the middle classes. His treatment of an historical subject—his psychic relation to history—here attains its highest achievement. Here at last he is plastic and picturesque, letting the characters portray themselves in action.

We have noted that Webster was his chief source, Tate and the Italian Leti having been used secondarily. But he criticized Webster's treatment sharply, which doubtless explains his deviations from the English dramatist. Where Webster seemed to him to have debased the heroine, he, without historical justification, has elevated and almost apotheosized her. He has also idealized Bracciano. He has given the heroine and her environment decided traits of Romantic culture and sociability.[27]

In numerous points he has deviated from the facts of history. Thus the heroine's family name was Accoramboni; it was her father who betrothed her to Peretti as a favor to the latter's powerful uncle Montalto; both Vittoria and Peretti seem to have been spendthrifts; after the death of Peretti Vittoria was in reality freed from prison through the influence of a cardinal; the action against her and Bracciano undertaken by Montalto after ascending the papal throne was prompted by revenge; finally the historical Bracciano died a natural death.

Recently the astonishing charge has been made[28] that the work is a plagiarization of an unpublished novel of Kleist. But no serious Kleist scholar or critic of Romanticism has been convinced by this assertion, which seems all the more preposterous since Tieck's work reveals hardly a trace of Kleistean spirit.

If Tieck had written the work in 1792, when and as originally conceived, it would probably have become a Romantic fairy play. But as we know it, it is unthinkable without the influence of the Young Germans, of Manzoni, the French Romanticists and Scott. In a sense it is a mature reflection of Friedrich Schlegel's ideas, as expressed in *Lucinde*, and a rejoinder to "das junge Deutschland," with their St. Simonistic ideas. "Emancipation" in the sense of freedom of action, Tieck would say, is undesirable and dangerous for a weak woman, such as the heroine of *Eigensinn und Laune* or Gutzkow's Wally, but is justifiable and indeed imperative for a strong, noble character—an exceptional woman—like Vittoria.

As a social novel, with sharp delineation of characters and events, emphasis upon individualism, richness of language, iconoclastic views, use of *mots propres*, it bears the impress of de Vigny, Balzac, Hugo and Merimée. But this is an influence of spirit more than of matter and would scarcely repay mathematical scrutiny. More marked is the impress of Manzoni's *I promessi sposi*, which Tieck rated even higher than he did any of Scott's writings, and of the Waverley novels of Scott himself.[29] His realistic method of treatment, suppression of excessive conversation, his plasticity, vastly improved characterization and regard for historical background are elements which he had learned from these two writers.

His lifelong love of the Middle Ages, manifested under various aspects in *Sternbald*, *Genoveva*, *Octavian*, *Pietro von Abano* and *Der Hexensabbath*, is here revealed, as it was in the two last-mentioned works, by an interest in the psychosis ascribed to medieval man. It is characterized by a tension between body and soul, a reflection of broken colors and tones, a depiction of a realm between the Here and the Hereafter, between day and night, between body and spirit. The society which he pictures is confused by ecclesiastical laws, mystic and social customs, unbridled passions. He has not stripped his characters of that demonism which he sensed as his own birthright.

Vittoria Accorombona is not without flaws. Several of the characters have no *raison d'être*, and the insanity of Vittoria's mother is poorly motivated. Tieck becomes guilty of anachronisms in his description of the salons, with their one-sided interest in literature, and of Vittoria's craving for rights which smack of the nineteenth century. Hebbel, although he deemed Tieck a better poet than himself, found that the work reveals his worst fault, lack of character.[30] Moreover, in the words of Carlyle, the novel is a bit "too showy in diamonds—Bristol diamonds —, tinsel and the precious metals . . . almost an opera. . . . Vittoria herself is . . . a right divine stage goddess."[31] This criticism is in striking agreement with the charge which a recent critic, Gundolf, raises against most of Tieck's works.

But, as Carlyle rightly added, *Vittoria Accorombona* contains much that is "true, genial, warm and very grand." For this reason it enjoyed considerable success and within a year went into a second edition, which came out with an enthusiastic epilog by Professor Braniss of Breslau. An Italian translation appeared in 1843, an English version in 1845. Many critics, among them Treitschke, Witkowski, Bartels, Berend and Gundolf, have agreed since Carlyle's time that it is the best work which Tieck had written for a generation.[32] Frances, the wife of Karl von Bunsen, wrote to Abeken that it contains the finest portrait of a woman, under infinitely complicated circumstances, that has ever come to her notice. She would never have thought Tieck capable of it.[33] Particular attention has been called by recent judges to the fact that the picture of the Renaissance world presented by him was clearly a model for the greatest German-speaking author of Renaissance novels, Conrad Ferdinand Meyer.[34] No one before the historian Burckhardt and the poet Meyer has recreated sixteenth century Italy as vividly as Tieck. Certainly the oblivion into which his novel has fallen is not altogether deserved.

For the student of Tieck this work is of monumental importance in offering a sort of reflex of the main problems which agitated him throughout his life: the problems of love and of faith, the conquest of the ego, and the place of evil in the scheme of things. All the steps of his development are here recapitulated, all his pitfalls, blind alleys and abysses. Love is seen as a demonic force. Bracciano's affection for Vittoria is defiled at the very start by the murder of his wife. She, in turn, has not shown enough humility in her relation to her first husband. Thus love leads to the vexing question: To what extent should man submit to fate?, and: Where is faith to begin, where to end? But Vittoria, far from committing Bracciano's sin, remains true to herself and refuses to stoop to divorce. In thus overcoming her ego, she achieves its noblest assertion.

Unhappily, however, Evil is often victorious over Good. This visible rent in the moral texture of the world, which Böhme had shown him over forty years before, is to Tieck as palpable as it is inscrutable. Should man bow before it in silence, he asks, and thus acknowledge the meaninglessness and vacuity of life? In bidding us ponder this question, he reverts to the basic problem of one of his earliest works, *Abdallah*. But he has risen in fifty years to a loftier point of vantage, from which, like Goethe, he can regard life more maturely, more tolerantly, more symbolically. In the very realization of the imperfections of this world, he has at length found his God. And so he could well afford to spend his last thirteen years in silence.[35]

Another blow, which made this silence all the deeper because it destroyed his creative power and killed the poet within him, was the death of Dorothea. She succumbed to a vicious attack of the measles on February 21, 1841. The report in Hebbel's diary (IV, 13), that she died of typhoid fever and that Tieck, fearing contagion, left his home before her death and did not return until after the funeral, is not trustworthy.

With the loss of this intelligent but reticent soul, who was patient and self-effacing and passionately religious, and who had been his ever ready helper since 1820, he felt that half of his own being had been torn from him. The shattering effect of her death is described by Köpke in the following words: "As never before he was shocked to the very core. A convulsive, compressing sensation of pain seized him, which vainly sought expression. Cold, rigid, tearless, unable to utter a word or a sound, he concealed himself in the most remote room. He refused to see anyone or to hear of any comfort. The hours, day and night, passed by indifferently and unnoticed, so far as he was concerned."[36] Tieck, writing to Count Yorck von Wartenburg in 1848, after the passing of the latter's two children, was undoubtedly thinking of his own experience: "There are in our mortal lives such sorrows as no man can comprehend or imagine, if he has not experienced them. At first dull, almost painless stupefaction takes hold of us, when all life, all brighter consciousness become torpid and vanish. Then an abyss of our sorrow opens at the terrible blow, an inmost trembling, so that we shudder before our very selves. These raging pains of our soul and existence yield finally, when the battle is waged, to true heavenly love, which purifies and transfigures us in sorrow. Then in our grief we experience divine love."[37]

To his sorrow Dorothea had with her mother embraced the Catholic faith early in life (1805) and, if we may judge by her splendid letters to Friedrich von Üchtritz,[38] lived almost the life of a saint. It was one of the saddest shocks of his career when Üchtritz, shortly after her death, foolishly permitted him to peruse these letters. They brought him the terrible disillusionment that despite her reverence and admiration for him, her attachment to Catholicism had surpassed this affection, that he never commanded her heart as did her mother, and that without his realizing it, she had fathomed his soul more thoroughly than perhaps he himself.[39]

His other daughter, Agnes, married her cousin Gustav Alberti, a son of an older brother of her mother, in 1842. She settled in Waldenburg in Silesia, where he owned a factory. Agnes probably had no children. A Dora von Treutler, née Alberti, who lived in Neu-Weissstein in Silesia, at the end of the nineteenth century, was apparently her stepdaughter.[40]

Of a family of five only two were now left, Tieck himself and the aging Countess Henriette, who was almost blind and whose fortune had dwindled.

CHAPTER EIGHTEEN

LAST YEARS IN BERLIN

ALTHOUGH as a "Dramaturg" Tieck had always worked with one eye on his native Berlin, yet his relations to King Frederick William III of Prussia were never good because of Kotzebue's intrigues, and Iffland's aversion to him. Only once, in 1816, had his help been solicited in Berlin for the presentation of a Shakespearean play. Early in June 1840 the Prussian king died. In July, urged by Alexander von Humboldt and Friedrich von Raumer, Tieck decided to approach the new ruler, Frederick William IV, who as crown prince had expressed great enthusiasm for his *Phantasus* and favored calling him to the University of Berlin after Solger's death. A lively interest in literature and art, which the monarch had developed in his youth, remained with him after his coronation and earned him the nickname of "the Romanticist on the throne." Such interest, centered on the most innocuous manifestations of Romanticism, on the ancient Greeks and Shakespeare, and unmindful of all writings dealing with live problems of the day, was combined in this weak ruler with a bigoted, ruthless ultraconservatism, which threw men like Kinkel into prison and drove thousands of the best citizens into exile or voluntary expatriation.

Upon the advice of his Berlin friends Tieck decided to present the new king with a copy of *Vittoria Accorombona* and to accompany it with a cordial note. Try as he would, however, he who had never turned to royalty before, could not phrase the note quite to his own satisfaction. Finally he appealed to Raumer in Berlin for help. On August 1 the latter sent him a proposed draft for his approval and transcription.[1] He copied Raumer's draft verbatim, adding only a brief introductory paragraph and a single unimportant word.[2] This brought a prompt and very cordial holograph from the king, a gift of one hundred Friedrichd'or and an invitation to Potsdam. And on August 28 the Berlin "Intendant," Count Redern, approached Tieck with the request for a prolog to commemorate the double celebration of the coronation and the king's birthday on October 15. About the same time he learned that he would receive an annual compensation of one thousand talers in addition to travelling expenses if he agreed to spend two months of each year at Sans Souci. He followed up this promising "lead" by composing the prolog. It found the ruler's favor and was spoken by

Auguste Crelinger in the royal Schauspielhaus antecedent to a festival performance of Goethe's *Tasso*.[3]

When Dorothea died a third of a year later, Tieck still had a six months' lease on his apartment at the Altmarkt. But he could not bear to remain in the abode in which he had experienced so much grief. He abandoned it and moved into a new apartment in Amalienstrasse 15.

Dresden had begun to pall upon him. The constantly increasing attacks of his opponents, the realization that his work as dramatic adviser was not appreciated, and the pettiness of his Dresden environment made life in that city odious to him. In this spirit he wrote to a Prussian courtier on December 7, 1841: "Here everything, important and unimportant, moves very slowly and has five rubber tires for every four wheels."[4] And to his friend F. A. Schulze he wrote in December 1843, soon after leaving Dresden: "I have wasted so many years in Dresden and have been able to accomplish but little on account of the wretched conditions here."[5]

A second more definite invitation from the Prussian king, which arrived soon after Dorothea's death and asked him to visit Potsdam in the summer and supervise the performance of an ancient Greek tragedy, must, then, have seemed a godsend. Not only did it offer an opportunity to break away from Dresden at least for a while; it also held forth new hope and the prospect of new activity in a larger field under more auspicious circumstances. In May, even before he was fully settled in his new apartment, he departed from Dresden, leaving explicit written instructions to Frau Solger, Bülow and Baron Wilhelm von Ungern-Sternberg for the arrangement of his huge library in the new quarters.[6] But he did not go to Berlin directly; at first he headed west, stopping at Heidelberg, Baden-Baden and Darmstadt.

In midsummer he finally arrived at Sans Souci, where he was well received by the monarch and often seen in his environment. Soon he was invited to give readings before court. They did not prove a success. The courtiers were bored, the ladies did needlework while he read (which would have been considered the height of impudence in Dresden), and the king himself made pencil sketches or followed the recitation with a copy of the text in his hand.[7] As his readings grew more frequent after his settling in Potsdam in 1842, they became more and more a travesty of the ceremonious occasions in Dresden and a source of silent martyrdom for him.

An incident related by Varnhagen von Ense in his Berlin papers shows how little knowledge and appreciation the king's unintelligent entourage had of Tieck and his poetry. Once at a royal banquet some young officers, nodding kindly, pledged their glasses to him with the toast "Oranien." For a long time he was puzzled, until it was explained to him that they had confused him with the poet Tiedge, whose chief work was *Urania!*

There was uncertainty which ancient Greek tragedy he should stage. At first one of the dramas of Euripides was thought of. But after he had read the *Antigone* of Sophocles at court and shown that this was the easiest ancient work for a modern Christian audience to understand, it was decided to put it on in Donner's translation. The performance took place on the stage of the Neues Palais on October 28, with choruses by Mendelssohn, and was a success, despite Tieck's admission that it was prepared hastily.

A book by A. Böckh, F. Förster and E. H. Tölckens, *Über die Antigone des Sophocles und ihre Darstellung auf dem königlichen Schlosstheater im Neuen Palais bei Sanssouci* (Berlin, 1842), describes the performance.[8] It was done without a curtain or any scenic simulation, and with permanent settings; almost the whole action took place far downstage in profile or bas relief, as it were (a favorite idea of Tieck); the actors entered not from wings but from the orchestra pit, which as a compromise was to suggest the ancient Greek orchestra and Tieck's mistaken notion that in the old Greek theater, as in the Shakespearean, the spectators witnessed the action going on in their midst. We have noted that Tieck believed he had discovered an historical relationship between these two theaters. As a token of his satisfaction with the performance, and to commemorate it, the king had a medallion struck bearing the images of both Tieck and Mendelssohn. There were sixty-two performances.

By the end of November Tieck was back again in Dresden, without having ascertained what his future relation to the Prussian ruler would be, whether he was to settle permanently in Potsdam or divide his time between Dresden and the Prussian residence. It seems that at first he preferred the latter arrangement, so as to be able to continue drawing his annual honorarium of eight hundred talers from the Saxon coffers.

Further correspondence with the Prussian court followed. Finally he was given the title of "Geheimer Hofrat," offered in addition to his pension of a thousand talers an annual emolument of 2200 talers for services to the royal Prussian theaters, with the understanding that he could spend a part of each year in Dresden and thus retain his income there. But the Dresden authorities were apparently not favorable to this arrangement, so that he had to break tent entirely in Dresden.

LAST YEARS IN BERLIN

In the spring of 1842 he returned to Sans Souci. Here the Romanticist among the princes (der Fürsten Romantiker) definitely allied himself with the prince of Romanticism, as Herwegh jokingly remarked. On his birthday he was decorated with the new order Pour le Mérite. According to a cabinet decree of June 22, he was assigned the duty of staging and artistically presenting ancient Greek and Shakespearean dramas, also other plays of his own selection. At the same time a new "Intendant," Karl Theodor von Küstner, assumed control of the royal Prussian theaters. Tieck was expected to work in harmony with him. While their relations were at first amicable, friction developed. Officially the "Intendant" informed the actors that they were to submit unconditionally to Tieck's orders, but in confidence he stressed the fact that Tieck's performances were of a private nature, to be presented on a private stage in the castle before the king and a personally invited audience, and to be given a public showing only in case of marked success. Küstner's hostile attitude, growing out of his conviction that Tieck's efforts would constitute only a waste of time, money and energy, was countered by Tieck with testiness and stubbornness. Cooperation proved out of the question, especially since the "Intendant" often deliberately granted leaves of absence to the actors whom Tieck needed. Had not the king, fairly "bewitched by Tieck," as the poet Rückert, another favorite, put it, done all in his power to coddle him, his position in Potsdam would have been unbearable.

In September 1842 Tieck made a final journey to Dresden to call for Henriette and arrange for the shipment of his effects by barge in spring. On his return to Potsdam late in the autumn he suffered a stroke and was on the point of death. Not until the end of the year could he, completely broken in health, move into his winter apartment in Friedrichstrasse No. 208, near Kochstrasse in the heart of Berlin.

Preparations for Tieck's next official task, the staging of Euripides' *Medea*, were begun in October during his absence, not requiring his immediate supervision because it was produced on the same stage and with the same architecture as had been used for *Antigone*. Since neither Mendelssohn nor Meyerbeer was willing to compose the music, the task was assigned to W. G. K. Taubert. Tieck supervised the later rehearsals; the first performance (there were seven in all) took place on August 7, 1843.[9]

But his most important achievement during his last thirteen years, and, from the point of view of the theater, the greatest accomplishment of his career, was the staging of *A Midsummer Night's Dream*, which went on at the Neues Palais on October 14. It represents the consummation of over fifty years of thought and planning about the Elizabethan theater and the best way of presenting Shakespeare.

The performance was not hastily arranged. At least a year before the king gave Tieck *carte blanche* for the necessary preparations. About 1828 Tieck had planned to stage this play in Dresden. Certain sketches which he showed or sent Goethe, subsequently found among the latter's papers, were obviously made under Tieck's supervision for this purpose. They agree in details with sketches he prepared for the Potsdam presentation in 1843.

The stage of the Neues Palais required alterations for the performance, which Tieck would have preferred to put on in a simple circular wooden structure of his own in the Tiergarten, with natural light from above. The plans for the settings were sketched under his instructions by Gerst, the scene painter of the royal theaters, and then adapted to the needs of the Neues Palais. The music, by Mendelssohn, was probably finished by 1841, the overture in 1827, the other passages in 1834. It was composed for a play of five acts; Tieck's method of division provided for only three. This made it necessary to insert some protracted and awkward pantomimes, so as to do justice to the surplus music. Otherwise, too, the music, as lovely and masterly as it is, hampered Tieck and forced him to make compromises.

Stage and auditorium, not separated by a curtain, were assimilated, the stage being arranged in two tiers or stories and a gallery on top. Each tier consisted of three square sections, in which different scenes were played. The two side sections of the lower tier consisted simply of stairways. No movable scenery was used; the single interior was indicated by a drop. One hundred persons took part and over thirty rehearsals were required.

The performance proved a success and was soon taken to Berlin, where it was given considerably more than one hundred fifty times during the next forty years. It furnished the model for other presentations in various German cities.[10]

Of course, Tieck's general solution of the problems of *A Midsummer Night's Dream* did not lead to anything approaching a scientific reconstruction of the Elizabethan stage. It was a compromise which combined Elizabethan and modern ideas, but it proved poetical and artistic. His ideas of fixed scenery, suggesting different elevations, his various small "cells" and his free open spaces eliminated scene shifting and made it possible conveniently to put on even long and complicated plays. Before the era of modern stage inventions, such as Reinhardt's

[328]

revolving stage, Tieck's method was the most logical and best. On small but progressive stages without modern devices its influence is felt to this day in numerous points, such as stairways, draperies, pillars and balconies. The wonder of it is, however, that even present-day stage managers are often unaware that Tieck is responsible for these features.

A Midsummer Night's Dream was the last play to enjoy the full benefit of his knowledge and experience as a production manager. His constantly failing health made it impossible thereafter to devote much time to the performance of plays. *The Frogs* of Aristophanes went on late in 1843. Tieck's own comedy, *Der gestiefelte Kater*, produced on April 20, 1844, but not at his suggestion, was only a moderate success, as he himself, prevented by illness from attending, admitted.[11] Varnhagen von Ense recorded that the audience, including the king and his entourage, were bored.[12] *Blaubart*, played on February 1, 1845, also without Tieck's sanction, proved a failure.[13] *Oedipus in Colonos* was staged on November 1, 1845, with music by Mendelssohn, but did not enjoy as much success as *Antigone*.[13] Racine's *Athalie* was produced on December 1 of the same year, and the *Hippolytus* of Euripides on April 26, 1851.[14] Tieck felt that the lack of competent actors made it difficult to stage such works. To Gustav Freytag he wrote on January 14, 1848, that the art of acting had sunk so low that Shakespeare was intolerable on the stage. And if Goethe and Schiller were not fixtures in the repertory, he thought, they too would disappear from the stage, where they are now "torn to pieces and bungled" (zerrissen und verhunzt).[15]

His health necessitated revivals of *Julius Caesar*, *Coriolanus*, *Much Ado about Nothing*, *A Comedy of Errors*, *Macbeth* (music by Spohr) and *Twelfth Night* without his assistance. Performances of the *Eumenides*, *Agamemnon* and the *Choephori* were planned but not carried out. According to Tieck's letter of January 16, 1844, to the king, he was preparing to do the *Eumenides* and studying the translations of Johannes Minckwitz and Karl Otfried Müller.

The reason why many of these performances failed to materialize lies in the unfavorable political conditions and in the strenuous objections to "learned but lifeless" dramatic experiments, which glorified the literatures of ancient Greece and Elizabethan England but offered no encouragement to the new generation of German authors. Tieck's correspondence with Heinrich Theodor Rötscher, from 1845 dramatic critic of the *Haude-Spenersche Zeitung* and proponent of a school for acting in Berlin, shows that he attached little hope to this new generation. In his letter of May 2, 1847, he condemned Gutzkow's *Zopf und Schwert*, *Richard Savage* and *Das Urbild des Tartuffe* and Laube's *Die Karlsschüler* as reversions to the "sorcery, unpoetic stuff and most insipid triviality of Iffland and Kotzebue," and included the plays of Mosen and Birch-Pfeiffer in this denunciation. He added: "Iffland, Kotzebue passed by, then Müllner, who deemed himself a dictator; and let us hope that Gutzkow, Laube, Birch-Pfeiffer, Töpfer and so forth will soon be passé. Lessing, Schröder, even Brandes will reappear, and Shakespeare, Goethe and Schiller will remain. Many English and even French writers who are now neglected will receive new coats."[16]

Only few of the young contemporary dramatists found Tieck's approval. He had a poor opinion of Hebbel's early dramas and doubted whether the author would ever win a hearing.[17] But to Freytag he wrote two warm, friendly letters in 1847 and 1848, respectively, praising his plays *Die Valentine* and *Graf Waldemar*. The former seemed to him "interesting, poetic and original," while the latter was "a wonderful phenomenon" in an age of "aridity and almost inexplicable lack of talent." He found in it a "truly deep ethical core, without flourishes, hypocrisy and conventional phrases."[17] But he was dead when *Die Journalisten* appeared. For the Viennese dramatist Eduard von Bauernfeld he also had words of praise.[18] But Grillparzer and Tieck always remained bitter enemies. Tieck, in his unpublished review of Schenk's *Belisar*, judged that Grillparzer's plays were weak and untrue to life. Grillparzer expressed his opinion of his adversary unequivocally. According to him Tieck was devoid of creative talent and of a sense for form—a clever mixer of paints (Farbenreiber), but no painter; he tried, in Grillparzer's opinion, to make good his deficiencies by using various props, now Shakespeare, now Calderon, now the minnesingers; he seemed deficient also in feeling but possessed a surplus of esprit; only in the comic-parodistic vein, which ridicules triteness and insipidness, did he reveal to Grillparzer special gifts; on the whole his influence upon German literature, like Jean Paul's, seemed bad.[19]

Tieck's work as a publicist during his last Berlin years was negligible, although Hebbel's remark that in his declining years he tolerated only mediocrity,[20] is not fair. Of the fifteen hundred pages of his *Kritische Schriften*, volumes 1 and 2 of which came out in 1848, and volumes 3 and 4 in 1852, only twenty-nine date from this period, namely twelve pages of *Bemerkungen über einige Schauspiele und deren Darstellung auf der Berliner Hofbühne* (1851)[21] and three prefaces. They introduced a German translation of Swedish sagas and folk songs (Leipzig, 1842); the *Gesammelte Schriften* of Friedrich Laun (the pseudonym of

Tieck's friend Friedrich August Schulze), which came out in Stuttgart in 1843; and Franz Fritze's translation of Sophocles (Berlin, 1845).[22]

Of these only the foreword to Schulze's works, which Tieck seems to have written before he left Dresden, has significance. It recalls the beginning of his friendship for that author in Dresden in 1801; breaks a lance for Goethe, whom he remembers he was one of the earliest to style the "greatest and most national" German poet; and ridicules the folly of those who, particularly in France, used Romanticism as a literary slogan after 1820, "as though we could have, since the Middle Ages, any other but Romantic poetry, in contrast to the Greeks!" As frequently, he seems tacitly to ignore his own share in this "folly."

Other brief prefaces and critical undertakings of his later years found no place in his *Kritische Schriften*. In 1843 he edited the poems of his friend Karl Förster, in 1844 *Goethes ältestes Liederbuch*.[23] In 1847 he wrote a foreword for a German translation of a collection of Norwegian folk tales. The next year witnessed the appearance of two prefaces, one for the *Lieder* of Dilia Helena (that is, Branco), the other for M. Wiener's translation of the dramatic works of John Ford. Finally he wrote a preface for the poems of Ferdinand Lehmann (Berlin, 1851) and one for the fairy tales of Ludwig Wahl (Berlin, 1852). They were all done perfunctorily and are the work of a famous man who, besieged by young authors and publishers, occasionally succumbs to their pleadings. Tieck succumbed frequently because he deemed it a moral duty to encourage that scant literary talent which he thought was left. His epilog for the celebration of the one hundredth anniversary of Goethe's birth in 1849 was not published.

One finished but unpublished literary undertaking of Tieck remains to be discussed. It is a translation of R. B. Sheridan's *The Rivals*, which he dictated to his secretary K. H. Dammas in 1850, probably for purposes of presentation in Berlin.[24] The rendering is done with care, and the manuscript contains corrections in Tieck's hand, probably for the printer. According to the original table of contents of the *Nachgelassene Schriften*, preserved in Köpke's hand, it was planned to publish the play in the second volume.

Generally Tieck follows Sheridan's text carefully. His translation is superior to the earlier one of W. Hoffmann[25] and not as free as that of Ernst von Wolzogen.[26] The British locale, Bath, becomes Pyrmont, and the characters are given German names. Thus Acres is Herr von Ackerland and Mrs. Malaprop Frau von Storrwald. Even English book titles are replaced by German works, which, however, are less apt. He makes a valiant but not always successful effort to imitate Mrs. Malaprop's

perversions of English: "inflammatory branches of learning"—
entzündlich; "supercilious knowledge in accounts"—artificiell; "the
contagious countries"—tropisch; "reprehend the true meaning"—
captierte; "superstitious article"—superficiell. Occasionally he omits a
passage or adds a clause. More frequently he conventionalizes Sheridan's racy language or misses part of his humor. Downright errors are
infrequent. Perhaps the worst occurs at the beginning of Act 3, where
Sir Anthony says of his son: "Who can he take after?" Tieck translates:
"Wem mag er wohl nachlaufen?"

On the whole this rendering, which concludes fifty-nine years of
desultory activity as a translator, is fluent, able and skilful, but shows
clearly that he never became a master of the English language. In
routine he has improved since 1791, when he did the latter part of
Middleton's *Life of Cicero*, but some earmarks of amateurishness
remain.

All his life Tieck was prolific in literary projects which never got
on paper. As early as 1800 he broached a host of plans to Cotta, among
them a list of dramas on German history and another on classical
themes. To the Schlegels he mentioned many other plans, among them
works on the Holy Grail and on Moses, as well as a marionette theater.
At the end of his career he was just as busy making plans, as his letter
of February 3, 1852, to Brockhaus shows.[27] His principal project at the
time was a volume of his own memoirs, a work which would have
served as an important source for the literary historian. A letter to
A. W. Schlegel of March 27, 1837, contains an early reference to this
plan. After he had settled in Berlin, the king instructed him to carry
it out, assigning Dammas as secretary for the purpose.

In 1847 Tieck's beloved Countess, the last member of his inner circle,
died. Thereafter he was quite alone. His closest friends and confidants,
besides Raumer, were now his biographer and literary testator-to-be,
Köpke, and Count Yorck von Wartenburg, the son of the field marshal
by the same name, whom he had met in Dresden as early as 1823.
Köpke made his acquaintance in 1849 and in long conversations was
initiated into so much of the poet's private life as the latter wished
posterity to know. These colloquies, supported by all the documents
and manuscripts still in Tieck's possession, formed the basis of his
biography.

Beginning in 1848, Count Yorck and Tieck wrote one another confidential and interesting letters, Tieck entrusting to him some of his
more intimate secrets, particularly concerning his relations to Sophie
and her sons, and to his brother Friedrich. Questions of spiritualism

were also touched. Occasionally Yorck helped him discreetly with money. After Tieck's famous library had been auctioned by Asher late in 1849, despite the mortgage held on it by Brockhaus, and the king had caused as much of it as possible (over eleven thousand volumes) to be repurchased and restored to Tieck, Yorck secretly paid six thousand talers to Tieck on condition that after their owner's death the books would pass into his possession.[28]

In Berlin Tieck no longer received as many visits from celebrities as in Dresden. But in 1852 Carlyle, who rated him far below Goethe yet revered him as one of the last surviving representatives of a great age, called upon him. The call was disturbed by strong disagreement concerning the merits of Coleridge, whom Carlyle detested.[29]

During the Berlin years Tieck came into closer contact with his own brother than ever before. As a young student Friedrich was referred to by Ludwig as "der Künstler" or "der Esel." They had met again at Munich in 1804, when Friedrich helped nurse Ludwig back to health and then accompanied him to Rome. Thereupon Friedrich spent about fourteen years in Italy and southern Germany. Not until 1818, when he returned to Berlin, eventually becoming head of the division of sculptures in the Berlin museums, did the brothers take up a regular correspondence. They never lost interest in one another's work; Friedrich read most of Ludwig's "novellen" while they were still in proof. But their sister stood between them and prevented a closer friendship, Ludwig feeling that Friedrich had sacrificed his career to her. After 1842 they saw each other frequently. It must have been a shock to Ludwig when his seventy-year-old brother, a confirmed bachelor, who had always led a lonely life, married a twenty-year-old girl, Marie Paetsch, in June 1846. This marriage proved unhappy.

A note among Varnhagen von Ense's Berlin papers relates how it came to pass. One day Friedrich was in the shop of a merchant whom he owed a large sum. Marie was also present. They became engaged in conversation, and Friedrich took an immediate fancy to her. After she had left, the merchant suggested that she would make him an excellent wife and, since she was the only daughter of wealthy parents, would furnish him the wherewithal to straighten out his finances. Finally Friedrich promised to pay off his debts to the man and give him two thousand additional talers if he would arrange the match. This was done. But Marie's parents, learning of the shameful barter, always remained hostile to their aged son-in-law and allowed Marie only an annuity during his life.

LUDWIG TIECK, THE GERMAN ROMANTICIST

The frequently repeated statement that Ludwig sold his library in 1849 to help pay the debts of Friedrich, who was as notoriously poor a business man as his brother, is probably true. Friedrich, still remembered for his able cooperation with Schinkel and Rauch in many works of sculpture and for his busts of Goethe, F. A. Wolf and Frederick William III,[30] died on May 12, 1851, a thoroughly unhappy man. He had much more in common with Sophie than with Ludwig. Goethe once called him selfish, informal and coarse, and the artist Riepenhausen found him unfriendly (zänkisch). Varnhagen remarked in unpublished notes that he was well read and intelligent, but quarrelsome, argumentative and stubborn.[31]

Tieck's last letters to the king are noted for their adulation, their pathetic confessions of utter physical disability, and the consequent fear that the king may withdraw his favor and the pension. And indeed, if we would trust Varnhagen, the monarch was gravely disappointed by Tieck's complete collapse.[32] On August 15, 1846, Tieck confessed to his royal patron that he had experienced "seit einem Jahre keine Stunde ohne Schmerz."

On October 15, the king's birthday, he admitted to him that he would henceforth be unable to do any work. A year later he penned a sonnet to Frederick William,[33] full of official flattery and of rueful confession of his own disability. It begins:

> Ill, aged, bowed, but seldom tired of life,
> My soul doth oft find peace with sweetness rife. . . .*

It ends joyfully with the Ambrosian paean and the Horatian "O et praesidium et dulce decus meum." Through an oversight the king was kept in ignorance of the poem and did not acknowledge it. Tieck, in dismay and fear that he had fallen into disfavor, turned to Alexander von Humboldt, who quickly cleared up the matter. In his last letter to the king, of October 15, 1852, Tieck, not far from death, showed more concern for the future of his faithful butler, Johannes Glaser, than for himself.

Occasionally the king's reactionary spirit and pietism were too much even for him, and he criticized them to his friends. To Varnhagen von Ense he remarked that such censorship as the king had introduced would have precluded the publication of most of his own works of two generations before.[34] Tieck had been a stanch supporter of the Polish cause in 1832, writing to Raumer that he deemed the Prussian policy

---

*Krank, alt, gebeugt, doch selten lebensmüde,
Erglänzt mir oft ein süsser Seelenfriede. . . .

"bad and arid" and condemning citizens who conceal or deny the evil deeds of their government.[35] But now he became an arch-conservative. When he learned that Johanna Steffens, the niece of his wife and the widow of his old friend, had expressed herself in favor of the revolutionary movement of 1848, he wrote her the angriest, most petulant letter of his whole career. "This so-called national assembly," he exclaimed, "is a disgrace to our times which cannot be blotted out. Nothing so stupid, mean, base and vulgar in its malice has ever existed before. One might feel ashamed of being a Prussian. That is no longer democratism or republicanism, but the most sinful rebellion, anarchy, rapine, murder, robbery. . . . What do women know about matters of state? Knitting, sewing, housekeeping are their vocations, in these they are to be revered."[36]

Under these circumstances it is not surprising that the liberals, not to mention a half-crazed individual like Skepsgardh,[37] were bitter against this "blue-eyed eagle with wings all shot to pieces,"[37] who looked like a child from another world. No wonder they relentlessly combated everything he had stood for. But it is a pity that their campaign was conducted with so little discrimination that it tended to destroy not only the reprehensible but also the better elements—the light buoyancy and charming winsomeness—of his finest poetry, and with them the high cultural values which had been in their ascendancy ever since 1748.

"Früh gesattelt und spät geritten," Tieck wrote of himself to Varnhagen von Ense on January 2, 1853, sensing that now at length the end was not far off. It came on April 28, soon after six in the morning, less than five weeks before his eightieth birthday. His daughter Agnes had arrived a few days before. The obituary notice bears her name. The burial, at which the liberal-minded Lutheran clergyman Sydow,[38] a pupil of Schleiermacher and friend of Tieck, officiated, took place in the plot of the Dreifaltigkeits-Kirche near the Hasenheide. An impressive assemblage of notable men, among them Alexander von Humboldt, as the delegated representative of the king, Schelling, Raumer, Eichendorff and Rauch, attended. The "Domchor" furnished fitting music. To the few for whom Romanticism still held a message in those unromantic days his passing made it doubly clear that with him a great era had died a belated death.[39]

Indeed, he had been forgotten by his countrymen before his end. A movement started a few months after by his friends, among them Herman Grimm, von der Hagen, Häring, Humboldt, Köpke, Rauch,

Raumer and Reimer, to raise funds, through public subscription, for a monument in his memory, failed.

And still some remained sanguine and felt that although Tieck had been eclipsed, he was certain to come into his own again. Hebbel, who rated him as one of the most important among the few great German poets, thought that his place in literature was secure, and believed that a reaction in his favor was as sure to follow "as the blossoms of the trees in springtime."[40]

Perhaps this conviction is based upon an exaggerated notion of Tieck's importance. Indeed, there are few indications that Hebbel's prophecy is to be literally fulfilled. And yet certain signs point to a gradual revival of interest in Tieck. Scarcely a year has passed during the last decade without the appearance of at least one important book on him. Moreover, the publishers report good sales for the two eclectic editions of his works which have appeared in this century—those of Witkowski and Berend—, as well as for the Reclam editions of many of his writings. More surprising, some dozen of his "novellen" and plays have come out in new French and Italian translations since 1930, not to mention various critical articles, among them one by the well known French publicist Edmond Jaloux.[41]

It may well be, then, that Tieck will after all come into his own again before the centenary of his death is commemorated.

EPILOG

IT HAS appeared from the preceding pages that but few German authors have produced more than Tieck. His published writings comprise over 15,000 octavo pages. Some thirty works, largely the product of his early youth and discussed in chapter 2, are still unpublished. These statistics do not take into account numerous published and unpublished translations, largely from the English, and almost a thousand letters.

Tieck has exercised an undisputed influence upon a host of German writers and upon an array of foreign authors as well. A list of those indebted to him in Germany would include Schiller, E. T. A. Hoffmann, Heine, Arnim, Brentano, Eichendorff, Uhland, Fouqué, Zacharias Werner, Immermann, Lenau, Mörike, Ludwig, Freytag, Hebbel and Richard Wagner, and, carried down to more recent times, Keller, Heyse, Wilbrandt and Gerhart Hauptmann. In Denmark it would record Heiberg and Oehlenschläger; in Russia Gogol; in France Verlaine; in England M. G. Lewis, Bulwer-Lytton, Felicia Hemans, Stevenson, Coleridge, Scott and Carlyle; in America Charles Brockden Brown, Hawthorne, Longfellow, Poe and Margaret Fuller.[1]

It cannot be gainsaid that he was a genuine poet—more a "Naturpoet" than a "Kunstpoet"—and one of that comparatively small number who transcend the ranks of the mere artisans and mechanics of literature. Drawing from a wellnigh inexhaustible store of imagination, he contributed great treasures to enrich literature with a wealth of poetic forms and concepts. Without him the "moon-illumined magic night," the emphasis of feeling, particularly the mood of vague but wistful longing, the love of the flowers and birds, the rippling silver waves, the thrill of solitary communion with the green forest, the glory of knighthood and of ancient castle ruins, the joy of wandering, singing and dreaming, and the spirit of "Romantic Irony" would not be commonplaces in German poetry today. Their impulse came from him. They are the liquid elements, so to speak, which have irrigated German Romanticism and kept it alive during the nineteenth century. And without him the history of the "novelle" and of the historical novel in Germany would probably tell a different tale.

His critical work, though its bulk may be incommensurate with its weight, enjoyed a real importance in its day. It received the highest praise from such a discriminating judge as Hermann Hettner,[2] but has often been underestimated in our own times. He has left a definite imprint upon the theater, especially as it developed after 1880;[3] did much to make English and Spanish literatures, in particular Shakespeare and Cervantes, at home in Germany; strove to reawaken popular interest in German literature of the Middle High German period and of the seventeenth century; and was the first to call the attention of his countrymen to Friedrich (Maler) Müller, Lenz, Wackenroder, Novalis and Kleist.

In 1797 August Wilhelm Schlegel,[4] and in 1800 Fichte,[5] placed him practically upon a par with Goethe. Thirty years later he was looked upon by many as the heir to Goethe's position of leadership in the field of German letters. In 1829 a German critical writer called him the "Novellen-Goethe."[6] Even bitter antagonists like Heinrich Laube styled him "one of our most important living poets."[7] After Goethe's death in 1832 it became a commonplace among Tieck's numerous friends to allude to him as the inheritor of Goethe's toga. This idea was widely reflected, even abroad. Carlyle referred to him in the same breath with Goethe and Schiller as one of the "Masters of Arts, the Saints of Poetry."[8] Henry Crabb Robinson[9] and Mrs. Jameson[10] spoke of him as Goethe's successor, as did also Amédée Prévost of Geneva in the *Revue de Paris*[11] (1832) and the American George Ticknor in his journals.[12] And the Dane Hans Christian Andersen addressed a letter in 1842: "An den Dichter Deutschlands Ludwig Tieck."[13] It is probably true, too, that Tieck was more widely read in Germany during the 'twenties than any other high-class author. In England he bid fair, during the 'thirties, to become the most popular German writer.[14]

Yet today, although new interest in him can be noted, his name is not inscribed by literary historians on the tablets reserved for the greatest poets, and but a modicum of his voluminous output has survived. Among the comparatively small number of his works which in a sense still live or retain their appeal we would class his early plays *Die Sommernacht* and *Der Abschied*, the satires *Der gestiefelte Kater* and *Leben und Tod des kleinen Rotkäppchens*, the tragedy *Leben und Tod der heiligen Genoveva*, the prolog of *Kaiser Octavianus*, all seven tales in the first volume of *Phantasus*, ten or a dozen of the later "novellen," including *Die Gemälde*, *Der Gelehrte* and *Des Lebens Überfluss*, and the two novels *Der Aufruhr in den Cevennen* and *Vittoria Accorombona*.

Critics have tried hard to explain this loss of popularity. They have ascribed it to the limited appeal of his work to a certain class and a given age. They find that he took his light and leading essentially from the cultural refinement of the metropolitan centers, which during his youth were beginning to assume prominence with the gradual disappearance of feudal, agrarian Germany. They detect in him too much of the *littérateur*, the artificer, and too little of the poet. Rudolf Haym, the historian of early German Romanticism, who has proved one of Tieck's severest critics, has another explanation for the instability of his fame. He has made the charge that it was his character to have had no character at all. Others add the accusation of opportunism.

While there is something to be said for these views, they do not tell the whole truth, or penetrate the surface, or fully elucidate the why and wherefore of the poet's waning prestige. In the course of our study we have endeavored to go into these matters with some care. A brief résumé will now perhaps be appropriate.

No German author before Tieck had recognized the changes wrought in literature and society by the development of the German bourgeoisie to intellectual maturity. He was the first German poet whose writings reflected such a modern society as only a metropolis can produce. He may, then, be styled the first urban poet, and consequently the first urbane poet and literary exponent of polite society. Though often characterized by lyricism, the works of this Poet of the City are without the relaxations of pastoral gaiety and the warm, rich pungency of the soil. For the most part his inspiration seems urban (particularly in his later works), with a thorough understanding of average cosmopolitan society, although he has the yearning of the city-bred man for rusticity and forest solitude.

Except for one brief lustrum—from his twenty-first to his twenty-sixth year—when it seemed as if immaturity, poverty and the temptings of unscrupulous teachers and publishers would make a hacking pot-boiler of him, he remained steadfastly true to the ideal which his mission prescribed: the propagation of a supreme social culture untrammelled by selfishness, petty prejudice or class distinction. Thus, particularly after he attained a belated maturity in his thirties, he became the untiring champion in the struggle of the upper middle classes against the curtailment of their intellectual prerogatives and of their hegemony in the field of arts and letters.

Certain basic facts, however, tended to frustrate his efforts toward a realization of his dreams. In his youth he was under the influence of Storm and Stress but did not accept it because it was too egocentric; he fought every phase of egoistic Rationalism, which, as a tool of the rabble, had become trivial, sordid and soul-deadening. His weapon was Romanticism, which was forced into a system by the Schlegels. Being by nature both of a poetic and an East Elbian, irrationalist mold, he was an ideal "romantischer Dichter," with a marked cleavage in his personality. Quick to realize this, the Schlegels, who themselves lacked creative ability, proclaimed him, more or less against his will, a poet laureate.[15] But for the first fifty years Tieck depended entirely upon literary work for a living. This made haste, shallowness and popularization necessary. Now since he was essentially a popularizer, he succeeded, as no greater poet than he could have, in "selling" Romanticism to the intelligent reading public. But in the hands of inferior writers it grew decadent and trite during the Napoleonic era, giving way to religious orthodoxy, superstition, claptrap, empty saccharine affectation and clannishness. Meanwhile Tieck was engaged in a persevering struggle to lessen the rift in his personality. With a highly elastic flexibility of endowment, he overcame a mysticism which threatened to subvert his poetry, dropped a great part of Romanticism, and took up the cudgels of a realistic, though purely theoretical bourgeois philosophy to batter down the excesses of a movement for whose origins he was responsible.

Then, while he was still developing this new philosophy, the spirit of the times changed and gave birth to practical bourgeois liberalism and modern industrialism—currents which remained distasteful riddles to him.

Further, patriotism had flared up in Germany during the Napoleonic era. The other Romanticists either suffered early tragic destruction, like Kleist, or adapted themselves to the change. Some turned seriously to religion (Friedrich Schlegel), others to scholarship (A. W. Schlegel), others became wrapt up in medieval German lore and knighthood (Fouqué), others again devoted their attention to patriotic agitation (Fichte). Tieck, though engaging in German medieval studies, never did so to the prejudice of Raphael, Shakespeare and Calderon. Though not without personal patriotism, he remained the cosmopolite and, with an ascetic horror of the realities of life, kept aloof from the spirit of his times. By doing so he ceased being a typical representative of his age.

Is it any wonder, then, that his writings were exposed to the charges of inconsistency and obsoleteness? One needs but turn the pages of the hostile reviews of his "novellen" during the 'thirties to see the changing attitude toward his work. His ideals were described there as "mere whims";[16] his ironical view of the world was called futile;[17] he was accused of abandoning true poetry in order to produce contemporary moral documents,[18] and was charged with failing to lay his finger upon the social realities and with losing contact with middle-class life.[18]

In Tieck's own eyes these charges seemed unfounded, for now as then his energies were bent toward a single principle: the best interests of the bourgeoisie as opposed to vulgarity and cheapness.

But he was burdened also with the graver accusation that he lacked character. No doubt this indictment was rooted in a well founded realization of his innate duality, or chameleonism, which caused Hebbel to call him a "Zwitter-Natur."[19] He was Democritus—genial, witty and loquacious—and Heraclitus—brooding, melancholy and mystic—all in one. He was extremely adaptable and, as a born actor, able to feel his way into the thoughts, emotions and situation of others. He possessed a passive, feminine temper. His intellectual and moral indifference usually made it easy to see both sides of a question and to ridicule even himself. No wonder this "problematic figure" proved too critical to please the poets, too poetical for the critics, too devout for the Rationalists, too Rationalistic for the Pietists, too reactionary for the liberals, and too liberal for the reactionaries.

And yet precisely because his was a mobile, unfettered and homeless nature, he succeeded better than any of his Romantic colleagues in mediating between Rationalism and Romanticism and, later, in finding at least a path to the new era of 1830. Thus he stood out all his life as a transitional figure. Though he would never admit it, his mentality during youth showed traits of Rationalism; later his ideas came remarkably close to those of the Young Germans. In his capacity as a mediator, more than in his poetry, Tieck's present-day importance lies.

Luckily he did not succumb to those dangerous tendencies besetting every drifter; he never consciously employed his chameleonism as the handmaid of selfishness or base purposefulness. He was often a propagandist and usually an improviser, but his instincts and motives remained above reproach. He always affirmed a noble humanism and idealism, combated his own duality in a brave and constant struggle, and never ceased fighting like a crusader against the sordid, the trifling, the egoistic. These vices signified to his truly religious soul what the devil signified to the medieval theologian—the incarnation of the principle of Evil.[20] The purity of his ethical and artistic character, at least, cannot be impugned. It is blindness to these factors that makes critics like Haym and Gundolf unfair to Tieck.

Among his other assets we find keen critical insight, an urbane style, a masterly humor, rich imagination, a very sensitive nature, and inexhaustible inventiveness. But he depended too much upon books—literature and history—for his inspiration, and too little upon life and direct experience. He was deficient in formative power, neither could he create characters nor give his works balance and proportion. His was a

more reproductive than creative talent. He also lacked depth of sentiment, the white heat of a ravishing emotion, and a uniformly compelling artistic purpose. Only on rare occasions and with the application
of great energy could he summon up all his powers at one time. Such
divine moments were his when he wrote the tales *Der blonde Eckbert*,
Der Runenberg and *Die Elfen* and the best of his later "novellen," like
Des Lebens Überfluss. On the other hand, his numerous unfinished
works—the treatises on Shakespeare, the Spanish theater, Goethe and
early German literature, a series of historical tragedies and the three
great torsos *Franz Sternbalds Wanderungen*, *Phantasus* and *Der
Aufruhr in den Cevennen*—are sad testimony of his inability to concentrate.

As a rule he took his poet's mission too seriously. In striving for universality he sacrificed homogeneity of purpose and symmetry of effect.
In some of his writings, as in *Der gestiefelte Kater* and *Die Vogelscheuche*, his head alone was at work, usually in the guise of wit and
irony. In others, as in *Genoveva* and *Octavian*, imagination ran riot in
wild orgies of color and melody. In others, for instance *Dichterleben*,
he let the subject matter control him completely, while in some—
witness *Vittoria Accorombona*—he sought to master it.

In old age he tended to become garrulous and prolix. Though himself under the spell of Walter Scott, he vainly tried to combat the
influence of this writer in the historical novel by substituting for his
description a dialog style which strikes most modern readers as more
tiresome and interminable than do Scott's descriptive eccentricities.

We believe we have stated those factors which should furnish the
reasons for Tieck's remarkable loss of prestige. This, then, was his
quandary. His duality made him poet and professional *littérateur* at
the same time. But because he depended upon his pen for a living and
by virtue of his great prolificness, tendency to improvise, and insistent
championship of the ideals of polite middle-class society, the *littérateur*
in him became more prominent than the poet. He deliberately wrote for
his age, not for posterity. He supported and popularized ephemeral
causes in an era of rapid social and political change, and lost touch
with the *Zeitgeist*. His Romanticism became too popular and fell into
the hands of trivializers. Finally he suffered from such radical defects
as bookishness, a surplus of reproductive talent but a dearth of original
creativeness, inability to concentrate and insufficient unity of artistic
purpose. In consequence some of the precious ore of poetry in his work
has been eclipsed, although German literature as it has developed since
his day would be unthinkable without him.

NOTES

INTRODUCTORY BIBLIOGRAPHICAL NOTE

For the principal published writings see *Ludwig Tiecks Schriften*, 28 vols., Berlin (Reimer), 1828-1854; *Novellen*, 7 vols., Berlin and Breslau, 1823-1828; *Gesammelte Novellen*, 14 vols., Breslau, 1835-1842 (vols. 1-4 were reprinted in 1838 and in 1847); *Nachgelassene Schriften* hrsg. v. Rudolf Köpke, 2 vols., Leipzig, 1855; *Gedichte*, 3 vols., Dresden, 1821-1823; *Gedichte*, Neue Ausgabe, Berlin, 1841; *Kritische Schriften*, Leipzig, 1848-1852 (vols. 3 and 4 ed. by Eduard Devrient); *Vittoria Accorombona, ein Roman*, 2 vols., Breslau, 1840; *Das Buch über Shakespeare. Handschriftliche Aufzeichnungen*...hrsg. v. Henry Lüdeke, Halle, 1920.

Editions of selected works of Tieck, with biographical and critical data, have been published by Jakob Minor, 2 parts, Berlin and Stuttgart [1885], *Deutsche National-Literatur*, vol. 144; *idem, Tieck und Wackenroder*, Deut. Nat.-Lit., vol. 145; Heinrich Welti, 6 vols., Stuttgart [1886-1888]; Gotthold Klee, 3 vols., Leipzig and Vienna, 1892; Georg Witkowski, 4 vols., Leipzig [1904]; Eduard Berend, 6 parts, Berlin, Leipzig, Vienna, Stuttgart, 1908.

In the new collection, *Deutsche Literatur*, edited by Heinz Kindermann in conjunction with Walther Brecht and Dietrich Kralik, and now appearing at Leipzig (Reclam), 22 vols., edited by Paul Kluckhohn, are being devoted to Romanticism. Among the works of Tieck to be included are *William Lovell* (selections) in vol. 2, the *Phantasien* in vol. 3, *Sternbald* in vol. 6, *Genoveva* in vol. 7, and various parodies, satires, comedies and tales.

For more complete, though not up-to-date bibliographical data on Tieck's writings see Rudolf Köpke, *Ludwig Tieck, Erinnerungen aus dem Leben des Dichters*, vol. 2, Leipzig, 1855, pp. 286 ff.; Klee, vol. 3; Karl Goedeke and Edmund Goetze, *Grundriss zur Geschichte der deutschen Dichtung*, vol. 6, 2nd ed., Leipzig, Dresden, Berlin, 1898, pp. 28-45 and 797 f.; and Rudolf Haym, *Die romantische Schule*, 5th ed. (by Oskar Walzel), Berlin, 1928.

For the translations see Köpke and Goedeke-Goetze. Among the unpublished translations in the *Tieck-Nachlass* (Handschriftenabteilung, Preussische Staats-bibliothek, Berlin) is a complete rendering of R. B. Sheridan's *The Rivals*.

For the letters see Karl von Holtei, *Briefe an Tieck*, 4 vols., Breslau, 1864; Goedeke-Goetze; E. H. Zeydel, *Nachträge zu Holteis Briefe an Tieck*, Modern Language Notes, Baltimore, Nov. 1928, pp. 459 ff.; H. Lüdeke von Möllendorff, *Aus Tiecks Novellenzeit. Briefwechsel zwischen Ludwig Tieck und F. A. Brockhaus*, Leipzig, 1928; E. H. Zeydel, *Die Briefe Ludwig Tiecks, ein literarisches Problem, Journal of English and Germanic Philology*, Urbana, Jan. 1929, pp. 72 ff.; E. H. Zeydel and Percy Matenko, *A Supplementary List of Published Letters from and to Tieck, Germanic Review*, New York, April 1930, pp. 182 f.; Marta Becker in *Deutsche Rundschau* 55, 144 ff.; Zeydel-Matenko, *Ludwig Tieck-Friedrich von Raumer Letters* (Germanic Review Texts 2), New York, 1930; Henry Lüdeke, *Ludwig Tieck und die Brüder Schlegel*, Frankfurt a.M., 1930; Percy Matenko, *Tieck and Solger*, New York and Berlin (Westermann), 1933.

LUDWIG TIECK, THE GERMAN ROMANTICIST

An edition of some five hundred unpublished Tieck letters is in preparation by R. H. Fife, Percy Matenko and E. H. Zeydel. The letters in this collection, frequently quoted in the present work, are here referred to as unpublished, with indication of their location.

Besides the letters, the most important sources for Tieck's life and the best general critical accounts of his work are the three *Vorberichte* by himself prefacing vols. 1 (40 pp.), 6 (50 pp.) and 11 (84 pp.) of his *Schriften*; R. *Kausler, Ludwig Tieck und die deutsche Romantik* (Mundts Freihafen, 2. Jahrgang, Altona, 1839); Köpke; J. L. Hoffmann, *Ludwig Tieck, eine literarische Skizze* (Album des literarischen Vereins in Nürnberg), Nürnberg, 1856; Haym; H. Freiherr von Friesen, *Ludwig Tieck. Erinnerungen eines alten Freundes aus den Jahren 1825-1842.* 2 vols., Vienna, 1871; Minor; Klee; Wilhelm Bernhardi in *Allgemeine Deutsche Biographie*, vol. 38, Leipzig, 1894, pp. 251 *ff.*; Goedeke-Goetze; Witkowski; Berend; Friedrich Gundolf in *Jahrbuch des freien deutschen Hochstifts*, Frankfurt a.M., 1929, pp. 99 *ff.* (also in *Romantiker, Neue Folge*, 1931).

INTRODUCTION

[1] A bibliography of German Romanticism would fill a stout volume. Consult Haym; G. Brandes, *The Romantic School in Germany (Main Currents)*, New York, 1924; J. Petersen, *Die Wesensbestimmung der deutschen Romantik*, Leipzig, 1926; Oskar Walzel, *Deutsche Romantik*, 5th ed., Leipzig, 1923 (English trans. by Alma E. Lussky, New York, London, 1932); L. A. Willoughby, *The Romantic Movement in Germany*, Oxford, 1930; J. G. Robertson, *A History of German Literature* (new and revised ed.), Edinburgh and London, 1931.

[2] *A. W. von Schlegels sämtliche Werke* XI, 136.

CHAPTER ONE

The principal source is Köpke's biography.

[1] cf. *Literarisches Echo* 6, 1099, and Berend's biographical introduction to his edition.

[2] *Tieck-Nachlass*, Box 8. Also E. A. Regener, *Tieck-Studien*, Rostock, 1903.

[3] J. G. Sulzer, *Allgemeine Theorie der schönen Künste*, 3. Teil, 2. Aufl., Leipzig, 1793, p. 507: "Als wirkende Ursache betrachtet, ist die Natur die Führerin und Lehrerin des Künstlers; als Wirkung ist sie das allgemeine Magazin, woraus er die Gegenstände hernimmt, die er zu seinen Absichten braucht. Je genauer der Künstler in seinem Verfahren oder in der Wahl seiner Materie sich an die Natur hält, je vollkommener wird sein Werk. ... Das Verfahren der Natur ist ... die eigentliche Schule des Künstlers, wo er jede Regel der Kunst lernen kann. ... Deswegen kann auch die Theorie der Kunst nichts anders sein, als das System der Regeln, die durch genaue Beobachtung aus dem Verfahren der Natur abgezogen werden."

[4] *ibid.*, 1. Teil, pp. 684-5: "Aber diese Dichtungskraft ist nur alsdenn wichtig, wenn sie von einem scharfen Verstand unterstützt wird. ... Darum muss in der Seele des Künstlers der Verstand eine völlige Herrschaft über die lebhafteste Wirksamkeit der Einbildungskraft behalten."

[5] *Gesammelte Novellen* II, Breslau, 1847, 10-11: "Am glänzendsten aber sind die Abendstunden, in welchen diese breite Strasse von vielen tausend Lichtern

NOTES

aus den Buden von beiden Seiten erleuchtet wird, dass fast eine Tageshelle sich verbreitet, die nur hie and da durch das Gedränge der Menschen sich scheinbar verdunkelt. . . . So wandeln denn Tausende, scherzend mit Planen zu kaufen, erzählend, lachend, schreiend an den süssduftenden mannigfaltigen Zucker- und Marzipangebäcken vorüber, wo Früchte, in reizender Nachahmung, Figuren aller Art, Tiere und Menschen, alles in hellen Farben strahlend, die Lüsternen anlacht."

[6] *Tieck-Nachlass*, Box 3.

[7] See *Aus meinem Bühnenleben*. Erinnerungen von Karoline Bauer, hrsg. v. Arnold Wellmer. Berlin, 1871, 336 *ff*. Also *Tiecks Schriften* VI, xii.

[8] F. H. von der Leyen, *Wackenroders Werke und Briefe* II, Jena, 1910, 143: "herrlich, göttlich."

[9] *Aus dem Leben Theodor von Bernhardis* II, Leipzig, 1893, 84 *f*. This work (vol. 1), contains the earliest known portrait of Ludwig and Sophie, by Friedrich.

[10] Köpke II, 269: "Johann Ludwig Tieck, aus Berlin, 19 Jahre alt, neun Jahre Gymnasiast, und seit vier Jahren ein Mitglied der ersten Classe. Er hat gute Fähigkeiten, und er hat sich durch seinen bei aller Einseitigkeit unverkennbaren Fleiss in mancher Rücksicht sehr gute Kenntnisse erworben, besonders hat er seinen Geschmack gut ausgebildet. Sein Betragen war lobenswert. Er wird in Halle Theologie studieren."

[11] *Tieck-Nachlass*, Box 1.

[12] *ibid*., Box 2.

[13] *ibid*., Box 24.

[14] *ibid*., Box 18. Published by Zeydel in *Publications of the Mod. Lang. Assoc. of Amer.* L, 2 (June 1935), 537 *ff*.

[15] Lüdeke, *L. T. und die Brüder Schlegel*, 65.

[16] Holtei IV, 159: "Ich habe an mir selbst und an Mitschülern in der Jugend die Erfahrung gemacht, dass diejenigen jungen Leute, die wirklichen Sinn für die Poesie hatten, lange Zeit den Alten keinen Geschmack abgewinnen konnten. Trifft es sich, wie es natürlich geht, dass wir unter den Neuern Lieblinge antreffen, und uns irgend einen grossen Dichter der neuern Zeit befreunden, so werden dadurch leicht die grössten Schönheiten des Altertums auf gewisse Weise verdunkelt, so dass uns erst späterhin wieder der Sinn für diese aufgeht. Dazu kommt, dass die einfache, rührende Grösse des Altertums erst recht einleuchtet, wenn wir vieles in uns überwunden, durchlebt, Irrtümer erfahren und abgelegt haben."

[17] *Solgers Nachgel. Schr. u. Briefw.* I, 411; Matenko, 229.

[18] *Schriften* VI, xii *f*.

[19] von der Leyen II, 148: "So viel ich die Minnesänger kenne, herrscht auch eine erstaunliche Einförmigkeit in allen ihren Ideen; es ist überhaupt schon gar keine Empfehlung für den poetischen Geist dieses Zeitalters, dass es nur diese eine Art von Gedichten gab, nur diesen Zirkel von Empfindungen."

[20] *ibid*., II, 165.

[21] *Tieck-Nachlass*, No. 6: "einen König absetzen! i da gehört dreimal mehr Verstand dazu, als ihn einsetzen, wir haben die Beispiele!"

[22] *Tieck-Nachlass*, Box 4.

[23] von der Leyen II, 161: "O, wenn ich izt ein Franzose wäre! Dann wollt' ich nicht hier sitzen, dann—Doch leider bin ich in einer Monarchie geboren, die

gegen die Freiheit kämpfte, unter Menschen, die noch Barbaren genug sind, die Franzosen ganz zu verachten."

[24] Zeydel, *L. T. and England*, Princeton, 1931, p. 3.

[25] von der Leyen II, 148: "Lieblingsdichter" . . . "göttlich."

[26] *Schriften* V, 450: "Es lässt sich nicht beschreiben, und nur wer in seiner Jugend eine ähnliche Begeisterung für die Magie der Bühne erfahren hat, kann den Zauber, die Wonne fassen, die aus den geringfügigsten, ja oft widerwärtigsten Dingen auf mich einströmten. Jeder Lampenputzer war mir geweiht."

[27] *Schriften* I, xiii *f.*: "In meiner früheren Jugend sah man in Berlin, neben manchen schwachen und unbedeutenden Versuchen deutscher Dichtkunst, viele französische Dramen und Lustspiele, die früheren Tragödien Schillers sehr häufig; eben so viele Werke Shakespeares, die, wenn auch in der Umarbeitung entstellt, das Gepräge der Grossheit behalten hatten. Andre englische Trauerspiele, wie Athelstan, Ethelwolf und ähnliche, wurden mit Beifall gegeben, so wie die gemilderten Comödien des Farquhar und Congreve. Emilie Galotti und Minna von Barnhelm erhielten sich ihre Verehrer, so wie Gotters fein ausgeführte Umarbeitungen. Lustige Possen ermunterten durch den Contrast, und, so viel zu wünschen blieb, so sprach doch die Bühne einen kräftigen, heitern und grossartigen Charakter aus."

[28] Karoline Bauer, as in note 7. Also Köpke I, 31.

[29] *Schriften* I, xiv: "mächtig, genialisch und kühn."

CHAPTER TWO

[1] *Tieck-Nachlass*, Box 8.

[2] In *Schiller und die Bühne*, Berlin, 1904, Appendix, Julius Petersen suggests that Tieck's version of *Die Räuber* was never complete. Köpke's notes prove otherwise.

[3] *Tieck-Nachlass*, Box 24.

[4] von der Leyen II, 5.

[5] *Tieck-Nachlass*, Box 3.

[6] Köpke II, 194.

[7] *Tieck-Nachlass*, Box 2. The plot of *Der doppelte Vater*: Young Baron Silbersen's sweetheart will not marry him until his severe stepfather has consented to the match, so the lover has his butler impersonate the gruff guardian. Trouble brews when the real stepfather also proposes to the girl. But in the end the young people are happily united.

[8] *ibid.*, Box 5. The plot of *Die Nebenbuhler*: Ahlfeld and Freundlich, not realizing that they are in love with the same girl, complain to each other of their unknown rivals. Each issues a challenge to his opponent, asking his friend to act as his second. Complications ensue when Ahlfeld dresses his servant Peter in a suit of mail and forces him to take his part in the duel. But the girl arrives in time to reveal to her two lovers what the audience knew from the outset.

[9] *ibid.*, Boxes 3 and 5. The plot of *Die Heirat*: In the shorter play Christian's marriage is opposed by a scheming rival, who tries to force a wedge between him and the girl's mother. But this plot is frustrated. In the longer one the marriage is opposed by Christian's mother and, less firmly, by his weak-kneed father, who wish him to marry another girl. The plans of Christian and his

NOTES

friends, among them a cobbler who disguises as the devil, to force his parents to relent, fail, until the other girl suddenly dies.

[10] *ibid.*, No. 6 and Box 18. The plot of *Der letzte Betrug*: Herr von Sondersheim, a stupid nobleman, hard of hearing, has promised his daughter to Peter von Lingen, who, though personally unknown to him, has won his respect exorcising the devil. A friend of Sondersheim, hearing this, poses as Peter and snatches the girl. Peter swears vengeance. He disguises as the devil and frightens Sondersheim, who is intoxicated, into cancelling the first match and promising his daughter to the genuine Peter. But Peter himself succumbs to the influence of drink and is tricked by the other suitor, who now in turn appears as the devil, into revealing his identity.

[11] *ibid.*, Boxes 4 and 8.

[12] *ibid.*, Box 2.

[13] *ibid.*, Box 3.

[14] *ibid.*, Box 2.

[15] *ibid.*, Box 5.

[16] *ibid.*, No. 6. Act 2 is extant in two copies.

[17] *ibid.*, Box 4.

[18] *Nachgel. Schr.* I, 183 *f.*

[19] *Tieck-Nachlass*, Box 1.

[20] *ibid.*, Boxes 1 and 8.

[21] *ibid.*, Boxes 7 and 8.

[22] *ibid.*, Boxes 4 and 6.

[23] *Nachgel. Schr.* I, 184 *ff.*

[24] *Tieck-Nachlass*, Box 4.

[25] *Nachgel. Schr.* I, 173 *ff.*

[26] *Tieck-Nachlass*, No. 6 and Box 24.

[27] von der Leyen II, 23.

[28] Frankfurt a.M.

[29] *Nachgel. Schr.* I, 3 *ff.*

[30] Zeydel, *L. T. and England*, 176 *f.* and 211 *ff.*

[31] *Tieck-Nachlass*, Box 1 and No. 6.

[32] *ibid.*, Box 7.

[33] This work has not before been noticed as revealing Gozzian influence. See A. Köster, *Schiller als Dramaturg*, Berlin, 1891, 222 *ff.*, and H. Rusack, *Gozzi in Germany*, New York, 1930.

[34] *Nachgel. Schr.* I, 21 *ff.*

[35] Zeydel in *Euphorion* 29, Heft 1-2, pp. 93 *ff.*

[36] *Schriften* XI, lii *ff.* A new edition (Bremen, 1807) calls the play *Prinz Aldrovan, oder das Ungeheuer.*

[37] Unpublished. Original: Walther de Gruyter collection, Berlin.

[38] The former in *Schriften* XI, 269 *ff.*, the latter *ibid.*, VIII, 259 *ff.* See also *Schriften* VI, ix and XI, xvi *f.*

[39] *Schriften* XI, xvii.

[40] *Nachgel. Schr.* I, 188 *ff.* The other three *Paramythien*, unpublished, are preserved in the *Tieck-Nachlass*, Box 1.

[41] *Nachgel. Schr.* II, 3 *ff.*

[42] *ibid.*, I, 195 *ff.*

[43] *Schriften* VIII, 279. Also *ibid.*, VI, ix *f.*

[44] von der Leyen II, 113.

[45] *Tieck-Nachlass*, Box 8.

[46] *ibid.*, Boxes 6 and 7.

[47] *ibid.*, Box 18. See note 14 to chap. 1.

[48] See *Schriften* I, xxxvii and XI, xxxviii.

[49] Karoline Bauer, *Aus meinem Bühnenleben*, 336 *ff.*

[50] *Schriften* XI, xxxviii.

[51] Jakob Minor in *Jahrb. d. Grillparzer-Gesell*, 9, 1 *ff.*

[52] J. Petersen, *Schiller und die Bühne.*

[53] von der Leyen II, 189.

[54] E. Sulger-Gebing in *Literaturblatt f. germ. u. roman. Philologie* 21, 329 *f.*

[55] *Schriften* VI, vii *f.*

[56] *ibid.*, viii *f.*: "Der junge Autor, dem sein Gegenstand sehr wichtig erschien, hatte alles und jedes mit gleicher Umständlichkeit, jeden Gedanken mit gleicher Kraft vortragen wollen. Er hatte es noch nicht gelernt, wie man Lichter und Schatten ausspart, und wie manches nur leicht angedeutet werden muss, um die beabsichtigte Wirkung hervor zu bringen. Das Gespenstische und Wilde, wenn es sich auch steigert, übersättigt endlich."

[57] Allgem. Deutsche Biographie *sub* Reichardt.

[58] *Nachgel. Schr.* I, 78.

[59] H. Hemmer, *Die Anfänge Ludwig Tiecks und seiner dämonisch-schauerlichen Dichtung*, Berlin, 1910, and M. Thalmann, *Probleme der Dämonie in Ludwig Tiecks Schriften*, Weimar, 1919.

[60] Erna Görte, *Der junge Tieck und die Aufklärung*, Berlin, 1926.

[61] Friedr. Gundolf, *Ludwig Tieck.*

CHAPTER THREE

The principal source is von der Leyen, *op. cit.*

[1] Tieck's letters to Sophie, unpublished, are mostly in the Sächsische Landes-bibliothek. Seventeen letters of Sophie to Ludwig are in the Preussische Staats-bibliothek. For Tieck and Wackenroder see also Helene Stöcker in *Vossische Zeitung*, Beilage 19, 1903.

[2] von der Leyen II, 58: "in einer ziemlich engen Strasse, im dritten Stock, was aber nicht sehr hoch ist." "nach vier Uhr, oft nach fünf erst."

[3] *ibid.*, p. 7: "Ich finde gewiss keinen Menschen wieder, der mich so ganz versteht, wie Du, der jeden meiner Gedanken behorchen kann, der der Dolmetscher aller meiner Empfindungen ist, der so fein, so zart fühlt, dessen Phantasie so ätherisch und geläutert wäre."

[4] *ibid.*, p. 15: "Wäre ich Alexander, so würde ich's mit der eben so machen, wie jener mit Pindars Hause. Sie müsste eine ewige Reliquie bleiben, wenn auch ganz Berlin unterginge. Ich werde die Stube nie ohne Rührung, nie ohne von wehmütigen Erinnerungen gepresst zu sein, ansehn."

[5] *ibid.*, p. 16: "Es ist bald 12 Uhr nachts. Ich lege mich jetzt schlafen. Ich merke, dass es eine wahre Wonne ist, an Dich zu schreiben. Selig, selig ist der Tag, den ich mit dem Gedanken an Dich beschliesse. Er wird mich auch im Schlafe nicht verlassen. Träume Du auch von mir. Denkst Du jetzt an mich?

NOTES

Oder träumst Du von mir? Eine allerliebste schmelzend-sanfte Elegie von Voss fängt an: 'Denkt mein Mädchen an mich?' Es ist eine höchst natürliche schöne Empfindung darin. Jetzt hat es grade 12 geschlagen. Gute Nacht. Tieck, fliege her, und ich drücke den feurigsten Kuss auf Deine Lippen. Gute Nacht, der Himmel sei mit Dir! Gute Nacht!"

[6] *Blütezeit der deutschen Romantik*, 5 Aufl., Leipzig, 1913. Also O. Walzel, *Deutsche Romantik*, and Marie Joachimi, *Die Weltanschauung der deutschen Romantik*, Jena and Leipzig, 1905.

[7] von der Leyen II, 20: "Wenn ich bedenke, wie viele hunderttausend Sachen es gibt, und wie viele tausend noch täglich erfunden werden, um uns die Zeit zu vertreiben, so ist mir manchmal, als bestünde das ganze Menschengeschlecht aus lauter Kindern, die vor Langeweile nicht wissen, was sie tun sollen. Die meisten Menschen werden kaum fünfzig Jahre alt, dreissig gehen mit Schlaf, Essen und Trinken dahin, die übrigen sind ein Opfer der Langeweile und nichtswürdiger Beschäftigungen, ich sollte es freilich nicht, aber das Gefühl dringt sich so oft unwiderstehlich mir auf, dass ich solche Menschen verachten müsste, diese Verachtung muss aber bald dem Mitleide den Platz machen."

[8] *ibid.*, p. 38: "Dass ich hier niemand habe, mit dem und in dem ich eigentlich lebe, das wirst Du mir wohl glauben. Schmohln habe ich Dir schon geschildert, er bleibt sich immer gleich, kleinlich, pedantisch und kalt, dabei ist er doch nicht von Affektation frei, er will nach Umständen den schönen Geist, den Empfindsamen, den Politiker und hundert andre Rollen spielen, die ihm alle gleich übel stehen, er geht so weit, dass er sich lächerlich macht, dabei, und dies ist mir das unausstehlichste, ist er eitler wie ein Frauenzimmer, wenigstens eitler als wir beide es selbst unsern Geliebten vergeben könnten, ein Bläschen im Gesicht kann ihn über eine Stunde beschäftigen, er kann sich drei- bis viermal am Tage von vorn anziehen, er ist nie glücklicher, als wenn er sich putzen kann. Und Bothe! Davon hast Du gar keine Idee. Du kannst und wirst es mir gar nicht glauben, Du wirst es für den Ausbruch meiner üblen Laune halten, allein Bothe ist noch eitler als Schmohl."

[9] *ibid.*, pp. 56 ff.: "ein göttlicher Abend . . . der Mond schien so hell, die Luft war so heiter und war der Himmel so blau. Ich begleitete mechanisch meine Gefährten bis zum Tor und kehrte dann um, ohne von ihnen eben bemerkt zu werden und ohne ein Wort zu sprechen. Ich forderte von der Natur Ersatz für die verlorenen Stunden und erhielt ihn, ich war wirklich einmal glücklich. Ich ging neben Gärten hin, wo mich der balsamische Duft von tausend Blumen umfing, die Lichter erloschen nach und nach in den Häusern, die Hunde bellten mir allenthalben nach, ich ging vor einer Wassermühle vorbei, deren schäumender Wasserfall wie Flammen in dem Strahl des Mondes flutete, alles war so schön, so abenteuerlich. Ich setzte mich oft nieder, die schöne Gegend zu übersehen. Die Saale glänzte vor mir wie ein grosser See, tausend kleine Sterne zitterten auf der ungewissen Oberfläche, ein leichter goldener Nebel ruhte über die ganze Gegend, die Wogen der Saale tönten in der einsamen Nacht wie die Schritte eines Wanderers, bald wie Harfentöne, bald wie das Rudern eines Schiffes. O wie oft dacht' ich an Dich, wie oft wünscht' ich Dich an meine Seite. Endlich stieg ich auf die Felsen, die schönste Gegend bei Giebichenstein, wie alles romantisch vor mir lag, mir war, als lebt' ich in der fernsten Vergangenheit, die Ruinen des Ritterschlosses blickten so ernsthaft nach mir hin, die

Felsen gegenüber, die Felsen über mir, die wankenden Bäume, das Hundebellen, alles war so schauerlich, alles stimmte die Phantasie so rein, so hoch. Oft sass ich halb im Traum, halb wachend, mit einem Auge süsse Träume sehend, mit dem andern in die schöne Gegend blickend. Rührend ist mir immer der Untergang des Mondes, er senkt sich so still, so bescheiden, einem Grösseren Platz zu machen . . . Das Heraufkommen des Tages ist mir immer so bang, so erwartungsvoll, die ganze Natur scheint aufmerksam. . . . Das Morgenrot glänzte um den ganzen Horizont—kurz, diese Nacht gehört zu den schönsten Stunden meines Lebens, sie wird mir unvergesslich sein, ich habe hier manches gelernt, manches empfunden, was ich vorher nicht wusste, nicht empfand."

[10] See Zeydel in *Modern Lang. Notes* XLI (Nov. 1926) 444 *ff.*

[11] von der Leyen II, 53 *f.*: "Ich war auf einige Sekunden wirklich wahnsinnig. Jetzt kam eine verlorene Idee zurück, ich stürzte vorüber, den Zügel wieder zu fassen, der Wagen stand, um Gotteswillen! ich werde rasend! rief ich und sank halb ohnmächtig nieder, alles gewann nach einem kleinen Kampfe seine natürlichen Umrisse wieder, ich fand mich selbst wieder. Ich war äusserst ermattet. Alle meine Pulse klopften hörbar. Meine Phantasie arbeitet aber immer noch . . . der Anblick des Weissen war mir besonders schrecklich. . . . Höchst ermattet legte ich mich endlich aufs Bette . . . über eine Stunde brachte ich in einem Zustande zu, der einer Ohnmacht des Körpers nahe war, indes alle meine Kräfte der Phantasie krampfhaft arbeiteten. Sobald ich die Augen zumachte, war mir, als schwämme ich auf einem Strom, ich löste sich mein Kopf ab und schwämme rückwärts, der Körper vorwärts, eine Empfindung, die ich sonst noch nie gehabt habe, wenn ich die Augen aufmachte, war mir's, als läg' ich in einem weiten Totengewölbe, drei Särge nebeneinander, ich sahe deutlich die weissen schimmernden Gebeine, alles drehte sich in eine fürchterliche Länge, alle meine Glieder waren mir selbst fremd geworden und ich erschrak, wenn ich mit der Hand nach meinem Gesicht fasste. . . . Einigemal schlief ich ein, Du weisst, dass das Einschlafen mit einer krampfhaften Zuckung anfängt, diese war aber so gewaltsam, dass ich davon fürchterlich in die Höhe geworfen wurde. Endlich schlief ich ein und erwachte äusserst ermattet. Ich konnte den ganzen Tag nicht ausgehn und mich kaum von einem Stuhl zum andern bringen."

[12] *Gedichte*, 1821-1823, II, 227; ed. of 1841, p. 3.

[13] For the first hallucination see Köpke I, 235, and *Abendgespräche* (*Ges. Nov.* X, 50) and an unpublished letter to Yorck-Wartenburg of 1853 (original: Preuss. Staatsbib.). The latter hallucination is recorded in the last-mentioned source. On his experience in the Harz see Friesen II, 138, and Köpke I, 143.

[14] von der Leyen II, 107.

[15] *Schr.* V, 441: "als ich mich eben so wenig zur Zunft der Studenten, als zu den Gewerben des bürgerlichen Lebens rechnete."

[16] von der Leyen II, 22.

[17] *ibid.*, 113: "ich lebe und webe jetzt im Shakespeare, ich habe ihn noch nie so fleissig als izt studiert, in acht Tagen habe ich mir den ganzen Sturm abgeschrieben und trage nun eine Menge Lesarten und Bemerkungen zusammen, ich studiere mich auch jetzt mehr in seine Sprache hinein, von meinen Grillen über ihn bin ich noch nicht abgewichen,—Romeo, Hamlet und Othello habe ich seit kurzer Zeit nun englisch durchgelesen, die Übersetzung gibt einem wirklich gar keine rechte Idee von Shakespeare."

NOTES

[18] Fritz Wölcken, *Shakespeares Zeitgenossen in der deutschen Literatur*, Berlin, 1929.

[19] See introductory bibliographical note.

[20] Zeydel, *L. T. and England*, p. 10, note 3.

[21] *Schr.* XI, xxv-xxvii.

[22] G. W. Whiting in *Publications of the Mod. Lang. Assoc. of Amer.* XLVI, 2 (June 1931), 605 *ff.*

[23] *Schr.* XI, xxvii-xxix.

[24] Stanger in *Studien zur vergleich. Lit.gesch.* I, 182 *ff.* and II, 37 *ff.* Also Lüdeke, *L. T. und das alte englische Theater*, Frankf. a.M., 1922, 264 *ff.*; and Zeydel, *L. T. and England*, 17.

[25] W. Fischer in *Jb. der deut. Shakes.-Gesell.* 62 (N. F. III, 1926), 98 *ff.*

[26] L. Fränkel in *Goethe-Jb.* 16, 200 *f.*

[27] *Schr.* IV, 15: "die berührigen, muntern Franken in ihrer romantischen, vielfach wechselnden Umgebung."

[28] G. Klee in *Forschungen zur deut. Philologie*, Festg. f. Rud. Hildebrandt, Leipzig, 1894, 180 *ff.*, and L. Assing, *Briefe v. Chamisso usw. nebst Briefen, Anmerkungen u. Notizen v. Varnhagen v. Ense*, Leipzig, 1867, I, 189 *ff.*

[29] von der Leyen II, 205 *ff.*

[30] *Episteln und Elegien*, Stuttgart, 1894, 34 *ff.*

[31] *Schr.* IV, 12: "wie gern schweifte ich durch die krummen Gassen, über die Brücken und Plätze, wo künstliche Brunnen, Gebilde aller Art, mich an eine schöne Periode Deutschlands erinnerten, ja! damals noch die Häuser von aussen mit Gemälden von Riesen und altdeutschen Helden geschmückt waren."

[32] G. Klee as in note 28 above: "Die Klöster müssen durchaus nicht ausgerottet werden, hier findet der Mensch, der die Welt, oder den sie von sich stösst, doch eine sichere, heilige Zuflucht." "es erregte sonderbare Empfindungen, eine Menge armseliger zu sehn, die aus Gewohnheit, aus Meinung (mir fehlen Worte, selbst blinder Instinkt ist hier wirklich noch zu viel) nach Maschinenart ihren Körper und Glieder wie am Draht zu leeren Zeremonien zogen, und doch scheint es mir wieder so schwer, ganz genau die Grenze zwischen der bedeutungslosen und bedeutenden Zeremonie zu finden,—die katholische hat wirklich so viel Schönes, Seelenerhebendes,—sie könnte auch auf gebildete Geister noch immer viel wirken,—aber jetzt schlägt sie (wie unsre ganze Religion) alle Seelenkräfte, alle Erhabenheit nieder, gewöhnt zur Knechtschaft und ist die hassenswürdige Dienerin des Despotismus unsrer Verfassungen."

[33] Köpke I, 105 *f.*: "Es war doch eine schöne Einrichtung des Mittelalters, dass man dem verwirrenden Lärm der Welt entfliehen konnte! Man ging in ein Kloster und war von allen Sorgen der Welt befreit. Welche tiefe Ruhe muss es geben, einem grossen Gedanken das ganze Leben zu widmen, in ihn alle andern, die uns tausendfach quälen, versenken zu können! Ich wünschte, auch wir hätten unsere Klöster!"

[34] *Schr.* V, 441 *ff.*

[35] *Schr.* XI, xxxvii *f.*

[36] von der Leyen II, 190. Also *Schr.* XI, xxxvii.

[37] A. W. *von Schlegels sämtl. Werke* XII, 35.

[38] J. Minor in *Jb. d. Grillparzer-Gesell.* 9, 1 *ff.*

[39] *Tieck-Nachlass*, Box 7.

LUDWIG TIECK, THE GERMAN ROMANTICIST

[40] Lüdeke, *L. T. und die Brüder Schlegel*, 36.

[41] See Tieck to Göschen, Feb. 23, 1794: *Aus den Briefen der Göschensammlung des Börsenvereins der deutschen Buchhändler zu Leipzig*, Leipzig, 1918.

[42] G. A. Danton, *Tieck's Essay on the Boydell Shakespeare Gallery*, Ottendorfer Memorial Fellowship Series No. 3.

[43] Lüdeke in *Jb. der deut. Shakes.-Gesell.* 55, 1 ff.

[1] Unpubl. Original: Sächs. Landesbib., Dresden.

[2] On Nicolai see M. Sommerfeld, *Friedrich Nicolai und der Sturm und Drang*, Halle, 1921.

[3] Köpke I, 201 f. Also C. G. von Maassen in *Der Grundgescheute Antiquarius* I, Breslau, 1921, 137 ff.; and *Schr.* XI, xxxi-xxxiv and xlvi-xlviii.

[4] See note 38 in chap. 3.

[5] *Schr.* XI, xlviii: "ohne Aufwand von Elend, Jammer und Liebe einen leichten Scherz wohl zu leicht auszuführen."

[6] *Schr.* VI, xxxi.

[7] *Briefwechsel zwischen Varnhagen v. Ense u. Rahel* I, 72. Also v. Maassen, as in note 3 above.

[8] *Schr.* XI, xxxii.

[9] *Schr.* XI, xxxiv, also xxxvi: "das eine der französischen Büchelchen zog mich so viel mehr an, dass ich mir eine freiere Form erlaubte, es in Kapitel teilte und es als kleinen Roman auftreten lassen wollte. Ich hatte den Helden der Erzählung mit dem trivialen Namen Friedrich Lebrecht genannt, und als mein Verleger diese Bogen durchsah, gefiel ihm der Schwank so sehr, dass er ihn seiner Familie vorlas. Der Sohn desselben, der selbst Verleger wurde, bemächtigte sich des Büchelchens, um es selbst in die Welt zu senden, der Vater überliess es ihm, und ich musste den Vornamen Friedrich in Peter umändern, um, den Titel, nach der Meinung meiner Beschützer pikanter zu machen. So wurde das Werkchen ausgegeben, das in manchem Zirkel Glück machte, und in vielen Journalen und Kritiken jener Tage als etwas Treffliches und Vielversprechendes gelobt wurde. Es sprach freilich die mittlere Bildung vieler Menschen, die leichte Aufklärung, den mässigen Spass und die sanfte Satire aus, die man verstand und billigte. Waren doch selbst manche Freunde der Meinung, diese Art und Weise sei mein Beruf, und andre Aufgaben, die ich mir gesetzt hatte, wären zu weit vom Wahren und Natürlichen entfernt."

[10] *Schr.* XI, xxxvi.

[11] *Krit. Schr.* I, 77 ff.: pp. 87 f.: "ist ohne Zweifel in seinen einzelnen Stellen ausserordentlich schön, aber ich gestehe Ihnen, dass ich, mit aller Anstrengung, keinen eigentlichen Plan darin habe finden können. Es sind Gedanken, die sich meistenteils in recht gut gewählten Bildern gegenüberstehen, die aber nicht untereinander zusammenhängen und sich noch weniger einander erläutern: mit einem Worte, ich vermisse hier einen lyrischen und poetischen Gang, und finde nur einen prosaischen vernünftigen Zusammenhang, eine Art von Streit oder Gespräch über die Würde der Weiber und die Schwächen der Männer." p. 90: "Was sagt diese spielende unpoetische Idee?" p. 88: "Die Beiträge von Kosegarten sind überhaupt nicht vorzüglich." p. 87: "bei deren Wiege aber weder Musen

NOTES

noch Grazien lächelten." p. 94: "wenn er sie uns nur nicht in seinen widrigen Reimen vororgeln wollte!"

[12] *Nachgel. Schr.* I, 125: "Sie wissen, Gottsched vertrieb mich, weil er allein meine Rolle spielen wollte. Die Gelehrten machten gemeinschaftliche Sache mit ihm, weil ich ihnen im Wege stand. Lessing und einige andere gute Leute nahmen sich meiner zwar an, allein es half nichts; die Stimmenmehrheit war gegen sie, ich musste fort. Traurig verliess ich mein Vaterland, schweifte in der ganzen Welt umher, war Soldat, Gelehrter, Schriftsteller. . . . Jetzt hat es nun einem ganz neuen Dichter gefallen mich zurückzurufen. . . . Ach, aber leider ist es nicht mehr der ordentliche Hanswurst! Kopf und Gliedmassen sind Holz, meine Herren Kollegen sind gar von Leder!"

[13] K. Hassler, *L. Ts. Jugendroman William Lovell und der Paysan Perverti von Restif de la Bretonne*, Greifswald, 1902. Also *Schr.* VI, xvi-xviii.

[14] *Schr.* VI, 178-9.

[15] *A. W. von Schlegels sämtl. Werke* XII, 35.

[16] Thalmann and Hemmer as in note 59, chap. 2.

[17] *Schr.* VI, xiv *ff.*

[18] *Solgers Nachgel. Schr. und Briefwechsel* I, 342; Matenko, 167.

[19] R. Steig, *Achim von Arnim und die ihm nahestanden* I (Achim von Arnim und Clemens Brentano), Stuttgart, 1894, p. 41.

[20] *Studien* I, Berlin, 1839, 277 *ff.*

[21] J. O. E. Donner in *Zeitschrift für vergleichende Literaturgeschichte* 10, 1 *ff.*; and Zeydel, *L. T. and England*, 14 *ff.*

[22] *Schr.* VI, xviii.

[23] H. Nehrkorn, *Heinse und sein Einfluss auf die Romantik* (Göttingen diss.), 1904.

[24] Zeydel in *Germanic Review*, III, 4 (Oct., 1928), 295 *ff.*

[25] P. Neuburger, *Die Verseinlage in der Prosadichtung der Romantik*, Leipzig, 1924.

CHAPTER FIVE

For the Volksmährchen see B. Steiner, *L. T. und die Volksbücher*, Berlin, 1893; also R. Fürst, *Die Vorläufer der modernen Novelle im 18. Jahrhundert*, Halle, 1897.

[1] *Schr.* XV, 21: "Die gewöhnlichen Leser sollten ja nicht über jene Volks-romane spotten, die von alten Weibern auf der Strasse für einen und zwei Groschen verkauft werden, denn der gehörnte Siegfried, die Heymonskinder, Herzog Ernst und die Genovefa haben mehr wahre Erfindung, und sind ungleich reiner und besser geschrieben, als jene beliebten Modebücher. Will der Leser mir nicht auf mein Wort glauben, so mag er jene schlecht gedruckten und ver-achteten Geschichten selber nachlesen, und wenn sein Geschmack noch nicht ganz und gar zu Grunde gegangen ist, so wird er diesen vor jenen den Vorzug geben."

[2] *Schr.* XV, 22: "Ich habe nämlich ein Manuskript liegen, welches nächstens im Druck unter dem Titel Volksmährchen erscheinen wird, und welches nichts als wunderbare und abenteuerliche Geschichten enthält. Der Leser muss dies für keinen Scherz aufnehmen, sondern es ist mein vollkommener Ernst, und das Buch wird selbst nächstens bei dem Verleger dieser Erzählung herauskommen . . . Wem

daher dieses Buch nicht gefällt, der mag mit jenem zukünftigen den Versuch machen."

[3] *Schr.* XI, xxxv.

[4] See the unpublished letters of Tieck to Nicolai in the Preuss. Staatsbib., especially that of July 5, 1797.

[5] Herford, *Studies in the Literary Relations of England and Germany during the Sixteenth Century.*

[6] F. Riederer, *L. Ts. Beziehungen zur deutschen Literatur des 17. Jahrhunderts,* Greifswald (diss.), 1915.

[7] *Schr.* XIV, 149 *ff.*: "Bin ich bezaubert, rief er aus, oder haben mich meine Träume und Phantasien verrückt gemacht? Ist es die wunderbare Wirkung der Einsamkeit, dass ich mich selber nicht wieder erkenne, oder schweben Geister und Genien um mich her, die meine Sinne gefangen halten? . . . Nun klang und tönte alles, tausend schöne Stimmen redeten durch einander, Gesänge lockten sich und Töne schlangen sich um Töne, und in dem niedersinkenden Abendrote wiegten sich unzählige blaue Schmetterlinge, auf deren breiten Flügeln der Schein funkelte. . . . In der Mitte strahlte ein Pallast mit tausend und tausend Farben. . . . Alle seine Sorgen, alle seine ehemaligen Erinnerungen waren abgeschüttelt; sein Inneres tönte von den Gesängen wieder, die ihn äusserlich umgaben; alle Sehnsucht war gestillt; alle gekannten und ungekannten Wünsche in ihm waren befriedigt."

[8] *Schr.* XIV, 160: "übermenschliche Lüsternheit nach übermenschlichen Gütern, dass wir nachher in einem schwermütigen Rausche die schöne Erde mit ihren herrlichen Gaben verachten."

[9] *Schr.* XI, xli-xlvi.

[10] *A. W. von Schlegels sämtl. Werke* XII, 30.

[11] *Schr.* VI, xxii.

[12] *Schr.* IX, 8: "Man suche ja zum Besten der Aufklärung und der Menschheit den Till Eulenspiegel, die Heymonskinder, den gehörnten Siegfried und dergleichen Bücher durch andere neuere, ungemein abgeschmackte zu verdrängen."

[13] *Schr.* IX, 69.

[14] *A. W. von Schlegels sämtl. Werke* XII, 29.

[15] Goethe, *Werke,* Weimar ed. I, 146 *f.*

[16] *Schr.* X, 319 *f.*

[17] On *Magelone* see *Schr.* I, vii *f.*

[18] Lüdeke, *L. T. und die Brüder Schlegel,* 34.

[19] *O'er the sea;* music by H. W. Loomis, Wa-wan Press, Newton Center, Mass., 1902.

[20] The first three in *Gedichte* I (1821), 115 *ff.*, and in the ed. of 1841, pp. 22 *ff.*; the fourth in the former ed. II, 199, and in the latter, p. 103; the fifth only in the former, III, 88.

[21] J. F. Hausmann in *Zeitschr. f. Aesthetik u. allgem. Kunstwissenschaft* 8, 606 *ff.*

[22] *Schr.* IV, 356: "Nach zweien Tagen war Peter wieder ganz zu Kräften gekommen. Er sass mit Magelonen, ohne dass er sie kannte, vor der Tür der Hütte. Bienen und Schmetterlinge schwärmten um sie, und Peter fasste ein Zutrauen zu seiner Verpflegerin, so dass er ihr seine Geschichte und sein ganzes Unglück erzählte. Magelone stand plötzlich auf und ging in ihre Kammer, da löste sie

NOTES

ihre goldenen Locken auf und machte sie von den Banden frei, die sie bisher gehalten hatten, dann zog sie ihre köstliche Kleidung an, die sie eingeschlossen hielt, und so kam sie plötzlich wieder vor die Augen Peters. Er war vor Erstaunen ausser sich, er umarmte die wiedergefundene Geliebte, dann erzählten sie sich ihre Geschichte wieder und weinten und küssten sich, so dass man hätte ungewiss sein sollen, ob sie vor Jammer oder übergrosser Freude so herzzerbrechend schluchzten. So verging ihnen der Tag."

[23] *Schr.* IV, 359: "wenn aber eine alte Erzählung einen so herzlichen Mittelpunkt hat, der der Geschichte einen grossen und rührenden Charakter gibt, so ist es doch wohl nur die Verwöhnung einer neuern Zeit und ihre Beschränktheit, diese Schönheit ganz zu verkennen und sie mit einer willkürlichen Abänderung verbessern zu wollen, durch welche das Ganze eben so wohl Mittelpunkt als Zweck verliert."

[24] *Schr.* IV, 360: "Das alte Gedicht ist eine Verherrlichung der Liebe und frommen Demut, die neuere Erzählung ist süss freigeisterisch und ungläubig."

[25] On *Blaubart* and the other *Märchendramen* see K. G. Wendriner, *Das romantische Drama*, Berlin, 1909, and K. Brodnitz, *Die vier Märchenkomödien von L. T.*, Erlangen, 1912. See also *Schr.* I, v *ff.*, and VI, xxiii.

[26] *Schr.* V, vi.

[27] *Schr.* I, vii.

[28] Hebbel, *Briefe* IV, 295.

[29] *Solgers Nachgel. Schr. u. Briefwechsel* I, 350; Matenko, 173.

[30] J. Budde, *Zur romantischen Ironie bei L. T.*, Bonn. 1907; E. Brüggemann, *Die Ironie als entwicklungsgeschichtliches Moment*, Jena, 1909; M. Pulver, *Romantische Ironie und romantische Komödie*, St. Gallen, 1912; A. E. Lussky, *Tieck's Romantic Irony*, Chapel Hill, N.C., 1931; C. Hille, *Die deutsche Komödie unter der Einwirkung des Aristophanes*, 1907; W. Süss, *Aristophanes und die Nachwelt*, 1911.

[31] H. Gumbel in *Romantik-Forschungen*, Deutsche Vierteljahrschr. f. Literaturwiss. u. Geistesgesch. hrsg. v. P. Kluckhohn u. E. Rothacker, 16. Bd. (Buchreihe), Halle, 1929, p. 63 *ff.*

[32] Tieck's theories on "Romantic Irony" are vague and of *ex post facto* construction. In *Schr.* VI, xxvii *f.* he distinguishes between "die ganz einfache Ironie, die Umkehrung der Sache," and "die höhere Ironie," in which the poet regards his own subjective work objectively. In another place (Köpke II, 173 *f.*) he differentiates between his early "unbewusste Ironie" (*William Lovell*) and his later "bewusste Ironie" (*Der gestiefelte Kater*). He also speaks of a "höhere Ironie" in *Blaubart* and *Fortunat*.

[33] *Schr.* VI, xxviii: "jene letzte Vollendung eines poetischen Kunstwerks, die Gewähr und den höchsten Beweis der ächten Begeisterung, jenen Äthergeist, der . . . doch befriedigt und unbefangen über dem Ganzen schwebt."

[34] *Schr.* VI, xxiv: "eine geistreiche, würdige Frau."

[35] *Schr.* VI, xxv: "ein Tummelplatz für Schalkheit, Spass, seltsame Begebenheiten, ja Kritik in dieser bizarren Form und Selbstparodie des Dargestellten."

[36] *Schr.* VI, xxvi. The epitaph, *Schr.* IX, 240: "Steh, Wandersmann! Hierunter liegt die grosse Seele, die sich ganz dem Studium der Weisheit ergab, und nur den Kopf, als den edelsten Teil ihres Körpers, ausbildete."

[37] Köpke I, 210.

LUDWIG TIECK, THE GERMAN ROMANTICIST

[38] Neuburger, *op. cit.*

[39] C. G. Schütz, *Darstellung seines Lebens* . . . hrsg. v. seinem Sohne F. K. J. Schütz, II, Halle, 1835, p. 175; Hebbel, *Briefe* IV, 295; H. Steffens, *Was ich erlebte* IV, Breslau, 1841, 269 f.

[40] Zeydel, *L. T. and England*, 182 *ff.*

[41] *Schr.* XI, xlvi.

[42] On *Der gestiefelte Kater* see *Schr.* I, viii-xxi.

[43] Lüdeke, *L. T. und die Brüder Schlegel*, 144.

[44] *Schr.* VI, xxxii: "Seichtigkeit, die ohne Sinn für Tiefe und Geheimnis alles, was sie nicht fassen konnte und wollte, vor den Richterstuhl des sogenannten gesunden Menschenverstandes zog."

[45] *Schr.* I, xvi: "Alle meine Erinnerungen, was ich zu verschiedenen Zeiten im Parterre, in den Logen, oder den Salons gehört hatte, erwachten wieder, und so entstand und ward in einigen heitern Stunden dieser Kater ausgeführt. Es kam mir nicht darauf an, irgend jemand durch Bitterkeit erniedrigen zu wollen, einen Satz eigensinnig durchzufechten, oder das Bessere nur anzupreisen, sondern das, was mir als das Alberne und Abgeschmackte erschien, wurde als solches mit allen seinen Widersprüchen und lächerlichen Anmassungen hingestellt, und an einem eben so albernen aber lustigen Kindermärchen deutlich gemacht."

[46] *A. W. von Schlegels sämtliche Werke* XI, 141.

[47] See *Schr.* I, xx, and J. Wolf in *Revue Germanique* V, 158 *ff.*

[48] Holtei III, 60: "wenn Sie z.B. im gestiefelten Kater auf hiesige Theater-Anekdoten anspielen, so ist's vielleicht schon für hiesige Leser, welche unbedeutende Theater- und Parterre-Anekdoten für armselig halten, nicht interessant; was sollen denn auswärtige Leser dabei denken, welche gar nicht wissen, was sie lesen?"

[49] O. Walzel, *Friedr. Schlegels Briefe an s. Bruder Aug. Wilh.*, Berlin, 1890, p. 306.

[50] See Maync, *Immermann* II, 254 *f.*

[51] *Schr.* I, xx.

[52] *Schr.* I, xxi.

[53] *Schr.* I, xxii.

[54] Jonas-Dilthey, *Aus Schleiermachers Leben. In Briefen* I, 2. Aufl., Berlin, 1860, 219.

[55] *Achim v. Arnim u. die ihm nahestanden* III, 269.

[56] *Solgers Nachgel. Schr. u. Briefw.* I, 396; Matenko, 210.

[57] G. Schumann in *Zeitschr. f. Bücherfreunde*, N. F. 10, 104, mentions such a play in another connection.

[58] Lüdeke, *L. T. und die Brüder Schlegel*, 34.

[59] *Schr.* VI, xxxi *ff.*

[60] *Schr.* VI, xxxix.

[61] *Schr.* X, 280 *f.*

[62] M. v.Collin, *Nachgel. Gedichte*, ed. J. v.Hammer I, Vienna, 1827, xxviii.

[63] H. Rusack, *Gozzi in Germany*, New York, 1930.

[64] *Solgers Nachgel. Schr. u. Briefwechsel* I, 502; Matenko, 335. See also E. Pfeiffer, *Shakespeare und Tiecks Märchendramen*, Bonn, 1933. She concludes that

NOTES

Shakespeare's baroque art reveals romantic traits, while Tieck's Romantic art contains baroque elements.

[65] Zeydel, *L. T. and England*, 40 f.

[66] H. Todsen, *Über d. Entwickl. d. romant. Kunstmärchens*, Berlin, 1906.

[67] A. Stoll, *Der junge Savigny*, Berlin, 1927, p. 66.

CHAPTER SIX

See P. Koldewey, *Wackenroder und sein Einfluss auf Tieck*, Leipzig, 1904; J. Minor, *Tieck und Wackenroder* (Deut. Nationallit. 145); von der Leyen; H. Hartmann, *Kunst und Religion bei Wackenroder, Tieck und Solger*, Solingen, 1916; K. Brömel, *L. Ts. Kunstanschauungen im Sternbald*, Weida in Th., 1928. See also *Deutsche Literatur*: Reihe Romantik, III (Andreas Müller, Leipzig, 1931, p. 307); and H. Kern, *Schöpferische Freundschaft*, Jena, 1932.

[1] Only *Sternbald* is published among Tieck's works (*Schr.* XVI); for the other two works see von der Leyen.

[2] von der Leyen I, 23: "Die Welt sucht viel Besonderes in meinen Bildern; und wenn man mich auf dies und jenes Gute darin aufmerksam macht, so muss ich manchmal selber mein Werk mit Lächeln betrachten, dass es so wohl gelungen ist. Aber es ist wie in einem angenehmen Traum vollendet, und ich habe während der Arbeit immer mehr an den Gegenstand gedacht, als daran, wie ich ihn vorstellen möchte."

[3] *ibid.*, 25: "An ihm mögen die lehrbegierigen Jünger der Kunst ersehen, dass es nicht damit getan sei, zu einer Fahne zu schwören, nur ihre Hand in gelenkiger Führung des Pinsels zu üben, und mit einem leichten und flüchtigen After-Enthusiasmus ausgerüstet, gegen das tiefsinnige und auf das wahre Fundament gerichtete Studium zu Felde zu ziehen. Ein solches Beispiel wird sie belehren, dass der Genius der Kunst sich nicht unwillig mit der ernsthaften Minerva zusammenpaart und dass in einer grossen und offenen Seele, wenn sie auch auf Ein Hauptbestreben gerichtet ist, doch das ganze vielfach zusammengesetzte Bild menschlicher Wissenschaft sich in schöner und vollkommener Harmonie abspiegelt."

[4] *ibid.*, 69: "Die Kunst stellt uns die höchste menschliche Vollendung dar. Die Natur, so viel ein sterbliches Auge sieht, gleicht abgebrochenen Orakelsprüchen aus dem Munde der Gottheit. Ist es aber erlaubt, also von dergleichen Dingen zu reden, so möchte man vielleicht sagen, dass Gott wohl die ganze Natur oder die ganze Welt auf ähnliche Art, wie wir ein Kunstwerk, ansehen möge."

[5] *ibid.*, 82: "sind nicht darum da, dass das Auge sie sehe; sondern darum, dass man mit entgegenkommendem Herzen in sie hineingehe, und in ihnen lebe und atme."

[6] G. Stefansky, *Das hellenisch-deutsche Weltbild*, Bonn, 1925, 154.

[7] von der Leyen I, 132: "Es war, als wenn sie losgebunden vom Körper wäre, und freier umherzitterte, oder auch als wäre sein Körper mit zur Seele geworden."

[8] Tieck's letters to Perthes are unpublished. Original: Staatsarchiv, Hamburg.

[9] von der Leyen I, 297. These verses were glossed by A. W. Schlegel in his brother's *Europa* I, 78 ff.

[10] W. Miessner, *L. Ts. Lyrik*, Berlin, 1902.

LUDWIG TIECK, THE GERMAN ROMANTICIST

[11] See O. Fischer in *Archiv f. d. Studium der neueren Sprachen* 123, 1 *ff.*; H. Thummerer, *Literarisches Echo* 14, 1028 *ff.*; W. Steinert, *L. T. und das Farbenempfinden der romantischen Dichtung*, Dortmund, 1910; J. F. Hausmann in *Zeitschr. f. Ästhetik und allgemeine Kunstwissenschaft* 8, 606 *ff.*; E. von Erhardt-Siebold in *Publicats. of the Mod. Lang. Assoc. of Amer.* XLVII, 2 (June 1932); E. V. Brewer in *Germanic Review* VII, 3, p. 173; W. Hilbert, *Die Musikästhetik der Frühromantik*, 1911; and H. Goldschmidt, *Die Musikästhetik des 18. Jahrhunderts und ihre Beziehungen zu seinem Kunstschaffen*, 1915.

[12] von der Leyen I, 236: "Schon oft habe ich Dich angeredet in Gedanken und laut, Du teures Angesicht, alle meine Sorgen, meinen Jammer habe ich Dir in schönen, abergläubischen Stunden geklagt, und dann schautest Du mich an, als wenn Du mich kenntest, als wenn Du mich besser verständest, als meine Freunde, die mich umgeben. Innig hat mich schon von meiner Kindheit der Klang Deines Namens ergötzt. Was ist es, das meine Seele zu Dir Unbekannten, der mir so befreundet ist, hinzieht? Immer red' ich zu Dir wie gegenwärtig, vertraulich bin ich in Deiner Nähe, alles, was ich denke, alles, was mir begegnet, erzähl' ich Dir, wie von einem lieben Herzensfreunde, nehme ich Abschied von Dir, und lege mich zur Ruhe."

[13] *ibid.*, 18: "jene Zeit, als die bewundernde Welt noch Raphael unter sich leben sah, dessen Name nicht leicht über meine Lippen geht, ohne dass ich ihn unwillkürlich den Göttlichen nenne,—zu jener Zeit—, o wie gern gäb' ich alle Klugheit und Weisheit der späteren Jahrhunderte hin, um in jenem gewesen zu sein."

[14] See H. Prodnigg, *Über Tiecks Sternbald und sein Verhältnis zu Goethes Wilhelm Meister* (Progr. d. Oberrealschule Graz), 1892; J. O. E. Donner, *Der Einfluss Wilhelm Meisters auf den Roman der Romantiker* (Helsingfors diss.), 1893; H. Roetteken in *Zeitschr. f. vergl. Literaturgesch.* 6, 188 *ff.*; L. Marchand in *Revue Germanique* 2, 522 *ff.*; K. Brömel, *L.Ts. Kunstanschauungen im Sternbald*, Leipzig, 1928; Paula Scheideweiler, *Der Roman der deutschen Romantik*, 1916.

[15] von der Leyen I, 197.

[16] H. Nehrkorn, *Heinse und sein Einfluss auf die Romantik.*

[17] *Letters of S. T. Coleridge*, ed. by E. H. Coleridge II, 683. For the favorable opinion of Mad. de Staël and Mrs. Austin see Zeydel, *L.T. and England*, 144 and 157. Longfellow found in it a delightful "Claude Lorraine atmosphere" (J. T. Hatfield, *New Light on Longfellow*, Boston and New York, 1933, p. 176).

[18] Friedr. Gundolf, *Ludwig Tieck.*

[19] *Schr.* XVI, 335: "tastet die Göttlichkeit unserer Religion an, die wie ein wunderbares Gedicht vor uns daliegt und nun einmal keinem andern verständlich ist, als der sie versteht." "Fülle einer göttlichen Religion." "dürre vernünftige Leerheit, die alle Herzen schmachtend zurücklässt, der ewige Strom voll grosser Bilder und kollosaler Lichtgestalten trocknet aus, die dürre gleichgültige Welt bleibt zurück, und einzeln, zerstückt und mit ohnmächtigen Kämpfen muss das wieder erobert werden, was verloren ist, das Reich der Geister ist entflohen, und nur einzelne Engel kehren zurück."

[20] *ibid.*, 337: "Franz trocknete sich die Tränen ab, er unterdrückte sein Schluchzen. Es war ihm, als drängte ihn eine unsichtbare Gewalt aufzustehn, die Hand des Unbekannten zu fassen, ihm in die Arme zu stürzen und auszurufen: Nimm mich zu Deinem Bruder an! Er fühlte die Einsamkeit, die Leere in seinem

eigenen Herzen, Ludoviko sprach die Wünsche aus, die ihn so oft in stillen Stunden geängstigt hatten, er wollte seinen Klagen, seinem Jammer den freien Lauf lassen."

[21] O. Walzel, *F. Schlegels Briefe an s. Bruder A. W.*, 414.

[22] Lüdeke, *L. T. und die Brüder Schlegel*, 45.

[23] H. Petrich, *Drei Kapitel vom romantischen Stil*, Leipzig, 1878.

[24] E. Wieneke, *Caroline u. Dorothea Schlegel in Briefen*, Weimar, 1914, 125 *f.* Goethe, *Briefe* 13, 267.

[25] *Schriften der Goethe-Gesell.* 13, Weimar, 1898, 290.

[26] Goethe, *Werke*, Weimar ed. 48, 122.

[27] *Der junge Tischlermeister* I, Berlin, 1836, preface.

[28] E. Ederheimer, *J. Böhme u. d. Romantiker*, Heidelberg, 1904; W. Feilchenfeld, *Der Einfluss J. Böhmes auf Novalis*, 1922; F. Strich, *Die Mythologie in der deutschen Literatur v. Klopstock bis Wagner*, 2 vols., Halle, 1910. No definite influence of Böhme on Tieck can be proved before 1796.

[29] *Schr.* XIII, 323.

[30] *Lebenserinnerungen u. Briefwechsel v. Friedr. v. Raumer*, 2. Teil, Leipzig, 1861, 77 *ff.*

[31] von der Leyen II, 67. But in the early essay *Über das Erhabene* he is already less hostile to allegory.

[32] *Solgers Nachgel. Schr. u. Briefwechsel* I, 538 *ff.*; Matenko, 361 *ff.* Ranftl, *L. Ts. Genoveva 'als romantische Dichtung*, denies that Böhme had much influence on Tieck and minimizes the crisis caused by the mystics, which he dates after 1802. But new sources not at Ranftl's disposal, especially Tieck's letters to Friedr. Schlegel, show that the mystics did serious havoc.

[33] Vol. 56, 198.

[34] *ibid.*, 199.

[35] Lüdeke, *L. T. und die Brüder Schlegel*; also Zeydel in *Journal of Engl. and Germanic Philol.* XXVII, 1 (Jan. 1928), 16 *ff.*, and *ibid.* (July 1928), 383 *ff.*

[36] *A. W. von Schlegels sämtliche Werke* XI, 136.

[37] Walzel, *op. cit.*, 303. The quotations from Friedrich's letters to his brother which follow are all in this work. "Er ist recht kindlich ungeschickt und unschuldig im merkantilischen Teil der Schriftstellerei." "In Gesellschaften, und besonders denen, die ich kenne, ist er gern gesehen. Dass er oft wunderlich und zuweilen langweilig sein kann, ersetzt er dadurch, dass er immer bescheiden und nicht selten sehr launig ist. Er hat sich aber sehr zurückgezogen, und lebt fast ganz in dem kleinen Kreise, den er um sich gebildet hat." "an Geist und Leib gleich mager." "nichts wie ein Junge." "ein ganz gewöhnlicher und roher Mensch." "Von Charakter ist auch noch nicht ein Krümchen sichtbar, und ich fürchte, ich fürchte, bei gänzlichem Mangel an Geschick, Klugheit und Weisheit —sinkt er mit eiligen Schritten in der Klasse der jungen Halunken der deutschen Literatur, der Woltmann usw. Er hat einen kleinen Instinkt von gentlemanity und honesty, aber wie bald kann der bei einem Charakterlosen im Gedränge verloren gehen."

[38] Matenko, 279. *Lebenserinnerungen u. Briefw. v. Fr. v. Raumer* II, 169 *ff.*: "Er sah damals gutmütig auf mich herab und ehrte mit fast ausschliessender Liebe mein Talent; aber mich eigentlich zu verstehen, hielt er doch nicht der Mühe wert, und wenn ich einmal den Ansatz nahm, ihn verstehen zu wollen, so

wandelte sich Spinozism, Fichtianism, Platonism und wie es Namen haben mochte, in Geheimniskrämerei, und ich wurde freundlich ironisch abgewiesen."

[39] Lüdeke, *L. T. und die Brüder Schlegel*, 185.

[40] J. Körner, *Briefe von u. an Friedr. u. Dorothea Schlegel*, Berlin, 1926, 30: "Mit Tieck spricht man sich so einen Winter hindurch gründlich zu Ende."

[41] Walzel, *op. cit.*, 335, 346; E. Schmidt, *Caroline* I, 518; Jonas-Dilthey, *Schleiermacher* III, 304.

[42] H. Mulert, *Briefe Schleiermachers*, Berlin, 1923, 92.

[43] J. Körner in *Zeitschr. f. deut. Philologie* 56, Heft 2 u. 3 (Oct. 1931), 371.

[44] A. W. *von Schlegels sämtl. Werke* XII, 36: "Er vergesse nicht, dass alle Wirkung der Kunst einem Brennpunkte gleicht, diesseits und jenseits dessen es nicht zündet, er behalte immer ihr Höchstes vor Augen und achte sein schönes Talent genug, um nichts Geringeres leisten zu wollen, als das Beste, was er vermag. Er sammle sich, er dränge zusammen und ziehe auch die äusseren Formen vor, welche von selbst dazu nötigen."

[45] Lüdeke, *L. T. und die Brüder Schlegel*, 36.

[46] *Achim v. Arnim u. die ihm nahestanden* I, 96: "Er denkt mit Unwill daran, dass sich die Schlegel par force seiner bemächtigt hatten, und dass durch ihr verfluchtes Posaunen der stille, bescheidene Gang seiner Kunst in einem elenden Gerücht gestört wurde."

CHAPTER SEVEN

On Tieck's relation to Spanish literature see J. J. A. Bertrand, *Cervantes et le romantisme allemand*, Paris, 1914; idem, *L. T. et le théâtre espagnol*, Paris, 1914; E. Münnig, *Calderon und die ältere Romantik*, Berlin, 1912.

[1] Maria Fehling, *Briefe an Cotta*, Stuttgart, 1925. This edition is not complete, however. The present writer has used the originals of the letters, in the possession of the Cotta firm in Stuttgart.

[2] Unpubl. letter in the Preuss. Staatsbib.

[3] Unpubl. letter (July 3, 1832), Staatsarchiv, Hamburg.

[4] Zeydel in *Modern Lang. Notes* XLII, 21 ff.

[5] Zeydel in *Publicats. of the Modern Lang. Assoc. of Amer.* XLIV (Sept. 1929), 891.

[6] B. Kronacher, *Bertuchs Don Quijote-Übersetzung unter Einbeziehung der ihm nächstfolgenden Übersetzungen von Tieck und Soltau* (Munich typewr. diss.), 1924.

[7] Grillparzer, *Sämtl. Werke*. 5. Ausg. hg. v. A. Sauer, XVII, 246: "Was Cervantes mit künstlerischer Weisheit nur aus dem Hintergrunde hervorblicken lässt: die von vorneherein edle Natur und die lichten Augenblicke seines Helden, möchte Tieck in den Vordergrund stellen."

[8] A. E. Lussky in *Publicats. of the Mod. Lang. Assoc. of Amer.* XLIII, 4 (Dec. 1928), 1082 ff. Also *Schr.* I, xxviii.

[9] *Solgers Nachgel. Schr. u. Briefw.* I, 374; Matenko, 182.

[10] On the dispute which arose as to the comparative merits of Tieck's and Soltau's translations see E. Schmidt, *Caroline* II, 602.

[11] Lüdeke, *L. T. und die Brüder Schlegel*, 60. To Frommann, *Euphorion* 20 (1913), 645.

NOTES

[12] See the discussion of *Der Schwärmer* and *König Braddeck* in chap. 2 above.

[13] *Solgers Nachgel. Schr. u. Briefw.* I, 538; Matenko, 361.

[14] Lüdeke, *L. T. und die Brüder Schlegel*, 149.

[15] See B. Golz, *Pfalzgräfin Genoveva in der deutschen Dichtung*, Leipzig, 1897; J. Ranftl, *L. Ts. Genoveva als romantische Dichtung betrachtet*, Graz, 1899; also *Schr.* I, xxvi-xxxvi. The best discussion of the play is found in W. Liepe, *Das Religionsproblem im neueren Drama v. Lessing bis zur Romantik*, Halle, 1914.

[16] M. v. Collin, *Nachgelassene Gedichte*, ed. Hammer I, xxviii, rightly says that Tieck is "mehr Natur- als Kunstpoet."

[17] *Schr.* II, 235.

[18] *Achim v. Arnim u. die ihm nahestanden* I, 72, 96.

[19] Holtei II, 43; *Schr.* I, xxix; also *Krit. Schr.* IV, 157. For evidence that Tieck thought for a while of an acting version of *Genoveva* see Körner-Wieneke, 92.

[20] *Schr.* I, xxx.

[21] The first letter in *Euphorion* 20 (1913), 644; the second unpublished. Orig.: Preuss. Staatsbib.: "meine Oper, das Mährchen."

[22] R. Mezleny, *F. Hebbels Genoveva*, Berlin, 1910; L. Gorm in *Euphor.* 17, 106 *ff.*; H. Kraeger in *Euphor.* 6, 304 *ff.*; H. Seyboth, *Dramatische Technik u. Weltanschauung in Ts. Genoveva u. Maler Müllers Golo und Genoveva*, Regensburg, 1928.

[23] Jonas-Dilthey I, 247. On Friedr. Schlegel see *ibid.* III, 171.

[24] Goethe, *Werke*, Weimar ed. XXXV, 85.

[25] F. Jonas, *Schillers Briefe* VI, 60.

[26] *ibid.* VI, 167; also 88 and 235: "Er ist eine sehr graziöse, phantasiereiche und zarte Natur; nur fehlt es ihm an Kraft und an Tiefe und wird ihm stets daran fehlen. Leider hat die Schlegelsche Schule schon viel an ihm verdorben; er wird es nie ganz verwinden. Sein Geschmack ist noch unreif, er hält sich nicht gleich in seinen Werken, und es ist sogar viel Leeres darin."

[27] See e.g. *Schr.* I, xxxii, and *Solgers Nachgel. Schr. u. Briefw.* I, 501; Matenko, 334. Caroline was not convinced of this; cf. E. Schmidt, *Caroline* II, 122.

[28] F. Jonas, *Schillers Briefe* VI, 270.

[29] *ibid.* VI, 324 *f.*, and VII, 14.

[30] *Solgers Nachgel. Schr. u. Briefw.* I, 463 *ff.* (Matenko, 302 *ff.*), 465 (304): "dass diese Sinnesart nicht ganz Ihr gegenwärtiger Zustand, vielmehr dieser eine tiefe Sehnsucht nach derselben gewesen ist."

[31] *ibid.*, 502, Matenko, 335: "Es gehört zu meinen Eigenheiten, dass ich lange Jahre den Pericles von Shakesp. vielleicht übertrieben verehrt habe; ohne diesen wäre Zerbino nicht, noch weniger aber Genoveva oder Oktavian entstanden. Ich hatte mich in diese Form wie vergafft, die so wunderbar Epik und Drama verschmilzt; es schien mir möglich, selbst Lyrik hineinzuwerfen, und ich denke mit wahrem Entzücken an jene Stunden zurück, in denen Genove. und später Oktav. mir im Gemüthe aufgingen: dies Entzücken wollt' ich wohl zu körperl. buchstäbl. hineinbringen, und so entstand manches Manirirte."

[32] *Schr.* XI, lxviii *f.*: "Unglaube, seichte Aufklärung, Unphilosophie, Hass alles Heiligen, Geheimnisvollen und aller Überlieferung, galt für Protestantismus."

[33] Köpke II, 283 *f.*

[34] E. Wieneke, *Caroline u. Dor. Schlegel*, 380.

[35] *Achim v. Arnim u. die ihm nahestanden* II, 342; E. Schmidt, *Caroline*, 547, 552.

[36] Robinson, *Diary and Reminiscences* I, 195 f.

[37] The two letters to Perthes are unpubl. Original: Staatsarchiv, Hamburg.

[38] Zeydel, *L. T. and England*, 99.

[39] *Moderne Charakteristiken* II, Mannheim, 1835, 145 ff.

[40] *Achim v. Arnim u. die ihm nahestanden* I, 97.

[41] E. Schmidt, *Caroline* II, 501.

[42] Holtei I, 305: "Deine Bekanntschaft hebt ein neues Buch in meinem Leben an."

[43] E. Wieneke, *op. cit.*, 12, 305, 307; also Jonas-Dilthey III, 129 and 133.

[44] P. Lersch, *Der Traum in der deutschen Romantik*, Munich, 1923.

[45] Lüdeke, *L. t. und die Brüder Schlegel*, 70: "Wenn ich von dem Einfluss, von dem Wirken der Gestirne auf mich und mein Leben gern überzeugt bin, wenn ich die Freundschaft der Pflanzen, des Himmels und Wassers zu mir empfinde, so muss ich ja noch inniger den unmittelbarsten notwendigsten Einfluss, den Atem fühlen, den befreundete Seelen in mich ergiessen."

[46] W. Schmidt in *Euphor.* 21, 251 ff.

[47] *A. W. von Schlegels sämtl. Werke* XI, 145: "Ich habe seitdem in den geistreichsten und gebildetsten Kreisen gelebt, viele der merkwürdigsten Zeitgenossen in Deutschland und im Auslande kennen gelernt; aber jener freien und fruchtbaren Gemeinschaft der Geister in dem hoffnungstrunkenen Lebensalter wendet sich meine Erinnerung noch oft mit Sehnsucht zu."

[48] Jonas-Dilthey III, 154.

[49] Friedr. Schlegel to Schleiermacher, *ibid.* III, 188.

[50] E. Wieneke, *op. cit.*, 12.

[51] *Propyläen*, Goethe, *Werke*, Weimar ed. 47, 196.

[52] G. Waitz, *Caroline, Briefe*, II, Leipzig, 1871, 121 and 151.

[53] E. Wieneke, *op. cit.*, 127 and *passim*. Also H. Jansen, *Briefe aus dem Stolberg- und Novalis-Kreis*, Münster, 1932, 25 ff.

[54] H. Mulert, *Briefe Schleiermachers*, 104.

[55] J. G. Fichte, *Briefwechsel*, Krit. Gesamtausg. v. Hans Schulz, 2nd ed. II, Leipzig, 1930, 192.

[56] *Aus Schellings Leben in Briefen* I, Leipzig, 1869, 245, 247.

[57] *ibid.*, 265.

[58] *ibid.*, 268 f.

[59] E. Schmidt, *Caroline* II, 55 and 660 f.

[60] Matenko, 370 f., 402.

[61] G. Klee in *Euphor.* Ergh. 3, 212 ff.: "Es ist um die Kreuzschwerenot zu kriegen, mit Erlaubnis sei's gesagt, wie die Bestie sich hier benimmt . . . die andern sind wie verzaubert, das macht, weil alles eine Einzige Schweinewirtschaft ausmacht. . . . Sonst macht Schelling der Schlegel die Cour, dass es der ganzen Stadt einen Skandal gibt, die Veit dem Wilhelm S. und so alles durcheinander, und die Weiber würden sich freuen, wenn wir mit darin hineingingen, Friedrich ist allen mit der Lucinde lächerlich, wie notwendig. Diese Menschen müssten gerade alles beobachten, weil sie die Moral verachten wollen, und weil mit ihrem Benehmen auch ihre Lehre fällt und für falsch gehalten wird. . . . Es ist zu bedauern, dass diese Menschen von den göttlichsten Anlagen zu wahren Affen

durch die abgeschmackten Weiber werden, denn seid nur überzeugt, dass die Schlegel (hier Caroline) eigentlich die Ursach aller Zänkereien ist, in welche die beiden jetzt verfangen sind, und wie sie es nicht merken, weil sie nachher immer die Weibliche spielt, und es mildern will, wenn es geschehn ist; sie sind hier fast durchgängig gehasst, nun will das freilich blutwenig sagen, weil das durchgängig meist aus Pöbel besteht. . . . Wilhelm gewinnt immer mehr, je länger man ihn sieht, er ist die Gutmütigkeit selber und möchte kein Wasser betrüben, nun aber unternimmt er eine Rolle, die sie eigentlich von mir abgesehen haben, und der Wilhelm durchaus nicht gewachsen ist. . . . Friedrich war in Berlin viel liebenswürdiger, wir kommen mehr auseinander. Die Veit ist unbeschreiblich brutal: Musikkennerin, Vertraute der Schlegel, Lucinde in einer Brechpotenz, eine wahre Polychrestpille, zu allen Dingen nutze, und die Schlegel ist auch mehr listig als klug, und mehr klug als verständig, und mehr verständig als edel, und mehr edel als eine Frau: man ist mit ihr wie . . . mit einem Hermaphrodit. Dass die beiden Weiber sind, fällt einem gar nicht ein. Man könnte ordentlich Juvenalisch über diese abgeschmackten Huren werden."

[62] "recht leidliche Natur." *Briefe* 14, 135.

[63] A. Stoll, *Der junge Savigny*, 138.

[64] *Krit. Schr.* III, 37 *ff.*; IV, 142 *ff.*, 220 *ff.*, 267 *ff.*

[65] F. Jonas, *Schillers Briefe* VI, 60.

[66] *Solgers Nachgel. Schr. u. Briefw.* I, 486; Matenko, 315.

CHAPTER EIGHT

[1] *Was ich erlebte* IV, 196, 368.

[2] E. Schmidt, *Caroline* II, 50, 153, 160, 343 and 545.

[3] E. Wieneke, *op. cit.*, 312. By July 11 Tieck was no longer in Jena. See Jonas-Dilthey III, 199.

[4] To Frommann, Jan. 30, 1801. *Euphorion* 20, 1913, 643.

[5] Lüdeke, *L. T. und die Brüder Schlegel.*

[6] *Lebenserinnerungen u. Briefw. v. Fr. v. Raumer* II, 169 *ff.*; *Euphorion* Ergh. 13, 61 *ff.*; L. H. Fischer, *Aus Berlins Vergangenheit*, Berlin, 1891, 177.

[7] *A. W. von Schlegels sämtl. Werke* XI, 144.

[8] Lüdeke, *L. T. und die Brüder Schlegel*, 186.

[9] Köpke I, 265.

[10] Erich Schmidt in *Festschrift zum 8. Okt. 1892*, pp. 1 *ff.*; T. Hertel, *Über Tiecks getreuen Eckart und Tannenhäuser* (Marburg diss.), 1917.

[11] *Schr.* IV, 184: "Bist du der Herzog von Burgund? redete dieser ihn an. Worauf der Herzog mit Ja antwortete. Und du hast meinen Sohn Dietrichen hinrichten lassen? Der Herzog sagte Ja. Und auch mein jüngstes Söhnlein Conrad, rief Eckart im Schmerz, ist dir nicht zu gut gewesen, und du hast ihn auch umbringen lassen? Worauf der Herzog wieder mit Ja antwortete."

[12] *Schr.* IV, 206 *f.*: "Ich halte Wache, sprach der Alte, denn meine Gattin sitzt noch immer neben mir. Meine Sinne vergingen, ich heftete meine Augen in einen Winkel, und nach kurzer Weile regte es sich wie ein Dunst, es wallte und wogte, und die bekannte Bildung meiner Mutter zog sich sichtbarlich zusammen, die nach mir mit ernsten Mienen schaute. Ich wollte fort, ich konnte nicht, denn die mütterliche Gestalt winkte und mein Vater hielt mich fest in den Armen, welcher mir leise zuflüsterte: sie ist aus Gram um dich gestorben."

[13] C. G. Schütz, *Darstellung seines Lebens* II, 175.

[14] See note 1 to Epilog.

[15] *Schr.* XI, lvii-lix.

[16] *Schr.* II, 357.

[17] *Romantische Dichtungen* II, Jena, 1800, pp. 507 *f.*: "Da so viele prosaische Gegenstände, als Politik, Oekonomie, bis auf den Akazienbaum hinunter, ihre eigenen Zeitschriften gefunden haben, so ist es vielleicht nicht unrecht, die Poesie auch einmal an der Spitze eines Journals anzukündigen, die so oft als Lückenbüsser in den Winkeln solcher beherbergt wird, wo sie nicht hingehört. Mein Hauptzweck wird sein, meine Gedanken über Kunst und Poesie, und zwar mehr darstellend als räsonnierend zu entwickeln. Sie werden sich daher vornehmlich an die Werke der anerkannt grössten Dichter der Neueren anknüpfen, von denen meine Betrachtungen immer ausgehn und darauf zurückzukommen pflegen. So werden z.B. Briefe über Shakespeare einen stehenden Artikel in jedem Stücke ausmachen, worin ich sowohl die Resultate meines Studiums seiner dramatischen Kunst mitteilen, als mich in historische und kritische Untersuchungen einlassen werde, die über die Werke dieses unerschöpflichen und immer noch nicht genug verstandenen Geistes Licht verbreiten. Aehnliche Aufsätze über die ältere englische und deutsche und die glänzenden Perioden der spanischen und italienischen Literatur sollen damit in Verbindung gesetzt werden und nach und nach ein Gemälde der echten und modernen Poesie (nicht dessen, was so oft dafür ausgegeben ist) darstellen. Diesem werde ich durch poetische Nachbildungen und Bearbeitungen fremder, besonders spanischer und englischer Geistesprodukte, die grösste Anschaulichkeit zu geben suchen." See also Lüdeke, *L. T. und die Brüder Schlegel*, 36.

[18] *Euphorion* 21 (1914), 230 *ff.* See also E. Schmidt, *Caroline* II, 306.

[19] *Gedichte*, 1841, pp. 551 *ff.*: "Die Atmosphäre wird ein duftend Meer" (553). "Den künft'gen Glanz in Farben zu verkünden" (557).

[20] *Krit. Schr.* I, 135 *ff.*

[21] *Schr.* XIII, 267 *ff.*; also *Schr.* XI, lix-lxxvii.

[22] E. Nippold, *Ts. Einfluss auf Brentano*, Jena, 1915; E. Wieneke, 327; *Achim v. Arnim u. die ihm nahestanden* I, 23.

[23] *Achim v. Arnim u. die ihm nahestanden* I, 27.

[24] A. Stoll, *Der junge Savigny*, 231 and 252.

[25] *ibid.* I, 106.

[26] *ibid.* I, 227 and 233.

[27] *Schr.* IX, 339, and VI, liii *f.*

[28] *Schr.* XII, 155.

[29] H. Lüdeke, *L. T. und das alte englische Theater*, index *sub* "Jonson."

[30] *Gedichte* II, 1821, pp. 71 *ff.*; *Gedichte*, 1841, p. 151 *ff.* The poem "Leben" is on p. 101 of the former and on p. 166 of the latter volume and edition.

[31] Lüdeke, *L. T. und die Brüder Schlegel*, 59.

[32] *Tieck-Nachlass*, Box 11 (on the first page of the MS. of the preface to *Altenglisches Theater*). In Box 16, *ibid.*, we find rough attempts at Shakespeare's first and second sonnets.

[33] *ibid.*, Box 17.

[34] E. Schmidt, *Caroline* II, 603.

[35] Lüdeke, *L. T. und die Brüder Schlegel*, 63.

NOTES

[36] *Nachgel. Schr.* II, 37: "die er mit sich auf einer Stufe der Bildung glaubt."

[37] Wieneke, 141 ; also Jonas-Dilthey III, 129.

[38] F. Dingelstedt, *J. V. Teichmanns Literar. Nachl.*, Stuttgart, 1863, 281.

[39] *Schr.* XI, lvi.

[40] Holtei II, 47: "Ihre literarische und physische Existenz, vielleicht sogar Ihr Name, ist dem Verfasser des Chamäleons gänzlich unbekannt. Ich wohne jezt mit Ihnen an einem Orte und habe nichts von Ihnen gelesen als Ihren Sternbald und Ihre beiden Briefe an mich. Die letztern hätte ich Ihnen gern erlassen."

[41] Dingelstedt, *op. cit.*, 284 ; E. Schmidt, *Caroline* II, 603.

[42] L. H. Fischer, *op. cit.*, 94 *ff*.

[43] E. Schmidt, *op. cit.*, II, 32.

[44] *Nachgel. Schr.* I, 127.

[45] *Achim von Arnim u. die ihm nahestanden* I, 131.

[46] *Schr.* I, xxxvii.

[47] *Schr.* I, 33.

[48] *Schr.* I, xxxviii: "allegorisch, lyrisch und dramatisch."

[49] *Schr.* I, 29.

[50] E. Hügli, *Die romanischen Strophen in der Dichtung der deutschen Romantiker*, Zürich, 1901.

[51] F. Eichler, *Das Fortleben des Hans Sachs*, Leipzig, 1904.

[52] M. v. Collin, *Nachgel. Gedichte*, ed. Hammer, I, xxviii: "Tieck . . . verhält sich leidend zur Begeisterung."

[53] Lüdeke, *L. T. und die Brüder Schlegel*, 66.

[54] To Frommann, Jan. 30, 1801, *Euphorion* 20 (1913), 644.

[55] Unpubl. (Dec. 1801) ; original : Preuss. Staatsbib.: "ich muss Ihnen überhaupt gestehen, dass ich eine gewisse Vorliebe für dieses Produkt empfinde, es ist möglich, dass ich mich täusche, aber ich bin mir bewusst, immer mit Liebe gearbeitet zu haben, ich bin immer sorgfältig geblieben und habe nichts übereilt."

[56] Varnhagen von Ense, *Tagebücher* 13, Hamburg, 1870, 252.

[57] J. Körner and E. Wieneke, *A. W. und Friedr. Schlegel im Briefwechsel mit Schiller und Goethe*, Leipzig, n.d., 130: "ein unvergleichliches Werk, ganz der Gegensatz der Genoveva, nur in seiner Art vielleicht noch vollendeter und energischer." Also p. 132. Goethe, *Briefe* 16, p. 75.

[58] Friedr. Ast, *System der Kunstlehre*, 1805, p. 307: "das vollendete Beispiel der modernen Poesie."

[59] Lüdeke, *L. T. und die Brüder Schlegel*, 113.

[60] *Achim v. Arnim u. die ihm nahestanden* I, 115.

[61] *ibid.* I, 96-7 and 116. In the former place: "Es ist überhaupt sehr keck und unvorsichtig, solche ganz vollendete Naturgedichte in Reime zu bringen, ein paar Jakob Böhmische Naturansichts-Rezepte dran zu rühren und einigen Lärm über Frühling und Wald zu machen. Die Assonanzen und die affektierte altteutsche Sprache steh auch wie Stier und Esel neben einander gespannt. Einige gemeine Charaktere sind ihm dennoch vortrefflich drinnen gelungen, doch alle die Hauptpersonen, und auch *wieder* ein Hofnarr, sind sehr langweilig."

[62] *Schr.* I, xl, and XI, lxxviii.

CHAPTER NINE

[1] W. Vollmer, *Briefwechsel zwischen Schiller und Cotta*, Stuttgart, 1876, 416

LUDWIG TIECK, THE GERMAN ROMANTICIST

and 427. For the genesis of the *Musenalmanach* see Lüdeke, *L. T. und die Brüder Schlegel.*

[2] *Gedichte* I, 1821, 48-9; *Gedichte*, 1841, 486.

[3] Lüdeke, *L. T. und die Brüder Schlegel*, 107: "rechne ich zu den göttlichsten und vollendetsten Werken."

[4] *Gedichte* I, 1821, 122 *ff.*; *Gedichte*, 1841, 142 *ff.*

[5] G. H. Danton, *The Nature Sense in the Writings of L. T.*, New York, 1907; W. Donat, *Die Landschaft bei L. T. und ihre historischen Voraussetzungen*, Frankfurt, 1925; M. Greiner, *Das frühromantische Naturgefühl in d. Lyrik v. T. u. Novalis*, Leipzig, 1930.

[6] *Gedichte* II, 1821, 96; and *Gedichte*, 1841, 162.

[7] *ibid.*, 97 and 163, respectively.

[8] *ibid.*, I, 185 *ff.*, and 351, respectively.

[9] *ibid.*, 172, 234, and 376, 384, respectively.

[10] According to notes of Köpke, *Tieck-Nachlass*, Box 8. See also *Schr.* XI, lxxviii. On Jan. 14, 1826, Tieck wrote to Raumer that he began it in 1797 (Zeydel-Matenko, *Germanic Review Texts* 2, p. 34).

[11] H. Gumbel in *Romantik-Forschungen*, Halle, 1929, 63 *ff.*

[12] *Aus dem Leben Theodor von Bernhardis*, Leipzig, 1893 *f.*

[13] E. Schmidt, *Caroline* II, 546, 554-5.

[14] The information about Bernhardi's character is found in a letter of Dec. 1930, from Anna Bernhardi (a descendant), of Rehbrücke bei Potsdam, to Professor Josef Körner of Prague.

[15] The writer owes this important information to Professor Körner, who has derived it from the unpublished Schlegel-Sophie correspondence which he discovered in Coppet and elsewhere. Twenty-five letters from Schlegel to Sophie (1804-1806) are now in the Preuss. Staatsbib.

[16] See also a note on her by Varnhagen von Ense among his papers in Berlin, *sub* Tieck.

[17] A. Aubert, *Runge und die Romantik*, Berlin, 1909; S. Krebs, *P. O. Runges Entwicklung unter dem Einfluss L. Ts.*, Heidelberg, 1909; W. Roch, *P. O. Runges Kunstanschauung und ihr Verhältnis zur Frühromantik*, Strassburg, 1909; P. F. Schmidt, *Ph. O. Runge*, Leipzig, 1923; J. B. C. Grundy, *Tieck and Runge*, Strassburg, 1930.

[18] von der Leyen I, 265: "Aber dennoch regiert gleichsam in den untersten geheimsten Tiefen der Erde eine andre unsichtbare Sonne." *ibid.*, 263: "Das Pflanzenreich und das Steinreich hängt mit Seel' und Leib unmittelbar mit der alles erzeugenden Erde zusammen."

[19] *Achim v. Arnim u. die ihm nahestanden* I, 128.

[20] Zeydel, *T. and England*, 173; on *Der Runenberg* see Max Diez in *Publicats. of the Mod. Lang. Assoc.* XLVIII, 3 (Sept. 1933), 877 *ff.*

[21] *Achim v. Arnim u. die ihm nahestanden* I, 102: "der öffentliche Undank für seine Kunst."

[22] *ibid.* I, 96.

[23] See chap. 6.

[24] Lüdeke, *L. T. u. die Brüder Schlegel*, 65.

[25] H. Gumbel in *Romantik-Forschungen*, 63 *ff.*

[26] Lüdeke, *L. T. u. die Brüder Schlegel*, 149 *f.*: "ohne diesen einfältigen Glau-

NOTES

ben . . . lockt mich alles, was da ist, nur in einen ungeheuren Abgrund von Wahnsinn."

[27] M. Thalmann, *Probleme der Dämonie in L. Ts. Schriften.*

[28] Lüdeke, *L. T. u. die Brüder Schlegel*, 145.

[29] von der Leyen I, 297.

[30] *Schr.* V, 95.

[31] *Krit. Schr.* I, 187 *ff.*

[32] *ibid.*, 204: "Die Poesie war ein allgemeines Bedürfnis des Lebens und von diesem ungetrennt, daher erscheint sie so gesund und frei, und so viel Kunst und strenge Schule auch so manche Gedichte dieser Zeit verraten, so möchte man doch diese Poesie nicht Kunst nennen; sie ist gelernt, aber nicht um gelehrt zu erscheinen, die Meisterschaft verbirgt sich in der Unschuld und Liebe, der Poet ist unbesorgt um das Interesse, daher bleibt er in aller Künstlichkeit so einfältig und naiv."

[33] Lüdeke, *L. T. u. die Brüder Schlegel*, 137 *ff.* and 155.

[34] G. Richert, *Die Anfänge der romanischen Philologie u. d. deut. Romantik*, Halle, 1914; L. Schmidt in *Anzeiger der Zeitschr. f. deut. Altertum* 29, 158 *ff.* Also *Krit. Schr.* I, ix, and L. Ranke in Scherer's *J. Grimm*, 12. Also Konrad Burdach in *Sitzungsberichte der Preuss. Akad. der Wissenschaften*, 1918, 845 *ff.*

[35] Hoffmann von Fallersleben in *Weimarisches Jahrbuch* II, 224.

CHAPTER TEN

[1] *Schr. der Goethe-Gesell.* 13, Weimar, 1898, p. 293 *f.*

[2] See *Deutsche Lit.denkmale des 18. u. 19. Jhdts.*, 139, Berlin, 1907.

[3] E. Joachim and M. Klinkenborg, *Familiengesch. des Gräfl. Finck v. Finckensteinischen Geschlechts*, Berlin, 2 Teile, 1920.

[4] *Gedichte* II, 1821, 1 *ff.*; *Gedichte*, 1841, 177 *ff.*

[5] See his letter to Raumer of 1829 publ. by Zeydel and Matenko in *Germanic Review Texts* No. 2, New York, 1930, p. 18.

[6] *Achim v. Arnim u. die ihm nahestanden* I, 97.

[7] Holtei, *Dreihundert Briefe aus zwei Jahrhunderten*, 4. Teil, 99: "Er mag in der langen Einsamkeit, von Menschen umgeben, die auf seine Worte schwören, ein wunderlicher Kauz geworden sein."

[8] An eight-page fragment of Tieck's diary of this trip, from June 21 (Dresden) to July 12 (Erlangen), is in the *Tieck-Nachlass*, Box 24.

[9] Lüdeke, *L.T. und die Brüder Schlegel*, 143.

[10] E. Schmidt, *Caroline* II, 554.

[11] Tieck practically fled from his wife. *Achim v. Arnim u. die ihm nahe standen* I, 124.

[12] See *Allgem. Deut. Biogr.* 38, Leipzig, 1894, 251 *ff.*; also E. Schmidt, *Caroline* II, 663.

[13] *Gedichte* III, 1823, p. 90 *f.*

[14] Publ. by O. Fiebiger in *Deut. Rundschau*, Aug. 1918, p. 214 *ff.*

[15] *Gedichte* III, 1823, 240; *Gedichte*, 1841, 306.

[16] Five letters from Rumohr to Tieck between 1807 and 1828 are in Holtei, III, 181 *ff.* Other letters, unpublished, chiefly from Tieck to Rumohr, are in the Staats- und Universitätsbib., Hamburg. Later relations: In 1831, when Rumohr came from Lübeck to live in Dresden, their friendship deepened. Under Tieck's

influence he turned from art to literature. But this proved fatal, for jealousy set in when Rumohr began to vie with Tieck as a writer.

[17] E. Guglia in *Allgem. Zeitung*, Beil. 112, 1898; G. Fornelli in *Rivista d'Italia*, Dec. 15, 1913.

[18] Matenko 283. Zeydel-Matenko, *L.T.-Friedr. v. Raumer Letters*, p. 2.

[19] Zeydel, *T. and England*, 71.

[20] H. C. Robinson, *Diary, Reminiscences and Correspondence* I, 195 f.

[21] *Achim v. Arnim u. die ihm nahestanden* I, 192.

[22] *Gedichte* III, 1823, 98 ff.; *Gedichte*, 1841, 215 ff.; also *L. Ts. Reisegedichte* hrsg. v. Georg Witkowski, Berlin, 1925.

[23] Lüdeke, *L. T. u. die Brüder Schlegel*, 194.

[24] O. Walzel in *Euphor.* 5 (1898), 149 ff.; E. Elster, *ibid.*, 1924, 63 ff.

[25] Unpubl. (Sächs. Landesbib.): "jenes leere Ideal, welches so viele Kunstfreunde wie ein Irrlicht hinter sich herzieht, so dass sie glauben, sie könnten ohne alle Zeit, allen Glauben, alle Eigentümlichkeit in einer Schönheitsregion, einem wahrhaften Jenseit schweben und leben, und um so mehr, um so mehr sie alle Stricke und Fäden, Erinnerungen und Gefühle hinter sich abschneiden, die sie an ihre Welt und Zeit binden."

[26] *Gedichte* III, 1823, Vorwort.

[27] *ibid.*, 210; *Gedichte*, 1841, 288.

[28] *ibid.*, the former, 116 ff.; the latter, 226 ff.

[29] *ibid.*, 178; 268.

[30] *ibid.*, 161 and 189; 257 and 275.

[31] *ibid.*, 190; 275.

[32] *Solgers Nachgel. Schr. u. Briefw.* I, 488; Matenko, 316.

[33] *Gedichte*, 216; 291: "die mir verhasste dreifarbige Schleife der Weltbeherrscher."

[34] G. Klee, *Zu L. Ts. germanistischen Studien*, Progr. Bautzen, 1895; also *Achim v. Arnim u. die ihm nahestanden* I, 192.

[35] *Krit. Schr.* I, 192: "Vieles vom Ton eines epischen Zeitalters." "eine Grösse und Erhabenheit."

[36] *Tieck-Nachlass*, No. 21.

[37] *Schr.* XIII, 171 ff. Arnim secured the selection from the publisher Zimmer.

[38] *Achim v. Arnim u. die ihm nahestanden* II, 45; I, 139 and 194. Matenko, 424, 436.

[39] The best account of the trial, by Varnhagen v. Ense, is among the latter's papers in Berlin *sub* Tieck. See also J. Körner, *Briefe von u. an A. W. Schlegel*, 1930, II, 111. Quotations from the unpublished letters of Bernhardi to Varnhagen (Varnh.-Samml., Preuss. Staatsbib., *sub* Bernhardi) will be of interest: Dec. 28, 1806: "Jene Menschen sind zu niederträchtig, als dass man nur noch ein einziges [winziges?] Vertrauen auf sie haben könnte. Tieck hat nicht geantwortet, nun habe ich noch an seine Frau geschrieben. Am 4. komme ich nach Berlin und finde ich da keine Antwort, so soll alles ein andres Ansehen gewinnen. Ich kann, Gott sey mein Zeuge, gegen diese Schurken nicht anders." Feb. 2, 1807: "Er [sc. der Termin] ist aber nicht zu Stande gekommen, indem die Instruction, welche Tieck an seinen Mandatarius eingesandt hat, so weitläufig gewesen ist, dass dieser nicht hat damit zu Stande kommen können. Vorläufig weiss ich, dass diese an Niederträchtigkeit alles übertreffen soll, was

man bis jetzt er— habe. Es hat jene beliebt, mich einer Notzucht und eines Duells oder wenigstens einer Aufforderung zu beschuldigen, welche ich soll haben an den ehrlosen Schurken Carl Gregor von Knorring ergehen lassen, die dieser Nichtswürdige aber nicht angenommen haben will, weil er Edelmann sey. . . . Unter diesen Umständen sehen Sie indessen [indes ein?], dass ich Tieck sen. und junior, A. W. Schlegel und Knorring für ehrlos und niederträchtig, für Schurken und Schufte erklären muss. . . . Denn Tieck sen. ist als Mensch ein Niederträchtiger, so wie Knorring, Schlegel und meine ehemalige Frau. Rasende Verblendete und darum Schändliche und Ehrlose. . . . Tieck, der das weiss und wissen soll, was ich vorhabe und auf den Antrag, die Sache in Güte abzumachen, wie ein ehrloser Schuft geantwortet hat, thut alles, um mich daran zu hindern. Es bangt dem jämmerlichen vor der Zerstörung seiner schändlichen Pläne und vor der Publicität, indessen soll er mich nicht hindern. Er erkauft die partielle Unterdrückung durch die Rückgabe der mir gestohlenen Kinder." Feb. 13, 1807: "Noch habe ich nicht des ehrlosen Tiecks Antwort auf meine Klage erhalten. Was Sie mir über seinen Umgang mit seiner Schwester schreiben [Varnhagen had suspected Tieck and Sophie of incest] glaube ich nicht, doch daraus folgt nichts, denn nicht den hundertsten Theil dessen, was ich jetzt weiss, glaubte ich, und hätte mir dies Jemand gesagt, ich hätte mich mit ihm geschossen."

On March 27, 1807 (Preuss. Staatsbib.) Schütz offered Tieck his mediation to quash the shameful litigation.

[40] Eight letters from v. d. Hagen to T. are in Holtei I, 265 *ff.* T's. letters to him, unpublished, are in the Preuss. Staatsbib.

[41] *Achim v. Arnim u. die ihm nahestanden* III, 12; I, 251.

[42] H. Lüdeke, *L. T. u. die Brüder Schlegel*, 121 *f.*

[43] *ibid.*, 148, where he wishes that Friedr. Schlegel had collaborated.

[44] As early as Sept. 26, 1805, the painter Riepenhausen predicted that unless constantly pressed Tieck would not finish the work. See O. Fiebiger in *Deut. Rundschau*, Aug. 1918, p. 224.

[45] For the occupation of the Romanticists with the *Nibelungenlied* see J. Körner, *Nibelungenforschungen der deut. Romantik*, Leipzig, 1911. See also J. Brüggemann, *L. T. als Übersetzer*, Trier, Progr., 1908.

[46] *Tieck-Nachlass*, Box 7.

[47] *ibid.*, Box 8.

[48] *Achim v. Arnim u. die ihm nahestanden* III, 26.

[49] *Kleine Schr.* I, 61.

[50] *Achim v. Arnim u. die ihm nahestanden* III, 28: "Das Verdienst, das Gedicht wieder hervorgezogen zu haben, konnte ich unmöglich Hagen zuschreiben, da es Tieck zugehört, und ich auch dieses anerkannt habe."

[51] *Krit. Schr.* I, 192: "ein wahres Epos, eine grosse Erscheinung. . . ein vollendetes Gedicht vom grössten Umfange." "reine Erhabenheit."

[52] *Solgers Nachgel. Schr. u. Briefw.* I, 538 *ff.*; Matenko, 361 *ff.*

[53] *Achim v. Arnim u. die ihm nahestanden* I, 192 *f.*; Lüdeke, *L. T. u. die Brüder Schlegel*, 157.

[54] *Tieck-Nachlass*, Boxes 7 and 13.

[55] Two copies in the *Tieck-Nachlass*, Boxes 7 and 8.

[56] *Gedichte* II, 1823, 272; *Gedichte*, 1841, 541.

[57] *Schr.* XIII, 193.

[58] *Schr.* XI, lxxxii.

[59] In a letter to his brother Friedrich of April 9, 1818 (unpubl.: Sächs. Landesbib.). See also the letter to Friedrich of Oct. 24, 1822, in the same place.

[60] *Achim v. Arnim u. die ihm nahestanden* I, 366.

[61] Unpubl. Orig.: Cotta firm, Stuttgart.

[62] *Solgers Nachgel. Schr. u. Briefw.* I, 269; Matenko, 94.

[63] *ibid.*, 488; Matenko, 317.

[64] Lüdeke, *L. T. u. die Brüder Schlegel*, 165.

[65] *Solgers Nachgel. Schr. u. Briefw.* I, 393; Matenko, 205.

[66] *Schr.* XIV, 338: "Geht ein frischer Geist durch alle ihre Länder, und zerreisst und verbindet, was noch nie vereinigt, was seit lange nicht getrennt war: so erwachen sie wohl und huldigen nun besonnen einer neuen Gewalt, die dazu bestimmt scheint, Europa zu beherrschen. Ja, gezwungen werden sie, statt des kleinstädtischen Provinz-Eigensinnes einen europäischen grossartigen Geist in sich zu bilden. Wie viel Gut gewinnen sie also, gegen den scheinbaren Verlust armseliger Schatten."

[67] W. Herzog, *Heinr. v. Kleist*, 2. Aufl., München, 1914, p. 448.

[68] J. Körner in *Zeitschr. f. deut. Philologie* 56, 2-3 (Oct. 1931), 370.

[69] E. Schmidt, *Caroline* II, 660-1.

[70] *ibid.*, 536 and 538.

[71] Wieneke, 261; E. Schmidt, *Caroline* II, 546: "ein anmutiger und würdiger Lump." "ein blinder Passagier."

[72] *Achim v. Arnim u. die ihm nahestanden* II, 244 and *passim*; Schmidt II, 546 and 553.

[73] *Gedichte* I, 1821, 240; *Gedichte*, 1841, 426. A love note from Bettina (Preuss. Staatsbib.) must date from this time.

[74] *Achim v. Arnim u. die ihm nahestanden* II, 263. A letter from Brentano to Arnim of April 2, 1805, in a copy in the Varnhagen-Samml., Berlin, *sub* Tieck, would date this love affair earlier. But probably Varnhagen erred in writing 1805 for 1809. A love letter (Tieck to Amalie, from Sandow to Ziebingen, Nov. 6, 1806, immediately after his first trip to Munich, unpubl.: Preuss. Staatsbib.) contains no sign of a rift; cf. Schmidt II, 555.

[75] Schmidt II, 555; also Hebbel, *Tagebücher* IV, 13; and Wilh. v. Chézy, *Erinnerungen aus meinem Leben* I, Schaffhausen, p. 196.

[76] Schmidt II, 546.

[77] *Achim v. Arnim u. die ihm nahestanden* II, 244.

[78] Schmidt II, 554.

[79] *ibid.*, 546 and 662.

[80] A. Stoll, *Der junge Savigny* 392.

[81] *ibid.*, 387.

[82] Unpubl. Orig.: Staatsarchiv, Hamburg: "Als ich in München Anno 09, 10 krank lag, habe ich sehr viel Ihren Freund, den herrlichen Jacobi, gesehen, mir eine der erfreulichsten und vielleicht die reinste und edelste Erscheinung der Menschheit; seine Bekanntschaft, hauptsächlich durch sein Dasein als Mensch . . . hat wirklich Epoche in meinem Leben gemacht."

[83] *Achim v. Arnim u. d. ihm nahestanden* II, 228, 242.

[84] Matenko, 361.

NOTES

[1] T's. rendering of these two acts is in the *Tieck-Nachlass*, Box 18. It is published in *Jb. d. deut. Shakesp.-Gesell.* 55.

[2] Zeydel, *L. T. and England*, 18.

[3] Körner-Wieneke, 91: "Cromwell und Oldcastle sind unstreitig aus seiner reifsten Zeit und gehören, wie mich dünkt, zu Shakespeares vorzüglichsten Stücken. Wenn Sie an die Lektüre kommen, werden Sie über die englische Blindheit staunen."

[4] Lüdeke, *L. T. u. d. Brüder Schlegel*, 129.

[5] *Festschr. f. W. Viëtor zum 25. Dez. 1910*, Marburg, 1910, 150 *ff.*

[6] *Lebenserinn. u. Briefw. v. Friedr. v. Raumer* II, 131 *ff.*

[7] Lüdeke, *Das Buch über Shakespeare*, Halle, 1920, 404: "Im ersten wird als Einleitung vom Geiste des Mittelalters, den grossen Erscheinungen seiner Literatur und Dichtkunst gesprochen werden, dem Untergang dieser Zeit und was ihn veranlasste, welche Wendung hierauf die Geschichte und mit ihr die Kunst nahm. Boccaz in Italien, Chaucer und Gower in England an der Grenzscheide der grössten Epoche. In England um diese Zeit ein neu aufblühendes Heldenalter und Rittertum, aber ohne sonderlichen Einfluss auf die Poesie, gleichsam ein Nachsommer. Auflodern eines Heldengeistes unter Heinrich V.; dann die Vorbereitung der Bürgerkriege, indem sich in Deutschland die Reformation vorbereitet. Einfluss dieser Umwandlung, die unmittelbar in einigen Ländern alle Lebensteile durchdringt. Untergang fast aller Poesie."

[8] *Krit. Schr.* I, 268.

[9] Lüdeke, *L. T. u. d. alte engl. Theater*, 117 *f.*: "Tiecks Werk, wäre es erschienen, hätte zweifellos epochemachend gewirkt. Sehr vieles von Tiecks Wissenschaft hätte freilich der fortschreitenden Forschung nicht lange Stand gehalten. Seine Liebhabereien wären gar zu leichte Ziele der Kritik geworden. Aber die grossartige Auffassung des Ganzen, die Einstellung Shakespeares in den grossen Gang der europäischen Geistesgeschichte, die Verbindung von reichen Kenntnissen und lebhafter Phantasie, die Tieck zur Wiederbelebung von Shakespeares Welt zu Gebote stand, das feine Empfinden für die Seelenregungen des andern,' das dem Dichter gegeben ist, und das gemeine Schauspielerblut hätten dem Werk einen eignen Reiz und Wert verleihen können, den noch keine Shakespearebiographie erlangt hat. Es wäre, wenn selbst wissenschaftlich unzulänglich, in der Absicht doch eine grosse Tat gewesen, und als solche hätte sie ihre Wirkung nicht verfehlt."

[10] Hillard, *Life, Letters and Journals of George Ticknor* I, Boston, 1876, 472.

[11] *Tieck-Nachlass*, Box 24: "ganz ohne Stimmung." "ohne Stimmung." "nichts, blieb unten, melancholisch." "krank und verstimmt." "war mein Geburtstag, war melancholisch, wie immer an diesem Tage."

[12] *Schr.* I, xxxiv; O. Heuer in *Jb. d. freien deut. Hochstifts* 1904, 376 *ff.; ibid.,* 1906, 282 *ff.*

[13] Lüdeke, *L. T. u. d. Brüder Schlegel*, 53, 121; also in an unpubl. letter to Cotta of 1800.

[14] *Schr.* I, xli *ff.*

[15] The charges of Caroline and her circle that there were promiscuous relations between the sexes in Ziebingen, particularly between Tieck and three daughters of Count Finckenstein, are mere balderdash (Schmidt II, *passim*).

[16] *Achim v. Arnim u. d. ihm nahestanden* III, 471.

[17] April 9, 1818. Unpubl. Orig.: Sächs. Landesbib.

[18] *Achim v. Arnim u. d. ihm nahestanden* I, 306, and III, 242.

[19] A possible relation between this character and Goethe's Euphorion is discussed by K. Francke in *Mod. Lang. Notes* 10, 129 *ff*.

[20] Lüdeke, *L. T. u. d. Brüder Schlegel*, 166.

[21] *Achim v. Arnim u. d. ihm nahestanden* III, 253.

[22] F. Strich, *Die Mythologie in d. deut. Literatur v. Klopstock bis Wagner.*

[23] Zeydel, *L. T. and England*, 182 *ff*.

[24] See Arnim, *Werke* XXII, 126, and Köpke I, 349.

[25] *Achim v. Arnim u. die ihm nahestanden* III, 242.

[26] *Schr.* IV, 283: "Diese Geschichten gehn zu schneidend durch Mark und Bein, und ich weiss mich vor Schauder in keinen meiner Gedanken mehr zu retten. Es ist geradezu abscheulich, dergleichen zu erfinden. Ich zittre und ängstige mich und vermute, dass aus jedem Busche, aus jeder Laube ein Ungeheuer auf mich zutreten möchte, dass die teuersten, bekanntesten Gestalten sich plötzlich in fremd gespenstische Wesen verwandeln dürften."

[27] *Schr.* I, xliii.

[28] *Solgers Nachgel. Schr. u. Briefw.* I, 301; Matenko, 106: "zu viel Symmetrie und zu wenig Harmonie."

[29] *ibid.*, 295; Matenko, 101.

[30] *Achim v. Arnim u. die ihm nahestanden* III, 269.

[31] *Gedichte*, 1841, 558 *ff*.

[32] Holtei, *Dreihundert Briefe*, 4. Teil, p. 100.

[33] *Schr.* I, lxiii *f*.

[34] Lüdeke, *L. T. u. die Brüder Schlegel*, 164. A new edition of Tieck's *Frauendienst* was published by A. R. Ruhemann (Leipzig, 1885).

[35] Tieck to von der Hagen, Nov. 7, 1813 (unpubl. See Meyer u. Ernst, *Versteigerungs-Kat.* 25, Berlin, 1932), where Tieck asks for "mein Mscpt. von Dietrich, damit ich die Umbildung vollenden kann, auch meine Nibelungen, wenn Sie diese nicht mehr brauchen."

[36] Unpubl. letter. The Mohr and Brentano letters are in the Preuss. Staatsbib.; the Friedrich Tieck letter in the Sächs. Landesbib.

[37] *Tieck-Nachlass*, Box 21.

[38] *Solgers Nachgel. Schr. u. Briefw.* I, 428; Matenko, 260.

[39] *ibid.*, 322; Matenko, 143: "Gewiss giebt es doch keinen schönern Genuss, als den Umgang mit einem wahren Freunde, der in den vorzüglichsten Ansichten des Lebens und der Kunst mit uns übereinstimmt."

[40] Köpke I, 367; *Solgers Nachgel. Schr. u. Briefw.* I, 689, 704; Matenko, 486, 509.

[41] Solger I, 538 *ff.;* Matenko, 361 *ff*.

[42] Wieneke, 442.

[43] *Briefw. zwischen Karoline v. Humboldt und Rahel*, 1896, p. 104; *Rahel, Buch des Andenkens* II, 128.

[44] *Euphor.* Ergh. 13, p. 69: "sah sie täglich und verhandelte viel mit ihr, oft bis in die Nacht hinein. Ich suchte ihr immer die haltungslose Willkür ihres Wesens und ihrer Denkweise deutlich zu machen."

[45] Unpubl. letter. Orig.: British Museum: "Von wenigen Gestorbenen kann

man so gewiss sagen, dass sie nicht ganz gestorben sind, wie von Ihrem edlen Sohn, der sich der heiligsten Sache zum Opfer gebracht hat."

[46] Unpubl. letter to Helmina von Chézy. Orig.: Preuss. Staatsbib. Personally, however, he and Helmina disliked each other. See Wilh. v. Chézy, *Erinnerungen aus meinem Leben* I, 195.

[47] K. Förster, *Biographische u. literar. Skizzen*, 209.

[48] Reprinted in *Krit. Schr.* I, 325 *ff.*

CHAPTER TWELVE

The chief sources are the travel diary of Burgsdorff, preserved in the *Tieck-Nachlass* No. 23, and published by A. F. Cohn in *Zeitschr. f. Bücherfreunde*, N.F. I, 1910, 343 *ff.*; Tieck's paper *Über das englische Theater*, *Krit. Schr.* IV, 317 *ff.*; the two prefaces of *Shakespeares Vorschule;* and Sadler, *Diary, Reminiscences and Correspondence of H. C. Robinson*, Boston, 1870. See especially Zeydel, *L. T. and England*, chap. 2.

[1] In a letter of Jan. 5, 1817 (Orig.: Preuss. Staatsbib.); also *Solgers Nachgel. Schr. u. Briefw.* I, 500; Matenko, 330, 333.

[2] Letter of Feb. 27, 1817, in possession of the Cotta firm, Stuttgart.

[3] Unpubl., March 10 (Orig.: Preuss. Staatsbib.).

[4] Unpubl., Feb. 28 (Orig. *ibid.*).

[5] Cohn, *op. cit.*

[6] *Achim v. Arnim u. die ihm nahestanden* III, 387.

[7] *Krit. Schr.* IV, 330: "Langsame, klagende Rezitation."

[8] Zeydel, *op. cit.*, 58.

[9] *Krit. Schr.* IV, 347: "elende Bearbeitung dieses mächtigen Schauspiels."

[10] Zeydel, *op. cit.*, 60.

[11] *Schr.* V, 476.

[12] Original, Sächs. Landesbib.: "Es ist mit dem englischen Theater fast doch noch schlimmer wie mit dem unsrigen bestellt . . . wer besucht in London das Theater? Die Kenner nicht."

[13] Orig.: Walther de Gruyter collection, Berlin.

[14] *Mucedorus* publ. by J. Bolte, Berlin, 1893; *Nobody and Somebody, Jb. d. deut. Shakesp.-Gesell.* 29-30 (1894); *The Fair Maid of Bristol, ibid.*, 31 (1895).

[15] Robinson, *Diary* I, 195 *f.*

[16] *ibid.* I, 360 *f.*

[17] J. M. Carré in *Revue germanique* VIII, Jan. 1912, 38 *f.*

[18] Robinson, *Diary* I, 364.

[19] See the letter from Robinson to Wordsworth of July 13, 1832, in Robinson, *Diary* II, 174.

[20] Some five hundred slips containing notes on expressions occurring in Elizabethan dramas and written in Tieck's hand (*Tieck-Nachlass* Box 20) probably represent his preliminary studies in this field. A few examples will show their unfinished state: "Apple-squire, Kuppler, Honest Whore 474. Auch einer, der zur Unzucht unterhalten wird, so Hall B. IV. S. 1. Woher der Ausdruck?" "Eggs for money, sprichwörtlich. Match at Midnight 432. Winter's Tale. Aber woher?" "Catastrophe: Tickles our catastrophe: was meint dieser Ausdruck eigentlich, der um 1600 Mode war? Scheint wohl die Nase zu sein. s. Henry IV. kommt sehr oft vor."

[21] Robinson, *Diary* I, 366.

[22] I, 376.

[23] *The Life of Wm. Godwin*, by Ford K. Brown. London, Toronto, New York, 1926, p. 310.

[24] *Solgers Nachgel. Schr. u. Briefw.* I, 550 *ff.*; Matenko, 370 *ff.*: "gestern spät . . . angekommen."

[25] *Ges. Novellen* vermehrt u. verbessert. Neuer Abdr. I, Berlin, 1847, 183: "das mir wegen Shakespeare als ein Heiligtum entgegenglänzte." "denn er wollte alles in einer Stunde abgemacht wissen."

[26] See note 24.

[27] Cohn, *op. cit.*: "Tieck war von Burgsdorff sehr gehetzt."

[28] Unpubl. Orig.: Sächs. Landesbib.: "sie ging selbst für einen Gesunden zu schnell."

[29] *ibid.*: "Ich nenne ihn unglücklich, weil der Arme doch in gar keiner Art sein Leben genossen hat."

[30] "Ich aber hatte mir vorgenommen, in dieser Geburtsstadt meines Lieblings einheimisch zu werden, und, ohne dass ich es wusste, wohnte ich schon neben dem Hause, in welchem er seine Knabenzeit und ersten Jugendjahre verlebt hatte. Wie oft war ich in den niedrigen Zimmern; das ganze Haus hat im wesentlichen noch dieselbe Einrichtung wie vor dreihundert Jahren. Es ist zu verwundern, dass sich das schwache Gebäude so lange erhalten hat, da jenes grössere, in welchem er nachher eigentlich lebte, nicht mehr steht, sondern durch Baulust eines spätern Besitzers, eines Geistlichen, eingerissen ward und ein anderes sich an derselben Stelle erhoben hat. Dieses Unglück, so muss ich es nennen, hat sich erst um 1750 ereignet. Der Eigentümer muss den Dichter wenig gekannt und noch weniger geliebt und verehrt haben." "Malone, der so viele schöne Stellen durch seine Erklärungen überstrichen und überweisset, aber nicht gelichtet hat."

[31] *Ges. Nov.* V, Breslau, 1838, p. 69: "Hier lässt uns die Natur frei dichten."

[32] *ibid.* VII, Breslau, 1838, p. 213.

[33] *ibid.* V, 69.

[34] I, 377.

[35] See note 24.

[36] See Uffo Horn in *Libussa*, Jahrb. f. 1842 hg. v. P. A. Klar, Prague, 1841.

[37] Holtei, *Dreihundert Briefe aus zwei Jahrhunderten* 4. Teil, 99.

[38] O. Walzel, *Friedr. Schlegels Briefe an s. Bruder Aug. Wilh.*, Berlin, 1890, 573.

[39] Wieneke, 495.

[40] *Solgers Nachgel. Schr. u. Briefw.* I, 553: Matenko, 372: "England hat mir in manchen Hinsichten gefallen, in andren nicht, und London hat mir ganz misfallen. Wie glücklich sind wir, mein Freund, dass wir als Deutsche geboren sind und in Deutschland leben: der wahre Geist, Freiheit und Gemüt ist nur bei uns zu finden, und ist das Höchste bei uns auch selten, so ist doch die Möglichkeit dafür da, und hierin sind wir einzig glücklich, was die meisten völlig verkennen."

[41] *Krit. Schr.* I, 245: "Gewiss ist es, abgesehen von aller poetischen Vorliebe für ältere Zeit, dass old England zu den Zeiten der Elisabeth ein weit lebenslustigeres Volk, zu Witz und Scherz mehr geneigt, auferzog, als wir es jetzt dort gewahr werden. Mit der puritanischen Revolution verschwand auch

NOTES

dieses Treiben und musste einer missverstandenen Frömmigkeit Platz machen. Der alte Sinn fand sich auch nach Herstellung der königlichen Würde nicht wieder, und so wie die Insel an Macht und Reichtum zugenommen hat, so hat sich auch mit diesen eine gewisse Pedanterie des Lebens dort entwickelt, die nach und nach in trockene Gleichförmigkeit alles Individuelle aufzulösen droht."

[42] The first, a four-page letter, is preserved. Orig.: Sächs. Landesbib. See Zeydel, *op. cit.*, 89.

[43] Zeydel, *op. cit.*, 41 *ff.* and 86 *ff.*

CHAPTER THIRTEEN

[1] Unpubl. Orig.: Preuss, Staatsbib.

[2] Unpubl. Orig.: Universitätsbib. Bonn.

[3] *Solgers Nachgel. Schr. u. Briefw.* I, 622; Matenko, 428: "Wäre er nie Gutsbesitzer geworden, oder vorher nicht Jurist gewesen, so würde er gewiss einer der gebildetsten und edelsten Menschen [geworden sein]."

[4] Letter to Friedr. Tieck of April 9, 1818.

[5] Solger I, 733.

[6] *ibid.*, 775 *f.*; Matenko, 568 *f.*: "ich hatte eine unglaubliche Sehnsucht nach Dresden: ich konnte die Ankunft hier nicht erwarten; gantz auf krankhafte Weise, die mir sonst gar nicht eigen ist, so dass ich oft fürchtete, diese Spannung sei Vorbote einer schweren tödl. Krankheit. Seit ich hier bin, bin ich heiterer, als seit vielen Jahren: alles kommt mir frisch und in neuem Gewande entgegen, und, was mich am meisten erstaunt, dieselben Gegenstände entzücken mich, die mich damals bedrängten und melankolisch machten, als ich im Jahre 1801 und 2 hier wohnte, jung und gesund, aber in einer Melankolie und Lebensüberdruss versunken, die ich jezt meiner Einbildungskraft kaum vergegenwärtigen kann. So steigen auch alle meine Plane mit neuer Kraft und frischen Farben in meinem Innern auf."

[7] Wilh. v. Chézy I, 195 *f.*

[8] See *Lebenserinn. u. Briefw. v. Friedr. v. Raumer; Literar. Nachlass v. Friedr. v. Raumer;* Zeydel-Matenko, *L. T.-Friedr. v. Raumer Letters;* also Zeydel in *Publicats. of the Mod. Lang. Assoc. of Amer.* XLIII, 3 (Sept. 1928), 863 *ff.* and Marta Becker in *Deut: Rundschau 55,* 144 *ff.*

[9] P. Heidelbach, *Deutsche Dichter u. Künstler in Escheburg,* Marburg, 1913. According to his article in *Taschenbuch Penelope* (1826), Tieck had planned to collaborate with Malsburg in translating Shakespeare's sonnets.

[10] See the unpubl. letter of T. to Müller of 1820: Orig.: Sächs. Landesbib. Two letters from Müller to T. are in Holtei III, 45 *f.*

[11] W. Steinert, *L. T. und das Farbenempfinden der romantischen Dichtung;* also Zeydel in *Mod. Lang. Notes* XLIII (Feb. 1928), 73 *ff.* (here four letters from Tieck to Carus are published). For three letters of Tieck to Jean Paul (1822-1824) see *Münchener Neueste Nachrichten,* Beilage 11, 1908; another of 1822 is in *J. Pauls Blätter der Verehrung,* Munich, 1865, p. 323; two from Jean Paul to Tieck are in Holtei. On their relations see also Eduard Berend, *Jean Pauls Persönlichkeit,* Munich and Leipzig, 1913, *passim.*

[12] Wilh. v. Chézy I, 196. Also Charlotte Ernst to A. W. Schlegel, Feb. 22, 1827 (unpubl., communicated by Josef Körner, Prague).

[13] Holtei II, 275: "unerreichbar am Dichterhimmel." "Wer hinanblickt, für den sind Sie da."

[14] *ibid.* II, 303: "Sie Lieber, Guter, Herrlicher, von dem ich nicht weiss, ob ich ihn lieber liebe oder bewundere, von dem geliebt zu sein mir aber eine Seligkeit ist."

[15] *ibid.* II, 321

[16] *ibid.* II, 241: "zu dem sich sein Verfasser [d. h. ich, Loebell] mehr als zu irgend einem der lebenden hingezogen fühlt."

[17] See the letter to Rumohr of Sept. 8, 1827. Unpubl. Orig.: Staats- u. Universitätsbib., Hamburg.

[18] Holtei I, 35.

[19] According to an unpubl. letter from T. to his nephew Gustav Waagen of about 1845 (in the present writer's possession). See also R. Altenheim, *L. T. als Berater der Jugend* (Bonn typewr. diss.), 1921.

[20] See introductory bibliographical note.

[21] Zeydel, *L. T. and England.*

[22] Zeydel in *Publicats. of the Mod. Lang. Assoc. of Amer.* XLIV, No. 3 (Sept. 1929), 879 *ff.* and *ibid.* XLVI, No. 3 (Sept. 1931), 946 *f.*

[23] Köpke II, 72.

[24] *Krit. Schr.* IV, 270. See also note 1 to Epilog and Zeydel in *Mod. Lang. Notes* XLIV (1929), 179 *ff.*

[25] E. Schmidt, *Caroline* II, 538; see *ibid.*, 536: "einen ganz einzigen Genuss."

[26] *ibid.* II, 660 *f.*: "königlicher Genuss."

[27] C. G. Carus in *Raumers histor. Taschenbuch* N.F. 6, Leipzig, 1845, 195 *ff.*: H. Steffens, *Was ich erlebte* IV; A. Meissner, *Geschichte meines Lebens* I, 2. Aufl., Vienna and Teschen, 1884; Karoline Bauer, *Aus meinem Bühnenleben*, hrsg. v. A. Wellmer, Berlin, 1871, 336 *ff.*; B. G. Niebuhr, *Lebensnachrichten über B. G. Niebuhr* aus dessen Briefen I, Hamburg, 1838, p. 534; H. C. Robinson, *op. cit.*; George Ticknor, *op. cit.*

[28] Köpke II, 178 *ff.*

[29] Steffens IV, 371.

[30] K. A. Varnhagen v. Ense, *Tagebücher* XII, Hamburg, 1870, 267.

[31] H. A. Krüger, *Pseudoromantik. F. Kind u. d. Dresdner Liederkreis*, Leipzig, 1904. Also H. Fleischhauer, *Theodor Hell (Winkler) und seine Tätigkeit als Journalleiter, Herausgeber, Übersetzer und am Theater*, Borna-Leipzig, 1930.

[32] Unpubl. letter from Schulze to Tieck of Sept. 1841 (Orig.: Sächs. Landesbib.); also one from Tieck to Schulze of Dec. 1843 (Orig.: Dresd. Stadtbib.).

[33] Unpubl. Origs. mostly in Sächs. Landesbib.

[34] H. Lüdeke v. Möllendorff, *Aus Ts. Novellenzeit*, Leipzig, 1928, 102 *f.*: "Will ich denn etwa ein blödsinniger Tory sein? Habe ich es denn gegen den Liberalismus? Oder gar gegen die ächte Freiheit? Unsinn! . . . Gegen diese elenden Stellvertreter der deutschen Freiheit habe ich es allerdings, diese Rasse, die weder Freie noch Deutsche sind. Sie glauben nicht, wie viele dieser schlechten Sekte sich mir aufgedrängt haben. . . . Diese Gutzkow usw.—wie ohne Gesinnung, Talent und Wissen; ja ohne alle Erziehung, von Bildung nicht einmal zu sprechen."

[35] Holtei II, 85.

[36] Heine, Walzel ed. VII, 82, 444; II, 66; VII, 427; I, 425; VIII, 174.

NOTES

[37] J. Dresch, K. Gutzkow u. L. Wienbarg, *Die deutsche Revue* (1835), Deut. Literaturdenkm., 1904.

[38] *Krit. Schr.* II, 157: "In Kunst, Poesie und Geschichte wollte man mit Willkür alte Zeiten wiederholen, und ein Mittelalter, wie es nie war, wurde geschildert, und als Muster empfohlen, Ritterromane, kindischer als jene veralteten, drängten sich mit treuherziger Eilfertigkeit hervor, predigten süsslich ein falschpoetisches Christentum, und lehrten mit dem steifsten Ernst eine Rittertugend und Vasallenpflicht, Ergebenheit unter Herrschern und Herzogen, Minne und Treue; in Ton und Gesinnung so über allen Spass des Don Quixote hinaus, dass Scherz und Satire eben deshalb keine Handhabe an diesen Dingen fanden, um sie von den Tischen der Modegöttin herabzuwerfen. Die alte, erst verkannte und geschmähte Kunst galt nun für die einzige, das Zufällige und Ungeschickte an ihr für die höchste Vollendung. Die erneute religiöse Gesinnung artete bald in Sektengeist und Verfolgung aus, und selbst Lehrer der Wissenschaft glaubten nur fromm sein zu können, wenn sie die Wissenschaft zu vernichten suchten, so wie sich Künstler fanden, die nur begeistert zu sein vermochten, wenn sie sich von der Schönheit und den Göttergebilden der Griechen mit einem heiligen Grauen abwendeten."

[39] Köpke II, 173: "Nachher hat man mich zum Haupte einer sogenannten Romantischen Schule machen wollen. Nichts hat mir ferner gelegen als das, wie überhaupt in meinem ganzen Leben alles Parteiwesen. Dennoch hat man nicht aufgehört, gegen mich in diesem Sinne zu schreiben und zu sprechen, aber nur, weil man mich nicht kannte. Wenn man mich aufforderte, eine Definition des Romantischen zu geben, so würde ich das nicht vermögen. Ich weiss zwischen poetisch und romantisch überhaupt keinen Unterschied zu machen." On Tieck's later relation to Romanticism see R. Lieske, *Tiecks Abwendung von der Romantik* (Teildruck, Berlin diss.), 1932.

[40] Solger I, 683; Matenko, 476: "kaum eine Spur von der grossen Vernunft, die Shak. so himmlisch und ächt human macht; nichts mehr von jener grossartigen Naivetät, die ich immer am Lope bewundern muss."

[41] *ibid.*, 696; Matenko, 493 *f.*: "Calderon ist ein vollendeter Manierist und in seiner Manier gross und unverbesserlich; es scheint mir aber doch noch ungewiss, ob nicht Lope der grössere Dichter sei, wenn er vielleicht auch nur wenig oder nichts vollendet hat. Aber auch Cald. hat seine grossen Schwächen."

[42] *Lebenserinn. u. Briefw.* II, 169: "Er verehrt jetzt nur die trunkene Poesie des Calderon und der Orientalen, die im berauschten Schwulst oft so unendlich nüchtern ist. Er wirft mir vor, ich hätte den Sinn für Calderon verloren: Er den für Shakespeare, was gewiss schlimmer ist."

[43] H. Lüdeke von Möllendorf, *op. cit.*

[44] The fullest discussion of Tieck's lyrics: W. Miessner, *L. Ts. Lyrik*, Berlin, 1902.

[45] *Schr.* I, xli: "weil es meine Absicht in der Poesie am deutlichsten ausspricht."

[46] Stoll, *Der junge Savigny*, 400.

[47] Holtei III, 216, and Zeydel-Matenko, *Germanic Rev. Texts* 2, p. 9.

[48] *Briefw. zw. Ed. v. Schenk und Ludwig I v. Bayern*, hg. v. Max Spindler, Munich, 1930, 160 *f.*; 420. See also J. Weyden, *E. v. Schenk, ein bayrischer Dichter und Staatsmann*, Graz, 1932.

[49] Unpubl. See J. A. Stargardt Katalog 278, 1928.

[50] A letter of Dec. 1930, by Anna Bernhardi (a descendant of Sophie's first husband), of Rehbrücke bei Potsdam, to Professor Josef Körner of Prague quotes a letter from Agnes to Fräulein Solger of May, 1871, to this effect. This Agnes letter, together with ten others (six from Agnes to Köpke, 1853-1855; one from Agnes to Holtei, 1854; one from Agnes to Bülow, no year; and two from Holtei to Agnes, 1864) are now in the Sophie Bernhardi-Nachlass, Preuss. Staatsbib., and deal chiefly with Tieck's "Nachlass" and his collection of letters. Apparently Agnes caused much trouble and misunderstanding incident to plans for publishing what became Köpke's edition of the *Nachgelassene Schriften* and Holtei's *Briefe an Tieck*.

[51] *Liter. Nachl. v. Friedr. v. Raumer* II, 148: "Ist es nicht die Seligkeit der wahren Freundschaft, dass wir von jedem echten Freunde auf eine ganz eigene andere Art geliebt werden, wie wir jedem denn auch mit einer eigentümlichen Liebe entgegenkommen.... Wie hätte z. B. W. Schlegel die Liebe brauchen können, mit welcher ich Novalis zugetan war? Wackenroder hätte mit meinen Solgerschen Geistes-Ergüssen nichts anzufangen gewusst, und Solger hätte sich gewiss zurück-gezogen, wäre ihm eine Freundschaft wie zu Wackenroder in mir entgegenge-treten; Sie und Solger sind sich verwandt, und doch lebe ich verschieden mit beiden. Diese notwendige, fast kunstmässige Verschiedenheit des Betragens wird von den Menschen zu wenig beachtet. Je mehr wahre Freunde der Mensch hat, je reicher gestaltet und entwickelt er sich."

[52] *Solger, Nachgel. Schr. u. Briefw.* I, 480; Matenko, 311.

[53] Lüdeke, *L. T. u. d. Brüder Schlegel*, 148.

[54] *Lebenserinn. u. Briefw.* II, 77: "Könnte ich doch nur Ihren oder unseres Solgers stetigen und ruhigen Fleiss gewinnen: allein seit meiner frühen Jugend ist dies eins meiner grössten Leiden, dass ich nur selten meiner Laune gebieten kann, in Träumen, Planen, Wünschen und oft unfruchtbaren Studien lebe, und dann plötzlich wie im Sturme und dann zu viel und zu schnell arbeite. Wenn Sie einen Sohn haben, erziehen Sie ihn zur Ordnung. Aber es hilft auch nicht immer; denn bei mir ist von der Seite meiner Eltern und Vorgesetzten das Hinlängliche geschehen, und doch ist es der Mangel dieser Fähigkeit, welcher mir so oft mein Leben am meisten verkümmert hat."

[55] Lüdeke, 147: "dass meine Heftigkeit mich in jedem Gedanken, in jeder Empfindung, in allen Entwicklungen bis an die Grenze des Wahnsinns reisst."

[56] *ibid.*, 142.

[57] *ibid.*, 143.

[58] *ibid.*, 145; "dergleichen inhaltleere und geschäftslose Briefe ... wie ich sie einzig nur schreiben kann und mag."

[59] *ibid.*, 148: "zage und bange."

[60] *ibid.*, 99: "für meine Werke sorgsamer."

[61] *Lebenserinn. u. Briefw.* II, 140 *ff.*: "Und warum ist so vieles und vielleicht das beste unterblieben? Wären es grosse eigentliche Schicksale, so könnte ich doch beruhigter sein: nein, Launen, Verwöhnungen, Aufschieben, Trägheit, Lust am Lesen, Schwelgen im Geist, Übermut im Projektieren, Spielen mit dem Leben, und hauptsächlich jener verächtliche Kleinmut, von dem Sie gar keine Vor-stellung haben, der mich immer wieder dahin bringt, mich und mein Leben auf Zeiten so platt hinfallen zu lassen."

[62] Lüdeke, 182: "ich . . . lese viel zu viel."

[63] *ibid.*, 82.

[64] *ibid.*, 165.

[65] *ibid.*, 146: "Es war mir von je an natürlich, ohne Schmerzen, ohne Unglück, ohne äusserliche Veranlassung das Leben selbst als eine drückende Bürde anzusehn."

[66] *ibid.*, 147; also Solger I, 541; Matenko, 363 *f*.

[67] Lüdeke, 176: "Schmerz und Leiden war eigentlich mein Lebenslauf."

[68] *ibid.*, 171: "Seit dem Jahr 1805 ist mein Gesundheits-Zustand so, dass ich fast immer zu klagen Ursach habe."

[69] *ibid.*, 145: "ja, ich möchte fast lieber sagen, in einem zeitlosen Zustande . . . fast in der schönen Einsamkeit eines Klosters."

[70] *ibid.*, 147.

[71] *ibid.*, 166.

[72] In the early unpubl. drama *König Braddeck*. See chap. 2.

[73] In *Blaubart*. See chap. 9.

[74] Lüdeke, 146.

[75] *Literar. Nachl. v. Friedr. v. Raumer* II, 173.

[76] Lüdeke, 53: "Wenn wir doch das Geld abschaffen könnten! Es drückt mich beständig, dass ich dafür arbeite."

[77] Zeydel, *L. T. and England*, 128 *ff*.

[78] Varnhagen v. Ense, *Tagebücher* XII, 280; also Varnhagen-Samml. *sub* Tieck.

[79] Lüdeke, 144.

[80] *ibid.*, 176: "Ich begreife andre Menschen nicht, die ihre Freunde wie ein Kleid wieder aufgeben oder vergessen können."

[81] *Literar. Nachl. v. Friedr. v. Raumer* II, 173.

[82] H. Jansen, *Briefe aus dem Stolberg- und Novalis-Kreis*. See also Josef Körner in *Preuss. Jahrbücher*, July 1933.

[83] E. Schmidt, *Caroline* II, *passim*.

[84] Wilh. v. Chézy, *Erinnerungen aus meinem Leben* I, 196.

[85] Sybel, *Erinnerungen an Friedr. v. Üchtritz u. seine Zeit*, 217 *ff*. Also F. Binder, *Luise Hensel*, Freiburg i. B., 1885, 310 *f*. But cf. a very friendly letter from Amalie to Henriette, June 27, 1828 (Preuss. Staatsbib.).

[86] This letter (unpubl., Preuss. Staatsbib.) is most personal, containing expressions like "ich küsse jede Zeile, jedes Wort von Deinen Händen, jeden Ausdruck, jede Spur Deines Daseins . . . ich kenne keinen andren Gedanken als nur Dich. . . . Du bist meine Seele." It is superscribed "An Alma"; perhaps he planned to use it for his novel by that name.

[87] Solger I, 538; Matenko, 361 *ff*.

[88] Lüdeke, 149.

[89] *ibid.*, 147: "Denn nichts habe ich von je an weniger begreifen können, als die Gleichgültigkeit der Menschen, die von Wundern allseitig umgeben, von Geistern und Erscheinungen umringt, den Einfluss, das ewige Sein aller magischen Kräfte fühlen, sich aber mit Zweifeln bedecken, und doch nicht ganz ihrem Zweifel sich zu eigen ergeben, die das Geheimnis verlieren, und auch kein Entgegengesetztes, kein Nichtgeheimnis gewinnen."

[90] *Literar. Nachl. v. Friedr. v. Raumer* II, 154 *f*.

[91] Unpubl. Orig.: Walther de Gruyter collection, Berlin: "meine Autorität und möglichen Einfluss auf mein Zeitalter."

CHAPTER FOURTEEN

[1] *Krit. Schr.* III, 5 *ff.* On this chapter generally see H. Bischoff, *L. T. als Dramaturg*, Brussels, 1897; H. Günther, *Romantische Kritik und Satire bei L. T.*, Leipzig, 1907; and O. Weissert, *L. T. als Kritiker d. Dramas u. Theaters*, Munich, 1928.

[2] *Krit. Schr.* III, 11 *ff.*: "die Aufführung so korrekt und präzis...wie ich noch keine gesehen habe."

[3] D. Salomon, Berlin, Katalog 55, 1931.

[4] *Krit. Schr.* II, 3 *ff.* When in proof, I heard of Professor Minde-Pouet finding a MS. of this essay in W. v. Schütz's hand. A *copy* of T's original?

[5] p. 671 *ff.*

[6] Unpubl. letter to Friedr. Tieck of Nov. 22, 1819.

[7] M. Beer, *Briefw.* hg. durch Ed. v. Schenk, 1837, p. 45.

[8] Holtei II, 245.

[9] See *Baltische Monatsschrift* 41. Jahrg XLVII, April 1899.

[10] *Lebenserinn. u. Briefw.* II, 77 *ff.*

[11] Köpke II, 188 *f.* See also note 9 to chap. 1.

[12] Unpubl. Orig.: Universitätsbib., Leipzig.

[13] K. Freye in *Zeitschr. f. Bücherfreunde* N.F. 4, 247 *ff.*

[14] *Krit. Schr.* III, 37 *ff.* (the M.S. of this paper, in the *Tieck-Nachlass*, Box 11, is dated Jan. 12 and 13, 1823); *Krit. Schr.* IV, 142 *ff.* (the M.S., *ibid.*, Box 11); *Krit. Schr.* IV, 267 *ff.* (the M.S., *ibid.*, Box 11).

[15] *Krit. Schr.* IV, 203 *f.*

[16] *ibid.* III, 39.

[17] *ibid.* IV, 149.

[18] *ibid.* IV, 204 *f.*

[19] *ibid.* III, 39 *ff.*

[20] *ibid.* IV, 149.

[21] *ibid.* III, 52, 59.

[22] *ibid.* IV, 208.

[23] *ibid.* IV, 149 *f.*

[24] *ibid.* III, 54.

[25] *ibid.* IV, 149 *ff.*

[26] *ibid.* IV, 210: "Wie sehr Schiller immer mehr das eigentliche Drama in seiner Jungfrau auflöste, noch mehr in den feindlichen Brüdern, es ebenfalls im Tell ganz in Rede, Gesinnung, Situation verwandelte." "niemals so schwach und ungenügend, dem Drama so völlig widersprechend . . . unsere Bühne aus allen Fugen."

[27] *ibid.* IV, 150: "mit kaltem Prunk."

[28] *ibid.* IV, 150 *ff.*; 267 *ff.*

[29] *ibid.* III, 40 *ff.*; IV, 210.

[30] *ibid.* III, 40: "der Dichter der Nation."

[31] *ibid.* IV, 157: "Dass es nicht meine Absicht sei, den auch von mir verehrten Dichter zu schmähen, füge ich kaum hinzu, denn wer mich und mein Bestreben so verkennen kann, sollte sich billig um meine Erörterungen nicht kümmern. Dass der Götzendienst mit Schillers Werken (wie jeder Götzendienst) unserer

NOTES

Literatur grossen Schaden getan hat, ist von Verständigen längst anerkannt und ausgesprochen worden."

[32] To Raumer in 1829. Zeydel-Matenko, p. 18.

[33] Köpke II, 193 *ff*.

[34] H. v. Sybel, *Erinnerungen an Friedr. v. Üchtritz u. s. Zeit*, 147 *ff*. Also Holtei IV, 104 *ff*.

[35] v. Sybel, 156 *ff*.

[36] *Krit. Schr.* IV, 98 *ff*.

[37] Holtei IV, 109.

[38] *Krit. Schr.* II, 315 *ff*.

[39] *ibid.*, 374: "die neuere sophistisierende, die Iffland hervorbrachte."

[40] M. Breuer, *Sophie Bernhardi geb. Tieck als romantische Dichterin* (Tübingen diss.), 1915.

[41] Lüdeke v. Möllendorff, *Aus Ts. Novellenzeit*, 121: "das schönste und reifste, was seit langer Zeit erschienen ist."

[42] Unpubl. letter of Nov. 5, 1836 (orig.: Preuss. Staatsbib.): "Gemüt, Liebe, Gesinnung, edelster Menschensinn, Wohlwollen, Reinheit, Tiefsinn, Beobachtung, milder Schmerz."

[43] See *Blätter für literar. Unterhaltung*, July 14, 1837.

[44] *Tieck-Nachlass*, Box 39.

[45] Unpubl. letter dated Feb. 26, 1839 (Orig.: Lehrbücherei d. Stadtgymnasiums, Linz, Austria).

[46] *Krit. Schr.* II, 391 *ff*.

[47] *ibid.* II, 397: "mit grösserm Vertrauen."

[48] J. Wetzel, *Adelheid Reinbold, die Schülerin Ts.*, Leipzig, 1911.

[49] *Krit. Schr.* IV, 270.

[50] Unpubl. Origs. mostly: Sächs. Landesbib.

[51] To Brockhaus on Feb. 3, 1852. Lüdeke v. Möllendorff, *Aus Ts. Novellenzeit*, 187: "Es ist das einzige Mal in meinem Leben, wo Freundschaft zu einem Autor und dessen Liebenswürdigkeit mich bestochen haben, ein zu günstiges Urteil über ihn zu fällen."

[52] *Tieck-Nachlass*, Box 18: "eine Tragödie, eine gute, wenn auch nicht die beste, wenn auch keine vollendete."

[53] See Prölss, *Geschichte des Hoftheaters in Dresden*, Dresden, 1877. For a general picture of theatrical conditions at the time see L. Wolff, *Almanach f. Freunde der Schauspielkunst*, and Martersteig, *Das deutsche Theater im 19. Jahrhundert*, 1904.

[54] Lüdeke v. Möllendorff, 47.

[55] *Krit. Schr.* III.

[56] *ibid.* III, 217: "Kritik wäre also bei diesen und ähnlichen Produkten verschwendet."

[57] *Krit. Schr.* IV, 3-98.

[58] Unpubl. Orig.: Preuss. Staatsbib. and Sächs. Landesbib.

[59] E. Devrient, *Geschichte d. deut. Schauspielkunst* V, Leipzig, 1874, 115.

[60] Hillard, *Life, Letters and Journals of George Ticknor* I, 469.

[61] Unpubl.: Sächs. Landesbib.

[62] According to unpubl. letters of Charlotte Ernst to A. W. Schlegel. Professor J. Körner of Prague has given this information.

⁶³ A. Stern in *Goethe-Jb.* 21, 173 *ff.*, and H. Brandt, *Gs. Faust auf der kgl. sächs. Hofbühne zu Dresden*, Berlin, 1921.

⁶⁴ Unpubl. letter of Dec. 10, 1825 (Preuss. Staatsbib.).

⁶⁵ Unpubl.: Preuss. Staatsbib.

⁶⁶ *Krit. Schr.* IV, 4 *ff.* and 72 *ff.* Grillparzer (*Tageb.* I, 120) ridicules the topics discussed by Tieck, suggesting as another: "Ob der Geist im Hamlet in einem geblümten oder gestreiften Schlafrock darzustellen sei."

⁶⁷ *ibid.* IV, 37 *ff.* and 79 *ff.*

⁶⁸ *ibid.* IV, 109 *ff.*

⁶⁹ *ibid.* IV, 132 *ff.*: "man muss beklagen, dass Autoren wie Castelli und T. Hell, die doch schon Besseres geleistet, mit diesen Übertragungen ihre Zeit verlieren und die flüchtigen Arbeiten nachher noch mit ihrem Namen drucken lassen."

⁷⁰ *ibid.* IV, 142 *ff.*: "Können wir nicht Shakespeare zum Grundstein unserer Bühne brauchen, Goethe, Schröder, Schiller, manche von den Tadelnswürdigen hinzufügend, Engländer, Italiener, Franzosen und selbst Spanier, aber mit Auswahl und besonnener Kritik, nutzen, so wird die Verirrung immer wilder und in schnelleren Verhältnissen sich steigern, und jedermann wird einsehen, dass wir Deutschen, mag unsere Literatur auch merkwürdig sein, doch keines eigentlichen Theaters bedürfen."

⁷¹ *Krit. Schr.* IV, 217 *ff.*

⁷² II, 384 *f.* Goethe's words: "Bei ihm ruht das Urteil auf dem Genuss, der Genuss auf der Kenntnis."

⁷³ Solger I, 538 *ff.*

⁷⁴ *ibid.*, 623.

⁷⁵ *Krit. Schr.* I, 240 *ff.*

⁷⁶ *ibid.* I, 242: "weil es diese Versuche sind, die das Volk und die nachfolgenden Schriftsteller stimmten, denen der grosse Dichter sich anschloss, indem er sie nachahmte, und welche seit mehr als zwei Jahrhunderten, ungeachtet mancher Widersprüche und vielfacher späterer Entartung, das begründet und ausgebildet haben, was wir die englische Schule der dramatischen Kunst nennen müssen; eine Schule und Form, die, wie ich schon sonst behauptet habe, sich uns Deutschen ebenfalls aneignet und uns die natürlichste ist, im Gegensatz des später ausgebildeten und beschränkten französischen oder spanischen Theaters."

⁷⁷ See note 14 to chap. 12.

⁷⁸ Lüdeke v. Möllendorff, 8 *ff.* In 1823-1824 Tieck also worked on a translation of *Six Old English Plays*. See Adolf Wagner to Tieck, Jan. 12, 1824 (Sächs. Landesbib.).

⁷⁹ M. Fehling, *Briefe an Cotta* I, 253. Tieck's letters to Cotta, some unpublished, are owned by the Cotta firm in Stuttgart. Tieck's relations to Cotta deserve some comment. In 1800, a year after the break with Nicolai, Tieck was introduced to Johann Friedrich Cotta by Fichte, who wrote a strong, enthusiastic letter recommending Tieck as a promising author. Cotta got in touch with Tieck, magnanimously giving the impecunious writer an advance of one hundred talers. Tieck sent Cotta a list of projects, among them a series of historical and classical dramas, the work on the Spanish theater, and the "dramatic novel" *Die Gartenwochen* (which became *Phantasus*). But to carry out this ambitious program, he asked for an annual salary of eight hundred talers for three years. Cotta did not comply. The only works of Tieck which he published were the Schlegel-Tieck

Musenalmanach of 1802, the version of *Frauendienst* (1812) and *Vier Schau-spiele von Shakespeare* (1836). Cotta wished Tieck to contribute to the literary and artistic supplements of his *Morgenblatt* and, in 1832, to write a biography of Goethe. Tieck wanted Cotta to publish an edition of his collected works down to 1819. In 1817 Tieck suggested a "Musenalmanach" to Cotta (Goethe, *Briefe* 28, 245). It is surprising that in almost every letter to Cotta Tieck, usually careless in pecuniary matters, referred to Cotta's one hundred taler gratuity of 1800 as "jene alte Schuld."

[80] H. Meisner and E. Schmidt, *Briefe an W. Menzel*, Berlin, 1908.

[81] Grillparzer, *Werke*, Sauer ed., XVIII, 81.

[82] *Krit. Schr.* III, 171 *ff.* and 226 *ff.*

[83] *Tieck-Nachlass*, Box 12. See *Nachgel. Schr.* II, 154 *ff.*

[84] The "Nachlass" contains a sketch by Tieck of the second sonnet (Box 16) and his almost finished rendering of the eighteenth (Box 11).

[85] *Tieck-Nachlass*, Box 17.

[86] Unpubl.: Goethe-Museum, Frankfurt.

[87] Zeydel, *L. T. and England*, 17 *ff.*, 22 *ff.* W. Schulz in *Zeitschr. f. deut. Phil.* 59, pp. 52 *ff.* studies the diaries of Baudissin and his part in the work. He finds that B. has been underestimated. The latter bore the brunt of the labors for the second edition (1839-1840).

[88] G. Hille in *Neues Archiv f. Theatergesch.* I, Berlin, 1929.

[89] See J. Petersen, *ibid.*, II, 176 *ff.*

[90] The last has not been printed. The rest are all in *Krit. Schr.* III.

CHAPTER FIFTEEN

[1] Lüdeke, *L. T. u. d. Brüder Schlegel*, 200.

[2] Köpke II, 202 *ff.*

[3] Lüdeke, *op. cit.*, 164, 169: "den ich für einen vollständigen Maniristen halte." "Widerschein von Widerschein, Hörensagen von einem gewissen fernen Hören-sagen." "Ich habe überhaupt keine Freude an allen den Sachen, die wir veran-lasst haben." Also Raich, *Dorothea v. Schlegel* II, Mainz, 1881, 277 *f.*

[4] Köpke II, 206. Also *Lebenserinn. u. Briefw. v. Friedr. v. Raumer* II, 298. In the former place: "ein kleines unruhiges Männchen mit dem beweglichsten Mienenspiel und stechenden Augen. Er hatte etwas Unheimliches, und fürchtete sich zuletzt selbst vor seinen eignen Gespenstern."

[5] To F. A. Schulze, Dec. 21, 1843 (unpubl.: Dresd. Stadtbib.). Tieck was not alone in his condemnation. Jean Paul told Rellstab in 1823 that he greeted Tieck's "novellen" as a quiet, artistic counterpart to Hoffmann's blatancy.

[6] *Ges. Novellen* II, 113: "eine schreckliche Angst ergreift uns, wenn so das Leben und alles, was den Inhalt desselben ausmachen kann, auf eine unsinnige Spitze hinaufgetrieben wird, um das als das Vergänglichste und Aberwitzigste hinzustellen, was als das Festeste und Notwendigste uns immerdar trösten und beruhigen muss."

[7] *Krit. Schr.* III, 205: "jenes [Volk], welches durch ein Buch die lästige Zeit vertreiben will. Und freilich erheben sich viele nicht höher, als dass sie über-zeugt bleiben, die Künste seien nur dazu erfunden und ausgebildet. Diesen muss ein solcher Autor willkommen sein."

[8] *ibid.* III, 217: "die Unnatur, die groben Widersprüche, den Mangel an Charakter und Zusammenhang."

[9] *Schr.* XI, lxxxiv-xc; also Friesen II, 312 *ff.* In the former place, p. lxxxvi: "Eine Begebenheit sollte anders vorgetragen werden als eine Erzählung, diese sich von Geschichte unterscheiden." "dass sie einen grossen oder kleinern Vorfall ins hellste Licht stelle, der, so leicht er sich ereignen kann, doch wunderbar, vielleicht einzig ist."

[10] Received Oct. 24, 1822. Unpubl.: Sächs. Landesbib.

[11] W. Greiner, *Die ersten Novellen Otto Ludwigs u. ihr Verhältnis zu L. T.* (Jena diss.), 1903.

[12] Solger I, 695; Matenko, 493: "ich habe in jeder Kunst einen Wendepunkt des Hasses, der mir unentbehrlich ist, um meine Liebe zu stützen."

[13] To Eduard Devrient, 1838. Unpubl. Orig.: Preuss. Staatsbib.

[14] *Schr.* XI, lxxxix *f.*: "Strebt die Tragödie durch Mitleid, Furcht, Leidenschaft und Begeisterung uns in himmlischer Trunkenheit auf den Gipfel des Olymp zu heben, um von klarer Höhe das Treiben der Menschen und den Irrgang ihres Schicksals mit erhabenem Mitleid zu sehn und zu verstehn; führt uns der Roman der Wahlverwandtschaften in die Labyrinthe des Herzens, als Tragödie des Familienlebens und der neuesten Zeit; so kann die Novelle zuweilen auf ihrem Standpunkt die Widersprüche des Lebens lösen, die Launen des Schicksals erklären, den Wahnsinn der Leidenschaft verspotten, und manche Rätsel des Herzens, der Menschentorheit in ihre künstlichen Gewebe hineinbilden, dass der lichter gewordene Blick auch hier im Lachen oder in Wehmut, das Menschliche, und im Verwerflichen eine höhere ausgleichende Wahrheit erkennt."

[15] J. A. Spaulding in *Journal of Engl. and Germanic Philol.* 21, 259 *ff.*

[16] Biedermeier was a comical figure in the poems which Ludwig Eichrodt published in the *Fliegende Blätter* in 1855. For a characterization of the age see G. Hermann, *Das Biedermeier im Spiegel seiner Zeit*, 1913; and H. H. Houben, *Der gefesselte Biedermeier*, 1924.

[17] *Krit. Schr.* II, 377 *ff.*

[18] To Josef Max. Unpubl. Orig. Preuss. Staatsbib.: "mir selbst wäre dies auch vielleicht bequemer gewesen, als den Gegenstand jedesmal so in die Kürze zu fassen." See also Lüdeke v. Möllendorff, 100.

[19] Hebbel, *Briefe* V, 253.

[20] *Schr.* XI, lxxxiv.

[21] Köpke II, 234: "Es ist nicht leicht zu sagen, was eigentlich die Novelle sei, und wie sie sich von den verwandten Gattungen, Roman und Erzählung, unterscheide. . . . Es ist zu viel, wenn man geradezu sagt, die Novelle müsse eine ausgesprochene Tendenz haben, aber doch erwartet man in ihr etwas Hervorspringendes, eine Spitze, in der man sich wiederfindet. Wenn ich meine Novellen übersehe, so muss ich sagen, ein grosser Teil davon hat eine solche Spitze; aber andere wieder nicht. . . . Man wird die scharfe, epigrammatische Pointe auch nicht zu sehr herausheben dürfen; dann würde etwa auch Wilhelm Meister eine Novelle sein, und die Wahlverwandtschaften gewiss, in denen eine so entschiedene Tendenz liegt. . . . Es ist sehr schwer, hier einen allgemeinen Begriff zu finden, auf den sich alle Erscheinungen dieser Art zurückbringen liessen." See Wendt to Tieck, Feb. 12, 1823 (Sächs. Landesbib.) for a trenchant critique of the early "novellen."

NOTES

[22] Adolf Stern, *Zur Literatur der Gegenwart. Studien.* Leipzig, 1880, pp. 1 *ff.*: "Gute Erziehung, Feinheit des Betragens ist mir immer das notwendige Element gewesen, um nur zum Bewusstsein zu kommen, dass ich eine Seele im Leibe habe."

[23] F. Th. Vischer, *Auch einer* II, 1902, p. 242.

[24] Hebbel, *Briefe* V, 304.

[25] M. Schaum, *Das Kunstgespräch in Ts. Novellen,* Giessen, 1925.

[26] Lüdeke v. Möllendorff, *Aus Ts. Novellenzeit,* 63.

[27] Oct. 23, 1823. Unpubl.: Sächs. Landesbib.: "Ist denn nicht alles echte Komponieren eine Wiederkehr und Belebung der Gegenwart und Wirklichkeit? Nur muss es freilich nicht auf die flache Weise geschehn."

[28] Goedeke's *Grundriss* does not record these reprints.

[29] For the sparse published letters of Tieck to Max see Geyder in *Deutsches Museum* v. Prutz, 1864, No. 25, 890 *ff.*, and Günther in *Euphor.* 21, 230 *ff.* The majority of Tieck's important letters to Max are unpublished (Preuss. Staatsbib.)

[30] H. Lüdeke v. Möllendorff, *Aus Ts. Novellenzeit.* For additional letters see Zeydel, *Germanic Review* V, 2 (April 1930), 193 *ff.*

[31] Only three letters from Tieck to Reimer have been published. See Zeydel, *Journal of Engl. and Germanic Philol.* 28, Jan. 1929, No. 1, p. 80. The originals of some seventy others, mostly of importance, are to a great extent owned by the publisher Walther de Gruyter, Berlin. On Tieck's original plans for his *Schriften* see his letter to Raumer of Nov. 19, 1824 (Zeydel-Matenko, *Germanic Review Texts* 2, p. 31).

CHAPTER SIXTEEN

[1] J. L. Hoffmann, *L. T., eine literarische Skizze.* Album d. literar. Vereins in Nürnberg f. 1856. 180 pp.

[2] J. Minor, *T. als Novellendichter.* Akadem. Blätter hrsg. v. Otto Sievers, Braunschweig, 1884, pp. 129-61 and 193-220.

[3] *Achim v. Arnim u. d. ihm nahestanden* III, 519.

[4] To Varnhagen v. Ense, June 26, 1836 (unpubl. orig.: Preuss. Staatsbib.).

[5] A. F. v. Schack, *Ein halbes Jahrhundert* I, Stuttgart and Leipzig, 1888, 321.

[6] Zeydel, *L. T. and England,* 182, 196.

[7] This correspondence is unpublished: Histor. Archiv d. Stadt Köln.

[8] Letter of 1815.

[9] To Friedr. Tieck, Oct. 23, 1823. Unpubl.: Sächs. Landesbib.

[10] J. J. A. Bertrand, *L. T. et le théâtre espagnol.*

[11] In *Oeuvres complètes de L. Tieck.* 2me livraison. Contes lunatiques: I, La maison de fous. Paris, C. Vimont, 1833.

[12] Lüdeke v. Möllendorff, 24: "Und es sind Worte recht zur Zeit gesprochen, denn in der Tat, es ist jetzt arg. Ob einer recht tut, seine Pflicht erfüllt, darauf wird weniger gesehen, als darauf, ob er die Äusserlichkeiten der Religion befolgt."

[13] Goethe, *Werke* 41², p. 84: "hat . . . das düstere Gewölk an die Berge geworfen . . . uns aber hat er wieder einen klaren blauen Himmel des Menschenverstandes und reiner Sitte zu eröffnen gewusst."

[14] Zeydel, *L. T. and England,* 182, 198.

[15] See also E. Eckertz in *Der Zeitgeist,* 1907, No. 39.

[16] J. Minor in *Euphor.* 3, 265 *ff.*

[17] Lüdeke, *L. T. u. d. Brüder Schlegel*, 177: "mit unendlichem Ergötzen." Also *Zeitschr. f. Bücherfreunde* N. F. XX, 18. For other reviews see H. W. Hewett-Thayer in *Germanic Review* III, 4 (Oct. 1928), p. 333.

[18] "Spielen wir selbst mit uns oder mischt eine höhere Hand die Karten? Vielleicht läuft in den recht wichtigen Lebensmomenten beides auf eines hinaus."

[19] O. F. Walzel in *Deut. Literaturzeitung* 25, 344 *ff.*

[20] Niebuhr, *Lebensnachrichten* III, 102.

[21] Zeydel, 183 *f.* and 195 *f.*

[22] *Krit. Schr.* I, 148.

[23] March 5, 1840. Unpubl. Orig.: Preuss. Staatsbib.

[24] April 4, 1842. Unpubl. *ibid.*: "späteres Verhältnis zu B. Jonson und den übrigen Dichtern, hauptsächlich aber die Geschichte des Essex und dessen vertrauten Sekretär Cuffe . . . zu diesem Werke liegen schon seit vielen Jahren die Bau-Materialien in Bereitschaft, und es ist wohl möglich, dass Sie, mein Freund, es in einem oder zwei Jahren verlegen."

[25] Lüdeke v. Möllendorff, 26, 39, 44. See also A. Eichler in *Engl. Studien*, 1922 (vol. 56), 254 *ff.*

[26] Hewett-Thayer, *loc. cit.*, 336 *ff.*

[27] Grimm: *Allgem. Zeitung*, Beil. 1892, No. 275, p. 4; Immermann: Holtei II, 52; Hebbel: *Tagebücher* I, 287. Also Hebbel, *Briefe* V, 263.

[28] Lüdeke v. Möllendorff, 44.

[29] Lüdeke, *L. T. u. d. Brüder Schlegel*, 177.

[30] Zeydel, 183, 198 *f.*

[31] *Digterliv, Novelle af Tieck*, overs. af P. J. T. Sehorn, Copenhagen, 1826.

[32] *Oeuvres complètes de L. Tieck*. 1er livraison. Contes d'artiste. Une fête à Kenilworth. Shakespeare et ses contemporains. Paris, C. Vimont, 1832. A. Cherbuliez, *Les matinées suisses*. 3me série continuée. Une vie de poète par Tieck. Paris, 1832.

[33] *Modern Lang. Review* 18, 235 *f.*

[33a] Wendt sent him a copy of *Histoire des Troubles* (Wendt's letter of Aug. 27, 1823; Stadtgeschichtl. Museum, Leipzig).

[34] J. H. Loewe, *J. E. Veith*, Weimar, 1879, p. 40.

[35] *Achim v. Arnim u. d. ihm nahestanden* I, 192 *ff.*

[36] H. Lebede, *Ts. Novelle Der Aufruhr in d. Cevennen*, Halle, 1909. Though overlooking Brentano's part in calling Tieck's attention to the subject, it is the best study of Tieck's "novelle." See also F. Conen, *Die Form der historischen Novelle bei L. T.*, Gladbach, 1914, and H. Schwarz, *Der Kamisardenaufstand in der deutschen Literatur des 19. Jahrhunderts*, Münster, 1912.

[37] Hewett-Thayer, *loc. cit.*, 338 *ff.*; also Lebede, *op. cit.*, 173 *ff.*

[38] Holtei II, 92.

[39] Holtei I, 254.

[40] Holtei III, 352.

[41] Holtei II, 6.

[42] To Kessler, Aug. 3, 1827.

[43] A. Stahr, *Kleine Schr.* I, 306.

[44] Unpubl. Orig.: Walther de Gruyter collection, Berlin.

[45] *L. Ts. ausgew. Werke*, Leipz., n. d., p. lxxxii.

NOTES

[46] Eduard Berend, *L. Ts. ausgew. Werke*, Berlin, Leipzig, Vienna, Stuttg., 1908, Introd.

[47] L. A. Willoughby, *The Romantic Movement in Germany*, Oxford, 1931. A still more recent critic, A. W. Porterfield (*The German Quarterly* VII, 2, March, 1934, pp. 58 *ff.*), also thinks highly of the work.

[48] *Zeitung für d. elegante Welt*, Dec. 15, 1826, No. 245, Col. 1961: "Bei wenig Dichtern erkennt man so wie bei ihm, wie wenig der Stoff und wie viel die Form, oder die Behandlungsart bedeutet."

[49] Unpubl. Orig.: Preuss. Staatsbib.

[50] Zeydel, *op. cit.*, 183 and 195. *Oeuvres complètes de L. T.* Contes d'artistes. 2me livraison. Paris, C. Vimont.

[51] Unpubl. (Michaelis-Tag 1829). Orig.: Frankf. Goethemuseum.

[52] See Hewett-Thayer, *loc. cit.*, 343 *f.* See esp. *Hallesche Allgem. Lit.zeitung.* Dec. 1830, No. 238, Col. 618.

[53] Zeydel, *op. cit.*, 166 *f.*

[54] *Zeitung f. d. elegante Welt*, Oct. 14, 1830, No. 262, Cols. 1609 *f.*

[55] *Jenaische Allgem. Lit.-Zeitung*, Nov. 1830, No. 217, p. 292.

CHAPTER SEVENTEEN

[1] Eitner, *Ein Engländer über deut. Geistesleben im ersten Drittel dieses Jahrhunderts*, Weimar, 1871, 83.

[2] Zeydel-Matenko, *Germanic Rev. Texts* 2, p. 13.

[3] *Lebenserinn. u. Briefw. v. Friedr. v. Raumer* II, 352 *ff.*: "Meinem Gefühl und meiner Einsicht nach gehört vieles, was Labitt spricht, zu dem Grossartigsten und Tiefsinnigsten, was jemals gedacht und ausgesprochen ist."

[4] *Le sabbat des sorcières; chronique de 1459.* E. Renduel, Paris, 1833.

[5] *Abendzeitung*, Dresden (Oct. 12, 1831, No. 183: *Der Wegweiser* No. 82, 325 *ff.*); Grillparzer (Sauer-Backmann) II. Abt., X, 161; *Goethe-Zelter-Briefw.* VI, Berlin, 1834, p. 347.

[6] Zeydel in *Germanic Review* II, 1927, p. 12 *ff.*; also *Literar. Nachl. v. Friedr. v. Raumer* II, 154 *f.*

[7] Zeydel, *L. T. and England*, 185 and 208-9.

[8] Hewett-Thayer, *loc. cit.*, 347 *f.*

[9] Zeydel, *L. T. and England*, 159.

[10] Hewett-Thayer, *loc. cit.*, 349 *ff.*

[11] L. H. Fischer, *Aus Berlins Vergangenheit*, 162 *ff.*

[12] J. Petersen, *Schiller u. d. Bühne*, 249 *f.*

[13] Hewett-Thayer, *loc. cit.*, 352 *ff.*

[14] L. H. Fischer, *op. cit.*, 162 *ff.* Tieck's letters to Count Yorck, unpublished, are in Schloss Wartenburg, Kleinöls, Silesia.

[15] *Tagebücher*, Feb. 16, 1839 (I, 333): "dass der reine Mensch dem Schicksal gegenüber immer seine Selbständigkeit zu behaupten vermag, wenn er Kraft genug besitzt, mit der ihm aufgebürdeten Last zu spielen." See also Hebbel, *Briefe* I, 379.

[16] Zeydel, *L. T. and England*, 184 *ff.*

[17] According to an unpubl. letter by Tieck in the possession of the present writer.

[18] *Nachgel. Schr.* II, 19 *ff.*

LUDWIG TIECK, THE GERMAN ROMANTICIST

[19] See Dorothea's account of the effect of Goethe's death on her father in H. v. Sybel, *Erinner. an Friedr. v. Üchtritz u. s. Zeit*, 165 ff.

[20] *Gedichte*, 1841, p. 165.

[21] The other extant letters from Sophie to Friedrich (Origs.: Sächs. Landesbib.) were not available at the time of writing.

[22] Lüdeke, *L. T. u. d. Brüder Schlegel*, 165.

[23] Of Feb. 1853. Unpubl. Orig. in Schloss Wartenburg, Kleinöls, Silesia.

[24] Unpubl. Orig.: Preuss. Staatsbib.

[25] Literar. *Nachl v. Friedr. v. Raumer* II, 173. See also Dorothea to Üchtritz, v. Sybel, 206 ff.

[26] April 10, 1840. Unpubl. Orig.: Preuss. Staatsbib.

[27] See M. Landau in *Euphor.* 9, 310 ff., also the typewr. Leipzig diss. of Paul Sieger, *Ts. Vittoria Accorombona u. ihre Quellen* (1923).

[28] Emil Schering in *Berliner Tageblatt*, Aug. 7, 1926. G. Witkowski in *Leipziger Neueste Nachr.*, Aug. 15, 1926, F. Droop, *ibid.*, Aug. 13, 1926, and K. Viëtor in *Jb. d. Kleistges.* 1925-1926.

[29] On T's. relation to Scott see Zeydel, *L. T. and England*, 41 ff.

[30] Hebbel, *Briefe* I, 397; II, 143.

[31] James A. Froude, *Thomas Carlyle. A History of his Life in London, 1834-1881*, vol. I, New York, 1904, p. 257 f.

[32] See also Wenger, *Historische Romane deutscher Romantiker* in Walzel's *Untersuchungen zur neueren Sprach- u. Lit.-Gesch.* 7, Bern, 1905.

[33] A. T. C. Hare, *Freifrau v. Bunsen, ein Lebensbild.* Deutsch v. H. Tharau. 6. Aufl. II, Gotha, 1890, p. 47.

[34] See also O. Weibel, *Ts. Renaissancedichtung in ihrem Verhältnis zu Heinse u. C. F. Meyer*, Bern, 1925; W. Rehm, *Das Werden des Renaissance-Bildes*, Munich, 1924, p. 129.

[35] See H. Gumbel in *Romantik-Forschungen*, 80 f.

[36] Köpke II, 99 f.: "Wie nimmer war seine Natur in ihren Grundlagen angegriffen worden, es fasste ihn ein krampfhaftes, zusammenpressendes Schmerzgefühl, das vergebens nach einem Ausdrucke rang. Kalt, starr, tränenlos, ohne ein Wort oder irgend einen Laut zu finden, verbarg er sich in dem entlegensten Zimmer. Keinen Menschen wollte er sehen, keinen Zuspruch hören; die Stunden, Tag und Nacht, gingen gleichgültig und unbemerkt an ihm vorüber."

[37] Unpubl. letter of Aug. 8, 1848. Orig.: Schloss Wartenburg: "Es gibt in unserem sterblichen Leben solche Leiden, die kein Mensch begreift, nicht denkt, wer sie nicht erfahren hat. Im Anfang ergreift uns dumpfe, fast schmerzlose Betäubung, wo alles Leben, alles hellere Bewusstsein in uns erstarrt und verschwindet. Dann tut sich vor dem entsetzlichen Schlage ein Abgrund unseres Jammers auf, ein tiefes Erbeben, so dass wir uns vor unserem eignen Wesen entsetzen. Dies Wut-Schmerzen unseres Geistes und Daseins macht dann, durchgekämpft, der wahren himmlischen Liebe Raum, die uns im Schmerz durchläutert und verklärt. Dann fühlen wir im Schmerz die göttliche Liebe!"

[38] H. v. Sybel, *op. cit.*

[39] See esp. her letter to Üchtritz of Jan. 7, 1839, v. Sybel, 217 ff., and Tieck's letter to Üchtritz of March 18, 1846, *ibid.*, 151.

[40] The writer owes this information to Professor J. Körner of Prague. See note 14, chap. 9.

NOTES

[1] The Raumer draft is publ. in *Literar. Nachl. v. Friedr. v. Raumer* II, 188 *f.*

[2] The note as Tieck wrote it (now in the Prussian archives) is publ. in L. H. Fischer, *Aus Berlins Vergangenheit*, 108 *f.*

[3] *L. Ts. Gedichte*, Berlin, 1841, pp. 596 *ff.* The MS. is in the *Tieck-Nachlass*, Box 10. A huge painting by F. W. Krüger, "Huldigung der Berliner an Friedrich Wilhelm IV," representing Tieck, rather youthful looking, in the foreground, commemorates the poet's attachment to the ruler.

[4] Unpubl. Orig.: Preuss. Staatsarchiv: "hier geht alles, Wichtiges und Unwichtiges, sehr langsam, und hat bei vier Rädern immer ·fünf Gummischuh."

[5] Unpubl. Orig.: Dresd. Stadtbib.: "Ich habe so viele Jahre in Dresden versessen und wegen der dortigen Armseligkeit nur wenig wirken können."

[6] Unpubl. Orig.: Sächs. Landesbib.

[7] *Tagebücher v. K. A. Varnhagen v. Ense* I, Leipzig, 1861, 329.

[8] See also *Krit. Schr.* IV, 371 *ff.*

[9] *ibid.*, 373 *f.*

[10] J. Petersen in *Neues Archiv. f. Theatergesch.* 2, 163 *ff.* Also *Krit. Schr.* IV, 375 *f.*

[11] *Krit. Schr.* IV, 377 *f.* It was given a second time on May 13.

[12] *Tagebücher* II, Leipzig, 1861, 287.

[13] *Krit. Schr.* IV, 379 *ff.*, but with incorrect date.

[14] *ibid.* IV, 382 *f.*, but with incorrect date.

[15] Unpubl. Orig.: Preuss. Staatsbib.

[16] Unpubl. Orig.: Preuss. Staatsbib.: "Zauberei, Unpoesie und nüchternste Trivialität." "Iffland, Kotzebue gingen vorüber, dann Müllner, der sich Diktator dünkte, so hoffentlich bald Gutzkow, Laube, die Birch-Pfeiffer, Töpfer etc.: und Lessing, Schröder, selbst Brandes werden wieder erscheinen, und Shakespeare, Goethe und Schiller stehen bleiben. Viele jetzt vernachlässigte, Engländer und selbst Franzosen werden neue Röcke bekommen."

[17] Tieck expressed his opinion of Hebbel in a letter to Theodor v. Küstner of Jan. 27, 1848. *Unveröffentlichte Briefe: Ludwig Tieck an Th. v. Küstner; Albert Niemann an Botho von Hülsen. Den Besuchern des Staatstheater-Museums. Der Generalintendant der Preuss. Staatstheater. n. d.* The letters to Freytag, unpubl., are of Nov. 4, 1847, and Jan. 14, 1848. Origs.: Preuss, Staatsbib. The quotations are from the letter of Jan. 14, 1848: "interessant, poetisch und originell." "wundersame Erscheinung in einem Zeitalter der Dürre und fast unerklärlichen Talentlosigkeit." "diese echte, tiefe Sittlichkeit des Ganzen, ohne Floskel, Heuchelei und Konventions-Phrasen."

[18] Unpubl. letter of Dec. 2, 1851. Orig.: Stadtbib., Vienna.

[19] Grillparzer (Sauer-Backmann) I. Abt., XIV, 109; XVI, 183; II. Abt., VIII, 123, 127.

[20] Hebbel, *Briefe* II, 209.

[21] *Krit. Schr.* IV, 371.

[22] *ibid.* II, 403 *ff.* The quotations are on pp. 405 and 406: "unser grösster und nationalster Dichter." "Als wenn wir seit dem Mittelalter, im Gegensatz der Griechen, irgend eine andere Poesie als die romantische haben könnten."

[23] Also in *Neues Jb. der Berlinischen Gesell. f. deut. Sprache u. Altertumskunde* 6, 272 *ff.*

LUDWIG TIECK, THE GERMAN ROMANTICIST

[24] *Tieck-Nachlass*, vol. 19. *cf.* Tieck's *Nebenbuhler* of 1789, pp. 16, 346 above.

[25] *Sheridan, Dramat. Werke* übers. v. W. Hoffmann, Gotha, 1828-1829.

[26] *Die Nebenbuhler*, frei übers. v. Ernst v. Wolzogen, Leipzig (Reclam), 1875.

[27] Lüdeke v. Möllendorff, 186 *ff.*

[28] See Zeydel, *L. T. and England*, 131 *f.* See also Zeydel in *Mod. Lang. Notes* XLII (Jan. 1927) p. 21 *ff.*, and Hewett-Thayer in *Germanic Review* IX (Jan. 1934), pp. 9 *ff.*

[29] *ibid.* (first work.)

[30] F. Hildebrandt, *Friedr. Tieck*, Leipz., 1907.

[31] Goethe, *Briefe* XV, 365; O. Fiebiger in *Deut. Rundschau*, Aug. 1918, 218 *f.* For the Varnhagen v. Ense note see his papers *sub* Friedrich Tieck in the *Handschr.-Abt.*, Preuss. Staatsbib.

[32] *Tagebücher* VII, Zurich, 1865, p. 166; also *ibid.*, XI, 322 and XII, 219.

[33] Tieck's letters to the king, also the sonnet, are unpubl.: Preuss. Hausarchiv, Brandenburg. For Tieck's relations to him see A. v. Reumont, *Aus König Friedrich Wilhelms IV. gesunden und kranken Tagen*, Leipzig, 1885.

[34] *Tagebücher* II, 171. *ibid.* III, 250 and 307.

[35] See the undated letter to Raumer publ. by Zeydel and Matenko in *Germanic Review Texts* 2, 21 *ff.*: "schlechte, aride Politik."

[36] Unpubl.: Preuss. Staatsbib.: "Diese sogenannte Nationalversammlung ist ein Schandfleck unserer Zeit, der nicht auszutilgen ist, so etwas Dummes, Niederträchtiges, Gemeines und Plattes in der Bosheit ist noch zu keiner Zeit dagewesen. Man möchte sich schämen, ein Preusse zu sein. Das ist nicht mehr Demokratismus, Republikanismus, sondern die sündlichste Rebellion, Anarchie, Plünderung, Mord, Raub . . . Was verstehn Weiber von Staatssachen? Stricken Nähen, Haushalten ist ihr Beruf, darin sind sie ehrwürdig." According to a letter to Johanna from the minister Uhden of Feb. 21, 1849, she was excluded from membership in a "Frauen-Kranken-Verein" because of her political views. See Varnhagen-Sammlung, Berlin, *sub* Ludwig Tieck. Was this due to Tieck's influence? To Ida Lüttichau (Preuss. Staatsbib., probably 1849) Tieck writes similarly.

[37] Otto v. Skepsgardh, *Drei Vorreden. Rosen u. Golem-Tieck*, Berlin, 1844. Hebbel, *Tagebücher* III, 440: "blauäugiger Adler mit zerschossenen Flügeln." Also *ibid.* IV, 34.

[38] *Worte am Sarge L. Ts. gesprochen am 1. Mai 1853 von Dr. A. Sydow, Prediger an der Neuen Kirche zu Berlin.* Berlin, 1853. Sydow emphasized Tieck's struggle against Rationalism, maintained that Romanticism is essentially a Christian product and asserted that Tieck had "proclaimed skepticism worthily," always remaining upon a Christian foundation. A reproduction of Tieck's death mask is in E. Friedell, *Das letzte Gesicht* (Zurich, Orell u. Füssli).

[39] See the Romantic "novelle" of Adolf Zeising, *Meister Ludwig Tiecks Heimgang*, Frankf.a.M., 1854. It revolves around Tieck's death and has a description of the funeral cortege. The grave, marked only by a plain brown stone with the inscription: "Ludwig Tieck, geb. 31. Mai 1773, gest. 28. April 1853" and hardly worthy of his memory, is well kept. On the sixth anniversary of his death a scrap of paper (now in the *Tieck-Nachlass*, Box 24) with these pencilled words in English was found in the iron grating: "Six years ago—no flower's on thy turf, to celebrate the awful memory of thy death. Oh how says Hamlet true,

NOTES

there's hope a great man's memory may outlive his death six months, no more. April 28, 1859."

[40] Hebbel, *Briefe* II, 6; IV, 296; VI, 332: "so sicher, als dass die Bäume wieder ausschlagen müssen, sobald es Frühling wird."

[41] See *Les Nouvelles Littéraires*, Paris, June 17, 1933.

EPILOG

[1] In the body of the book many of these influences have been dealt with. Only a brief bibliography of Tieck's influence on some of the authors can be given here.

Schiller: Sulger-Gebing in *Euphorion* 19, 148 *ff.*

Hoffmann: Otto Fischer in *Archiv f. d. Studium d. neueren Sprachen*, vol. 123, 1 *ff.*

E. Ellinger in *Deutsche Dichtung* 7.

F. Leppmann, *Kater Murr und seine Sippe*, Munich, 1908.

W. Jost, *Von Ludwig Tieck zu E. T. A. Hoffmann*, Frankf.a.M., 1921.

Heine: O. zur Linde, *H. Heine u. d. deutsche Romantik*, Freiburg, 1899.

Arnim: Gundolf, and F. Schönemann, *L. A. v. Arnims geistige Entwicklung*, Leipzig, 1912.

Eichendorff: Gundolf.

Fouqué: Max Koch in *Deut. Nat.-Lit.* 146.

Werner: F. Poppenberg. *Z. Werner, Mystik und Romantik in den Söhnen des Tals*, Berlin, 1894.

Brentano: W. Steinert, *Ludwig Tieck und das Farbenempfinden der romantischen Dichtung*, Dortmund, 1910.

H. Amelung, *Ein neues Drama Clemens Brentanos*, Frankf. Zeitung, 1912, No. 260.

E. Nippold, *Tiecks Einfluss auf Brentano*, Jena, 1915.

Immermann: O. Wohnlich, *Tiecks Einfluss auf Immermann, besonders seine epischen Produktionen*, Tübingen, 1913.

W. Küper, *Immermanns Verhältnis zur Frühromantik unter besonderer Berücksichtigung seiner Beziehungen zu Tieck*, Münster, 1913.

K. L. Wittsack, *K. L. Immermann als Dramaturg*, Greifswald, 1914.

Lenau: Gundolf.

Mörike: Gundolf.

Ludwig: W. Greiner, *Die ersten Novellen O. Ludwigs und ihr Verhältnis zu Ludwig Tieck*, Jena, 1903.

R. M. Meyer in *Jahrbuch der deutschen Shakespeare-Gesellschaft* 37, 59 *ff.*

R. Müller-Ems, *O. Ludwigs Erzählungskunst*, Berlin, 1905.

Freytag: Klee, vol. 3.

Hebbel: Emil Kuh, *Kritische und literarische Aufsätze* hrsg. v. A. Schaer, Weimar, 1910.

C. von Klenze in *Euphorion* 20, 165 *f.*

H. W. Hewett-Thayer in *Germanic Review* 2, 16 *ff.*

LUDWIG TIECK, THE GERMAN ROMANTICIST

Wagner: F. Muncker, *R. Wagner, eine Skizze seines Lebens und Wirkens*, Bamberg, 1891.

E. von Komorzynski in *Euphorion* 9, 189 *f.*

Keller: Albert Ludwig in *Literarisches Echo* 24, 4.

Emil Ermatinger, *Gottfried Kellers Leben, Briefe u. Tagebücher* I, 2. Aufl., Stuttg. u. Berlin, 1916, *passim* (see index, vol. III).

Heyse: Berend and Gundolf.

Wilbrandt: *Die Grenzboten* 2.

Hauptmann: A. Thimme in *Preussische Jahrbücher* 103, 161.

Heiberg: G. Brandes, *Skandinavische Persönlichkeiten*, Munich, 1902 (Gesammelte Schriften 2).

Oehlenschläger: L. H. Fischer, *Aus Berlins Vergangenheit*, Berlin, 1891.

A. Sergel, *Oehlenschläger in seinem persönlichen Verhältnis zu Goethe, Tieck und Hebbel*, Rostock, 1907.

Gogol: A. Stender-Petersen in *Euphorion* 24, 628 *ff.*

Verlaine: J. Thorel in *Revue politique et littéraire* 3, 95 *ff.*

For the British and American influences see C. F. Schreiber and F. E. Pierce, *Fiction and Fantasy of German Romance*, New York, 1927; E. H. Zeydel, *L. T. and England*; and (for Coleridge and Scott) F. W. Stokoe, *German Influence in the English Romantic Period*, Cambridge, 1926.

[2] *Kleine Schriften von Hermann Hettner*, Braunschweig, 1884, 513 *ff.*

[3] E. Kilian, Beilage der *Allgemeinen Zeitung*, Nos. 219 and 221, 1890. E. Drach, *Ludwig Tiecks Bühnenreform*, Berlin, 1909. E. Gross, *Die ältere Romantik und das Theater*, Leipzig, 1910. J. Petersen in *Neues Archiv für Theatergeschichte* 2, 163 *ff.*

[4] Lüdeke, *L. T. und die Brüder Schlegel*, 33; also *A. W. von Schlegels sämtliche Werke* hrsg. v. E. Böcking, XII, Leipzig, 1847, 34 *f.*

[5] J. G. Fichte, *Briefwechsel*. Kritische Gesamtausgabe v. Hans Schulz, II, 2nd ed. Leipzig, 1930, 286 *f.*

[6] *Mitternachtsblatt*, Dec. 11, p. 790.

[7] H. Laube, *Moderne Charakteristiken*, II, Mannheim, 1835, 145 *ff.*

[8] T. Carlyle, *Critical and Miscellaneous Essays*, I, 3rd ed., London, 1847, 62 *f.*

[9] Zeydel, *L. T. and England*, 98.

[10] Anna B. Jameson, *Visits and Sketches Abroad*, II, 2nd ed., London, 1835, 148 *ff.*

[11] pp. 141-9.

[12] Hillard, *Life, Letters and Journals of George Ticknor*, 2 vols., Boston, 1876.

[13] Holtei, I, 7.

[14] Zeydel, *L. T. and England*, 219 *f.*

[15] But the Schlegels (August Wilhelm, at least) did not intend to oppose Tieck to Goethe. They thought of them as co-founders of a new school ("so dass nun von beiden gemeinschaftlich eine Dichterschule ausgehen kann"—*A. W. Schlegels sämtl. Werke* XII, 35.).

[16] *Abendzeitung* (Literarisches Notizblatt No. 68, Nov. 24, 1832).

[17] *Jahrbücher für wissenschaftliche Kritik*, 1834, No. 90, Cols. 753 *ff.*

[18] *ibid.*, 1837, No. 35, Cols. 275 *ff.* Also T. Mundt, *Charaktere und Situationen*, Wismar and Leipzig, II, 1837, 259 *ff.* In 1830 Menzel called Tieck a literary Burke, powerful but conservative (See Löbell to Tieck, May 10, 1835—Univers.-Bibl., Bonn).

NOTES

[19] Hebbel, *Briefe* VII, 155.

[20] To Friedrich Schlegel, Dec. 16, 1803: "das Böse, das in allem menschlichen Tun, vorzüglich aber in der Kunst seinen Geist sichtbar macht." Lüdeke, *L. T. und die Brüder Schlegel*, 147. See also *Solgers Nachgel. Schr. u. Briefw.* hrsg. v. L. Tieck u. Fr. v. Raumer, I, 541; Matenko, 363.

INDEX

INDEX

INDEX

INDEX

INDEX

INDEX

INDEX

INDEX

INDEX

INDEX

INDEX

INDEX